CIVIL WAR
VOLUNTEER SONS
OF CONNECTICUT

CIVIL WAR
VOLUNTEER SONS
OF CONNECTICUT

BLAIKIE HINES

AMERICAN PATRIOT
PRESS

Civil War Volunteer Sons of Connecticut

Blaikie Hines

American Patriot Press
44 Fluker Street
Rm 157
Thomaston, Maine, 04861

Copyright © 2002

FIRST EDITION

Editor: Blaikie Hines
Copy Editors: Richard Oliver and Gordon Hines
Art Director: Blaikie Hines
Consultants:
Robert Bee 20th Infantry, Dale Call 17th Infantry, Dave Corrigan Connecticut State Library, Ross S. Dent New England Civil War Museum, Randy Hackenburg US Army Military Institute, Scott Holmes 16th Infantry, Kevin Johnson 29th Infantry, Lawrence Matthew 26th Infantry, Matt Minor 2nd Heavy Artillery, Dave Naumec 14th Infantry, Jim Naumec Connecticut Rifles, Dean Nelson Museum of Connecticut History, Kim Perlotto 8th Infantry, Michael Thomas 5th Infantry, Crawford Westbrook 21st Infantry, Mark Wicander 5th Infantry, Mary Witkowski Bridgeport Public Library
Special Contributors:
Bridgeport Public Library, Ellen/Peter Burnham, Connecticut Historical Society, Connecticut State Library, Darien Public Library, Mike Flanagan, Tom Geary, Stephen Hatch, Priscilla B. Hines, Kevin Kerrigan, Raymond Johns, Bob/Priscilla Marshall, Norman/Karen Meares, New Canaan Public Library, Gary Paxton, Chris Rector, Stamford Public Library Historical Collection, George Willis

Publisher's - Cataloging in Publication Data
Hines, Blaikie, 1949-
    Civil War Volunteer Sons of Connecticut/ Blaikie Hines
        p.   cm.
Includes bibliographical references.
Index
ISBN 0-9709888-7-7
1. United States -- History -- Civil War, 1861-1865
-- Regimental histories -- Connecticut
I. Hines, Blaikie, 1949 - Civil War Volunteer Sons of Connecticut.
II. Title.
973.7
Manufactured in the United States of America
10 9 8 7 6 5 4 3 2 1

Front Cover: Photo collection of author, inset photo: Nathan Gillette, 1st Light Battery
Title Page: Captain John H. Burton, Battery No. 8 in front of Petersburg, VA 1864

To my understanding wife Judith and
daughter Christina

To my Father, Gordon Hines, who planted the seeds for my interest in the
Civil War

★★★★★★★★★★★★★ CONTENTS ★★★★★★★★★★★★★

CONTENTS

USAMHI

FIRST REGIMENT CONNECTICUT VOLUNTEER
HEAVY ARTILLERY
PORTION OF COMPANY A AT FORT BLENKER (REYNOLDS)
1863

VOLUNTEERS.

ATTENTION!

Volunteers wanted immediately to join a Company to be attached to one of the Regiments called for by the Executive of this State

THE SONS OF CONNECTICUT

now in the Field battling for our Common Cause are anxiously awaiting our response. Let it be such as shall gladden their hearts and nerve their arms for the contest. Let us fly promptly to their relief and close this unholy rebellion, that we may soon again enjoy the blessings of peace together.

COMPENSATION

Government Pay	per month	$ 15.00	Each Volunteer will receive, in advance, upon	
" Bounty		100.00	being mustered into service one month pay	$15.00
State Bounty by act of 1861	" year	30.00	One fourth of Government pay	25.00
" pay to wife	" month	6.00	One third of State Bounty by act of Legisla-	10.00
" " " " and one child	" "	8.00	ture of 1861	
" " " " " two children " "		10.00	State Bounty by act of 1862	50.00
" Bounty by act of 1862 in advance		50.00	Recruiting Bounty by order of Sec'y of War	2.00
			Bounty from Town	50.00

Let there be no bickerings among ourselves as to this or that policy, but placing confidence in the Government let us give it our united support.

JULIUS BASSETT, *Recruiting Officer*

West Meriden, July 16th, 1862

INTRODUCTION

This book includes the only concise and comprehensive history of every Connecticut Civil War regiment and the casualties credited to each incorporated town. The regiments are presented in numerical order from the first numbered regiment to the last. Each history details the total number of recruits, its senior officers and dates of service. Using charts and maps based on the Federal pension records; every regimental casualty is catalogued by date and geographical location. Every significant regimental engagement is highlighted and every troop movement is listed and mapped.

Additionally, a Connecticut map showing the borders for each incorporated town from the Civil War period accompanies each history. The map indicates the total number of soldiers credited from each town and in the legend lists the total number of men from every other state who served in that Connecticut regiment.

In the town history section, every enlistment credited to each town is catalogued by regiment and every credited casualty is listed by regiment and place. The most significant day of the war for each town is identifed based on the total credited casualties and a complete statistical summary is presented.

The statistical foundation is the revised catalogue of THE RECORD OF SERVICE OF CONNECTICUT MEN DURING THE WAR OF THE REBELLION, published in 1889. The idea of a revised catalogue came into being when, in 1885, it became apparent to the General Assembly of the State of Connecticut that a complete and accurate record of Connecticut service in the Civil war was needed. Three catalogues listing the records of Connecticut Volunteers had

already been published in 1869. However, errors relating to regimental and company organizations and more importantly damaging inaccuracies in the records of individual soldiers, compelled the State to look into revising the catalogues and to make an accurate record of the service of all the men who were credited to Connecticut in the Civil War.

Problems had occurred when an aged parent, whose son was listed in the official catalogues of 1869 as a "deserter", presented undeniable proof that their son had served honorably and heroically in a Connecticut regiment but had been captured and had died in a southern prison. Naturally, the individual service record was amended but the State was powerless to correct the record in the many published copies that had been widely distributed.

On March 10, 1886, the Connecticut General Assembly unanimously adopted an Act to provide funding for the publication of an accurate record of Connecticut Volunteers. The work was begun at once and steps were taken to secure access to the records of the Adjutant General's office in Washington, D.C. This was considered to be the only way of gathering complete individual service records. Previously, all applications by State officials for Washington records had been denied by the Adjutant General of the Army because of the amount of clerical time needed to respond to the State's requests.

Fortunately, individual soldiers or their families seeking individual records were not treated in this way. Finally, the Connecticut State legislature pressed the matter all the way up to Secretary of War William C. Endicott. Congressional Connecticut Senators Orville Platt and Joseph Hawley forcibly seconded the

State's position. A compromise was eventually reached in which the State of Connecticut and not the War Department paid for the clerical work needed to collate the information.

Each of the 4,500 original State muster rolls was critically examined and it was found that more than 10,000 Connecticut individual service records were either incomplete or contradictory. In December 1888, a more accurate revised Connecticut catalogue was completed and was published the following year. The Connecticut regimental histories that accompanied the rosters in the revised catalogue were prepared by members of the various organizations and were published as written without further revision other than a verification of dates by comparison with official records.

An attempt to gather the records of Connecticut men who served in regiments of other states and in the Navy and the Marine Corps was made with great difficulty These records are not to be considered complete. However, Connecticut men who served in the regular army were secured directly from the War Department and are accurate.

Other than the numerous published Connecticut regimental histories, the only comprehensive history written about Connecticut regiments during the Civil War is Crofut & Morris' THE MILITARY AND CIVIL HISTORY OF CONNECTICUT DURING THE WAR OF 1861-65. The book was published in 1869, which was the same year as the first catalogues of Connecticut soldiers. It presents the war chronologically and although indexed by regiment there are no concise, comprehensive regimental histories or accurate casualty records presented. However, a summary of the histories of the various Connecticut organizations can be constructed by

using the regimental index.

The only other attempt to create a comprehenive Connecticut Civil War history was made in 1865 when THE CONNECTICUT WAR RECORD WAS published. This book is a bound edition made up of letters, testimonials, and partial histories written in a newspaper format by various members of Connecticut organizations and sent to the publisher as the events of the war occurred. Although an index exists for each soldier and organization mentioned, the book is incomplete for most regiments. The project was abandoned because of the lack of funds before the war had ended in 1865 and although it contains a lot of valuable information it does not fully cover the history of each Connecticut regiment.

In September 1997, I began to write concise, detailed, and comprehensive Connecticut regimental histories using the summaries written in THE RECORD OF SERVICE..., the Crofut & Morris book plus THE CONNECTICUT WAR RECORD as a framework. The information that I gathered from the above sources was combined with Connecticut inf-ormation extracted from the official records CD-ROM, from the published individual Connecticut regimental histories, and from microfilm newspaper accounts from Bridgeport, Danbury, Hartford, Norwich, and Stamford, Connecticut.

Using Dyer's COMPENDIUM, I also began to make detailed maps that listed and indicated every geographic movement made by each Connecticut regiment. In addition, I began the creation a computer database derived from the revised 1889 Connecticut catalog. The completed database lists every soldier who served in a Connecticut regiment. It includes his name, dates of service, highest rank, regiment, company, town of residence or enlistment, and casualty if any.

Every casualty figure listed in the casualty tables for each regiment in this book is based on the numbers generated from the database. For the first time, extremely accurate casualty figures are presented for each Connecticut regiment and battlefield. These figures are not based on official battlefield reports but come from the pension records themselves.

What had been known to historians, is that Connecticut supplied the Union Army with 28 regiments and 3 battalions of infantry, 2 regiments of heavy artillery, 3 light batteries, 1 regiment of cavalry, and 1 squadron of cavalry.

What was not known, until now, because the analysis was impossible without the aid of a computer, is that 39,395 men from 400 different American towns served in these organizations. They came from every incorporated Connecticut town plus 19 other states and the District of Columbia. Not all men listed in the record actually served. Some men were unassigned. 4,454 (11%) men served in more than one military organization, 218 men served in three and only 2 men served in four.

Although most men who enlisted more than once, or had an officer's commission in more than one regiment, served in other Connecticut regiments, many volunteered in regiments from 12 other states. A significant number also served in regular army units and departments, "colored" regiments, the invalid corps, and in the Navy and Marine Corps. In fact Connecticut men served in 157 different state and federal military organizations.

Since this book deals exclusively with Connecticut regiments, the total number of men listed in the regimental casualty tables, when all added together, does not in fact represent the total number of

Connecticut men who were casualties in the war. That number, which has not been determined, would have to also include all of the various other Federal and other state units where Connecticut men served. That record is not complete.

As previously mentioned, each regimental history in the book has a casualty table. It is important to understand the meaning of the various casualty classifications.

The category titled "K" in each regimental casualty table counts only those that were directly killed in the war. It includes not only those killed directly on the battlefield but also those killed directly by accidents, murder, and drowning. Soldiers who died from wounds either accidentally or on the battlefield, or from injuries from accidents, or in Confederate captivity, or from disease are not included in this category.

The category titled "M" in the regimental casualty tables represent the missing and presumed dead. The category has a different meaning from that definition of "missing" that is generally associated with the official battlefield reports. The vast majority of the missing recorded in the official reports were captured and although many may have died in captivity they were not presumed dead. In this publication, missing means presumed dead.

Another area of potential confusion in the regimental casualty tables is the category titled "W". This category is associated with wounds both accidental and battlefield related. It does not include soldiers who were wounded and subsequently captured.

5,918 (15%) soldiers in Connecticut regiments were wounded. 353 men were wounded twice, 23 three times, 3 four times and one 6 times. Of all the wounded soldiers, 884 (15%) eventually died. This book has no category called "mortally wounded" for the mere fact that finding a suitable definition for the category was hard to determine. In my research I found many instances when wounded soldiers died after hours, days, weeks, months, years and yes even decades later. So said some of the Union widows. For this reason there is no "mortally wounded" category for this publication.

Soldiers that died from wounds are not listed as killed but as died. The figures listed in the regimental summaries as "died" are a total of the wounded dead and those who died in captivity or not, from disease, injuries from accidents, suicide, and execution.

The category with the "W/C heading designates those soldiers who were wounded and captured in the same engagement or day of battle.

The meaning of the category titled "C" presented in the regimental casualty tables includes any Conn-ecticut soldier who was captured by the Confederates and imprisoned. It does not include soldiers that were wounded and subsequently captured.

4,075 (10%) men in Connecticut regiments were captured and 119 were captured more than once. Many of the captured were paroled within days or weeks after capture although a significant number served long prison terms particularly in Virginia, Georgia, and North and South Carolina. Of those captured 807 (20%) eventually died before the war ended. Some actually died in prison and many died after release due to the harsh conditions of prison life. Over 300 Connecticut men died at Andersonville Prison alone.This was more dead than on any single battlefield by far. Many also died at Libby Prison, VA, at Millen, GA, at Salisbury, NC, at Florence, SC and other places.

4,277 (10%) men died indirectly while in the service of a Connecticut regiment. Combined with the total directly killed of 1,349 (3%) and missing and presumed dead of 117 (less than .3%). The grand total of men who were killed or died while serving in Connecticut regiments is 5,743 (15%)

5,461 (14%) men deserted from Connecticut regiments. Nearly 95% of the deserters served in only one regiment. Less than 5% (289) of these deserters served in more than one. Not all deserters were cowards. Some left service for reasons due to illness or injury or for family concerns only to join another regiment at a later date. A few deserters left one regiment to join another to be with family or friends. Contrary to some preconceived notions most deserters did not leave their regiments immediately preceeding or at the height of a battle but grew despondant and left their units after months of boredom and drudgery associated with camp life.

In summary, 39,395 men served in Connecticut Civil War regiments and they accounted for 43,837 enlistments. Over 85% of the men survived the terrible hardhips associated with the war. Almost all became ill at one point in their service and in many respects miserable camp life and exhaustive marching proved to be at least as great a threat to their health as Confederate bullets.

ABBREVIATIONS

K = KILLED

M = MISSING

W = WOUNDED

WC = WOUNDED & CAPTURED

C = CAPTURED

Rank of Connecticut Oragnizations

The State of Connecticut had 43,837 volunteer enlistments in Connecticut volunteer organizations by 39,395 men. There were 4184 men who served in more than one regiment.

REGIMENT	Number of Recruits
1st Heavy Artillery	3190
2nd Heavy Artillery	2447
11th Infantry	2022
14th Infantry	1966
7th Infantry	1916
1st Cavalry	1833
10th Infantry	1820
5th Infantry	1754
8th Infantry	1622
6th Infantry	1610
15th Infantry	1560
13th Infantry	1480
20th Infantry	1395
12th Infantry	1362
29th Infantry	1249
9th Infantry	1223
18th Infantry	1192
17th Infantry	1167
16th Infantry	1091
21th Infantry	1023
22th Infantry	940
23th Infantry	847
27th Infantry	829
1st Infantry	820
25th Infantry	816
26th Infantry	815
2nd Infantry	793
3rd Infantry	781
28th Infantry	678
24th Infantry	669
12th Battalion Infantry	492
30th Infantry	469
13th Battalion Infantry	448
9th Battalion Infantry	431
1st Light Battery	291
2nd Light Battery	230
1st Squadron Cavalry	157
3rd Light Battery	152

CONNECTICUT CASUALTIES RANKED BY TOTAL AND PLACE

Connecticut suffered over 11,000 casualties in 220 different places on over 1200 different days during the war. The top 50 places are listed below.

RANK	PLACE	DATE	TOTAL	K	M	W	W/C	C
1	Antietam (Sharpsburg), MD	Sep 16-17, 1862	689	131	2	515	19	22
2	Chancellorsville, VA	May 1-5, 1863	677	40	1	153	50	433
3	Drewry's Bluff, VA	May 12-16, 1864	634	64	3	290	36	241
4	Petersburg, VA	Jun 15, 1864-Apr 1, 1865	612	96	17	446	3	40
5	Winchester (2nd Battle), VA	Jun 15, 1863	592	23	0	8	41	520
6	Cold Harbor, VA	May 31-Jun 3, 1864	557	118	12	422	1	4
7	Port Hudson, LA	May 24-Jul 9, 1863	520	64	0	444	2	10
8	Kinston (2nd Battle), NC	Mar 8-10, 1865	494	21	3	12	49	409
9	Plymouth, NC	Apr 20, 1864	433	1	2	0	12	418
10	Cedar Creek, VA	Oct 19, 1864	415	48	2	203	10	152
11	Gettysburg, PA	Jul 1-3, 1864	360	46	7	203	9	94
12	Winchester (Opequan), VA	Sep 19, 1864	274	37	0	207	0	30
13	Fredericksburg, VA	Dec 12-15, 1862	257	41	5	203	2	6
14	Fort Wagner, SC	Jul 18- Sep 18, 1863	252	35	9	121	21	66
15	Bermuda Hundred	Jun 2–Feb 10, 1864	216	28	1	98	8	81
16	Cedar Mountain, VA	Aug 9, 1862	173	35	0	74	8	56
17	Piedmont, VA	Jun 5, 1864	156	21	1	82	25	27
18	Irish Bend, LA	Apr 14, 1863	144	18	0	117	0	9
19	Deep Run, VA	Aug 14-16, 1864	143	17	2	112	2	10
20	Morton's Ford, VA	Feb 6, 1864	109	5	3	84	2	15
21	Peach Tree Creek, GA	Jul 19-20, 1864	108	21	0	85	0	2
22	Wilderness, VA	May 6-12, 1864	81	14	4	63	0	0
23	Kell House, VA	Oct 27, 1864	80	14	0	66	0	0
24	Fort Gregg, VA	Apr 2, 1865	79	13	0	66	0	0
25	James Island, SC	Jun 16, 1862	77	11	0	64	0	2
26	Walthall Junction, VA	May 7-9, 1864	71	1	1	63	3	3
27	Deep Bottom, VA	Aug 14-16, 1864	68	10	2	52	0	4
28	Bull Run, VA	Jul 21, 1861	66	4	1	24	4	33
29	Pocotaligo, SC	Oct 22, 1864	65	7	0	58	0	0
30	Darbytown Road, VA	Oct 13, 1864	64	9	1	49	2	3
31	Resaca, GA	May 15, 1864	63	8	0	55	0	0
32	Bristoe, Station, VA	Oct 13-15, 1863	62	12	0	18	0	32
33	New Market, VA	May 15, 1864	60	2	1	30	5	22
	Fort Harrison, VA	Sep 29, 1864	60	9	1	46	0	4
	Olustee, FL	Feb 20-23, 1864	60	6	0	35	6	13
34	Roanoke Island, NC	Feb 8, 1862	56	4	0	52	0	0
35	New Bern, NC	Mar 14, 1862	52	13	0	39	0	0
36	Spottsylvania, VA	May 6-18, 1864	51	4	1	36	0	9
37	Ream's Station, VA	Jun 29, 1864	49	3	3	8	2	33
38	Ream's Station, VA	Aug 25, 1864	47	6	1	18	2	20
39	Craig's Church, VA	May 5, 1864	43	0	0	5	0	38
40	Welaka, FL	May 19, 1864	42	0	0	1	0	41
	Morris Island, SC	Jul 1- Oct 14, 1863	42	3	0	36	1	2
41	Ashland, VA	Jun 1, 1864	41	4	0	13	5	19
42	Chaffin's Farm, VA	Sep 29- Oct 1, 1864	40	1	0	38	0	1
43	Bentonville, NC	Mar 19, 1865	39	4	0	32	0	3
44	Dunn's Lake, FLA	Feb 4-5, 1865	36	1	0	0	1	34
45	Snicker's Ford, VA	Jul 18, 1864	34	6	0	27	0	1
	Pattersonville, LA	Mar 27-29, 1863	34	0	0	2	1	31
46	Cedar Run Church, VA	Oct 17, 1864	33	1	0	3	1	28
47	Brashear City, LA	Jun 21-26, 1863	31	6	0	4	0	21
48	Boydton Plank Road, VA	Oct 27, 1864	27	1	1	13	1	10
49	Bolivar Heights, VA	Jul 14, 1863	26	0	0	0	1	25
50	Dallas, GA	May 25-27, 1864	25	1	2	22	0	0
	Cane River, LA	Apr 23, 1864	25	2	0	23	0	0

ABBREVIATIONS

K = KILLED   M = MISSING

W = WOUNDED   WC = WOUNDED & CAPTURED

C = CAPTURED

CONNECTICUT CASUALTIES RANKED BY TOTAL AND DATE

Connecticut suffered over 11,000 casualties in 220 different places on over 1200 different days during the war. The top 50 dates are listed below.

RANK	DATE	TOTAL	K	M	W	W/C	C
1	September 17, 1862	686	131	2	514	19	20
2	June, 15, 1863	595	23	0	11	41	520
3	May 3, 1863	577	36	1	138	29	372
4	May 16, 1864	560	52	3	224	38	243
5	March 8, 1865	496	22	3	12	49	410
6	April 20, 1864	433	1	2	0	12	418
7	October 19, 1864	417	48	2	204	10	153
8	June 1, 1864	374	89	10	246	6	23
9	September 19, 1864	279	38	0	209	0	32
10	December 13, 1862	253	40	5	200	2	6
11	June 14, 1863	217	32	0	179	1	5
12	June 3, 1863	196	24	2	168	0	2
13	August 9, 1862	175	35	0	74	8	58
14	June 5, 1864	166	22	1	89	25	29
15	August 16, 1864	163	18	4	125	2	14
16	July 1, 1863	157	18	4	70	8	57
17	April 14, 1863	147	18	0	120	0	9
18	May 27, 1863	145	13	0	132	0	0
19	May 15, 1864	143	14	1	100	5	23
20	July 18, 1863	141	18	9	84	7	23
21	October 27, 1864	130	18	1	94	1	16
22	May 2, 1863	121	8	0	30	21	62
23	June 2, 1864	118	9	0	39	7	63
24	July 30, 1864	118	26	14	70	3	5
25	July 20, 1864	116	23	0	91	0	2
26	September 29, 1864	114	12	1	94	0	7
27	April 2, 1865	113	14	1	97	0	1
27	July 3, 1863	112	14	1	92	0	5
28	February 6, 1864	109	5	3	84	2	15
29	July 11, 1863	108	19	0	29	15	45
29	July 2, 1863	108	14	2	55	1	36
30	December 14, 1862	104	15	0	89	0	0
31	May 14, 1864	85	13	0	69	0	3
32	May 7, 1864	80	4	1	69	3	3
33	October 13, 1864	79	11	1	62	2	3
34	June 16, 1862	78	11	0	64	0	3
35	June 18, 1864	77	7	1	53	0	16
35	May 6, 1864	77	12	3	55	1	6
36	June 17, 1864	68	11	1	28	0	28
37	July 21, 1861	66	4	1	24	4	33
38	October 14, 1863	65	13	0	19	0	33
38	October 22, 1862	65	7	0	58	0	0
39	May 25, 1862	64	1	0	10	3	50
40	May 10, 1864	60	5	0	55	0	0
40	May 5, 1864	60	4	0	11	1	44
41	August 25, 1864	58	6	1	26	2	23
42	June 29, 1864	56	3	3	12	3	35
42	February 20, 1864	56	6	0	32	6	12
42	February 8, 1862	56	4	0	52	0	0
43	March 14, 1862	53	13	0	40	0	0
44	March 25, 1865	51	10	0	31	0	10
45	May 19, 1864	49	1	0	7	0	41
46	August 14, 1864	45	7	0	38	0	0
47	February 5, 1865	43	2	0	5	1	35
48	May 20, 1864	42	3	0	34	0	5
48	May 12, 1864	42	6	2	26	0	8
49	June 22, 1864	41	9	0	26	1	5
49	March 19, 1865	41	4	0	33	0	4
50	July 18, 1864	37	6	0	30	0	1

TOTAL ENLISTMENTS CREDITED TO TOWNS IN CONNECTICUT VOLUNTEER ORGANIZATIONS

There were 39,395 men who served from 400 different American towns. They came from every incorporated Connecticut town plus 19 other states and the District of Columbia. 4,184 (11%) men served in more than one military organization. 218 men served in three and only 2 men served in four.

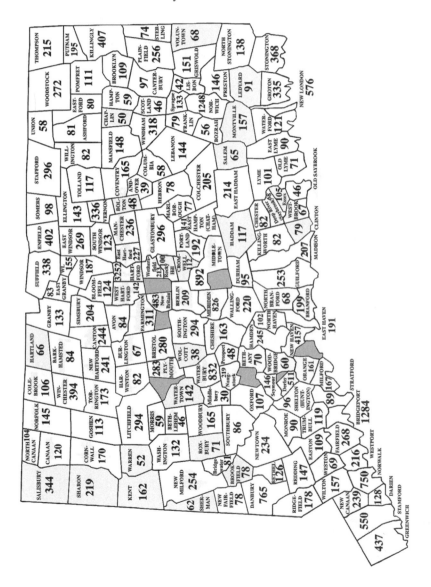

THE CONNECTICUT
VOLUNTEER ORGANIZATIONS

FIRST REGIMENT
CONNECTICUT VOLUNTEER INFANTRY
APRIL 23, 1861 - JULY 31, 1861
(THREE MONTHS)
820 RECRUITS
7 WOUNDED, 6 CAPTURED

USAMHI

Daniel Tyler of Norwich, the only professional soldier in the first three month regiments, was appointed Colonel of the 1st Connecticut Infantry. After reaching Washington, DC, he was appointed Brigadier General of Volunteers and commanded the First Division at the Battle of Bull Run on July 21, 1861

The 1st Regiment Connecticut Volunteer Infantry was recruited under the proclamation of President Abraham Lincoln issued on Monday, April 15, 1861 and from the call of Governor William Buckingham the following day.

Rifle Company A of Hartford, with George S. Burnham as Captain and Joseph R. Hawley as 1st Lieutenant, was the first company to complete its organization with full ranks. This company and Infantry Company A, also from Hartford, commanded by Captain John C. Comstock, left for NEW HAVEN on April 20. A regiment was quickly organized with Daniel Tyler of Norwich, as Colonel, George S. Burnham of Hart-ford, as Lieutenant Colonel, and John L. Chatfield of Waterbury, as Major.

The 1st Connecticut Infantry was well armed and equipped. Eight of the companies were issued Springfield rifles and the two flank companies were armed with Sharps. Many of the uniforms however, were inferior, although all possible effort was made to remedy the defects. A few of the companies were old militia organizations who preferred their old regimental letters. This led to some confusion in identifying the companies.

The regiment was at first housed in buildings at Yale University. However, all the men soon went into camp on a vacant lot in the western part of the town.

The 1st Connecticut Infantry was mustered into United States service on April 23, 1861.

On May 10, the regiment left New Haven on the steamer *Bienville* for

WASHINGTON, DC

On that same day, Colonel Tyler, who was a West Point graduate and who had been in the regular army, was made Brigadier General of Volunteers. Lieutenant Colonel Burnham was promoted to the position of Colonel of the regiment, John Chatfield was promoted to Lieutenant Colonel and John Speidel of Bridgeport, to Major.

The 1st Connecticut Infantry arrived in Washington, on May 13, by way of the Chesapeake Bay and the Potomac River. They went at once to camp on the grounds of the Corcoran estate at Glenwood, situated about two miles north of the Capitol.

On May 31, Lieutenant Colonel Chatfield was promoted to Colonel of the 3rd Connecticut Infantry after Colonel John Arnold of New Haven, had resigned. Major Spiedel was made Lieutenant Colonel of the 1st Infantry and Captain Theodore Byxbee of Meriden, was promoted to Major.

There were many days of intense excitement. On May 24, Washington was alarmed by a report that Confederate troops were near. The long roll was sounded, and the 1st Connecticut Infantry, along with its brigade, was ordered out and marched to the Long Bridge. When the alarm subsided the regiment was ordered back to camp. At midnight, on June 1, the regiment broke camp at Glenwood and crossed the Long Bridge into

VIRGINIA

They marched to Roach's Mills located on the Alexandria and Leesburg Railroad, where they relieved the 12th New York Infantry and established a camp.

On June 16, a detachment of the 1st Connecticut Infantry, commanded by Colonel Burnham, was ordered up the rail line as an escort to Brig. General Tyler's scouting expedition. The train was made up of dilapidated cars and the couplings parted so frequently that the detachment was forced to return after passing a short distance beyond Vienna. As the train was passing Vienna on its return, it was ambushed and Private George H. Bugbee of Infantry Company A was severely wounded. The first Connecticut blood shed in the war, however, had happened at Big Bethel seven days earlier. This was, however, the first casualty in a Connecticut regiment.

The following day, the 1st Connecticut Infantry was relieved by the 1st and 2nd Ohio Infantry regiments. The regiment went back to the area of the Long Bridge where, with a large number of other regiments, were reviewed by Secretary of War Simon Cameron. As the review closed, the 1st Connecticut Infantry was ordered to the relief of the Ohio regiments who had come under fire at Falls Church. Their position was considerably in advance of the main Union lines. The Confederates could have easily reached the rear of the Ohio regiments by way of Balls or Bailey's Cross Roads.

On June 18, the 2nd Connecticut Infantry joined with the 1st and then later with the 3rd Connecticut Infantry and the 2nd Maine Infantry. They were organized as a brigade under the command of Colonel Erasmus D. Keyes, a regular army officer..

On July 16, the entire army, under the immediate command of Brig. General Irwin McDowell, began its advance toward

MANASSAS

The Keyes Brigade was designated the 1st Brigade, 1st Division and had the advanced position. The 1st Connecticut covered the right side. They slept the first night at Vienna, the second at Germantown, and arrived in Centreville on the third.

At midnight, on Saturday, July 20, 1861, the brigade advanced up the Warrenton Road toward

BULL RUN

stream. The 1st Connecticut Infanty was ordered to guard the road at Sudley Ford during the departure of the flanking column. The regiment remained in this position until about 10 AM, July 21, when fire from a Confederate artillery battery forced the regiment to move across the stone bridge spanning Bull Run. They formed a line of battle in an open field nearly half a mile west beyond Young's Branch.

The regiment soon met and drove back a force of Confederate cavalry and infantry. At several other encounters, at different parts of the line, the Confederates constantly retreated before them. The regiment advanced with the Keyes Brigade toward a Confederate battery posted near Henry House Hill. The 1st and 2nd Connecticut Infantry halted near the Robinson House while the 3rd Connecticut Infantry and 2nd Maine Infantry attempted to charge the battery. They had little success.

During this time, the regiment was unaware of what was happening on the other parts of the field. Things were not going well and they were ordered to re-cross Bull Run and retreat. A half-hour earlier the regiment had assumed that victory was theirs. The regiment had 5 wounded and 6 captured at the Battle of Bull Run.

Before nightfall, the entire brigade reached its former campground at Centreville. At 10PM, orders came to continue the retreat to Falls Church. The road was comparatively clear as the disorganized part of the Union army was already far on its way to Washington. At about 9AM, the next day, July 22, the regiment arrived at Falls Church and, in a drenching rain, packed their tents and sent off their equipment together with that of the 2nd Maine Infantry.

The three Connecticut regiments marched to the deserted camp of the 1st and 2nd Ohio Infantry. They stayed there that night and spent all day Tuesday, July 23, in packing and sending to Alexandria the equipment of the Ohio regiments, leaving not a trace of anything useful that could fall into the hands of the Confederates.

The regiment remained in Washington until July 27 even though their term of service had expired five days earlier on July 22. The 1st Connecticut Infantry started for New Haven and arrived three days later on July 30.

The 1st Connecticut Volunteer Infantry was mustered out on July 31, 1861 after 3 months service. Nearly 180 men from the regiment eventually held officer commissions in other Connecticut volunteer organizations.

BATTLE OF BULL RUN
JULY 21, 1861
The First Connecticut Infantry fought near the Robinson House. It was here that they received severe fire from an eight gun Confederate battery strongly posted on Henry House Hill.

BATTLE AND LEADERS

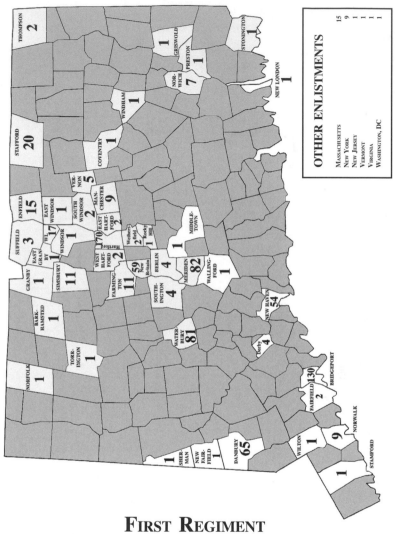

OTHER ENLISTMENTS

MASSACHUSETTS	15
NEW YORK	9
NEW JERSEY	1
VERMONT	1
VIRGINIA	1
WASHINGTON, DC	1

FIRST REGIMENT
CONNECTICUT VOLUNTEER
INFANTRY

FIRST REGIMENT

CONNECTICUT VOLUNTEER HEAVY ARTILLERY

MAY 23, 1861 - SEPTEMBER 25, 1865

(FOUR YEARS, FOUR MONTHS)

3,190 RECRUITS

35 KILLED, 1 MISSING, 192 DIED, 132 WOUNDED, 5 WOUNDED & CAPTURED, 29 CAPTURED

HISTORY OF THE FIRST REGIMENT HEAVY ARTILLERY

Robert O. Tyler of Hartford, was commissioned Colonel of the undisciplined 1st Connecticut Heavy Artillery in September 1861 and was credited with making the men of the regiment "true soldiers". He was eventually promoted to Brigadier General, then Major General of Volunteers in November 1862

The 1st Regiment Connecticut Volunteer Heavy Artillery was originally organized, in May 1861, as the

4TH CONNECTICUT VOLUNTEER INFANTRY

They formed in response to the first call (April 15, 1861) for three-month soldiers. Its companies gathered in

HARTFORD

expecting to be included among those accepted, but the State quota had already been filled.

On May 3, there was another call, this time for three-year men. The regiment was reorganized and was mustered into the United States service on May 22-23. It was the first three-year regiment in the State ready for field service.

Levi Woodhouse of Hartford was appointed Colonel, Nelson L. White of Danbury, was appointed Lieutenant Colonel, and P. L. Cunningham of Norwalk, was appointed Major.

Colonel Woodhouse had served in the Mexican War. Lieutenant Colonel White was a prominent Danbury lawyer and had been a Major in the 3rd Connecticut Infantry before being promoted to Lieutenant Colonel. Major Cunningham had no prior military service.

The regiment left Hartford on June 10 and arrived in Jersey City, New Jersey that evening. The following day they arrived in Philadelphia, and then went on to join Robert Patterson's command at

CHAMBERSBURG, PA

On June 12, the regiment was camped at Hagerstown, Maryland and was assigned to the 2nd Division (W. H. Keim) and 6th Brigade (J. J. Abercrombie) consisting of the 1 WS, 11 PA, and 2 MA. On June 17, the left wing of the regiment was detached to Williamsport to hold a ford on the Potomac River. They were relieved on August 9 and ordered to Frederick. The right wing of the regiment joined the left wing on August 17 and went into camp at White Oak Springs near Frederick.

Dissatisfaction among the men had been silently growing and it finally erupted into a crisis. The regiment had not been paid and their uniforms were so worn by three months service that hardly any two men had hats or shirts alike. Coats had long been discarded and many were forced to appear, even in dress parade, in simple under-clothing. So bitter was the discontent that on August 23, about 200 men marched out with their arms, formed in line, and facing the camp announced that they were going home. Colonel Woodhouse directed the senior captain to arrest them and shoot them if necessary.

All ended peacefully with the ringleaders being arrested. Active resistance was quelled but discontent continued. Within a week there were 18 desertions. A week later came pay day.

On September 6, the regiment was ordered to report to Maj.Gen. Nathaniel

BANKS COMMAND AT DARNESTOWN, MARYLAND

where they were assigned to the 2nd Brigade (Abercrombie). On September 9, Colonel Woodhouse resigned because of poor health. Lieutenant Colonel White was placed in command until September 26 when Robert Tyler, a Hartford native and in the regular army, took over.

At this point there was little doubt that the men were undisciplined and poorly instructed and that the regiment was in need of a competent commander. With Colonel Tyler the men were turned into true soldiers. The regiment was ordered to

WASHINGTON, DC

and began the march on October 2. On the way, the State gray uniform was exchanged for the army blue. On October 7, they camped near the Capitol and on October 9 the regiment crossed the Potomac and went into camp for the winter. They worked on finishing and garrisoning Forts Richardson, Scott and Barnard.

On January 2, 1862, the organization of the regiment was changed to artillery. Two new companies, L and M, were formed and the recruits for the regiment arrived on March 15. The name of the regiment was changed from the 4th Connecticut Volunteer Infantry to 1st Connecticut Volunteer Heavy Artillery. The winter was spent in exhaustive study and drilling in artillery procedure and tactics.

On April 3, the regiment, with 1,400 men left for the

PENINSULA CAMPAIGN

in Virginia and arrived at Cheeseman's Landing near Yorktown on April 11. The regiment was detailed to serve the siege artillery train. The following was the assignment to batteries: Company B to No. 1 (two 200-pounder and five 100-pounder Parrotts); Companies A and H to No.2 (five 4½-inch ordnance guns and five 30-pounder Parrotts); Companies F and G to No.4 (ten 13-inch mortars); Company C to No.6 (six 10-inch mortars); Companies D and E to No.9 (ten 10-inch mortars); and Company I to No.10 (five 4½-inch ordnance guns).

From April 30 to May 3, Battery No.1 was in action firing 141 shots. The other batteries were ready to fire on May 4 but Yorktown was evacuated by the

Union force, before they went into action.

On May 20, ten companies from the 1st Heavy Artillery went with Colonel Tyler to White House Landing to serve as infantry. Companies L and M remained in batteries near Yorktown. The ten companies were assigned to a brigade in Syke's Division of the 5th Army Corps and were employed in scouting and destroying bridges across the Pamunkey River and at Hanover Court House. The regiment marched 42 miles in 37 hours in pursuit of Confederate General J.E.B. Stuart's cavalry after his raid in the rear of the Union army.

On June 2, a detachment from the regiment was ordered to supply deficiencies in the batteries. They performed active service during the Peninsula campaign and rejoined their regiment later.

On June 20, Colonel Tyler was ordered to bring up five 4½-inch guns and five 30-pounder Parrotts from White House Landing. On June 24, they were in position near New Bridge, under Major Elisha Kellogg. On June 25-26, they fired effectively and later moved across the

CHICKAHOMINY

to Golding's farm where they were re-enforced by two 10-pounder Whit-worths. They were heavily engaged on June 27 at

GAINES MILLS

and that night were withdrawn. The regiment pushed across White Oak Swamp and joined the rest of the artillery train under Captain Leverett G. Hemingway. He had two 8-inch howitzers, two 10-pounder Whitworths and nine heavy guns near Seven Pines and in the depot at Orchard Station.

The united artillery train was then moved to Turkey Bend. During the night of June 30, a part of the 1st Connecticut

Artillery placed, with great difficulty, five 4½-inch ordnance guns, five 30-pounder Parrorts, two 8-inch howitzers and two 10-pounder Whitworths in position on

MALVERN HILL

The guns were used in the battle of July 1. During the battle the men suffered from a rear fire from Union gunboats. Two men of the regiment were wounded, both mortally. During the following night the artillery train was retired to Westover Landing.

In the artillery attack upon Harrison's Landing on the night of August 1, three companies of the regiment replied promptly with fire from five 30-pounder Parrots and four 10-pounder Whitworths. The guns had been placed on the river bank to repel an expected attack from a Confederate ironclad.

Of the 26 heavy guns brought from Yorktown, 25 arrived safely at Harrison's Landing. At the end of the Peninsula campaign, the 1st Connecticut Heavy Artillery was authorized to place on its colors "Siege of Yorktown, Hanover Court House, Chickahominy, Gaines' Mills, and Malvern".

On August 12, the regiment left on ships for

ALEXANDRIA

Virginia where they were posted at Fort Scott and Fort Ward. Most of the regiment remained at the forts until 1864. On November 29, 1862, Colonel Tyler was promoted to Brigadier General of Volunteers. He was succeeded by Henry L. Abbot. Except when the depot of the Army of the Potomac at Alexandria was threatened by raiding parties in the Gettysburg campaign, the regiment was mostly inactive until December.

On December 5, 1862, Major Thomas Trumbull of Hartford, with

Companies B and M were detached with seven 4½-inch guns for duty at Fredericksburg. They fired 357 rounds in the Battle of

FREDERICKSBURG

Afterward, the companies joined the Artillery Reserve of the Army of the Potomac at Falmouth where they were equipped as light artillery batteries of four 4½-inch siege guns.

Companies B and M followed the movements of the army during 1863, marching more than 500 miles. Company B was engaged at Fredericksburg in June with a 100-pounder Parrot and at Wolf Run Shoals on November 30, 1863. Company M was engaged at Fredericksburg from April-June, at Kelly's Ford, and at Mine Run. The use of such heavy guns with a marching army was an experiment. They were never allowed to fall behind. The companies rejoined the regiment in April 1864.

On April 20, 1864, Colonel Abbot was ordered to organize a large siege artillery train. The regiment was ordered to report for temporary duty as infantry to Maj. Gen. Benjamin Butler's

ARMY OF THE JAMES

who were advancing from Bermuda Hundred toward Richmond. The regiment arrived on May 13 with 1,700 men and reinforced the 85th Pennsylvania who was holding the line against an expected attack from the direction of Petersburg. On May 16, the Army of the James fell back to the earthworks at Bermuda Hundred and the 1st Connecticut Artillery was placed in charge of its 17 siege guns.

During the next month they fired 25 tons or 1,971 rounds. On May 20, the regiment went into action when a demonstration was made against their position. On May 23, an incident occurred involving six soldiers returning

from veteran furlough. They were passing Wilson's Landing in a boat when an attack was made upon a small force stationed there. The boat landed and the six men manned an abandoned 10-pounder Parrot until the Confederates were repelled. On June 2, Company I, stationed in the advanced redoubt Dutton, repulsed an assault by the 22nd South Carolina. On June 21, the regiment open fired at Confederate rams who had engaged the land batteries and the Union Fleet in the James River.

On June 23, the regular artillery train arrived from Washington and the

SIEGE OF PETERSBURG

began in earnest. During these operations, the siege artillery train was organized as a separate brigade under Colonel Abbot. The train contained 3,500 men, 127 guns and 73 mortars. The line of batteries was 17 miles long. Over 1,200 tons of ammunition (63,940 rounds) were hauled by wagon an average distance of seven miles to be fired during the siege.

The artillery depot was at Broadway Landing on the Appomattox River and the wharves and earthworks had to be built. The guns not in use were kept on twenty schooners and barges. They were moved to land by a steam tug and pulled to the firing line by over 50 wagons. Four light artillery teams of the 1st Pennsylvania Artillery moved the guns.

The first siege operations ended in the

BATTLE OF THE CRATER

on July 30, 1864. On this occasion, the 1st Connecticut Artillery and 4th New York Artillery manned 81 guns and mortars. About 75 tons (3,833 rounds) were fired in the battle and 225 tons (12,229 rounds) were fired in the lead up to the battle. The battle was probably the first in which spherical case shot was used from mortars. The novel use of putting thirty, 12-pound canister shot under the bursting charge of a 10-inch shell proved very effective.

Immediately after the battle, the movement of the Army of the Potomac required that 52 heavy guns and mortars and all the ammunition be quickly moved a distance of eight miles from the fronts of the 5th, 9th, and 18th Corps to the artillery depot. This was accomplished in 27 hours with twenty-two light artillery mule teams and 170 wagons. The total weight moved was 225 tons. The Confederates did not discover the movement.

The Siege of Petersburg now took the form of bombardment. From August 1864 to February 1865, 793 tons (37,264 rounds) were fired from the Union batteries. Sudden artillery battles occurred at all hours of the day and night and often involved the entire line. To stop the Confederate fire from the left bank of the the Appomattox River, a 13-inch seacoast mortar was mounted on a railroad platform car. This novelty was widely known as the "Petersburg Express" or the "Dictator". There was also much firing at the

DUTCH GAP CANAL

At the canal, Company C fired about 4,000 shots. On October 21, the company surprised the Confederate fleet lying in Graveyard Bend on the James River. Three 30-pounder and four 20-pounder Parrotts were placed in position at night and they opened fired at daylight at a range of 1,500 yards. A gun carriage was struck on the gunboat *Drewry* and the ironclad *Virginia* was struck seven times. The ironclad *Richmond* was struck more frequently with her smokestack being shot away. The ironclad *Fredericksburg* fared still worse.

On January 23, 1865, the Confederate fleet made a determined attempt to pass down the James River to destroy the Union base at City Point. The only Union monitor present withdrew and left the defense to the four land batteries unsupported. The 1st Connecticut Artillery posted one company in each of the batteries. The fire from the Confederate land batteries was very heavy but it did not divert attention from the Union fire on the Confederate fleet. The gunboat *Drewry* was sunk and the torpedo launch *Wasp* was destroyed before the fleet retreated.

Three companies of the 1st Connecticut Artillery, under Henry Abbot, accompanied Alfred Terry's expedition to Fort Fisher, North Carolina in January 1865. The fort was stormed before the artillery train could be landed and the detachment returned to the lines before Richmond.

The assault on Confederate

FORT STEDMAN

on March 25, was the next notable incident in the history of the regiment. The fort was 200 yards from the Confederate lines and Union Brig. Gen. George H. Gordon's columns poured over the parapet at 4 AM. The heavy guns brought to bear were manned by the 1st Connecticut Artillery and the light batteries. They delivered such a heavy fire that the Confederates were driven into their bombproof and the fort was finally captured about 8AM. Company L joined the charge and captured 13 prisoners of the 26th Georgia with their battle flag. A Medal of Honor was awarded to Private G. E. McDonald.

On April 2, the final assault was made upon the Confederate works. The 1st Connecticut Artillery occupied eleven forts and batteries and manned 49 guns and mortars, firing 4,257 rounds. A special detail of 100 men from five companies armed with muskets and equipped with lanyards, fuses, and primers joined the assaulting column near Battery No.20 and entered the Confederate works. They immediately reversed four captured light 12-pounder guns and opened fired on the retreating Confederates, almost before they were out of the works. These guns and two others were moved across the battery under a line of fire, where they were manned by the detachment, firing over 800 rounds during day and night. The men not required at the guns, using their muskets, captured about 15 prisoners in different assaults on their position.

Before daylight on April 3, the Confederates evacuated their lines and for the 1st Connecticut Artillery the war ended.

The removal of the artillery train and the captured ordnance, which consisted of 176 guns and mortars, consumed their time until July 13 when the regiment was transferred to the Defenses of Washington.

On September 25, the regiment was mustered out of service. They left for Connecticut and were finally discharged on October 1, 1865.

LIBRARY OF CONGRESS

FORT BRADY
CO. C AT A BATTERY OF 30-POUNDER PARROTT GUNS NEAR PETERSBURG, VA IN OCTOBER 1864

TOTAL CASUALTIES 1ST HEAVY ARTILLERY

DATE	PLACE OF CASUALTY	TOTAL	K	M	W	W/C	C
1861							
May 15	New Haven, CT	1			1		
June 28, July 4	FT. Richardson, VA	2			2		
June 12	Rail Road Accident	1	1				
June 15, July 3	Williamsport, MD	2			1		1
June 17, August 1	Hagerstown, MD	3			3		
July 26	Harper's Ferry, WVA	1			1		
August 17	Silver Spring, MD	1			1		
1862							
April 1	FT. Richardson, VA	1			1		
April 15	Arlington Heights, VA	1			1		
May 1, 18	Yorktown, VA	2			2		
May 24	Old Church, VA	1			1		
June 1	Malvern Hill, Va	1			1		
June 15	Williamsport, VA	1					1
June 20, 27,29	Gaines Mills, VA	4	1			1	2
June 23, 27, 28	**Cold Harbor, VA**	**12**				**1**	**11**
June 25	Chickahominy, VA	1			1		
June 27	Unknown	2					2
June 27	Goldings Farm, VA	2	1				1
June 28	Richmond, VA	2			1	1	
June 29	Unknown	1					1
June 30	Savage Station, VA	1					1
July 1	Malvern Hill, VA	4			2	1	1
July 1	Haxall's Landing, VA	1				1	
July 15	Richmond, VA	1		1			
1863							
January 9	Rappahannock, VA (Drowned)	1	1				
January 29	Rail Road Accident	1	1				
March 2	Alexandria, VA	1	1				
April 1	Fredericksburg, VA	1			1		
November 20	Arlington Heights, VA	1			1		
November 30	Mine Run, VA	1			1		
December 18	Culpeper Court House, VA	1			1		
1864							
January 25	Ball's Cross Roads, VA	1			1		
March 5,9	Petersburg, VA	2	1		1		
May 1	Bermuda Hundred, VA	1			1		
May 10	Petersburg, VA	1			1		
May 18, 20,24, 30	Bermuda Hundred, VA	5	3		2		
June 2,18,27,30	**Petersburg, VA**	**11**			**11**		
June 1	Point of Rocks, VA	1			1		
June 9	Bermuda Hundred, VA	1	1				
July 1,2,5, 6,9,10,12,15,19,20	**Petersburg, VA**	**16**	**3**		**13**		
July 23	Battery Stevenson, VA	1			1		
July 23,24	Petersburg, VA	8	1		7		
July 29	FT Dutton, VA	1			1		
July 30	Petersburg, VA	3	1		2		
August 1,2,5,6	Petersburg, VA	5			5		
August 13	Dutch Gap, VA	1			1		
August 16	Petersburg, VA	2			2		
August 16	Deep Bottom, VA	1	1				
August 17	Battery Morton, VA	1	1				
August 17,18,19,24	Petersburg, VA	5			5		
August 29	James River, VA	1	1				
August 29	Petersburg, VA	1			1		

DATE	PLACE OF CASUALTY	TOTAL	K	M	W	W/C	C
August 31	Dutch Gap, VA	1			1		
September 9,12,19,20,23,29	Petersburg, VA	6	2		4		
September 17	Antietam, MD	1			1		
September 19	Winchester, VA	1			1		
October 3,4	Petersburg, VA	2			2		
October 12	Battery Morton, VA	1			1		
October 15	Petersburg, VA	1			1		
October 24	Battery Morton, VA	1			1		
October 24	Dutch Gap, VA	1	1				
October 24	Petersburg, VA	1			1		
November 2,4,5	Petersburg, VA	4	3		1		
November 26	Battery Morton, VA	2			2		
November 27,28	Petersburg, VA	2			2		
December 16	Battery Anderson, VA	1			1		
December 17	Petersburg, VA	1			1		
1865							
January 1	FT. Brady, VA	1			1		
January 16	Petersburg, VA	1	1				
March 5,15	Petersburg, VA	4			2		
March 25	FT. Stedman, VA	3					3
March 25	**Petersburg, VA**	**24**	**6**		**12**		**6**
March 25	Petersburg VA	1					1
March 28	Petersburg, VA	3	1		2		
March 29	Petersburg, VA	2			2		
March 30	Petersburg, VA	1			1		
April 1	Richmond, VA	6			1		5
April 2	FT. Mahone, VA	1			1		
April 2	Battery Anderson, VA	1			1		
April 2,3	Petersburg, VA	7	1		6		
May 3	James River, VA (Drowned)	1	1				
June 1	Richmond, VA	1	1		1		

LIBRARY OF CONGRESS

CONGRESSIONAL MEDAL OF HONOR WINNER

Private George E. McDonald, Company L, 1st Connecticut Heavy Artillery
Place and Date: At Fort Stedman, Va., 25 March 1865
Date of Issue: 21 July 1865
Citation: Capture of flag

TROOP MOVEMENTS 1ST HEAVY ARTILLERY

DATE	PLACE
1861	
June 10	Left State for Chambersburg, PA
Until July 4	Duty at Chambersburg & Hagerstown, MD
Until August 16	Duty at Williamsport, MD
September 5	Duty at Frederick, MD
September 6	Duty at Darnestown, MD
October 2	Moved to Washington, DC
Until April 1862	Defenses of Washington (FT. Richardson)
1862	
April 2	Ordered to Peninsula, VA
April 12-May 4	Siege of Yorktown
May 27	Battle of Hanover Court House
May 27-29	Operations about Hanover Court House
June 25-Julu 1	Seven days before Richmond
June 27	Gaines Mill
July 1	Malvern Hill
Until August 15	At Harrison's Landing
August 16-27	Moved to Alexandria
Until May 1864	Defenses of Washington, DC
December 12-15	Co. B/M Detached for Battle of Fredericksburg, VA
April 27-May 6 1863	Chancellorsville Campaign (Co. B. & M)
1863	
May 1-5	Battle of Chancellorsville, VA (Co. B & M)
June 12	Stafford Heights (Co. B & M)
July 1-3	Battle of Gettsyburg (Co. B & M)
October 9-22	Bristoe Campaign (Co. B & M)
November 7-8	Advance to line of the Rappahannock (Co. B & M)
November 8	Brandy Station (Co. B & M)
November 26-December 2	Mine Run Campaign (Co. B & M)

TROOP MOVEMENTS 1ST HEAVY ARTILLERY

DATE	PLACE
1864	
January	Co. B & M joined regiment at Washington, DC
May 13	Regiment ordered to Bermuda Hundred
May-April 1865	Siege of Petersburg
June 2, 21	Assault on Fort Dutton (Co. L)
May 18-21,25,27,30,31, June 1,2,5,9,18,20,23	Attacks on lines
July 30	Mine explosion, Petersburg
November 17,18, 28	Attacks on lines
1865	
January 23-24	Repulse of Confederate fleet on James River
January 3-15	Expedition to FT. Fisher, NC (Co. B,G,L)
January 15	Capture of Fort Fisher (Co. B, G, L)
April2	Assault and fall of Petersburg
July 11	Duty in Dept. of Virginia
Until September	Moved to Washington, DC
September 25	Mustered out

CHEESEMAN'S LANDING

CO. D MANNING BATTERY 4 OF 13-INCH SEACOAST MORTARS
NEAR YORKTOWN, VIRGINIA IN APRIL 1862

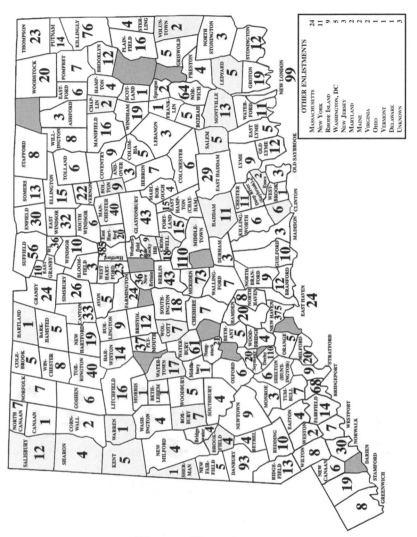

FIRST REGIMENT
CONNECTICUT VOLUNTEER HEAVY ARTILLERY

FIRST REGIMENT
CONNECTICUT VOLUNTEER CAVALRY
OCTOBER 26, 1861 - AUGUST 18, 1865
(THREE YEARS, NINE MONTHS)
1,833 RECRUITS
30 KILLED, 10 MISSING, 163 DIED, 98 WOUNDED,
286 CAPTURED, 16 WOUNDED & CAPTURED

USAMHI

Judson M. Lyon of Woodstock commanded the 1st Connecticut Cavalry in the days before its organization as a regiment when it was a battalion of four companies. He resigned in April 1862

The 1st Regiment Connecticut Volunteer Cavalry was originally organized as a battalion of four companies, with one company coming from each congressional district in the State. The call for volunteers was issued on October 1, 1861 and on the 23rd they assembled at Camp Tyler, **WEST MERIDEN** with full ranks. The Battalion remained in camp until February 20, 1862 when, under the command of Major Judson M. Lyon of Woodstock, they moved to Wheeling

WEST VIRGINIA

arriving there on the 24th. On March 27, they were assigned to the brigade of Brig. General Robert C. Schenck and were ordered to Moorefield, West Virginia to fight Confederate guerillas.

In early May, the brigade moved up the

SHENANDOAH VALLEY and on May 8 was at the Battle of

McDowell

The Battalion covered the rear of the Union army as it fell back.

They repelled an attack by Turner Ashby's cavalry near Franklin on May 11. Confederate General Stonewall Jackson had driven the Union forces under Maj. General Nathaniel Banks from Strasburg and Union Maj. General John C. Fremont hurried to intercept Jackson. The Battalion led Fremont's advance over the mountains.

At daylight on May 30, they met and pushed back the Confederate cavalry at Wardensville. On June 1, the Battalion overtook and charged Jackson's rear at Strasburg.

In the Union Army's pursuit of Jackson up the Shenandoah, the 1st Connecticut Cavalry was constantly in the advance. They joined in the cavalry fight near

Harrisonburg

on June 6, where Confederate General Ashby was killed and were at Fremont's battle at

CROSS KEYS

two days later. On June 9, they made a dash to save the brigade from a Confederate attack at

Port Republic

but were too late. The Union army retired down the Shenandoah and on July 10 they crossed the mountains at Sperryville. At about this time, Major Lyon resigned and Captain Louis Middlebrook, from Bridgeport, assumed command of the Battalion.

The Battalion was next assigned to Maj. General Franz Sigel's Corps. They arrived at Cedar Mountain, Virginia on August 9, 1962 just as the battle raged, and after the Union defeat they joined in the pursuit of Jackson to the Rapidan River. With its brigade, under Colonel John Beardsley of the 9th New York Cavalry, the Battalion fought through Maj. Gen. John Pope's disastrous

BULL RUN CAMPAIGN

and helped to cover the shattered fragments of his army on its retreat. The Battalion was now badly used up and to a large extent without horses. They remained with

SIGEL'S CORPS

in camp near Washington, DC for three months. During this time, the Battalion received about 100 new recruits and was entirely refitted and remounted. In December 1862, they moved with the corps to

Stafford Court House

where they stayed for a month on scouting and picketing duty. The Battalion then was assigned to provost duty and was eventually brought up to regimental strength.

During this period, the headquarters of the Battalion was at Camp Cheesebrough,

Baltimore

Maryland. Major William Fish of Stonington, was the provost marshal. Large details of the men were constantly on provost duty in the city and on provost and scouting expeditions to various parts of Maryland. Captain Charles Farnsworth of Norwich, had charge of the camp. The men rebuilt the barracks and erected officers quarters, paved the company streets with brick, and graded and turfed the ground between. They built barns, a hospital, and a chapel. On July 5, 1863 Captain Farnsworth was ordered with 180 men to Harper's Ferry, West Virginia, which was occupied by the Confederates. On July 14, he attacked a group of 200 Confederate pickets with 49 men on

BOLIVAR HEIGHTS

The captain's horse was disabled and he was captured along with more than half his men.

In August, the Battalion took part in an expedition under Colonel F. L. Vinton of the 6th Michigan, that was surprised in camp and driven off at night near

WATERFORD

Virginia. Later, the 1st Connecticut Cavalry, under Lieutenant Joab Rogers, surprised a Confederate camp in the same region and captured a large number of prisoners. Afterward, along with other troops, they made two expeditions to Winchester. One expedition in November lasted 15 days and skirmished with the Confederates near Harrisonburg.

Meanwhile, large additions of new recruits were being added to the regiment. In January 1864 its ranks were full and Major Erastus Blakeslee, who had been on recruiting service for some time, was ordered to Baltimore to assume command. The detachment at Harper's Ferry was sent back and the new recruits were put under rigid drill. The regiment was mounted and fully equipped on March 8 and with 675 strong moved to join the

ARMY OF THE POTOMAC

They arrived at Stevensburg, Virginia on March 24, 1864 and were assigned to the First Brigade, Third Division,

CAVALRY CORPS

Army of the Potomac where they served until the end of the war. During the summer of 1864, General J. H. Wilson commanded the division and General J. B. McIntosh the brigade.

On May 4, the Union army crossed the Rapidan River. The next morning the 1st Connecticut Cavalry, as advance guard, met Longstreet's advance at

CRAIG'S CHURCH

opening the Wilderness battles on the Union left. Major George Marcy with about 200 men was on a scouting expedition when he was cut off from the Union lines. As the only chance of escape, he ordered sabers drawn and charged through the Confederates. There were 40 Connecticut men lost in this engagement. The Union division fell slowly back to

TODD'S TAVERN

with the 1st Connecticut Cavalry covering the rear. The division made a stand and stopped the Confederates. When the terrific, two day infantry fighting ended, the 1st Connecticut Cavalry led the advance in Grant's movement toward

SPOTTSYLVANIA COURT HOUSE

Early in the morning of May 6, the 1st Connecticut charged into the town, drove the Confederates out and captured 35 prisoners. But support failed to come up, so the Union division withdrew. That night, the regiment received Spencer and Sharps carbines to replace their Smith carbines.

At daybreak of May 9, the cavalry started on

SHERIDAN'S RAID TO RICHMOND

Confederate General J.E.B. Stuart followed and engaged the Union cavalry at

BEAVER DAM STATION

on May 10 and the next day, at

YELLOW TAVERN

General Stuart was killed. On May 12, the corps, with the 1st Connecticut in the extreme advance near Richmond, fought all day within the defenses of the city. That night, the Union cavalry withdrew across Meadow Bridge. On the 15th, the 1st Connecticut Cavalry met the supply steamers at Haxall's Landing on the James River and then rejoined the army at

HANOVER COURT HOUSE

on the 25th. The 1st Connecticut Cavalry lost about 150 horses in the raid. At dusk on May 31, 1864, the brigade charged on foot up a steep slope and drove the Confederates at all points. The 1st Connecticut Cavalry had been on the skirmish line away from their horses nearly all day and stayed there all night. The next day at

ASHLAND

while in the woods, the brigade was surprised by an attack on its rear. The 1st Connecticut had orders to support Fitz Hugh's mounted battery and was the only force between the battery and Confederate General W.H.F. Lee's cavalry division. The Confederates charged furiously on the brigade pack train in the rear of the 1st Connecticut causing the horses and mules to stampede through the regiment. The regiment quickly rallied and stopped the Confederates after having lost about 20% of its men. Lieutenant Colonel Blakeslee was wounded and Major Marcy assumed command.

The division was now on the extreme right of the army and remained on duty as rear guard during Grant's hazardous movement across the James River. On June 17, the worn out division crossed the James River at 1 AM. On the 22nd, they started on a

RAID AGAINST THE SOUTH SIDE RAILROAD

Without rest, the regiment marched for 24 hours to Ford's Station, fourteen miles west of Petersburg, and tore up the railroad track. A few miles west, at Nottoway Court House, heavy fighting occurred while the 1st Connecticut Cavalry was tearing up the track toward Danville. An attempt to destroy the great bridge across the Staunton River at Roanoke Station failed and a detachment from the 1st Connecticut Cavalry was called to burn it. The order was eventually revoked. The retreat to Stony Creek on the Weldon Railroad now began. The 1st Connecticut distinguished itself in the unsuccessful attempt to break through the Confederate lines. They then covered the rear in a perilous withdrawal to

REAM'S STATION

The Confederates were met in force on June 29. The command was in great danger and a detachment from the 1st Connecticut and 3rd New York Cavalry, dashed though the Confederate lines to reach headquarters but it was too late. The Union command had left its ambulances, spiked its guns and retreated in great haste. The Confederates pressed on every side and turned the retreat into a rout. The 1st Connecticut Cavalry was the first regiment to make a stand against the Confederates. It formed a line, rallied the stragglers, and held the Confederates back while covering the retreat of the rest of the division. This desperate rear guard action continued all night and cost the 1st Connecticut over 60 men.

The command re-crossed the Nottoway River and with a detour of 100 miles reached

PETERSBURG

on July 2. The 300 mile expedition had lasted ten days, destroyed 60 miles of railroad track, fought four battles and many skirmishes, and rested at no place for more than six hours. The regiment next went into camp for a month and was placed on picket duty in the rear of the Union army at Petersburg. The regiment with its division was then ordered to the

SHENANDOAH VALLEY

Colonel Blakeslee rejoined the regiment on route to Washington, DC where they were remounted, thoroughly refitted and were fully armed with Spencer carbines.

The campaign in the Shenandoah under Sheridan was a busy one. On August 16, 1864, the 1st Connecticut Cavalry, fighting dismounted, was cut off and almost surrounded by a large body of Confederate infantry. The regiment escaped disaster aided by darkness and a swamp, which hindered the Confederate column. On the 25th, the regiment fought at

KEARNEYSVILLE

On September 14, a squadron from the regiment helped to surround and capture the 8th South Carolina. Colonel Blakeslee, suffering the effects of wounds, left Major Marcy in command. The regiment opened the battle of

WINCHESTER

on September 19, 1864. They crossed the Opequan River at dawn and drove the Confederates back to their earthworks. The whole brigade, with the 1st Connecticut Cavalry in the center, charged up the slope and went over the breastworks and captured 100 prisoners. The brigade held its position until the infantry came up. They were ordered to charge the Confederate breastworks and were repelled. At sunset, the works were charged again and 5,000 Confederate prisoners were captured.

On April 9, 1865, Sheridan saw that the end was near. He had cut off the Confederate way of retreat and advanced for a grand final charge. A flag of truce appeared asking for a cessation of the hostilities. Soon after, the regiment was detailed to escort General Grant to receive Lee's surrender at

APPOMATTOX

The regiment next went to Danville and then marched back to

WASHINGTON, DC

took part in the grand review and stayed in the city performing provost duty until August 1865. A battalion of the 1st Connecticut Cavalry was sent to

GETTYSBURG

for the laying of the comer stone of the soldier's monument there on July 4, 1865.

When the regiment was mustered out, they were allowed to return to Connecticut mounted, a privilege granted to no other regiment in the service. The regiment was mustered out on August 18, 1865 in New Haven.

LIBRARY OF CONGRESS

CONGRESSIONAL MEDAL OF HONOR WINNERS

1st Lieutenant Aaron S. Lanfare, Company B, 1st Connecticut Cavalry
Place and Date: At Sailors Creek, Va., 6 April 1865
Date of Issue: 3 May 1865
Citation: Capture of flag of 11th Florida Infantry (C.S.A.).

Private Charles H. Marsh, Company D, 1st Connecticut Cavalry
Place and Date: At Back Creek Valley, Va., 31 July 1864
Date of Issue: 23 January 1865
Citation: Capture of flag and its bearer.

Captain Edwin M. Neville, Co. C, 1st Connecticut Cavalry
Place and Date: At Sailors Creek, Va., 6 April 1865
Date of Issue: 3 May 1865.
Citation: Capture of flag.

TOTAL CASUALTIES 1ST CAVALRY

DATE	PLACE OF CASUALTY	TOTAL	K	M	W	W/C	C
1862							
April 3	Moorefield, WVA	2			2		
May 8	McDowell, VA	3			1		2
May 11	Franklin, VA	1			1		
May 14	McDowell, VA	1					1
June 6	Harrisonburg, VA	1					1
June 6	MT. Jackson, VA	1			1		
June 8	Cross Keys, VA	8			1		7
June 12	Harrisonburg, VA	1					1
June 22	Moorefield, WVA	2					2
July 16	Sperryville, VA (Lightning)	1	1				
July 29	Madison C H, VA	2					2
August 6	Sperryville, VA	2			1		1
August 7	Gordonville, VA	1				1	
August 9	Cedar Mountain, VA	1			1		
August 9	Cedar Run, VA	2					2
August 30	Bull Run, VA	1			1		
1863							
January 3	Stafford Court House, VA	1	1				
March 20	Baltimore, MD (Thrown from Horse)	1	1				
June 20	Frederick, MD	3					3
July 1	Fairfax, VA	1			1		
July 14	**Bolivar Heights, VA**	**26**				**1**	**25**
August 7	**Waterford, VA**	**8**	**1**			**1**	**6**
October 13	Upperville, VA	1					1
1864							
January 15	Unknown	1		1			
January 24	Winchester, VA	1					1
March 29	Bristoe Station, VA	1					1
March 29	Grove Church, VA	5			4		1
April 1	Stevensburg, VA	1			1		
April 1	Grove Church, VA	1			1		
May 1	Grove Church, VA	1			1		
May 5	**Craig's Church, VA**	**43**			**5**	**1**	**37**
May 5	Mine Run, VA	1					1
May 5	Winchester, VA	1					1
May 10	Beaver Dam Station, VA	1			1		
May 12	Mechanicsville, VA	1					1
May 12	Meadow Bridge, VA	5			4		1
May 12	Spottsylvania, VA	1			1		
May 12	Cold Harbor, VA	1			1		
May 12	Strawberry Hill, VA	1	1				
May 13	Mechanicsville, VA	1					1
May 18	White House, VA	1					1
May 23	Gaines Mills, VA	1					1
May 23	White House, VA	1					1
May 27	Butler's Mills, VA	1					1
May 31	Hanover Court House, VA	2	1		1		
June 1	**Ashland, VA**	**40**	**4**		**12**	**6**	**18**
June 1	Winchester, VA	1					1
June 10	Ashland, VA	1					1
June 10	**Old Church Tavern, VA**	**11**	**1**		**2**		**8**
June 13	James City, VA	1					1
June 15	White Oak Swamp, VA	1					1
June 16	Savage Station, VA	1	1				
June 17	Bermuda Hundred, VA	1			1		

TOTAL CASUALTIES 1ST CAVALRY

DATE	PLACE OF CASUALTY	TOTAL	K	M	W	W/C	C
June 17	Little Shop, VA	1					1
June 18	Snicker's Gap, VA	1			1		
June 21	Ream's Station, VA	1		1			
June 23	Hungertown, VA	1					1
June 24	Notoway Court House, VA	1					1
June 25	Staunton, VA	1					1
June 26	Roanoke Station, VA	1					1
June 27,28,29,30	**Ream's Station, VA**	**53**	**3**	**3**	**10**	**2**	**35**
June 28, 29	Stony Creek, VA	7			2		5
June 29	Cold Harbor, VA	1				1	
June 30	Cabin Point, VA	1					1
July 1	Ream's Station,, VA	5					5
July 1	Andersonville, GA	1			1		
July 3	Winchester, VA	1					1
July 12	Rockville, MD	1			1		
July 17	Light House Point, VA	1			1		
July 28,29	Ream's Station, VA	2		1	1		
July 28	Unknown	1			1		
August 15	Berryville, VA	1					1
August 16, 18	Winchester, VA	2			1		1
August 24	Berryville, VA	1					1
August 25	Kearneyville, VA	1			1		
August 25	Shepardstown, VA	3			1		2
September 1,7,12	Berryville, VA	3					3
September 13	Winchester, VA	1	1				
September 19	Winchester, VA	3	1		2		
September 21	Luray Valley, VA	1					1
September 24	Front Royal, VA	3					3
September 25	Spring Valley, VA	1					1
September 25	New Market, VA	1					1
September 28	Waynesboro, VA	1					1
October 1	Unknown	1					1
October 5	Harrisonburg, VA	1					1
October 6	Bunker's Hill, VA	1			1		
October 12	Florence, SC	1			1		
October 17	**Cedar Run Church, VA**	**32**	**1**		**2**		**29**
October 19	Cedar Creek, VA	8			2		6
November 1	Cedar Creek, VA	1					1
November 4	Fisher's Hill, VA	1					1
November 7,10,12	**Cedar Creek, VA**	**30**	**1**		**5**		**24**
November 11	Unknown	1		1			
December 7	Charlestown, VA	1	1				
December 12	Cedar Creek, VA	1				1	
1865							
January 30	Winchester, VA	2					2
March 2	Unknown	1		1			
March 2	Waynesboro, VA	1					1
March 3	Columbia, VA	1				1	
March 8	Fisherville, VA	1					1
March 8	Railroad Accident	1	1				
March 9, 10	New Market, VA	4					4
March 11	Ashland, VA	1					1
March 12	Frederick Hall, VA	1					1
March 14, 15, 16	**Ashland, VA**	**15**	**1**	**1**			**13**
March 19	King Wilhelm Court House, VA	1					1
March 31	Dinwiddie Court House, VA	1			1		
April 1	Harper's Ferry, VA	1			1		
April 1	FT Gregg, VA	2	2				
April 1	Dinwiddie Court House, VA	1			1		
April 1	Five Forks, VA	3			3		
April 3	Farmville, VA	1			1		
April 6	Harper's Farm, VA	7	5		2		
April 6	Sailor's Creek, VA	1			1		
April 6	South Side Railroad, VA	1			1		
April 13	Unknown	1	1				
July 4	Gettysburg, PA	1			1		
Unknown	Unknown	4			4		

TROOP MOVEMENTS 1ST CAVALRY

DATE	PLACE
1862	
Until May 1862	Operations in Hardy County, WVA
April 3	Action at Moorefield, WVA
May 2-7	March to Milroy
May 8	McDowell, VA
May 10-12	Franklin
May 24	Strasburg
May 28	Wardensville
May 30	Raid to Shaver River
June 1	Strasburg
June 5	New Market
June 7	Harrisonburg
June 8	Cross Keys
June 9	Port Republic
June 10-July 28	Movement to Madison Court House
June 22-30	Scout from Strasburg (Co B)
Until August	Scouting near Madison CH
August 16-September 2	Pope's Campaign in Northern VA
August 27-30	Provost duty during battle of Bull Run
Until December	Duty at Tenallytown, Fairfax CH, Kalorama Heights and Hall's Farm
Until January 1863	March to Fredericksburg duty at Stafford CH
December 20-22	Kelly's Ford
Until March 1864	Moved to Baltimore, MD (CO A B C D)
1863	
July 5	Moved to Harper's Ferry, WVA until January 1864
August 8	Skirmish at Waterford, VA (Detachment)
October 18	Berryville
November 15-18	Expedition from Charlestown to New Market
1864	
January 27-February 7	Operations in Hampshire and Hardy Co, WVA
February 4	Moorefield, WVA (Detachment)
Until March	Regimental organization complete at Baltimore
March 8	Moved to Annapolis Junction
March 15	Moved to Brandy Station and joined Brigade
April 1	Rappahannock
May-June	Rapidan Campaign
May 5	Craig's Meeting House
May 5-6	Todd's Tavern
May 8	Alsop's Farm, Spottsylvania
May 9-24	Sheridan's raid to James River
May 9-10	North Anna River
May 11	Ground Squirrel Bridge and Yellow Tavern
May 12	Brook Church or fortifications of Richmond
May 12	Strawberry Hill
May 26	Demonstration on Little River
May 28-31	Line of Totopotomoy
May 31	Mechump's Creek and Hanover CH
June 1	Ashland
June 2	Totopotomoy and Gaines' Mills
June 3	Haw's Shop
June 3-12	Cold Harbor
June 11	Bethesda Chruch
June 13	St. Mary's Church
June 18	Cold Harbor
June 20-30	Wilson's raid on South Side and Danville RR
June 23	Black and White Station and Nottaway CH

TROOP MOVEMENTS 1ST CAVALRY

DATE	PLACE
June 25	Staunton Bridge or Roanoke Station
June 28-29	Sappony Church or Stony Creek
June 29	Ream's Station
Until August	Siege of Petersburg
August-December	Sheridan's Shenandoah Valley Campaign
August 17	Winchester
September 13	Abraham's Creek
September 19	Battle of Opequan (Winchester)
September 20	Near Cedarville
September 21	Front Royal Pike
September 22	Tom's Brook
October 8-9	"Woodstock Races"
October 10-13	Cedar Creek
October 17	Cedar Run Church
November 12	Newtown, Cedar Creek
November 22	Rude's Hill, near MT Jackson
December 19-22	Raid to Lacy Springs
December 21	Lacy Springs
1865	
February 4-6	Expedition from Winchester to Moorefield, WVA
February 27-March 25	Sheridan's Raid
March 2	Occupation of Staunton
March 2	Waynesboro
March 3	Charlottesville
March 15	Ashland
March 28-April 9	Appomattox Campaign
March 30-31	Dinwiddie Court House
April 1	Five Forks
April 2	Fall of Petersbrug
April 3	Namozine Church
April 6	Sailor's Creek
April 8	Appomattox Station
April 9	Appomattox Court House, surrender of Lee's Army
April 23-29	Expedition to Danville
May 23	Grand Review Washington, DC
Until August	Provost duty
August 2	Mustered out

SHERIDAN'S CAVALRY CORPS BADGE

WILSON'S CAVALRY CORPS BADGE

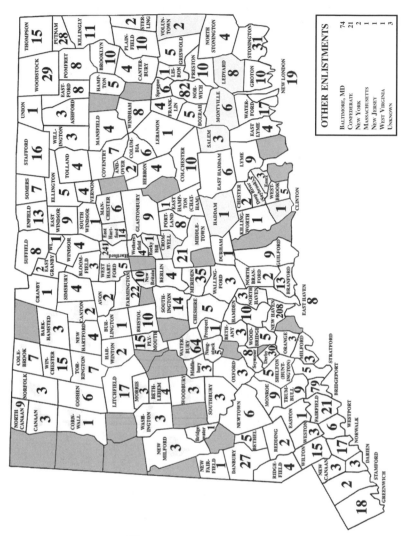

FIRST REGIMENT
CONNECTICUT VOLUNTEER CAVALRY

FIRST BATTERY

CONNECTICUT VOLUNTEER LIGHT ARTILLERY

OCTOBER 26, 1861 - JUNE 11, 1865

(THREE YEARS, EIGHT MONTHS)
291 RECRUITS
2 KILLED, 20 DIED, 20 WOUNDED

HISTORY OF THE 1ST HEAVY ARTILLERY

Alfred P. Rockwell of Norwich was appointed Captain of the 1st Connecticut Light Battery in January 1862. He was appointed Colonel of the 6th Connecticut Infantry in June 1864

The 1st Connecticut Volunteer Light Battery was organized in September 1861. On October 18, about 100 men went into camp at Hanover Village **MERIDEN** On October 26, they were mustered into the United States service.

That same day, they elected Selden T. Porter of Andover, and John S. Cannon of New Haven, 1st Lieutenants, and William T. Seward of Guilford, and George T. Metcalf of Hartford, 2nd Lieutenants. Guns and horses were furnished and artillery practice began at once. Soon the number of men in the battery numbered 156.

On January 13, 1862, the battery broke camp and marched to New Haven with full ranks. On their arrival they were met by the Second Company Governor's Horse Guard and then were escorted by the 13th Connecticut Infantry to the steamer *Elm City*. The battery left for New York City.

On January 21, Captain Alfred P. Rockwell of Norwich, assumed command of the Battery and on the same day they began boarding the ship *Ellwood Walter*. At sunrise on Monday the 27th, the ship sailed from New York Harbor bound for Port Royal, South Carolina as part of **SHERMAN'S EXPEDITIONARY CORPS** They arrived at Hilton Head, South Carolina on February 4. The following day, the battery went up the Broad River to **BEAUFORT, SOUTH CAROLINA** and landed on February 6. Several days were spent in unloading and getting settled in camp. On February 18, the first mounted drill took place. Through March and April, Captain Rockwell made sure the Battery was thoroughly instructed in tactics. On May 3, two howitzers arrived and were placed in the center section of the battery.

On May 29, the Battery had its first engagement (without loss) at

Pocotaligo Bridge

Their next service was in the

First Movement Against Charleston

under Major General David Hunter. The 1st Battery took part in the engagements of June 2, 3 and 14 on

James Island

and in the attack on the Confederate fort at

Secessionville

on June 16. The battle was one of the most severe for the Battery and although several horses were killed, not a man was injured. On July 4, the Battery was transferred to Beaufort. On September 30, the left section of the Battery took part in an

Expedition to Florida

and assisted in the capture of St. John's Bluff. Nothing more of note occurred until April 1863 when a

Second Movement Against Charleston

was made in which the Battery, although present, took no active part and soon returned to Beaufort.

In June, one section, without horses, under First Lieutenant J. B. Clinton, boarded the steamer *Governor Milton* and went on an expedition under the command of Colonel Higginson of the 1st South Carolina Colored Volunteers to destroy the railroad bridge over the Pompon River near Willtown. The movement was not a success and on the return the steamer ran aground. It was impossible to get her free, so she was set on fire. The two guns of the Battery were sunk in the river to prevent the Confederates from taking them.

In July 1863, the Battery took part in the

Third Movement Against Charleston

On the morning of June 16, the Confederates made a surprise attack. They were turned away and the Battery was highly complimented by Maj. General Alfred Terry. Shortly after, the Battery was transferred to

Folly Island

where, for nine months, it formed a part of the reserve force under Maj. General Quincy A. Gillmore in the Siege of Charleston. In December 1863, while on Folly Island, forty-six men re-enlisted as veterans.

On April 18, 1864 the Battery boarded the *General Meigs* and *Ella Knight* bound for Fort Monroe,

Virginia

They arrived there on April 22 and camped for a few days at Gloucester Point. The Battery joined the 1st Division of the

10th Corps

On May 4 they joined Maj. General Benjamin Butler's force at Bermuda Hundred on the James River.

On May 10, the Battery was engaged in the Battle of

Chester Station

The Battery had 2 wounded. On the 13th, they were called into action near the Halfway House on the Richmond and Petersburg Turnpike. The Battle of

Proctor's Creek

occurred the next day. In this engagement Lieutenant George Metcalf and Private Henry L. Wilmot were killed, nine men were wounded and ten horses killed. The Battery was also in action at the same place on the 15th and 16th.

After a short and sharp campaign, the Battery retired to the earthworks at Bermuda Hundred. Captain Rockwell was promoted to Colonel of the 6th Connecticut and 1st Lieutenant James B. Clinton of New Haven assumed command of the Battery. The Battery remained at Bermuda Hundred for six weeks and engaged in the Battle of

WARE BOTTOM CHURCH

under Alfred Terry. The Battery moved from there to Deep Bottom and then to the earthworks in front of

PETERSBURG

They remained there from August 30 to September 23 under constant fire, day and night.

On September 27, the Battery moved with the 10th and 18th Corps across the James River and were stationed near Fort Harrison. They were next transferred to the Light Artillery Brigade, 25th Army Corps under Brig. General Godfrey Weitzel in front of Richmond. The Battery was engaged in sharp fighting near Chaffin's Farm on October 7, at Darbytown Road on the 13th and at Charles City Road on the 27th.

In November, the six-pounder James rifles were exchanged for light twelve-pounder Napoleon guns because it was almost impossible to get ammunition for the rifled guns. The winter was enlivened occasionally with some skirmishes.

On April 2, 1865, orders were issued to attack the Confederate lines near Fort Buchanan at daybreak the following morning. Near midnight, however, the plan of attack was modified. It was thought that the Confederates were preparing to abandon the defenses of Richmond. Soon, heavy and repeated explosions and the sight of bright fires confirmed the suspicion. At daybreak, the Battery moved with the 25th Corps through and over the Confederate works and on to

RICHMOND

The Battery entered the city early in the morning amid burning buildings and the explosion of shells at the burning arsenal. While in Richmond, the news of the surrender of Lee and his army reached the Battery. The war had ended. In a few days the Battery was ordered to Petersburg and then on May 3 to City Point.

On June 1, the battery moved to Manchester, near Richmond, where on June 11, 1865 the men were mustered out of the United States service. The horses, guns, and stores were turned over to the government officers at Richmond.

On Monday morning June 12, the men started for Connecticut and arrived at New Haven two days later. The 1st Connecticut Battery was the first organization of veteran troops to return to the State.

TOTAL CASUALTIES 1ST LIGHT BATTERY						
DATE	PLACE OF CASUALTY	TOTAL	K	M	W	C
1861						
December 20	Meriden, CT	1			1	
1862						
January 1	USS Elwood Water	1			1	
May 8	Beaufort, SC	1			1	
September 1	Beaufort, SC	1			1	
1863						
June 1	Pompon, SC	1			1	
July 16	James Island, SC	1			1	
1864						
May 6	James River, VA	1	1			
May 10	Chester Station, VA	2			2	
May 14 –15	**Proctor's Creek, VA**	**11**	**2**		**9**	
July 10	Unknown	1				1
April 13	Unknown	1	1			
1865						
February 1	Richmond, VA	1			1	

First Light Battery Conn. Vols

DEEP BOTTOM, VA AUGUST 1864

TROOP MOVEMENTS 1ST LIGHT BATTERY

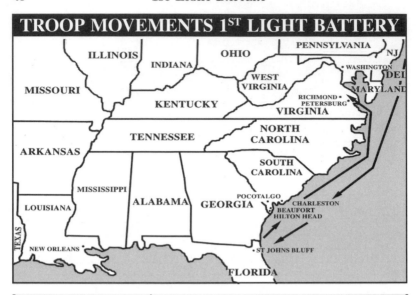

DATE	PLACE
1861	
January 13	Left State for Hilton Head, SC
Until May 1862	Duty at Hilton Head
1862	
May 31-June 28	Expedition to James Island
June 16	Battle of Secessionville
May 28-July 7	Evacuation of James Island/moved to Hilton Head
September 30-October 13	Expedition to St John's Bluff, FLA
October 21-23	Expedition to Pocotaligo, SC
October 22	Frampton's Plantation, Pocotaligo
Until June 1863	Duty at Hilton Head & Beaufort
1863	
July 9-16	Moved to Folly Island, Expedition to James Island
July 10	Williston Bluff, Pon Pon River
July 16	Action on James Island
Until April 1864	Siege operations against Charleston
1864	
April 18-23	Moved from Folly Island to Gloucester Point, VA
May 4-June 21	Butler's operations on South Side of James River
May 10	Chester Station
May 12-16	Operations against Fort Darling
May 14-16	Battle of Proctor's Creek
May 17-June 21	On Bermuda Hundred front
June 16-17	Port Walthall
June 16-April 2, 1865	Siege operations against Petersburg/Richmond
June 21-August 25	Duty at Deep Bottom
July 21, 27-28	Actions at Deep Bottom
August 14-18	Strawberry Plains, Deep Bottom
August 25-September 28	Duty in trenches before Petersburg
September 28	Moved to Deep Bottom
September 29-30	Battle of Chaffin's Farm, New Market Heights
Until April 1865	Duty in trenches before Richmond
1865	
April 3	Occupation of Richmond
Until June	Duty at Richmond and Manchester
June 11	Mustered out

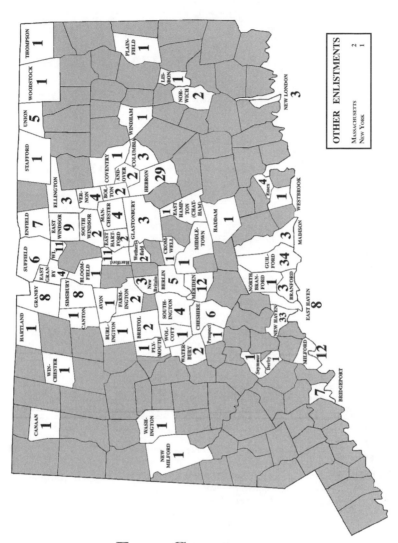

FIRST CONNECTICUT
VOLUNTEER LIGHT BATTERY

FIRST SQUADRON

CONNECTICUT VOLUNTEER CAVALRY

AUGUST 13, 1861 - JUNE 23, 1865

(THREE YEARS, TEN MONTHS)

157 RECRUITS

11 KILLED, 1 MISSING, 31 DIED, 8 WOUNDED,
1 WOUNDED & CAPTURED, 25 CAPTURED

MILITARY AND CIVIL HISTORY OF CONNECTICUT...

The 1st Squadron Connecticut Volunteer Cavalry was organized in August 1861. This was at the same time that the 6th to 11th Connecticut Volunteer Infantry Regiments were forming. The squadron was to be the Connecticut portion of a proposed cavalry regiment for the regular army that was to be formed of six squadrons from six states. Major William H. Mallory of Watertown, who had served in Duryea's 5th New York Zouaves, received authority to recruit a squadron in Connecticut.

The squadron was recruited in

HARTFORD

and after 13 days was mustered into United States service on August 13, 1861. They left for New York and rendezvoused with six other New York

William H. Mallory of Watertown, and a former Major in the 5th New York Infantry organized the First Squadron Cavalry in August 1861. The squadron was eventually consolidated into the 2nd New York Cavalry. Mallory served as Captain of Company C and rose to the rank of Major

companies. All of the companies were assigned to New York as a state regiment and became the

2ND NEW YORK CAVALRY

or the "Harris Light Cavalry". The War Department no longer recognized the squadron as a Connecticut organization.

The Connecticut squadron formed companies C and D of the 2nd New York Cavalry with William Mallory as Captain of Company C and T. Bradley Thornett of Hartford, as Captain of Co. D.

On September 8, the regiment left for

WASHINGTON, DC

by rail. Near Cockeysville, MD, the engineer, who was a Confederate sympathizer, tried to throw the rear cars of the train from the track at a high rate of speed. Two Connecticut soldiers from the regiment were killed in attempting to stop the train.

At its arrival in Washington, the regiment went into camp on Arlington Heights and remained several months attached to McDowell's Division,

ARMY OF THE POTOMAC

It was among the very first of the volunteer cavalry regiments in United States service. Judson Kilpatrick, who later commanded a division of the Cavalry Corps, was appointed Colonel.

From March 10 to 16, 1862 the regiment advanced toward Manassas with King's 3rd Division, 1st Army Corps, Army of the Potomac

On April 17, they moved near Falmouth and were engaged in a skirmish that drove the Confederates from their camp. The regiment moved toward Fredericksburg then toward Hanover Court House. On July 23, they were in another skirmish near the Confederate camp near Carmel Church. The camp was destroyed along with seven rail cars of grain. The regiment did not lose any men or horses. Following the engagement, the regiment returned to their camp near Fredericksburg

In August, the regiment went on an expedition to Frederick's Hall Station and then moved to Thornburg and was near but not engaged at the battle of Cedar Mountain on August 9. They next joined Pope's Campaign in Northern Virginia from August 16 to September 2. From September 16 to19, the regiment was on a reconnaissance from Upton's Hill to Leesburg and was involved in a skirmish with light casualty. They drove about 200 Confederate cavalry and 500 infantry troops from the town.

The men moved to Warrenton on September 29 and then on to Dumfries, Hazel River, Aldie, Mountsville, Sudley Church, New Baltimore, Salem and then back to Warrenton, arriving on November 4. They next moved to Rappahannock Station, Aldie and Stafford Court House. They arrived at Fredericksburg on December 12 but were not engaged in that battle. They went into winter quarters near Rappahannock Station with the 3rd Division of the Cavalry Corps.

On April 16, 1863, they moved to Warrenton then back to Rappahannock Station three days later. On May 3, as part of the

STONEMAN RAID

they were ordered to destroy the railroad bridge on the Chickahominy and to inflict as much damage to the Confederates as possible. The following day, they destroyed the depot and tracks at Hungary, moved on and arrived in Hanovertown on May 5. They burned the ferry and 30 rail cars loaded with bacon. They surprised a force of 300 cavalry at Atlett's Depot, captured 35 men, burned 56 wagons, and the depot containing about 60,000 barrels of corn and wheat. They crossed the Mattaponi and destroyed a ferry, a wagon train and a depot a few miles above Tappahannock. On May 7, they arrived at Gloucester Point and the safety of the Union lines. The loss to the regiment was 35 men.

On May 20, the regiment left Gloucester Point on an expedition into Matthews County and returned the next morning without the loss of a single man. They captured 300 horses and mules, 150 head of beef cattle and 150 sheep. Large quantities of grain and forage were destroyed.

On June 9, the regiment took part in the cavalry action at

BRANDY STATION

with 48 casualties. It was the largest single mounted battle ever fought on the American continent. Of the 20,000 troops that were engaged, 17,000 were mounted. The Union force was obliged to pull back from the stronger Confederate defenses. The day long battle with 868 Union and 515 Confederate casualties pointed to the rise of the Union cavalry over the proud but dwindling Confederate cavalry.

The regiment next moved toward Maryland in pursuit of Lee and on June 28 were positioned near Rockville, Maryland. A battalion from the regiment was detached and participated in Dix's fruitless Peninsula Campaign from June 24-July 7. The regiment saw very limited service at the battle of Gettysburg, July 1-3. After the battle, the regiment followed Lee's army. They moved to Monterey Gap then to Smithburg, Emmettsburg and Hagerstown. On July 14 they were at Williamsport, Maryland. They crossed the Potomac and moved toward Falling Waters, Berryville and Bristerburg. Gradually moving east, they crossed the mountains at Thoroughfare Gap on August 5. A detachment from the regiment went on a scouting expedition near Hopewell in the Bull Run Mountains on August 14. They had very limited contact with the Confederates, so they pushed on to Aldie. On August 22, they were at U. S. Ford on the Rappahannock River.

The regiment went on an expedition to Port Conway during the first couple of days in September. They were part of the advance of Union forces from the Rappahannock to the Rapidan River September 13-15. They engaged the Confederates at Culpeper Court House on September 19 with slight losses. The regiment spent the fall and winter of 1863 moving through Virginia destroying tracks and Confederate stores, zig zagging from depot to depot and from ford to ford.

In February 1864, Division Head-quarters was at Stevensburg and on the 28th the regiment participated in

KILPATRICK'S EXPEDITION AGAINST RICHMOND

but was not part of the main column. The expedition crossed the Rapidan and swept around the right flank of Lee's army by way of Spottsylvania Court House; then pushed rapidly toward Richmond and struck the Virginia Central Railroad at Beaver Dam Station. They then crossed the South Anna, cut the Fredericksburg and Richmond Railway and on March 1 halted within 3 miles of Richmond. The grand object of the expedition was to liberate the Union captives from Libby prison. The Union army was eventually repulsed and was forced to retreat toward the Chickahominy. The regiment was at Stevensville on March 3. They moved to Carrollton's Store on March 11 and from May to June were part of the Campaign from the Rapidan to the James River.

From June 13 to July 31 the regiment was in the reserve picket during the

RICHMOND CAMPAIGN

They manned a picket post near Temple House on July 27. In August, the regiment was transferred to the Shenandoah Valley and was held in reserve as a support to the artillery. Near Columbia Furnace they met a small force of Confederates on October 11. The regiment captured four prisoners and lost seven wounded.

On October 18, the command was camped near

CEDAR CREEK

and participated in the Union victory of October 19. They had 1 killed, 3 wounded, and 8 captured. Two days later they went on a scouting expedition to Fisher's Hill, and then moved on to Middletown. At Mount Zion Church, near Cedar Creek, Colonel Hull was killed while leading a charge at the head of the regiment. Thirty-nine men of the regiment were casualties. The command next moved toward Woodstock and met the Confederates near Mount Jackson on November 21. The casualties numbered 15. On December 2, they went into camp at Moorefield, West Virginia.

From February 27-March 25, 1865 the regiment participated in Sheridan's raid from Winchester to Petersburg. They saw action at Waynesboro on March 2 and participated in the

APPOMATTOX CAMPAIGN

from March 28-April 9. The regiment was at Appomattox Court House for Lee's surrender on April 9 and participated in the Grand Review at Washington, DC on May 23. They were mustered out on June 5 and were discharged from service on June 23, 1865.

TOTAL CASUALTIES 1ST SQUADRON CAVALRY

DATE	PLACE OF CASUALTY	TOTAL	K	M	W	W/C	C
1861							
September 8	Railroad Accident	2	2				
October 12	Washington, DC (Accident)	1	1				
1862							
April 17	Falmouth, VA	1	1				
August 20,23	Rappahannock Station, VA	2	1			1	
August 29	Gainesville, VA	1	1				
September 7	Unknown	1			1		
1863							
June 1	Unknown	1					1
June 9	Brandy Station, VA	2					2
June 17	**Aldie, VA**	**4**	**3**		**1**		
July 1	New Baltimore, VA	3					3
July 3	Gettysburg, PA	1		1			
July 4	South Mountain, MD	1					1
July 4	Smithburg, VA	2					2
July 6	Hagerstown, MD	1					1
September 1	Sailor's Creek, VA	1			1		
September 14	Rapidan, VA	1	1				
September 22	Liberty Mills, VA	1					1
September 22	White's Ford, VA	1			1		
October 12	Brandy Station, VA	2					2
October 19	New Baltimore, VA	1					1
December 1	Unknown	1			1		
1864							
March 1	**Richmond, VA**	**5**	**1**				**4**
March 1	Rapidan, VA	1			1		
May 5	Todd's Tavern, VA	3			2		1
June 29-30	Ream's Station, VA	3					3
Unknown	Unknown	3					3

SOLDIER IN OUR CIVIL WAR

TROOP MOVEMENTS 1ST SQUADRON CAVALRY

DATE	PLACE
1862	
Until March	Duty in Defenses of Washington, DC
April 3-18	Advance on Falmouth, VA
May 5	Near Fredericksburg
May 11	Bowling Green
July 4	Flipper Orchard
July 19-20	Expedition Fredericksburg to Hanover Junction
July 20	Beaver Dam Station
July 22-24	Reconnoissance to James City
July 23	Mt. Carmel Church
August 5-8	Expedition to Frederick's Hall Station
August 5	Thornburg or Massaponax Church
August 8	Orange Court House
August 9	Battle of Cedar Mountain
August 16-September 2	Pope's Campaign in Northern Virginia
August 18	Near Rapidan Station
August 20	Brandy Station
August 21-23	Fords of the Rappahannock
August 21	Kelly's Ford
August 22	Catlett's Station
August 23	Culpeper
August 23	Waterloo Bridge
August 24	Sulphur Springs
August 26	Manassas Junction
August 28	Thoroughfare Gap
August 29	Groveton
August 30	Bull Run
August 31	Germantown
August 31	Centreville and Chantilly
September 1	Little River Turnpike
September 14	South Mountain, MD
September 1 7	Goose Creek
September 16-19	6 Companies Action at Leesburg
September 29	Warrenton
October 5	Dumfries
October 31	Hazel River, Aldie, Mountsvillie
November 3	Sudley Church
November 4	New Baltimore, Salem, Warrenton, Upperville
November 8-9	Rappahannock Station
November 25	Aldie
December 7	Stafford Court House
December 12-15	Fredericksburg
1863	
April	Rappahannock Station
April 16	Warrenton
April 19	Rappahannock Station
May 2	Louisa Court House
May 3	Ashland and Hanover Station
May 4	Glen Allen
May 5	Aylett' s

TROOP MOVEMENTS 1ST SQUADRON CAVALRY

DATE	PLACE
1863	
May 6	King and Queen Court House
May 6	Centreville
May 10	Morrisville
May 19-20	Expedition from Gloucester into Matthews County
June 1	Falmouth
June 3	Brandy Station
June 9	Beverly Ford and Brandy Station
June 17	Aldie
June 19	Middleburg
June 21	Upperville
June 28	Rockville, MD
June 24-July 7	Dix's Peninsula Campaign (Battalion)
June 29	Cooksville
July 1-3	Battle of Gettysburg
July 4	Monterey Gap
July 5	Smithburg
July 5	Emmettsburg
July 6	Hagerstown and Williamsport
July 8	Boonsborough
July 10-13	Jone's Cross Roads
July 11-13	Hagerstown
July 14	Williamsport
July 14	Falling Waters
July 16	Berryville
July 27	Bristerburg
August 3	Fairfax
August 5	Thoroughfare Gap
August 12-14	Near Aldie
August 22	U.S.Ford
September 1-3	Expedition to Port Conway
September 1	Lamb's Creek
September 13-17	Advance from the Rappahannock to the Rapidan
September 13	Culpeper Court House
September 14	Somerville Ford
September 16	Robertson's Ford
September 17	U.S. Ford
September 19	Culpeper
September 21	Madison Court House
September 21-22	White's Ford and Liberty Mills
September 27-28	Scout to Hazel River
October 2	Hazel Run
October 6	Hazel River
October 7	Culpeper
October 9-22	Bristoe Campaign
October 10	James City, Robertson's River Bethesda Church
October 11	Near Culpeper
October 11 - 12	Brandy Station
October 14	Gainesville
October 17-18	Groveton
October 19	Haymarket. Buckland's Mills. New Baltimore
November 4	Catlett's Station

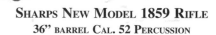

SHARPS NEW MODEL 1859 RIFLE
36" BARREL CAL. 52 PERCUSSION

TROOP MOVEMENTS 1ST SQUADRON CAVALRY

DATE	PLACE
November 7	Stevensburg
November 7-8	Advance to line of the Rappahannock
November 15	Hartwood Church
November 18	Germania Ford
November 26-December 2	Mine Run Campaign
November 26	Morton's Ford
November 27	New Hope Church
November 29	Robertson's Tavern
December 2	Germania Ford
December 5	Raccoon Ford
December 18	Somerville
1864	
January 12	Kelly's Ford
January 17	Ellis Ford
January 19	Stevensburg
January 19	Ely's Ford
February 28-March 3	Kilpatrick's Raid to Richmond
February 29	Beaver Dam and Frederick's Hall Station
March 1	Defenses of Richmond
March 2	Old Church and King and Queen
March 2	Near Walkertown
March 3	Near Tunstall Station (Detachment)
March 3	New Kent Court House and Stevensville
March II	Carrollton's Store
May-June	Rapidan Campaign
May 5	Craig's Meeting House
May 5-6	Todd's Tavern
May 6-7	Wilderness
May 8	Spottsylvania, Alsop's Farm
May 9-24	Sheridan's Raid to James River
May 9-10	North Anna River
May 11	Ground Squirrel Church and Yellow Tavern
May 12	Brook's Church of fortifications of Richmond
May 12	Strawberry Hill
May 23	Polecat Station
May 26	Demonstration on 1~ittle River
May 28-31	Totopotomoy
May 29-30	Hanover Court House
May 31	Mechump's Creek
June 1-12	Cold Harbor
June 2	Totopotomoy and Gaines' Mill
June 3	Hawe's Shop
June 3	Via's House
June 10-11	Old Church
June 11	Bethesda
June 12	Riddell's Shop and Long Bridge
June 14	Malvern Hill
June 15	Smith's Store near St. Mary's Church
June 22-30	Wilson's Raid to south side and Danville RR
June 23	Noteway Court House
June 28	Sapponay Church or Stony Creek

SPENCER CARBINE MODEL 1860
CAL. 52 RIMFIRE

TROOP MOVEMENTS 1ST SQUADRON CAVALRY

DATE	PLACE
August 7-November 28	Sheridan's Valley Campaign
August 17	Near Winchester
August 21	Summit Point, Charlestown
August 25	Near Kearneysville
September 2	Waynesboro
September 4	Berryville
September 9	Near Winchester
September 13	Abram's Creek
September 19	Battle of Opeguan, Winchester
September 20	Near Cedarville
September 21	Fishers Hill
September 21	Front Royal Pike
September 22	Milford
September 26	Staunton
September 29	Waynesboro
September 30	Mt. Crawford
October 2	Bridgewater and Woodstock
October 6	Brock's Gap
October 7	New Market
October 8	Fisher's Hill
October 8-9	Tom's Brook 'Woodstock Races"
October 13	Cedar Run
October 19-November 7	Battle of Cedar Creek
November 12	Nineveh
November 22	Mt. Jackson
November 23	Hood's Hill
November 28-December 2	Expedition from Kernstown to Moorefield
December 3	Moorefield
December 19-22	Expedition to Lacy Springs
December 21	Lacy Springs
December 21	Mt. Jackson
1865	
February 27-March 25	Sheridan's Raid from Winchester
March 2	Occupation of Staunton
March 2	Action at Waynesboro
March 3	Charlottesville
March 15	Ashland
March 28-April 9	Appomattox Campaign
March 30-31	Dinwiddie Court Rouse
April 1	Five Forks
April 2	Fall of Petersburg
April 3	Namozine Church
April 6	Saylor's Creek
April 8	Appomattox Court House
April 23-29	Expedition to Danville
May 23	March to Washington and Grand Review
June 5	Mustered out
June 23	Discharged from service

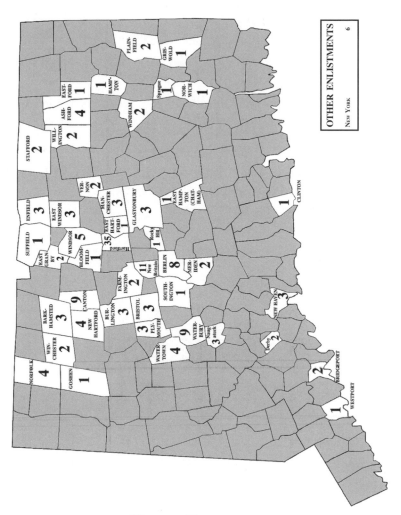

OTHER ENLISTMENTS

NEW YORK 6

PLAINFIELD	2
GRISWOLD	1
HAMPTON	1
EASTFORD	1
SPRAGUE	1
NORWICH	1
ASHFORD	4
WINDHAM	2
WILLINGTON	2
STAFFORD	2
VERNON	2
MANCHESTER	3
GLASTONBURY	3
EAST HAMPTON (CHATHAM)	1
CLINTON	1
ENFIELD	3
EAST WINDSOR	3
EAST HARTFORD	3
SUFFIELD	1
WINDSOR	5
HARTFORD	35
ROCKY HILL	1
EAST GRANBY	2
BLOOMFIELD	1
NEW BRITAIN	11
BERLIN	8
MERIDEN	2
FARMINGTON	2
SOUTHINGTON	3
BARKHAMSTED	3
CANTON	9
NEW HARTFORD	4
BURLINGTON	3
BRISTOL	3
NEW HAVEN	3
WINCHESTER	2
PLYMOUTH	3
WATERBURY	9
NAUGATUCK	3
DERBY	2
NORFOLK	4
GOSHEN	1
WATERTOWN	4
BRIDGEPORT	2
WESTPORT	1

FIRST SQUADRON
CONNECTICUT VOLUNTEER CAVALRY

SECOND REGIMENT
CONNECTICUT VOLUNTEER INFANTRY
MAY 7, 1861 - AUGUST 7, 1861
(THREE MONTHS)
793 RECRUITS
1 KILLED, 2 DIED, 5 WOUNDED, 15 CAPTURED, 1 WOUNDED & CAPTURED

USAMHI

Alfred H. Terry of New Haven, was appointed the Colonel of the 2nd Connecticut Infantry. Before the war, he was the popular Colonel of the 2nd Regiment of the State Militia. Terry eventually served as Colonel of 7th Connecticut Infantry and later became Major General of Volunteers

The 2nd Regiment Connecticut Volunteer Infantry was organized after President Lincoln's first call for troops on April 15, 1861. The first company to enlist was the *Buckingham Rifles* from Norwich. The company was originally formed to be in the 1st Connecticut, however that regiment was full so they became the first to join the 2nd Connecticut. The *Mansfield Guard* of Middletown, the *New Haven Grays* and the *National Guard of Birmingham* from Derby were the next companies to enlist. All were experienced and well drilled popular militia organizations and formed the core companies of the 2nd Connecticut Regiment.

The 2nd Connecticut Infantry was fortunate in that most of its officers had been trained in the State Militia. Colonel Alfred Terry of New Haven, had served as Colonel, Lieutenant Colonel David Young of Norwich, as Brigadier General, Major Ledyard Colburn of Derby, as Major, and Adjutant Charles Russell also from Derby, as Adjutant. Many of its captains and lieutenants had served as line officers.

Eight companies of the regiment were armed with Model 1855 percussion rifles and the two flank companies were armed with Sharps rifles. On Monday, May 6, the 2nd Connecticut Infantry joined with the 1st at Brewster Park,

NEW HAVEN

The regiment was mustered into the United States service the following day. The 2nd Connecticut Infantry left on the steamer *Cahawba* for

WASHINGTON, DC

on May 10, and reached there on May 14. The regiment camped next to the 1st Connecticut Infantry two miles north of the Capitol at Glenwood on the pleasant grounds of the wealthy banker William Corcoran. They remained there and drilled until ordered into

VIRGINIA

At midnight on June 16, the regiment crossed the Long Bridge and marched, during intermittent showers, nine miles to a camp at Roach's Mills. After reaching camp, the regiment was ordered to the support of the 1st Ohio Infantry of Schenck's Brigade that had been attacked at Vienna Station. The Confederates had retreated before the arrival of the 2nd Connecticut Infantry.

The regiment continued to march for about five miles to Taylor's Tavern on Oak Hill, near Falls Church. The 2nd Connecticut Infantry joined with the 1st and 3rd Connecticut Infantry and performed picket and outpost duty until the advance on

BULL RUN

The regiment was assigned to a brigade with the 1st and 3rd Connecticut Infantry and 2nd Maine Infantry. The brigade was supported by Tompkins' New York Cavalry and Berrian's New York Battery. Brigadier General Daniel Tyler, from the 1st Connecticut Infantry, was appointed brigade commander. General Tyler was eventually assigned to the command of the First Division and Colonel Erasmus D. Keyes, a former instructor of artillery and cavalry from West Point, was put in command of Tyler's brigade.

From July 18 to 20, the Union army, under Irwin McDowell, gathered on the outskirts of Centreville, Virginia. On Sunday morning, July 21, General Tyler began the battle when he fired the first

gun near the Stone Bridge across the Bull Run stream. The Confederates opened fired on the Keyes Brigade, who were guarding the Warrenton Turnpike, with 20 to 30 artillery shells from a battery across the Run.

The 2nd Connecticut Infantry, along with its brigade, crossed the stream farther west and fell into line next to Sherman's Brigade, beyond Youngs Branch. The Confederate battery retreated to Henry House hill behind the Robinson House. The 1st and 2nd Connecticut Infantry remained in place as the 3rd Connecticut Infantry and 2nd Maine Infantry pressed their regiments up the hill for about 100 yards and then halted and laid down. The 1st and 2nd Connecticut followed. The forward regiments re-loaded their weapons and advanced again in the face of a moveable battery of 8 pieces and a large body of Virginia infantry.

The fighting continued when suddenly there was a lull in the Union artillery fire and to the surprise of everyone in that section of the field, the Union force was ordered to retreat. Moving back down the hill and marching across the level fields, they had reached the woods when Confederate cavalry bore down on them. Facing to the rear rank, the regiments repelled them. As the Keyes Brigade approached Cub Run the bridge across it was so crowded that the troops had to ford the stream.

The 2nd Connecticut Infantry fell back to Centreville, and later continued its march to the camp at Oak Hill. They arrived the following morning. The regiment had 1 killed, 2 wounded, 13 captured, and 1 wounded & captured in the battle. For the greater part of the next two days, the regiment was employed in packing its tents and the tents of several other brigades. The tents had been left standing and deserted by the retreating Union soldiers. Large quantities of arms, ammunition, camp equipment and stores waited for transportation back to the Capitol. Telegrams were sent to Union headquarters that brought the necessary trains. The men of the three Connecticut regiments loaded, guarded, and escorted the trains over the Potomac River back to Washington.

After the return from Bull Run, the regiment remained in Washington for a few days and at the expiration of its term of service, the 2nd Connecticut Infantry returned to New Haven and were mustered out on August 7.

Two hundred veterans of the 2nd Connecticut Infantry became valuable officers in the other Connecticut organizations that were recruited throughout the war.

LIBRARY OF CONGRESS

BATTLE OF BULL RUN
JULY 21, 1861

THE 2ND CONNECTICUT INFANTRY (KEYES BRIGADE) SUFFERED ITS GREATEST LOSS OF THE WAR NEAR THE ROBINSON HOUSE ON THE HENRY HOUSE HILL. THE KEYES BRIGADE WAS LOCATED TO THE LEFT OF THE SHERMAN BRIGADE. TWO COMPANIES WERE ARMED WITH SHARPS RIFLES AND EIGHT COMPANIES WERE ARMED WITH MODEL 1855 PERCUSSION RIFLES.

SHARPS NEW MODEL 1859 RIFLE
36" BARREL CAL. 52 PERCUSSION

MODEL 1855 US PERCUSSION RIFLE
CAL. 58

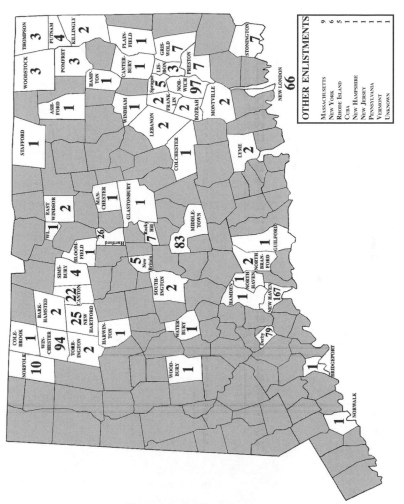

SECOND REGIMENT
CONNECTICUT VOLUNTEER
INFANTRY

SECOND REGIMENT
CONNECTICUT VOLUNTEER HEAVY ARTILLERY
SEPTEMBER 11, 1862 - AUGUST 18, 1865
(TWO YEARS, THREE MONTHS)
2,447 RECRUITS
146 KILLED, 14 MISSING, 270 DIED, 567 WOUNDED
3 WOUNDED & CAPTURED, 69 CAPTURED

USAMHI

The 2nd Regiment Connecticut Volunteer Heavy Artillery was originally organized in July 1862 as the **19TH REGIMENT CONNECTICUT VOLUNTEER INFANTRY** They formed in response to Governor William H. Buckingham's call for three-year soldiers and were also known as the *Litchfield County Regiment.*

On August 24, 815 men gathered on the farm of Cyrus Catlin, a mile east of Litchfield at South Chestnut Hill. Sheriff Leverett W. Wesells of Litchfield, was commissioned Colonel and Major Elisha S.

Elisha S. Kellogg of Derby, was at first commisioned Lieutenant Colonel however, he assumed command of the regiment from nearly the beginning. He was promoted to Colonel when Wessells resigned in September 1863. Colonel Kellogg was killed on June 1, 1864 at the Battle of Cold Harbor

Kellogg of Derby and in the 1st Connecticut Heavy Artillery was appointed Lieutenant Colonel. Nathaniel Smith of Woodbury, was appointed Major.

On September 10, Mrs. William Curtis Noyes presented the regiment with a beautiful stand of Colors. The following day, they were mustered into United States service and on September 15 left in 23 railroad cars for **WASHINGTON,DC**

The regiment arrived on September 19. They were equipped with "A" tents and Enfield Rifles and were assigned to Brig. General John P. Slough's Brigade which was located at **ALEXANDRIA** Virginia.They relieved the 33rd Massachusetts from the disagreeable task of patrolling the hostile Confederate city. Due to typhoid fever and malaria, the health of the men quickly deteriorated. Colonel Wessells and a large number of other men fell ill and by the end of the month 16 had died.

Because the Colonel was so sick, Lieutenant Colonel Elisha Kellogg assumed command of the regiment. On January 12, 1863, they were assigned to the Military Defenses of Alexandria and were placed in a Brigade with the 1st Connecticut Heavy Artillery under Connecticut General Robert O. Tyler. The regiment moved to Fort Worth near Fairfax Seminary and the health of the men gradually improved.

Five months later, the companies of the regiment were distributed for garrison duty at Fort Ellsworth, Redoubts A, B, C, and D, and at the Water Battery on the Potomac, below Alexandria. On September 16, Colonel Wessells resigned due to poor health, and on October 23, Elisha Kellogg was promoted to Colonel. On November 23, the organization of the regiment was changed from infantry to heavy artillery. They assumed the name of the 2nd Regiment Connecticut Volunteer Heavy Artillery and recruiting was begun to raise two more companies.

On November 30, several officers of the regiment were ordered to Connecticut on recruiting service. By March 1, 1864, the regiment numbered 1,800. On May 17, the regiment was ordered to the Army of the Potomac as infantry and was assigned to Emory Upton's 2nd Brigade, Wright's 1st Division,

6TH ARMY CORPS

under Major General John Sedgwick. The corps was located near Spottsylvania and on May 22 crossed the North Anna River. Two days later, the regiment while on the skirmish line had its first man killed. From May 24 to 30, the regiment was occupied with destroying the railroads at various places. On May 29, they were on picket duty near Totopotomy Creek, and the following day were near Hanover Court House where they had 6 wounded. At

COLD HARBOR

on June 1, the regiment was deployed as infantry into three lines and advanced to take the heavy Confederate earthworks. The regiment managed to take the first line of works and captured over 300 prisoners. They moved forward again with intervals of less than 100 yards between the three regimental lines and passed through a stiff abatis 20 yards in front of the Confederate main lines. The regiment was met by terrific fire from the front and left flank but pressed on with some of the regiment mounting the top of the works. Nothing could withstand the overwhelming fire and the first two lines of the regiment fell back to a somewhat less exposed position held by the third regimental line.

The regiment left 322 men on the field with 129 of them dead or mortally wounded. Among the dead was Colonel Kellogg who fell riddled with bullets in the advance of the first line. Captain Luman Wadhams and Major William B. Ellis were severely wounded. The regiment held their position under constant fire until June 12.

On June 6, Captain Ronald S. Mackenzie, of the U.S. Engineer Corps, took command of the regiment after Lieutenant Colonel James Hubbard of Salisbury, declined the promotion.

On June 16, the regiment boarded ships in the James River and moved to Bermuda Hundred. On the 19th, they crossed the Appomattox River with Upton's Brigade and relieved Hinds Colored Brigade and the 11th Connecticut in the rifle pits in front of

PETERSBURG

On June 20 to 21, they made cautious and slight advances.

On June 22, they engaged Hill's Division losing 6 killed, 9 wounded and 3 captured.The regiment captured a position that was held by the Union army as the advance line until the close of the war. On July 9, the regiment marched through stifling dust to City Point and boarded steamboats. On July 12, they arrived in Washington, DC and marched to Tennallytown. On July 16, they forded the Potomac at Edward's Ferry, crossed the Blue Ridge Mountains and Shenandoah River on July 20 and camped near Berryville. The regiment did not engage the Confederates and at midnight they began the return march to Tennallytown and reached there on July 23. Two days later, they crossed Aqueduct Bridge to Fort Corcoran and relieved an Ohio regiment. The following day, the regiment crossed the Potomac and rejoined the 6th Corps who were attempting to block Confederate General Jubal Early's advance into Maryland and Pennsylvania. The regiment crossed the Potomac at Harper's Ferry on July 29 and was occupied in continual skirmishing up and down the

SHENANDOAH VALLEY

until September 11 when Early was pushed to near Cedar Creek. The regiment camped with the 1st Division near Clifton.

On September 19, the regiment was called into action to halt the Confederates who had broken through the Union lines near

WINCHESTER

With Upton's Brigade (2nd Connecticut Heavy Artillery, 65 NY, 121NY, 95 PA) the regiment restored the line of battle until Crook and Merritt's Divisions, with

Averill's Cavalry sent the Confederates through Winchester. The regiment lost 14 officers and 107 enlisted men killed and wounded. Among the killed was Major James Rice of Goshen. Colonel Mackenzie was among the slightly wounded.

On September 22, the 6th Corps advanced directly up the seemingly impassable face of

FISHER'S HILL

and arrived at the summit just as the 8th Corps struck the Confederate right flank causing them to retreat in confusion. The 2nd Connecticut lost 1 killed and 16 wounded.

On September 25, at Harrisonburg, the regiment was faced toward the Potomac with orders to destroy everything left behind that could give aid and comfort to the Confederates and reached Ashby's Gap on October 13. The following day, Major General Philip Sheridan learned that Confederate General Jubal Early was once again in the Shenandoah Valley and once more headed his army up the valley and camped near

CEDAR CREEK

On October 19, the Union force was surprised and driven back three miles. At about 4PM, Sheridan rallied his troops, a new line was established and the Confederates were driven back and scattered. The 2nd Connecticut lost 22 killed, 112 wounded, 50 captured, and 2 wounded & captured at Cedar Creek. Companies E and L, under Lieutenant Henry Skinner, were captured while on picket duty and not released until April 1865.

On November 9, the regiment camped at Kernstown. On December 2, the regiment left by rail for Washington, DC and then by boat to City Point, VA. They moved on to comfortable winter quarters at Parke Station and performed picket duty with the occasional un-explained movements to the right or left.

On December 28, Colonel Mac-kenzie was promoted to Brigadier General, and Lieutenant Colonel James Hubbard was promoted to Colonel on January 7, 1865.

On February 5, the regiment participated in an affair at

HATCHER'S RUN

and passed the day massed and ready for a charge in a drizzling, freezing rain, with shots from the artillery of both armies passing over them. The regiment finally engaged near dusk for a short while. They eventually returned to winter quarters on February 8. The casualties in the regiment were 1 killed, 1 missing and 6 wounded.

On March 25 at the Petersburg front, the regiment moved to Fort Stedman, which the Union Army had re-captured just as the 6th Corps had arrived. The regiment next advanced toward Petersburg in front of Fort Fisher. Their brigade passed a line of rifle pits, captured the Confederate occupants, and then advanced to an unsupported position. The regiment was pushed back and returned to their former line with 3 killed and 14 wounded.

At about midnight on April 1, the brigade formed in front of the breastworks during the heaviest cannonading it had ever witnessed and at dawn the following day, charged over the Confederate works and into their deserted camps. The casualties to the regiment were Lieutenant Colonel Jeffrey Skinner and 12 enlisted men wounded.

The regiment was ordered to report to Major General John G. Parke, who commanded the 9th Corps, and to march to the right to Fort Hell. They were moved by a covered way to the Confederate works that had been captured earlier in the day by the 9th Corps. On April 3, with the 2nd Connecticut Heavy Artillery leading the brigade, the Union army entered the city of Petersburg. Colonel Hubbard was made provost marshal, only to be relieved when the brigade was ordered to join the 6th Corps on April 4. The regiment followed the fleeing Confederate army on April 5-6 and had its last fight at

SAILOR'S CREEK

where they had 7 wounded. The regiment captured one battle flag, the headquarters train of Confederate Major General William Mahone's Division, and a large number of prisoners.

On April 7, the regiment was near Farmville. The following day it was near New Store and on April 9 near Clover Hill, where Colonel Joseph E. Hamblin, who now commanded the Brigade, announced the news of Lee's surrender.

On April 23, while camped at Burkeville, the 6th Corps was ordered to Danville to prepare to operate with General William T. Sherman against Confederate General Joesph E. Johnston's army in North Carolina. The march of 105 miles was accomplished in less than 5 days with the 6th Corps arriving at Danville on April 27 only to learn that Johnston had already surrendered his army.

On May 2, the regiment, with the exception of Companies F, G, and K, was detailed as guard to the wagon train on the return march to Burkeville. They arrived there on May 6 and remained until May 18 when the corps moved (the 2nd Connecticut by rail) to Manchester, opposite Richmond.

On May 24, the regiment marched through Richmond and arrived at Fredericksburg on May 29. Then on June 1, they moved to Bailey's Cross Roads where they stayed until June 8. The regiment received the "new men" of the 14th Connecticut when the veterans of the 14th were mustered out.

On June 8, the regiment took part in a troop review in Washington. On June 16, the regiment was assigned to the 3rd Brigade, Hardin's Division, 22nd Army Corps and was ordered to garrison 11 forts on the north side of the Potomac.

On June 27, they were transferred to Forts Ethan Allen, Marcy, Albany, and Battery Martin Scott, on the south side of the Potomac.

On July 7, the remaining members of the original regiment were mustered out, and left for home. On July 20, the 12 companies were consolidated to 8 (I, K, L, M ceased to exist). On August 18, 1865, the eight companies were mustered out at Fort Ethan Allen and received their final discharge at New Haven on September 5, 1865.

CONGRESSIONAL MEDAL OF HONOR WINNERS

Sergeant Wesley Gibbs, Co. B, 2d Connecticut Heavy Artillery
Place and date: At Petersburg, Va., 2 April 1865
Date of issue: 10 May 1865
Citation: Capture of flag

Corporal Elijah A. Briggs, Co. B, 2d Connecticut Heavy Artillery
Place and date: At Petersburg, Va., 3 April 1865
Date of issue: 10 May 1865
Citation: Capture of battle flag

LIBRARY OF CONGRESS

BATTLE OF COLD HARBOR
JUNE 1, 1864

THE 2ND CONNECTICUT HEAVY ARTILLERY WAS ACTING AS INFANTRY IN THE SIXTH CORPS (WRIGHT), 1ST DIVISION (RUSSELL), 2ND BRIGADE (UPTON) WHEN COLONEL ELISHA S. KELLOGG LED THEM TO HIS DEATH IN THE CHARGE ON THE CONFEDERATE EARTHWORKS MANNED BY HOKE'S DIVISION. THE REGIMENT SUFFERED 322 CASUALTIES (23%).

TOTAL CASUALTIES 2ND HEAVY ARTILLERY

DATE	PLACE OF CASUALTY	TOTAL	K	M	W	W/C	C
1862							
October 15	Alexandria, VA	1			1		
Unknown	Unknown	1					1
Unknown	Railroad Accident	1	1				
October 24	Alexandria, VA	1			1		
November 20	Alexandria, VA	1			1		
1863							
July 1	FT. Lyon, Ward, VA	2			2		
August 15	FT. Lyon, VA	1			1		
Unknown	FT. Williams, VA	1			1		
October 1	FT. Ellsworth, VA	1			1		
1864							
March 25	Petersburg, VA	1			1		
April 1	Petersburg, VA	1			1		
April 8	Cedar Creek, VA	1			1		
May 6	Spottsylvania, VA	1			1		
May 20	Hanover Court House, VA	1			1		
May 22-26	North Anna River, VA	6	1		5		
May 24	Fontaine, VA	1			1		
May 26	Noel's Station, VA	1			1		
May 29	Totopotomy, VA	3			3		
May 29-30	Hanover Court House, VA	3			3		
June 1	**Cold Harbor, VA**	**322**	**85**	**11**	**223**	**1**	**2**
June 1	FT. Ellsworth, VA	1			1		
June 1	Petersburg, VA	1			1		
June 2	Cold Harbor, VA	2			2		
June 2	Gaines Mills, VA	1					1
June 3	Cold Harbor, VA	8	2		6		
June 5	Cold Harbor, VA	2			2		
June 5	Rapidan, VA	1					1
June 6,8,10,14,16	Cold Harbor, VA	6			3		3
June 14	Ford's Mills, VA	1					1
June 19-30	Petersburg, VA	33	7		22		4
July 2	Petersburg, VA	1			1		
July 21, 24	Snicker's Ford, VA	2					2
July 21	Leesburg, VA	1					1
July 27	Harper's Ferry, WVA	1			1		
August 19	Strasburg, VA	1					1
August 31	Petersburg, VA	1			1		
September 2	Fisher's Hill, VA	1	1				
September 18-19	**Winchester, VA**	**121**	**21**		**100**		
September 20	Cedar Creek, VA	1			1		
September 21-22	Strasburg, VA	3			3		
September 21-22	Fisher's Hill, VA	17	1		16		
September 22	Winchester, VA	1			1		
September 24	Strasburg, VA	1					1
October 19	**Cedar Creek, VA**	**186**	**21**	**1**	**112**	**2**	**50**
October 19	Strasburg, VA	1			1		
October 19	Middletown, VA	1					1
1865							
February 2, 6	Hatcher's Run, VA	8	1	1	6		
March 5,6	Petersburg, VA	2			2		
March 25-26	Petersburg, VA	18	4		14		
April 2	Petersburg, VA	14		1	13		
April 4	Amelia Court House, VA	1			1		
April 6	Sailor's Creek, VA	7			7		
July 7	Shenandoah Valley, VA	1			1		
July 27	Potomac River, VA (Drowned)	1	1				

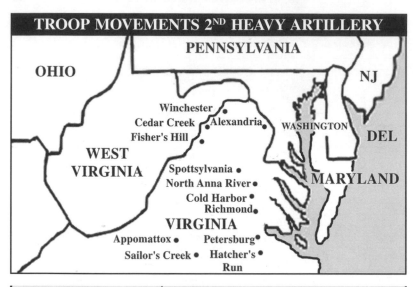

DATE	PLACE
1862	
September 15	Left State for Washington, DC
Until January 1863	Guard Duty at Alexandria, VA
1863	
Until May 1864	Garrison duty at Fort Worth, Williams, Ellsworth
1864	
May 17-19	Moved to Spottsylvania Court House, VA
Until May 21	Duty at Spottsylvania Court House
May 23-26	North Anna River, VA
May 26-28	On line of the Pamunkey
May 28-31	Totopotmoy
May 29	Hanover Court House, VA
May 31-June 12	Cold Harbor, VA
June 18-July 10	Before Petersburg, VA
June 22-23	Jerusalem Plank Road, VA
July 10-12	Moved to Washington, DC
July 12	Repulse of Early's attack on Washington, DC
August-December	Sheridan's Shenandoah Valley Campaign
September 19	Battle of Oquequan, Winchester, VA
September 22	Fisher's Hill, VA
September 23-24	New Market, VA
September 25	Woodstock, VA
October 19	Battle of Cedar Creek, VA
Until December	Duty at Winchester and Shenandoah Valley
December 1-5	Moved to Petersburg, VA
December 5-April 5-7, 1865	Siege of Petersburg, VA
1865	
March 28-April 9	Appomattox Campaign
April 2	Assault on and fall of Petersburg, VA
April 3-9	Pursuit of Lee
April 6	Sailor's Creek, VA
April 9	Appomattox Court House, VA
Until April 23	At Farmville, Burkesville, VA
April 23-27	March to Danville, VA
May 24-June 3	March to Richmond then to Washington, DC
June 8	Corps review
Until August	Duty at Washington
August 18	Mustered out

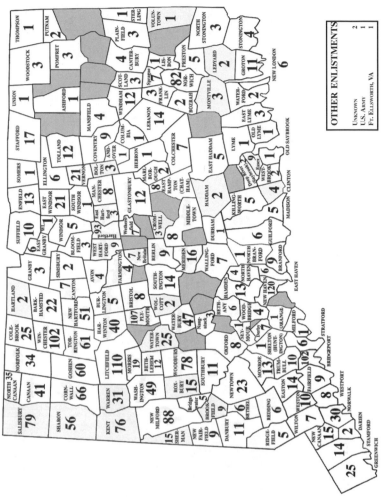

OTHER ENLISTMENTS

UNKNOWN	2
U.S. ARMY	1
FT. ELLSWORTH, VA	1

SECOND REGIMENT
CONNECTICUT VOLUNTEER HEAVY ARTILLERY

SECOND BATTERY

CONNECTICUT VOLUNTEER LIGHT ARTILLERY

SEPTEMBER 10, 1862 - AUGUST 9, 1865

(TWO YEARS, ELEVEN MONTHS)
230 RECRUITS

2 KILLED, 18 DIED, 5 WOUNDED

COLLECTION OF THE AUTHOR

The 2nd Connecticut Volunteer Light Battery was organized in **BRIDGEPORT** in August 1862 and was mustered into the United States service for three years on September 10. John S. Sterling of Bridgeport, was appointed Captain.

The Battery, which was composed of portions of two batteries of the State militia, gathered at Camp Buckingham, Seaside Park, Bridgeport. They left for Washington, DC on October 15 numbering 115 men. The Battery marched as far as New York City and then traveled by rail to the Capitol. In Washington, they went to "Camp Barry" at Bladensburgh Toll Gate.

On December 12, the Battery armed with four 6-pounder James Rifles and two 12-pounder Howitzers marched to Fairfax Court House, Virginia and joined the

DEFENSES OF WASHINGTON

They were placed in the Second Brigade of General Silas Casey's Division under the command of Brigadier General Edwin H. Stoughton. At Fairfax, the battery participated in repelling a night attack of Confederate General J. E. B. Stuart's cavalry.

At the end of January 1863, they were ordered to Wolf Run Shoals and stayed until June 25. The camp was pleasantly located however, four men died from disease.

In the summer of 1863, the Army of the Potomac pursued the Confederates into Maryland and Pennsylvania. On June 25, the Battery was ordered to the Artillery Reserve, under the command of General Robert O. Tyler. They joined the Reserve at Edwards Ferry and marched by way of Frederick, Maryland Taneytown to

GETTYSBURG

Before the Battery had left Wolf Run Shoals, they were ordered to destroy 1,100 rounds of ammunition. The Battery arrived at Gettysburg during the second day of the battle on Friday, July 2. They were re-supplied and ordered into position to the left center of the Union line off the Taneytown Road near the 2nd Corps.

The Battery was in position for 56 hours and escaped without any casualties at Gettysburg. They did lose three horses and one caisson however, when a Confederate shell exploded near their position.

The battery left Gettysburg for Frederick, Maryland on July 5. They reached there the next day and camped with the 7th New York State Militia. The Battery stayed in Frederick until the 18th. Next, they moved to Washington, DC, reached there two days later and went into camp at "Camp Barry".

On August 18, the Battery left on ships from Alexandria, Virginia for

NEW YORK

to aid in enforcing the draft. They reached New York on the 22nd, went into camp at City Hall Park, and then in sections, the Battery was sent to East New York, Troy, Albany, Kingston, and Tarrytown.

Up to this date, the Battery had lost five men by death from disease, six by desertion, fifteen by discharge and fifteen were sick in the hospital.

After the draft in New York had taken place, the Battery went to

BALTIMORE

Maryland, and on January 27, 1864 left on the steamship *Argo* for New Orleans

LOUISIANA

The Battery arrived there on February 5 and went into camp at Algiers. On March 1, they were ordered to Brashear City

where they remained until June 17 with one section at Thibodeaux. On July 30, under the command of Lieutenant Walter Hotchkiss of Bridgeport, the Battery left Algiers for Dauphin Island, Mobile Harbor,

ALABAMA

Captain Sterling, the original commander, was in the hospital in Louisiana.

The Battery reached Dauphin Island on August 3 and two days later participated in the attack on Forts Gaines while Union Admiral David Farragut led his fleet into Mobile Bay past Fort Gaines and Morgan. The fleet attacked and captured the Confederate ram *Tennessee*. The Battery witnessed the surrender of Fort Gaines.

On August 20, they crossed to the rear of Fort Morgan and assisted in the bombardment of the fort. For 24 hours shot and shell was poured into the fort from land and sea. The citadel was set on fire in the night and at dawn the next day the fort surrendered.

On August 28, the Battery crossed Mobile Bay to Cedar Point and on September 10, returned to Algiers

LOUISIANA

and went into winter quarters on St. Charles Street in New Orleans. On November 15, the Battery was ordered to the mouth of the White River,

ARKANSAS

and went into camp five days later..

The Battery left White River on January 19, 1865 and went into camp at Kennerville, ten miles above New Orleans. They remained there until February 10 when they were ordered to Greenville. On the 19th, they broke camp at midnight and before daylight the next morning had moved to Hickock's Landing on Lake Pontchartrain. Next, the Battery was dismounted and transported to Fort Morgan, arriving there on the 22nd. The Battery sailed for Barrancas,

FLORIDA

on February 26 and stayed until March 11 when they marched to Pensacola.

The Battery began its march to Blakely

ALABAMA

on March 20 and passed through the Black Swamp. After crossing Pine Barren Creek, the Battery came upon and captured 100 prisoners from a Confederate brigade under the command of Brigadier General James H. Clanton. The rest of the Confederate brigade escaped across the Escambia River after burning the bridge behind them.

The Battery stopped at the abandoned town of Pollard the following day and then moved to the head of the Perdido River. On the morning of April 2, Confederate skirmishers were encountered in the vicinity of Blakeley and were pursued into their fortifications. The Union lines were gradually drawn closer and on April 8 the Confederate works were charged and captured. Mobile surrendered to the Union army ending one of the last battles of the war. The Battery lost one man when a torpedo went off in the fort after it had been taken. The following day Lee surrender to Grant at Appomattox Court House, Virginia.

On April 20, the Battery boarded boats for Mobile and the next day started up the Alabama River. The Battery went on to Selma, reached there on the 27th, remained until May 12 and then returned to Mobile.

In July 1865, the order came for the Battery to return to Connecticut to be mustered out. Their guns were turned over to the United States Quartermaster in New Orleans.

The Battery left on ships for Connecticut and arrived in New Haven on July 31 under Captain Walter S. Hotchkiss' command. The Battery was officially welcomed by New Haven Mayor E. C. Scranton and were mustered out on August 9.

During its three year service, the Battery traveled or marched about 6,000 miles, serving in New York, Pennsylvania, Maryland, Virginia, Louisiana, Alabama, Arkansas and Florida. The Battery used 387 horses and never lost a gun or a flag. Its property had been so well taken care of that the Battery returned home with the same harnesses that were first issued.

The Battery had entered into service with the 6-pounder James Rifle and the 12-pounder howitzer. When they were in the Department of the Gulf they exhanged these guns for the three-inch ordnance rifle gun. It is a remarkable that during its three years of active service not a member of the Battery was killed in battle.

CAISSON

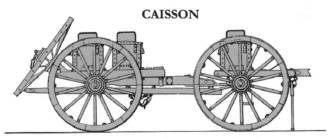

TOTAL CASUALTIES 2ND LIGHT BATTERY						
DATE	PLACE OF CASUALTY	TOTAL	K	M	W	C
1862						
September 20	Bridgeport, CT	1			1	
October 1	Bridgeport, CT	1			1	
December 15	Washington, DC	1			1	
1863						
February 1	Wolf Run Shoals, VA	1			1	
1864						
July 23	Rodney, MS	1			1	
December 22	At Sea (Drowned)	1	1			
1865						
April 9	Blakely, AL	1	1			

LIBRARY OF CONGRESS

12 POUNDER BRONZE HOWITZER
73 INCHES; 778 POUNDS; RANGE 1100 YARDS

LIBRARY OF CONGRESS

6 POUNDER BRONZE JAMES GUN
74 INCHES; 860 POUNDS; RANGE 1520 YARDS

TROOP MOVEMENTS 2ND LIGHT BATTERY

DATE	PLACE
1862	
October 15	Left State for Washington, DC
Until January 1863	Duty at Camp Barry
1863	
Until June 1863	Duty at Wolf Run Shoals
July 1-4	Battle of Gettysburg, PA
Until August 15	Duty at Washington, DC
August 15	Moved to New York City
Until October 12	Duty in New York at various locations
October 12	Moved to Washington, DC
Until January 1864	Duty at Washington, DC
1864	
January	Moved to New Orleans, LA
Until June 17	Duty at Brashear City
Until July 31	Duty at Algiers
July 31-September 8	Expedition to Mobile Bay, AL
August 2-8	Operations against Fort Gaines
August 9-23	Operations against Fort Morgan
Until September 8	Duty at Fort Gaines
September 8	Moved to Algiers
September 19	Moved to New Orleans
Until November 13	Duty at New Orleans
November 13	Moved to mouth of White River, ARK
Until February 1865	Duty at White River
1865	
March 11-April 1	Expedition to Fort Blakely, Mobile Bay
March 27	Occupation of Canoe Station, AL
April 1-9	Siege of Fort Blakely, AL
April 9	Assault & capture of Fort Blakely
April 12	Occupation of Mobile, AL
Until July	Duty at Mobile and Selma, AL
July 31	Moved to New Orleans & New Haven, CT
August 9	Mustered out

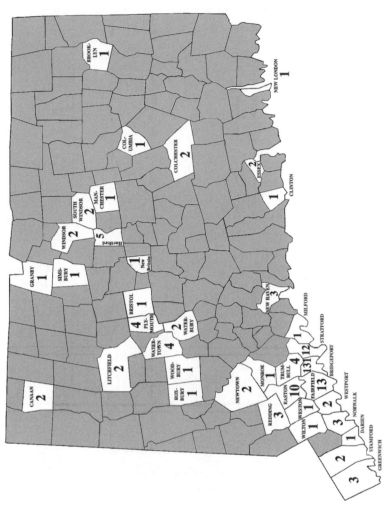

SECOND CONNECTICUT
VOLUNTEER LIGHT BATTERY

THIRD REGIMENT

CONNECTICUT VOLUNTEER INFANTRY
MAY 14, 1861 - AUGUST 12, 1861
(THREE MONTHS)
781 RECRUITS
4 KILLED, 1 MISSING, 16 WOUNDED,
3 WOUNDED & CAPTURED, 15 CAPTURED

USAMHI

John L. Chatfield of Waterbury, was the third Colonel appointed to the 3rd Connecticut Infantry and led the regiment at the Battle of Bull Run in July 1861. Chatfield was also the Colonel of the 6th Connecticut Infantry. He died while leading the 6th Connecticut at the assault on Fort Wagner, SC in July 1863

The 3rd Regiment Connecticut Volunteer Infantry began their organization almost simultaneously with that of the 1st and 2nd Connecticut Infantry Regiments.

The original call of President Lincoln, on April 15, 1861, requested only one regiment from Connecticut but the eagerness of Connecticut men to enlist caused Governor William Buckingham to personally intercede with the President to accept at least three regiments. This request was granted and the 3rd Connecticut was soon filled to the maximum.

The regiment went into camp at the Fair Grounds on Albany Avenue in

HARTFORD

and on May 14, 1861 was mustered into the service of the United States.

Levi Woodhouse of Hartford, was appointed Colonel but was later transferred to the command of the 4th Connecticut (1st Heavy Artillery). He was succeeded by John Arnold of New Haven. Allen G. Brady of Torrington was appointed Lieutenant Colonel and Alexander Warner of Woodstock was appointed Major.

About a week before they left Hartford, the regiment received US Model 1842 percussion muskets with flint locks altered to percussion. On May 19, they were ordered to Washington, DC and the next day they struck their tents and marched into Hartford. The regiment received their Colors from the hands of

Governor Buckingham in front of the State House.

They left Hartford, by rail, for New Haven that same day. The regiment sailed from New Haven, for the Capitol on the steamer *Cahawba*, by way of the Chesapeake Bay and the Potomac River. They arrived in

WASHINGTON, DC

on May 23, and went into camp at the Corcoran Estate of Glenwood. They were near the 1st and 2nd Connecticut Infantry. The regiment was assigned to a brigade with the two other Connecticut regiments and the 2nd Maine Infantry. The brigade was at first commanded by Brigadier General Daniel Tyler, who had been promoted from Colonel of the 1st Connecticut. Tyler was eventually replaced as brigade commander by Erasmus Keyes, a regular army officer, when he was promoted to division commander

Colonel Arnold proved to be incompetent and resigned at the end of May. Lieutenant Colonel John Chatfield, of the 1st Connecticut, was appointed Colonel. Chatfield was chosen because he had the advantage of a long experience as a militia officer. He was also an excellent drillmaster and disciplinarian, and did not tolerate insubordination in any form.

Lieutenant Colonel Brady considered the commissioning of Colonel Chatfield over himself a violation, by the Governor, of the regulations of the State militia. Brady refused to recognize Colonel Chatfield as his superior officer. For this insubordination, Lieutenant Colonel Brady was put under arrest for mutiny.

Although there was never a trial, for the next three months he was deprived of his command. He was however, honorably mustered out when the regiment's term of service expired in July. Lieutenant Colonel Brady's impetuous indiscretion was atoned for by his subsequent honorable and extremely efficient service in the 17th Connecticut Infantry, and in the Veteran Reserve Corps.

On June 24th, the 3rd Connecticut followed the other Connecticut regiments across the Long Bridge to

VIRGINIA

and camped beside them at Falls Church. At that time their position was the extreme and much exposed outpost of the Union lines.

On July 16, the regiment moved, with its brigade, at the head of the column, through Vienna and then to the outskirts of Centreville. The First Division halted on the heights and then with Richardson's Brigade pushed forward and encountered Longstreet's Confederate division at Blackburn's Ford on

BULL RUN

In the slight conflict that resulted, the Ford was held for the next two days. From July 18 to 20, the Union army continued to gather at Centreville.

On July 21, the Keyes Brigade was ordered to guard the Warrenton turnpike on the west side of Centreville. They had reached the Stone Bridge across Bull Run at about 10AM. At 2PM, General Tyler ordered the brigade to attack a battery on the Henry House hill near the Robinson House on its front. The Confederate battery, with 8 guns had fired 20 to 30 rounds and was strongly posted and supported by infantry.

A building, fence and a hedge sheltered the battery. Colonel Charles D. Jameson of the 2nd Maine and Colonel Chatfield of the 3rd Connecticut pressed their regiments forward about 100 yards up to the base of the hill. The regiments were ordered to lie down and to load their rifles. They then advanced toward the top of the hill and after a short while retreated without success. Suddenly, the Union artillery in other parts of the field fell silent and to the surprise of the Keyes Brigade they were ordered to retreat.

The 3rd Connecticut retreated to Centreville with the rest of the brigade. They had lost 3 killed, 1 missing, 15 wounded, 14 captured, and 3 wounded & captured. The regiment was prepared to sleep that night on the ground that they had left on the morning of the battle. At about 10PM, after the routed portion of McDowell's army was far on its way toward Washington, orders were given to continue the march to Falls Church.

For the next two days, the 3rd Connecticut was engaged in saving the equipment and stores that had been abandoned by the other troops.

The regiment eventually made their way back to the Capitol. For the next three weeks, they remained in camp near Washington, and at the termination of its service headed for home.

The 3rd Connecticut Volunteer Infantry returned to Hartford and was mustered out of service on August 12, 1861. By the end of the war 140 of its men were commisioned as officers in various Connecticut volunteer organizations.

USAMHI

THIRD CONNECTICUT VOLUNTEER INFANTRY

A PORTION OF THE 3RD CONNECTICUT INFANTRY POSED FOR THIS PHOTOGRAPH PRIOR TO THE BATTLE OF BULL RUN ON JULY 21, 1861. THE REGIMENT JOINED THE KEYES BRIGADE (TYLER'S DIVISION) ALONG WITH THE 1ST AND 2ND CONNECTICUT INFANTRY AND 2ND MAINE INFANTRY. THE REGIMENT WAS ENTIRELY ARMED WITH 1842 SMOOTHBORE MUSKETS ALTERED TO PERCUSSION.

US MODEL 1842 PERCUSSION MUSKET
.69 CAL. SMOOTHBORE

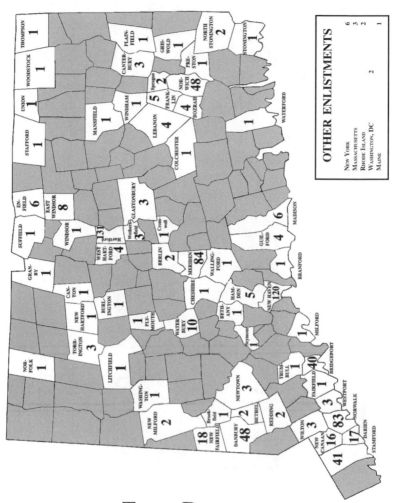

OTHER ENLISTMENTS

NEW YORK	6
MASSACHUSETTS	3
RHODE ISLAND	2
WASHINGTON, DC	2
MAINE	1

THOMPSON 1
WOODSTOCK 1
PLAIN-FIELD 1
CANTER-BURY 3
GRIS-WOLD 1
NORTH STONINGTON 2
STONINGTON 1
UNION 1
PRE-STON 1
SPRAGUE 2
NOR-WICH 48
WINDHAM 1
FRANK-LIN 5
MANSFIELD 1
STAFFORD 1
BOZRAH 4
LEBANON 4
COLCHESTER 1
WATERFORD 1
1
EN-FIELD 6
EAST WINDSOR 8
GLASTONBURY 3
SUFFIELD 1
WINDSOR 1
Hartford 131
Wethersfield 3
Crom-well 1
MADISON 6
WEST HART-FORD 4
GUIL-FORD 4
GRAN-BY 1
CAN-TON 1
BERLIN 2
MERIDEN 84
WALLING-FORD 1
BRANFORD 1
NEW HARTFORD 1
BURL-INGTON 1
CHESHIRE 1
HAM-DEN 5
NEW HAVEN 120
PLY-MOUTH 1
BETH-ANY 1
NOR-FOLK 1
TORR-INGTON 3
WATER-BURY 10
MILFORD 1
LITCHFIELD 1
WASHING-TON 1
TRUM-BULL 1
FAIRFIELD 40
BRIDGEPORT
NEWTOWN 3
FAIRFIELD 1
WESTPORT
NEW MILFORD 2
Brook-field 1
BETHEL 1
REDDING 2
WILTON 3
NORWALK 83
NEW FAIRFIELD 18
DANBURY 48
NEW CANAAN 16
DARIEN 17
STAMFORD
41

THIRD REGIMENT
CONNECTICUT VOLUNTEER
INFANTRY

THIRD BATTERY

CONNECTICUT VOLUNTEER LIGHT ARTILLERY
SEPTEMBER 1864 - JUNE 23, 1865
(NINE MONTHS)
152 RECRUITS

3 DIED, 2 WOUNDED

COLLECTION OF THE AUTHOR

T he 3rd Connecticut Volunteer Light Battery was recruited during the summer and fall of 1864. The Battery was organized and its officers commissioned by Special Order No. 126 from Headquarters of the Volunteer Recruitment Service of Connecticut.

Thomas S. Gilbert of Derby, was appointed Captain. He had been Captain of Company A in the 1st Connecticut Heavy Artillery.

Some of the recruits of the 3rd Battery enlisted for one year and others for two. A number of men had served in other commands, notably the 1st Connecticut Heavy Artillery.

On November 2, 1864, they left Connecticut for

VIRGINIA

The Battery reported at Broadway Landing on November 10, to Colonel Henry L. Abbot, commander of the 1st Connecticut Heavy Artillery. Captain Gilbert was instructed to move the Battery to

CITY POINT

near the line of artillery defenses on the

PETERSBURG

front. On November 26, the Battery was assigned to the defenses as a permanent garrison and occupied Redoubts No 2, 5, 7, and 8.

The 3rd Connecticut Battery was divided into detachments that were under the command of Lieutenants. Lieutenant Henry Middlebrook of Derby, with a detachment of 23 men and armament of 10-Pounder Parrott guns, was assigned on the right of the line at Redoubt No. 2.

Redoubt No. 5, near the railroad depot, was made the Headquarters of the 3rd Connecticut Battery. At Headquarters, Captain Gilbert was assisted by Lieutenant Nelson B. Gilbert of Chester, who acted as adjutant of the command. The redoubt was armed with four 4½-inch siege guns that covered a wide range on either side of the tracks.

Lieutenant William C. Beecher of Derby, commanded Redoubt No. 7 with a detachment of 20 men. They were equipped with six 10-Pounder Parrott guns.

Redoubt No. 8 was under the command of Lieutenant Richard E. Hayden of Naugatuck, with a force of 20 men and armament of six 4½- inch Rodman guns. All of the 3rd Connecticut Battery was also armed with muskets and infantry equipment.

The redoubts were complete fortifications that were connected by a line of infantry parapet. They were furnished with excellent magazines and a full set of ammunition.

Since all of the officers and most of the non-commisioned officers, and many of the enlisted men of the Battery had been in service before, they were familar with the duties and trials of camp and field. The Battery drilled constantly. Every man was taught the special duty that he would have to perform in any emergency. The 3rd Connecticut Battery was part of the defenses that protected the vast army stores, hospitals, charitable commissions, and the Headquarters of General Grant at City Point.

The Battery drilled and worked under the observant eyes of the senior command of the Union Army. The officers kept the redoubts neat and their personnel free from reproach. To "be always ready" was the brief instruction given to them. No pains were spared to obey this injunction. The men were instructed to maneuver the guns, to fix and prepare ammunition and were taught military bearing and conduct. They were also instructed in sanitation and to be alert and vigilant. The Battery watched and waited.

On January 24 and 25, 1865, when Confederate iron clads attempted to force a passage by the James River batteries, a section of the Battery, with four 4½-inch siege guns, was stationed in front of General Grant's headquarters and covered the wharves and storehouses, ready for action. The Confederate attempt did not succeed, and the battery was returned to the redoubts.

On the morning of April 2, 1865, when two Federal Corps made attacks at different points along the Confederate defenses, the Union earthworks were strengthened by the addition of a section of the light guns that could be easily moved along the line of breastworks that adjoined the redoubts. The entire line was left completely dependent on the officers and the men of the 3rd Connecticut Battery. That night, Lee began withdrawing his forces from the city to the north side of the Appomattox River. The Confederates began their westward movement and a week later they surrendered at Appomattox Courthouse.

The 3rd Connecticut Battery was ordered to work with a battalion of the 1st Connecticut Artillery, commanded by Major Albert F. Brooker, to dismantle the Confederate fortifications in the vicinity of Chaffin's Bluff on the James River. On June 22, Captain Gilbert was directed by the Commissary of Musters, Department of Virginia, to prepare muster out rolls of all the enlisted men of the Battery whose terms of service expired before October 1, 1865. The rolls contained the names of 93 men. The muster out rolls were sent to Headquarters the following day. The battery was mustered out with the exception of 27 men, who were transferred to the 1st Connecticut Heavy Artillery.

On June 24, a steamer took the Battery to New York, and then on to New Haven. The men were met at the dock by the New Haven Grays under the command of Colonel Samuel E. Merwin.

They were escorted in a drenching rain, to a splendid feast at the Union House.

On July 3, 1865, the officers and men of the Battery were paid and the command was disbanded. The Battery had lost no men in battle. Three men died of exposure or disease during its period of service. Only one man was wounded in combat. He was severely burned by the bursting of a buried shell in front of one of the Confederate works near Richmond.

LIBRARY OF CONGRESS

WHARFS AT CITY POINT, VIRGINIA 1864

THE 3RD LIGHT BATTERY WAS DIVIDED INTO DETACHMENTS AND ASSIGNED TO REDOUBTS NEAR THE PETERSBURG FRONT. THE BATTERY WAS PART OF THE LINE OF ARTILLERY THAT PROTECTED THE VAST ARMY STORES, HOSPITALS, CHARITABLE COMMISSIONS AND THE HEADQUARTERS OF GENERAL GRANT

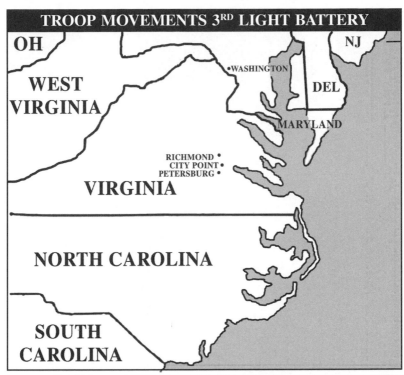

TROOP MOVEMENTS 3RD LIGHT BATTERY

DATE	PLACE
1864	
November 16-19	Moved to City Point, VA
Until December	Attached to defenses of City Point
Until June 1865	Siege Artillery Army of James & Potomac
1865	
January-June	Duty in redoubts 2,5,7,8
January 24-25	Repulse of attack on City Point by ironclads
June 23	Mustered out

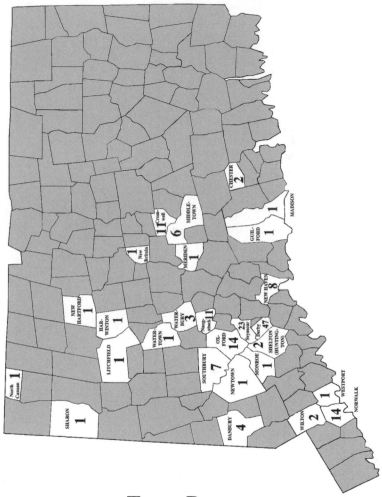

CHESTER 2

MIDDLE-TOWN 6

Crom-well 1

New Britain 1

MERIDEN 1

GUIL-FORD 1

MADISON 1

NEW HAVEN 8

NEW HARTFORD 1

HAR-WINTON 1

WATER BURY 3

Naug-atuck 11

Seymour 23

Derby 47

SHELTON (HUNTING-TON) 1

WATER-TOWN 1

LITCHFIELD 1

OX-FORD 14

MONROE 2

North Canaan 1

SOUTHBURY 7

NEWTOWN 1

SHARON 1

DANBURY 4

WILTON 2

WESTPORT 1

NORWALK 14

THIRD BATTERY
CONNECTICUT VOLUNTEER LIGHT ARTILLERY

FIFTH REGIMENT

CONNECTICUT VOLUNTEER INFANTRY

JULY 23, 1861 - JULY 19, 1865

(FOUR YEARS)
1,754 RECRUITS
81 KILLED, 2 MISSING, 107 DIED, 254 WOUNDED
201 CAPTURED, 14 WOUNDED & CAPTURED

The 5th Regiment Connecticut Volunteer Infantry was organized in the spring and summer of 1861. It was generally made up of the companies that did not serve under Governor William Buckingham's April 15th call for three months troops.

On May 4, after President Lincoln's call for 75,000 three years troops, the companies began to re-enlist. The men started gathering in HARTFORD on May 14, and were organized as fast as they arrived into the

1ST REGIMENT COLT'S REVOLVING RIFLES

On May 16, Samuel Colt of Hartford, inventor of the revolver bearing his name, was appointed Colonel.

The men were housed in the buildings and on the grounds of the Colt Patent

USAMHI

Orris S. Ferry of Norwalk, was appointed Colonel of the 5th Connecticut when Samuel Colt resigned. Ferry, a Congressman and lawyer, was eventually appointed Brigadier General of Volunteers in March 1862.

Fire Arms Company. They drilled until June 20, when once again they broke up primarily because of Colonel Colt's insistence that the regiment enlist as a regular United States Army regiment. A vote was taken and the men decided to form their own Connecticut volunteer regiment. They reorganized as the 5th Regiment Connecticut Volunteer Infantry, with Congressman Orris S. Ferry of Norwalk, as Colonel.

The following day, the regiment moved from Colt's meadows to a field on the southeast corner of Bond and Webster Streets in Hartford. Colonel James Loomis, United States Army, mustered the regiment into service on July 22 and 23.

The 5th Connecticut started for the

front on July 29 and arrived at Sandy Hook, Maryland, opposite

HARPER'S FERRY

West Virginia on the night of July 31.

The regiment's first service, was primarily in picketing and guarding along the Upper Potomac River in the area around Harper's Ferry. They covered the territory on the Maryland side north to Sir John's Run and south to Muddy Branch.

On the night of October 22, the regiment made a forced march of 20 miles from Darnestown to Ball's Bluff, arriving at dawn the following day. Orders were received for the regiment to cross the river at once, but after waiting two hours for transportation the order was changed.

Eventually, passage for one company was furnished and Co.I was sent. It was posted at the extreme right of the Union line in breastworks built of earth, fence rails, and bags of grain from adjacent mills.

Under the direction of Captain Griffin A. Stedman of Hartford, the breastworks were built from the river on the right of the Union line up to and over the crest of the bluff on the left side of the line. A picket line was established in front and was maintained until near daylight of October 24. After Company I was recalled to the Maryland side, they found, somewhat to their chagrin, that they had been used to cover the withdrawal of other Union troops from a dangerous position, rather than as pioneers to a real attack.

On October 26, the regiment camped at Muddy Branch, Maryland and remained there until December 4. Their duty, once again, was in picketing four miles along the Potomac River. During the month of December the 5th Connecticut was almost constantly on the move. They headed off Stonewall

Jackson's Confederates, who were active on the Virginia side of the Potomac, in attempting to destroy the Chesapeake & Ohio Canal and the B & O Railroad.

On December 20, Companies E and F had a skirmish with the Confederates who were trying to blow up Dam No. 5. The companies of the regiment, with others, assisted in driving the Confederates off with musketry and received a lively shelling in return. This was the first introduction of the regiment to Jackson and his Stonewall Brigade. The 5th Connecticut was in opposition to every movement of the Stonewall Brigade until the Battle of Chancellorsville in May 1863 when Stonewall Jackson lost his life.

On January 1, 1862, Jackson started from Winchester, Virginia and moved up the Potomac River with a Confederate force of 8,500. Three days later, the Confederates drove out the Union forces at Bath and chased some to Sir John's Run and the remainder to Hancock, Maryland. The next day, the Confederates burned the B & O Railroad Bridge over the Cacapon River, shelled Hancock, and then moved toward Romney, West Virginia.

The 5th Connecticut had left Hancock a few days earlier and had moved 60 miles down the river to Frederick. On January 5, they were ordered to return. The regiment broke camp in a blinding snowstorm and in the dead of night made its way through deep snow over the Blue Ridge and back into the Alleghenies. They reached Hancock on January 8 and stayed for the winter.

The regiment suffered considerable depletion in the ranks due to the hardships of cold and exposure. Similarly, Jackson's winter campaign had completely used up his men, and he was forced to go into winter quarters at Romney, nearly opposite Hancock.

Peace in western Virginia was kept until spring.

On March 2, 1862, the 5th Connecticut crossed into Virginia from Williamsport, Maryland, with Nathaniel Banks command. After moving about four miles, there was a skirmish with the Confederates at Falling Waters. The Union force continued to advance and had moved about 30 miles further when Confederate pickets were driven back at Bunker Hill. Finally, the 5th Connecticut was in the advance that drove the Confederates from Winchester on March 12. This was the regiment's first appearance in Winchester.

After the Union force had gained possession of the city, the regiment camped on the grounds of James M. Mason's estate. Mason was known as the surveyor of the Mason Dixon Line and Colonel Ferry occupied the Mason residence as regimental headquarters.

Nine companies of the regiment left Winchester with Banks army on March 22 and moved east toward Manassas. Winchester was left to the command of Brig. General James Shields who had recently moved his force from Romney. Shields main body of troops was lying at Stevenson's Station about four miles to the north of the city. At about 2PM that afternoon, Jackson's cavalry and Turner Ashby's artillery attacked the Union troops at Kernstown, a place just below Winchester. Company D of the 5th Connecticut had been left behind as train guards and was one of four companies that quickly established a skirmish line to meet the Confederates. Two hours later, Shields brought his forces down. The following day, Company D stayed at Kernstown and was placed into the Union battle line at three different points in the Union victory.

The other companies of the regiment returned the following morning, and joined in the pursuit of Jackson for 100 miles up the Shenandoah Valley. The regiment took part in skirmishes at Mount Jackson, Big Spring, and near Harrisonburg.

On April 16, at Hudson's Corner's, details from Companies E and F formed the major part of a detachment that made an all night march into the Confederate lines. They surprised and captured 59 men of Company H of Ashby's cavalry along with their horses, arms, accoutrements, and stores.

On May 3, Companies H and I drove the Confederates from Peaked Mountain and, after a sharp skirmish in which they had one wounded, they established a signal station. Colonel Ferry was appointed Brigadier General of the Brigade in Shields Division and Lieutenant Colonel George D. Chapman of Hartford, assumed command of the regiment. On May 5, after Shields division was withdrawn from the Shenandoah Valley, Banks began falling back with the remainder of his command.

On May 23, they were camped a few miles above Strasburg near Fisher's Hill. On that day, men of the 5th Connecticut were fired on while bathing in the Shenandoah River. The next day, the Confederates appeared in force, coming down the Valley Pike and the Luray Valley. Banks army was soon in full retreat. The regiment was engaged alternately in opening the way in front and for defenses in the rear.

On the Front Royal Road in front of

WINCHESTER

on May 25, the regiment had a sharp engagement with Trimble's brigade of Ewell's Division and the Confederates were pushed back with heavy loss. On the Strasburg Road however, George H. Gordon's Brigade was opposing Jackson's main and superior force. The

Union brigade retreated. The 5th Connecticut was forced to abandon its strong position and to retreat with the rest of Banks command.

The regiment moved off to the east of Winchester because the city was already in possession of the Confederates. For several hours, the regiment marched rapidly on roads and across fields. They out ran all pursuers and at 9 PM crossed the Potomac into Maryland near Sharpsburg. The exhausted regiment had in the previous 36 hours, fought for several hours, counter marched for many miles and had covered 65 miles of retreat. The 5th Connecticut suffered 1 killed, 9 wounded, 52 captured and 3 wounded & captured

On June 3, they crossed again into Virginia with the 1st Brigade, 1st Division, 2nd Corps, Army of Virginia and followed Jackson up the valley as far as Front Royal. The regiment, as part of a larger force, made a reconnaissance on June 30, and had a skirmish with the Confederates that cleared them out of Luray.

On July 7, the regiment crossed the Blue Ridge and joined Popes' army near Warrenton. On August 9, at

CEDAR MOUNTAIN

the 5th was in the very thickest of the fight. As part of Crawford's Brigade, Williams Division of Bank's 2nd Corp and in company with the 28 NY, 16 PA, and 10 ME, the regiment broke entirely through the Confederate infantry lines. The small brigade scattered and routed ten regiments of Confederate troops and carried the most commanding position on the field. The Union force however, was greatly outnumbered and not supported. After a hard struggle they fell back from the Confederates.

The 5th Connecticut had its heaviest loss for any single day of its service at Cedar Mountain. Out of nearly 380 men

engaged, the regiment had 35 killed, 71 wounded, 51 captured and 8 wounded & captured. Major Edward F. Blake of New Haven was killed, along with Adjutant Heber S. Smith of Hartford. Colonel Chapman and the wounded Lieutenant Colonel Henry B. Stone of Danbury, were captured. Henry Stone died from his wound and after being released from a long imprisonment, Colonel Chapman resigned. Warren W. Packer of New London, assumed command of the regiment.

Of the eight companies engaged in the battle, all but three officers, were killed, wounded, or captured. The two companies not engaged at Cedar Mountain were detailed elsewhere. Company F had been detached 6 miles away, guarding a signal station on Thoroughfare Mountain and Company H had been on provost duty in Culpeper.

On Sunday, August 17, Lee's army came into sight as they passed over the hills between Gordonsville and Orange Court House. The following day the Union army, under Pope, began falling back. All of the baggage teams were sent on to Alexandria and were not accessible again for a month. The month of August was hot, wretched, and uncomfortable. The hungry men of the 5th Connecticut were full of rage.

The regiment was with Pope's reserve force at the Battle of 2nd Bull Run on August 28-30 and during all the disheartening retreats and defeats that followed. They were under artillery fire at Rappahannock Station, White Sulfur Springs, Bristoe Station, and Chantilly and suffered only slight loss.

The 5th Connecticut participated in part of the Maryland campaign that followed. On September 15, the day before the battle of South Mountain, the regiment was detached from the main column. They performed provost duty at

Frederick, Maryland and remained there until December 10 when they joined the

12TH CORPS

of the Army of the Potomac in front of Fredericksburg, Virginia. The regiment did not participate in the Battle of Fredericksburg. They camped near Stafford Court House during the winter of 1862-1863.

The regiment broke camp on April 27 and with the 1st Brigade (Knipe), 1st Division (A.S. Williams), 12th Army Corps (Slocum) they arrived at

CHANCELLORSVILLE

on May 1. The regiment, with its brigade, built breastworks along their front. They then advanced about a mile further to support Sickles' movement near Hazel Grove. When they returned later that night, they found their works occupied by the Confederates, who were part of Stonewall Jackson's flank movement. A large number of men on the regiment's right side were captured when they charged the works. It was in the darkness and confusion of this counter charge that Jackson was fatally wounded. The 5th Connecticut had 1 killed, 22 wounded, and 27 captured.

Following the Union defeat at Chancellorsville, Lee and his Confederate force began to move north. On June 28, Lee learned, to his dismay, that the 95,000 man Army of the Potomac, led by its new commander George G. Meade, had crossed the Potomac and might soon strike his scattered force in Pennsylvania. As part of the 12th Corps the regiment reached the field at

GETTYSBURG

on the evening of July 1. It was put into the line of battle on the right of Culp's Hill on the morning of the 2nd. They built strong earthworks at once along their whole front. Toward evening the regiment was moved to the left to support

Sickles 3rd Corps after he had fallen back to his new line. The 5th Connecticut was ordered to return to their previous works and position in the line. Once again, as at Chancellorsville, the regiment found its position in the possession of the Confederates. In attempting to retake it, the regiment had 3 men wounded and 7 captured.

The next morning, while the 1st Division was storming and retaking the works, the 5th Connecticut was detached and sent farther to the right side to support a battery, at first, and later to support the cavalry. The Union victory at the Battle of Gettysburg ended with the 5th Connecticut in this position. During Lee's retreat, the regiment was in the advance of the pursuit as far as Warrenton, Virginia.

On September 25, the 11th and 12th Corps were consolidated into the

20TH CORPS

under Major General Joseph Hooker. The regiment was sent to join the Department of the Cumberland at

COWAN, TENNESSEE

and arrived on October 10 and finished their three-year term of service as railroad guards. The veterans went on furlough to Connecticut from January 13 to March 9, 1864.

When the veterans returned, the regiment was immediately launched into the

ATLANTA CAMPAIGN

With the 20th Corps, they participated in most of the victories of that arduous struggle, and suffered its share of losses. They were engaged at Resaca, Cassville, Dallas, Lost Mountain, Kenesaw, Culp's Farm, Peach Tree Creek, and the Siege of Atlanta. On May 14, at

RESACA

the 5th Connecticut was held in reserve until 4 PM when it was ordered to the extreme left to support Howard's position. Their entire march was in the rear of the fighting line but within range of the Confederate artillery. As part of Knipe's 1st Brigade, the regiment arrived in time to relieve the 4th Corps, and to drive the Confederates back to their works.

At about 1 PM the following day, the line in front of the 5th Connecticut was advanced at the double quick to the crest of a hill. The regiment had just gained a good position at the top of the hill when the Confederates charged up the slope in front. The order to fire came quickly, and the first volley brought the Confederates to a halt. The second volley sent them back into their works. While all this was going on, the regiment began singing "The Battle Cry of Freedom". Troops on the left and right picked up the tune. The color guard advanced well to the front waving the flag in the faces of the Confederates. The effect was magical. The Confederates charged again and again without effect. They became convinced at last that the flag, with the rifles of the 5th Connecticut behind it, would wave as long as they wished. The regiment had 8 killed and 40 wounded.

On June 22, at

CULP'S FARM

the regiment was held in reserve and built earthworks. At 2 PM, they were ordered to take a position at the extreme left of the entire Union army. When the regiment arrived, they opened fire at once on the advancing Confederates. The Southerners pressed on persistently, and at one time charged very near, as if they intended to use their bayonets. The Union bullets finally kept them off the line and pushed them back. In the fight, each man in the 5th Connecticut used 60 rounds. The regiment also captured many prisoners and one set of colors.

They had 3 killed, 11 wounded, 2 wounded & captured.

On July 20, the battle at

PEACH TREE CREEK

opened very suddenly for the 5th Connecticut. The regiment had been lying and waiting in the woods for orders to attack the Confederate lines, when Confederate General John B. Hood, with all his available force, surprised the Union lines by charging. The regiment moved quickly into position. The effect of the Confederates first volley was lost because they were charging up hill and had fired too high. The battle eventually settled down into a stand up fight for three hours. The Confederates hopelessly charged again and again. The regiment lost 13 killed, 38 wounded and 1 captured.

On September 1, 1864, the regiment in the advance, had the honor of being the first Union regiment to march through the city of Atlanta. During the 116 days of the Siege of Atlanta, the regiment had been under constant fire, had moved forward, made defenses, fought at every opportunity and had held their ground in every instance. On November 15, the regiment left Atlanta with Sherman on his

"MARCH TO THE SEA"

and took an active part in the Siege of Savannah.

The 5th Connecticut participated in the battles of Chesterfield Court House, South Carolina, and in Averysborough, and Bentonville, North Carolina. On March 16, 1865, at Silver Run the regiment participated in the defeat and surrender of Confederate General Joseph E. Johnston's Army.

The regiment next marched through Richmond and the familiar fields of northeastern Virginia. The 5th Connecticut participated in the Grand Review at Washington, DC on May 23 and was mustered out of service at Alexandria, Virginia on July 19, 1865.

BATTLE OF CEDAR MOUNTAIN, VIRGINIA

THE 5TH CONNECTICUT VOLUNTEER INFANTRY HAD ITS GREATEST NUMBER OF CASUALITIES (165) FOR ONE DAY WITH THE 1ST BRIGADE (CRAWFORD), 1ST DIVISION (A.S. WILLIAMS), 2ND CORPS ARMY OF VIRGINIA (BANKS) ON AUGUST 9, 1862

SOLDIER IN OUR CIVIL WAR (DETAIL)

US MODEL 1861 PERCUSSION RIFLE MUSKET

USAMHI

TOTAL CASUALTIES 5TH INFANTRY

DATE	PLACE OF CASUALTY	TOTAL	K	M	W	W/C	C
1861							
Unknown	Hyattstown, MD	1			1		
October 8	Unknown	1			1		
November 1	Muddy Branch, MD	1			1		
1862							
February 22	Buckingham Co., VA	1					1
April 21	Edinburgh, VA	1					1
April 21	Woodstock, VA	1					1
April 22	Buckingham Co., VA	1					1
May 1	Shenandoah Valley, VA	1			1		
May 3	Harrisonburg, VA	2			1		1
May 23	Front Royal, VA	1					1
May 24	Winchester, VA	7					7
May 24	Strasburg, VA	1					1
May 25	**Winchester, VA**	64	1		8	3	52
May 25	Middletown, VA	1			1		
June 10	Chickahominy, VA	1					1
June 30	Luray Valley	1					1
July 26	Little Washington, VA	1					1
August 9	Cedar Creek, VA	1			1		
August 9	**Cedar Mountain, VA**	165	36		70	8	51
August 9	Culpeper, VA	5					5
August 12	Culpeper Court House, VA	1					1
August 17	Virginia	1					1
Unknown	Unknown	2					2
August 20	Culpeper, VA	1					1
August 20	Beal's Station, VA	3				1	2
August 28	Warrenton, VA	1					1
August 30	2nd Bull Run, VA	3					3
September 1	Manassas Junction, VA	1					1
September 4	Darnestown, MD	1					1
1863							
May 1	Hagerstown, MD	1			1		
May 2-3	**Chancellorsville, VA**	50	1		22		27
July 2-3	**Gettysburg, PA**	10			3		7
July 10	Danville, VA	1					1
July 11	Darnestown, MD	1					1
July 21	Loudon County, VA	1					1
July 28	Manassas Gap, VA	1					1
August 1	Virginia	1					1
August 4	Fairfax Court House, VA	1					1
August 4	Kelly's Ford, VA	1					1
August 12	Kelly's Ford, VA	1	1				
September 27	Railroad Accident	1	1				
October 5	Railroad Accident	1	1				
November 23	Unknown	1			1		
December 24,30	Cowan, TN (Accident)	2	2				
1864							
February 17	Railroad Accident	1	1				
February 28	Putnam, CT	1	1				
May 15	**Resaca, GA**	49	8		41		
May 25	Near Atlanta, GA	2			1		1
May 25-June 3	**Dallas, GA**	29	2	2	25		
June 3	Georgia	1			1		
June 16-17	Pine Mountain, GA	2			2		
June 19	Kenesaw Mountain, GA	1			1		
June 19	Marietta, GA	1			1		
June 22	**Culp's Farm, GA**	16	3		11	2	
July 19-20	**Peach Tree Creek, GA**	54	13		40		1
July 20	Atlanta, GA	7	1		6		
July 22	Tennessee	1			1		
July 30-August 1	Atlanta, GA	9	3		6		
August 16, 26	Atlanta, GA	2			1		1
November 15	Georgia	1					1
November 18-20	Madison, GA	9					9
November 19, Dec 11	Savannah, GA	2					2
1865							
January 10	Steamer "Fulton" (Drowned)	2	2				
February 28	Liberty Hill, SC	1					1
March 2	Chesterfield Court House, SC	1					1
March 5	Wadesboro, NC	2					2
March 6	Pedee River, NC	1					1
March 7	Fayetteville, NC	1					1
March 10	Averysboro, NC	1			1		
March 16	Silver Run, NC	5	4		1		
March 19	Bentonville, NC	1					1
March 19,23	Goldsboro, NC	2			1		1
August 1	Atlanta, GA	1			1		

DATE	PLACE
1861	
July 29	Left State
July 30	Moved to Harper's Ferry, WVA
Until August 16	Duty at Harper's Ferry
Until February 1862	Duty on the Upper Potomac
October 20-24	Operations near Edward's Ferry
December 17-20	Operations about Dam No. 4, 5
1862	
March 1-12	Advance on Winchester, VA
March 5	Near Winchester
March 12	Occupation of Winchester
March 18	Ordered to Manassas, VA
March 19	Returned to Winchester
March 24-April 27	Pursuit of Jackson
April 17	Columbia Furnace
May 20	At Strasburg
May 20-25	Retreat to Winchester
May 23	Action at Front Royal
May 24	Middletown
May 24-25	Battle of Winchester
May 25-June 6	Retreat to Martinsburg, WVA/Williamsport, MD
Until June 10	At Williamsport
June 10-18	Moved to Front Royal
June 29-30	Reconnaissance to Lurray
July	Moved to Warrenton, Gordonsville, Culpepper
July 28	Reconnaissance to Raccoon Ford (Co I)
August 6-September 2	Pope's Campaign in Northern Virginia
August 9	Battle of Cedar Mountain
August 29-30	Battle of Bull Run
September 2-12	Moved to Washington, then Frederick, MD
Until December 10	Duty at Frederick, MD
December 10-14	March to Fairfax Station
Until January 19	Duty at Fairfax Station
1863	
January 19-23	Moved to Stafford Court House, VA
Until April 27	Duty at Stafford Court House, VA
April 27-May 6	Chancellorsville Campaign

TROOP MOVEMENTS 5TH INFANTRY

DATE	PLACE
May 1-5	Battle of Chancellorsville
June 11-July 24	Gettysburg Campaign
July 1-3	Battle of Gettysburg
July 12	Funkstown, MD
July 21	Snicker's Gap
Until September 24	Near Raccoon Ford, VA
September 24-October 3	Brandy Sta., Bealeton, VA Stevenson, AL
Until April 1864	Duty along Nashville & Chattanooga RR (Cowan)
1864	
May-September	Atlanta Campaign
May 8-11	Demonstration on Rocky Faced Ridge
May 14-15	Battle of Resaca
May 19	Cassville
May 25	New Hope Church
May 26-June 5	Battles Dallas, New Hope Church, Allatoona
June 10-July 2	Operations about Marietta, Kenesaw MT.
June 11-14	Pine Mountain
June 15-17	Lost Mountain
June 15	Gilgal or Golgotha Church
June 17	Muddy Creek
June 19	Noyes Creek
June 22	Culp's Farm
June 27	Assault on Kenesaw
July 4	Ruff's Station. Smyrna Camp Ground
July 5-17	Chattahoochee River
July 19-20	Peach Tree Creek
July 22-August 25	Siege of Atlanta
August 16	Allatoona
August 26-September 2	Operations at Chattahoochee River Bridge
September 2- November 15	Occupation of Atlanta
November 15-December 15	"March to the Sea"
December 9	Monteith Swamp
December 10-21	Siege of Savannah
January-April 1865	Campaign of the Carolinas
1865	
March 2	Thompson's Creek (Chesterfield CH, SC)
March 3	Near Cheraw
March 16	Averysboro, NC
March 19-21	Battle of Bentonville
March 24	Occupation of Goldsboro
April 9-13	Advance on Raleigh
April 26	Bennett's House
April 29	Surrender of Johnston's Army
April 30-May 20	March to Washington, DC via Richmond, VA
May 24	Grand Review
July 19	Mustered out (old members July 22)

CONGRESSIONAL MEDAL OF HONOR WINNER

Captain George W. Corliss , Co. C, 5th Connecticut Infantry
Place and date: At Cedar Mountain, VA 9 August 1862
Date of issue: 10 September 1865
Citation: Seized a fallen flag of the regiment, the color bearer having been killed, carried it forward in the face of a severe fire, and though himself shot down and permanently disabled, planted the staff in the earth and kept the flag flying.

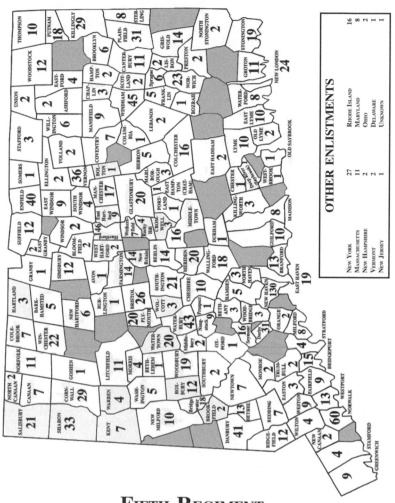

FIFTH REGIMENT
CONNECTICUT VOLUNTEER
INFANTRY

SIXTH REGIMENT

CONNECTICUT VOLUNTEER INFANTRY

SEPTEMBER 13, 1861 - AUGUST 21, 1865

(THREE YEARS, ELEVEN MONTHS)
1,610 RECRUITS
56 KILLED, 15 MISSING, 179 DIED, 379 WOUNDED
11 WOUNDED & CAPTURED, 99 CAPTURED

The 6th Regiment Connecticut Volunteer Infantry was organized in August 1861 under the leadership of John L. Chatfield of Waterbury. Chatfield had been Colonel of the 3rd Connecticut Infantry

The 6th Connecticut was the third regiment furnished by Connecticut under the first call for three-year volunteers.

The 4th Connecticut was the first of the three-year regiments to be recruited. It eventually became the 1st Heavy Artillery. The 5th Connecticut was the second regiment recruited.

The men of the 6th Connecticut camped at Oyster Point, **New Haven**

USAMHI

John L. Chatfield of Waterbury, was the first Colonel of the 6th Connecticut Infantry. He had been the controversial Colonel of the 3rd Connecticut Infantry who fought at the Battle of Bull Run in July 1861. Colonel Chatfield died from wounds received while leading the 6th Connecticut at the assault on Fort Wagner, SC on July 18, 1863

and were mustered into the United States service on September 13, 1861.

On September 17, the regiment numbering 1,008 left New Haven for **WASHINGTON, DC** and arrived two days later. In Washington, the 6th Connecticut camped on Meridian Hill and was assigned with the 7th Connecticut, 9th Maine and 4th New Hampshire to the Third Brigade of **SHERMAN'S EXPEDITONARY CORPS**

The third brigade was under the command of Brig. General Horatio G. Wright, from Orange and Clinton, Connecticut. The regiment left Washington for Annapolis, MD on October 8 where they joined over 12,000 soldiers who were being organized under Brig. General Thomas W. Sherman and Admiral Samuel F. Dupont for an expedition to the

SOUTH CAROLINA

coast. The expedition sailed on October 19 and eventually encountered a terrific storm off Cape Hatteras, North Carolina. A number of ships were wrecked or disabled before the fleet arrived off Port Royal, South Carilina on November 4.

THE BOMBARDMENT OF FORTS WALKER AND BEAUREGARD

began on November 7. The engagement lasted five hours and at its close the 6th and 7th Connecticut regiments were landed in small boats and took possession of the forts. For the next few months, the regiment was engaged in rebuilding the walls and in making raids upon the surrounding country.

In January 1862, the regiment took part in a failed expedition through Warsaw Sound to capture Savannah, Georgia. The 6th Connecticut was kept on board a small, overcrowded boat for 16 days without cooked food or any vegetables. The hard tack was full of vermin and the water supply was stored in empty kerosene barrels. In addition, there was not enough room on the boat for all of the men to lie down at once. Spotted fever eventually broke out and many lives were unnecessarily lost.

In March 1862, the 6th Connecticut was engaged in the Union victory at the

SIEGE OF FORT PULASKI

on the Savannah River, Georgia. The regiment participated in the construction and maintenance of a battery on Jones Island which was located between the fort and the City of Savannah. The purpose of the battery was to prevent the reinforcement of the fort and to stop the Confederate ironclad *Atlanta* from passing down the river. Because the island

was covered with water at high tide, the duty was laborious as well as dangerous. On April 11, Fort Pulaski surrendered and the regiment returned to more pleasant quarters on Dawfuski Island.

The regiment took part in the second expedition against Charleston in June. They marched over John's Island, suffered many hardships and were without food for three days because their wagon trains were cut off. The regiment finally arrived at James Island on June 10 and two days later were engaged in a skirmish that left 3 men of the regiment wounded.

The 6th Connecticut took a small part in the Union loss on June 16 at the

BATTLE OF SECESSIONVILLE

The regiment had no casualties and after the battle went into camp at Beaufort, South Carolina and performed picket and guard duty until October 22, when they were engaged in the Union defeat at the

BATTLE OF POCOTALIGO

The regiment suffered its first casualties with 5 killed and 30 wounded. Among the severely wounded were Colonel Chatfield, who had been commanding the 1st brigade, and Lieutenant Colonel John Speidel, who had been commanding the regiment.

The 6th Connecticut returned to Beaufort and from there were transferred to Jacksonville, Florida on March 18, 1863. The regiment participated in the fortification and defense of the town.

On April 1, they left Jacksonville and after a short stay at Hilton Head, Beaufort, and on some of the islands along the coast they landed on Folly. Island on May 1. The regiment participated in the second attack on Charleston and Fort Sumter, this time attacking by way of Morris Island. The regiment worked nights for three weeks, without being discovered, in constructing ten batteries and mounting 48 heavy siege guns all within 400 yards of the Confederate works.

At midnight on July 9, the regiment went up the Folly River in boats with Strong's Brigade and at daybreak, under intense fire, landed on Morris Island in the face of the Confederate guns. They charged, carried the fortifications, captured 125 prisoners, and two battle flags. The 6th Connecticut was at the front and lost 1 killed and 11 wounded.

On July 18, Strong's Brigade led the disasterous charge on the sea face of

FORT WAGNER

Colonel Chatfield, who had resigned from the command of the brigade to lead his regiment, was mortally wounded. The Connecticut men held an angle of the fort for three hours almost unaided. Since they were not supported they were forced to retire after a portion of the regiment had been captured. The 6th Connecticut took about 400 men into the charge and its losses were 16 killed, 9 missing, 83 wounded, 23 captured and 6 wounded & captured

The loss to the regiment at Fort Wagner was so great that they were sent to Hilton Head to recuperate. Colonel Chatfield died of his wounds, and Lieutenant Colonel Speidel, because of his wounds, was transferred to the Invalid Corps.

During the fall and winter of 1863, many of the men re-enlisted. The regiment was engaged in routine duty. Adjutant Redfield Duryee was promoted to Colonel.

In April 1864, the regiment, as part of the

10TH ARMY CORPS

1st Division, 2nd Brigade was transferred to Virginia and took part in the campaign under the command of Maj. General Benjamin Butler's

ARMY OF THE JAMES

On May 9 and 10, they were engaged in the

ACTION AT CHESTER STATION

on the Petersburg Road. On May 16, the regiment was engaged in the

BATTLE OF DREWRY'S BLUFF

on Proctor's Creek and on May 20 and June 2 in skirmishes at Bermuda Hundred. On May 27, Colonel Duryee resigned and subsequently so did his replacement Alfred P. Rockwell. On June 9, the regiment took part in an attack on Petersburg, under Maj. General Q. A. Gillmore.

On June 17, the 6th Connecticut advanced from

BERMUDA HUNDRED

and tore up some of the track of the Petersburg railroad They came under attack from the Confederate army that was on its way to Petersburg to defend the city against General Grant. The Confederates were eventually driven back into their earthworks. The regiment lost 184 men in several engagements from May 10 to June 18.

On June 25, the 6th Connecticut crossed the James River and covered the movement of Maj. General Sheridan who was returning from his famous cavalry raid around Richmond.

From June 25 to August 13, the 6th Connecticut was in the earthworks at Bermuda Hundred doing picket duty and guarding the Union line. On August 14, they crossed the James River to

DEEP BOTTOM AND DEEP RUN

and were engaged in the Battle of Strawberry Plains. They captured a line of earthworks, 200 prisoners, and two stands of colors.

The regiment was then ordered to

PETERSBURG

and was engaged in the siege of that city. They were on the front line until September 27. The regiment performed picket duty and built Fort Haskell, which was one of the largest and strongest forts on the Union line. The men slept in holes in the ground and the luxury of a cooked meal was rare. The exposure and hardships on the Petersburg line involved more danger than pitched battle because the canon fire was continuous both day and night.

On September 11, when their terms of service had expired, the men of the 6th Connecticut who did not re-enlist, were discharged while on the frontline of Petersburg. On September 28, the regiment marched to the north side of the James River and near

RICHMOND

was engaged in the Battle of Fort Harrison, New Market Road, and Chaffin's Farm. They advanced up the Darbytown Road to within three miles of Richmond. On October 1, the regiment was once again engaged in a skirmish on the Darbytown Road at Laurel Hill Church.

On October 7, the Confederates made an attack on the Union lines on the New Market Road. The brunt of the battle fell upon the 1st Division (Ames) of the 10th Army Corps that included the 6th Connecticut. The Southern attacks were repelled and the Confederates fell back. On October 13, the regiment was engaged at Darbytown Road and on October 27 at the Charles City Road.

Prior to the presidential election of November 1864, the 6th Connecticut, along with other regiments, were ordered to New York in anticipation of riots. The Union force was stationed in boats at different points on the East and Hudson Rivers.

Although within a few miles from home and loved ones, the men were not permitted to visit them, but were returned to their camp on the Petersburg front after not landing in New York.

When the regiment returned to Virginia, their time was spent in camp and picket duty until the later part of December 1864, when the regiment was ordered to take part in the second attack on

FORT FISHER

The regiment accompanied Major General Alfred Terry's 10th Corps on the expedition to North Carolina and witnessed the bombardment of the fort. On January 16, 1865, they were part of the successful assault.

After the capture of Fort Fisher, the regiment took part in the operation to capture Wilmington that opened a base for Maj. General William T. Sherman in North Carolina. They were involved in a skirmish on January 19 near Fort Fisher

CAPTURE OF WILMINGTON

on February 21, and a skirmish at the Northeast Branch of the Cape Fear River on February 22.

The 6th Connecticut was next engaged in garrison duty along the line of the Wilmington & Weldon Railroad from Wilmington, to Goldsboro until August.

The regiment returned to New Haven on July 28 and was finally mustered out of United States service on August 21, 1865. Of its orginial members 205 re-enlisted and 600 recruits were credited to the regiment.

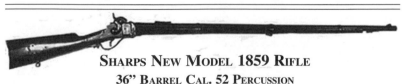

SHARPS NEW MODEL 1859 RIFLE
36" BARREL CAL. 52 PERCUSSION

TOTAL CASUALTIES 6TH INFANTRY

DATE	PLACE OF CASUALTY	TOTAL	K	M	W	W/C	C
1862							
Unknown	Johns Island, SC	1			1		
January 1	FT. Wagner, SC	1			1		
March 1	FT. Pulaski, GA	1			1		
April 8	Savannah River, SC	1			1		
April 15	Dawfuskie Lake, SC (Drowned)	1	1				
June 8	North Edisto River, SC (Drowned)	1	1				
June 12	James Island, SC	2			2		
June 15	Hilton Head, SC	1			1		
October 19	Lady's Island, SC	1					1
October 19	Cheatham Island, SC	3					3
October 19	Chisholm, SC	2					2
October 22	**Pocotaligo, SC**	**35**	**5**		**30**		
1863							
March 1	Jacksonville, FL	1			1		
April 1	Fall Island, SC	1			1		
June 14	Deep Bottom, VA	1			1		
July 1	FT. Wagner, SC	1			1		
July 8	Long Island, SC	1					1
July 10, 18, 25	**Morris Island, SC**	**16**	**2**		**14**		
July 11,14,18,25	**FT. Wagner, SC**	**140**	**17**	**9**	**85**	**6**	**23**
1864							
May 3	Bermuda Hundred, VA	1			1		
May 3	Proctor's Creek, VA	2			2		
May 9-10	Bermuda Hundred, VA	3			3		
May 9-10	Petersburg, VA	3	1		2		
May 10, 16	**Chester Station, VA**	**13**	**1**		**12**		
May 10, 13-16, 20	**Drewry's Bluff, VA**	**99**	**6**		**60**	**4**	**29**
May 18, 20	**Bermuda Hundred, VA**	**31**	**2**		**26**		**3**
May 20	Wire Bottom Church, VA	2			2		
May 20	Petersburg, VA	1					1
May 20,23	Proctor's Creek, VA	2			2		
May 30, June 1,6,9	**Bermuda Hundred, VA**	**8**	**2**		**6**		
June 17,19,20	**Bermuda Hundred, VA**	**38**	**5**	**1**	**15**		**17**
June 17	Hatcher's Run, VA	2			2		
June 29	Bermuda Hundred, VA	1			1		
June 29	Ream's Station, VA	1		1			
July 7	James River, VA (Drowned)	1	1				
July 7	FT. Stevens, DC	1			1		
August 1	Dutch Gap, VA	1			1		
August 14,16	**Deep Bottom, VA**	**16**		**2**	**13**	**1**	
August 14-18	**Deep Run, VA**	**68**	**5**	**2**	**54**		**7**
August 23	Bermuda Hundred, VA	1			1		
August 24	Unknown	1			1		
August 26-September 22	**Petersburg, VA**	**10**	**2**		**8**		
September 1	Newmarket Road, VA	1			1		
September 28	Deep Bottom, VA	1			1		
October 1	Newmarket Road, VA	1					1
October 1,7	Richmond, VA	8			6		2
October 2	Osborne Pike, VA	1					1
October 7	Darbytown Road, VA	4	2		2		
October 19	Cedar Creek, VA	2			1		1
October 27	Richmond, VA	1			1		
Unknown	Virginia	1			1		
1865							
January 13-16	Fort Fisher, NC	5	2		3		
January 18	Federal Point, NC	2					2
January 18-22	Wilmington, NC	5	1		3		1
March 1	Petersburg, VA	1			1		
March 6	Brunswick, NC	2					2
March 6	Unknown	1					1
April 1	Wilmington, NC	1			1		
April 8	Burgan, NC	2					2
April 22	North East Bridge, NC	1			1		
June 15	Unknown	1	1				
July 14	Goldsboro, NC	1			1		
Unknown	Unknown	2			2		

DATE	PLACE
1861	
September 17	Left Connecticut for Washington
October 5	Moved to Annapolis, MD
October 21-November 7	Sherman's expedition to South Carolina
November 7	Capture of Forts Walker/Beauregard
November 8	Reconnaissance on Hilton Head
November 10-11	Expedition to Braddock's Point
Until January 20, 1862	Duty at Hilton Head
1862	
January 20-February 27	Expedition to Warsaw Sound
Until March 20	Duty at Hilton Head
March 20-April 11	Siege operations against Fort Pulaski,GA
April 10-11	Bombardment/capture of Fort Pulaski
June 1-28	Operations on James Island, SC
June 10	Grimball's Plantation
June 16	Battle of Secessionville
June 28-July 7	Evacuation of James Island
Until October	Duty at Hilton Head
October 22	Action At Frampton's Plantation, Pocotaligo, SC
Until March 1863	Duty at Beaufort, SC
1863	
April 1863	Duty at Jacksonville, FL
Until June	Duty at Hilton Head, SC
June 3-July 10	Occupation of Folly Island, SC
July 10	Attack on Morris Island, SC
July 18	Attack on Fort Wagner, SC
July 25-April 1864	Duty at Hilton Head, SC
1864	
April 27-May 1	Moved to Gloucester Point, VA
May 4-28	Operations on south side of James River

TROOP MOVEMENTS 6TH INFANTRY

DATE	PLACE
1864	
May 9-10	Swift Creek or Arrowfield Church
May 10	Chester Station
May 12-16	Operations against Fort Darling
May 13	Proctor's Creek
May 14-16	Battle of Drewry's Bluff
Until August 13	At Bermuda Hundred
May 20	Ware Bottom Church
June 9	Petersburg
June 16-17	Port Walthall
June 16-January 3, 1865	Siege against Petersburg/Richmond
June 20	Ware Bottom Church
August 13-20	Demonstration north side of James River
August 14-18	Battle of Strawberry Plains, Deep Bottom
August 16	Deep Run
August 25-September 27	In trenches before Petersburg
September 27-28	Moved to north side of James River
September 28-30	Battle of Chaffin's Farm, New Market Heights
October 7	Darbytown and New Market Roads
October 13	Darbytown Road
October 27-28	Battle of Fair Oaks
October 31-November 2	In front of Richmond
November 2-17	Duty at New York City, Presidential election
Until January 3	Duty in trenches before Richmond
1865	
January 3-15	2nd expedition to Fort Fisher, NC
January 19	Half Moon Battery,
February 11, 18	Sugar Loaf Battery, Fort Anderson
February 22	Capture of Wilmington/North East Ferry
Until June	Duty at Wilmington
Until July	Duty at Goldsboro
August 21	Mustered out

BATTLES AND LEADERS

FORT WAGNER (BATTERY WAGNER)
ASSAULT OF JULY 18, 1863

THE 6TH CONNECTICUT INFANTRY HAD ITS MOST CASUALTIES FOR ONE DAY (137) AT
THE DISTASTEROUS CHARGE UPON THE SEAFACE WITH THE 2ND BRIGADE (STRONG), 2ND
DIVISION (SEYMOUR), 10TH CORPS DEPARTMENT OF THE SOUTH (GILLMORE)

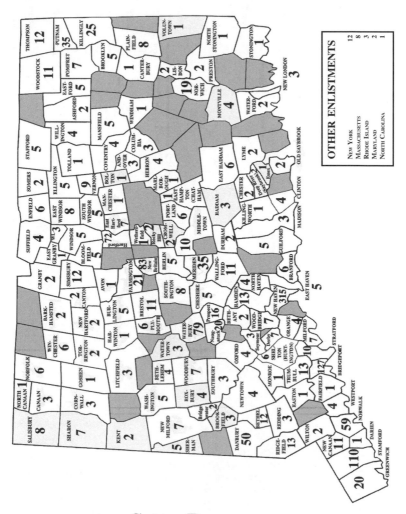

OTHER ENLISTMENTS

NEW YORK	12
MASSACHUSETTS	8
RHODE ISLAND	3
MARYLAND	2
NORTH CAROLINA	1

SIXTH REGIMENT
CONNECTICUT VOLUNTEER INFANTRY

SEVENTH REGIMENT
CONNECTICUT VOLUNTEER INFANTRY

SEPTEMBER 17, 1861 - JULY 20, 1865
(THREE YEARS, TEN MONTHS)
1,916 RECRUITS
107 KILLED, 3 MISSING, 238 DIED, 392 WOUNDED
44 WOUNDED & CAPTURED, 213 CAPTURED

USAMHI

Alfred Terry of New Haven, was the first Colonel of the 7th Connecticut. He had been the Colonel of the 2nd Connecticut Infantry and had led them at the Battle of Bull Run in July 1861. He was eventually appointed Major General of Volunteers and commanded the 10th Corps

The 7th Regiment Connecticut Volunteer Infantry was organized in New Haven during August 1861. A large percentage of the recruits were men who had recently been discharged from the three-month regiments.

Alfred H. Terry of New Haven, who had been the Colonel of the 2nd Connecticut Infantry, was commissioned Colonel. Joseph R. Hawley of Hartford, who had been a captain in the 1st Connecticut Infantry, was appointed Lieutenant Colonel and George F. Gardiner of New Haven was appointed Major.

The regiment, numbering 1,018, was mustered into the United States service in **NEW HAVEN** on September 17, 1861 and started for Washington, DC the following day.

The 7th Connecticut was assigned to Brigadier General Horatio G. Wright's Third Brigade of **SHERMAN'S SOUTH CAROLINA EXPEDITIONARY CORPS** The other regiments in the brigade at that time, included the 6th Connecticut, 9th Maine and 4th New Hampshire.

The regiment moved to Annapolis, Maryland after three weeks of constant drill and on October 29 boarded a steamer headed for Fort Monroe, Virginia which was the gathering place for the expedition. A series of heavy gales wrecked some of the ships and scattered the fleet after they had left Fort Monroe. The regiment finally arrived off Port Royal, South Carolina on November 4.

On November 7, the 6th and 7th Connecticut were the first regiments ashore and their colors were the first to float over South Carolina since her secession after the Union army and navy successful five hour

BOMBARDMENT OF FORTS WALKER AND BEAUREGARD

On December 19, following six weeks of heavy work on the huge fortifications being built at Hilton Head, the 7th Connecticut occupied Tybee Island at the mouth of the Savannah River, Georgia.

The regiment devoted the entire winter to the building of masked batteries for the capture of Fort Pulaski, which was situated on Cockspur Island. The work was difficult due to the swampy nature of the soil and because of the close proximity of the fort.

The men worked at night on the batteries while the days were devoted to the landing of artillery and ordnance stores and in drilling as heavy artillerists. The work of hauling timber for the batteries as well as moving the immense guns and mortars more than two miles through deep, shifting sands and bottomless swamps was completed in April 1862.

The first 13-inch mortars used during the war were mounted and manned by the men of the 7th Connecticut. During the

BOMBARDMENT OF FORT PULASKI

on April 10-11, the regiment manned nine of the eleven batteries engaged and was under fire for more than thirty hours. The regiment was transformed from artillerists into expert bricklayers after the surrender of the fort. Every available man was employed either in rebuilding the fort, so badly battered down, or in removing the heavy guns from the batteries on Tybee Island.

On May 19, Colonel Terry was promoted to Brigadier General of Volunteers and Lieutenant Colonel Hawley was elevated to the position of Colonel. The regiment left Fort Pulaski on June 1 and on June 6 occupied James Island south of Charleston, South Carolina. Frequent skirmishes and the incessant shelling of the Union lines reached a climax on June 16 with the

BATTLE OF SECESSIONVILLE

or James Island. The 7th Connecticut was one of the leading regiments to attack and one of the last to retreat. They lost 11 killed, 62 wounded, 1 captured, and 2 wounded & captured.

The regiment left James Island after this bloody defeat and returned to Hilton Head on July 20. Offensive operations at various points in the Department of the South kept the 7th Connecticut constantly employed with little loss until October 22, when they were engaged in another Union loss at the

BATTLE OF POCOTALIGO

The regiment had 2 killed and 29 wounded.

Frequent expeditions all along the coast from Charleston to St. Augustine, Florida divided the regiment into small battalions for many months. On July 10, Lieutenant Colonel Rodman led Companies A, B, I, and K in charges at Morris Island, South Carolina and at Fort Wagner on July 11, 1863.

The attack on Fort Wagner was made at night and the 7th Connecticut was one of few regiments that gained and carried one face of

FORT WAGNER

Unfortunately, the supporting regiments were unable to endure the heavy fire and fell back in disorder before reaching the battalion from the 7th regiment. They held their position for more than an hour and were nearly surrounded and outnumbered five to one.

Their only field officer, Lieutenant Colonel Rodman was seriously wounded and no re-enforcement was sent to their aid. The 7th Connecticut eventually retreated two miles down an open beach without cover and under a raking fire of artillery and infantry. The regiment lost 18 killed, 23 wounded, 42 captured and 16 wounded & captured.

The regiment was strengthened by the arrival, from Florida, of Jospeh Hawley with the remaining six companies.

The 7th Connecticut took a prominent part in the

SIEGE OF FORTS WAGNER, GREGG, AND SUMTER

They participated in the building of the *Swamp Angel Battery* and furnished details of men for artillerists. The regiment had charge of the 300-pounder rifled Parrott which was the heaviest gun on the island.

Five distinct lines of earthworks were finally erected at Fort Wagner after the Union force had pushed their trenches forward under a very heavy and continuous fire. The final Union line was established within thirty yards of the fort. Preparations were made for storming the fort when the Confederates evacuated the island on the night of September 7, and left the Union army in possession of their works.

Under the concentrated fire from ten Confederate batteries, the fort was rebuilt to face the other way. Heavy guns were eventually mounted that could reach the entire City of Charleston as well as the whole line of Confederate batteries. After having participated in stopping all offensive Confederate demonstrations in the Charleston area, the 7th Connecticut returned to Hilton Head

on October 16. The regiment had been in the trenches and under constant fire for 98 days.

They camped next on St. Helena Island, near Beaufort, South Carolina, and began to drill as "boat infantry". The men manned a fleet of flat bottom boats that carried 20 each. To insure a quiet movement, six paddles on each side propelled the boats instead of oars.

The regiment had gained sufficient proficiency in amphibious warfare after two weeks and was sent back to Folly Island, under special orders. They were held from October 30 until November 17 for a night attack on Fort Sumter. The project was eventually abandoned. The regiment returned to St. Helena Island and was relieved from boat infantry duty and resumed infantry drill.

Early in December 1863, their old Enfield rifles were exchanged for Spencer repeating carbines. New recruits from the North filled their sadly thinned ranks to the maximum and drilling was continued with increased vigor. During December, 333 original members of the regiment re-enlisted for three years under the provisions of the Veterans Act. On January 13, 1864, the veterans went back to Connecticut for a furlough of thirty days.

The remainder of the regiment was sent on an expedition into Florida and along with Hawley's Brigade (7th CT, 7th NY, 8th US Colored Infantry) was engaged in the Union loss at the

BATTLE OF OLUSTEE

on February 20,1864. During the inland march from Jacksonville to Olustee, the 7th Connecticut was in the advance, and was on the skirmish line the following day when the battle opened. The regiment was actively engaged until the battle closed and lost 6 killed, 34 wounded, 14 captured and 6 wounded & captured.

The 7th Connecticut acted as rear guards for 18 miles on the return march from Olustee. On the second day of the march, the regiment pushed several abandoned railroad cars filled with valuable stores all the way to Jacksonville. The 7th Connecticut camped at Six-Mile Creek, Florida and was joined by the returning veterans in March 1864.

On April 13, the 7th Connecticut was transferred to the 10th Army Corps on the Bermuda Hundred, Virginia front. They spent their time constantly scouting and skirmishing until April 17. The regiment was engaged at various points in the advance on Richmond and lost 151 men from May 14 -16 at the

BATTLE OF DREWRY'S BLUFF

On June 2, the regiment was in action on the

BERMUDA HUNDRED FRONT

again and had 79 more casualties. On June 17, they had another 17 casualties.

Constant skirmishing and outpost duty, with frequent casualties, gave the regiment no rest. On August 13, they crossed to the north bank of the James River. The 7th Connecticut was in action at

DEEP BOTTOM

on August 14 and 15 and at the action nearby a Deep Run on August 16 and 18. There was a total loss of 41 men.

On September 17, 1864, Colonel Hawley, who had commanded brigades for months was promoted to Brigadier General. Lieutenant Colonel Rodman had been disabled early in May and Major Sanford had been captured on June 2, so the 7th Connecticut was virtually commanded by line officers during the greater part of the battle summer of 1864.

From September 29 to October 27, the regiment participated in five engagements

BEFORE RICHMOND

losing 79 men from a small battalion of less than 200.

On November 2, the regiment joined a detachment sent to New York in anticipation of riots during the Presidential elections but none of the force was landed. They remained on ships in New York Harbor until November 14, and then returned to the Richmond front.

The 7th Connecticut closed out the month of December 1864 doing outpost duty living in shelter tents.

On January 3, 1865, the 7th Connecticut was in Abbott's Brigade, 24th Army Corps when they accompanied Alfred H. Terry on the

2ND ATTACK ON FORT FISHER

North Carolina. The brigade led the final and victorious charge after the attack by sailors and marines had been repulsed with heavy loss. A series of minor engagements during the hotly contested advance on Wilmington, resulted in the

CAPTURE OF WILMINGTON

on February 21-22. The Confederates were steadily pushed back toward Raleigh when the surrender of General Joseph Johnston virtually ended the war in North Carolina.

The 7th Connecticut was mustered out of service at Goldsboro on July 20, 1865. They returned by rail to City Point, Virginia and then travelled by steamer to New Haven. They arrived on July 29 and went into camp at Grapevine Point until discharged on August 11, 1865.

SPENCER CARBINE MODEL 1860
CAL. 52 RIMFIRE

TOTAL CASUALTIES 7TH INFANTRY

DATE	PLACE OF CASUALTY	TOTAL	K	M	W	W/C	C
1861							
October 26	Hampton Roads, VA	1	1				
November 3	Boyne Island, NC	1			1		
November 3-4	Wreck "Union", NC	6					6
1862							
February 6	Stoddard's Plantation, SC	1			1		
February 10	Dawfuskie Island, SC	1			1		
March 1-April 1	Tybee, GA	3			3		
June 1-14	James Island, SC	5			4		1
June 16	**James Island (Secessionville)**	**77**	**11**		**63**	**2**	**1**
June 17	James Island, SC	1			1		
June 18	Tallahatchie, FL	1			1		
June 28	James Island, SC	1			1		
June 30	James Island, SC	1			1		
October 22	**Pocotaligo, SC**	**31**	**2**		**29**		
1863							
February 10	Gloucester Point, VA	1					1
July 10, 11	Morris Island, SC	8			8		
July 11	**Ft. Wagner, SC**	**99**	**18**		**23**	**16**	**42**
July 13-October 14	Morris Island, SC	10			10		
July 18- October 8	Ft. Wagner, SC	6			5	1	
August 11,12,22	James Island, SC	3	3				
August 20	Charleston, SC	2					2
October 10	Fort Sumter, SC	1					1
December 20	Helena Island, SC	1			1		
1864							
February 20-24	**Olustee, FL**	**60**	**6**		**34**	**6**	**14**
May 1, 6	Petersburg, VA	2	1		1		
May 10,14	Chester Station, VA	8			8		
May 10,13,16	Bermuda Hundred, VA	3			3		
May 13-15	Drewry's Bluff, VA	49	6		41		2
May 16	**Drewry's Bluff, VA**	**106**	**17**	**2**	**28**	**5**	**54**
May 14,18	Petersburg, VA	3	2		1		
May 16	Spottsylvania, VA	1					1
May 31	Bermuda Hundred, VA	5	3		2		
June 2	**Hatcher's Run, VA**	**13**				**1**	**12**
June 2	**Bermuda Hundred, VA**	**77**	**5**		**17**	**9**	**46**
June 2,6,9,16	Petersburg, VA	5	1		2		2
June 13	Proctor's Creek, VA	1		1			
June 17	Chester Station, VA	1					1
June 17	Hatcher's Run, VA	1					1
June 20	Petersburg, VA	1			1		
June 15-18, July 26	**Bermuda Hundred, VA**	**26**	**6**		**8**	**2**	**10**
August 14-18	**Deep Bottom/ Deep Run, VA**	**45**	**10**		**31**	**2**	**2**
August 15	Andersonville, GA	1			1		
August 25,26,31	Petersburg, VA	3			3		
September 1	Bermuda Hundred, VA	1			1		
September 20	Petersburg, VA	1			1		
September 20	Richmond, VA	1					1
September 29	Dutch Gap/Laurel Hill, VA	2			2		
September 29	New Market Road, Chaffin's Farm, VA	6			6		
September 29	Drewry's Bluff, VA	1			1		
September 29	Deep Bottom, VA	3			3		
October 1	Darbytown Road, Newmarket Road, VA	3					3
October 1	Petersburg, VA	1			1		
October 1	Richmond, VA	7	1		2		4
October 7	Chaffin's Farm, VA	2			2		
October 7	Newmarket Road, VA	8	1		6		1
October 7	Richmond, VA	2			2		
October 13	Darbytown Road, VA	5	1		4		
October 13-15	Richmond, VA	9	5		4		
October 15,27	Petersburg, VA	2	1		1		
October 27	Charles City Road, VA	2			2		
October 27	Chaffin's Farm, VA	1			1		
November 15	Richmond, VA	1			1		
December 1	Columbia, SC	1			1		
December 10,11	Deep Bottom, VA	2			2		
1865							
January 14-20	**FT. Fisher, NC**	**11**	**2**		**8**		**1**
February 22	Wilmington, NC	1			1		
April 1	Chinquenpin, NC	1			1		
April 24, May 2, June 16	Drowned Potomac River (1) Wilmington, NC (2)	3	3				
July 3	Goldsboro, NC	1	1				

TROOP MOVEMENTS 7TH INFANTRY

DATE	PLACE
1861	
September 13	Left for Washington, DC
October 5	Moved to Annapolis, MD
October 21-November 7	Sherman's Expedition to Port Royal, SC
November 7	Capture Forts Beaureguard and Walker
November 7- December 18	Duty at Hilton Head, SC
November 8	Reconnaissance on Hilton Head
November 10-11	Expedition to Braddock's Point, SC
December 18-April 1862	Moved to Tybee Is. GA
1862	
March 20-April 11	Co. B,G,I on Dawfuski Is., GA
April 10-11	Bombardment of Fort Pulaski
April 11-May 27	Garrison duty at Fort Pulaski
June 1-28	Operations on James Island, SC
June 16	Battle of Secessionville
June 28-July 7	Evacuation of James Island
July 8-September 30	Duty at Hilton Head, SC
September 30-October 13	Expedition to St. John's Bluff, FL
October 21-23	Expedition to Pocotaligo, SC
October 22	Action at Frampton's Plantation, Pocotaligo
October 23-January 8	Duty at Hilton Head and Beaufort, SC
1863	
January 13-April 12	Moved to Fernandia, FL
April 13-August 2	Duty at St Augustine, FL
August 13	Co A,B,I,K moved to Morris Island, SC
June 3	Occupation of Folly Island, SC
July 10	Attack on water batteries, Morris Island
July 11	Assault on Fort Wagner
July 11-September 7	Siege of Fort Wagner
August 5	Regiment joins from St. Augustine, FL
September 7	Capture of Ft Wagner, Gregg, Morris Is,SC
September 7-October 16	Operations against Charleston, SC
October 16	Moved to St Helena Island, SC
October 29-November 17	Boat duty at Folly Island, SC
November 18-February 1864	Duty at St Helena Island, SC
1864	
January 15-February 27	Veterans on furlough in Connecticut
February 5-7	Moved to Jacksonville, FL
February 8-28	Expedition into Central FL
February 20	Battle of Olustee, FL

TROOP MOVEMENTS 7TH INFANTRY

DATE	PLACE
Feb 21-April 13	Duty at Jacksonville, FL
April 12-20	Moved to Gloucester Point, VA
May 4-28	Operations on south side of James River
May 9-10	Swift Creek or Arrowfield Church
May 10	Chester Station
May 12-16	Operations against Fort Darling
May 13	Proctor's Creek
May 14-16	Battle of Drewry's Bluff, VA
May 16-August 13	On Bermuda Hundred lines
June 2	Attack on picket line
June 9	Petersburg
June 14	Bermuda Hundred
June 16-17	Port Walthall
June 16- January 3 1865	Siege operations Petersburg/Richmond
August 13-20	Demonstration on north side of James
August 14-18	Battle Strawberry Plains/Deep Bottom
August 25-September 28	In Trenches before Petersburg
September 28	Moved to north side of James
September 28-30	Battle of Chaffin's Farm/New Market Heights
October 7	Darbytown and New Market Roads
October 13	Darbytown Road
October 27-28	Battle of Fair Oaks
November 2-7	Duty at New York, Presidential elections
November 8-January 3, 1865	Duty in trenches before Richmond
1865	
January 3-15	2nd expedition to Fort Fisher, NC
January 15	Assault and capture of Fort Fisher
January 19	Half Moon Battery
February 11	Sugar Loaf Battery
February 18	Fort Anderson
February 22	Capture of Wilmington, NC
February 22	North East Ferry
February 23-June	Duty at Wilmington
July	Duty at Goldsboro
July 20	Mustered out at Goldsboro
August 11	Discharged at New Haven CT

CONGRESSIONAL MEDAL OF HONOR WINNER

1st Serg. Frederick R. Jackson, Co. F, 7th Connecticut Infantry
PLACE AND DATE: At James Island, S.C., 16 June 1862
DATE OF ISSUE: 1863
CITATION: Having his left arm shot away in a charge on the enemy, he continued on duty, taking part in a second and a third charge until he fell exhausted from the loss of blood

USAMHI

DREWRY'S BLUFF MAY 16, 1864

THE 7TH CONNECTICUT INFANTRY HAD ITS MOST CASUALTIES FOR ONE DAY (106) WITH THE 2ND BRIGADE (HAWLEY), 1ST DIVISION (TERRY), 10TH CORPS ARMY OF JAMES (GILLMORE)

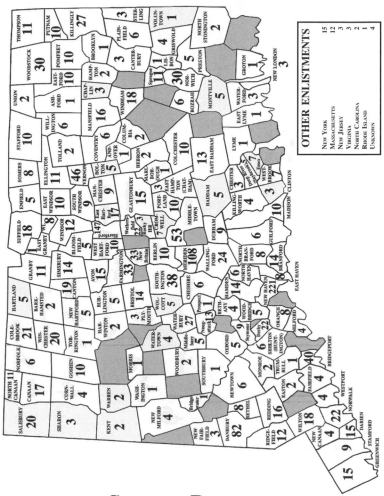

Map of Connecticut towns with enlistment numbers:

THOMPSON 11 · PUTNAM 10 · KILLINGLY 27 · STERLING 1 · VOLUNTOWN 1 · NORTH STONINGTON 2 · WOODSTOCK 30 · POMFRET 10 · PLAINFIELD 6 · BROOKLYN 3 · EAST FORD 10 · HAMPTON 3 · CANTERBURY 3 · LISBON 5 · GRISWOLD 4 · PRESTON 1 · GROTON 1 · NEW LONDON 3 · UNION 2 · ASHFORD 1 · CHAPLIN 2 · WINDHAM 18 · Sprague 11 · NORWICH 30 · BOZRAH 6 · MONTVILLE 1 · WATERFORD 3 · STAFFORD 10 · WILLINGTON 6 · MANSFIELD 16 · COLUMBIA 2 · HEBRON 2 · COLCHESTER 10 · EAST HADDAM 13 · LYME 1 · EAST LYME 1 · SOMERS 8 · ELLINGTON 11 · TOLLAND 2 · COVENTRY 6 · ANDOVER 5 · MARLBOROUGH 3 · BOLTON 5 · VERNON 46 · MANCHESTER 9 · GLASTONBURY 15 · PORTLAND 3 · EAST HAMPTON (CHATHAM) · HADDAM 5 · CHESTER 3 · WESTBROOK 4 · CLINTON · MADISON · ENFIELD 5 · EAST WINDSOR 10 · SOUTH WINDSOR 12 · East Hartford 17 · CROMWELL 7 · MIDDLETOWN · KILLINGWORTH 4 · DURHAM 9 · GUILFORD 6 · SUFFIELD 18 · WINDSOR 12 · BLOOMFIELD 5 · WEST HARTFORD 10 · Wethersfield 22 · Rocky Hill 3 · BERLIN 10 · NORTH BRANFORD · BRANFORD 14 · EAST GRANBY 8 · Hartford 147 · New Britain 33 · MERIDEN 108 · NORTH HAVEN 8 · EAST HAVEN · GRANBY 11 · SIMSBURY 14 · AVON 15 · FARMINGTON 33 · SOUTHINGTON 38 · CHESHIRE 6 · WALLINGFORD 24 · NORTH HAVEN · NEW HAVEN 221 · HARTLAND 5 · BARKHAMSTED 2 · CANTON 19 · BRISTOL 14 · WOLCOTT 5 · HAMDEN 14 · COLEBROOK 21 · WINCHESTER 20 · NEW HARTFORD 5 · BURLINGTON 5 · PLYMOUTH 3 · WATERBURY 27 · PROSPECT 1 · BETHANY 1 · WOODBRIDGE 5 · ORANGE 8 · MILFORD 4 · NORFOLK 6 · TORRINGTON 1 · HARWINTON 2 · Middlebury 5 · Naugatuck 13 · Seymour 1 · DERBY 22 · SHELTON (HUNTINGTON) 4 · NORTH CANAAN 11 · CANAAN 17 · GOSHEN 10 · MORRIS 1 · WOODBURY 2 · SOUTHBURY 1 · OXFORD 5 · MONROE 2 · TRUMBULL 2 · BRIDGEPORT 40 · CORNWALL 4 · WARREN 2 · WASHINGTON 1 · NEW MILFORD 4 · NEWTOWN 6 · EASTON 2 · FAIRFIELD 4 · WESTPORT 4 · SALISBURY 20 · SHARON 3 · KENT 2 · NEW FAIRFIELD 3 · Bridgewater 1 · BETHEL 8 · REDDING 16 · WILTON 18 · NORWALK 22 · DANBURY 82 · RIDGEFIELD 12 · NEW CANAAN 4 · DARIEN 15 · STAMFORD 15 · GREENWICH 9

SEVENTH REGIMENT
CONNECTICUT VOLUNTEER
INFANTRY

EIGHTH REGIMENT
CONNECTICUT VOLUNTEER INFANTRY

OCTOBER 5, 1861 - DECEMBER 12, 1865
(FOUR YEARS, TWO MONTHS)
1,622 RECRUITS
75 KILLED, 1 MISSING, 180 DIED, 405 WOUNDED, 23 WOUNDED & CAPTURED, 61 CAPTURED

MILITARY AND CIVIL HISTORY OF CONNECTICUT...

The 8th Regiment Connecticut Volunteer Infantry was organized at Camp Buckingham, **HARTFORD** in September 1861. Edward Harland of Norwich, who had recently returned from three months service as a Captain in the 3rd Connecticut Infantry was appointed Colonel. Peter Cunningham of Norwalk, was appointed Lieutenant Colonel and Andrew Terry of Plymouth, was appointed Major.

The regiment was mustered into United States service on October 5, 1861.

The 8th Connecticut left Hartford on October 17 and was in a camp of instruction at Jamaica, Long Island, New York for two weeks. On November 1,

Edward Harland of Norwich, who was a popular Captain in the 3rd Connecticut Infantry, was appointed Colonel of the 8th Connecticut. Later as a Brigadier General, he commanded The Harland Brigade in the 9th Army Corps. The Brigade at times was made up of the 8 , 11, 15, 16, 21st Connecticut Infantry and 4th Rhode

they moved to Annapolis, Maryland. The regiment sailed with the **BURNSIDE NORTH CAROLINA EXPEDITION** early in January 1862. After a difficult and stormy passage, the Union army finally landed and the Confederate forces on Roanoke Island, were attacked and defeated on February 7. The 8th Connecticut was held in reserve and suffered no loss.

After about a month at Roanoke Island, Burnsides's forces moved by water toward New Bern. The 8th Connecticut landed 18 miles below the city and marched up the south bank of the Neuse River to Slocum's Creek. The

Confederates were attacked at

NEW BERN

on March 14, 1862. The regiment assisted in the capture of about 500 Confederates. This was the regiment's first involvement in combat and they lost 2 killed and 4 wounded.

The next advance of the regiment was on March 19 to engage in the

SIEGE AT FORT MACON

The 8th Connecticut moved by steamer back to Slocum's Creek and then marched along the rail lines to the fort on Bogues Banks. The siege of Fort Macon ended during the last week in April 1862.

During the greater part of the siege, Colonel Harland was sick with typhoid fever and the regiment was under the command of Lieutenant Colonel Hiram Appelman of Groton. Appelman received a painful though not dangerous wound from a canister shot.

Soon after the surrender of Fort Macon, the 8th Connecticut went by steamer back to New Bern where the regiment enjoyed two months of rest and recuperation.

On July 2, 1862, the regiment moved by rail to Morehead City and then by the steamer *Admiral* to Newport News, Virginia where they camped for the remainder of the month of July. On August 1, in company with the 11th Connecticut, the 8th Connecticut went by water to Aquia Creek and then by rail to Fredericksburg. They went into camp in front of the Lacey House in Falmouth across the Rappahannock River from the city. The month of August was spent doing picket duty every other day west of Fredericksburg.

The Union forces left Fredericksburg on September 1, and were ordered to Washington, DC. The regiment arrived on September 3 and rested on Capitol

Hill until September 8 when they began the march into Maryland that led to the

BATTLE OF ANTIETAM

on September 17, 1862. The regiment had its greatest loss of the entire war with 33 killed, 145 wounded, 9 captured and 14 wounded & captured.

As part of Cox's 9th Army Corps, Rodman's 3rd Division,

HARLAND'S 2ND BRIGADE

the 8th Connecticut suffered its casualties on the battlefield south of Sharpsburg, on the extreme left of the Union lines at the area below the Lower Bridge over Antietam Creek. Lieutenant Colonel Appelman, five captains, and four lieutenants were listed as casualties.

Six weeks after the battle, the Union army slowly pursued the Confederates. They moved from a camp in Pleasant Valley, Maryland, just below Harper's Ferry, West Virginia and passed southwest on the east side of the Blue Ridge Mountains. The 8th, 11th, and 16th Connecticut moved together. The 15th and 21st Connecticut joined the Harland Brigade later.

In November, Ambrose Burnside assumed command of the Army of the Potomac and he directed them toward

FREDERICKSBURG

The 8th Connecticut reached Falmouth on November 19, and pitched their shelter tents in front of the Lacey House again, within a short distance of its camp of the previous August.

After weeks of delay, a general attack on the Confederate positions at Fredericksburg was planned. The laying of pontoon bridges across the Rappahannock River began on December 11. Fire from Confederate sharpshooters, entrenched on the opposite shore of the river, was distastrous for the Union bridge builders. Ninety men from the 8th Connecticut responded to the call for volunteers and went down to the riverbank to assist in the terrible ordeal. They came back alive (2 wounded) because the chief of the engineer corps decided that it was useless to slaughter a hundred men in a vain attempt to lay the pontoons. The Confederate sharpshooters could only be silenced by Union artillery.

The bridges were finally completed and on December 12, Harland's Brigade, with the 8,11,16th Connecticut and 4th Rhode Island, crossed into the city and slept on Caroline St. The brigade was spared from the fruitless attack on the Confederate's entrenched positions that brought a loss of more than 12,000 casualties to the Union army. The 8th Connecticut lost 1 killed and 2 wounded.

After the battle, the regiment re-crossed the Rappahannock and went back into their old camp. A little more than a month later, the regiment participated in the pointless "Mud March" of January 1863.

Early in February, Harland's Brigade went down the Potomac River and spent a month at Newport News housed in comfortable barracks. In the middle of March, they moved to Suffolk and Harland's Brigade was assigned to Peck's Division. The 8th Connecticut had little to do except when six companies under Colonel John E. Ward made an attack on a Confederate battery on the Nansemond River. The battery was captured by complete surprise without firing a shot. The regiment remained in the vicinity of Portsmouth during the summer of 1863 and was occasionally called out on short raids in various directions.

In December, 310 of the original members of the 8th Connecticut re-enlisted as veterans and in January 1864 went to Connecticut on veteran furlough. March 1 found the regiment back in the field and ready for duty.

On March 13, they were ordered to Deep Run and on April 21, they went to Yorktown. From May 7- 9, they participated in the

BATTLE OF WALTHALL JUNCTION

The regiment assisted in the destruction of the railroad tracks and had 1 killed, 63 wounded, 3 captured and 3 wounded & captured.

The regiment was transferred to the First Division (Brooks), 2nd Brigade (Burnham) of the

18TH CORPS

On May 13, the corps moved up the south side of the James River and on the 16th, the 8th Connecticut fought in the fog at the

BATTLE OF DREWRY'S BLUFF

The regiment occupied the left center of the Union line. The men could not see more than 10 paces in front and eventually the order was given to retreat after they had lost 5 killed, 27 wounded, 23 captured and 5 wounded & captured.

June 1, 1864 was the beginning of the fighting at the

BATTLE OF COLD HARBOR

The regiment's losses were comparatively light. They were held in reserve for most of the engagement. Two weeks later the regiment began the movement toward

PETERSBURG

after having lost 8 killed and 32 wounded. The Petersburg campaign would last nearly all summer. On June 16, the regiment lost 2 killed and 17 wounded. There was a loss of 20 from Confederate artillery and sharpshooters during the next month.

On September 26, the 18th Corps was sent back across the James River to operate in Major General Benjamin Butler's move toward

RICHMOND

In a successful charge on

FORT HARRISON

on September 29 the 8th Connecticut suffered 9 killed, 1 missing, 51 wounded, 3 captured. The charge upon Fort Harrison was the last fighting for the decimated 8th Connecticut.

On April 3, 1865 the regiment was with the advance when the Union army made its final move on to Richmond.

After the close of the war, the 8th Connecticut went to Lynchburg and performed guard and police duty. The regiment was mustered out in Hartford with the 11th Connecticut Infantry on December 12, 1865.

LIBRARY OF CONGRESS

BATTLE OF ANTIETAM, SEPTEMBER 17, 1862

THE 8TH CONNECTICUT INFANTRY CROSSED ANTIETAM CREEK SOUTH OF THE LOWER BRIDGE WITH THE 2ND BRIGADE (HARLAND), 3RD DIVISION (RODMAN), 9TH CORPS (COX) AND PROCEEDED TO A MEADOW ON THE CORNER OF THE 40 ACRE CORNFIELD NEAR THE HARPER'S FERRY ROAD. THE REGIMENT SUFFERED 201 CASUALTIES, ITS GREATEST NUMBER FOR ANY ONE DAY OF THE WAR.

SHARPS NEW MODEL 1859 RIFLE
36" BARREL CAL. 52 PERCUSSION

US MODEL 1861 PERCUSSION MUSKET
40" BARREL CAL. 58 PERCUSSION

TOTAL CASUALTIES 8TH INFANTRY

DATE	PLACE OF CASUALTY	TOTAL	K	M	W	W/C	C
1861							
October 16	Long Island, NY (Accident)	1			1		
October 21	Jamaica, NY (Accident)	1			1		
November 6	Annapolis, MD (Accident)	1			1		
December 1	Annapolis, MD (Accident)	1			1		
1862							
January 30	Albemarle Sound, NC (Drowned)	1	1				
February 8	Roanoke Island, NC	1			1		
March 14	New Bern, NC	6	2		4		
April 12	FT. Macon, NC	1			1		
April 26	FT. Macon, NC	1			1		
August 31	Aquia Creek, VA	1			1		
September 7	Virginia	1			1		
September 14	Bolivar Heights, VA	1			1		
September 14	South Mountain, VA	1			1		
September 16-19	Antietam, MD	201	33		145	14	9
November 16	Fauquier, VA	1					1
December 11-13	Fredericksburg, VA	3	1		2		
1863							
April 11	Suffolk, VA	1			1		
April 12-19	FT. Hugar, VA	6	1		5		
August 1	Getty's Station, VA	1			1		
August 25	South Mills, NC	1					1
1864							
February 24	New Haven, CT (Accident)	1			1		
March 17	Unknown	1			1		
April 20	Plymouth, NC	1					1
May 7	Petersburg, VA	1			1		
May 7	Swift's Creek, VA	3	3				
May 7-9	Walthall Junction, VA	70	2		62	3	3
May 9	Swift's Creek, VA	1	1				
May 9	Petersburg, VA	1			1		
May 11-16	Drewry's Bluff, VA	61	6		27	5	23
May 16	City Point, VA	1					1
May 16	Proctor's Creek, VA	2				1	1
June 1-9	Cold Harbor, VA	40	8		32		
June 14-September 18	Petersburg, VA	55	7		43		5
August 1	City Point, VA	1			1		
August 25-September 16	Cox's Mills, VA	6					6
September 18-19	FT. Powhatan, VA	5					5
September 29-October 3	FT. Harrison, VA	64	9	1	51		3
September 29-October 4	Chaffin's Farm, VA	12	1		11		
October 9	Richmond, VA	1			1		
October 27-29	Fair Oaks, VA	3			1		2
1865							
February 21	Wilmington, NC	1			1		
April 1	Richmond, VA	1			1		
August 27	Petersburg, VA	1			1		
October 1	Richmond, VA	1			1		

CONGRESSIONAL MEDAL OF HONOR WINNER

Corporal Nathan E. Hickok, Co. A, 8th Connecticut Infantry
Place and Date: At Chaffin's Farm, Va., 29 September 1864
Date of Issue: 6 April 1865
Citation: Capture of flag.

TROOP MOVEMENTS 8ᵀᴴ INFANTRY

OH
WEST VIRGINIA
VIRGINIA
NORTH CAROLINA
SOUTH CAROLINA
NJ
DEL
MARYLAND

ANTIETAM
ANNAPOLIS
WASHINGTON
FREDERICKSBURG
COLD HARBOR
RICHMOND
LYNCHBURG
PETERSBURG
SUFFOLK
NEWPORT NEWS
YORKTOWN
PORTSMOUTH
ROANOKE ISLAND
NEW BERN
MOREHEAD CITY

DATE	PLACE
1861	
October 17	Left Connecticut for Annapolis, MD
Until January 6 1862	Duty at Annapolis, MD
1862	
January 7-February 8	Burnside's expedition to North Carolina
February 8	Battle of Roanoke Island
Until March 11	At Roanoke Island
March 11-13	Moved to New Bern
March 14	Battle of New Bern
March 23-April 26	Operations against Fort Macon
April 26	Capture of Fort Macon
Until July	Duty at New Bern
July 2	Moved to Morehead City
July 3-5	Moved to Newport News, VA
Until August 1	Duty at Newport News
August 1-5	Moved to Fredericksburg, VA
Until August 31	Duty at Fredericksburg
August 31-September 3	Moved to Brooke Station/Washington, DC
September 14	Turner's Gap, South Mountain
September 16-17	Battle of Antietam
Until October 27	Duty in Pleasant Valley
October 27-November 19	Movement to Falmouth, VA
December 12-15	Battle of Fredericksburg
1863	
January 20-24	Burnside's 2ⁿᵈ Campaign, "Mud March"
February 6-9	Moved to Newport News, VA
March 13	Moved to Suffolk
April 12-May 4	Siege of Suffolk
April 19	Fort Hugar
April 24	Edenton Road
May 3	Nansemond River
June 24-July 7	Dix's Peninsula Campaign
July 1-7	Expedition from White House to South Anna Riv.

TROOP MOVEMENTS 8TH INFANTRY

DATE	PLACE
Until March 1864	Moved to Portsmouth and duty there
October 12-14	Expedition to South Mills
1864	
March 13-April 18	Outpost duty at Deep Creek
April 18-21	Moved to Yorktown, VA
May 4-28	Operations south side of James River
May 7	Walthall Junction, Chester Station
May 9-10	Swift Creek, or Arrowfield Church
May 9-10	Operations against Fort Darling
May 14-16	Battle of Drewry's Bluff
May 27-June 1	Moved to White House Landing
June 1-12	Battles about Cold Harbor
June 15-16	Assaults on Petersburg
June 16-April 2, 1865	Siege operations against Petersburg and Richmond
August 25-September 27	On Bermuda Hundred front
September 28-30	Ft. Harrison, New Market Heights, Chaffin's Farm
Until April 1865	Duty in trenches before Richmond
October 27-28	Battle of Fair Oaks
1865	
April 3- December	Occupation of Richmond and duty there
December	Duty at Lynchburg and muster out

EARTHWORKS OUTSIDE CAPTURED   LIBRARY OF CONGRESS
CONFEDERATE FORT HARRISON, VIRGINIA
SEPTEMBER 29- OCTOBER 3, 1864

THE 8TH CONNECTICUT WAS A PART OF SMITH'S 18TH ARMY CORPS, BROOKS' 1ST
DIVISION, BURNHAM'S 2ND BRIGADE ON THE PETERSBURG FRONT

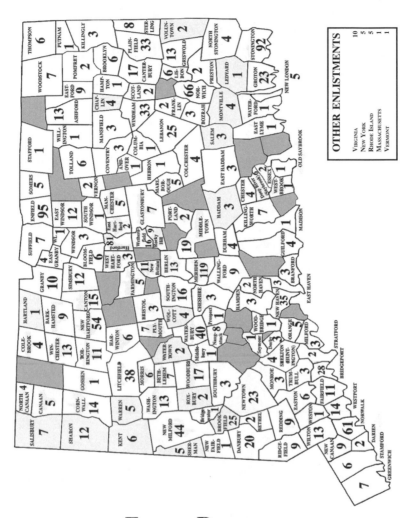

OTHER ENLISTMENTS

VIRGINIA	10
NEW YORK	5
RHODE ISLAND	5
MASSACHUSETTS	1
VERMONT	1

EIGHTH REGIMENT
CONNECTICUT VOLUNTEER
INFANTRY

NINTH REGIMENT
CONNECTICUT VOLUNTEER INFANTRY

NOVEMBER 1, 1861 - AUGUST 3, 1865
(THREE YEARS, NINE MONTHS)
1,560 RECRUITS
13 KILLED, 2 MISSING, 239 DIED, 48 WOUNDED, 19 CAPTURED

HISTORY OF THE 9TH CONNECTICUT ...

The 9th Connecticut "Irish Regiment" was commanded by Thomas W. Cahill of New Haven who had been a Captain of the Emmett Guards in the State Militia. He served for three years and was discharged after the Battle of Cedar Creek in October 1864

The 9th Regiment Connecticut Volunteer Infantry was organized in September and October 1861, at Camp English, **NEW HAVEN** and was composed mostly of men of Irish birth or parentage.

The regiment was commanded by Colonel Thomas W. Cahill of New Haven, Lieutenant Colonel Richard Fitzgibbons, and Major Frederick Frye of Bridgeport. All had the benefit of previous military experience. The Colonel as Captain of the Emmett Guards in the State Militia and the two others as captains of companies in the 1st and 3rd Connecticut Infantry.

Recruiting for the 9th Connecticut proceeded slowly and was somewhat hampered by the lack of proper clothing and equipment. From the beginning, the regiment had been destined to be a part of Major General Benjamin

BUTLER'S EXPEDITION FOR THE CAPTURE OF NEW ORLEANS

On November 4, with insufficient uniforms and without arms, the 9th Connecticut left New Haven, by rail for Lowell, Massachusetts which was the gathering place of Butler's **NEW ENGLAND BRIGADE**

The regiment joined with the 26th Massachusetts Infantry and on November 21 was ordered to Boston.

On November 26, the regiment left on the steamer *Constitution* for Ship Island, Mississippi. General Butler accompanied the expedition which arrived at Ship Island on December 3, 1861. The 9th Connecticut went into camp and received inadequate tents and arms.

The regiment remained at Ship Island for four months and then, with a section of the 6th Massachusetts Battery, was ordered to Biloxi, Mississippi. The regiment found the town deserted and on the night of April 2, 1862 returned to their steamer anchored in the harbor.

At 4AM the following morning, three Confederate gunboats attacked the steamer. The Union gunboats *New London* and *Jackson* came to their rescue and the Confederates were driven off.

The 9th Connecticut, under a convoy of the gunboats, steamed for Pass Christian, Mississippi and reached there at 11AM. They landed and started at once with a section of the 6th Massachusetts Battery in pursuit of the Confederates. After firing a few shots, the entire camp and the flag of the 3rd Mississippi regiment was captured. The camp was burned and the 9th Connecticut returned to its camp at Ship Island.

On April 15, the 9th Connecticut boarded the steamer *Matanzas*, with the 12th Connecticut in tow on board the *E.W. Farley*. On the 17th, the *Matanzas* anchored at South West Pass and remained there until after the capture of Forts Jackson and St. Philip, at the mouth of the Mississippi. The regiment next went up the river to New Orleans and occupied the Reading Cotton Press. The 9th Connecticut paraded through some of the principal streets of New Orleans. The regiment performed provost duty in the city and had its camp on Lafayette Square.

Colonel Cahill was assigned to the command of the defenses of the city. Captain Silas Sawyer was assigned to the command of the city below the mint, Captain Lawrence O'Brien to the Parish of St. James and Captain John G. Healy, with companies C and F, to Lake Pontchartrain.

The 9th Connecticut joined the expeditionary corps in June, under Brig. General Thomas Williams, for the destruction of the Confederate "Camp Moore". The regiment moved to a location on the Mississippi River opposite

VICKSBURG

On June 25, 1862, they were put to work in cutting the canal that was expected to isolate Vicksburg. The hope was that the river could be diverted away from the wharves and that the city would be unapproachable to shipping. During this period, a group of 20 men from the 9th Connecticut crossed the river and for eight days remained in the swamp under the Confederate guns of Vicksburg. The canal work was finally abandoned though not until the regiment had suffered severe loss due to the disease infested swamps and from the lack of food and water.

The regiment returned to Baton Rouge. On July 20, they left by steamer for Ellis Cliffs, Mississippi, located below Natchez. Their purpose was to break up a Confederate camp. They arrived on the 22nd with the 30th Massachusetts, 4th Wisconsin and six guns of Nim's and Everett's batteries. After a march of several miles, they received the news that the Confederates with two guns and 90 mounted men had left their camp only hours before. Two days later, the Confederates were encountered at Hamilton near the Port Gibson railroad. The engagement resulted in the loss to the Confederates of three killed and five captured with no loss to the Union force.

After five days, the 9th Connecticut boarded a steamer on the morning of June 29 and entered Bayou Pierre. They had passed up the bayou for about nine miles when the troops were landed at Barry's Plantation, four miles from Grand Gulf. Once again, the Union force found that the Confederates had left their camp leaving only a few sick. The regiment returned to Baton Rouge.

The next action in which the 9th Connecticut was engaged was at the

BATTLE OF BATON ROUGE

on August 5, 1862. At 3AM, they took a position on the extreme left of the Union line an hour later the battle began. The 9th Connecticut was eventually moved to support the center of the line and later to a cemetery on the left. Thirty-five men of the regiment were detailed as artillerists to Nim's and Everett's Batteries. The casualties of the regiment were 3 wounded and 1 missing. The brigade commander Brig. General Thomas Williams was killed and the command fell upon Colonel Cahill. Lieutenant Colonel Richard Fitzgibbons assumed the command of the regiment.

About a month later, the regiment under Major Frye, participated in an expedition to the vicinity of St. Charles Court House. The purpose of the expedition was to capture or to break up a camp of 2,000 Confederate infantry and cavalry.

The 9th Connecticut and the 14th Maine landed at dawn on September 8, at a point above Carrollton and advanced west. They moved up the river for about six miles. The Confederate camp was discovered and the Union artillery shelled the woods but failed to dislodge them. The Union regiments were thrown forward as skirmishers and the

Confederate cavalry attempted to break through in their direction. The cavalry was driven back, abandoned their equipment, and fled into an almost impenetrable swamp. The Union force captured 40 prisoners and almost 200 horses fully equipped.

The regiment returned to New Orleans where its headquarters remained for the rest of 1862. The companies of the 9th Connecticut were separated doing duty at different points.

During the fall of 1862, a scouting was made of the country north of Manchac Pass on Lake Pontchartrain and several companies of the regiment participated. One company of the 9th Connecticut was stationed at the North Pass, dividing Jones Island from the swamp land and another company was placed with two rifled guns along the road leading to Pontchaloula. From October 20-21, the regiment had 3 casualties and the Confederates lost 3 killed and 11 wounded. Among the Confederate prisoners were 22 Choctaw Indians.

In March 1863, the 9th Connecticut was assigned to the Second Brigade of General Cuvier Grover's Fourth Division, 19th Corps. The regiment was scattered in various locations. That summer, the 9th Connecticut was in an engagement at La Fourche Crossing on June 20-21 with no loss, and at Chacahoula Station on June 24, in which they had 4 wounded and 2 captured.

In April 1864, the veterans of the 9th Connecticut started for New Haven on their veteran furlough and arrived on April 15. The recruits not on furlough were transferred to the Department of the East in

VIRGINIA

When the veterans returned from leave on July 18 they were assigned to the

10TH CORPS

The regiment arrived on July 24 at Bermuda Hundred and then to Deep Bottom on the 29th.

On July 30, the regiment sailed for Washington, DC and arrived on August 1. The next day, they marched through Georgetown to Tennallytown. The regiment remained there until August 14, then they crossed the Chain Bridge and marched to Leesburg, Virginia and through Snickers Gap to Berryville and into the Shenandoah Valley. As part of Henry Birge's First Brigade, Curvier Grover's Second Division, William Emory's

19TH CORPS

the 9th Connecticut participated in the victory at the

THIRD BATTLE OF WINCHESTER

on September 19, 1864 with two wounded and then in the victory at

FISHER'S HILL

on September 22 with 2 killed and 2 wounded. In October, the men who had not re-enlisted as veterans left the service and the remainder were organized as a battalion of four companies under the command of Captain John G. Healy. The

9TH BATTALION

bore a conspicuous part in the Union triumph at the

BATTLE OF CEDAR CREEK

on October 19. Their flag was one of the first planted on the recaptured Confederate works. In this desperate action, the 9th Connecticut suffered its greatest loss for the war, with 1 missing, 13 wounded, and 9 captured.

The battalion remained in Virginia until January 7, 1865 when it was ordered to Baltimore, Maryland. They boarded the steamer *General Sedgwick* with the 175th New York and headed for Fort Monroe, Virginia. From there, the 9th Battalion went to Savannah, Georgia and arrived on January 17. In April, the battalion, under Lieutenant Colonel Healy, was ordered to Dawfuski Island where it dispersed a Confederate guerilla force who were oppressing and murdering blacks. The regiment returned to Savannah and was ordered to Hilton Head, South Carolina. They remained in service, with Quincy. A. Gillmore's 10th Corps, until the close of active service.

On August 3, 1865 the regiment left for Connecticut, arrived in New Haven on August 8 and were mustered out.

HISTORY OF THE NINTH CONNECTICUT VOLUNTEERS

US NAVAL HISTORICAL CENTER

MISSISSIPPI RIVER, LOUISIANA
1863

TOTAL CASUALTIES 9TH INFANTRY

DATE	PLACE OF CASUALTY	TOTAL	K	M	W	C
1862						
January 5	Madisonville, LA	1			1	
February 1	Ship Island, MS	1			1	
April 3	Pass Christain, LA	1			1	
April 14	Unknown (Accident)	1	1			
May 1	FT. Jackson, MS	1			1	
May 4	New Orleans, LA	1	1			
June 1	Vicksburg, MS	1			1	
June 5	Carlington, LA	1			1	
August 3	New Orleans, LA	1			1	
August 4-5	**Baton Rouge, LA**	**4**		**1**	**3**	
September 8	Camp Parapet, LA	1			1	
October 1	St. James Parish, LA	1			1	
October 19	St. John's Parish, LA	3	1		2	
October 20	Bona Casa, LA	2	1		1	
1863						
February 1	Baton Rouge, LA	1			1	
April 18	Pass Manchac, LA	2				2
April 19	Lake End, LA (Drowned)	1	1			
May 16	Tickfaro Bridge, LA	1				1
May 27	Railroad Accident	1	1			
June 24	**Chacahoula Station, LA**	**6**			**4**	**2**
September 30	Unknown (murdered)	1	1			
October 5	**Bay St. Louis, MS**	**7**			**4**	**3**
November 29	FT. Jefferson, FL	1	1			
1864						
June 25	Ranch La Russias, TX	1				1
June 26	Grand Gulf, MS	1			1	
August 26	Bolivar Heights, VA	1			1	
September 5	Berryville, VA	1			1	
September 19	Winchester, VA	2			2	
September 21	Cedar Creek, VA	1	1			
September 21	Strasburg, VA	3			3	
September 21-22	**Fisher's Hill, VA**	**4**	**2**		**2**	
October 10	Cedar Creek, VA	1				1
October 16-19	**Cedar Creek, VA**	**24**	**2**	**1**	**11**	**9**
November 1	Cedar Creek, VA	1			1	
Unknown	Unknown	2			2	

CEDAR CREEK, VIRGINIA OCTOBER 19, 1864

USAMHI

THE 9TH CONNECTICUT INFANTRY SUFFERED ITS GREATEST NUMBER OF CASUALTIES (24) FOR ONE DAY WITH THE 1ST BRIGADE (BIRGE), 2ND DIVISION (GROVER), 19TH CORPS (EMORY)

TROOP MOVEMENTS 9TH INFANTRY

DATE	PLACE
1861	
September 26	Moved to Lowell, MA
November 4	Moved to Boston, MA
November 25	Boarded Steamer Constitution for Ship Island, MS
December 3	Arrived Ship Island, MS
1862	
April 2-5	Expedition to Biloxi and Pass Christian, MS
April 3	Biloxi, MS
April 4	Pass Christian, MS
April 15-28	Operations against Forts St. Philip and Jackson, LA
April 29-May 1	Moved to New Orleans
May 1	Occupation of New Orleans, LA
May 9-10	Expedition to New Orleans and Jackson RR, LA
May 13	Moved to Baton Rouge, LA
May 14-29	Reconnoissance to Warrenton, LA
June 20-July 23	William's expedition to Vicksburg, MS
June 22	Ellis Cliffs, MS
June 24	Hamilton Plantation, near Grand Gulf, MS
June 25	Arrived at Vicksburg, MS
June 26-July 23	Fatigue duty on Vicksburg Canal
July 23-26	Moved to Baton Rouge, LA
July 27-August 21	On duty in Baton Rouge, LA
August 5	Battle of Baton Rouge
August 21-22	Moved to Carrollton, LA
September 7-8	Expedition to St. Charles Court House, LA
September 9-April 1864	Duty in the defense of New Orleans, LA
October 19	At New Orleans, Algiers, Bonnet Carre, St. John Baptist District
1863	
March 21-30	Expedition to Ponchatoula, LA (Detachment)
March 24	Capture of Ponchatoula (Detachment)
June 24	Action at Chacahoula Station (Co. C,E,G,I,K)

TROOP MOVEMENTS 9TH INFANTRY

DATE	PLACE
1864	
January 3	Expedition to Madisonville, SC
April 15-July 16	Veteran furlough in Connecticut
July 16-20	Moved to Bermuda Hundred, VA
July 20-28	On Bermuda Hundred front
July 28-29	Deep Bottom
July 30-August 1	Moved to Washington, DC
August-December	Sheridan's Shenandoah Valley Campaign, VA
September 19	Battle of Opequan, (3rd Winchester), VA
September 22	Fisher's Hill
October 19	Battle of Cedar Creek
October 20-January 1865	Duty in the Shenandoah Valley
1865	
January 6-20	Moved to Savannah, GA
January 21-May 24	On Duty in Savannah
May 24	Moved to Hilton Head, SC
August 3	Mustered out at Savannah

BATTLE OF BATON ROUGE LOUISIANA
AUGUST 4-5, 1864

CURRIER & IVES

CONGRESSIONAL MEDAL OF HONOR WINNER

Serg. Major John C. Curtis, 9th Connecticut Infantry
Place and Date: At Baton Rouge, La., 5 August 1862
Date of Issue: 16 December 1896
Citation: Voluntarily sought the line of battle and alone and unaided captured two prisoners, driving them before him to regimental headquarters at the point of the bayonet.

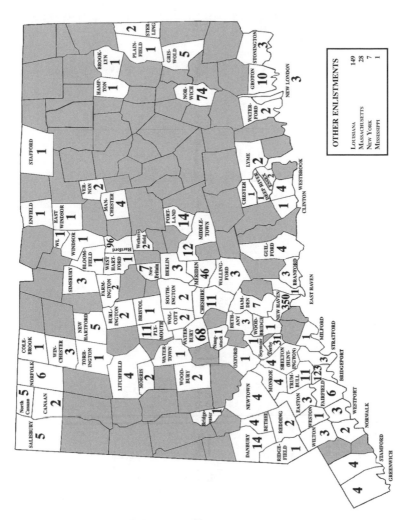

OTHER ENLISTMENTS

LOUISIANA	149
MASSACHUSETTS	28
NEW YORK	7
MISSISSIPPI	1

NINTH REGIMENT
CONNECTICUT VOLUNTEER
INFANTRY

TENTH REGIMENT
CONNECTICUT VOLUNTEER INFANTRY

SEPTEMBER 30, 1861 - SEPTEMBER 5, 1865
(FOUR YEARS)
1,820 RECRUITS
71 KILLED, 7 MISSING, 199 DIED, 441 WOUNDED, 8 WOUNDED & CAPTURED, 32 CAPTURED

USAMHI

Charles L. Russell of Derby was the first Colonel of the 10th Connecticut. Colonel Russell died in the regiment's first engagement at the Battle of Roanoke Island, North Carolina on February 8, 1862

The 10th Regiment Connecticut Volunteer Infantry was organized late in the summer of 1861 and was mustered into United States service on September 30, at Camp Buckingham,

HARTFORD

The regiment organized quickly with good discipline and enthusiasm.

On October 31, they left for Annapolis, MD on the steamers *Granite State* and *Mary Burton*. The regiment was under the command of Colonel Charles L. Russell of Derby, Lieutenant Colonel Albert W. Drake of Hartford, and Major Ira W. Pettibone of Winchester.

Colonel Russell had previously served as Adjutant in the 2nd Connecticut Infantry. Lt. Colonel Drake had been a 1st Lieutenant in Company A of the 1st Connecticut Infantry and this was Major Pettibone's first service.

The regiment was assigned to the 1st Brigade, (J. G. Foster), of Burnsides' Division. The 8th, 10th, and 11th Connecticut regiments waited patiently in Annapolis for two months.

On January 2, 1862, the Connecticut regiments left on the

BURNSIDE EXPEDITION TO NORTH CAROLINA

They were on board ships with miserable provisions for over five weeks and eventually landed at Roanoke Island on February 7. The following day, the regiment fought in the Union victory to sieze the Confederate fortifications at the

BATTLE OF ROANOKE ISLAND

The 10th Connecticut lost 4 killed and 51 wounded. It was the heaviest loss sustained by any regiment engaged. Colonel Russell was killed and Lieutenant Colonel Albert W. Drake succeeded him.

On February 11, the regiment boarded ships once again and this time remained on board for over a month. They eventually landed at Slocum's Creek on March 13, and after a hard march and a night spent sleeping in the mud, were under fire on the morning of 14th in the Union victory at the

BATTLE OF NEW BERN

The regiment lost 5 killed and 20 wounded. Colonel Drake died on June 5 from disease and Major Ira W. Pettibone succeeded him.

The 10th Connecticut remained in North Carolina throughout the summer of 1862 and took part in all of the movements of the army.

They were sent back to Roanoke Island to suppress a mutiny and a battalion from the regiment was sent to Plymouth to take part in capturing some Confederate earthworks on the Roanoke River.

The whole regiment took part in the Trenton and Tarboro expeditions and met the Confederates at Rawle's Mills, Hamilton, and Williamstown.

On July 22, all Union troops in North Carolina were organized into a new military organization,

THE 9TH CORPS

under Major General Ambrose Burnside. On November 15, Colonel Pettibone resigned and the command of the regiment fell for a short time on Lieutenant Colonel Benjamin Pardee of Hamden, and from then on to Major Robert Leggett of New London.

During the Goldsboro Expedition on December 14, 1862, there was a sharp engagement at

KINSTON

The Confederates occupied the town with about 6,000 men and one of their brigades under Nathan Evans was posted at a strong position on the opposite side of the Neuse River. The Confederate brigade was in place to defend the approach to the bridge. Several Union regiments had attempted to take the Confederate position but were repelled.

The 10th Connecticut was sent from the rear and passed, on its way to the front, one Union brigade and three regiments of another. When they had arrived near the bridge, the regiment charged the Confederates after having passed by three Union regiments who were lying down in line of battle. They captured the bridge which was on fire and was being shot at by four cannons. They drove the Confederates from their position and pursued them to the Neuse River. The regiment captured 500 prisoners, a number of small arms, and eleven pieces of artillery.

The 10th Connecticut had a loss of 15 killed and 88 wounded. This was the greatest loss the regiment sustained in a single day of the war.

On December 16, the regiment took part in the engagement at Whitehall and on the 18th at Goldsboro with no loss. Major General John G. Foster commanded the expedition and the department and T. G. Stevenson of the 24th Massachusetts commanded the brigade. On December 24, all of the troops in North Carolina were, by order of the President, made into the

18TH ARMY CORPS

with Major General Foster in command. On January 29, 1963, General Foster led a division of his troops including the 10th Connecticut to

SOUTH CAROLINA

The purpose of the move was to make an attack on Morris Island and

Charleston. Foster's troops landed on St. Helena Island. On February 13, Major John L. Otis of Manchester, was commissioned Colonel of the 10th Connecticut and assumed command of the regiment.

While on the island, General Foster, with 30 men from the 10th Connecticut, made a complete scouting of

MORRIS ISLAND

and declared a small force could easily capture it. But difficulties with Union Major General David Hunter and his staff arose which resulted in General Foster's forced return to New Bern. Stevenson's Brigade along with the 10th Connecticut was assigned to Brig. General Orris S. Ferry's Division of the

10TH CORPS

On April 9, 1863, the brigade left St. Helena Island for Edisto Inlet. The next day, the 10th Connecticut landed under the guns of Union Captain John Rodgers' monitors and drove the Confederates from Seabrook Island.

While stationed on the island, the regiment was ordered to make a scouting of Johns Island. The Confederates had taken up the planks of the bridge connecting the two islands and had a large force of infantry, artillery, and cavalry stationed there to prevent the repair to the bridge. Colonel Otis and the 10th Connecticut were alone. The Colonel sent for another regiment of infantry and a section of artillery for support. Meanwhile the Confederates crossed to Seabrook Island with the hope of capturing the regiment before the reenforcements could arrive. They were too late and the Confederates were attacked and driven back from the island, pulling up the bridge planks after them.

On July 14, Stevenson's Brigade boarded boats for

JAMES ISLAND

and landed there on the 16th and was assigned to Major General Alfred Terry's Divison, Tenth Corps.

On the 17th, the Confederates drove the 55th Massachusetts from their position where they were holding one of the causeways and marched five regiments of infantry, a battery, and a squadron of cavalry on to the island and formed their line of battle. The 10th Connecticut was positioned on the right and to the rear of the Union line. The Union force outnumbered the Confederates more than two to one and faced them at not more than 250 yards.

Colonel Otis asked for permission to attack the Confederate right and rear but permission was refused. The two sides faced each other for a few minutes without a shot being fired. The Confederates then faced to the right, marched deliberately past the Union front, and moved over one of the causeways without any Union response. Colonel Otis was ordered to follow closely but in no case was he to bring on any action.

On the morning of July 18, the regiment with Terry's Division, marched across Coles Island to a position opposite Folly Island. They boarded boats for Morris Island after several hours delay. The Union force arrived just in time to participate in the

ATTACK ON FORT WAGNER

The order to charge was changed just as the regiment came under fire. The next morning, the Chaplain and Adjutant of the 10th Connecticut were captured trying to help the wounded. Two weeks later Colonel Otis was detailed for special duty, and with Lieutenant Colonel Robert Leggett severely wounded, the command of the regiment fell upon Major Edwin. S. Greeley of New Haven. Although the regiment suffered little loss on Morris Island its service was hard and trying. When the regiment was ordered to

ST. AUGUSTINE

after the capture of Fort Wagner, sixty percent of the men were on the sick list.

In November 1863, Colonel Otis was relieved from special duty, resumed the command of the regiment, and was placed in charge of the Post and District of St. Augustine. On December 30, while the regiment was stationed there, a force of 160 Confederate cavalry ambushed a detail of 35 woodcutters from the 10th Connecticut. Of the Connecticut detail, 1 was killed, 1 was missing, 1 was wounded, and 17 were captured.

On April 18, 1864, the regiment boarded boats for

VIRGINIA

and reported at Gloucester Point on the 25th. The 10th Connecticut was assigned to the Third Brigade (Hawley), First Division (R.S. Foster),

10TH CORPS ARMY OF THE JAMES

The army was composed of the 10th Corps under Major General Quincy Gillmore and the 18th Corps under Major General William F. Smith. The whole command was under Major General Benjamin F. Butler.

On May 7, the regiment took part in the affair at

PORT WALTHALL JUNCTION

that drove the Confederates away from the railroad. The regiment destroyed the telegraph while other troops tore up the track. On May 13-15, the regiment took an active part in all the preliminary movements and skirmishing proceeding the

BATTLE OF DREWRY'S BLUFF

on the 16th. The right flank of the 18th Corps should have rested on the James River but it did not. The Confederates marched a large force between that flank and the river and captured two Union

brigades. This left the right side of the Union line in such a condition that the 10th Corps, which was forcing back the Confederate right side, was ordered to withdraw and was sent to re-enforce the 18th Corps.

The 10th Connecticut was assigned the duty of holding the Confederates in check while Joesph Hawley's Brigade on its right and Francis B. Pond's Brigade on its left withdrew. The moment that this was accomplished, the regiment was sent farther to the right with orders to hold the Confederates in check until other troops could gain a safe position. When this was done, Colonel Otis was ordered to take his own, and another regiment of infantry, and a section of artillery to the Halfway House and to hold a position on the Richmond & Petersburg Pike until the last of the 18th Corps had passed to the rear. The Confederates with infantry and artillery attempted to take the position but failed completely.

The 10th Connecticut was then sent far out to the right of the retreating Union army to protect its flank and remained there until all had passed to the rear. The regiment then became the rear guard back to Bermuda Hundred.   The regiment lost 36 men in these movements. At three different times during May 16 they had been in danger of capture while the 18th Corps was retreating.

Early in June 1864, the regiment took part in repelling the attack of Confederate General P.T.G. Beauregard on the

BERMUDA HUNDRED

lines. On June 15, the 10th Connecticut was on duty near Ware Bottom Church with Major Edwin S. Greeley in command. At about 3AM, signs of Confederate troop movement were observed. A Union skirmish line soon found out that the Confederates were retiring. The main body of the 10th Connecticut advanced so rapidly that they captured the famous Confederate Howlett House Battery.

On the evening of June 20, the 10th Corps, under Alfred Terry, moved down to Jone's Landing on the James River with orders to cross by pontoon bridge and to capture

DEEP BOTTOM

only nine miles from Richmond. There was so much delay with the pontoons that the General, fearing that daylight would reveal the movement before the bridge could be completed, ordered Colonel Otis to select another infantry regiment, in addition to his own, to cross the river in boats and to capture the position. The 11th Maine was selected, the movement was promptly executed, and the Confederate position was captured at 2AM.

At daylight, the Confederates appeared in force, with infantry and artillery, to retake their old position but were repelled. From this time until the end of the war, Deep Bottom was the base of operations against Richmond. A few days later, two detachments from the regiment were sent out to go within the Confederate lines, and to capture and destroy a large grain mill. They were also ordered to capture a torpedo station and to bring away the machinery. Both expeditions were completely successful.

On July 26, Colonel Otis was again ordered to take the 10th Connecticut and the 11th Maine and to cross from Deep Bottom to

STRAWBERRY PLAINS

to retake a position that a brigade of the 19th Corps had been driven from the evening before. The two regiments recovered the position, forced the Confederates back into their earthworks, and held the position through the night within fifty yards of the Confederates. In the morning, the two regiments joined a brigade of the 2nd Corps in charging the Confederate works. The 10th Connecticut and 11th Maine carried an angle of the works and captured three field guns. The loss to the regiment was nine casualties.

On October 1, Union Major General David Birney found that the Confederates were moving across the front of the 10th Corps. He ordered the 10th Connecticut to advance without support and to attack the marching column of the Confederates. General Birney personally thanked the regiment for the quickness and coolness it had displayed in attacking and keeping inactive, for two hours, a Confederate force that out numbered them ten to one.

On September 30, 1864, the three-year term of the regiment expired. Losses in battle, by disease, and the mustering out of the non re-enlisted men had reduced the command to a little more than 100 men present for duty.

On October 7, the 10th Connecticut was located on the extreme right of the Union Army when they were attacked by a Confederate brigade that had been pushed forward to turn the Union flank. The regiment stood its ground and drove back the entire brigade in confusion. The Confederates rallied and again advanced and were driven back with heavy loss.

The loss to the 10th Connecticut was eight killed or wounded. Colonel Harris M. Plaisted said in his official report, "that the conduct of the Tenth Regiment when the troops on its right broke and fled saved the Army of the James from disaster".

On October 13, the regiment, with 90 men in its ranks, was ordered to join Pond's Brigade in charging a heavy and well manned line of Confederate earthworks on the

DARBYTOWN ROAD

five miles from Richmond. The force sent in was entirely inadequate and met with a bloody repulse. The 10th Connecticut lost 5 killed, 1 missing, 38 wounded and 5 captured.

On October 18, Colonel Otis was mustered out at the expiration of his term of service and the command fell upon Edwin S. Greeley of New Haven.

On October 27, the 10th Connecticut under Greeley's command had a sharp skirmish near the Gerhardt Plantation with a loss of 5 wounded and near the Johnson Place on the 29th with one wounded.

The following week, the 10th Connecticut was one of the regiments selected to go to New York City to preserve order in the event of riots during the upcoming Presidential election. The regiment returned to Virginia without having left their boats anchored in New York harbor.

In November and December 1864, the regiment was replenished with about 800 recruits. On March 28, 1865, Colonel Greeley was absent on leave and the regiment under the command of Lieutenant Colonel Ellsworth Goodyear broke camp north of the James River with orders to march to the extreme left of the Union line south of Petersburg. They reached Dinwiddie Court House on the evening of the 29th. On the 31st the regiment arrived at

HATCHER'S RUN

and the next morning, at 4AM, were attacked by a brigade of North Carolina troops. They managed to beat back the attack and took a number of Confederate prisoners.

On April 2, while four companies of the regiment were on picket duty, Lieutenant Colonel Goodyear was ordered to take the other six companies to join in the

ASSAULT ON FORT GREGG

a key to the inner defenses of Petersburg. After a march of three hours, they joined the assaulting column, which had advanced under the fire of Fort Gregg, Bradley, and from Cemetery Hill.

The 10th Connecticut charged and carried the southern angle of the works. The State flag, with 23 bullet holes through it and three through the staff, was the first banner planted on the parapet. Out of the 13 officers and 180 men engaged, the regiment had 8 officers and 71 men as casualties.

The corps commander, Major General John Gibbon, presented the regiment a bronze eagle in recognition of its service on the occasion. Lieutenant Colonel Goodyear was severely wounded in the charge and the command of the regiment fell on the most senior captain of the 10th Connecticut, Captain Francis Hickerson of Derby.

The Confederate plan near Appomattox Court House was to defeat the Union cavalry and escape around the flank of the Army of the Potomac. They had already broken through the cavalry when the infantry of the 24th Corps, after a hard march, formed across their path. The Army of the James combined with the new 24th Corps proved an impassable barrier.

The Confederates advanced on the infantry and, after some sharp fighting had taken place, they were nearly surrounded. Flags of truce brought the fighting to a halt. The 10th Connecticut had several men wounded and captured.

After General Lee surrendered, on April 15, 1865, Colonel Greeley assumed command of the regiment. The 10th Connecticut Infantry moved to Richmond and stayed until August 25.

The regiment was ordered home, arrived in Hartford and was mustered out of service on September 5, 1865.

CONGRESSIONAL MEDAL OF HONOR WINNER

Sergeant Allen Tucker, Co. F, 10th Connecticut Infantry
Place and Date: At Petersburg, Va., 2 April 1865
Date of Issue: 12 May 1865
Citation: Gallantry as color bearer in the assault on Fort Gregg.

LIBRARY OF CONGRESS

PETERSBURG, VIRGINIA 1864-1865

THE 10TH CONNECTICUT INFANTRY WAS ASSIGNED TO THE 10TH ARMY CORPS ARMY OF THE JAMES AND PARTICIPATED IN ACTIONS IN THE PETERSBURG CAMPAIGN FROM MAY 1864 TO APRIL 1865

TOTAL CASUALTIES 10TH INFANTRY

DATE	PLACE OF CASUALTY	TOTAL	K	M	W	W/C	C
1862							
February 5	Roanoke Island, NC	55	4		51		
March 8	New Bern, NC	1			1		
March 14	New Bern, NC	25	5		20		
April 3	North Carolina	1	1				
April 4	North Carolina	1			1		
May 6	New London, CT (Drowned)	1	1				
June 1	New Bern, NC	1			1		
October 31	Manassas, VA	1					1
December 14	Kinston, NC	103	15		88		
1863							
March 14	New Bern, NC	1			1		
March 28	Seabrook Island, SC	1				1	
May 1	Seabrook Island, SC	1			1		
July 1	Morris Island, SC	1			1		
July 18	Stono Inlet (Drowned)	1	1				
July 19	Morris Island, SC	2					2
July 26	Morris Island, SC	1			1		
September 27	Morris Island, SC	1			1		
September 30	St. Augustine, FL	1					1
October 23	Trumbull, CT (Drowned)	1	1				
December 30	St. Augustine, FL	21	1	1		2	17
1864							
May 6	Gloucester Point, VA	1			1		
May 7	Walthall Junction, VA	1		1			
May 13-17	Drewry's Bluff, VA	31	6		25	1	
May 14	Bermuda Hundred, VA	1			1		
May 16	Proctor's Creek, VA	2	1			1	
May 16	Deep Run, VA	1			1		
May 20	Bermuda Hundred, VA	1			1		
May 25	Unknown	1			1		
June 1	Richmond, VA	1			1		
June 2, 18	Bermuda Hundred, VA	2	1		1		
July 26-27	Strawberry Plains, VA	7			7		
July 26	Haxall's landing, VA	1			1		
July 27	New Market, VA	1			1		
August 1	Deep Bottom, VA	3			3		
August 14,16	Deep Bottom, VA	33	6		25		2
August 14,16	Deep Run, VA	42	4		37		1
August 16	White's Tavern, VA	1			1		
August 16	Drewry's Bluff, VA	1			1		
August 16	Darbytown Road, VA	1			1		
August 27-31	Petersburg, VA	3			3		
September 1	Petersburg, VA	4			4		
September 13-15	Petersburg, VA	11	1		10		
September 20	Petersburg, VA	1			1		
October 1	Richmond, VA	1			1		
October 2	New Market, VA	1			1		
October 7	New Market Road, VA	3	2		1		
October 7	New Market, VA	4			4		
October 7	Laurel Hill, VA	1			1		
October 12-13	Darbytown Road, VA	46	5	1	35	3	2
October 13	Deep Bottom, VA	1			1		
October 13	New Market Road, VA	1			1		
October 13	Richmond, VA	1			1		
October 27	Darbytown Road, VA	6			6		
1865							
March 13	Hatcher's Run, VA	2	1		1		
March 30-April 2	Hatcher's Run, VA	13	1	1	10		1
March 31	Unknown	1			1		
April 2	FT. Gregg, VA	79	13		66		
April 2	Petersburg, VA	13			13		
April 3	Richmond, VA	1			1		
April 6-7	Burksville, VA	3		2			1
April 9	Appomattox CH, VA	4					4
April 15	Petersburg, VA	1		1			
July 15	Fredericksburg, VA	1			1		
Unknown	Petersburg, VA	1	1				
Unknown	Unknown	2			2		

DATE	PLACE
1861	
October 31	Left Connecticut for Annapolis, MD
Until January 1862	On duty at Annapolis
1862	
January 7-February 8	Burnside's expedition to North Carolina
February 8	Battle of Roanoke Island
Until March 11	On duty at Roanoke Island
March 11-13	Moved to New Bern
March 14	Battle of New Bern
Until October	Duty at New Bern
October 30-November 12	Expedition from New Bern
November 2	Action at Rawle's Mills
December 11-20	Foster's expedition to Goldsboro
December 14	Kinston
December 16	Whitehall
December 17	Goldsboro
1863	
January 26-29	Moved from New Bern to Hilton Head, SC
Until March 27	Camp at St Helena Island, SC
Until July 6	Camp at Seabrook Island, SC
June 18	Skirmish Edisto Island
July 9-16	Expedition to James Island
July 16	Battle of Secessionville
July 18	Assault on Fort Wagner, Morris Is. SC
July 18-September 7	Siege against Ft Wagner, Gregg, Sumpter
September 7	Capture of Ft Wagner and Gregg
Until October 25	Operations against Ft Sumpter, Charlestown
October 26-April 1864	Moved to St Augustine, FL

TROOP MOVEMENTS 10TH INFANTRY

1864	
April 20	Moved to Gloucester Point, VA
May 5-28	Operations on south side of James River
May 5	Operations on Bermuda Hundred
May 7	Port Walthall Junction, Chester Station
May 12-16	Operations against Fort Darling
May 14-16	Battle of Drewry's Bluff
May 17-July 21	On Bermuda Hundred front
June 2	Action Bermuda Hundred
June 9	Petersburg
June 16-17	Walthall Junction
June 16-April 2, 1865	Siege against Petersburg, Richmond
July 27-29	Demonstration on north side of James River
July 27-28, August 1	Deep Bottom
August 14-18	Strawberry Plains
August 25- September 27	Duty in trenches before Petersburg
September 27-28	Movement to north side of James River
September 28-29	Chaffin's Farm, New Market Heights
October 7	Darbytown and New Market Roads
October 13	Reconnoissance on Darbytown Road
October 27-28	Battle of Fair Oaks
October 29	Johnston's Plantation
November 2-17	Duty at New York Harbor, Presidential election
November 17-March 27, 1865	Duty in trenches before Richmond
1865	
March 27-28	Movement to Hatcher's Run
March 28-April 9	Appomattox Campaign
April 2	Assault on Petersburg
April 3-9	Pursuit of Lee
April 6	Rice's Station
April 9	Appomattox Court House
Until August	Duty at Richmond
August 15	Mustered out

NEW BERN, NORTH CAROLINA 1862

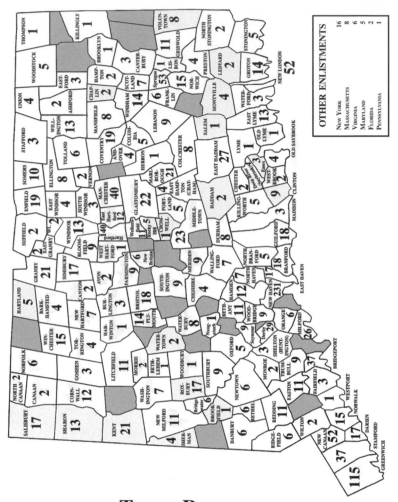

TENTH REGIMENT
CONNECTICUT VOLUNTEER
INFANTRY

ELEVENTH REGIMENT
CONNECTICUT VOLUNTEER INFANTRY

NOVEMBER 27, 1861 - DECEMBER 21, 1865
(FOUR YEARS, ONE MONTH)
2,022 RECRUITS
94 KILLED, 6 MISSING, 214 DIED, 391 WOUNDED,
16 WOUNDED & CAPTURED, 142 CAPTURED

The 11th Regiment Connecticut Volunteer Infantry was organized in September 1861. The first companies reported at Camp Lincoln, near the arsenal, in **HARTFORD** Enlistments and recruiting continued throughout October.

Henry W. Kingsbury of Lyme, was commisioned Colonel but declined the position to accept a command in the 14th Regulars and was he succeeded by Lieutenant Colonel Thomas H.C. Kingsbury from Franklin and the 5th Connecticut Infantry. Charles Matthewson of Pomfret, was appointed Lieutenant Colonel and Griffin A. Stedman Jr. of Hartford, was trans-

USAMHI

Griffin A. Stedman Jr of Hartford was the third Colonel appointed to the 11th Connecticut but the longest serving. He had been a Captain in the 5th Connecticut Infantry. Stedman rose to Brigade Commander in the 18th Corps and was promoted to Bvt. Brigadier General on the day he died. General Stedman was killed on August 5, 1864 in front of Petersburg, Virginia

ferred from the 5th Connecticut to be Major. Matthewson had not previously served in a Connecticut volunteer regiment.

The 11th Connecticut was mustered into United States service in Hartford on November 27, 1861.

The regiment remained in camp until December 16 when they were ordered to Annapolis, Maryland and left Hartford with 927 men. A set of regimental colors was presented to them in New York the following day. The regiment moved to Annapolis and was assigned to

BURNSIDE'S EXPEDITIONARY CORPS TO NORTH CAROLINA

On January 1, 1862, in company with the 8th and 10th Connecticut, they left Annapolis and headed to Fort Monroe, Virginia. One half of the regiment was placed on board the gunboat *Sentinel* and the other half was placed on the bark *Voltigeur*.

The expedition sailed the next day and was battered by a huge storm that lasted for many days. The *Voltigeur* was carried up on the beach by a tremendous wave at Cape Hatteras. After being on ships for 29 days, the regiment reunited and finally camped near Hatteras.

After the Battle of Roanoke Island, the regiment moved on to the island in March 1862 and joined the forces preparing to operate against

NEW BERN

On March 14, they had an active part in the attack on the city and were at the center of the Union line for the victory. In the final charge, their colors were among the foremost on the Confederate works. The regiment lost 6 killed and 16 wounded. After the battle, the regiment camped on the Trent River until July when they were ordered to join the

ARMY OF THE POTOMAC

located at Fredricksburg, Virginia. Colonel Kingsbury and Lieutenant Colonel Mathewson resigned shortly afterward and Henry W. Kingsbury was appointed Colonel and Griffin A. Stedman, Lieutenant Colonel.

The Union army evacuated Fredericksburg on the last day of August, crossed the Rappahannock River and burned the bridges behind them. The regiment moved north to Washington, DC and eventually joined the army under Maj. General George B. McClellan for the start of the Maryland Campaign. They were assigned to the 9th Corps (Reno), 3rd Division (Rodman)

HARLAND'S 2ND BRIGADE

The brigade (8th,11th,16th Connecticut,

and 4th Rhode Island) moved toward Frederick, Maryland and on September 12 the skirmish line of the 11th Connecticut entered the city on the heels of the Confederates. The Union army marched the following day and the Confederate forces were pushed back to Turner's Gap,

SOUTH MOUNTAIN

A battle took place in the late afternoon of September 14. The 11th Connecticut was under fire but its casualties were light (1 wounded) and the Union army advanced the next day. On September 16, the Confederates were found to be concentrated across Antietam Creek near Sharpsburg.

THE BATTLE OF ANTIETAM

began early on September 17, and in the afternoon the 11th Connecticut was placed on the left side of the Union line for the capture of the lower bridge.

Two detached companies of the regiment, under Captain John Griswold, plunged into the Antietam below the bridge and into a literal "valley of death". Griswold was killed in midstream and Colonel Kingsbury was mortally wounded. The regiment however, held its ground until support arrived. A general charge was eventually made across the bridge that drove the Confederates from the stone wall and the heights beyond. The regiment was nearly out of ammunition when they were relieved, but before the ammunition boxes could be filled, the regiment was called upon to support a Union battery with their bayonets.

The Confederate army was eventually pushed back across the Potomac River but not before the 11th Connecticut had lost 36 killed and 112 wounded, including every field officer. After the battle, the regiment went into camp at Pleasant Valley, Maryland. Griffin Stedman was promoted to Colonel.

On November 5, Harland's Brigade broke camp, crossed the Potomac at Berlin, Maryland and marched south into Virginia until November 9 when Ambrose Burnside assumed command of the Army of the Potomac.

The direction of the army was changed to Falmouth and they arrived ten days later. Harland's Brigade camped in the Stafford hills until December 12, then moved across the Rappahannock River into

FREDERICKSBURG

and slept on the streets. When the fog lifted the following morning, a battle began that raged until dark with Harland's Brigade not actively engaged. The 11th Connecticut supported the pickets connecting Sumner's line with that of Franklin's and had one casualty in the Union loss at Fredericksburg.

The following day, Maj. General Ambrose Burnside decided to renew the attack by putting himself at the head of his old 9th Corps and the 11th Connecticut was selected to lead the advance. Burnside was eventually persuaded to abandon the desperate scheme and the regiment was saved. Harland's Brigade quietly re-crossed the pontoon bridges on the night of December 14 and returned to their camp in the Stafford hills.

On February 6, 1863, the 11th Connecticut moved to Newport News where they remained until March 13, when they were assigned to Gettys 2nd Division, Harland's 2nd Brigade. The regiment was ordered to

SUFFOLK

to help build fortifications. On about April 10, the Confederates occupied Suffolk and Harland's Brigade took an active part in the siege of that city.

On April 11, the 11th Connecticut led a reconnaissance that captured a part of the Confederate advance line. Another reconnaissance in force was made on May 3. The siege was ended on May 4 when the Confederates abandoned Suffolk and the brigade moved back to Portsmouth. On June 30, as part of

DIX'S PENINSULA CAMPAIGN

Harland's Brigade was ordered to advance on Richmond. They marched up the Peninsula in a fierce sun and many suffered sunstroke. The Union advance continued until July 4, when Harland's Brigade was held at Taylor's Plantation as a reserve while the rest of their division made an unsuccessful attempt to destroy the Richmond & Fredericksburg Railroad. The entire Union force was eventually ordered back down the Peninsula and the campaign was viewed as a failure.

The 11th Connecticut went to Portsmouth and remained until October when they moved to Gloucester Point, occupied Fort Keyes, and then performed guard duty at Yorktown.

In January 1864, the term of service expired for the original members of the regiment. Two hundred-sixty-eight men re-enlisted for three years, received 30 day veteran furloughs to Connecticut, and arrived in New Haven on January 15.

After the expiration of the furloughs, the regiment regrouped, sailed south, arrived at Williamsburg, Virginia on March 3, and was assigned to the 2nd Brigade (Stedman), 2nd Division (Weitzel),

18TH CORPS

On May 4, they boarded ships and followed the Union gunboats up the James River and landed at

BERMUDA HUNDRED

On May 9, the Union army secured the Richmond & Petersburg Railroad and the Confederates were forced back across Swift's Creek toward Petersburg. The regiment lost 2 killed and 15 wounded. On May 13, the 18th Corps made an advance in force toward Richmond, the Confederates were forced back to a line of works near

DREWRY'S BLUFF

and many were captured. In the fog on May 16, the Confederates counter attacked and came very close to getting into the rear of the Union lines. The 11th Connecticut stopped them on its front, but because they were nearly surrounded Colonel Stedman ordered the regiment to fall back. The regiment lost 9 killed, 1 missing, 46 wounded, 119 captured and 16 wounded & captured. The Union army fell back and threw up a line of breastworks from the James to the Appomattox River. The regiment worked day and night until the works were completed.

On May 31, 1864, the 18th Corps was sent to reinforce General Grant at

COLD HARBOR

The 11th Connecticut arrrived on June 1, was sent out at once to the front as skirmishers, and met with small loss on that day (3 wounded). On June 3, the 11th Connecticut was at the front in the grand, early morning bayonet charge on the line of the Confederates breastworks. The charged was repulsed with a loss of several hundred in Colonel Stedman's Brigade.

The 11th Connecticut lost 18 killed, 2 missing, 86 wounded and 1 captured. Major Joseph Converse, Captain Amos Allen and Adjutant Samuel Barnum were mortally wounded. After the regiment was repelled, they threw up breastworks dug with tin cups.

After remaining 10 days under continuous fire, the 18th Corps moved back to Bermuda Hundred. On June 14 they advanced toward

PETERSBURG

and captured an important line of works

with several pieces of artillery. The 11th Connecticut had an active part in the siege of the city and was under nearly continuous fire until late August.

From May 1 until the end of August, the regiment lost about half its officers and over 400 men in action.

On August 5, Colonel Stedman was killed and Lieutenant Colonel William Moegling was mortally wounded. On August 31, the regiment moved to the Bermuda Hundred front, and later, went north of the James River to the Union lines near Richmond.

On the death of Colonel Stedman and Lieutenant Colonel Moegling, Captain R.H. Rice of Plainfield, became Colonel and Captain Charles Warren of Stafford, was made Lieutenant Colonel.

On March 1, 1865, Miss Julia A. Beach of Wallingford presented the regiment with a beautiful stand of national colors in memory of its late commander, Griffin Stedman. It bore upon its folds the names of eleven battles.

The 11th Connecticut was next assigned to the 1st Brigade (E.M. Cullen), 3rd Division (Devens),

24TH CORPS

and was in the triumphal advancce on April 3 into

RICHMOND

The regiment was sent to aid in putting out the fires that swept through the city. Lieutenant Colonel Warren was appointed provost marshal and the regiment was detailed for provost duty.

Eventually, the regiment was sent to southwestern Virginia and performed police duty until November. The 11th Connecticut was then ordered to Hartford and was finally mustered out on December 21, 1865 after a service of four years and one month.

TOTAL CASUALTIES 11TH INFANTRY

DATE	PLACE OF CASUALTY	TOTAL	K	M	W	W/C	C
1862							
March 1	New Bern, NC	2			2		
March 13	Slocum's Creek, NC	1			1		
MARCH 14	NEW BERN, NC	22	6		16		
March 20	New Bern, NC	3			1		2
June 1	Antietam, MD	1			1		
July 3	New Bern, NC	1	1				
July 27	Newport News, VA	1			1		
August 13	Drowned "West Point"	1		1			
September 14	South Mountain, MD	1			1		
SEPTEMBER 17	ANTIETAM, MD	148	36		112		
September 20	Antietam, MD	1			1		
December 13	Fredericksburg, VA	1			1		
1863							
April 24	Suffolk, VA	2	1		1		
May 3-4	Providence Church Road, VA	2			2		
May 4	Suffolk, VA	1					1
June 1	Portsmouth, VA	1			1		
July 2	Brandywine Creek, VA	1					1
July 5	King William Court House, VA	1					1
July 6	Hanover Court House, VA	1					1
Unknown	Unknown	2					2
1864							
January 24	Connecticut (Accident)	1	1				
May 4	Suffolk, VA	1			1		
MAY 9	SWIFT'S CREEK, VA	17	2		15		
May 12	Proctor's Creek, VA	2	1				1
May 14	Drewry's Bluff, VA	1			1		
May 15	Petersburg, VA	2			1		1
MAY 16	DREWRY'S BLUFF, VA	191	9	1	46	16	119
May 16	Petersburg, VA	1					1
May 16	Bermuda Hundred, VA	1			1		
May 16	Deep Bottom, VA	1			1		
May 20	Bermuda Hundred, VA	2			1		1
May 31	Bottom Bridge, VA	1			1		
June 1	Cold Harbor, VA	3			3		
June 1	Mechanicsville, VA	1			1		
June 2	Cold Harbor, VA	2			2		
JUNE 3	COLD HARBOR, VA	107	18	2	86		1
June 3	Petersburg, VA	4			4		
June 4,6,9	Cold Harbor, VA	3	1		2		
June 15,16	Petersburg, VA	11	1		10		
June 18	PETERSBURG, VA	54	5	1	39		9
JUNE 19-SEPTEMBER 11	PETERSBURG, VA	40	9		30		1
September 29	Chaffin's Farm, VA	1			1		
October 2	Petersburg, VA	1			1		
November 10	Broadway Landing, VA	1			1		
1865							
January 15	Chaffin's Farm, VA	1			1		
February 3	Unknown	1	1				
April 15	Richmond, VA	1			1		
April 20	Unknown	1	1				
October 9	Salem, VA	1	1				
Unknown	James River, VA	1		1			

CONGRESSIONAL MEDAL OF HONOR WINNER

Captain Samuel B. Horne, Co. H, 11th Connecticut Infantry
Place and Date: At Fort Harrison, Va., 29 September 1864
Date of Issue: 19 November 1897
Citation: While acting as an aide and carrying an important message, was severely wounded and his horse killed but delivered the order and rejoined his general

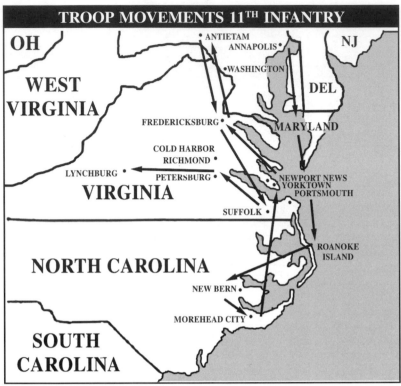

DATE	PLACE
1861	
December 16	Left Hartford for Annapolis, MD
1862	
January 7-February 8	Burnside's expedition to North Carolina
February 8	Battle of Roanoke Island
Until March 11	At Roanoke Island
March 11-13	Moved to New Bern
March 14	Battle of New Bern
Until July	Duty at New Bern
July 2	Moved to Morehead City
July 3-5	Moved to Newport News, VA
Until August 1	Duty at Newport News
August 1-6	Moved to Fredericksburg
Until August 31	Duty at Fredericksburg
August 31-September 3	Moved to Brooke Station then Washington
September-October	Maryland Campaign
September 14	Battle of South Mountain
September 16-17	Battle of Antietam
Until October 27	Duty at Pleasant Valley, MD
October 27-November 19	Moved to Falmouth, VA
December 12-15	Battle of Fredericksburg
1863	
January 20-24	Burnside's "Mud March"
February 6-9	Moved to Newport News, VA
March 13	Moved to Suffolk

TROOP MOVEMENTS 11TH INFANTRY

DATE	PLACE
1863	
April 12-May 4	Siege of Suffolk
April 24	Edenton Road
May 3	Providence Church Road, Nansemond River
May 4	Siege of Suffolk raised
June 9-16	Reconnaissance to Chickahominy
June 24-July 7	Dix's Peninsula Campaign
July 1-7	Expedition from White House to S. Anna
Until October	Moved to Portsmouth and duty there
October 1	Moved to Gloucester Point
Until April 1864	Duty at Gloucester point
1864	
May 4-28	Operations on south side of James River
May 5	Occupation of Bermuda Hundred
May 7	Port Walthall Junction, Chester Station
May 9-10	Swift Creek or Arrowfield Church
May 12-16	Operations against Fort Darling
May 12-16	Battle of Drewry's Bluff
May 17-27	On Bermuda Hundred
May 27-31	Moved to White House, then to Cold Harbor
June 1-12	Battles about Cold Harbor
June 15-18	Before Petersburg
June 16, 1864-April 2, 1865	Siege against Petersburg, Richmond
July 30	Mine explosion Petersburg (Reserve)
August 25-December	On Bermuda Hundred front
Until April 1865	North side of James before Richmond
1865	
April 3	Occupation of Richmond
Until December	Duty at Richmond, Lynchburg, VA

USAMHI

THE BATTLE OF DREWRY'S BLUFF
MAY 16, 1864

THE 11TH CONNECTICUT INFANTRY SUFFERED ITS GREATEST NUMBER OF CASUALTIES (191) FOR ONE DAY WITH THE 2ND BRIGADE (STEDMAN), 2ND DIVISION (WEITZEL), 18TH CORPS (W.H. SMITH)

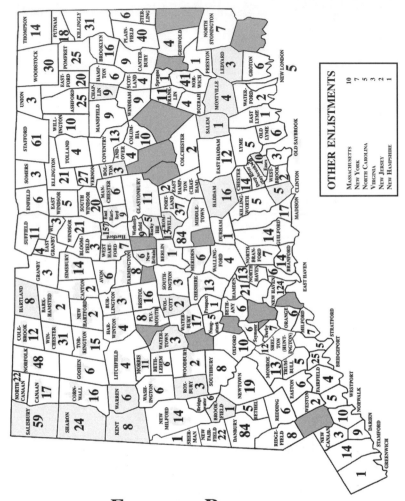

OTHER ENLISTMENTS

MASSACHUSETTS	10
NEW YORK	7
NORTH CAROLINA	5
VIRGINIA	3
NEW JERSEY	2
NEW HAMPSHIRE	1

ELEVENTH REGIMENT
CONNECTICUT VOLUNTEER
INFANTRY

TWELFTH REGIMENT
CONNECTICUT VOLUNTEER INFANTRY

DECEMBER 31, 1861 - AUGUST 12, 1865
(THREE YEARS, EIGHT MONTHS)
2,065 RECRUITS
58 KILLED, 205 DIED, 252 WOUNDED,
11 WOUNDED & CAPTURED, 136 CAPTURED

USAMHI

Frank H. Peck of New Haven went out with the 12th Connecticut as Major. As Colonel, he was the only regimental commander that the 12th ever intimately knew because Colonels Deming and Colburn had been on nearly constant detached service. Peck was severely wounded at Port Hudson, Louisiana and commanded a brigade at New Iberia. He was killed at Winchester, Virginia on September 19, 1864

The 12th Regiment Connecticut Volunteer Infantry was recruited in **HARTFORD** and was known as *The Charter Oak Regiment.* It was especially popular with young, pro war Democrats.

They were organized on September 16, 1861 to be a part of the "New England Division" of Maj. Gen. Benjamin F. Butler's **EXPEDITION FOR THE CAPTURE OF NEW ORLEANS** Henry C. Deming, the Mayor of Hartford, was selected by General Butler to be its Colonel and Ledyard Colburn of Derby, who had been a Major in the 2nd Connecticut Infantry, was appointed Lieutenant Colonel. On January 20, 1862, Frank H. Peck of New Haven, be- came its Major.

The recruits for the regiment came together on November 11, 1861 when four companies reported. Their camp was named "Camp Lyon" and was located in West Hartford, about two miles west of the State House, near Farmington Avenue.

The men lived in Silbey tents on the snow covered ground until the regiment was fully recruited and equipped. The 12th Connecticut left West Harford for New York City on February 24, 1862 with 1,008 men.

On February 27, they departed on the steamship *Fulton* and arrived at Ship Island, Mississipppi on March 8.

The regiment was assigned to a brigade commanded by Brigadier General

John W. Phelps. They remained at Ship Island until April 16 when they boarded the ship **E. Wilder Farley** bound for the Mississippi River.

They lay in the river just below Forts Jackson and St. Philip for several days awaiting the result of Admiral David Farragut's attack on the forts. Eventually two companies of the regiment were landed and ordered into the captured Fort Jackson. Before others could be landed however, news of the capture of New Orleans changed General Butler's plans and the two companies were recalled and the regiment was ordered to

NEW ORLEANS

They arrived on April 30 and camped in Lafayette Square the following day.

On May 5, the regiment, with its brigade, went to occupy an extensive earthworks known as "Fort John Morgan". The earthworks were located about ten miles above New Orleans and had been built by the Confederates as one of the defenses of the city. The Union forces renamed the earthworks "Camp Parapet". Shortly afterward, the regiment was placed under the command of Lieutenant Colonel Colburn when Colonel Deming was detached to act as Mayor of New Orleans.

The 12th Connecticut remained at Camp Parapet through the summer of 1862. In July, an expedition consisting of five companies and a section of Holcomb's 2nd Vermont Battery, all under the command of Major Frank H. Peck, was sent out on the gunboat **Grey Cloud** to destroy railroad bridges and to break up Confederate camps of mounted rangers and bushwhackers. The expedition destroyed bridges at Pass Manchac and North Pass and then sailed through Lakes Pontchartrain and Borgne up the Pearl River. They landed at Covington, Louisburg, Madisonville, Pass Christian and other points. After ten days, they re-turned to Camp Parapet having suffered little loss.

On September 29, the regiment was transferred to the "Reserve Brigade" commanded by Brig. General Godfrey Weitzel and went into camp at "Camp Kearney" in Carrollton. On October 24, the brigade, consisting of four regiments of infantry, two batteries and four troops of cavalry, left Carrollton on ships for an expedition to breakup the Confederate forces under Richard Taylor who occupied the La Fourche District. The Confederate force was found posted on both sides of La Fourche Bayou at

GEORGIA LANDING

An attack was made on October 27 and the Confederates were driven off after a sharp fight. The 12th Connecticut in this its first engagement had 17 casualties. The brigade next went into camp near Thibodeaux. Lieutenant Colonel Colburn was detached to act as Superintendent of the New Orleans & Opelousas Railroad and Major Peck was placed in command of the regiment.

In January 1863, the brigade moved up the Teche River to destroy the

CONFEDERATE GUNBOAT
COTTON

which was attacked on January 14. Infantry, artillery, cavalry, and gunboats were engaged on both sides. The gunboat **Cotton** was destroyed and the Confederate force was scattered. The brigade soon returned to Thibodeaux.

On March 27, Company A, under the command of Lieutenant William S. Bulkley, was captured with other troops aboard the

GUNBOAT *DIANA*

on the Teche River near Pattersonville. The Confederates paroled the enlisted men and sent the officers as prisoners to Texas. Company A lost 1 wounded, 1 wounded & captured and 32 captured.

On April 6, a large Union force under the command of Major General Nathaniel P. Banks crossed Berwick Bay and moved up the Atchafalaya and Teche Rivers. They found the Confederates strongly posted and supported with gunboats behind entrenchments at

CENTREVILLE, BISLAND AND BETHEL PLACE

A two day engagement began on April 13 that ended when the Confederates pulled out in the night. The 12th Connecticut, commanded by Lieutenant Colonel Peck, was actively engaged with losses of 2 killed and 11 wounded.

On April 14, General Banks started in pursuit of the retreating Confederates and with occasional skirmishing reached Opelousas on April 20. The regiment was placed on picket duty for several days.

On May 4, the 12th Connecticut joined in the advance on

ALEXANDRIA

up the Red River, 96 miles away. They reached the city on May 7 and two days later marched 36 miles to Piney Woods. They returned to Alexandria on May 12 and remained there on provost duty until the 17th. The regiment then marched to Simsport, on the Atchafalaya River and moved on the transport *Laurel Hill* to St. Francisville located above Port Hudson. They arrived there on May 25.

Two days later, the regiment joined in the general attack on

PORT HUDSON

that drove the Confederates into their last line of earthworks. The Union force had silenced four pieces of artillery and had reached the Confederate earthworks when the brigade was withdrawn and replaced by another. The regiment fell back and took a position about 150 yards from the Confederate earthworks where, under cover of hastily constructed breastworks, they remained under continuous fire doing duty as sharpshooters until the surrender of Port Hudson on July 8, 1863.

During this period, the regiment took part in two general attacks on the Confederates. One on June 10 and the other on the 14th. Its losses during the 42 days under fire at Port Hudson were 111 casualties.

After the fall of Port Hudson, the regiment was sent by water to Donaldsonville and then on to New Orleans. From there, they went by way of the Gulf of Mexico to Brashear City on Berwick Bay.

Accompanied by gunboats and the 13th Connecticut, the regiment under the command of Lieutenant Colonel Peck arrived on July 25 and occupied the city. The regiment was soon greatly reduced by malaria and was so incapacitated that it was difficult to find enough men to perform the required duties.

On September 2, the regiment went to Algiers, opposite New Orleans, and prepared to join an expedition against Galveston, Texas under Major General William B. Franklin. The ship that was selected for transport was found to be not seaworthy. The expedition was cancelled before another ship could be procured when news was received of the capture at Sabine Pass of the Union gunboats accompanying the expedition.

In October 1863, the regiment with its brigade, and a large force under General Franklin, penetrated the western part of Louisiana and reached Opelousas. The regiment remained in that section until the fall and eventually built comfortable winter quarters at New Iberia.

In February 1864, a large percentage of the regiment re-enlisted as veterans. They were the first regiment in the Department of the Gulf to take that step. In March they were sent home to Connecticut to enjoy their veteran furlough.

May 1864, found the regiment once again in Louisiana, this time on provost duty at Carrollton. They were next ordered to Morganzia and were attached to the 1st Division, 2nd Brigade

19TH ARMY CORPS

Brigadier General James W. McMillen commanded the 2nd Brigade. The 19th Corps was sent to Fort Monroe, Virginia in July and then on to Bermuda Hundred. The regiment remained there for two days and then was sent to Washington, DC.

On August 7, the 19th Corps became a part of the army commanded by Major General Philip H. Sheridan in the Shenandoah Valley. The regiment had traveled over 5,000 miles in a period of three months. The 12th Connecticut participated in the battle fought by General Sheridan's army at

WINCHESTER

on September 19, 1864. Colonel Peck was mortally wounded while leading the regiment and the command fell upon Captain Sidney E. Clark, Company F of New Haven, because Lieutenant Colonel George N. Lewis of Hartford, was absent due to a wound received at Port Hudson.

At one time during the afternoon of September 19, the 12th Connecticut and the 8th Vermont were left alone at the front when the regiments on either side were withdrawn. The 8th Corps on the extreme right of the Union line was just coming into action and had turned the left flank of the Confederates when the 12th Connecticut along with the 8th Vermont made a bayonet charge. The surprised Confederate force was pushed back into Winchester. The loss to the regiment was 9 killed and 61 wounded.

On September 25, the regiment was engaged with no casualties at

FISHER'S HILL

At the Battle of

CEDAR CREEK

on October 19, the regiment was led by Lieutenant Colonel George Lewis who had rejoined the regiment only a few days earlier. He bore a conspicuous part in another bayonet charge. At one point during the battle, the 12th Connecticut was surrounded and with the other regiments of the 2nd Brigade held off the Confederate divisions of Gordon and Kershaw. Eventually, the Union regiments defiantly fought their way to the rear.

Later in the day, the depleted 12th Connecticut joined in the grand charge that swept the Confederates from the Shenandoah. The loss to the regiment, in the battle, was 168 casualties.

The Battle of Cedar Creek ended the fighting days of the regiment. Because of the severe losses to the 12th Connecticut in battle, from disease, and the muster out at the end of term of service of those who did not reenlist, the regiment was consolidated into the

12TH BATTALION

on December 2, 1864.

The battalion went into winter quarters at Summit Point, Virginia. They remained there until April 30, 1865, moved to Washington, DC and participated in the Grand Review of May 23.

On June 1, they were sent to Savannah, Georgia and remained there until August 12 when they were mustered out. On August 22, the battalion was sent to Hartford where they were paid off and discharged.

TOTAL CASUALTIES 12TH INFANTRY

DATE	PLACE OF CASUALTY	TOTAL	K	M	W	W/C	C
1862							
February 11	West Hartford, CT (Accident)	1			1		
March 12	Ship Island, MS	1			1		
June 14	Mississippi River, LA (Drowned)	1	1				
October 27	Bayou La Fourche, LA	1			1		
OCTOBER 27	**GEORGIA LANDING, LA**	17	3		13		1
November 8	Unknown Location	1	1				
1863							
January 14	Brashear City, LA	2			2		
January 14	Bayou Teche, LA	2			2		
February 22	La Fourche Crossing, LA	1	1				
MARCH 27-29	**PATTERSONVILLE, LA**	35			3		32
March 27	Port Hudson, LA	1					1
March 28	Gunboat "Diana", LA	1					1
March 30	Unknown Location	1					1
April 13-14	Bethel Place, LA	2			2		
APRIL 13-14	**BISLAND, LA**	13	2		11		
April 14	Irish Bend, LA	1	1				
May 16	Alexandria, LA	2					2
May 27	**Port Hudson, LA**	21	2		19		
May 28	Port Hudson, LA	6	1		5		
May 29	Port Hudson, LA	4	2		2		
May 30-June 9	Port Hudson, LA	7	2		5		
June 4	Franklin, LA	1					1
June 10	**Port Hudson, LA**	31	1		31		
June 11	Port Hudson, LA	2	1		1		
June 13	Port Hudson, LA	2			2		
JUNE 14	**PORT HUDSON, LA**	19	1		18		
June 15,17,18,19,22	Port Hudson, LA	5	2		3		
June 23, 26	Brashear City, LA	10	1				9
June 27	Port Hudson, LA	4			2		2
June 28, 30	Port Hudson, LA	2			2		
July 3,5,8,9	Port Hudson, LA	6			5	1	
July 13	Donaldsonville, LA	1			1		
July 13	Port Hudson, LA	1			1		
July 23	Mississippi River, LA (Drowned)	2	2				
October 20	Carrion Crow Bayou, LA	1					1
1864							
January 1	Summit Point, VA	1			1		
April 8	Lakeport, LA	1			1		
May 3	Unknown Location (Shot while deserting)	1	1				
May 5	Railroad Accident	1	1				
September 4, 11,12	Charlestown, VA	3					3
SEPTEMBER 19	**WINCHESTER, VA**	70	9		61		
OCTOBER 19	**CEDAR CREEK, VA**	168	23		55	9	81
November 4	Newtown, VA	1					1
1865							
February 2	Summit Patrick, VA	1			1		
February 5	Waynesboro, NC	1			1		
March 6	Natural Bridge, FLA	1			1		
March 15	Wallingford, CT (Accident)	1			1		
March 18	Unknown Location (Drowned)	1	1				

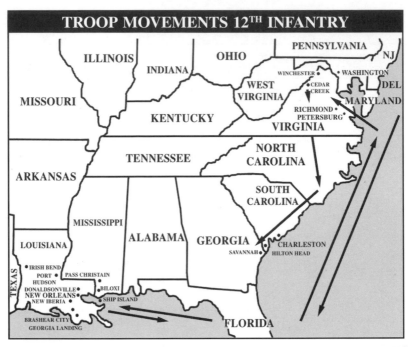

DATE	PLACE
1862	
February 24	Left State for New York City
February 27	Left New York for Ship Island, MS
March 8	Arrived Ship Island, MS
Until April 16	At Ship Island, MS
April 15-28	Operations against Forts St Philip & Jackson
May 1	Occupation of New Orleans, LA
Until October	Duty at Camp Parapet and Carrollton
July 25-August 2	Expedition to Pontchartrain, Pass Manchac, Teche/Pearl Rivers
July 27	Skirmishes at Madisonville near Covington
October 24-November 6	Operations in District of La Fourche
October 25	Occupation of Donaldsonville
October 27	Action at Georgia Landing, Labadieville
Until February 1863	Duty in District of La Fourche
1863	
January 13-15	Expedition to Bayou Teche
January 14	Action with steamer "Cotton"
Until March 1863	Duty at Brashear City
March 7-27	Operations against Port Hudson
March 28	Pattersonville (Detachment)
April 9-May 14	Operations in Western Louisiana
April 11-20	Teche Campaign
April 12-13	Port Bisland, Centreville
April 14	Irish Bend
April 20	Opelousas
May 5-18	Expedition to Alexandria and Simsport
May 18	Near Cheyneyville
May 22-25	Movement to Bayou Sara

TROOP MOVEMENTS 12TH INFANTRY

DATE	PLACE
1863	
May 25-July 9	Siege of Port Hudson
May 27 and June 14	Assaults on Port Hudson
July 9	Surrender of Port Hudson
July-September 1863	Operations in W. Louisiana
September 4-11	Sabine Pass, TX Expedition
October 3-November 30	Teche Campaign
Until January 1864	Duty at New Iberia
1864	
Until May	Move to New Orleans & Veteran furlough
Until July	Duty at Carrollton
July 5-13	Moved to Fort Monroe, VA then Washington
July 14-23	Snicker's Gap expedition
August-December	Sheridan's Shenandoah Valley Campaign
September 19	Battle of Opequan (Winchester)
September 25	Fisher's Hill
October 19	Battle of Cedar Creek
Until April 1865	Duty at Winchester, Newtown, Summit Point
1865	
April 21- June	Moved to Washington, DC
May 23-24	Grand Review
June 1-5 until August	Moved to Savannah, GA
August 12	Mustered out

USAMHI

THE BATTLE OF CEDAR CREEK
OCTOBER 19, 1864

THE 12TH CONNECTICUT INFANTRY SUFFERED ITS GREATEST NUMBER OF CASUALTIES (168) FOR ONE DAY WITH THE 2ND BRIGADE (THOMAS), 1ST DIVISION (MCMILLAN), 19TH ARMY CORPS (EMORY)

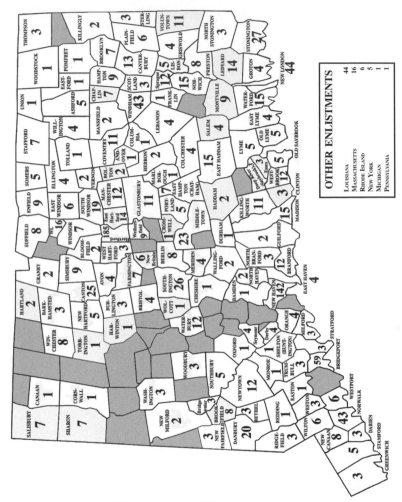

OTHER ENLISTMENTS

LOUISIANA	44
MASSACHUSETTS	16
RHODE ISLAND	6
NEW YORK	5
MICHIGAN	1
PENNSYLVANIA	1

TWELFTH REGIMENT
CONNECTICUT VOLUNTEER INFANTRY

THIRTEENTH REGIMENT
CONNECTICUT VOLUNTEER INFANTRY

FEBRUARY 18, 1862 - APRIL 25, 1866
(FOUR YEARS, THREE MONTHS)
1,480 RECRUITS
38 KILLED, 157 DIED,179 WOUNDED,
1 WOUNDED & CAPTURED, 58 CAPTURED

The 13th Regiment Connecticut Volunteer Infantry was organized in the fall of 1861. The headquarters were established in Durham & Booth's Carriage Factory, Chapel St. **NEW HAVEN** on November 25, 1861. The regiment remained in barracks at New Haven all winter.

Henry W. Birge of Norwich, was appointed Colonel. He was a Major in the 1st Connecticut Heavy Artillery. Alexander Warner of Woodstock, was appointed Lieutenant Colonel. He had served as a Major in the 3rd Connecticut Infantry and Richard E. Holcomb of East Granby, was appointed Major. He had served in the 3rd Connecticut Infantry as Quartermaster.

USAMHI

Henry W. Birge of Norwich, was promoted from Major in the 1st Connecticut Heavy Artillery to Colonel of the 13th Connecticut Infantry. Birge was appointed Brig. General U. S. Volunteers in October 1863 and Major General by Bvt. in February 1865. Colonel Birge assumed command for the defenses of New Orleans in 1862 and led divisions at Port Hudson,Louisiana in 1863 and in the battles in the Shenandoah Valley Virginia in 1864

The barracks occupied by the 13th Connecticut were poorly warmed and ventilated. Small pox eventually broke out and the knowledge of it was kept from the soldiers and the citizens of New Haven. Before the regiment left Connecticut, a dozen men had died from the disease.

On March 17, 1862, The 13th Connecticut left New Haven for New York City with 1,000 soldiers. The following day, they boarded the ship *City of New York* which was lying off the Battery in New York harbor. The regiment was assigned to Major General Benjamin Butler's

EXPEDITION FOR THE CAPTURE OF NEW ORLEANS

Because of bad weather conditions, the ship did not leave until Sunday, March 23. After a rough voyage with two severe gales and a narrow escape from shipwreck on the Florida coast, the regiment arrived at Ship Island, Mississippi on Sunday, April 13, and reported to General Butler.

The regiment left Ship Island on May 4, and reached

NEW ORLEANS

on May 12. They were housed in the Custom House and assigned to provost duty. Colonel Birge was given the command of the Defenses of New Orleans.

During the summer of 1862, companies of the 13th Connecticut were occasionally sent up the river on scouting or foraging expeditions. On September 11, Company A was stationed on outpost duty at Lake End on Lake Pontchartrain and remained there until October 4.

On September 29, a brigade was formed known as the "Reserve Brigade". It consisted of the 12th and 13th Connecticut, 1st Louisiana (commanded by Colonel Holcomb, the original Major of the 13th Connecticut), 75th New York, 8th New Hampshire, four companies of cavalry, and two batteries. The brigade was formed at Camp Kearney in Carrollton and Brig. General Godfrey Weitzel was put in command.

On October 24, the brigade started up the Mississippi by boat to break up the Confederate forces under Richard Taylor. They landed at Donaldsonville the next day and marched down Bayou La Fourche. On October 27, the

BATTLE OF GEORGIA LANDING

(or Labadieville) occurred and ended when the Confederates were driven off. The 13th Connecticut lost one killed and three wounded.

The regiment reached Thibodeaux on October 28, and formed Camp Stevens on the 30th. On November 7, an explosion of ammunition occurred on a train from New Orleans just as it reached La Fourche Crossing. Seven men from the 13th Connecticut were casualties.

The regiment broke camp on December 27, 1862 and reached

BATON ROUGE

on December 31. They went into camp on the Arsenal grounds on January 1, 1863. On March 13, the regiment moved with Maj. General Nathaniel Banks' army to the rear of Port Hudson and made a feint to assist Admiral Farragut's run past the fort. The next morning, the regiment hastily retraced their steps back to Baton Rouge. On March 28, the 13th Connecticut left Baton Rouge for the

FIRST RED RIVER CAMPAIGN

to take western Louisiana from the Confederates. Colonel Birge was in command of the brigade and Lieutenant Colonel Alexander Warner commanded the regiment. On April 13, they were engaged in a skirmish at Sand Beach, and on April 14 in the Union victory at

BATTLE OF IRISH BEND

The regiment lost 8 killed and 42 wounded. On April 17, they were also engaged in a skirmish at Vermilion Bayou. On April 20, the regiment camped at Washington, LA, and from April 30 to May 5 they were at Barre's Landing. On May 11, they reached Stafford's Plantation and were 13 miles from Alexandria, LA. They then returned, by way of the Atchafalaya River and Bayou Sara to the rear of Port Hudson. The regiment took part in the

SIEGE OF PORT HUDSON

from May 24 to July 9, 1863 with Captain Apollos Comstock of New Canaan, in command of the regiment. The 13th Connecticut took part in the assaults of May 27 and June 14.

After the disasterous assault of June 14, General Banks called for a storming column of 1,000 men. He promised a Medal of Honor to every soldier and a promotion to every officer who volunteered. Colonel Birge was selected to lead the column and 16 officers and 225 men of the 13th Connecticut volunteered. The promises of medals and promotions were not kept.

The capture of Vicksburg, Mississippi by Union General Grant made the surrender of Port Hudson inevitable and therefore the storming column was not called upon. When the surrender of Port Hudson took place on July 8, the storming column under Colonel Birge, with the colors of the 13th Connecticut, had the distinquished position on the right of the line, followed by the remainder of the 13th Connecticut.

On July 13, the regiment took part in the final skirmish against General Richard Taylor's forces at Donaldsonville. Next, the 12th and 13th Connecticut left for Brashear City and arrived on July 25. They remained on outpost duty until August 19 when they returned to camp at Carrollton and for the first time in five months went into tents. On August 30, the regiment went into camp at Thibodeaux, on the Bayou La Fourche.

Early in January 1864, Joseph Selden arrived as recruiting officer. He recruited 400 of the 406 men present for duty at that time to re-enlist for 3 years. On March 19, 1864, the regiment started on the

SECOND RED RIVER CAMPAIGN

Colonel Charles Blinn of Cornwall, was in command of the regiment. On March 28, they reached Alexandria where they were detailed to do garrison duty. On April 7 and 8, the regiment was held in reserve in the engagements at Sabine Cross Roads and Pleasant Hill. On April 12, the regiment reached Grand Ecore.

On the evening of April 20, the regiment moved in the advance toward

CANE RIVER CROSSING

but halted because of a Confederate battery on a bluff across the river. While scouting the situation, Union Brigadier General Henry Birge, his staff and a detachment from the 13th Connecticut were ambushed (18 out of 30 were killed or wounded). The remainder of the 13th Connecticut charged with their brigade up the bluff but before they reached the top, the Confederate battery had broken and run. The loss to the regiment was 2 killed and 22 wounded.

On April 29, the regiment returned to Alexandria and was stationed as an outpost across the river at Pineville. They remained there until a dam had been completed. On May 21, the regiment reached Morganzia near the junction of the Mississippi and Red Rivers. The regiment remained there until July 2, when they traveled to New Orleans and then left for home on veteran furlough of 30 days. The veterans arrived in New Haven on July 27, 1864.

In August, the 13th Connecticut, with Colonel Blinn in command, joined the

19TH ARMY CORPS

2nd Division (Grover), 2nd Brigade (Molineux), under General Philip Sheridan for the 1864 Shenandoah Valley Campaign. The regiment took part in the Union victory at the

BATTLE OF OPEQUAN (THIRD WINCHESTER)

on September 19, 1864. The loss to the regiment was 6 killed, 41 wounded, 1 wounded & captured, and 29 captured. It was the greatest number of casualties for the regiment for one day. Two days later, the regiment participated (1 casualty) in the battle and victory at

FISHER'S HILL

On October 19, the 13th Connecticut took part in the victory at

BATTLE OF CEDAR CREEK

The regiment lost 2 killed, 20 wounded and 9 captured. Major Appolos Comstock was wounded.

The regiment next went into barracks at Camp Russell, near Winchester, and remained there until December 1, when they were sent to Martinsburg, West Virginia. On December 15, those who had not re-enlisted (125) were discharged and the remainder became known as the

VETERAN BATTALION OF THE 13TH CONNECTICUT VOLUNTEERS

In January 1865, the battalion, with Captain William Bradley of New Cannan, in command was sent to

SAVANNAH

Georgia where they remained until March 12. Next, they were sent to

NEW BERN

North Carolina where the battalion performed provost duty until the close of the war.

In May 1865 the battalion was sent to Augusta,

GEORGIA

with Lieutenant Colonel Homer B. Sprague of New Haven, in command. They remained there, on provost duty, until August 25, 1865, when they moved to Gainesville to suppress Confederate guerillas. On October 17, the battalion was ordered to Athens and was housed in the college buildings at the University of Georgia. Companies of the battalion were detached for duty at Washington, Carnesville, and Lexington. On December 23, 1865, headquarters were moved to the Arsenal at Augusta and on January 3, 1866, the battalion was ordered to the district of Allatoona, with headquarters at Atlanta.

On April 13, 1866, the battalion was ordered to Fort Pulaski and Captain J. H. Butler, USA, mustered them out of United States service on April 25, 1866. The battalion reached Hart Island, New York on May 1, were paid, and disbanded between May 5 and 7, 1866.

TOTAL CASUALTIES 13TH INFANTRY

DATE	PLACE OF CASUALTY	TOTAL	K	M	W	W/C	C
1862							
March 11	New Haven, CT	1			1		
Unknown	Steamer "New York"	1			1		
May 14	Ship Island, MS	1			1		
August 1	Unknown	1			1		
September 1	New Orleans, LA	1			1		
October 27	Georgia Landing, LA	4	1		3		
October 27	La Fourche District, LA	1					1
November 7	La Fourche District, LA	1	1				
November 7	Algiers & Opelousas RR, LA	1			1		
November 7	New Orleans, LA	1			1		
November 7	Terre Bonne Station, LA	1			1		
November 7	Thibodeaux, LA	2	2				
November 7	Unknown	1	1				
November 17	Thibodeaux, LA	1			1		
1863							
February 1	Indian Bend, LA	1			1		
March 26	Baton Rouge, LA	1			1		
APRIL 13-14	**IRISH BEND, LA**	**50**	**8**		**42**		
April 16	Unknown	1	1				
April 20	Opelousas, LA	2					2
April 27	Washington, LA	1	1				
May 9	Bayou Boeuf, LA	1			1		
May 14	Alexandria, LA	1					1
May 21	Washington, LA	4					4
May 22,24	Port Hudson, LA	5	1		3		1
May 26	Bayou Sara, LA	1					1
May 27-29	Port Hudson, LA	4			4		
June 13	Irish Bend, LA	1			1		
JUNE 14	**PORT HUDSON, LA**	**25**	**7**		**18**		
June 19	Port Hudson, LA	1			1		
June 21	Brashear City, LA	1	1				
June 27	Port Hudson, LA	2			1		1
July 22	New Orleans, LA (Drowned)	1	1				
August 18	Winchester, VA	1			1		
August 23	New Orleans, LA (Drowned)	1	1				
1864							
April 11	Alexandria, LA	1	1				
April 14	Unknown	1			1		
April 21	Grand Ecore, LA	2					2
APRIL 23	**CANE RIVER, LA**	**24**	**2**		**22**		
April 23	Cloutierville, LA	1					1
April 23	Monett's Ferry, LA	1					1
May 16	Marksville, LA	1					1
June 2	Mississippi River, LA (Drowned)	1	1				
Unknown	Red River, LA	1			1		
August 23	Charlestown, VA	1					1
September 8	Berryville, VA	1					1
September 18	Cedar Creek, VA	1			1		
SEPTEMBER 19	**WINCHESTER, VA**	**77**	**6**		**41**	**1**	**29**
September 22	Fisher's Hill, VA	1			1		
October 7	Hawkinstown, VA	1					1
October 8	Newmarket, VA	1					1
OCTOBER 19	**CEDAR CREEK, VA**	**31**	**2**		**20**		**9**
1865							
June 1	Atlanta, GA	1			1		
1866							
March 5,18	Atlanta, GA	2			2		
Unknown	Unknown	2			2		

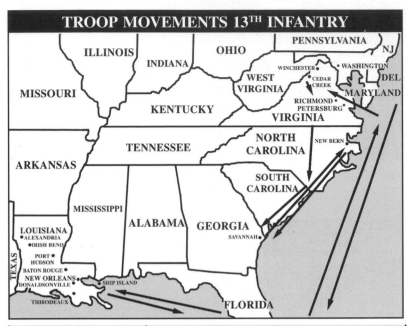

TROOP MOVEMENTS 13TH INFANTRY

DATE	PLACE
1862	
March 17	Left State for New York City
March 23	Left New York for Ship Island, MS
April 15-28	Operations against Forts St. Philip & Jackson
May 1	Occupation of New Orleans, LA
Until October	Duty at Camp Parapet and Carrollton, LA
September 13-15	Expedition to Pass Manchac and Pontatoula
September 14-15	Ponchatoula
October 24-November 6	Operations in District of La Fourche
October 25	Occupation of Donaldsonville, LA
October 27	Action at Georgia Landing (Labadieville)
October 28	Thibodeaux
Until December 27	Duty at Thibodeaux
December 27	Moved to Baton Rouge
1863	
Until March 1863	Duty at Baton Rouge
March 7-27	Operations against Port Hudson
March 28	Moved to Donaldsonville
April 9-May 14	Operations in W. Louisiana
April 11-20	Teche Campaign
April 13-14	Irish Bend
April 17	Bayou Vermillion
May 5-18	Expedition to Alexandria and Simsport
May 21-26	Expedition Barre's Landing to Brashear City
May 26-July	Siege of Port Hudson
May 27, June 14	Assaults on Port Hudson
July 9	Surrender of Port Hudson
July 11	Moved to Donaldsonville
Until March 1864	At Thibodeaux

TROOP MOVEMENTS 13TH INFANTRY	
DATE	PLACE
1864	
March 25-May 22	Red River Campaign
April 28	Monett's Bluff, Cane River Crossing
April 30-May 10	Construction of dam at Alexandria
May 13-20	Retreat to Morganza
May 16	Mansura
Until July 3	Duty at Morganza
July-August	Veterans on furlough
August-December	Sheridan's Shenandoah Valley Campaign
September 19	Battle of Opequan (Winchester)
October 19	Battle of Cedar Creek
Until January 1865	Duty at Kernstown and Winchester
1865	
January 5-22	Moved to Savannah, GA
Until March 8	Duty at Savannah
Until May	Duty at Morehead City and New Bern, NC
Until April 1866	Duty at Savannah, Augusta, Athens, Gainesville, and District of Allatoona, GA
1866	
April 25	Mustered out Fort Pulaski, GA

USAMHI

THE BATTLE OF WINCHESTER (OPEQUAN)
SEPTEMBER 19, 1864

THE 13TH CONNECTICUT INFANTRY SUFFERED ITS GREATEST NUMBER OF CASUALTIES (77) FOR ONE DAY WITH THE 2ND BRIGADE (MOLINEUX), 2ND DIVISION (GROVER), 19TH ARMY CORPS (EMORY)

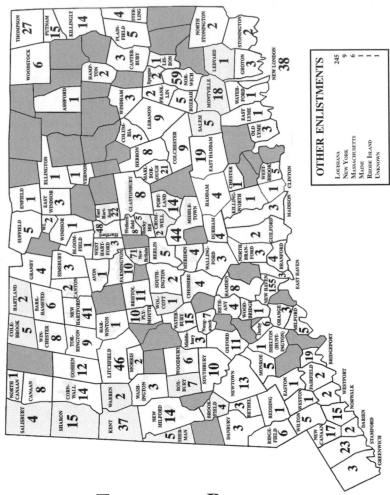

OTHER ENLISTMENTS

LOUISIANA	245
NEW YORK	9
MASSACHUSETTS	6
MAINE	1
RHODE ISLAND	1
UNKNOWN	1

THIRTEENTH REGIMENT
CONNECTICUT VOLUNTEER
INFANTRY

FOURTEENTH REGIMENT
CONNECTICUT VOLUNTEER INFANTRY

AUGUST 23, 1862 - MAY 31, 1865
(TWO YEARS, NINE MONTHS)
1,966 RECRUITS

118 KILLED, 15 MISSING, 263 DIED, 614 WOUNDED
14 WOUNDED & CAPTURED, 173 CAPTURED

USAMHI

Theodore G. Ellis of Hartford, was mustered into the regiment as Adjutant. He was promoted to Major in April 1863, and assumed command of the regiment for the battles of Chancellorsville, Gettysburg and every other major confrontation the regiment participated in from 1863-1865. He was appointed Colonel in October 1863 and Bvt. Brig. Gen. in March 1865

The 14th Regiment Connecticut Volunteer Infantry was organized following the May 22, 1862 call to furnish Connecticut's quota of the 50,000 men. Recruitment for the regiment progressed slowly until after the Union reverses on the Peninsula in Virginia. President Lincoln then called for 300,000 volunteers for three years or for the length of the war.

The regiment filled up rapidly and was first to complete its organization under that call. The men came from every part of the State and gathered at Camp Foote, in HARTFORD

Dwight Morris of Bridgeport, was appointed Colonel of the regiment and Dexter R. Wright of Meriden, was ap-

pointed Lieutenant Colonel. Wright held the commission for a short while and was then appointed Colonel of the 15th Connecticut. Sanford H. Perkins of Torrington, was appointed Major. He had been promoted from Captain of Company I of the 1st Heavy Artillery.

The 14th Connecticut was mustered into the United States service on August 23, 1862.

The regiment left Connecticut on August 25 with 1,015 soldiers. They arrived in WASHINGTON, DC and crossed the Potomac River to Arlington, VA on August 28. The next morning they went by forced march to Fort Ethan Allen, located near the Chain

Bridge. The regiment remained there until September 7 and held a part of the defensive lines of Washington, DC during the alarm caused by the Second Battle of Bull Run. Cyrus C. Clark, of Middletown, was appointed Major after Sanford Perkins was promoted to Lieutenant Colonel.

The 14th Connecticut with the 108th New York and 130th Pennsylvania, formed the 2nd Brigade (Morris) of the 3rd Division (French),

SECOND ARMY CORPS
ARMY OF THE POTOMAC

Colonel Morris was promoted to commander of the 2nd Brigade and the command of the regiment fell upon Lieutenant Colonel Perkins. The regiment entered into the Maryland campaign in pursuit of Confederate General Robert E. Lee.

On September 17, the 14th Connecticut, with little training, was plunged into the

BATTLE OF ANTIETAM

Their location on the battlefield was at the Roulette farm and near the "Sunken Road". The regiment was heavily engaged for several hours and was under fire all that day and the following. The regiment lost 19 killed, 1 missing, and 103 wounded.

On September 22, the regiment marched to Bolivar Heights near Harper's Ferry, West Virginia. They remained there for picket and special duty until October 30, when they went down the Loudon Valley, Virginia and reached Falmouth near Fredericksburg on November 17. The next day, the 14th Connecticut was sent, with the brigade, to Belle Plain on the Potomac for guard and fatigue duty. On December 6, the regiment rejoined the division at Falmouth and on December 11 moved toward

FREDERICKSBURG

They crossed the Rappahannock River and moved into the city. On December 13, the regiment charged the stonewall at the foot of Marye's Heights three times. Lieutenant Colonel Perkins was severely wounded while leading the regiment on its third charge.

The 14th Connecticut was among the last regiments to leave Fredericksburg on the evening of December 15. They returned to their old camp about two miles north of Falmouth. The regiment had suffered 23 killed, 3 missing, 96 wounded, 2 captured, and 2 wounded & captured. For a short while after the battle, the regiment was commanded by Captain Samuel H. Davis, of New London.

The regiment remained in camp during the winter and spring of 1863 doing picket duty along the Rappahannock, opposite Fredericksburg. The losses to the regiment were greatly increased during the winter by death or discharge for wounds and disabilities.

On April 28, 1863, the regiment under the command of Major Theodore Ellis, of Hartford, moved with the 2nd Corps on the

CHANCELLORSVILLE

Campaign. Once again the regiment saw hard service and had serious losses. On the night of May 2, they were sent with the brigade to the right of the Union line to hold the ground after the rout of the 11th Corps the day before. At the Union defeat at Chancellorsville, the regiment had 2 killed, 1 missing, 44 wounded, 2 wounded & captured, and 10 captured. On May 6, the 14th Connecticut returned to camp near Falmouth. The regiment stayed there until June 14 when they started on the

GETTYSBURG

Campaign. The regiment under the command of Major Ellis, reached Gettysburg on July 1, 1863 and on the next day were placed on Cemetery Ridge at the center of the 2nd Corps. On July 3, armed with their Sharps rifles, the regiment was part of the Union force that repelled Picket's grand charge of the afternoon.

The regiment captured five battle flags and more than 200 prisoners. During the morning of July 3, eight companies of the regiment captured the large brick barn and house of William Bliss from Confederate sharpshooters. They held the buildings until ordered to burn them after having lost several men. The regiment lost 10 killed, 57 wounded, and 4 captured.

On July 6, the regiment started with the Army of the Potomac in pursuit of Lee. On the 14th, they were lightly engaged at Falling Waters, near Williamsport, Maryland. On August 6, the regiment received its first installment of recruits, conscripts, and substitutes from the draft in Connecticut. In a few months the depleted ranks of the 14th Connecticut were swelled to the numbers of a large regiment.

The 14th Connecticut next, went by way of Harper's Ferry and the Loudon Valley, to the vicinity of Catlett's Station, Virginia. From August 31–September 3, the regiment was on an expedition to Hartwood Church. The purpose of the expedition was to support a force designed to move against Confederate gunboats on the Rappahannock River. The regiment also moved along Elk Run, Cedar Run, and near Bristerburg doing picket duty until September 12.

On September 13, the regiment crossed the Rappahannock and moved to Culpeper, Virginia and on the 16th advanced, by way of Cedar Mountain, to the Rapidan River. They did picket duty until October 10. On September 18, two deserters from the regiment were shot in the presence of the whole division.

The Army of the Potomac then moved north to intercept the Confederates who were attempting to capture Washington, DC. Major Ellis was promoted to Colonel. On October 14, the regiment was engaged in a skirmish at Auburn, Virginia and later that same day was in a sharp fight at

BRISTOE STATION

They lay on the north bank of Bull Run until October 20 and were engaged in a light skirmish at Blackburn's Ford on the 17th.

The 14th Connecticut then headed south, and from October 23 to November 7 camped near Warrenton and from November 10 – 26 near Stevensburg. From November 27 to December 2, the regiment was in the

MINE RUN

Campaign. On the morning of November 30, the 14th Connecticut was under orders, and fully expected, to engage in one of the most desperate charges the men ever contemplated. It appeared so hopeless and the chances of survival so slight that the men pinned on their uniforms papers on which they had written their names for their identification. Fortunately and mercifully, the order to advance was withheld.

On December 2, the regiment returned to its former camp near Stevensburg and remained in the vicinity until the 29th when winter quarters were fixed at Stony Mountain. The quarters were located on a point near the Rapidan River, far in advance of the main line of the army.

In February 1864, an expedition was organized as a diversion to aid a cavalry movement to the rear of the Confederate lines. The expedition was poorly planned and on February 6, 1864, the regiment was engaged in the battle of

MORTON'S FORD

The 14th Connecticut waded the icy

waters of the Rapidan, charged under the fire of artillery and infantry, and fought a hand to hand fight at night. The 14th Connecticut lost about one half of the number of men lost by the whole division. The regiment had 5 killed, 3 missing, 84 wounded, 14 captured and 3 wounded & captured.

When the army was reorganized in March, the regiment became a part of the Third Brigade (Morehead), Second Division (Gibbon), Second Army Corps.

On May 4, the regiment crossed the Rapidan River and the great forward movement of the army toward Richmond began. From May 5 to June 10, the 14th Connecticut engaged at

WILDERNESS, LAUREL HILL, SPOTTSYLVANIA, NORTH ANNA RIVER, TOTOPOTOMY, AND COLD HARBOR

and had 191 casualties.

On June 14, the regiment crossed the James River and reached the outskirts of Petersburg the next day. Until early August, the 14th Connecticut was occupied in various siege operations at the front. The regiment moved to Prince George Court House from June 27-29 and was on an expedition to Deep Bottom from July 26-30, changing camp continually. From August 12-21, the regiment participated in the second expedition to Deep Bottom and was involved in hard marching and severe skirmishing in the mid summer's heat.

On returning to Petersburg, the 14th Connecticut moved out for the destruction of the Weldon Railroad with only a few hours rest. On August 24, the men were busy destroying the railroad line and on the 25th they were engaged at

REAM'S STATION

in one of the harshest fights the 14th Connecticut ever experienced. The regiment had the singular experience of being under attack from three directions and of fighting some of the time from the reverse side of their own breastworks. That night, the troops returned to the earthworks near Petersburg, having lost 6 killed, 1 missing, 18 wounded, 20 captured, and 2 wounded & captured.

The regiment remained under daily artillery fire and did hazardous picket duty, close to the Confederates works, while building or strengthening the Union breastworks. On September 15-24, the regiment went on an expedition to Prince George Court House and on October 25-29 engaged in an action at

BOYDTON PLANK ROAD

In early November, the 14th Connecticut was on duty near Fort McGilvery and on the 29th they moved to relieve a part of the 9th Corps. On December 6, they went to relieve a portion of the 5th Corps. After December 13, the 14th Connecticut had a period of comparative rest while they camped near Fort Clark.

On February 5, 1865, the regiment was ordered out of their comfortable quarters to participate in another action at Hatcher's Run. They remained on the field until February 10, when the regiment went into camp.

On March 25, the 14th Connecticut with three other regiments of the brigade, all under the command of the 14th Connecticut's Lieutenant Colonel Samuel Moore of New Britain, made a demonstration at the left of the 2nd Corps line. They captured the Confederate works on the far side of Hatcher's Run and about 70 prisoners. This movement was made as a diversion at the time of the Confederate attack on Fort Stedman.

The regiment rested for two days and then entered the final campaign of the Army of the Potomac. On March 28, the 2nd Corps left their earthworks and from that day on until the surrender of Lee at

Appomattox, the regiment was engaged in forced marches, skirmishing, charging earthworks and lines of battle, and pressing the fleeing Confederates. The regiment was at the actions at HIGH BRIDGE AND FARMVILLE on April 7, 1865. From April 14 to May 2, the 14th Connecticut spent their time at Burksville, Virginia guarding captured stores. On April 15, the regiment went into camp at Alexandria, Virginia. On May 23, 1865, they took part in the Grand Review of the Armies in Washington, DC.

On May 30, the recruits of the 14th Connecticut were transferred to the 2nd Connecticut Heavy Artillery and the following day the original members were mustered out of service near Alexandria. On June 1, the regiment began their return home and reached Hartford two days later.

The 14th Connecticut was in the greatest number of battles of any Connecticut regiment and lost the largest percentage of men killed or died in service. They were in 34 battles and skirmishes with some of the battles ranked as the greatest of the war.

CONGRESSIONAL MEDAL OF HONOR WINNERS

Private Elijah W. Bacon Co. F, 14th Connecticut Infantry
Place and Date: At Gettysburg, Pa., 3 July 1863
Date of Issue: 1 December 1864.
Citation: Capture of flag of 16th North Carolina regiment (C.S.A.).

Corporal Christopher Flynn, Company K, 14th Connecticut Infantry
Place and Date: At Gettysburg, Pa., 3 July 1863
Date of Issue: 1 December 1864
Citation: Capture of flag of 52d North Carolina Infantry (C.S.A.).

Serg. Maj. William B. Hincks 14th Connecticut Infantry
Place and Date: At Gettysburg, Pa., 3 July 1863.
Date of Issue: 1 December 1864. Citation: During the highwater mark of Pickett's charge on 3 July 1863 the colors of the 14th Tenn. Inf. C.S.A. were planted 50 yards in front of the center of Sgt. Maj. Hincks' regiment. There were no Confederates standing near it but several were lying down around it. Upon a call for volunteers by Maj. Ellis, commanding, to capture this flag, this soldier and 2 others leaped the wall. One companion was instantly shot. Sgt. Maj. Hincks outran his remaining companion running straight and swift for the colors amid a storm of shot. Swinging his saber over the prostrate Confederates and uttering a terrific yell, he seized the flag and hastily returned to his lines. The 14th Tenn. carried 12 battle honors on its flag. The devotion to duty shown by Sgt. Maj. Hincks gave encouragement to many of his comrades at a crucial moment of the battle.

SHARPS NEW MODEL 1859 RIFLE
36" BARREL CAL. 52 PERCUSSION

TOTAL CASUALTIES 14TH INFANTRY

DATE	PLACE OF CASUALTY	TOTAL	K	M	W	W/C
1862						
SEPTEMBER 17	**ANTIETAM, MD**	123	19	1	103	
September 23	Fort Ethan Allen, VA	1			1	
October 27	Snicker's Gap, VA	1				
November 17	Warrenton, VA	1				
November 19	Falmouth, VA	1				
November 22	London County, VA	1				
DECEMBER 13	**FREDERICKSBURG, VA**	125	23	3	96	2
1863						
MAY 2-3	**CHANCELLORSVILLE, VA**	59	2	1	44	2
May 3	Fredericksburg VA	1				
JULY 2-3	**GETTYSBURG, PA**	71	10		57	
July 20	Warrenton, VA	2				
September 1	Culpeper, VA	1				
October 11	Culpeper, VA	1				
October 13-15	**BRISTOE STATION, VA**	65	12		18	1
October 13	Rappahannock River, VA	1				
October 14	Lexington, VA	1				
October 14	Auburn, VA	1	1			
October 14	Cedar Creek, VA	1				
November 17	Orange Court House, VA	1				
November 27 – December 2	Mine Run, VA	8			2	
December 1	Orange Court House, VA	1				
December 1	Rapidan, VA	12				
December 2	Hartwood Church, VA	1				
December 3	Rapidan, VA	1				
1864						
FEBRUARY 6	**MORTON'S FORD, VA**	109	5	3	84	3
February 6	Rapidan, VA	1				
March 31	Hatcher's Run, VA	1			1	
April 1	Alexandria, VA	1			1	
April 24	Railroad Accident, VA	1			1	
May 2	Unknown	1				
May 4	Brandy Station, VA	1				
May 4	Unknown	1			1	
MAY 5-7	**WILDERNESS,VA**	77	11	3	62	1
May 5-6	Winchester, VA	9				
May 8-9	Ely's Ford, VA	2				
May 10	Pomfret River, VA	1			1	
May 10	Laurel Hill, VA	19	1		18	
MAY 10-19	**SPOTTSYLVANIA, VA**	48	5	1	34	1
May 10	Unknown	1			1	
May 10	Po River, VA	1			1	
May 11	Wilderness, VA	1	1			
May 24,27	Hanover Junction, VA	2			1	
May 24-27	North Anna River, VA	15	6		8	
June 3-9	**COLD HARBOR, VA**	14	5		9	
June 16-22	**PETERSBURG, VA**	12	2		9	
July 26	Strawberry Plains, VA	1			1	
August 2	Hartford, CT (Drowned)	1	1			
August 15-17	Deep Bottom, VA	9	2		7	
AUGUST 25	**REAM'S STATION, VA**	47	6	1	18	2
September 5 – October 27	Petersburg, VA	6			5	
October 14	North Anna River, VA	1				
October 25	Ream's Station, VA	1		1		
OCTOBER 27	**BOYDTON PLANK ROAD, VA**	25	1	1	12	2
October 27,28	Stony Creek, VA	2				
October 27	Deer Creek, VA	1			1	
October 27	Petersburg, VA	1				
October 27,28	Hatcher's Run, VA	3	1		1	
October 28, November 1	Unknown	2			1	
October 28	Dinwiddie Court House, VA	1				
1865						
February 5-7	Hatcher's Run	6	1		5	
March 3	Lyme, CT (Drowned)	1	1			
March 25	Hatcher's Run, VA	7			6	
April 6	Farmville, VA	1			1	
May 31	Wilderness, VA	1	1			
Unknown year	Unknown	16			3	

DATE	PLACE
1862	
August 25	Left State for Washington, DC
August 28	Arrived Washington, DC
Until September 7	Camp at Arlington, VA
September 7-8	Moved to Rockville, MD
September 16-17	Battle of Antietam, MD
September 22	Moved to Harper's Ferry, WVA
Until October	Duty at Harper's Ferry, WVA
October 16-17	Reconnaissance to Charlestown
October 30-November 17	Movement to Falmouth, VA
December 12-15	Battle of Fredericksburg, VA
Until April 27, 1863	Duty at Falmouth, VA
1863	
April 27-May 6	Chancellorsville Campaign
May 1-5	Battle of Chancellorsville
June 11-July 24	Gettysburg, PA Campaign
September 13-17	Advance from Rappahannock to Rapidan River
October 9-22	Bristoe Campaign
October 14	Action at Bristoe Station
November 7-8	Advance to Rappahannock
November 26-December 2	Mine Run Campaign
Until April 1864	At Stevensburg, VA
1864	
February 6-7	Demonstration on Rapidan
May-June	Campaign from Rapidan to James River
May 5-7	Battles of Wilderness
May 8-12	Spottsylvania Court House
May 12	Attack on the salient, Spottsylvania
May 23-26	North Anna River
May 26-28	Line of the Pamunkey
May 28-31	Totopotomy
June 1-12	Cold Harbor
June 16-18	Before Petersburg
June 16-April 2 1865	Siege of Petersburg
June 22-23	Jerusalem Plank Road
July 27-29	Demonstration north side of James River
August 14-18	Strawberry Plains, Deep Bottom
August 25	Ream's Station
October 27-28	Boydton Plank Road, Hatcher's Run

TROOP MOVEMENTS 14TH INFANTRY	
DATE	PLACE
1865	
February 5-7	Dabney's Mills
March 25	Watkin's House
March 28-April 9	Appomattox Campaign
March 31	Crow's House
April 2	Assault on Petersburg
April 6	Sailor's Creek
April 7	High Bridge and Farmville
April 9	Appomattox Court House
May 2	Surrender of Lee's army
May 2	At Burkesville
May 2-15	Moved to Washington, DC
May 2-15	Grand Review , Washington, DC
May 21	Old members mustered out
May 30	Veterans and recruits transferred to 2nd Conn. Heavy Artillery

BATTLE OF FREDERICKSBURG, DECEMBER 13, 1862

USAMHI

THE 14TH CONNECTICUT INFANTRY CROSSED THE RAPPAHANNOCK RIVER WITH THE 2ND BRIGADE (PALMER), 3RD DIVISION (FRENCH), 2ND ARMY CORPS (COUCH)

HISTORY OF THE 14TH CONNECTICUT INFANTRY...

THE REGIMENT CHARGED NEAR THE "FAIRGROUNDS" AND SUFFERED ITS GREATEST NUMBER OF CASUALTIES (125) FOR ANY SINGLE DAY OF THE WAR

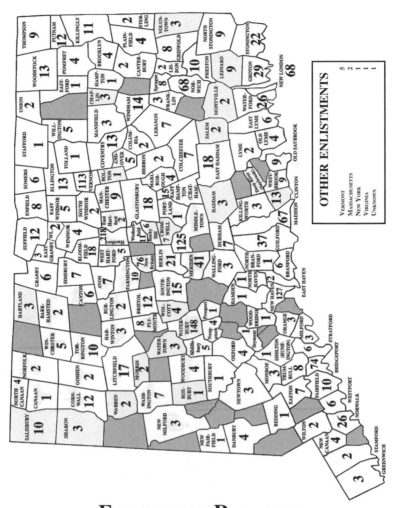

FOURTEENTH REGIMENT
CONNECTICUT VOLUNTEER INFANTRY

FIFTEENTH REGIMENT
CONNECTICUT VOLUNTEER INFANTRY

AUGUST 25, 1862 - JULY 12, 1865
(TWO YEARS, TEN MONTHS)
1,560 RECRUITS

26 KILLED, 4 MISSING, 156 DIED, 35 WOUNDED, 49 WOUNDED & CAPTURED, 421 CAPTURED

USAMHI

Dexter R. Wright of Meriden, was originally commissioned Lieutenant Colonel of the 14th Connecticut Infantry but before the regiment left the State he was apponted Colonel of the 15th Connecticut. He led the regiment until February 1863, when he was forced to resign due to poor health from malaria that he had contacted while the regiment was performing guard duty at Long Bridge, Washington, DC

The 15th Regiment Connecticut Volunteer Infantry was recruited in New Haven County in July and August, 1862 and was mustered into United States service at Oyster Point,

NEW HAVEN

on August 25th. Dexter R. Wright of Meriden, was appointed Colonel, Samuel Tolles of New Haven, Lieutenant Colonel, and E. Walter Osborn also of New Haven, Major.

Dexter Wright had been commissioned Lieutenant Colonel in the 14th Connecticut but was appointed Colonel of the 15th before the 14th Connecticut departed the State. Lieutenant Colonel Tolles had been a Captain with the State militia, **New Haven Grays** and Major Osborn had seen prior service in the war, as Captain of Company C, 2nd Connecticut Infantry.

On August 28, without firearms, but with a fine stand of colors presented by the ladies of Meriden, the regiment left New Haven for

WASHINGTON, DC

They arrived on the 30th and went into camp on Arlington Heights, VA. The regiment spent the first day and night without firearms or tents and listened to the artillery of the 2nd Battle of Bull Run, only 20 miles away. The regiment finally received their arms and camp equipment the following day and was assigned to guard the Long Bridge.

On September 5, the regiment received orders to join the Union forces hurrying into Maryland to repel the invasion of Lee's army. However, the orders were countermanded and the 15th Connecticut continued to guard the Long Bridge.

They camped near the unfinished Washington Monument and at Camp Chase on Arlington Heights. The regiment remained on duty in Washington until November. The malarial atmosphere of the Potomac mud flats seriously affected the health of the men.

During November 1862, the regiment camped at Fairfax Seminary, Virginia attended numerous parades and reviews, and suffered from the

MALARIA

contracted while on duty at Long Bridge.

On December 1, the 15th Connecticut recrossed Long Bridge into Washington and began to march south along the Maryland side of the Potomac. On December 6, they had reached a point nearly opposite Aquia Creek, VA. They crossed the river to the Virginia side and camped in 8 inches of snow without tents or cooking utensils. Four days later, the 15th Connecticut was part of

HARLAND'S CONNECTICUT BRIGADE

and camped at Falmouth opposite Fredericksburg. Harland's Brigade, at that time, consisted of the 8th, 11th, 15th, 16th and 21st Connecticut regiments and were designated the 2nd Brigade, 3rd Division (Getty)

9TH ARMY CORPS

Union Maj. General Ambrose Burnside's attack on

FREDERICKSBURG

began with heavy artillery on December 11. The following day, the 15th Con-

necticut crossed with its brigade into the town. They slept in the streets with the artillery from both armies flying or bursting over head.

On December 13, the regiment saw repeated and desperate assaults upon the Confederate lines that were repulsed with dreadful loss, but the regiment was not actively engaged. At about 6 PM, the Harland Brigade marched out and spent the night within short range of the silent Confederate guns that had so effectively defended Marye's Heights.

With the dawn of Sunday, December 14, the brigade fell back into the main streets of Fredericksburg. The regimental and company officers were soon called to headquarters, and on their return the brigade was called into line to await orders for a grand assault upon the Heights. It was to be headed by the old Ninth Corps, with General Burnside personally in command. During six hours of suspense, the men stood in line fully realizing what was before them. The wise council of corps commanders eventually averted the potential slaughter.

At midnight the next day, Harland's Brigade was silently wending its way over the pontoon bridge away from Fredericksburg. Daylight found it at its former camp in Falmouth ready for picket duty on the same lines as before the battle.

The 15th Connecticut had borne its share of marching and suspense, but its casualties in this terrible contest amounted to only nine wounded. By being held in reserve for the final assault, Harland's Brigade had unwittingly been kept out of active participation in the bloodiest part of the fight.

After the disaster at Fredericksburg, the 15th Connecticut was occupied with camp duties and ordinary alarms until February 6, 1863 when Harland's Brigade broke camp and headed for

NEWPORT NEWS

The regiment went into comfortable barracks on February 8. After a pleasant month, the 15th Connecticut left on ships for Norfolk on March 14. They moved to

SUFFOLK

and went into camp west of town. Charles L. Upham, of Meriden, was promoted from Lieutenant Colonel of the 8th Connecticut and assumed command of the regiment after Colonel Wright resigned because of sickness contracted at Long Bridge.

The post at Suffolk was commanded by Maj. General John James Peck, and he soon had all of the Union troops shoveling dirt and making gabions in defense of a place which seemed as destitute of strategic importance as any in the Confederacy. But the work went on, despite grumbling, and by April 10, the reason for it was apparent.

Confederate General James Longstreet besieged Suffolk and held the town as if in a vise. On May 3, the 15th Connecticut participated in a mission that discovered that the Confederate force was preparing to retreat. Longstreet was given no rest and on May 4 he hurried his main force across the Black Water River, leaving many of his rear guard to fall into Union hands.

From the raising of the siege until June 20, the regiment was very pleasantly quartered in various camps in or near Suffolk. On June 22, they boarded railroad cars for Portsmouth and soon after arriving joined

DIX'S PENINSULA CAMPAIGN

The purpose of the campaign was to draw Lee from Pennsylvania by threatening Richmond. The raid left White House Landing on July 1, on a forced march in the hottest season of the year to the vicinity of Richmond.

On July 4, 1863, the Union forces were within twelve miles of Richmond, but Lee was already fleeing from Gettysburg and it became too late to take Richmond by surprise. Terrible as the strain of this march was upon the men, it really accomplished nothing in a military sense. On July 14, the regiment was back in camp at Portsmouth in a most dilapidated and exhausted condition. They had marched a distance of 120 miles.

The 15th Connecticut was occupied with camp and picket duty at Portsmouth and South Mills until January 21, 1864 when they boarded a steamer for Morehead City

NORTH CAROLINA

They arrived on January 23 and went at once to New Bern, then to Plymouth, and back again to New Bern on February 3. On April 18, they started for Little Washington and arrived on the 19th.

On the following day, April 20, 1864, Confederate General Robert F. Hoke captured Plymouth and its garrison including the 16th Connecticut. On April 27, Hoke's force appeared in front of Little Washington. He left without a serious attack and on April 29 Harland's Brigade was ordered to dismantle the forts at Little Washington, to burn the government buildings, and to board ships for New Bern as fast as possible.

The 15th Connecticut arrived in New Bern and was assigned to provost duty. The town was threatened for several days with the prospect of a siege but nothing materialized after General Hoke realized he could not take the Union force by surprise.

The 15th Connecticut passed the time with ordinary camp duty and the occasional raid until the last days of August 1864, when the Union force at New Bern as struck with

YELLOW FEVER

In a short time more than half of the regiment were down with the disease. Soon, the muffled drums of the burial parties were sounding constantly from sunrise until dark. For more than two months the regiment employed every known means to eliminate the disease. The city was fumigated as effectively as possible by huge bonfires, commissary buildings were burned, and every unsanitary place was cleansed, but there was no relief until frost came in November. During this terrible ordeal, 70 men of the 15th Connecticut died and about the same number were disabled by the fever.

On December 9, a brigade consisting of the 15th Connecticut and other regiments under the command of Colonel Upham started in the direction of Kinston on short notice. Its object was to surprise Kinston by fording the Neuse River, destroy a Confederate ram lying there, and to generally draw the attention of the Confederates while Union General Grant extended his lines in the direction of Weldon. The brigade was barely out of New Bern before a heavy winter rain came on ending in snow. The Union soldiers attempted to cross the Neuse River at Jackson's Creek but were prevented by the high water due to rain. Confederate reinforcements were hurried up from Goldsboro and Colonel Upham had no alternative but to retire to New Bern. The regiment continued on provost duty at New Bern through the winter. It eventually received a large number of recruits.

Early in February 1865, the rapid accumulation of stores at New Bern indicated that important movements were to be made from that place. Union Maj. General John M. Schofield was assigned to the command of the Department of North Carolina and his army corps, the 23rd, began to arrive. With it came a large number of recruits from the West to join regiments in Maj. General William T. Sherman's force. Nearly 300 of these Western recruits were temporarily assigned to the 15th Connecticut.

The regiment was enlarged and divided into two battalions commanded respectively by Lieutenant Colonel Tolles and Major Osborn. The battalions were incorporated into a provisional brigade that included the 27th Massachusetts Infantry, a section of a New York battery, and a detachment of cavalry. The brigade was placed under the command of Colonel Upham of the 15th Connecticut. The advance encountered no serious opposition until March 7, when they reached the Confederate entrenched line at South West Creek near

KINSTON

The brigade was placed within short range of the Confederate lines and waited for further orders from Maj. General Jacob D. Cox. Skirmishing became lively and on the morning of March 8, a determined Confederate line appeared in Colonel Upham's immediate front. His nearest support was two miles in the rear. Fighting continued until the afternoon, when suddenly a furious attack on the left and the rear showed that the brigade was surrounded by an immensely superior force. Confederate General Robert E. Hoke, with his entire division, had reached the rear by the left and was dealing the little Union brigade an overwhelming blow in the belief that he was attacking Schofield's entire force.

The two battalions of the 15th Connecticut and the 27th Massachusetts fought desperately for an hour changing front first to left and then to rear until almost in the form of a hollow square the doomed brigade was receiving a murderous fire from all directions. There was no surrender; it was simply a capture.

When it was over, Confederate General Hoke realized for the first time that he had been fighting a small fraction of the Union force in his front. The Confederates made a second attack two days later, but this time they found the entire Union force ready to receive them. The Confederates were repulsed with crippling losses. This left the way open for General Schofield to join Generals William T. Sherman and Alfred Terry at Goldsboro.

The men of the 15th Connecticut spent a short time as prisoners of war and were paroled from Libby Prison, Richmond, Virginia on March 26, 1865. They were soon back at Kinston on provost guard duty. They remained there until June 6, 1865, when the regiment was ordered to New Bern for mustering out.

All members of the regiment whose terms of service did not expire prior to September 30, 1865 were transferred to the 7th Connecticut. On June 30, the 15th Connecticut boarded ships for New Haven, arrived on July 4 and was mustered out July 12.

THE SOLDIER IN OUR CIVIL WAR

THE BATTLE OF KINSTON
MARCH 8, 1865

THE 15TH CONNECTICUT INFANTRY SUFFERED ITS GREATEST LOSS FOR ONE DAY (499) AT THE BATTLE OF KINSTON. THE REGIMENT WAS SURROUNDED, CAPTURED AND SENT TO LIBBY PRISON, VIRGINIA.

MODEL 1863 RIFLE MUSKET, TYPE II
CAL. 58

DATE	PLACE
1862	
August 28	Left State
August 30	Arrived Washington, DC
Until September 17	Defenses of Washington, DC
Until November 3	At Arlington Heights, VA
Until December 1	At Fairfax Seminary, VA
December 1-6	March to Fredericksburg, VA
December 12-15	Battle of Fredericksburg, VA
1863	
January 20-24	Burnside's 2nd Campaign "Mud March"
February 6-9	Moved to Newport News, VA
March 13	Moved to Suffolk, VA
April 12-May 4	Siege of Suffolk
April 24	Edenton Road
May 3	Providence Church Road, Nansemond River
May 4	Siege of Suffolk raised
June 9-17	Reconnaissance to the Chickahominy
June 24-July 7	Dix's Peninsula Campaign
July 1-7	Expedition from White House to South Anna River
Until January 1864	Moved to Portsmouth, VA and duty there
September 20	5 companies moved to South Mills
1864	
January 20	Skirmish Harrellsville (Detachment)
January 21	Moved to New Bern, NC
January 24	Moved to Plymouth, NC
January 29	Expedition up Roanoke River (Detachment)
January 30	Windsor (Detachment)
February 3	Moved to New Bern
Until March 1865	Duty at New Bern
June 20-23	Expedition to near Kinston
June 22	Southwest Creek
1865	
March 8-10	Battle of Wise's Forks
March 14	Occupation of Kinston
Until June	Provost duty at Kinston and New Bern
June 27	Mustered out
July 12	Discharged at New Haven

TOTAL CASUALTIES 15TH INFANTRY

DATE	PLACE OF CASUALTY	TOTAL	K	M	W	W/C	C
1862							
DECEMBER 12-17	FREDERICKSBURG, VA	9			9		
1863							
February 3	Unknown location (poisoned)	1	1				
February 15	Newport News, VA (suicide)	1	1				
April 24	Edenton Road, VA	2			2		
April 24-May 25	Suffolk, VA	6			6		
May 3	Providence Church Road, VA	2	1		1		
July 20	Unknown Location	1			1		
1864							
April 20-21	Plymouth, NC	8					8
September 27	North Carolina (unknown)	1		1			
December 27	New Bern, NC	1	1				
1865							
March 6	Bachelor's Creek, NC	1			1		
MARCH 8	**KINSTON, NC**	**499**	**22**	**3**	**12**	**49**	**413**
May 21	Railroad Accident, North Carolina	1	1				
Unknown Year	Unknown	1			1		
Unknown Year	Wisepoint, NC	1			1		
Unknown Year	Colerain, NC	1			1		

LIBBY PRISON 1865
RICHMOND, VIRGINIA

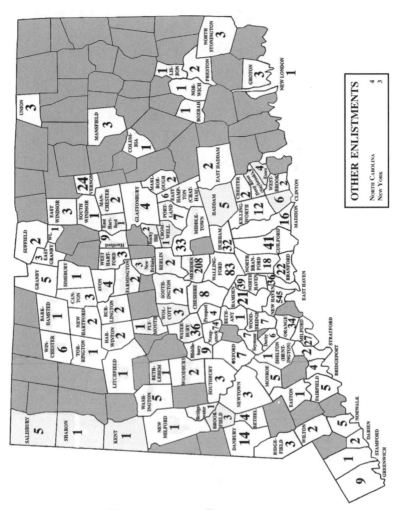

OTHER ENLISTMENTS

NORTH CAROLINA	4
NEW YORK	3

FIFTEENTH REGIMENT
CONNECTICUT VOLUNTEER INFANTRY

SIXTEENTH REGIMENT
CONNECTICUT VOLUNTEER INFANTRY

AUGUST 24, 1862 - JUNE 24, 1865
(TWO YEARS, TEN MONTHS)
1,091 RECRUITS

58 KILLED, 3 MISSING, 265 DIED, 178 WOUNDED, 16 WOUNDED & CAPTURED, 439 CAPTURED

The 16th Regiment Connecticut Volunteer Infantry was organized in August of 1862. All of the senior field officers were from Hartford. Francis Beach, a regular army officer, was commissioned Colonel. Frank W. Cheney was the Lieutenant Colonel and George A. Washburn was appointed Major. Washburn had been quartermaster in the 1st Connecticut Heavy Artillery.

The regiment gathered in **HARTFORD** at Camp Williams and was mustered into the United States service on August 24. The regiment, numbering 1,010, boarded the steamers *City of Hartford* and *Collins* and departed for New York City. They then boarded the

USAMHI

At the Battle of Antietam in September 1862, John H. Burnham of Hartford was the Adjutant. By December 1862, he had jumped ahead of 8 to 10 more senior officers to become Lieutenant Colonel. He effectively commanded the regiment from this position for the remainder of the war. He was wounded at Suffolk, Virginia in May 1863 and was captured at Plymouth, North Carolina in April 1864

steamer *Kill Von Kull* arrived in Elizabeth, New Jersey and then departed by rail for Baltimore, Maryland by way of Harrisburg, Pennsylvania. The regiment moved from Baltimore to **WASHINGTON, DC** arrived on August 29 and went into camp on Arlington Heights, near Fort Ward.

After a few days, the regiment was hurried forward, by forced marches, to join the Army of the Potomac which was located near Sharpsburg, MD. On September 16, the regiment was placed in the Second Brigade (Harland), Third Division (Rodman), **NINTH CORPS** The brigade was commanded by Colonel Edward Harland, of Norwich. It consisted of the 8th, 11th and 16th Connecticut Infantry and 4th Rhode Island Infantry. The regiment had received no drill, or discipline, instructions and only a few in marching. On the following morning the

BATTLE OF ANTIETAM

began. The regiment was kept back, under a heavy artillery fire, until late afternoon when they crossed Antietam Creek below the lower bridge and moved against the extreme right of the A. P. Hill's Confederate infantry that was positioned behind stonewalls and fences.

As the regiment entered the fated 40 acre cornfield on the Harper's Ferry Road, it was met by a terrific volley of musketry. The slaughter was appalling. Men fell by the score and the regiment eventually broke and fled toward the lower bridge. The 16th Connecticut lost 44 killed, 1 missing, 159 wounded, 15 captured, and 4 wounded & captured. Lieutenant Colonel Cheney and Major Washburn were severely wounded and both resigned at the end of the year.

Six weeks after the battle, the Union Army slowly pursued the Confederates. The regiment moved from camp to camp and eventually reached Falmouth, VA on November 19.

On December 12, the 16th Connecticut, as a part of Harland's Brigade, moved across the Rappahannock River into

FREDERICKSBURG

They were not actively engaged in the battle and had one man wounded. After General Burnside was relieved of the command of the Army of the Potomac, the Ninth Army Corps was detached and ordered to

NEWPORT NEWS

After a stay of about five weeks, the regiment was ordered with the rest of the Harland's Brigade to

SUFFOLK

They saw active service during the siege of the city by Confederate General James Longstreet. The 16th Connecticut was engaged at Edenton Road on April 24, 1863 (1 killed, 5 wounded) and at Providence Church (2 killed, 7 wounded) on May 3.

On June 16, the regiment moved to Portsmouth and on the 22nd was engaged, with other troops, in Maj. General John A.

DIX'S PENINSULA CAMPAIGN

The purpose of the expedition was to destroy communication between Lee's army and Richmond and to draw Lee away from Pennsylvania. The attempt proved fruitless and was given up. The expedition was known as the "Blackberry Raid" and involved the most severe marching of any campaign in which the regiment participated. After the "Blackberry Raid", the regiment enjoyed several months of quiet in camp near Portsmouth.

On September 6, five companies were detailed to go to South Mills for two weeks of picket duty. On January 21, 1864, the regiment was ordered to Plymouth on the coast of

NORTH CAROLINA

They arrived two days later. The regiment made several raids into the interior, breaking up Confederate cavalry camps and capturing or burning large quantities of cotton and tobacco. On March 3, the regiment was ordered to

NEW BERN

and went into barracks near the Neuse River. Company G was sent to Fort Stevenson to relieve a company of the 21st Connecticut.

On March 20, the regiment took the steamer *Thomas Collyer* and returned to

PLYMOUTH

The ship narrowly escaped shipwreck in

a storm off Roanoke Island. The steamer *General Berry* rescued the men.

On April 17, Plymouth was garrisoned by 1,600 soldiers under Brig. General Henry W. Wessells. The garrison was attacked by an overwhelming force of 12,000 Confederates, under R. D. Hoke. They were assisted by the ironclad ram *Albemarle*. The fighting continued until noon of the 20th when the town was forced to surrender.

The Confederates mercilessly shot down any black soldiers found in uniform in a repeat of what happened earlier at Fort Pillow. The losses in the 16th Connecticut were 1 killed, 2 missing, 422 captured, and 12 wounded & captured. For the remainder of 1864, the captured suffered confinement in various prisons of the South. A large number of them were imprisoned at

ANDERSONVILLE PRISON

Georgia and Florence, SC. Nearly one half of the captured 16th Connecticut soldiers died in prison.

The story of the preservation of the colors of the 16th Connecticut was, at that time, widely known. When every hope of escape from Plymouth was gone, the color guard took each flag from its staff and tore it into shreds and distributed them among the members of the regiment. The shreds were concealed in various ways through the weary days of their imprisonment.

In 1879, as many of these remnants as could be obtained from the survivors of the regiment were gathered and made up into the shape of a shield. It was mounted below an eagle that had been sewn on a white silk banner trimmed with gold fringe. The banner in letters of gold bore this inscription:

ANTIETAM, FREDERICKSBURG, EDENTON ROAD, SIEGE OF SUFFOLK, NANSEMOND, PLYMOUTH.

THE DEVICE ON THE FLAG IS COMPOSED

ENTIRELY OF FRAGMENTS OF THE OLD COLORS OF THE SIXTEENTH REGIMENT CONNECTICUT VOLUNTEERS. THEY WERE TORN INTO SHREDS BY THE OFFICERS AND MEN AND CONCEALED ON THEIR PERSONS IN ORDER TO SAVE THEM FROM THE ENEMY, AT THE BATTLE OF PLYMOUTH, NC, APRIL 20, 1864, WHERE TOGETHER WITH THE WHOLE UNION AT THAT POST, THE REGIMENT AFTER THREE DAYS' FIGHT AGAINST OVERWHELMING NUMBERS WAS COMPELLED TO SURRENDER. MANY OF THE MEN BEARING THESE RELICS WERE TAKEN TO SOUTHERN PRISONS, WHERE UNDER UNTOLD PRIVATIONS THEY STILL SACREDLY WATCHED OVER AND KEPT THEIR TRUSTS, SUBSEQUENTLY RETURNING THEM TO THEIR NATIVE STATE"

The restored banner was deposited with the battleflags of the State at the Capitol on "Battle Flag Day", September 17, 1879.

Captain Joseph H. Barnum of Company H, had escaped capture at Plymouth because he had been detached to Roanoke Island. He was left with the command of the 16th Connecticut, which was made up mostly of the few who had escaped, and of those that had been sick, absent or on special duty.

During December 1864, the greatly diminished 16th Connecticut moved from Plymouth on an expedition to Foster's Mills. The mills were destroyed and a large quantity of grain was taken along with various other spoils of war.

On another occasion, the regiment went to Hertford where they captured large quantities of cotton, tobacco, finished carriages and buggies, several thousand feet of lumber, several mules, and forty freed slaves. On another night, 60 men of the regiment went by steamer up the Alligator River and captured a barge and three small sailboats containing 2,500 bushels of shelled corn, and 15 men with mules and carts.

The regiment participated in raiding expeditions to Columbia and Edenton until March 4, 1865, when they were ordered to New Bern to join up with the released prisoners.

A number of men who were returning to the regiment, after having been released from prison, were on a steamer going down the Potomac River on the night of April 24 when the boat collided with the steamer *Black Diamond*. The regiment lost six in the collision.

The 16th Connecticut remained on provost duty at New Bern. In April, the regiment acted as personal escort for General Grant when he visited General Sherman at Raleigh.

The regiment was mustered out of the service of the United States on June 24, 1865. More soldiers died at Andersonville prison from the 16th Connecticut Infantry than from any other Connecticut regiment.

USAMHI

ANDERSONVILLE PRISON
GEORGIA

THE 16TH CONNECTICUT INFANTRY SUFFERED ITS GREATEST LOSS OF LIFE IN THE WAR AT ANDERSONVILLE PRISON, GEORGIA WHERE 98 MEN DIED OUT OF THE 422 WHO HAD BEEN CAPTURED AT PLYMOUTH, NORTH CAROLINA ON APRIL 20, 1864

TOTAL CASUALTIES 16TH INFANTRY

DATE	PLACE OF CASUALTY	TOTAL	K	M	W	W/C	C
1862							
SEPTEMBER 17-18	ANTIETAM, MD	223	44	1	159	4	15
September 28	Winchester, VA	2					2
November 1	Harper's Ferry, WVA	1			1		
December 4	Unknown	1			1		
Unknown	Unknown	2			2		
December 17	Fredericksburg, VA	1			1		
1863							
April 24	Suffolk, VA	6	1		5		
May 3	Suffolk, VA	1			1		
May 3	Providence Church Road, VA	9	2		7		
1864							
March 8	Albemarle Sound, NC (Drowned)	1	1				
APRIL 20	PLYMOUTH, NC	437	1	2		12	422
April 24	Suffolk, VA	1			1		
1865							
February 20	Charlotte, NC	1	1				
March 31	USS Lyons (Drowned)	1	1				
April 20	Potomac River (Drowned)	1	1				
April 24	Potomac River (Drowned)	6	6				

BATTLE OF ANTIETAM
SEPTEMBER 17, 1862

THE 16TH CONNECTICUT INFANTRY CROSSED ANTIETAM CREEK BELOW THE LOWER BRIDGE WITH HARLAND'S 2ND BRIGADE, RODMAN'S 3RD DIVISION, COX'S 9TH ARMY CORPS AND MOVED TO THE 40 ACRE CORNFIELD ON THE HARPER'S FERRY ROAD. THE REGIMENT SUFFERED 44 KILLED, 1 MISSING, 159 WOUNDED, 15 CAPTURED, AND 4 WOUNDED & CAPTURED

TROOP MOVEMENTS 16TH INFANTRY

DATE	PLACE
1862	
August 29	Left State for Washington DC
August 31	Arrived at Washington, DC
September-October	Maryland Campaign
September 16-17	Battle of Antietam
Until October 27	Duty at Pleasant Valley, MD
October 27-November 17	Movement to Falmouth, VA
December 12-15	Battle of Fredericksburg
1863	
January 20-24	Burnside's 2nd Campaign "Mud March"
February 6-9	Moved to Newport News, VA
March 13	Moved to Suffolk
April 12-May 4	Siege of Suffolk
April 24	Edenton Road
May 3	Providence Church RD and Nansemond River
May 4	Siege of Suffolk raised
June 9-17	Reconnaissance to Chickahominy River
June 24-July 7	Dix's Peninsula Campaign
July 1-7	Expedition from White House to S. Anna River
Until January 1864	Duty at Portsmouth and Norfolk
1864	
January 20	Skirmish at Harrellsville (Detachment)
January 24-28	Morehead City, New Bern, Plymouth, NC
January 30	Skirmish at Windsor, NC
February 2-March 20	Duty at New Bern
Until April	Duty at Plymouth
April 17-20	Siege of Plymouth
April 20	Captured
Until March 1865	Prisoners of war
1865	
Until June	Those not captured on duty at New Bern, Roanoke
June 24	Mustered out

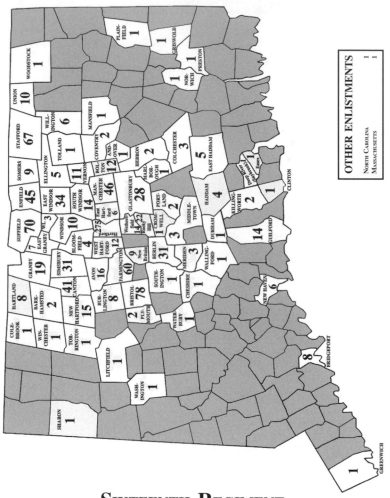

Map labels:

OTHER ENLISTMENTS

NORTH CAROLINA   1
MASSACHUSETTS   1

PLAINFIELD 1
GRISWOLD 1
PRESTON 1
NORWICH 1
WOODSTOCK 1
UNION 10
MANSFIELD 1
STAFFORD 67
WILLINGTON 6
TOLLAND 1
COVENTRY 2
ANDOVER 3
HEBRON 2
COLCHESTER 3
EAST HADDAM 5
SOMERS 9
ELLINGTON 11
VERNON 1
BOLTON 12
MANCHESTER 46
GLASTONBURY 28
MARLBOROUGH 2
HADDAM 4
Essex 1
DEEP RIVER 1
CLINTON
ENFIELD 45
EAST WINDSOR 34
SOUTH WINDSOR 14
PORTLAND 2
KILLINGWORTH 2
SUFFIELD 70
W. 3
WINDSOR 10
East Hartford 6
MANCHESTER
Rocky Hill 1
CROMWELL 1
MIDDLETOWN
DURHAM 1
GUILFORD 14
EAST GRANBY 3
BLOOMFIELD 4
Hartford 275
Wethersfield 12
22
GRANBY 7
WEST HARTFORD 12
New Britain 9
BERLIN 31
MERIDEN 3
WALLINGFORD 1
SIMSBURY 31
AVON 16
FARMINGTON 60
SOUTHINGTON 1
CHESHIRE 1
NEW HAVEN 6
GRANBY 19
CANTON 41
BURLINGTON 8
BRISTOL 78
WATERBURY 1
HARTLAND 8
BARKHAMSTED 2
NEW HARTFORD 15
PLYMOUTH 2
BRIDGEPORT 8
COLEBROOK 1
WINCHESTER 1
TORRINGTON 1
LITCHFIELD 1
WASHINGTON 1
SHARON 1
GREENWICH 1

SIXTEENTH REGIMENT
CONNECTICUT VOLUNTEER
INFANTRY

SEVENTEENTH REGIMENT
CONNECTICUT VOLUNTEER INFANTRY

AUGUST 28, 1862 - JULY 19, 1865
(TWO YEARS, ELEVEN MONTHS)
1,167 RECRUITS

28 KILLED, 9 MISSING, 100 DIED, 127 WOUNDED,
32 WOUNDED & CAPTURED, 218 CAPTURED,

USAMHI

William H. Noble of Bridgeport, was the first and only Colonel of the 17th Connecticut. He had a shaky start because of his lack of military experience but eventually became a brigade commander and Bvt. Brigadier General.. He was wounded at Chancellorsville in May 1863 and was captured in Florida in 1864. He spent time at Macon and Andersonville prisons, Georgia

The 17th Connecticut Volunteer Infantry was organized in the summer of 1862. The regiment was mostly composed of Fairfield County men.

William Noble of Bridgeport, was appointed Colonel on July 22. Charles Walter, also from Bridgeport, was appointed Lieutenant Colonel and Allen G. Brady of Torrington, was appointed Major.

Charles Walter had been a Lieutenant in the 1st Connecticut Infantry and Allen Brady had been a Colonel in the State Militia and was also the Lt. Colonel of the 3rd Connecticut Infantry.

The regiment gathered at Camp Aiken in what is now Seaside Park,

BRIDGEPORT

and was mustered into United States service on August 28, 1862.

The 17th Connecticut left by rail for New York City on September 3. They thought they were going straight to Virginia to join Major Gen. Franz Sigel's Corps. However, upon their arrival at

BALTIMORE

they found the city alarmed by a threat from Confederate calvary. The regiment was detained by Maj. Gen. John E. Wool, who was in command of the defenses of Baltimore.

After a delay of a couple of days, the 17th Connecticut was ordered to Fort Marshall as auxiliary to the garrison. The fort was an important earthwork and barracks just east of Baltimore. It overlooked the city and harbor, and commanded a wide view of the surrounding countryside.

Neither the work given the regiment, nor the duties imposed, nor their military associations were pleasing to the 17th Connecticut. Consequently, Colonel Noble sought a transfer from the War Department to the regiment's original destination, Sigel's Corps. When General Wool heard of this it so angered him that late on the night of October 14, 1862, he ordered Colonel Noble to have the 17th regiment outside the city limits of Baltimore before noon the next day or face the consequences. At 11:30 AM the following day, the regiment and all its belongings were speeding by rail to

WASHINGTON, DC

They arrived at night and were ordered to Fort Kearney, one of the northwest defenses of the Capitol. After about two weeks, the regiment was ordered to report to General Sigel, at Gainesville, Virginia. His corps held Thoroughfare Gap in the Bull Run Mountains.

After reaching Gainesville on November 5, the 17th Connecticut was placed in the Second Brigade (McLean), First Division (Stahel)

11TH CORPS

In addition to the 17th Connecticut, the Second Brigade was made up of four Ohio regiments - 25th, 55th, 75th, and 107th. The five regiments served together for the rest of the war in Virginia, South Carolina, and Florida.

After the 17th Connecticut had joined the 11th Corps, they moved to Hopewell Gap, then two weeks later moved to Chantilly. On December 6, the regiment began a difficult seven day winter march through slush and snow toward Fredericksburg. The corps was held at Brooke Station as a reserve to the advance of Maj. General Burnside's Army of the Potomac.

After the disaster at the Battle of Fredericksburg, the 17th spent the winter in camp at Stafford Court House, Belle Plain, and Brooke Station. All of the posts were near landings on the Potomac and the railroad from Aquia Creek to Falmouth.

At the end of April 1863, orders were given to move the 11th Corps (now under command of Maj. General Oliver Otis Howard) to the area near

CHANCELLORSVILLE

The weather was very warm and before Chancellorsville was reached the road was strewn with surplus belongings.

The 11th Corps crossed the Rappahannock River by pontoons at Kelly's Ford and the Rapidan River at Germania Ford by a temporary bridge and by wading the river. The 17th Connecticut was stationed near the extreme right of the Union line.

Two of its companies were on picket duty in the Wilderness when Confederate General Stonewall Jackson surprised and routed the 11th Corps on May 2. At the time, General Howard was two miles away at the Chancellor House. This was the first time the 17th Connecticut was under fire.

The regiment spent the next two days in the rear guarding the road to the U.S. Ford on the Rappahannock River.

The regiment had 106 casualties in the battle. Most of them were on May 2. Lieutenant Colonel Charles Walter was killed. He had been captured at First Bull Run, and had been released from prison just in time to receive the appointment of Lieutenant Colonel of the regiment. Colonel Noble was severely wounded and his horse was shot out from under him.

After the withdrawal of the Union troops from the battlefield, the regiment and its corps rested near Brooke Station until the Army of the Potomac began following Lee's advance into Pennsylvania. The result was the Battle of

GETTYSBURG

The regiment reached the battlefield at the height of the fight on July 1, 1863. They were pushed forward to the extreme right of the Union line. Two of its companies were sent to the outer flank as volunteer sharpshooters. An overwhelming force, under Confederate General John B. Gordon, struck the regiment at Oak Hill, now known as Barlow's Knoll. It was here that the regiment lost most of its 26 killed.

Overwhelmed and repulsed by the superior Confederate force, the 11th Corps retreated to Cemetery Hill. The 17th Connecticut was posted, in its brigade line, at its eastern foot. They held this place through the next two days. The regiment's position was charged many times, but the Confederates never completely broke through their ranks.

The total number of casualties for the regiment was 206. Lieutenant Colonel Douglas Fowler was killed, and Major Allen G. Brady was severely disabled by a shell splinter that broke his collarbone.

One of the 17th Connecticut monuments at Gettysburg stands at Oak Hill, and looking from Cemetery Hill north it is a conspicuous landmark. The other monument is at the foot of East Cemetery Hill. There is also a flagpole that was erected by the veterans association of the 17th Connecticut.

Following the battle, the Union army began pursuing the escaping Confederate force on July 6. The regiment was at times, close to the Confederate pickets, and at Hagerstown, Maryland, was right in front of their breastworks. However due to many delays, the Confederates crossed the Potomac back into Virginia before any attack could be made. The 11th Corps eventually crossed on pon-

toons then rested, and replaced their tattered uniforms from Gettysburg.

In early August at Catlett's Station, the 17th Connecticut with George H. Gordon's Division was ordered to take trains for Alexandria and then ships for

SOUTH CAROLINA

The regiment reached Folly Island on August 12. Their brigade, under Brig. General Adelbert Ames, was soon transferred to Morris Island. At that time, Confederate shell and round shot was reaching nearly the whole island. The regiment saw the first gun fired in Union Maj. General Quincy Gillmore's bombardment of Fort Sumter. The southwest wall of the fort was eventually severely battered.

The 17th Connecticut was in the siege works approaching Fort Wagner for several days. One of its men was killed and several wounded. For the next two weeks, the regiment was under constant fire from Forts Wagner, Moultrie, Johnson, and from the batteries near Charleston.

Worn out by long and hard service, the regiment then joined with the 6th and 7th Connecticut in Brig. General Alfred Terry's Division. Terry, who was next in command under General Gillmore, had a plan to assault Fort Wagner in three columns. The Confederates gave up the fort on September 6 before the planned attack.

Following the fall of Fort Wagner, the 17th Connecticut remained camped on Folly Island. From February 6-14 1864, the regiment went on an expedition to John's and James Island. On February 22, an order came for the Ames Brigade to leave for Jacksonville,

FLORIDA

The Union defeat at the Battle of Olustee, a few days earlier, threatened to drive the Union forces out of that area in Florida. On their arrival at Jacksonville, Colonel Noble assumed command of the 2nd brigade when Ames was promoted to division commander. Captain Albert Wilcoxson of Norwalk, was promoted to Lieutenant Colonel

After about a month without incident, the whole Union force at Jacksonville was broken up, and most of the re-enlisted regiments were sent north to the Army of the Potomac. However, the 17th Connecticut relieved the 10th Connecticut at St. Augustine while the Ohio regiments of their brigade remained at Jacksonville. Headquarters of the 17th Connecticut were at

ST AUGUSTINE

until the end of the war. One company was garrisoned at Ft. Marion and the rest were used on raids and were scattered at various outposts.

The primary foe of the 17th Connecticut during this time was the cavalry force under Captain. J. J. Dickison

On April 25, Colonel Noble started on a forging raid with a large part of his brigade, including the 17th Connecticut, to Volusia, 75 miles up the St Johns River. Three days later they captured a large amount of cotton and 1,000 head of cattle. They returned to St Augustine three days later.

On May 19, Company B was captured at an outpost near

WELAKA

The force of 40 men and two officers were taken to Andersonville prison. Two companies posted at Volusia held on until relieved.

At the end of May, Brig. General George H. Gordon, the commander of the District Florida, placed Colonel

Noble in charge of all the territory east of the St. John River. This brought Lieutenant Colonel Albert Wilcoxson of Norwalk, into immediate command of St. Augustine and the regiment.

Generals William Birney, George Gordon, and John P. Hatch, who commanded Florida during 1864, sent the regiment and other forces under Colonel Noble on various raids throughout the state. The result of these raids, though successful, were of no great military importance, but subjected the regiment to the trying effects of the climate, and planted the seeds of disease.

On December 24, 1864, Colonel Noble was captured while returning from a court martial hearing that he was presiding over at Jacksonville. He was imprisoned at Macon and Andersonville prisons until the end of the war.

On February 4, 1865, Lieutenant Colonel Wilcoxson was mortally wounded and Adjutant H.Whitney Chatfield was killed at

DUNN'S LAKE

while on an expedition to Braddocks Farm, about 50 miles from St. Augustine. Thirty men were also captured and taken to Andersonville Prison.

The 17th Connecticut served, without incident, for the remainder of the winter and spring of 1864-65. In June 1865, the 17th Connecticut was ordered to Jacksonville and then moved to Hilton Head, South Carolina where they were mustered out on July 19, 1865.

The 17th Connecticut regiment arrived in New Haven on August 3 and was disbanded.

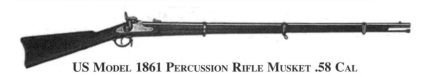

US MODEL 1861 PERCUSSION RIFLE MUSKET .58 CAL

TOTAL CASUALTIES 17TH INFANTRY

DATE	PLACE OF CASUALTY	TOTAL	K	M	W	W/C	C
1862							
November 14	Antioch, VA	1			1		
December 5	Chantilly, VA	1			1		
December 16	Stafford Court House, VA	1			1		
December 19	Dumfries, VA	1					1
December 27	Dumfries, VA	1					1
1863							
MAY 1	CHANCELLORSVILLE, VA	1			1		
MAY 2	CHANCELLORSVILLE, VA	97	7	1	24	20	45
MAY 3	CHANCELLORSVILLE, VA	7					7
MAY 5	CHANCELLORSVILLE, VA	1	1				
JULY 1	GETTYSBURG, PA	147	16	5	62	9	55
JULY 2	GETTYSBURG, PA	47	2	3	22	1	19
July 3	GETTYSBURG, PA	12			8		4
July 21	Loudon County, VA	1					1
August 1	Morris Island, SC	1			1		
August 16	Morris Island, SC	1			1		
August 19	Fort Wagner, SC	1			1		
August 20	Morris Island, SC	2	1		1		
September 6	Fort Wagner, SC	1			1		
November 18	James Island, SC	1			1		
1864							
MAY 19	WELAKA, FL	42				1	41
December 24	St. John County, FL	1					1
1865							
February 1	St. Augustine, FL	1					1
February 4	Dunn's Lake, FL	1					1
FEBRUARY 5	DUNN'S LAKE, FL	31	1			1	29
February 4	St. Augustine, FL	10					10
February 5	St. Augustine, FL	1					1
February 5	Braddock Farm, FL	1					1
May 15	Camp Finnagan, FL	1			1		

LIBRARY OF CONGRESS

BATTLE OF GETTYSBURG
FOOT OF EAST CEMETERY HILL

THE 17TH CONNECTICUT INFANTRY SUFFERED ITS GREATEST LOSS OF THE WAR (206) WITH THE 2ND BRIGADE (HARRIS), 1ST DIVISION (AMES), 11TH ARMY CORPS (HOWARD) FIRST ON JULY 1 AT BARLOW'S KNOLL (147) AND LATER FROM JULY 2-3 AT THE FOOT OF EAST CEMETERY HILL (59)

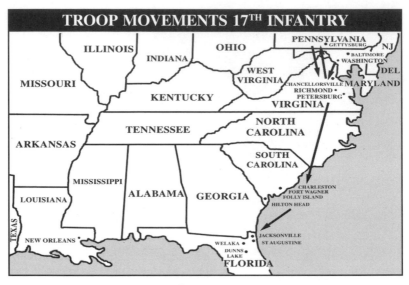

TROOP MOVEMENTS 17TH INFANTRY

DATE	PLACE
1862	
September 3	Left State for Baltimore
Until October	Duty at Fort Marshall, Baltimore, MD
October 15-November 3	At Tennallytown, building Fort Kearney
November 3-12	March to Thoroughfare Gap and Chantilly, VA
December –April 1863	Duty at Brooke Station, VA
1863	
January 20-24	Burnsides's 2nd campaign "Mud March"
April 27-May 6	Chancellorsville, VA
May 1-5	Battle of Chancellorsville
June 11-July 24	Gettysburg, PA Campaign
July 1-3	Battle of Gettysburg
July 11-13	Hagerstown, MD
August 1-12	Folly Island, SC
August 15-September 7	Siege operations against Ft. Wagner, Gregg, Sumpter, Charleston
September 7	Capture of Forts Wagner and Gregg
Until February 1864	Duty at Folly Island, SC
February 6-14	Expedition to John's and James Island
February 22	Moved to Jacksonville, FL
Until April 15	Duty at Jacksonville, FL
April 15-17	Moved to St. Augustine, FL
Until June 1865	Duty at St. Augustine, FL
May 19	Action at Welaka, FL (Detachment)
May 31-June 3	Expedition to Camp Milton
June 2	Action at Milton
July 24	Whitesville
July 18-February 1865	Co. A,C,I,K at Picolata, St John's River
July 22	Co A,E,F,H moved to Jacksonville
July 23-28	Expedition to Baldwin
September 28	Expedition to Enterprise
1865	
May-June	Co C,F,H at Lake City
May-June	Co G,I at Tallahatchie
June 9	Regiment moved from St. Augustine to Jacksonville
Until July 7	Duty at Jacksonville
July 19	Musterd out at Hilton Head, SC

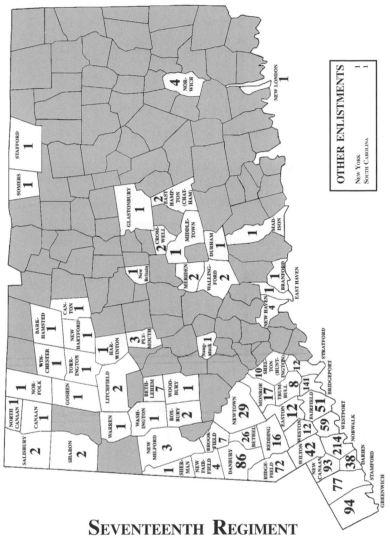

OTHER ENLISTMENTS

NEW YORK	1
SOUTH CAROLINA	1

NOR-WICH 4
NEW LONDON 1
STAFFORD 1
SOMERS 1
GLASTONBURY 1
EAST HAMP-TON (CHAT-HAM) 2
CROM-WELL 2
MIDDLE-TOWN 1
DURHAM 1
MAD-ISON 1
New Britain 1
MERIDEN 2
WALLING-FORD 2
BRANFORD 1
EAST HAVEN
NEW HAVEN 4
NAUGA-TUCK 1
BARK-HAMSTED
CAN-TON 1
NEW HARTFORD 1
WIN-CHESTER
TORR-INGTON 1
HAR-WINTON 1
PLY-MOUTH 3
STRATFORD
SHEL-TON (HUNT-INGTON) 10
TRUM-BULL 12
BRIDGEPORT
NORTH CANAAN 1
NOR-FOLK 1
GOSHEN 1
LITCHFIELD 2
BETHE-LEHEM 7
WOOD-BURY 1
MONROE 17
TRUM-BULL 8
FAIRFIELD 141
WARREN 1
WASH-INGTON 1
ROX-BURY 2
NEWTOWN 29
EASTON 12
WESTON 51
WESTPORT 59
SALISBURY 2
CANAAN 1
SHARON 2
NEW MILFORD 3
BROOK-FIELD 7
BETHEL 26
REDDING 16
WILTON 12
NEW CANAAN 42
NORWALK 214
DARIEN 38
SHER-MAN 1
NEW FAIR-FIELD 4
DANBURY 86
RIDGE-FIELD 72
NEW CANAAN 93
STAMFORD 77
GREENWICH 94

SEVENTEENTH REGIMENT
CONNECTICUT VOLUNTEER
INFANTRY

EIGHTEENTH REGIMENT
CONNECTICUT VOLUNTEER INFANTRY

AUGUST 22, 1862 - JUNE 27, 1865
(TWO YEARS, TEN MONTHS)
1,192 RECRUITS

53 KILLED, 2 MISSING, 98 DIED, 137 WOUNDED, 107 WOUNDED & CAPTURED, 552 CAPTURED,

USAMHI

The 18th Regiment Connecticut Volunteer Infantry was organized under the supervision of Brig. Gen. Daniel Tyler at Camp Aiken in **NORWICH** on August 4, 1862. The camp was located on the old fair grounds about 1 mile west of Norwich on the old Salem turnpike.

General Tyler had been Colonel of the 1st Connecticut Infantry and was a division commander at the battle of First Bull Run in July 1861.

On August 11, William G. Ely of Norwich, was promoted from Lieutenant Colonel of the 6th Connecticut Infantry to Colonel of the 18th. Monroe Nichols of Thomp-

William G. Ely of Norwich, was appointed Colonel of the 18th Connecticut Infantry after having been the Lieutenant Colonel in the 6th. He was captured at the Battle of Winchester in June 1863 and was imprisoned at Libby Prison until March 1864. He was wounded at Lynchburg, VA in June 1864 and was promoted to Bvt. Brigadier General in March 1865.

son, was appointed Lieutenant Colonel and Ephriam Keech Jr. of Killingly, was appointed Major.

The regiment was mustered into United States service on August 22 and left Norwich by boat with a regiment composed mostly of New London and Windham County men. They marched under elegant colors presented by the ladies of Norwich.

Two days later, the 18th Connecticut was camped at Fort McHenry **BALTIMORE** Maryland. The following day, four companies were detached as railroad guards at Havre de Grace, Maryland.

When the 17th Connecticut left Fort Marshall on October 15, the 18th Connecticut was transferred to Fort Marshall from Fort McHenry. Three companies of the regiment remained at Havre de Grace and one company was detached to Upper Marlborough, Maryland. The regiment remained divided all winter in Maryland with its headquarters at Fort Marshall.

On May 22, 1863, the regiment was ordered to take the railroad to the

SHENANDOAH VALLEY

They joined the command of Major General Robert H. Milroy's 2nd Division,

8TH ARMY CORPS AT WINCHESTER

The regiment was placed in the 2nd brigade and Colonel Ely was appointed brigade commander. The regiments of the 2nd brigade were the 18CT, 87PA, 1WVA Cavalry Co. K, 3WVA Cavalry Co. D, E, and 5th US Artillery Battery L.

On about June 9, the Confederates pushed silently and swiftly north through the Shenandoah toward Pennsylvania. On June 13, the Union pickets were driven toward Winchester and brisk skirmishing ensued. Within two days, the 18th Connecticut was engulfed in the

BATTLE OF SECOND WINCHESTER

The engagement was disastrous for the Union force. Milroy had 7,000 men, and his opponent, led by Ewell's corps of Early's division, had 30,000 and 87 field guns.

The 18th Connecticut was praised by General Milroy for its desperate fighting. In a third and last charge on June 15, the regiment completely disabled a confederate battery, but it had charged into the center of Major General Edward Johnson's Division which numbered 9,000. Within a short while, 511 men of the 18th Connecticut were captured.

Brig. General James A. Walker, of Stonewall Jackson's Brigade, generously praised the valor and discipline of the 18th Connecticut, and returned Colonel Ely's sword to him on the battlefield. Color Sergeant George Torrey of Woodstock, escaped with the regimental flags.

Although General Milroy with his little army had held in check the advance of Lee's army at Winchester for three days, the 18th Connecticut had its worst day of the war with 23 killed, 7 wounded, 511 captured, and 42 wounded & captured.

Two hundred twenty men of the regiment avoided being captured and eventually gathered, under Major Henry Peale of Norwich, at Maryland Heights, near Harper's Ferry, West Virginia.

After three weeks, Peale and his men were ordered to move toward Lee's Confederate army which was retreating from the Battle of Gettysburg. They marched to Snicker's Gap and captured many Confederates prisoners. Then acting as provost guards the small Connecticut battalion moved to Sharpsburg then to Hagerstown, Maryland.

The 18th Connecticut prisoners from the Battle of Winchester were marched to Richmond and put into

LIBBY AND BELLE ISLE PRISONS

On July 2, 1863, the privates were released. They were taken to City Point and then sent to Annapolis, Maryland. While at Annapolis, they stayed at Camp Parole. In October 1863, they were exchanged for Confederate prisoners and were returned to the regiment. Twenty-four officers of the regiment, however, were detained in Libby prison until March 1864.

The exchanged prisoners, when released from Camp Parole, increased the number in the regiment to eight officers and six hundred men. On October 3, 1863, they forded the Potomac and advanced to

MARTINSBURG

West Virginia. Comfortable quarters were established and the regiment spent a mostly uneventful winter.

In February 1864, Colonel Ely escaped from Libby prison with 108 other officers. They had dug a tunnel that took 55 days to complete. About 60 men were eventually captured, including the Colonel.

In March, Colonel Ely and seven other 18th Connecticut officers were paroled. The sixteen remaining officers of the regiment were taken to Danville, Virginia on May 7 and then after a few days were transferred to the new stockade prison at Macon, Georgia. In December, five more were paroled. In February 1865, the remaining eleven officers of the 18th were sent to Charlottesville, Virginia. Two of the eleven escaped and finally in March 1865, the remaining prisoners were paroled. All of the 18th Connecticut officers that had been been captured at the Battle of Second Winchester survived captivity.

On March 7, 1864, the 18th Connecticut moved to Harper's Ferry and camped for a time at Bolivar Heights. On March 28, the regiment was given a furlough and the men started for Connecticut. On April 9, they were back at Bolivar Heights.

The regiment moved to Martinsburg on April 28, and the next day, 10 officers and 600 men, under Major Peale, joined a large corps, under Major General Franz Sigel. They moved to Bunker Hill and Winchester. On May 9, they pushed toward New Market. The 18th Connecticut was detached to Edinburgh to support the 28th Ohio. On May 15, the regiment was involved, with Sigel's corps, in the battle near

NEW MARKET

and had 2 killed, 1 missing, 25 wounded,

13 captured, and 11 wounded & captured. The defeated Union force retreated to the east side of Cedar Creek and went into camp on May 17.

Following the defeat at New Market, Colonel Ely returned to the regiment and assumed command. Lieutenant Colonel Nichols, who had also been imprisoned, resigned due to ill health. General Sigel was replaced by Major General David Hunter, and the small army started again up the Shenandoah Valley.

On June 4, they crossed the river at Port Republic on pontoons and marched toward Staunton. The next morning, the Union force found the Confederates strongly posted on the high ground at

PIEDMONT

Both armies threw out strong lines of skirmishers and soon a pitched battle raged. By 5 PM, the Confederate army was routed. The 18th Connecticut had suffered terribly with 21 killed, 1 missing, 59 wounded, 6 captured, and 47 wounded & captured.

The 18th now greatly reduced in numbers and much exhausted pushed on to Staunton the next morning. On June 10, General Hunter was re-enforced by the commands of Crook and Averill. The Union army pushed through Lexington the following day.

On June 14, they arrived at Buchanan, a town on the James River 20 miles west of Lynchburg. They crossed the river and the next day climbed into the Blue Ridge Mountains. On June 18, there was an artillery duel at Lynchburg and the Confederates made two charges at the Union line. Colonel William Ely was wounded along with 2 other soldiers. In addition 5 were wounded and captured, and 2 others were captured only. The Confederates were reinforced and Hunter's army fell back across the James, and retired to the north into West Virginia.

The next ten days brought the severest trials to the regiment. There were tedious marches with little sleep and less food. By July 3, the regiment had retreated to Parkersburg and then moved to Martinsburg.

The 18th Connecticut had been reduced to 150 men and officers. Confederate General Early had brought his Corps forward to sweep Hunter's shattered army out of Virginia. On July 14, the 18th Connecticut, in Crook's column, passed from Harper's Ferry down the Potomac and pushed south through the Loudon Valley. They moved on toward Snicker's Gap and reached there on July 18.

The Confederates were found posted across the Shenandoah River. The regiment attempted to cross two miles down river at

SNICKER'S FORD

They had just crossed, when they were met by a crossfire that left 6 killed, 27 wounded, and 1 captured.

Colonel Ely had been appointed to the command of the 2nd brigade, 2nd division of Crook's 8th Corps and Major Peale had assumed the command of the regiment. After Snicker's Ford, the regiment now numbering less than 100, passed slowly westward to Winchester.

On July 24, the 18th Connecticut was on the west side of the Strasburg Pike when they found the Confederates advancing in force. Soon, they were furiously attacked and lost another 8 casualties.

The Union army was once again in full retreat. It reached Martinsburg the next morning, forded the Potomac and arrived in Williamsport, Maryland on July 26. The regiment remained along the Potomac in the vicinity of Harper's Ferry for several days.

General Grant was determined to push the Confederates at all points and ordered aggressive movements in the Shenandoah. Hunter was relieved of his command and Philip Sheridan was appointed his successor The new commander was given 3 infantry corps (6th, 8th, 19th) and 10,000 cavalry. The 18th Connecticut was a part of Crook's

8TH CORPS

The regiment was with the 8th Corps until September 12, when, after a sharp and successful skirmish at Berryville, they were detached to recuperate. The regiment was ordered to Martinsburg and was not engaged in the battles in the Shenandoah Valley in the autumn of 1864.

Colonel Ely resigned and was promoted to Bvt. Brigadier General. Captain Martin Tiffany of Norwich, assumed command of the regiment while Major Peale was temporarily absent.

In November 1864, the regiment had its headquarters at Halltown, West Virginia. Two companies were detached at Duffield Station and one was at Harper's Ferry. Major Peale was promoted to Lieutenant Colonel and was again in command of the regiment. The regiment was at Halltown until March 1865, when they moved back to Martinsburg for provost duty until June 1865.

On June 27, the regiment was mustered out at Harper's Ferry. The regiment returned to Connecticut by steamboat and arrived in Hartford on June 29. The men were escorted up State Street and formed in line on Central Row where they were received by Governor William Buckingham and many dignitaries.

TOTAL CASUALTIES 18TH INFANTRY

DATE	PLACE OF CASUALTY	TOTAL	K	M	W	W/C	C
1862							
December 4	Stemmer's Run, MD	1			1		
1863							
January 4	Havre De Grace, MD	1			1		
January 5	Harewood Station, MD	1	1				
May 14	Havre De Grace, MD	1			1		
June 10	Winchester, VA	1			1		
June 12	Unknown	1			1		
Unknown	Winchester, VA	1					1
JUNE 15	**WINCHESTER, VA**	**583**	**23**		**7**	**42**	**511**
1864							
February 7	Martinsburg, WVA	1			1		
March 5	Martinsburg, WVA	1			1		
MAY 15	**NEW MARKET, VA**	**52**	**2**	**1**	**25**	**11**	**13**
May 25	Cedar Creek, VA	1			1		
May 29	New Market, VA	1					1
May 29	Newtown, VA	1					1
May 30	Strasburg, VA	1					1
June 1	Harrisonburg, VA	1					1
June 1	Staunton, VA	1					1
JUNE 5	**PIEDMONT, VA**	**134**	**21**	**1**	**59**	**47**	**6**
June 8	Unknown	1					1
June 9	Staunton, VA	1					1
June 10	Staunton, VA	2					2
June 10	Piedmont, VA	1					1
June 11	Staunton, VA	2				1	1
June 14, 18, 19	Lynchburg, VA	12			4	5	3
June 29	Salem, VA	1					1
July 8	Staunton, VA	1					1
July 18	Lynchburg, VA	1			1		
July 18	Simsbury, CT	1			1		
JULY 18	**SNICKER'S FORD, VA**	**34**	**6**		**27**		**1**
July 24-25	Winchester, VA	8			2	1	5
September 4	Unknown	1			1		
October 15	Railroad Accident	1			1		

USAMHI

SECOND BATTLE OF WINCHESTER JUNE 15, 1863

WHAT WAS LEFT OF THE 18TH CONNECTICUT INFANTRY RETREATED DOWN THE VALLEY PIKE FOLLOWING THE BATTLE AFTER THE REGIMENT SUFFERED ITS GREATEST LOSS FOR ONE DAY (583) WITH THE 2ND BRIGADE (ELY), 2ND DIVISION (MILROY), 8TH CORPS (SCHENCK)

DATE	PLACE
1862	
August 22	Left State for Baltimore, MD
August 24	Arrived Baltimore, MD
Until May 1863	Duty at Forts McHenry, Marshall
1863	
May 22	Moved to Winchester, VA, Milroy's Command
June 13-15	Battle of Winchester
June 15	Mostly captured
July 2 and October 1	Privates exchanged
Until September 30	Duty at Hagerstown, MD
Until March 1864	Duty at Martinsburg, WVA
1864	
March 7-28	At Bolivar Heights
March 16-18	Reconnaissance toward Snicker's Gap, VA
April 29-May17	Sigel's expedition from Martinsburg to New Market
May 15	Battle of New Market
May 26-July 1	Hunter's expedition to Lynchburg, VA
May 26-June 5	Advance on Staunton, VA
June 5	Action at Piedmont, Mount Crawford
June 6	Occupation of Staunton, VA
June 17-18	Lynchburg
July 1-18	Moved to Camp Piatt, then to Parkersburg, Cumberland, MD, Martinsburg, Harper's Ferry, Snicker's Ford
July 18	Snicker's Ford
July 24	Battle of Kernstown, Winchester, VA
July 25	Martinsburg, WVA
Until October At	Charlestown, WVA
October 1-19	At Martinsburg
Until November 11	Moved to New Haven
November 11-13	Moved to Martinsburg
November 23	Moved to Halltown
1865	
Until March 1865	Duty at Halltown
Until June	Duty at Martinsburg
June 27	Mustered out at Harper's Ferry

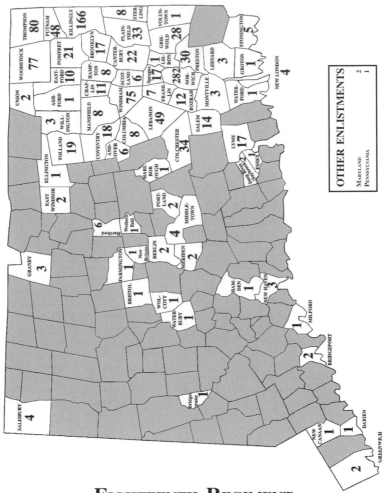

OTHER ENLISTMENTS

MARYLAND	2
PENNSYLVANIA	1

EIGHTEENTH REGIMENT
CONNECTICUT VOLUNTEER
INFANTRY

TWENTIETH REGIMENT
CONNECTICUT VOLUNTEER INFANTRY

SEPTEMBER 8, 1862 - JUNE 13, 1865
(TWO YEARS, NINE MONTHS)
1,395 RECRUITS

61 KILLED, 1 MISSING, 110 DIED, 223 WOUNDED, 22 WOUNDED & CAPTURED, 91 CAPTURED,

USAMHI

Samuel Ross of Hartford was the first and only Colonel of the 20th Infantry. He was a captain in the 14th US Infantry before his appointment. Colonel Ross was wounded at the Battle of Chancellorsville on May 3, 1863. Later on in the war he served as a brigade commander and was promoted to Brig. General by brevet in April 1865

The 20th Regiment Connecticut Volunteer Infantry was organized in the summer of 1862. The regiment was composed mostly of men from New Haven and Hartford Counties and the squads and companies began to gather at Oyster Point, **NEW HAVEN** on August 27. Uniforms and a few old muskets were furnished, a camp was laid out and regular military life began.

Governor William Buckingham appointed Samuel Ross, of Hartford and a Captain in the 14th US Infantry, Colonel. William B. Wooster of Derby, was appointed Lieutenant Colonel and Philo B. Buckingham of Seymour, was appointed Major.

The regiment was mustered into United States service on September 8, 1862

On September 11, Colonel Ross received orders to move his regiment to **WASHINGTON, DC** They reached the Capitol two days later and camped at first on the grounds of East Capitol Hill.

On September 15, the regiment moved to Arlington Heights, Virginia and Camp Chase. The 20th Connecticut took part in the defenses of Washington until the Confederates had moved to Culpeper, following the Battle of Antietam.

On September 29, they were ordered to move to Frederick, Maryland. On October 2, the 20th Connecticut was again under marching orders for Harper's Ferry, West Virginia. The regiment was placed in the Second Brigade (Ross), First Division (Williams),

12TH CORPS

Army of the Potomac. The 5th Connecticut Infantry was also in the 12th Corps and from then on they were together.

On November 1, the regiments north of the Potomac crossed the river and advanced into

VIRGINIA

The 20th occupied Keyes Ford and Mannings Ford on the Shenandoah River.

On November 9, they moved east over the mountains passing through Hillsborough, Wheatland, Leesburg, Chantilly, and Fairfax Court House.

On November 14, they reached Fairfax Station on the Orange and Alexandria Railroad. They crossed the Occoquan the next morning at Wolf Run Shoals and for two days pushed on through rain and mud. Two days later, they turned back to Fairfax Station and began to make a winter camp. The men built log huts and had begun to settle in when orders were received to march to Stafford Court House. The soldiers were, for most of the time, on half rations. The great wagons were loaded and dragged on through the mud at a rate of four miles a day. At

STAFFORD COURT HOUSE

full rations were restored and the regiment found rest. They built log huts once more and occupied them until April 1863.

On April 27, the Army of the Potomac was under the command of Maj. General Joseph Hooker. The 12th Corps crossed the Rapidan River at Germania Ford and marched toward Chancellorsville, reaching there on April 30. On May 1, the Battle of

CHANCELLORSVILLE

began with a furious Confederate attack on the 11th Corps. For the next two days, the 20th Connecticut was held in reserve with the 2nd brigade and occupied a position on the right of the 2nd division of the 12th Corps. The regiment suffered most of its casualties on the Union retreat of May 3. The results of the three day battle were disastrous for the Union Army. The 20th Connecticut suffered 26 killed, 49 wounded, 22 wounded & captured, and 73 captured. Of the wounded 16 died. The regiment had lost one third of its number. Colonel Ross, who commanded the 2nd brigade, was wounded and Lieutenant Colonel Wooster, who commanded the regiment, was captured for a short while. Major Buckingham was on detached duty and the command of the regiment eventually fell upon Captain Sanford E. Chaffee of Derby .

On May 6, the regiment returned to Stafford Court House and Major Buckingham took command of the regiment for a short while. They held the same relative position as before Chancellorsville, except that the 5th and 20th Connecticut were now in the same brigade of the 12th Corps.

Lee did not wait for the Union army to reorganize and began to move his army north to Maryland. Hooker moved his army toward Warrenton, covering Washington on the one hand and pressing the Confederate flank on the other. The 12th Corps left its camp on June 13 and pushed north arriving in Dumfries in the early morning the following day. The Union army followed closely. The 2nd Corps was the last to leave the line of the Rappahannock River. The regiment continued to press on and reached Fairfax Court House on June 15. Two days later, they had reached Dranesville. They moved toward Leesburg and remained there for nearly a week. On June 26, the 12th Corps crossed the Potomac at Edwards Ferry and arrived in Frederick, Maryland.

On July 1, Maj. General George Meade, now in command of the Army of the Potomac, pushed toward

GETTYSBURG

The 20th Connecticut was among the first regiments to arrive and acted on the defense until the commanding general had reached the town. The 12th Corps was then placed on the extreme right of the Union line at Rock Creek and then later at Cemetery Hill.

With Brig. General A.S. Williams commanding the 1st Division of the 12th Corps, the 20th Connecticut held Confederate General Ewell's force at bay. The regiment was commanded by Lieutenant Colonel Wooster and had 5 killed and 31 wounded.

After Gettysburg, General Meade continued to follow Lee but without any engagement. On July 16, the regiment was in camp at Pleasant Valley, Maryland on the same ground that they had occupied in October 1862.

On September 25, the regiment was at Brandy Station with the 12th Corps, when they were ordered to join the

ARMY OF THE CUMBERLAND

at Chattanooga,

TENNESSEE

under U. S. Grant, who had replaced William Rosecrans.

The Battle at Lookout Mountain was fought on November 24, 1863. During the battle, the 20th Connecticut was guarding supplies along the rail line from Stevenson, Alabama to Cowan, Tennessee. They remained there during the winter and engaged in frequent skirmishes with Confederate guerrillas. In an attack on Tracy City, Tennessee on January 20, 1864, Captain Andrew Upson of Company K was mortally wounded.

On April 11, 1864, an order was issued that combined the 11th and 12th Corps into the

20TH CORPS

On April 27, the 20th Connecticut moved to Lookout Valley, Tennessee to join the Second Brigade (Ross), Third Division (Butterfield), 20th Corps (Hooker). On May 2, they moved out of the valley and concentrated at Ringold,

GEORGIA

All Union forces began to concentrate for an assault on Atlanta. On May 7, the army was put into motion and the 20th Corps passed through Taylor's Ridge at Gardner's Gap to a fortified hill called Boyd's Trail. This position was taken after a sharp contest. On the night of May 10, the regiment moved down to the support of Maj. General James B. McPherson at Snake Creek Gap where the Confederates were concentrated. In the four day engagement at

RESACA

the 20th Connecticut had 15 wounded. On May 19, along with the 19th Michigan, the 20th Connecticut captured Cassville and remained there for three days. After the crossing of the Etowah River was completed between Allatoona and Rome, a two-hour battle at Pumpkinvine Creek ensued. The 20th Corps was exclusively engaged in this victory.

The regiment took an active part in all of the marches, skirmishes, and battles for the next two months. The 20th Connecticut did garrison duty at Marietta, and on about July 10 they drove the Confederates from their earthworks on the Chattahoochee River. The

SIEGE OF ATLANTA

began on the morning of July 20 with the Battle at

PEACHTREE CREEK

The regiment distinquished itself with a gallant charge that drove the Confederates from the field and captured prisoners and arms. The regiment lost 9 killed, 46 wounded and 1 captured. The Siege of Atlanta lasted until September 2, when the city surrendered to the Union army.

The 20th Connecticut remained at Atlanta doing fatigue duty and building fortifications until November 15. Under the command of Lieutenant Colonel Buckingham (Colonel Ross was brigade commander) the regiment moved with Maj. General Sherman's army on its

"MARCH TO THE SEA"

They arrived in front of Savannah on December 10. The regiment remained engaged in siege operations until December 20, when the 20th Corps entered Savannah. The force captured a large amount of artillery and ordnance stores, together with 30,000 bales of cotton.

On January 4, 1865, the regiment crossed the Savannah River and camped six miles north on Hardee's Plantation. They remained there until January 16, when the regiment broke camp the following morning and marched ten miles to Hardeesville where they stayed until January 20. The 20th Connecticut then continued its march through South Carolina and into

NORTH CAROLINA

where they met a Confederate force around

SILVER RUN

on March 14 - 16, 1865. After a sharp engagement, the Confederates were driven from their line of works. The regiment lost 2 killed, 17 wounded, and 3 captured.

On March 19, the regiment took part in the Battle of

BENTONVILLE

and lost 4 killed, 32 wounded, and 2 captured. After the battle, the 20th Connecticut continued its march to join the Army of the Potomac. They arrived in Raleigh on April 16. On April 30, they moved by land and passed through Richmond, Virginia on May 11, 1865. They eventually reached Washington, DC on May 20.

After participating in the Grand Review on May 23-24, the regiment camped near Fort Lincoln on the Bladensburg Road until they were mustered out on June 13, 1865 and returned to New Haven two days later.

USAMHI

THE BATTLE OF CHANCELLORSVILLE
MAY 3, 1863
THE 20TH CONNECTICUT INFANTRY SUFFERED ITS GREATEST NUMBER OF CASUALTIES (170) FOR ONE DAY WITH THE 1ST BRIGADE (KNIPE), 1ST DIVISION (A.S. WILLIAMS), 12TH CORPS (SLOCUM)

TOTAL CASUALTIES 20TH INFANTRY

DATE	PLACE OF CASUALTY	TOTAL	K	M	W	W/C	C
1862							
February 1	Stafford Court House, VA	1			1		
September 10	New Haven, CT	1			1		
September 30	Railroad Accident	1	1				
November 1	Harper's Ferry, WVA	1			1		
November 1	Loudon Heights, VA	1			1		
December 1	Stafford Court House, VA	1			1		
1863							
January 1	Stafford Court House, VA	1			1		
January 4	Fairfax, VA	1			1		
January 21	Dumfries, VA	2			1		1
January 28	Stafford Court House, VA	1	1				
April 29	Kelly's Ford, VA	1					1
MAY 3	**CHANCELLORSVILLE, VA**	**170**	**26**		**49**	**22**	**73**
June 13	Unknown	1			1		
JULY 2-3	**GETTYSBURG, PA**	**36**	**5**		**31**		
August 16	New Haven, CT	1			1		
November 11	Railroad Accident	1	1				
December 2	Stafford Court House, VA	1	1				
1864							
January 20-21	Tracy City, TN	2	1		1		
MAY 15	**RESACA, GA**	**15**			**15**		
May 19	Cassville, GA	4			4		
June 6	Unknown, GA	1					1
July 2-4	Ackworth, GA	3					3
JULY 20	**PEACH TREE CREEK, GA**	**56**	**9**		**46**		**1**
JULY 21-AUGUST 21	**ATLANTA, GA**	**20**	**4**	**1**	**15**		
August 27, 30	Turner's Ford, GA	4	2		1		1
October 4	Marietta, GA	1	1				
November 11	Railroad Accident	1	1				
1865							
March 14	Iversbury, NC	1			1		
March 14	Silver Run, NC	1			1		
March 14	Fayetteville, NC	4			1		3
March 15	Averysboro, NC	1			1		
March 16	Averysboro, NC	5	1		4		
March 16	Fayetteville, NC	1			1		
March 16	Silver Run, NC	10	1		9		
March 19	**Bentonville, NC**	**38**	**4**		**32**		**2**
March 24	Averysboro, NC	1					1
March 24	Goldsboro, NC	3					3
March 25	Goldsboro, NC	1					1
March 25	Pikeville, NC	1	1				
April 15	Raleigh, NC	1			1		
June 4	Washington, DC (Drowned)	1	1				

US MODEL 1861 PERCUSSION RIFLE MUSKET .58 CAL

DATE	PLACE
1862	
September 11	Left State for Washington, DC
September 13	Arrived at Washington, DC
Until September 29	Duty in Defenses of Washington
September 29	Moved to Frederick, MD
October 2	Moved to Sandy Hook, MD
December 10	March to Fredericksburg, VA
December 14-January 19, 1863	Duty at Fairfax Station, VA
1863	
January 19-23	Moved to Stafford Court House, VA
Until April	Duty at Stafford Court House
April 27-May 6	Chancellorsville Campaign
May 1-5	Battle of Chancellorsville, VA
June 11-July 24	Gettysburg Campaign
July 1-3	Battle of Gettysburg, PA
Until September 24	Near Raccoon Ford
September 24-October 3	Moved to Brandy Station, Bealton, Stevenson, AL
1864	
Until April	Guard duty along Nashville & Chattanooga RR
January 20	Action at Tracy City, TN (Co B)
May-September	Atlanta Campaign
May 8-11	Demonstration on Rocky Faced Ridge, GA
May 8-9	Buzzard's Roost Gap, GA
May 10	Boyd's Trail
May 14-15	Battle of Resaca
May 19	Cassville
May 24-June 13	Guard Ordinance trains
Until July 8	Provost duty at Ackworth, GA
July 16	At Marietta, GA
July 19-20	Peach Tree Creek, GA
August 26-September 2	Operations at Chatahoochee River Bridge
September 2-November 15	Occupation of Atlanta
November 15-December 10	March to sea
December 10-21	Siege of Savannah
1865	
January 4-16	At Hardee's Plantation
January-April	Campaign of Carolinas
February 2	Lawtonville, SC
March 14	Reconnaissance to Silver Run, NC
March 16	Averysboro or Taylor's Hole Creek, NC
March 19-21	Battle of Bentonville
March 24	Occupation of Goldsboro
April 14	Raleigh
April 26	Bennett's House
April 29	Surrender of Johnston's Army
April 30-May 20	March to Washington, DC
May 24	Grand Review
Until June 13	Camp near Fort Lincoln
June 13	Mustered out

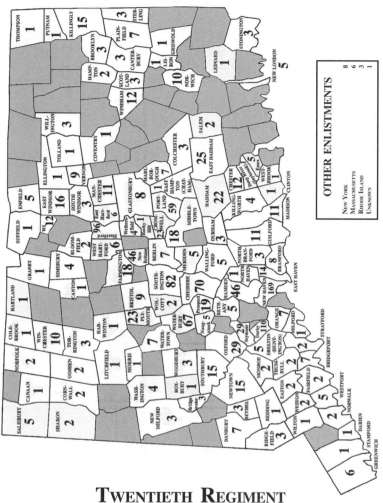

OTHER ENLISTMENTS

NEW YORK	8
MASSACHUSETTS	6
RHODE ISLAND	3
UNKNOWN	1

TWENTIETH REGIMENT
CONNECTICUT VOLUNTEER
INFANTRY

TWENTY-FIRST REGIMENT
CONNECTICUT VOLUNTEER INFANTRY

SEPTEMBER 5, 1862 - JUNE 16, 1865
(TWO YEARS, NINE MONTHS)
1,023 RECRUITS

28 KILLED, 147 DIED, 219 WOUNDED,
8 WOUNDED & CAPTURED, 34 CAPTURED

USAMHI

The 21st Regiment Connecticut Volunteer Infantry was recruited mostly in Eastern and Central Connecticut during August 1862.

Arthur H. Dutton of Wallingford, a lieutenant in the regular army was commissioned Colonel. Thomas F. Burpee of Vernon, was appointed Lieutenant Colonel and Hiram B. Crosby of Norwich, was appointed Major.

Thomas Burpee had been a captain in the 14th Connecticut Infantry and Hiram Crosby had been a private in the 18th Connecticut Infantry. The men established a camp in **NORWICH** and were mustered into United States service on September 5, 1862.

The regiment left Connecticut with 965 men on September 11 and reached

Arthur H. Dutton of Wallingford, was the only Colonel of the 21st Connecticut. He served as brigade commander several times and was promoted Bvt. Brig. General in May 1864. He was wounded on the Bermuda Hundred front the same month and died on June 5, 1864.

WASHINGTON, DC
on September 13. They spent the first couple of days near the 20th Connecticut on East Capitol Hill and then went into camp on September 17, at Camp Chase in Arlington Heights, Virginia

The regiment was part of the defenses of Washington until November 7, when they marched to Falmouth, Virginia and were assigned to the 2nd Brigade (Harland), 3rd Division (Getty),

9TH CORPS
Army of the Potomac, six weeks after the 9th Corps had fought at the Battle of Antietam. The 2nd Brigade was commanded by Connecticut Colonel Edward Harland and eventually included the 8th, 11th, 15th, 16th, 21st Connecticut, and 4th Rhode Island.

On December 12, 1862, the regiment crossed the Rappahannock River at the lower bridge for the Battle of

FREDERICKSBURG

The 2nd brigade was held in reserve and was not actively engaged in the battle although artillery shells rained down upon them. On the night of December 13, after many unsuccessful Union assaults, commanding Maj. General Ambrose Burnside decided to make a final attack the following day.

Burnside selected 18 regiments from his old 9th Corps (including the 21st Connecticut) to make a final charge at Marye's Heights. The assault was to be made at 10 AM on December 14. Every man realized that it would be a charge to almost certain death. The chosen time arrived and passed. After a long and painful period of suspense, the news came that the attack had been abandoned. Under cover of darkness, the Union army withdrew across the Rappahannock River and the 21st Connecticut returned to its old camp at Falmouth.

The men of the 21st Connecticut would never forget the suffering of the winter of 1862-1863 at Falmouth. The regiment lived without tents during most of the winter and was exposed to terrible storms. The men lay down at night on the frozen ground or in the plastic mud of Virginia with no covering other than blankets. The experience tried the endurance of every man to the utmost and planted the seeds of disease and death. The camp of the 21st Connecticut had the appropriate title of "Camp Death".

From January 20-24 they participated in Burnside's hopeless

"MUD MARCH"

which was a complete failure. On February 7, 1863, the 9th Corps joined the

ARMY OF THE JAMES

at Fort Monroe and moved by ships to Newport News. The 21st Connecticut went into camp until March 13 when they were ordered to the

SIEGE OF SUFFOLK

The 21st Connecticut joined the 3rd Brigade (21CT, 13NH, 25NJ, 4RI), 2nd Division (Getty),

7TH CORPS

Colonel Dutton was appointed brigade commander. During the siege, the regiment was under the command of Major Crosby. On May 3, the regiment was ordered to cross the Nansemond River, seize Reed's Ferry, and open communication with the 4th Rhode Island. The successful operation dispersed the Confederate cavalry at Chuckatuck and resulted in the capture of the ferry and 16 prisoners. The Seige of Suffolk was lifted on May 4.

In June 1863, the 21st Connecticut was ordered to Portsmouth to join

DIX'S PENINSULA CAMPAIGN

The expedition was also known as the "Blackberry Raid" to White House Landing. The regiment served as provost guard for Maj. General John A. Dix's command. The purpose of the raid was to disrupt Confederate communication and railroads to Richmond and to draw Lee away from Pennsylvania. The weather was brutally hot and the expedition was mostly unsuccessful. The regiment returned and was assigned to provost duty at Norfolk. After nearly five months, the regiment returned to Newport News.

On January 24, 1864, a part of the regiment, along with 132 marines, made a successful raid on Brandon Farms where they captured a large supply of Confederate stores.

The regiment was ordered to Morehead City,

NORTH CAROLINA

and arrived on February 3. They proceeded to Newport Barracks and Little Washington. After aiding in repelling the Confederates, the regiment was sent to New Bern where they remained until April.

The regiment returned to Portsmouth,

VIRGINIA

and left for Bermuda Hundred on April 29. They joined the 3rd Brigade (Sanders), 1st Division (Brooks),

18TH CORPS

On May 13, the Union army moved in force toward Richmond. On May 16, the 21st Connecticut occupied an important position in the Battle of

DREWRY'S BLUFF

The Confederates had fallen back to a line stretching from Fort Darling to the railroad. On the morning of the 16th, under cover of a very thick fog, they made a determined dash against the right side of the Union line.

After long and hard fighting, Brooke's 1st division with the 21st Connecticut, was forced to retreat. There was a simultaneous attack on the left side of the Union line with similar results.

The Union troops fell back to their original lines and began strengthening their earthworks that stretched from the James to the Appomattox Rivers. The Confederates advanced then occupied and repaired the railroad from Richmond to Petersburg. The regiment suffered 16 killed, 71 wounded, 8 wounded & captured and 15 captured.

On May 26, Colonel Dutton commanding the 3rd brigade consisting of the 21st Connecticut, 40th Massachusetts, 92nd New York, 58th & 188th Pennsylvania, and 19th Wisconsin was mortally wounded while leading a scouting party on the right of the Confederate position at Bermuda Hundred near Port Walthall.

The command of the brigade then fell upon Lieutenant Colonel Burpee who received orders to retreat. The regiment returned to White House Landing on May 29, joined the Army of the Potomac and participated in the fierce engagements around

COLD HARBOR

They had 50 wounded, and 1 captured on June 3. On the morning of June 9, Lt. Colonel Burpee, while acting as brigade officer of the day, was mortally wounded by a Confederate sharpshooter.

After Cold Harbor was evacuated, the Union army swung around in front of

PETERSBURG

and the 21st Connecticut participated in the first engagements. On June 17, the regiment was ordered to support a charge on the inner lines of the Confederate defenses.

Brooks' 1st Division, containing the 8th and 21st Connecticut was relieved and held in reserve. The regiment was under the command of Captain James F. Brown of North Stonington, because Lieutenant Colonel Crosby as well as Major Charles F. Stanton were in the hospital.

The 8th, 11th, and 21st Connecticut stayed under constant fire along the Petersburg front, as part of the 18th Corps. At the explosion of the mine at the Battle of the Crater on July 30, 1864, the 21st Connecticut was stationed well forward in support of the assaulting party.

Over the next few weeks, the regiment lost Captain Francis S. Long of Windam, along with 3 killed and 11 wounded. The regiment remained in front of Petersburg performing picket and skirmish duty until September 3. The 21st Connecticut lost 49 men during this period. The regiment was next ordered within the defenses of

BERMUDA HUNDRED

Their trenches were in the open, fully exposed to rifle fire and the scorching sun. On September 28, marching orders were received once again. The regiment crossed the James River at Aiken's Landing and assisted in the capture of

FORT HARRISON

and 22 pieces of artillery. On September 29-30, the regiment was engaged at

CHAFFIN'S FARM

The regiment had 16 wounded. The 21st Connecticut went into winter quarters following this engagement..

Hiram Crosby, who had been promoted to Lieutenant Colonel, and was in command of the regiment resigned because of fever. The regiment was then commanded by James F. Brown of North Stonington.

On March 4, 1865, the regiment was selected along with the 40th Massachusetts, 2nd New Hampshire, and 58th and 188th Pennsylvania to participate in a secret expedition to Fredericksburg. The purpose of the expedition was to break up an extensive illicit traffic in tobacco that had been smuggled across the river in exchange for supplies. The expedition resulted in the capture of thirty Confederate soldiers and the destruction of 82 carloads of tobacco.

The 21st Connecticut, along with the 1st Connecticut Battery, and 8th Connecticut Infantry participated in the advance toward

RICHMOND

in April 1865. Its stay in Richmond was brief and on April 28 the regiment was ordered to Columbia, a village 50 miles west of Richmond on the James River. The regiment was ordered to establish a military post to preserve order.

They arrived on May 1 with Lieutenant Colonel Brown in command. Several companies were assigned to provost duty in other towns. Some went to Palmyra and others went to Bremo Bluff and Goochland.

The 21st Connecticut was finally mustered out of United States service on June 16, 1865. They were ordered home and arrived in New Haven on June 22.

The regiment was entertained at the State House in Hartford and then travelled to Norwich, which was the local headquarters of the regiment. The 21st Connecticut Volunteer Infantry was received with a great reception, paid and discharged on July 6.

USAMHI

BATTLE OF DREWRY'S BLUFF, MAY 16, 1864

THE 21ST CONNECTICUT SUFFERED ITS GREATEST LOSS FOR ONE DAY AT DREWRY'S BLUFF (109) WITH THE 3RD BRIGADE (SANDERS), 1ST DIVISION (BROOKS), 18TH CORPS (W.F. SMITH)

TOTAL CASUALTIES 21ST INFANTRY

DATE	PLACE OF CASUALTY	TOTAL	K	M	W	W/C	C
1862							
August 16	Norwich, CT	1			1		
September 15	Drewry's Bluff, VA	1			1		
September 18	Washington, DC	1			1		
October 26	Arlington Heights, VA	1			1		
December 10-14	**FREDERICKSBURG, VA**	**10**			**10**		
December 30	Fredericksburg, VA	1			1		
1863							
January 18	Newport News, VA	1			1		
April 26	Unknown	1			1		
May 3	Suffolk, VA	3	1		2		
July 9	Burnt Ordinary, VA	6					6
July 11	Sherman's Mills, VA	1					1
July 14	Burnt Ordinary, VA	1					1
July 30	Portsmouth, VA	1			1		
1864							
February 1	Smithfield, VA	5				1	4
February 1	New Bern, NC	1					1
February 3	Newport News, VA (Drowned)	1	1				
February 17	New Bern, NC	1			1		
March 1	Little Washington, NC	1			1		
March 12	New Bern, NC	1			1		
May 1	Little Washington, NC	1			1		
MAY 16	**DREWRY'S BLUFF, VA**	**109**	**16**		**71**	**7**	**15**
May 19	Bermuda Hundred, VA	1			1		
May 26	Petersburg, VA	1			1		
JUNE 3, 9	**COLD HARBOR, VA**	**53**	**1**		**51**		**1**
JUNE 15-SEPTEMBER 1	**PETERSBURG, VA**	**50**	**6**		**44**		
September 27, 29	Fort Harrison, VA	4			3		1
SEPTEMBER 29-OCTOBER 30	**PETERSBURG, VA**	**11**	**3**		**7**		**1**
SEPTEMBER 29-OCTOBER 1	**CHAFFIN'S FARM, VA**	**17**			**16**		**1**
October 1-2	Petersburg, VA	1			1		
October 29	Fair Oaks, VA	1					1
1865							
June 3	Richmond, VA	1			1		

CONGRESSIONAL MEDAL OF HONOR WINNERS

Private Wallace A. Beckwith, Co. F Connecticut Infantry
Place and Date: At Fredericksburg, Va., 13 December 1862
Date of Issue: 15 February 1897
Citation: Gallantly responded to a call for volunteers to man a battery, serving with great heroism until the termination of the engagement

Corporal Clarence F. Buck, Co. A, 21st Connecticut Infantry
Place and Date: At Chaffins Farm, Va., 29 September 1864
Date of Issue: 6 April 1865
Citation: Although wounded, refused to leave the field until the fight closed.

Sergeant Robert A. Gray, Company C, 21st Connecticut Infantry
Place and Date: At Drurys Bluff, Va., 16 May 1864
Date of Issue: 13 July 1897
Citation: While retreating with his regiment, which had been repulsed, he voluntarily returned, in face of the enemy's fire, to a former position and rescued a wounded officer of his company who was unable to walk.

Capt. William S. Hubbell, Co. A, 21st Connecticut Infantry
Place and Date: At Fort Harrison, Va., 30 September 1864
Date of Issue: 13 June 1894
Citation: Led out a small flanking party and by a clash and at great risk captured a large number of prisoners.

Corporal John Gideon Palmer, Co. F, 21st Connecticut Infantry
Place and Date: At Fredericksburg, Va., 13 December 1862
Date of Issue: 30 October 1896
Citation: First of 6 men who volunteered to assist gunner of a battery upon which the enemy was concentrating its fire, and fought with the battery until the close of the engagement. His commanding officer felt he would never see this man alive again.

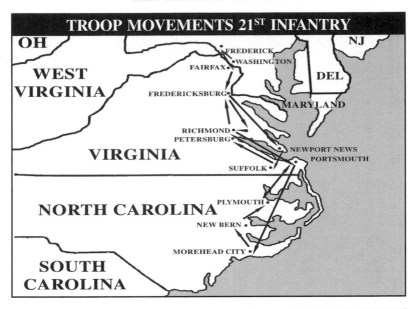

TROOP MOVEMENTS 21ST INFANTRY

DATE	PLACE
1862	
September 11	Left State for Washington, DC
September 13	Arrived Washington, DC
September 30	Washington, DC
October 1	Frederick City, MD
October 4	Sandy Neck, VA
October 6-28	Pleasant Valley, MD
October 29	Lovettsville, VA
October 30	Wheatland, VA
November 2	Unionville, VA
November 3	Ashby's Gap, VA
November 5	Oak Hill, VA
November 6	Orleans, VA
November 7	Warrenton, VA
November 16	Near Fairfax, VA
November 18	Cedar Grove, VA
November 19	Falmouth, VA
December 11-15	Battle of Fredericksburg, VA
1863	
January 20-24	Burnside's 2nd Campaign "Mud March"
February 6-9	Moved to Newport News, VA
March 13	Moved to Suffolk, VA
April 12-May 4	Siege of Suffolk
May 2	Chuckatuck and Reed's Ferry, Nansemond
May 4	Siege of Suffolk raised
May 25	Moved to White House
June 22	Moved to Yorktown, VA
June 26	White House Landing, VA
July 8	Marched down peninsula
July 13	Hampton, VA
July 14	Returned to Portsmouth
September 29	Moved to Norfolk
December 11	Moved to Newport News

TROOP MOVEMENTS 21ST INFANTRY

DATE	PLACE
Until February 1864	Duty at Newport News, VA
1864	
January 25	Expedition up James River to Fort Powhatan
February 1	Action at Smithfield
February 3	Moved to Morehead City, NC
February 13	Moved to New Bern
Until April	Duty at Plymouth and Washington, NC
April 5	Near Blount's Creek
April 28	Sailed to Fort Monroe, VA
May 2	Portsmouth, VA
May 9-10	Left for Bermuda Hundred, VA
May 10-28	Operations on south side of James River
May 10	Swift Creek, or Arrowfield Church
May 12-16	Operations against Fort Darling
May 14-16	Battle of Drewry's Bluff, VA
May 17-28	At Bermuda Hundred
May 29-31	Moved to White House and Cold Harbor
June 1-12	Battles about Cold Harbor
June 15-18	Before Petersburg
June 16	Action at Hare's Hill
June 16-April 2, 1865	Siege operations against Petersburg/Richmond
August 26-September 27	In trenches at Bermuda Hundred
September 28	Battle of Fort Harrison, VA
September 28-30	Chaffin's Farm, New Market Heights
October 27-28	Fair Oaks
Until March 1865	Duty in trenches before Richmond at Chaffin's Farm
1865	
March 4-8	Expedition to Fredericksburg
March 13-18	Moved to White House
March 24-26	Moved to Signal Hill, before Richmond
March 27	Moved to Spring Hill
April 3	Occupation of Richmond
April 25	Moved to Manchester
April 28	Moved to Columbia
April 30	Moved to Georges Tavern
June 16	Mustered out at Columbia
June 21	Discharged in Connecticut

USAMHI

PETERSBURG, VIRGINIA FRONT 1864

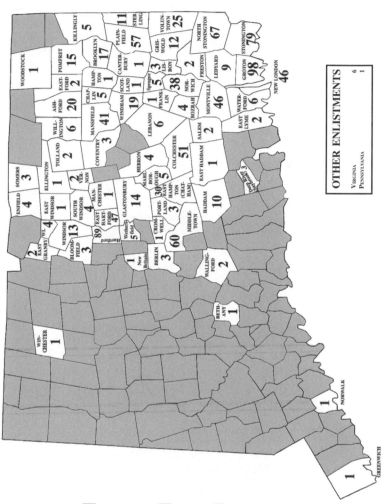

OTHER ENLISTMENTS

VIRGINIA	6
PENNSYLVANIA	1

TWENTY-FIRST REGIMENT
CONNECTICUT VOLUNTEER
INFANTRY

TWENTY-SECOND REGIMENT
CONNECTICUT VOLUNTEER INFANTRY

SEPTEMBER 20, 1862 - JULY 7, 1863
(TEN MONTHS)
940 RECRUITS
2 KILLED, 17 DIED

USAMHI

George S. Burnham had served as Colonel in the 1st Connecticut Infantry before he was elected to Colonel of the 22nd

The 22nd Regiment Connecticut Volunteer Infantry was organized in August 1862. Nearly 1,000 men, mostly from Hartford and Tolland Counties, gathered on September 3 at "Camp Halleck"

HARTFORD

The regiment was recruited to serve for ninth months and was technically a militia organization. Many of the members of the regiment were young farmers who had finished their haying and had calculated that they would return in time to take part in the hard work of the following summer.

All of the officers, both field and line, were chosen by election. The enlisted men designated the line officers and then the line officers elected the field command.

George S. Burnham of Hartford, was elected Colonel. He had been Colonel of the 1st Connecticut Infantry. Ellsworth N. Phelps of Windsor, was elected Lieutenant Colonel and Herman Glafcke of Hartford, was elected Major. Major Glafcke had been a First Lieutenant in the 1st Connecticut Heavy Artillery.

First Lieutenant Watson Webb of the 3rd US Artillery mustered the regiment into United States service on September 20.

On October 2, they left Hartford for New York City on the steamer *Granite State*. The regiment boarded trains in New York for

WASHINGTON, DC

They suffered their first casualty when a soldier was killed in a railroad accident on the way to the Capitol. The 22nd Connecticut arrived in Washington on October 5 and camped at East Capitol Hill.

The regiment entered the part of the Army of the Potomac that was assigned to the defenses of Washington under Major General Samuel Heintzelman. They joined Abercrombie's Division, Second Brigade commanded by General Robert Cowdin and later by Colonel Burr Porter of the 40th Massachusetts. The other regiments of the brigade were the 40th Massachusetts, 16th West Virginia, and the 114th New York. The 22nd Connecticut served its entire term in this brigade.

After two days on East Capitol Hill, the regiment marched to Georgetown, then crossed the chain bridge into

VIRGINIA

and rested at Fort Ethan Allen. The next morning, they moved a half mile and camped in a peach orchard.

On October 22, the regiment marched to Miner's Hill near Falls Church. They camped in shelter tents until they had built 113 log cabins, each measuring 10 by 14 feet. The regiment alternated with the other regiments of the brigade in picketing the line along the Vienna and Falls Church Roads and in responding to the occasional danger calls that occurred.

On December 12, the day before the Battle of Fredericksburg, the regiment was ordered to prepare to leave by rail for the front. After waiting two hours, the order was countermanded and the 1st brigade, which included the 27th Connecticut Infantry, was sent instead.

On December 29, the regiment marched eight miles to intercept Confederate General J.E.B. Stuart's cavalry. They marched back after 24 hours having made no contact.

In early February 1863, the regiment

was ordered to Hunter's Chapel near Arlington to assist in the construction of Forts Craig, McDowell, and McClellan. The regiment was placed into the newly created

22ND CORPS
DEPARTMENT OF WASHINGTON

and were also detailed as guards for the Long Bridge.

They suffered their only other casualty on April 12 when one soldier was killed in another accident.

The regiment boarded a steamer in Alexandria and left for Norfolk on April 14. From Norfolk they traveled by rail to Suffolk. The regiment participated in the

SIEGE OF SUFFOLK

They worked on Fort Connecticut and on the Nansemond sand batteries. The 22nd Connecticut supported the 8th and 21st Connecticut Infantry regiments and a Michigan battery. For weeks the regiment was required to stand "under arms" for two hours before daybreak in anticipation of an attack. The siege was raised on May 4 and the regiment was transported to

WEST POINT

on the York River. They arrived at night and joined the

4TH CORPS

Earthworks and rifle pits were quickly thrown up in anticipation of a night attack. After three weeks, the post was abandoned and the entire force was transported to

YORKTOWN PLAINS

The regiment camped directly in front of massive Union earthworks that were in sight of the old Revolutionary War rifle pits.

On June 9, the regiment formed a part of the advance column on Richmond. They moved along the Williamsburg and Chickahominy Rivers to Diascund Bridge and Chickahominy Church.

Later in the month, the army of Maj. General John Dix joined with the Union force. The unsuccessful expedition was known as the

DIX'S PENINSULA CAMPAIGN
"BLACKBERRY RAID"

Its purpose was to disrupt communication and rail traffic into Richmond and to draw Lee's army away from Pennsylvania.

The 22nd Connecticut eventually returned to Yorktown and on June 26 left by steamer for home.

The regiment stopped at Philadelphia, Pennsylvania and Jersey City, New Jersey. They arrived in Hartford on June 29 and were mustered out of service on July 7, 1863. Fortune favored this regiment in that none of its members were killed, wounded or captured in battle.

HARPER'S HISTORY OF THE CIVIL WAR

TROOP MOVEMENTS OF THE 22ND INFANTRY

PLACE	PLACE
1862	
October 2	Left State for Washington, DC
October 5	Arrived in Washington, DC
Until October 22	Duty at Langley, VA
Until February 12	Duty at Miner's Hill, Falls Church, VA
December 29-30	Expedition to intercept Stuart's cavalry
Until April 14, 1863	Fatigue duty, Defenses of Washington, DC
1863	
April 14-16	Moved to Suffolk, VA
April 16-May 4	Siege of Suffolk
May 4	Siege of Suffolk raised
May 5	Moved to West Point, York River, VA
Until June 9	Duty at West Point
June 9-10	Reconnaissance to Chickahominy
June 26	Left Yorktown for home
July 7	Mustered Out

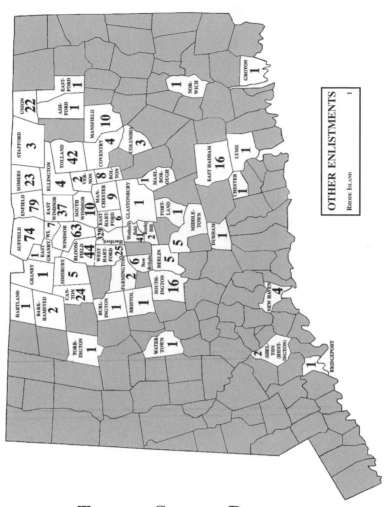

OTHER ENLISTMENTS

RHODE ISLAND 1

TWENTY-SECOND REGIMENT
CONNECTICUT VOLUNTEER
INFANTRY

TWENTY-THIRD REGIMENT
CONNECTICUT VOLUNTEER INFANTRY

NOVEMBER 14, 1862 - SEPTEMBER 1, 1863
(TEN MONTHS)
847 RECRUITS

8 KILLED, 50 DIED, 24 WOUNDED, 16 CAPTURED

COLLECTION OF THE AUTHOR

The 23rd Regiment Connecticut Volunteer Infantry was organized in August and September 1862 and was mostly made up of men from Fairfield and New Haven Counties.

The regiment was recruited for nine months and was technically a militia organization. Companies A, D, E, and G belonged to the State Militia. All of the line and field officers were elected.

Charles E. L. Holmes of Waterbury, was elected Colonel. Charles W. Wordin of Bridgeport, was elected Lieutenant Colonel and David H. Miller of Redding, was elected Major. All of the field officers and most of the line officers were connected with the active State militia. The men gathered at Camp Terry,

NEW HAVEN

and were mustered into the United States service on November 14, 1862.

The regiment remained in camp drilling and performing guard duty until No-vember 17 when they left on the steamer *Elm City* for Camp Buckingham at Centreville Race Course, Long Island, New York.

The regiment remained there until November 30 when they marched, with the 28th Connecticut, to the Atlantic Ferry, Brooklyn and boarded the steamer *Che Kiang*.

The regiment was assigned to Maj. General Nathaniel Banks

EXPEDITION TO NEW ORLEANS

Because of the crowded condition on the steamer, Companies A, H and I with two companies from other regiments were transferred to the Park Barracks, New York. The other companies of the regiment set sail with the flotilla.

They encounterd severe storms off Capt Hatteras, North Carolina. The *Che Kiang*, with 1,000 soldiers on board, arrived safely at Torugas on the Florida Keys, and eventually arrived at Ship Island, Mississippi on December 11. After a few days rest, they set sail again and passed up the Mississippi River to

NEW ORLEANS

The 23rd and 28th Connecticut were ordered to Camp Parapet and arrived at the northern defenses of the city on December 17. They formed a part of the

INDEPENDANT BRIGADE
DEPARTMENT OF THE GULF

The 23rd Connecticut had the unfortunate experience of being divided into three detachments since their departure from Long Island. Subsequently, the companies of the regiment were never together long enough to acquire any proper pride of organization.

The portion of the regiment, under the command of Major Miller, that had been left in New York boarded the ship *Planter* on December 30. On January 14, 1863, the ship wrecked on Sanger's Key, Bahama Islands without any casualties. The men of the 23rd Connecticut were rescued and they finally arrived in New Orleans on March 4.

In the mean time, all that were present in the regiment were assigned to Brig. General Godfrey Weitzel's

EXEDITION TO BERWICK BAY

On January 11, the regiment left Camp Parapet. They were expected to join in on the attack on the Confederate gunboat *Cotton* but because the organization of the regiment was incomplete they were ordered to do guard duty at Brashear City.

On February 9, the regiment was ordered to march to the Opelousas railroad. Most of the men were distributed as train guards from Berwick Bay to Jefferson, a town which was nearly opposite New Orleans. Companies B and E were detached to headquarters at La Fourche Crossing.

On June 1, the Confederates attacked the hospital opposite Brashear City.

Companies C, G, I, and K, under the command of Captain George S. Crofut of Bethel, were sent across the bay. They drove the Confederates off and protected the soldiers that were removing the sick and government property.

On June 18, Colonel Holmes resigned because of illness. Lieutenant Colonel Worden was also sick and the command of the regiment went to Major Miller. Regimental headquarters were at Brashear City. On June 22, the regiment received notice that the Confederates were about to attack the Union force at

LA FOURCHE CROSSING

A portion of the regiment was sent to re-enforce Companies B and E stationed there. Shortly after their arrival, Confederate cavalry attacked and following a sharp conflict the cavalry was driven back.

On June 21, the Confederates under Richard Taylor appeared and attacked with artillery and infantry. A determined fight ensued that lasted 40 minutes. The Confederates advanced up to and seized some the Union guns but they were eventually driven back with great loss. A breastwork, that had been hastily thrown up, protected the Union line. The loss to the regiment was 1 killed and 13 wounded.

On June 22, the Confederates sent in a flag of truce and the Union side delivered to them 108 dead and 40 prisoners.

The following day, the regiment was ordered to fall back to New Orleans. They camped there until June 26, when ordered to Camp Fair, Metaire Race Course. After the defeat at La Fourche Crossing, the Confederates retreated down the rail line to

BRASHEAR CITY

and captured the small Union detachments that were guarding the different stations along the way.

Captain Julius Sanford of Company C stationed at Bayou Boeuf, set fire to the sugar house that stored a large quantity of officer's baggage and regimental stores belonging to the troops engaged at Port Hudson. He did this in order to prevent them falling into Confederate hands.

Six captains and 5 Lieutenants were captured in the Lafourche District. They were sent to the stockade prison called Camp Ford at Tyler, Texas and were held captive for fourteen months.

On July 1, the regiment was in camp at Congo Square, New Orleans. Three days later, the City of New Orleans braced itself for a Confederate attack. The 23rd Connecticut was put on duty patrolling the city and the attack never happened. Two days later, the regiment was ordered to camp at Bonne Carre.

On August 7, the regiment left Bonne Carre on the steamer *Chancellor* headed for Cairo, IL. From Illinois they headed by train to New Haven and arrived there on August 28. The regiment was mustered out of service on September 1, 1863, after having suffered greatly from the heat and disease of the Louisiana summer.

NEW ORLEANS LEVEE IN 1862

TOTAL CASUALTIES 23RD INFANTRY

ALONG THE MISSISSIPPI RIVER IN 1863

THE 23RD CONNECTICUT INFANTRY SERVED ENTIRELY IN THE DEPARTMENT OF THE GULF AND FOR MOST OF THE TIME WAS DIVIDED INTO THREE DETACHMENTS. SUBSEQUENTLY, THE COMPANIES OF THE REGIMENT WERE NEVER TOGETHER LONG ENOUGH TO ACQUIRE MUCH PRIDE OF ORGANIZATION

NAVAL HISTORICAL CENTER

DATE	PLACE OF CASUALTY	TOTAL	K	M	W	C
1862						
October 28	New Haven, CT	1			1	
December 1	Steamer to New Orleans	1			1	
1863						
March 8	St. Charles, LA	1	1			
May 1	La Fourche, LA	1			1	
June 2	Brashear City, LA	1			1	
June 6	Bayou Boeuf (Drowned)	1	1			
June 12	Berwick, LA	1			1	
JUNE 20-24	**LA FOURCHE, LA**	**19**	**2**		**14**	**3**
JUNE 22-24	**BRASHEAR CITY, LA**	**17**	**4**		**4**	**9**
June 23	Alexandria, LA	1			1	
June 24	Bayou Boeuf, LA	4				4

TROOP MOVEMENTS 23RD INFANTRY

DATE	PLACE
1862	
November 17	Left State for Long Island, NY
November 29	Part of regiment left Long Island for Ship Island, MS
Until January 11	Duty at Camp Parapet, Defenses of New Orleans, LA
1863	
Until February 9	Provost duty at Brashear City, LA
Until June	Duty along Opelousas RR (Berwick to Jefferson)
	Headquarters at La Fourche
	Co. D at Jefferson
	Co. G at St. Charles
	Co. F at Boutte Station
	Co. C at Bayou des Almands
	Co. H at Raceland
Until April 1	Co. B at Lafourche, then Napoleonville, Terre Bonne
Until March 1	Co. K at Tigersville
	Co. A at Bayou Boeuf
April 1	Co. A moved to Bayou des Allemands, Labadievvle
Until March 1	Co. E at Bayou Romans
March 1	Co. E,I at Lafourche
June 16	Co. A moved to Bayou Boeuf
June 16	Co. B,E at Lafourche
June 1	Action at Beriwck (Co. I,G,K)
June 16	Regiment moved to La Fourche Crossing
June 20-21	Action at La Fourche Crossing
June 23	Brashear City (Co. A,C,H captured)
June 26	Captured companies paroled
Until August	Regiment on guard duty in lowlands of Louisiana
August 31	Mustered out

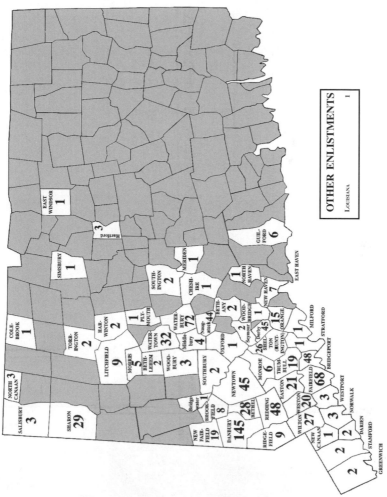

OTHER ENLISTMENTS

LOUISIANA 1

EAST WINDSOR 1

Hartford 3

GUIL-FORD 6

SIMSBURY 1

MERIDEN 1

EAST HAVEN

SOUTH-INGTON 2

CHESHIRE 1

NORTH HAVEN 1

NEW HAVEN 7

COLE-BROOK 1

HAR-WINTON 2

PLY-MOUTH 1

BETH-ANY 2

WOOD-BRIDGE 1

ORANGE 15

MILFORD

STRATFORD

TORR-INGTON 2

WATER-BURY 72

Nau-gatuck 44

Seymour

Derby 45

SHEL-TON (HUNT-INGTON) 26

ORANGE 1

LITCHFIELD 9

WATER-TOWN

Middle-bury 4

OXFORD 1

TRUMA-BULL 19

FAIRFIELD 48

BRIDGEPORT

NORTH CANAAN 3

MORRIS 5

BETH-LEHEM 2

WOOD-BURY 3

SOUTHBURY 2

NEWTOWN 45

MONROE 6

EASTON 21

WESTON 20

WESTPORT

SALISBURY 3

SHARON 29

Bridge-water 1

BROOK-FIELD 8

REDDING 28

BETHEL 145

DANBURY 145

RIDGE-FIELD 9

WILTON 27

NEW CANAAN 1

NORWALK 3

DARIEN 2

STAMFORD 2

NEW FAIR-FIELD 19

GREENWICH 2

TWENTY-THIRD REGIMENT
CONNECTICUT VOLUNTEER
INFANTRY

TWENTY-FOURTH REGIMENT
CONNECTICUT VOLUNTEER INFANTRY

NOVEMBER 18, 1862 - SEPTEMBER 30, 1863
(TEN MONTHS)
669 RECRUITS

15 KILLED, 59 DIED, 59 WOUNDED

MIDDLESEX COUNTY HISTORICAL SOCIETY

Samuel M. Mansfield of Middletown, was the Colonel of the 24th Connecticut Infantry. He had been a 2nd Lieutenant in the Engineer Corps of the regular army and was the son of Major General Joseph K.F. Mansfield

The 24th Regiment Connecticut Volunteer Infantry was organized in September 1862. Six Companies were recruited in Middlesex County and the four others in Hartford, New Haven, and Fairfield Counties.

The regiment gathered at **MIDDLETOWN** with Colonel E.W.N. Starr as post commander.

The regiment was recruited for nine months and was technically a militia organization. All of the line and field officers were elected.

On October 13, Samuel M. Mansfield, First Lieutenant in the regular army, and a son of Major General J.K.F. Mansfield, was elected Colonel. John D. Allsion of Middletown, was elected

Lieutenant Colonel and Patrick Maher of New Haven was elected Major.

The regiment was mustered into the United States service on November 18 and left Middletown with 681 officers and men for Centreville, Long Island.

On November 29, the regiment broke camp to join Major General Nathaniel Banks

EXPEDITION TO NEW ORLEANS

They left on the steamer *New Brunswick* along with a company of the 50th Massachusetts. The steamer was overloaded with men and freight. The soldiers suffered greatly from the lack of water and ventilation.

The secret expedition sailed on December 2 and the following day the sealed orders were opened which showed its destination to be Ship Island, Mississippi. On December 5 and 6, they encountered a gale and for 24 hours, the *New Brunswick* was in great danger. The steamer was a small, side wheel, riverboat, with wide, overhanging guards and was completely unsuitable for a winter voyage at sea.

The regiment arrived at Dry Tortugas, Florida on December 9 and loaded coal on to their steamer. On December 12, they finally arrived at Ship Island. The following day, they were ordered to

NEW ORLEANS

and arrived on the 14th. Two days later, they received their weapons and steamed up the river in the company of nine ships and four gunboats with orders to occupy

BATON ROUGE

Firing from Union gunboats dispersed a small group of Confederates before the 24th Connecticut landed. The regiment camped on the United States Arsenal grounds and remained there until January 21, 1863.

The 24th Connecticut, along with the 9th Connecticut and the 41st and 42nd Massachusetts, formed the 2nd Brigade of the 4th Division (Grover),

19TH CORPS

The Brigade commander was Colonel Thomas Cahill of the 9th Connecticut. On January 21, the regiment moved out to a new camp in a magnolia grove on the old battlefield of Baton Rouge. The formation of the brigade was changed by the substitution of the 91st New York for the 9th Connecticut. Colonel J. Van Zant of the 91st New York was made brigade commander.

On March 1, the regiment was consolidated into a battalion of eight companies because of sickness. Major Maher assumed command.

On March 13, the regiment moved toward

PORT HUDSON

The object of the movement was to act as a diversion in the rear of the city while Union Admiral David Farragut and his fleet steamed by the Confederate river batteries in front.

On March 15, the regiment was ordered back to Baton Rouge with one wounded soldier. They spent that night in a swamp, drenched in ankle deep water, sleeping on stumps and fence rails. The following day they camped on the banks of the Mississippi River.

On March 17, in company with two other regiments, the 24th Connecticut went on a cotton expedition toward Port Hudson and captured 100 bales. On March 20, the regiment was ordered back to Baton Rouge and reached their old camp ground weary and blistered.

On March 26, the 12th Maine, took the place of the 91st New York and changed the formation of the 2nd Brigade once again. This time, Colonel William K. Kimball of the 12th Maine was brigade commander.

On March 28, the regiment left with Grover's 4th Division on the steamer *Morning Light*, went down river and landed at Donaldsonville. On March 31, they started marching down Bayou La Fourche and passed through Napoleonville, Labadieville and Thibodeaux. They finally arrived at Terre Bonne on April 2. Two days later, the regiment went by rail to Bayou Boeuf.

On April 9, Grover's Division moved to Brashear City on a hot and dusty 10-mile march. Two days later, the regiment boarded the steamer *St. Mary*. They were ordered up to Grand Lake to cut off the retreat of the Confederates who were fortified at Camp Bisland, under the command of General Richard Taylor. On April 13, the division landed at Hutchin's

Point, marched two miles and camped on Madame Porter's Plantation. The next day, they were ordered to advance and found the Confederates in the woods. The battle of

IRISH BEND

was fought and the Union army lost over 300 killed or wounded. The 24th Connecticut was held in reserve and so had no casualties. The Confederates escaped and on April 15, the Union army began to pursue them toward the

RED RIVER

The regiment passed through Martinsville and New Iberia.

At New Iberia a detachment of 75 men from the 24th Connecticut was sent to assist in the destruction of the Confederate salt works on Petite Anse Island. On April 20, the regiment moved to Vermillionville. Six days later, they broke camp and marched to Barre's Landing. On May 5, the march toward the Red River was resumed.

After reaching a point within 15 miles of Alexandria a return march was made to the Atchafalaya River. They crossed the river at Simsport on May 17 and on May 21, the regiment left on ships and landed at midnight at Bayou Sara on the Mississippi River.

On May 22 and 23, they marched to the rear of

PORT HUDSON

The following day, the regiment was in the advance as skirmishers. They drove the Confederates from their rifle pits and held their position until morning. The regiment lost one man killed and three wounded. On May 25, five companies engaged in skirmishing and two men were killed. On May 26, four companies were detailed as sharpshooters. The next day, the sharpshooters were called in and the regiment moved with its division to support Brig. General Godfrey Weitzel's column. On May 31, the regiment was ordered to support the batteries on the right of the Union line.

The 24th Connecticut was at Port Hudson from June 1 to 13 with the reserve of the right wing of the Union army. The regiment took part in the second assault on the Confederate lines on June 14.

Each man was ordered to carry two 30 pound gunny sacks of cotton and to fill a ditch in their front with them so that the advancing Union troops could pass over them as a bridge. Tremendous fire from the Confederate works stopped those that had been detailed as sharpshooters and bearers of hand grenades and the plan failed. However, the 24th Connecticut rushed to the crest of a little hill within 50 yards of the Confederate works and thrust their cotton bags in front of them to form a breastwork. The construction of this light breastwork saved many lives in the retreating, forward Union regiments.

The Union forces that were pinned down, constructed an earthwork under the cover of darkness. Division commander Brig. General Cuvier Grover mistakenly thought that it had been constructed by the Confederates and ordered a battery to shell it. Fortunately the mistake was discovered in time and no harm was done. The newly constructed Union line was a valuable strategic point for further operations and from it a zig zag approach was dug close to a ditch that ran just in front of the main Confederate lines.

A tunnel 42 feet long was eventually dug under the Confederate works and was held by the 24th Connecticut until the surrender of Port Hudson, 25 days later, on July 8. The regiment had 8 killed and 29 wounded on June 14.

Because of sickness and casualties, only half of the regiment was on duty at Port Hudson each 24 hours. After the surrender of Port Hudson, the 24th Connecticut was complimented for its coolness and perseverance. Major General Nathaniel Banks ordered that "Port Hudson" be inscribed on the 24th's regimental flag.

On July 11, the regiment left the Union earthworks, departed by steamer, and reached

DONALDSONVILLE

that same day. The Confederate forces of General Taylor were close to the town and a sharp fight took place on the 13th with no casualties to the regiment.

On July 29, the 24th Connecticut went by boat to Carrollton and on August 6, sailed for Ship Island where they remained doing regular camp and picket duty until September 9. There were several deaths because of the heat, poor water, and the lack of vegetables.

On September 9, the regiment left for New Orleans. On September 15, they sailed for New York on the steamer *Continental* and arrived on September 24. The following day they left on the steamer *Granite State* bound for Middletown. They arrived there on the morning of the 26th. On September 30, 1863 the 24th Connecticut Volunteer Infantry was mustered out.

USAMHI

EARTHWORKS AT PORT HUDSON, LOUISIANA
1863

TOTAL CASUALTIES 24TH INFANTRY

DATE	PLACE OF CASUALTY	TOTAL	K	M	W	C
1863						
March 13	Port Hudson, LA	1			1	
MAY 24-29	PORT HUDSON, LA	12	3		9	
May 28	Baton Rouge, LA (Drowned)	1	1			
JUNE 14	PORT HUDSON, LA	37	8		29	
JUNE 15-JULY 6	PORT HUDSON, LA	22	2		20	
August 4	Unknown (Drowned)	1	1			

TROOP MOVEMENTS 24TH INFANTRY

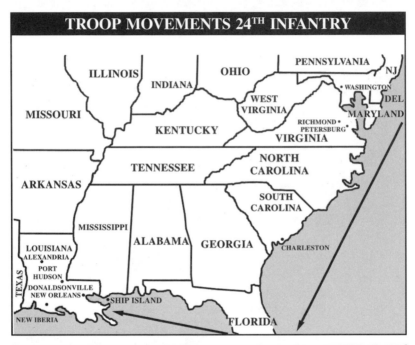

DATE	PLACE
1862	
November 18	Left State of East New York
November 29	Sailed for New Orleans
December 17	Arrived December 17
Until March 1863	Duty at Baton Rouge
1863	
March 7-27	Operations against Port Hudson, LA
March 28	Moved to Donaldsonville
April 9-May 14	Operations in Western Louisiana
April 14	Irish Bend
April 17	Bayou Vermillion
May 5-18	Expedition to Alexandria and Simsport
May 18	Destruction of Salt Works, New Iberia
May 22-25	Moved to Bayou Sara then Port Hudson
May 25-July 9	Siege of Port Hudson
July 9	Surrender of Port Hudson
July 11	Duty at Plaquemine
September 30	Mustered out

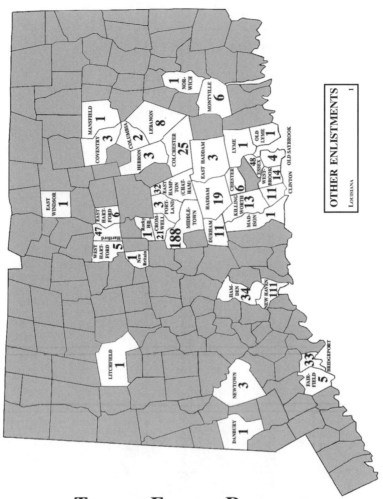

OTHER ENLISTMENTS

LOUISIANA 1

TWENTY-FOURTH REGIMENT
CONNECTICUT VOLUNTEER INFANTRY

TWENTY-FIFTH REGIMENT
CONNECTICUT VOLUNTEER INFANTRY

NOVEMBER 11, 1862 - AUGUST 26, 1863
(NINE MONTHS)
816 RECRUITS

15 KILLED, 72 DIED, 126 WOUNDED, 18 CAPTURED

USAMHI

The 25th Regiment Connecticut Volunteer Infantry was organized in the summer and fall of 1862 and was mostly made up of men from Hartford and Tolland Counties.

The companies reported to Camp Halleck in **HARTFORD** from August 20 to November 11. The regiment was recruited to serve for nine months and was technically a milita organization. All of the line and field officers were elected.

George P. Bissell of Hartford, was elected Colonel. Daniel H. Stevens of Glastonbury, was elected Lieutenant Colonel and Moses E. St. John of Simsbury, was

George P. Bissell of Hartford, was elected Colonel of the 25th Connecticut. He was taken ill while on duty in Louisana and assumed command of the regiment intermittantly

elected Major.

The regiment was mustered into United States service on November 11 and numbered 837 men.

On November 14, they sailed from Hartford to Centreville, Long Island in order to join Major General Nathaniel Banks

EXPEDITION TO NEW ORLEANS

The regiment left in two divisions. One division of five companies, under the command of Colonel Bissell, was placed on the steamer *Mary Boardman* and the other companies, under the command of Lieutenant Colonel Stevens, was placed on the *Che Kiang*.

The destination

of the expedition was unknown when the ships sailed. The sealed orders were not to to be opened until the ships had sailed for 24 hours to the south and east. When opened, the orders had the expedition reporting to Ship Island, Mississippi.

After a long and hazardous journey, the ships proceeded at once up the Mississippi River to New Orleans instead of to Ship Island. They arrived on December 14 and two days later, the *Mary Boardman* and several other ships went on to Baton Rouge. The *Che Kiang* landed the left wing of the regiment at Camp Parapet just above New Orleans. The command of the 25th Connecticut was divided for weeks between Baton Rouge and New Orleans.

After a brief bombardment of the city, the Union force landed at

BATON ROUGE

The five companies of the 25th Connecticut went into camp, first on the grounds of the United States Arsenal and later near the cemetery. The two wings of the regiment were joined together later and were a part of Cuvier Grover's U.S. Forces at Baton Rouge. Other Connecticut regiments at Baton Rouge were the 13th and 24th Connecticut Infantry. In January, the regiment was reassigned to the

19TH CORPS

4th Division, 3rd Brigade. Lieutenant Colonel Stevens and Major St. John were discharged and their positions were taken by Mason C. Weld, and Thomas McManus, of Hartford.

The 3rd Brigade was commanded by Colonel Henry W. Birge of the 13th Connecticut. The 25th Connecticut was with the 26th Maine, 159th New York and 13th Connecticut. The regiment served their entire service under Birge's command. In February, Major General Nathaniel Banks took command of the troops at Baton Rouge.

On March 9, 1863, Colonel Bissell was put in command of the advance guard with directions to repair the roads and bridges toward

PORT HUDSON

Colonel Bissell's command included the 25th Connecticut, two detachments of cavalry and a regular army battery.

The small Union force occupied Bayou Montesano, constructed earthworks and built a bridge across Bayou Sara. The regiment was seven miles in front of the Union army and was in a very exposed and dangerous position until the main column moved up to join them. Colonel Bissell was taken ill and the regiment was turned over to Major McManus because Lieutenant Colonel Weld was in the hospital at the time.

On March 13, the regiment moved to the rear of Port Hudson as part of a diversion to assist Union Admiral David Farragut's fleet in the running of the Confederate batteries in front of the city. From the banks of the Mississippi River, the 25th Connecticut witnessed the grand bombardment of Port Hudson and the burning of the frigate *Mississippi*.

The regiment eventually returned to Baton Rouge on a misrable, stormy, and muddy march. The men were upset with what seemed to them a foolish and pointless expedition that returned with 1,500 bales of cotton for the effort.

After a few days rest in new Silbey tents, the regiment made another advance with its division on the west bank of the Mississippi. On March 28, the regiment sailed down the river in a thunderstorm to Donaldsonville. They pitched their tents and on March 31 started down the road which leads along the bayou toward southern Louisiana.

On April 2, they marched through Thibodeaux to Terre Bonne, and then took a train west with the 12th Connecticut of Weitzel's Division. After reaching the Atchafalaya River, 50 miles west of New Orleans, Grover's Division steamed up Lake Chestimache while Weitzel's moved toward Franklin to attack the Confederates who were strongly posted there.

The Union assault was made on April 12 and the Confederates retreated toward Grover's Division near a place called

IRISH BEND

The Confederates slipped past in the night but the next morning they returned to engage the Union force. The regiment, along with the 13th Connecticut, was in its first real battle. The 24th Connecticut arrived toward the close of the fighting but was not under fire. The 25th Connecticut went into action with 350 men and suffered 10 killed, 79 wounded and 9 captured in the Union victory. Colonel Bissell who had recovered from his illness gallantly led the regiment.

From Irish Bend, the regiment with 20,000 soldiers of the 19th Corps marched up to within six miles of the Red River and pushed the Confederates through the Teche River valley. The Union troops reached the mouth of the Red River on May 18. Four days later, the entire corps sailed down the Mississippi to Bayou Sara, 20 miles above

PORT HUDSON

On May 24, sharp skirmishing began. The 13th and 25th Connecticut advanced in Birge's brigade. The 24th Connecticut was posted farther to the right of the Union line and the 26th Connecticut was on the left. They chased the Confederates through the woods and took possession of their earthworks.

On May 27, Birge's Brigade was ordered to the right to support Weitzel's postion and to carry a redoubt on the northeast angle of the Confederate works. Advancing under a severe cross fire through a ravine, waist deep in wa-

ter, the column halted at the abatis at the foot of a slope leading to the redoubt. The brigade managed to take the redoubt but were stopped a short while later by unrelenting fire at an impenetrable ravine. After two attempts, the regiment retired under cover of darkness.

The regiment rested in the rear and then numbering only 95 men, participated in an unsuccessful assault on June 14 that left them with 13 wounded. Ravines covering the front of the Confederate works were obstructed with felled trees and brush. A murderous fire from rifle pits and artillery swept the ground in front of the works.

Although other assaults were planned, it was not until July 8, when Port Hudson surrendered, that the Union army was able to enter the Confederate works. The surrender came when Vicksburg fell to the Union and Port Hudson lost its strategic importance. On June 23, the regiment participated in an engagement at

BRASHEAR CITY

with 3 captured and at Bayou Boeuf the following day with similar casualties. On June 27, the regiment had 11 wounded near Port Hudson

On July 11, the regiment left its camp outside Port Hudson and boarded the steamer *Laurel Hill* for

DONALDSONVILLE

So reduced had the Connecticut regiments become, that the relatively small steamer carried the 13th, 24th, and 25th Connecticut as well as two others. The 25th Connecticut was ordered to a point about a half mile below the town and remained there until the following afternoon when they were orderd to

BAYOU LA FOURCHE

Lieutenant Colonel Mason C. Weld, who had commanded the 25th during the entire siege of Port Hudson, assumed command of the brigade as senior officer.

Colonel Birge commanded the division. On the 13th, the Confederates made a dash for the Union lines on both sides of the bayou.

Lieutenant Colonel Weld led the skirmishers from the 25th Connecticut to the front but the Confederates had retreated without further engagement.

On July 16, Colonel Bissell rejoined the regiment and took command of the brigade after recovering from his long illness.

Following the surrender of Port Hudson on July 8, the regiment returned to Donaldsonville where it camped until the expiration of its term of service. The regiment left New Orleans by ship and returned to Hartford and were met by waving flags and cheers of welcome. They were mustered out on August 26, 1863.

HARPER'S PICTORIAL HISTORY OF THE CIVIL WAR

SURRENDER OF PORT HUDSON, LOUISIANA JULY 8, 1863

US MODEL 1861 PERCUSSION RIFLE MUSKET .58 CAL

TOTAL CASUALTIES 25TH INFANTRY

DATE	PLACE OF CASUALTY	TOTAL	K	M	W	C
1862						
December 1	Port Elizabeth, NJ	1			1	
December 1	Long Island, NY	1			1	
December 10	Park Barracks, NY	1			1	
1863						
February 15	Port Hudson, LA	1	1			
March 9	Baton Rouge, LA	1			1	
March 10	Bayou Sara, LA	1			1	
April 12	Brashear City, LA	3				3
April 14	Port Hudson, LA	1			1	
APRIL 14	**IRISH BEND, LA**	**98**	**10**		**79**	**9**
April 25	Port Hudson, LA	1			1	
May 3	Port Hudson, LA	2			2	
May 12	Port Hudson, LA	1			1	
May 27	Port Hudson, LA	9	3		6	
May 28	Port Hudson, LA	2	1		1	
May 31	Port Hudson, LA	4			4	
June 1	Port Hudson, LA	1			1	
June 6	Port Hudson, LA	1			1	
JUNE 14	**PORT HUDSON, LA**	**13**			**13**	
June 23	Brashear City, LA	3				3
June 23-24	Bayou Boeuf, LA	3				3
June 27	Port Hudson, LA	11			11	

CAMPFIRE AND BATTLEFIELD

BATTLE OF IRISH BEND, LOUISIANA
APRIL 14, 1863

THE 25TH CONNECTICUT SUFFERED ITS GREATEST LOSS FOR ONE DAY AT IRISH BEND (98) WITH THE 3RD BRIGADE (BIRGE), 4TH DIVISION (GROVER), 19TH CORPS (BANKS)

TROOP MOVEMENTS 25TH INFANTRY

DATE	PLACE
1862	
November 14	Left State for Long Island, NY
November 19	Sailed for New Orleans, LA
December 14	Arrived at New Orleans
December 16	Moved to Baton Rouge
Until March 1863	Duty at Baton Rouge
1863	
March 7-27	Operations against Port Hudson, LA
March 28	Moved to Donaldsonville
April 9-May 14	Operations in Western Louisiana
April 11-20	Teche Campaign
April 13	Porter's & McWilliams Plantation, Indian Bend
April 14	Irish Bend
April 17	Bayou Vermillion
May 5-28	Expedition to Alexandria and Simsport
May 22-25	Moved to Bayou Sara, Port Hudson
May 25-July 9	Siege of Port Hudson
May 27, June 14	Assaults on Port Hudson
July 9	Surrender of Port Hudson
July 11	Moved to Donaldsonville
Until August	Duty in Plaquemine District
August 26	Mustered out

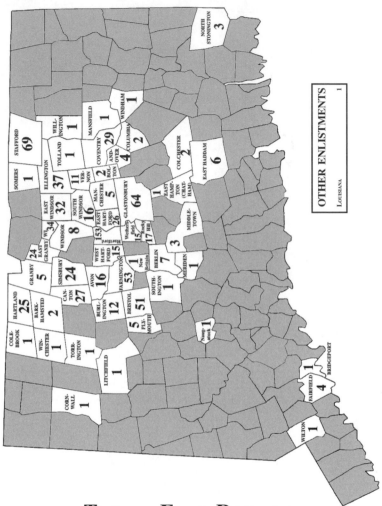

TWENTY-FIFTH REGIMENT
CONNECTICUT VOLUNTEER
INFANTRY

TWENTY-SIXTH REGIMENT
CONNECTICUT VOLUNTEER INFANTRY

NOVEMBER 10, 1862 - AUGUST 19, 1863
(NINE MONTHS)
815 RECRUITS

16 KILLED, 117 DIED, 180 WOUNDED

COLLECTION OF THE AUTHOR

T he 26th Regiment Connecticut Volunteer Infantry was organized in the late summer of 1862. From about August 22 until September 10 men mostly from New London and Windham Counties gathered at Camp Russell in **NORWICH** The regiment was recruited to serve for nine months and was technically a militia organization. All of the line and field officers were elected.

On September 19, the field officers were elected by the line officers and Thomas G. Kingsley of Franklin was elected Colonel. He had served for eight years as Colonel of the 3rd Regiment of the State Militia. Joseph Selden of Norwich was elected Lieutenant Colonel and Henry Stoll of New London, was elected Major.

The regiment was formally mustered into United States service on September 25 but the rolls were not signed. On November 10 and 11, the regiment was mustered into United States service

again, this time the rolls were signed.

Orders were received on November 12 to break camp. At 3PM the following day, the regiment eagerly left camp with full ranks, marched through the crowded streets of Norwich and boarded the steamer *Commodore* for New York City.

The regiment arrived in Brooklyn on November 14 and marched to the Centreville Race Course, Long Island. The 26th Connecticut was the first Connecticut regiment to arrive and Colonel Kingsley assumed command of the post.

He asked for and received permission to rename the camp "Camp Buckingham", a designation which had by this time ceased to be original or novel, but never ceased to be popular. Every regiment named several of its stopping places after the Connecticut governor until Camps "Buckingham" were scattered all over Virginia and extended down the Atlantic coast and up the Mississippi River.

The regiment left Camp Buckingham and went back to Brooklyn on December 4. That same evening, they boarded the steamer *Empire City.* The regiment remained in New York harbor until the morning of December 6. The steamer put to sea under sealed orders that were not opened for several days. The regiment soon learned that they were part of Major General Nathaniel Banks

EXPEDITION TO NEW ORLEANS

They arrived at Ship Island, Mississippi on December 14 and within hours moved toward New Orleans. On December 18, the regiment pitched their tents with the 23rd Connecticut at "Camp Parapet", Carrollton, a few miles above New Orleans.

The regiment became a part of General T. W. Sherman's Division. Firearms were issued for the first time and the men and officers eagerly studied and practiced the manual of arms. In no time malaria appeared in the camp and soon the hospital was more than full and many died.

On March 13, 1863, Union Admiral Farragut moved up the Mississippi with his fleet, and successfully passed Port Hudson. It became evident to the 26th Connecticut that they were soon going to participate in more active warfare at the front.

On May 20, eight companies of the regiment boarded the steamer *Crescent* and two companies boarded the *Creole* and both headed for Baton Rouge. Two days later they landed about six miles above the city at Springfield Landing. The regiment had a full view of the earthworks around

PORT HUDSON

which like Vicksburg, was a high bluff at a bend in the Mississippi. The area was strongly fortified on the river front and also had a parapet several miles in length in the rear which passed over and across ravines, gulches and woods. The parapet enclosed a Confederate camp of many acres. The works were garrisoned by about 6,500 troops under Confederate Major General Frank Gardner. The 26th Connecticut was at this time attached to the First Brigade (Dow), Second Division (T.W. Sherman),

19TH CORPS

After arriving at Springfield Landing, the regiment was ordered to report immediately to division headquarters at the front. The Union mortar fleet below Port Hudson kept up a continual shelling of the Confederate works with the missiles flying directly over the regiment.

The regiment joined the left wing of the 19th Corps on May 24. The Confederates were driven into their inner works during the afternoon after abandoning their rifle pits and ten separate lines of outer works. That evening, the regiment was ordered to establish a communication line at the extreme front between Sherman's and Auger's division on the Union left. A detachment from the 26th Connecticut was selected and by 10PM the mission was accomplished.

May 25 and 26 was spent in preparation for the first assault by the entire Union corps against the Confederate works. At 10:30 AM on May 27, the bugle called Sherman's Division into line but it was not until 1:30 PM that all was ready for the charge. The 26th Connecticut occupied the right center of Dow's Brigade. With great enthusiasm, General Sherman led the column across an open field until he lost his leg, and his horse from a Confederate shell.

Eventually, the Union force held an advanced position. The 26th Connecticut held the picket line in front of Dow's Brigade. The regiment had 6 killed, and 103 wounded on the first assault on Port Hudson. Colonel Kingsley was listed among its wounded.

The entire command was under continual fire, both day and night, from May 27 until June 14. On the afternoon of June 13, a heavy skirmish line was thrown out on Sherman's front. The 26th Connecticut lost 1 killed and 8 wounded.

A second general assault was ordered on June 14. Brig. General William Dwight had succeeded General Sherman who had been wounded on May 27. He selected a position closer to the Mississippi River and on the extreme right of the Confederate force. The result of this assault was similar to that of the first. The charge was made in the early morning. The 26th Connecticut numbered 235 men and its total casualties were 8 killed and 59 wounded. Of this number, 4 were killed and 16 wounded by a single shell.

The siege of Port Hudson continued from June 16 to July 8. On July 7, news was received of the surrender of Vicksburg and on the 8th Port Hudson surrendered with 6,408 Confederate pris-oners.

Total Union casualties during the siege were 500 killed and 2,500 wounded. The 26th Connecticut had borne a conspicuous part and was acknowledged by being selected as one of ten regiments to receive the terms of surrender of the Confederate fort. On July 9, the regiment was assigned to the second post of honor on the left of the line.

The regiment performed provost and guard duty at Port Hudson from July 10 to July 25. On the 25th, orders were received to break camp, board the steamer *St. Maurice* and return to Connecticut for muster out.

The regiment left Port Hudson on July 26, 1863 by way of the Mississippi River to Cairo, Ill. then by rail to Chicago and New York. They traveled by steamer from New York to Norwich and arrived on August 7 to a huge reception.

The 26th Connecticut Infantry reassembled again on August 19 at its original Camp Russell and was mustered out and paid off.

SIEGE OF PORT HUDSON, LOUISIANA MAY-JULY 1863 USAMHI

TOTAL CASUALTIES 26TH INFANTRY

DATE	PLACE OF CASUALTY	TOTAL	K	M	W	C
1862						
November	New York, NY	1			1	
1863						
February 22	Camp Parapet, LA	1			1	
May 22	Port Hudson, LA	1			1	
May 24	Port Hudson, LA	1			1	
MAY 27	**PORT HUDSON, LA**	**109**	**6**		**103**	
May 28	Port Hudson, LA	1			1	
June 13	Port Hudson, LA	9	1		8	
JUNE 14	**PORT HUDSON, LA**	**67**	**8**		**59**	
June 15	Port Hudson, LA	1			1	
June 25	Port Hudson, LA	1			1	
June 27	Port Hudson, LA	1			1	
July 1	Port Hudson, LA	2			2	
July 6	Port Hudson, LA	1	1			

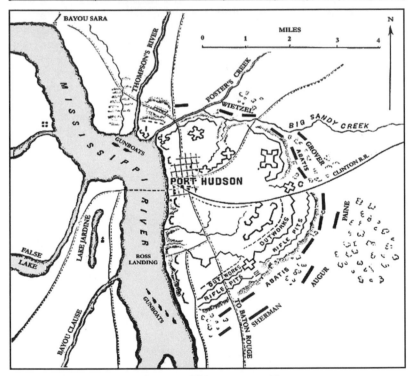

SIEGE OF PORT HUDSON, LOUISIANA
MAY - JULY 1863

Prior to the assault of May 27, 1863, the 26th Connecticut Infantry was placed in Sherman's Division closer to the Clinton Railroad tracks in the area between Auger and Paine. The map above shows their troop deployment in Sherman's Division prior to the assault of June 14.

TROOP MOVEMENTS 26TH INFANTRY

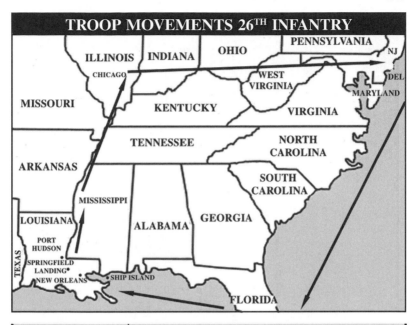

DATE	PLACE
1862	
November 12	Left State for Long Island, NY
November 19	Sailed for Ship Island, MS & New Orleans, LA
December 16	Arrived at New Orleans
Until May 1863	Duty at Camp Parapet, Carrollton, LA
1863	
May 20	Moved to Springfield Landing
May 22-July 9	Siege of Port Hudson, LA
May 27	Assault on Port Hudson
June 14	Assault on Port Hudson
July 9	Surrender of Port Hudson
August 17	Mustered out

SOLDIER IN OUR CIVIL WAR

PORT HUDSON, LOUISIANA

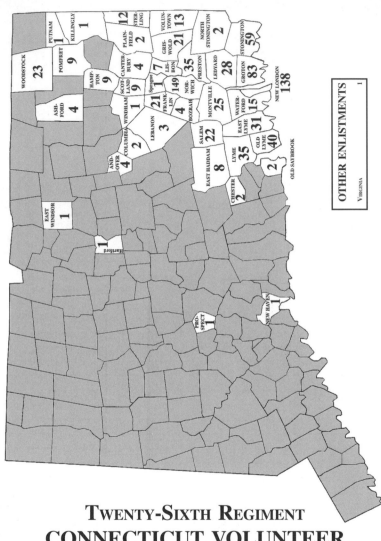

OTHER ENLISTMENTS

VIRGINIA   1

TWENTY-SIXTH REGIMENT
CONNECTICUT VOLUNTEER
INFANTRY

TWENTY-SEVENTH REGIMENT
CONNECTICUT VOLUNTEER INFANTRY

OCTOBER 22, 1862 - JULY 27, 1863
(NINE MONTHS)
829 RECRUITS

30 KILLED, 3 MISSING, 38 DIED, 129 WOUNDED, 7 WOUNDED & CAPTURED, 279 CAPTURED,

COLLECTION OF THE AUTHOR

The 27th Regiment Connecticut Volunteer Infantry was organized in early July 1862 and was mostly made up of men from New Haven County. Five hundred men came from New Haven alone.

The regiment was recruited to serve for nine months and was technically a militia organization. All of the line and field officers were elected.

The regiment went into camp at Camp Terry in

NEW HAVEN

at the end of August and by the end of September all of the companies were nearly full.

Richard S. Bostwick of New Haven, was elected Colonel. He had been a private in the 2nd Connecticut Infantry. Henry C. Merwin also from New Haven and a former Sergeant in the 2nd Connecticut Infantry, was elected Lieutenant Colonel and Theodore Byxbee of Meriden, a former Major in the 1st Connecticut Infantry was elected Major.

All of the field officers and most of the company officers had seen prior service in other Connecticut regiments.

The regiment was mustered into United States service on October 22, 1862 and started for Washington, DC with 829 men.

The regiment left New Haven for New York City on the steamer *Quaker City*. They boarded a train in New York that passed through Baltimore, Maryland and arrived in

WASHINGTON, DC

on October 25. The regiment initially camped at Camp Seward, which was in the peach orchard on Confederate General Robert E. Lee's former estate at Arlington Heights, Virginia.

On October 27, the regiment was ordered to move a few miles up the Potomac to join the 24 NJ, 28 NJ and 127 PA. The four regiments formed a brigade of Brig. General John J.

Abercrombie's Division for the

DEFENSES OF WASHINGTON

On November 30, the regiment received marching orders and the following day, the 27th Connecticut crossed the Chain Bridge and passed through Georgetown. After five days of marching down the Maryland side of the Potomac, they crossed in a blinding snowstorm from Liverpool Point to Aquia Creek, Virginia.

The regiment left Aquia Creek for Falmouth on December 8, and arrived the following day. They reported to Maj. General Darius Couch, who at that time commanded the

2ND ARMY CORPS

The 27th Connecticut was assigned to the 3rd Brigade (S.K. Zook) of the 1st Division (W. S. Hancock). The Army of the Potomac was divided into three Grand Divisions: Right, Left and Center. The 27th Connecticut became a part of the Right Grand Division, commanded by Maj. General Edwin V. Sumner.

The regiment, with the exception of the flank companies, was furnished with inferior Austrian rifles. Hardly one of them was without some defect. Brigade Commander Colonel Zook was quoted as saying "Boys, if you cannot discharge them, you can use the bayonet". In January 1863, the regiment would receive Whitney muskets.

On December 10, Union Maj. General Ambrose Burnside began his attack to take the city of

FREDERICKSBURG

Early in the morning of December 12, 375 men of the 27th Connecticut moved from a point near the Philips House and crossed into Fredericksburg. A detachment of 250 from the regiment was left to perform picket duty on the Falmouth side of the Rappahannock River.

On the morning of December 13, the 27th Connecticut with the other regiments in Hancock's Division formed on Caroline Street as artillery shells crashed among the houses and plowed through the street. The division was called upon to cross an open plain and to take the Confederate fortifications on Marye's Heights. Maj. General Hancock rode up to the 27th and leaning forward with his right arm raised said, "You are the only Connecticut regiment in my division. Bring no dishonor upon the State you represent."

The order was given to advance. The division filed out of Caroline Street and was met by terrific artillery fire. It formed a line of battle on the open plain between the city and Marye's Heights. Those who survived the artillery were soon met by overwhelming musket fire from the Confederate forces massed behind a stonewall in a sunken road at the base of the Heights.

A wooden fence running parallel and less than 100 yards from the stonewall stopped the advance of the few Union commands that reached that far. The Union dead and the wounded soon formed windrows across the field, and among them were many of the 27th Connecticut. The utter hopelessness of dislodging the Confederates was soon apparent to all. When night fell one-third of the regiment lay dead or wounded on the field or in the hospital.

On the night of December 14, Burnside withdrew his army from the Fredericksburg side of the river and the regiment went into winter quarters at Falmouth. Maj. General Joseph Hooker succeeded Burnside and the regiment was transferred to the 4th Brigade (John R. Brooke).

Another forward movement by the Army of the Potomac began about April 15, 1863 that culminated in the Battle of

CHANCELLORSVILLE

The battle began on May 1 and the regiment was actively engaged until May 3. On that morning, the regiment (with the exception of Companies D and F) with a small detachment of the 100 PA, 45PA, and 2 DE, numbering less than 400 men, was ordered to re-occupy the works that had been lost on May 1.

The works formed a part of the former picket line of the Union army. As the regiment advanced, at double time, down a hill and into a ravine, they were met by heavy musket fire. Also, unseen Confederate batteries opened fire in their rear. Colonel Bostwick sent Major Coburn to General Hancock for re-enforcements. The Confederates captured the Major and the re-enforcements never arrived.

Eventually the shelling ceased and an officer appeared on the Confederate front waving a flag of truce. He advanced slowly and waited for Union recognition. At this point the firing stopped. When the flag of truce had nearly reached the Union works the officer stopped to wait for Colonel Orlando H. Morris of the 66th NY who commanded the entire Union line. He could not be found and the responsibility of receiving the flag of truce fell upon Colonel Bostwick of the 27th.

The Confederate officer identified himself as Lieutenant Bailey of Georgia and stated that he had been directed to inform the commanding officer of the Union picket line that his force was entirely surrounded, and that there was no possibility of escape. He urged the Union force to surrender. Colonel Bostwick at first declined the truce.

Soon the Confederates came pouring in on both flanks and the desperate position of the little band of Union troops became apparent. The first impulse among the Union officers was to attempt to force their way through the Confed-

erates. However, cooler heads prevailed and a Union surrender was agreed upon.

The position of the regiment in a ravine surrounded by dense woods had made it impossible for them to see the movements going on other parts of the battlefield. The surging conflict had gradually pushed Hooker back and late in the afternoon of May 3 the Union army retreated to a position in the rear of the Chancellor House. The Confederates, aware of Hooker's retreat, and knowing the situation of the exposed Union force, immediately formed a skirmish line and pushed forward with all possible speed.

General Hancock subsequently stated that orders were sent for the 27th to fall back when Hooker had established the new line of battle, but the order was never received, so the regiment remained in the extreme front of the old line entirely unaware of this change of position.

As soon as the Union surrender was consummated, the captured troops were marched up the road to General Lee's headquarters, where their knapsacks, rubber blankets, shelter tents, and canteens were taken. They were marched off in the direction of Spottsylvania Court House.

The roads were full of Confederates who were moving to the rear. A portion of the 27th reached Spottsylvania that evening and slept in the Court House yard, while the other part of the regiment slept in the vicinity of the battlefield and in the Court House yard the following night.

The prisoners reached Guinea's Station the following evening and stayed there until May 7. The Union prisoners suffered under the intense sun in a large open lot. A terrific thunderstorm in the evening was followed by steady rain. Through all of this, the captured companies of the 27th Connecticut had no shelter and the only ration served was three pints of flour per man that was mixed with water and dried before a fire.

The regiment resumed its march on the morning of May 7. The heavy rains had made the roads almost impassable. After a tiresome march over the muddy roads and through swamps the prisoners reached Richmond on the evening of May 9. They were put in a tobacco factory opposite

LIBBY PRISON

The commissioned officers had been sent by rail from Guinea's Station and were already in Libby Prison.

After several days of prison life, the non-commissioned officers and privates of the regiment were paroled and were sent to the Union Convalescent Camp at Annapolis, Maryland. The commissioned officers were detained in Libby Prison for several days after the departure of the others. Two officers of the regiment were accused of being spies and were to be executed.

It was announced a few days later that two other solders from Tennessee were selected for execution instead. The officers of the regiment received their parole on May 23. That afternoon they began a forced march to City Point, where they boarded a U. S. steamer. They arrived in Annapolis on May 25.

Companies D and F had been detached when the other eight companies of the regiment were ordered forward on May 3. Consequently, they were not captured and remained with Hooker's army. From the remnants of the captured companies and from those in hospital or detailed for special service a new company was formed under the command of 1st Lieutenant Jedediah Chapman, of New Haven. The three companies numbering 75 men were under the overall command of Captain Joseph R. Bradley of Company F until the exchange and return of

Lieutenant Colonel Merwin on June 11. Colonel Bostwick, in poor health, returned to the regiment much later.

The three small companies of the regiment continued to maintain an active position within the Army of the Potomac while the others recovered in Annapolis.

The 2nd Corps was the last to leave the line of the Rappahannock in pursuit of General Lee who was heading north. On June 8, the regiment received orders to be ready to march any time. On June 14, the regiment moved to Banks Ford then moved toward Stafford Court House.

The regiment passed through Dumfries, Occoquan, Fairfax Court House and arrived in Centreville on June 19. On June 20, the regiment passed through the Blue Ridge at Thoroughfare Gap. On June 26, they crossed the Potomac at Edwards Ferry with the 2nd Corps and after a forced march reached

GETTYSBURG

during the evening of July 1. At dawn on July 2, they moved forward to take a place in the line of battle. The three companies of the 27th Connecticut were stationed about a mile and a half south of Cemetery Hill in the line occupied by the 2nd Corps.

That afternoon, the 3rd Corps advanced from its position on the left of the 2nd Corps toward the Emmettsburg Road and was soon engaged. Its thin line faltered under the force of a terrific Confederate attack. The 27th Connecticut with the rest of the 1st Division, was hurried forward to its support. When they entered the Wheat Field, the broken and disordered columns of the 3rd Corps were slowly retiring to the rear. They were followed closely by the Confederates.

As the 27th Connecticut, with others of the 4th Brigade, moved forward, the men became exposed to a sweeping fire. Lieutenant Colonel Merwin fell mortally wounded while leading the regiment. Major James H. Coburn of New Haven, assumed command.

The line pressed forward at double time and forced the Confederates from the Wheat Field and into the woods beyond. A ravine, rising into a precipitous ledge on its far side, checked the advancing line. The Union men climbed up the steep rocky ledge with great difficulty. As they appeared on the crest, the Confederates delivered a withering fire. Brooke's Brigade soon discovered that they had no support on either flank and the shattered line fell back.

The 27th Connecticut had gone into this action with 75 men and at 5PM had 27 casualties. Among those killed were Lieutenant Colonel Merwin and Captain Jedediah Chapman.

The following morning, General Hancock visited the brigade and its commander Colonel John R. Brooke. The Colonel called the General's attention to the little remnant of the 27th Connecticut. The position held by the regiment on July 3 was in the main line on Cemetery Ridge, a few yards to the left of the point attacked by the Confederates in Pickets Charge.

On July 5, following the Battle of Gettysburg, the regiment moved from Cemetery Ridge and left Gettsyburg by the Taneytown Road. They passed through Frederick, Maryland and crossed the Blue Ride Mountains at Crampton's Gap. The regiment, with the 4th Brigade, was ordered to Falling Waters, Virginia, located below Williamsport, Maryland. They arrived in time to participate in the capture of more than 1,000 of the Confederate rear guard. Next the regiment left Falling Waters and moved with the 2nd Corps down the Potomac to Harper's Ferry, West Virginia.

On July 18, the 27th Connecticut left the Army of the Potomac. The paroled prisoners of the regiment at Camp Convalescent joined the detachment in Baltimore on July 22. The surviving members of the regiment, numbering about 400, returned to New Haven and were mustered out on July 27, 1863.

BATTLES & LEADERS

**BATTLE OF FREDERICKSBURG, VIRGINIA
DECEMBER 13, 1862**

TOTAL CASUALTIES 27ᵀᴴ INFANTRY

DATE	PLACE OF CASUALTY	TOTAL	K	M	W	W/C	C
1862							
November 5	Arlington Heights, VA	1			1		
November 30	Washington, VA	1			1		
December 13	Fredericksburg, VA	113	17	2	90		4
December 21	Falmouth, VA	1			1		
1863							
May 3	Chancellorsville, VA	293	3		13	5	272
July 2-3	Gettysburg, PA	40	10	1	23	2	4

SOLDIER IN OUR CIVIL WAR (DETAIL)

BATTLE OF CHANCELLORSVILLE MAY 1-3, 1863

THE 27TH CONNECTICUT INFANTRY CROSSED THE RAPPAHANNOCK RIVER AT THE UNITED STATES FORD WITH THE 3RD BRIGADE (ZOOK), 1ST DIVISION (HANCOCK), 2ND CORPS (COUCH) AND SUFFERED ITS GREATEST NUMBER OF CASUALTIES (293) OF THE WAR ON MAY 3

BATTLE OF GETTYSBURG JULY 2-3, 1863
VIEW OF THE WHEAT FIELD

LIBRARY OF CONGRESS

TROOP MOVEMENTS 27TH INFANTRY

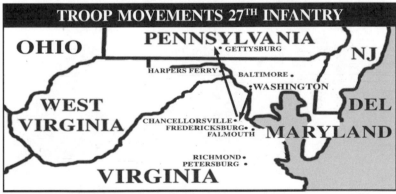

DATE	PLACE
1862	
October 22	Left State for Washington, DC
Until November	Defenses of Washington
November 7-19	Advance to Falmouth, VA
December 12-15	Battle of Fredericksburg
1863	
January 20-24	"Mud March"
Until April 27	At Falmouth
April 27-May 6	Chancellorsville, VA Campaign
June 11-July 24	Gettysburg, PA Campaign
July 1-3	Battle of Gettysburg
July 27	Mustered out

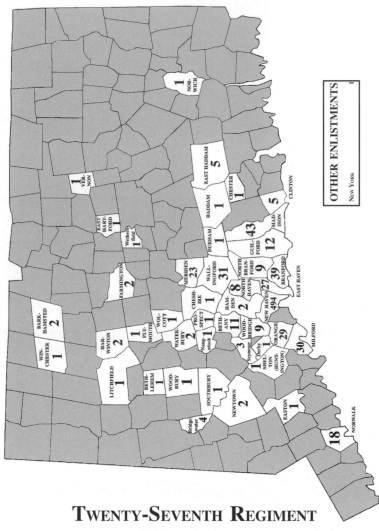

OTHER ENLISTMENTS

NEW YORK [1]

NOR-WICH **1**

VER-NON **1**

EAST HADDAM **5**

CHESTER **1**

EAST HART-FORD **1**

HADDAM **1**

CLINTON

Wethers-field **1**

DURHAM **1**

43

MAD-ISON **5**

GUIL-FORD **12**

FARMINGTON **2**

MERIDEN **23**

WALL-INGFORD **31**

NORTH BRAN-FORD **9**

BRANFORD **39**

EAST HAVEN

BARK-HAMSTED **2**

CHESH-IRE **1**

NORTH HAVEN **8**

NEW HAVEN **27**

NEW HAVEN **494**

WIN-CHESTER **1**

HAR-WINTON **2**

PLY-MOUTH **1**

WOL-COTT **1**

PROS-PECT **1**

HAM-DEN **2**

WOOD-BRIDGE **9**

ORANGE **29**

MILFORD

WATER-BURY **2**

Naug-atuck **1**

BETH-ANY **11**

Seymour **3**

Derby **1**

30

LITCHFIELD **1**

BETH-LEHEM **1**

WOOD-BURY **1**

SOUTHBURY **1**

SHEL-TON (HUNT-INGTON) **1**

EASTON **1**

NORWALK

Bridge-water **4**

NEWTOWN **2**

18

TWENTY-SEVENTH REGIMENT
CONNECTICUT VOLUNTEER INFANTRY

TWENTY-EIGHTH REGIMENT
CONNECTICUT VOLUNTEER INFANTRY

NOVEMBER 15, 1862 - AUGUST 28, 1863
(NINE MONTHS)
678 RECRUITS

10 KILLED, 96 DIED, 51 WOUNDED,
1 WOUNDED & CAPTURED, 6 CAPTURED

The 28th Regiment Connecticut Volunteer Infantry was the last Connecticut regiment organized under the call for nine months volunteers.

The regiment was technically a militia organization and was recruited in the Fourth Congressional District. It was composed of only eight companies. Five companies came from Fairfield County and three companies from Litchfield County. All of the field and line officers were elected.

Samuel P. Ferris of Stamford, a graduate of West Point, and 1st Lieutenant in the 8th U.S. Infantry was elected Colonel. Wheelock T. Batcheller of Winchester, was elected Lieutenant Colonel. He had been a 1st Lieutenant in the 2nd Connecticut Infantry. William B. Wescomer of Greenwich, was elected

USAMHI

Samuel P. Ferris had graduated from the United States Military Academy in 1861 and had entered the service as a 1st Lieutenant in the 8th US Infantry when he was elected Colonel of the 28th Connecticut Infantry in November 1862

Major.

The 28th Connecticut Infantry began gathering on September 15, 1862 at Camp Terry in NEW HAVEN and was in tents and barracks for about two months.

The regiment was mustered into United States service on November 15. Three days later they left New Haven by boat and headed for New York City.

On November 19, the regiment went into camp at Centreville, Long Island for ten days. The 23rd, 24th, 25th, 26th, and 28th Connecticut Regiments camped together.

On November 29, six companies of the regiment boarded the steamer *Che Kiang* and joined a portion of the 23rd Connecticut under the command of Colonel Charles Holmes of Waterbury. The two companies not on board the steamer joined the regiment weeks later after a very difficult passage.

The men formed a part of a secret

EXPEDITION TO NEW ORLEANS

organized by Major General Nathaniel Banks. The *Che Kiang* sailed from New York harbor on December 3, 1862 and after a very rough passage, including a terrible storm off Cape Hatteras, North Carolina reached Ship Island, Mississippi on December 12.

The regiment remained only long enough to recover from seasickness and then boarded the steamer again on December 17. On December 19, they landed at Camp Parapet in Carrollton, Louisiana a few miles above New Orleans. The regiment remained there for a short time, boarded ships once again and on December 22 left for

PENSACOLA

Florida. They arrived on December 29.

The 28th Connecticut had a long and pleasant stay in the Department of the Gulf. The companies were housed in homes that had been abandoned by their owners when the Confederates left the area. Drill and guard duties occupied the troops much of the time. The warm winter climate added to making the stay of the regiment memorable.

Expeditions into the interior and along the coast were made occasionally. They served to break the monotony of camp and guard duty. Once in a while the cry "Steamer coming" would cause the men to hurry to the rooftops in order to catch a glimpse of the welcome visitor, but too often the cry was only raised by some practical joker. When a steamer did arrive with the mail there was a busy time in reading the news from home and writing to friends and loved ones before the steamer's departure.

The 28th Connecticut left Pensacola on March 20, 1863, moved to Barrancas and into tents. Camp duties were about the same as in Pensacola with an occasional expedition that served to give variety to camp life.

On May 10, the regiment left Barrancas by steamer and landed at Brashear City, Louisiana two days later. They left there without regret on May 23 and arrived at Springfield Landing on the 25th and then moved to

PORT HUDSON

on May 26. While the regiment was at Port Hudson, the 28th Connecticut, with the 1st Brigade (Ingraham/Ferris), 3rd Division (Paine),

19TH CORPS

was under continual fire in the trenches. They assisted in all of the various siege operations.

In the assault on June 14, the regiment furnished 100 men and had 8 killed, 43 wounded, 5 captured, 1 wounded & captured.

At the surrender of Port Hudson on July 8, the 28th Connecticut moved to inside the fortifications and remained there until they departed for home on August 7, 1863. Several men died on the way home, after having been weakened by the climate and the disease that was prevalent around Port Hudson.

The 28th Connecticut travelled home by way of the Mississippi River to Cairo, Illinois and then by rail to New Haven. On August 28, 1863 the men were mustered out of service at New Haven.

19TH CORPS BADGE

TOTAL CASUALTIES 28TH INFANTRY

DATE	PLACE OF CASUALTY	TOTAL	K	M	W	W/C	C
1863							
March 22	Pensacola, FLA	1			1		
March 26	Peridita River, FLA (Drowned	1	1				
May 22	Port Hudson, LA	1			1		
June 6	Port Hudson, LA	1			1		
June 7	Port Hudson, LA	1			1		
JUNE 14	**PORT HUDSON, LA**	**57**	**8**		**43**	**1**	**5**
June 17	Port Hudson, LA	1	1				
June 21	Port Hudson, LA	1					1
July 1	Port Hudson, LA	2			2		
July 4	Port Hudson, LA	1			1		
July 8	Port Hudson, LA	1			1		

USAMHI

SIEGE OF PORT HUDSON, LOUISIANA
MAY 22 - JULY 9, 1863
CONGRESSIONAL MEDAL OF HONOR WINNER

Private Nicholas Fox, Co. H, 28th Connecticut Infantry
Place and Date: At Port Hudson, La., 14 June 1863
Date of Issue: 1 April 1898
Citation: Made two trips across an open space, in the face of the enemy's concentrated fire, and secured water for the sick and wounded.

TROOP MOVEMENTS 28TH INFANTRY

DATE	PLACE
1862	
November 17	Left State for Long Island, NY
December 3	Sailed for Ship Island, MS New Orleans, LA
December 17	Arrived at New Orleans
Until February 1863	Duty at Camp Parapet
1863	
Until May	Duty at Ft. Barrnacas, FLA (Pensacola)
May 10-12	Moved to Brashear City, LA
May 24-July 9	Siege of Port Hudson, LA
May 27	Assault on Port Hudson
June 14	Assault on Port Hudson
July 9	Surrender of Port Hudson
Until August 7	Duty at Port Hudson
August 28	Mustered out

USAMHI

PORT HUDSON, LOUISIANA MAY-AUGUST 1863

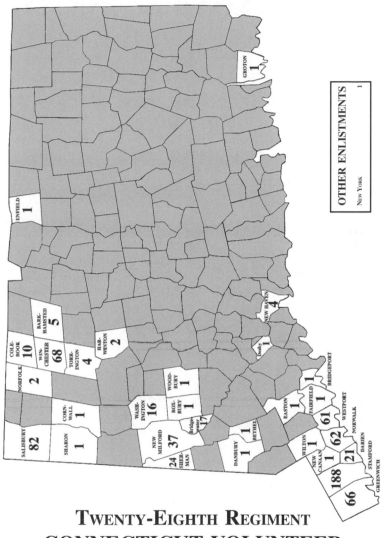

OTHER ENLISTMENTS

NEW YORK 1

GROTON 1

ENFIELD 1

BARK-HAMSTED 5

HAR-WINTON 2

COLE-BOOK 10

WIN-CHESTER 68

TORR-INGTON 4

NEW HAVEN 4

Derby 1

NORFOLK 2

WOOD-BURY 1

BRIDGEPORT

SALISBURY 82

CORN-WALL 1

WASH-INGTON 16

ROX-BURY 1

EASTON 1

FAIRFIELD 1

WESTPORT

SHARON 1

NEW MILFORD 37

Bridge-water 17

BETHEL 1

NORWALK 61

24 SHER-MAN

DANBURY 1

WILTON 1

NEW CANAAN 1

62

DARIEN 21

STAMFORD

188

66

GREENWICH

TWENTY-EIGHTH REGIMENT
CONNECTICUT VOLUNTEER
INFANTRY

TWENTY-NINTH REGIMENT
CONNECTICUT VOLUNTEER COLORED INFANTRY
MARCH 8, 1864 - NOVEMBER 25, 1865
(ONE YEAR, NINE MONTHS)
1,249 RECRUITS

29 KILLED, 199 DIED, 159 WOUNDED, 1 CAPTURED

MILITARY AND CIVIL HISTORY OF CONNECTICUT...

T he 29th Regiment Connecticut Volunteer Infantry was the first Afro-American regiment recruited from Connecticut. The earliest recruit was enlisted on August 11, 1863 however, most of the men came to the regiment at its camp in **FAIR HAVEN** during the last three months of the year. The required number of men and more was reached in January 1864.

The organization was indepted to Captain Charles L. Norton of Farmington who provided the disciplne and training through the winter of 1863. Because of the lack of officers, the regiment was not mustered into the United States service until March 8, 1864.

Four days later, William B. Wooster of Derby, who had been the Lieutenant Colonel of the 20th Connecticut Infantry was appointed Colonel. Henry C.

William B. Wooster of Derby, was appointed Colonel of the 29th Connecticut after having served as Lieutenant Colonel in the 20th Connecticut Infantry

Ward of Hartford, the adjutant of the 25th Connecticut was appointed Lieutenant Colonel and David Torrance of Norwich who had served as a Sergeant in the 18th Connecticut was appointed Major.

After the presentation of a flag by the Afro-American ladies of New Haven, the regiment left Connecticut on the steamer *Warrior* for **ANNAPOLIS** on March 19. They arrived on March 22 and pitched their tents near Camp Parole.

It was not until April 6 that the regiment was furnished with Springfield muskets.

The 29th Connecticut was assigned to the

9TH CORPS

and on April 9, sailed on two ships for Hilton Head,

SOUTH CAROLINA

They arrived on April 13 and were ordered to

BEAUFORT

The regiment performed drill, picket, and guard duty for nearly four months. The strength of the regiment was depleted by sickness. On August 8, orders came for the regiment to leave for Virginia and the following day they sailed for

BERMUDA HUNDRED

and arrived on August 14. A part of the regiment was immediately sent with a portion of the 10th Corps on a scouting mission.

The regiment was assigned to Brig. General William G. Birney's First Brigade in Maj. General D.B. Birney's Third Division of the

10TH CORPS

The 29th Connecticut was part of a brigade that included the 7th, 8th, and 9th United States Colored Infantry. They were engaged in an advance at

DEEP BOTTOM

under Maj. General Benjamin Butler and repulsed a Confederate attack on August 16 and 17. The regiment returned to the Bermuda Hundred front and camped near Point of Rocks. On August 24, the 10th Corps relieved the 18th in the trenches in front of

PETERSBURG

The 29th Connecticut remained under constant and wearing duty until September 24 when the entire 10th Corps was ordered to the rear for rest and to replace its worn and scant clothing. On September 28, the regiment marched to Deep Bottom and the next day, with the 18th Corps, engaged in taking

FORT HARRISON

about 8 miles from Richmond. An unsuccessful but persistent attack was made upon Fort Gilmer, the next fort in line, but in the evening the corps retired to the trenches in the rear. The following day the Confederates with heavy re-enforcement attempted to dislodge the Union force without success.

On October 7, the regiment assisted in repelling an attempt by the Confederates to turn the right of the Union line.

The 29th Connecticut constituted the 2nd Brigade, 3rd Division, 10th Corps along with the 8th and 45th United States Colored Infantry. On October 13, the brigade joined in a scouting party toward the right of the Union line across and beyond the New Market Road to the

DARBYTOWN ROAD

There was some sharp fighting and considerable loss of men.

On October 27 and 28, the 10th and 18th Corps, in conjunction with a forward movement of the Army of the Potomac, attacked along their entire front. The 29th Connecticut formed the skirmish line of its division and drove the Confederates into their works and kept them there. The regiment was the only one that had any casualties near the

KELL HOUSE

on October 27. Captain Frederick E. Camp, of Middletown, commanded the regiment with 584 men. They had 14 killed and 65 wounded. Afterward, the regiment was placed in the First Brigade and was assigned the duty of garrisoning the line of forts along the New Market Road.

On December 5, the 10th and 18th Corps were reorganized into a corps of Afro-American troops called the

25TH CORPS

The 29th Connecticut was placed in the Second Brigade, First Division and moved into the line on the left of Fort Harrison. The regiment remained there during the winter performing picket duty and building forts and roads in preparation for the spring campaign.

Late in March 1865, the regiment was

moved into Fort Harrison and witnessed the last Confederate dress parade on the afternoon of Sunday, April 2, 1865.

Early the next morning, the explosion of Confederate gunboats in the James River, of magazines in Fort Darling, and the rush of Confederate deserters toward the Union lines began to signal to the Union forces that the Confederates were evacuating their defensive positions.

The 29th Connecticut was in marching order and was eager for the pursuit. The men were soon over the breastworks, through the bristling abatis, the thickly planted torpedoes and into the deserted Confederate fort. An exciting race began to see who would be the first Union regiment to reach the burning City of

RICHMOND

Companies C and G of the 29th Connecticut were ordered forward as skirmishers and were the first infantry to reach the city. Union cavalry scouts had preceded them and were stationed at the entrance of the city to halt all stragglers. The regiment was placed in Batteries 5,6,7,and 8 of the interior line of the defenses of the city.

On April 13, the regiment moved to and through Petersburg and camped near Patrick's Station on the City Point railroad. On the 18th they marched to City Point and sailed to Point Lookout, Maryland where they were engaged in guarding the general depot for 20,000 Confederate prisoners of war. On May 28, the regiment was transferred to City Point to await transportation. On June 10, they sailed with the 25th Corps for

TEXAS

stopping at Mobile, Alabama and New Orleans, Louisiana. The regiment arrived at Brazos de Santiago, Texas on July 3, 1865. They marched to Brownsville and remained in camp until ordered to Connecticut for muster out on October 14, 1865.

The 29th Connecticut travelled to New Orleans and waited from October 27 until November 11 for transportation home. The regiment boarded a steamer for New York and Hartford. They arrived in Hartford on November 24, 1865 and were paid off and discharged.

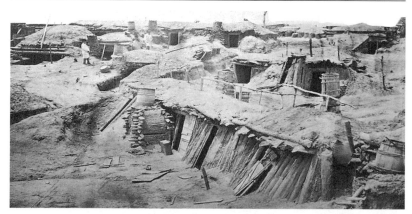

PETERSBURG, VIRGINIA FRONT **1864**

TOTAL CASUALTIES 29TH INFANTRY

DATE	PLACE OF CASUALTY	TOTAL	K	M	W	C
1864						
February 4	Unknown	1	1			
April 9	Unknown	1			1	
Unknown	Beaufort, SC	1			1	
July 5	Petersburg, VA	1			1	
August 1	Petersburg, VA	2			2	
August 1	Unknown	1			1	
August 20	Petersburg, VA	2			2	
August 25	Petersburg, VA	2			2	
August 26	Petersburg, VA	1				1
August 27	Petersburg, VA	3			3	
August 29	Petersburg, VA	4	1		3	
September 1	Petersburg, VA	3	2		1	
September 1	Fort Harrison, VA	1			1	
September 1	Deep Bottom, VA	1			1	
September 3-8	Petersburg, VA	5	1		4	
September 19-27	Petersburg, VA	5	2		3	
September 29-30	Chaffin's Farm, VA	6			6	
September 29-30	Petersburg, VA	7			7	
SEPTEMBER 29-30	RICHMOND, VA	15	1		14	
October 1-2	Chaffin's Farm, VA	2			2	
October 1	Petersburg, VA	1			1	
October 1	Richmond, VA	4			4	
October 4	Richmond, VA	1			1	
October 12-13	Chaffin's Farm, VA	2			2	
OCTOBER 13	DARBYTOWN ROAD, VA	13	3		10	
OCTOBER 13	RICHMOND, VA	6	1		5	
October 18	Fort Hurricane, VA	1			1	
October 24, 27	Fair Oaks, VA	2			2	
Unknown	Fair Oaks, VA	1			1	
October 27	Strawberry Plains, VA	1			1	
October 27	Richmond, VA	3	1		2	
October 27	Malvern Hill, VA	1			1	
OCTOBER 27	KELL HOUSE, VA	79	13		66	
November 10	Fort Harrison, VA	1			1	
November 24	Chaffin's Farm, VA	1			1	
1865						
February 18	Dutch Gap, VA	1			1	
April 1	Petersburg, VA	2			2	
April 1	Appomattox, VA	1			1	
April 3	Richmond, VA	1			1	
July 5, 10	Brownsville, TX (Drowned)	2	2			
August 28	Brownsville, TX (Drowned)	1	1			

TROOP MOVEMENTS 29TH INFANTRY

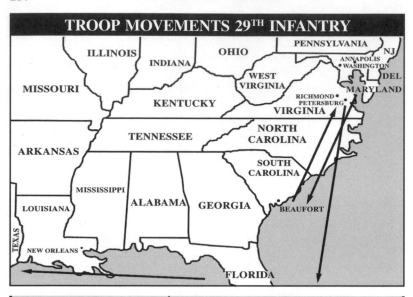

DATE	PLACE
1864	
March 19	Left State for Annapolis, MD
April 8-13	Moved to Beaufort, SC
Until August 8	Duty at Beaufort, SC
August 8-13	Moved to Bermuda Hundred, VA
August 13-April 2 1865	Siege operations Petersburg & Richmond
August 13-20	Demonstration North Side of James River
August 14-18	Deep Bottom, Strawberry Plains
August 25-September 24	Duty in trenches before Petersburg
September 28-29	New Market Heights & Fort Harrison
September 29-30	Chaffin's Farm
October 13	Darbytown Road
October 27-28	Battle of Fair Oaks
Until April 1865	Duty in trenches before Richmond
1865	
April 3	Occupation of Richmond
April 18	Moved to City Point then Point Lookout
Until May 28	Duty guarding prisoners at Point Lookout
May 28-30	Moved to City Point
June 10	Sailed for Texas
July 3	Arrived Brazos Santiago
Until October	March to Brownsville and duty there
October 24	Mustered out
October 27-November 11	At New Orleans, LA
November 25	Disharged at New Haven, CT

MODEL 1863 RIFLE MUSKET, TYPE II
CAL. 58

OTHER ENLISTMENTS

NEW YORK	2
MINNESOTA	1
NEW HAMPSHIRE	1
PENNSYLVANIA	1
TEXAS	1
VIRGINIA	1

TWENTY-NINTH REGIMENT
CONNECTICUT VOLUNTEER
COLORED INFANTRY

THIRTIETH REGIMENT
CONNECTICUT VOLUNTEER COLORED INFANTRY
MARCH 1864 - DECEMBER 1, 1865
(ONE YEAR, NINE MONTHS)
469 RECRUITS

19 KILLED, 14 MISSING, 60 DIED, 49 WOUNDED, 3 WOUNDED & CAPTURED, 4 CAPTURED

COLLECTION OF THE AUTHOR

The 30th Regiment Connecticut Volunteer Infantry was the second Afro-American regiment recruited in Connecticut. They gathered slowly at **FAIR HAVEN** during January 1864. In February, the famous orator Frederick Douglas addressed the men. Progress was being made in filling up the regiment, but the need for troops at the front was so urgent that, on June 4, the four companies that had been organized were sent to Cold Harbor **VIRGINIA** They were combined with other companies and formed the **31ST REGIMENT UNITED STATES COLORED INFANTRY** The regiment was assigned to the Third Brigade, Fourth Division, **9TH CORPS** and were detailed as a guard for 3,000 Confederate prisoners.

The regimental field and staff were not fully organized until November 1864 when Lieutenant Colonel Henry C. Ward of Hartford, and of the 29th Connecticut took command.

During its earlier months of service, Lieutenant Colonel W. E. W. Ross, of the regular army was in command. The only Connecticut men associated with him on the staff were Adjutant George Greenman and Regimental Quartermaster Dee Laroo Wilson of Norwich.

During June and July 1864, the regiment was constantly active with its corps on front of **PETERSBURG** On July 30, the regiment participated in the charge through the crater in the Confederate earthworks caused by the famous **EXPLOSION OF THE MINE** In the action, the Connecticut members of the 31st U.S. Colored Infantry lost 17 killed, 14 missing, 44 wounded, 4 captured, and 3 wounded & captured. Both

Lieutenant Colonel Ross and Major Wright were wounded.

The regiment followed the movements of the army along the South Side Railroad, while Union General Grant was trying to extend the left of his lines around Petersburg. On October 27, the regiment participated in a severe skrimish near Fort Sedgewick losing 21 men (None from Connecticut).

On Novmber 6, the number of men in the regiment had risen to nearly the same strength as when Colonel Ward had taken command the year before.

They were camped near Poplar Grove Church on the extreme left flank of the Army of the Potomac. Next, the regiment moved to the

BERMUDA HUNDRED

front betweeen the James and Appomattox Rivers Their duty was to relieve a brigade, and to re-establish a picket line that had been lost. The regiment was in very active service, under constant fire, on the right of the Bermuda Hundred line until late December.

On December 25, the regiment joined the

25TH CORPS

Army of the James near Fort Harrision, and continued in active duty there until spring. The regiment sent detachments for duty to the Dutch Gap Canal. On March 27, 1865, the regiment crossed the James River and took a position at Hatcher's Run on the left of Union line

of the Army of the Potomac.

The regiment was under constant fire in the operations southwest of Petersburg until April 1865 when the Confederate lines at Petersburg and Richmond were broken and abandoned on April 1 to 2.

On April 3, the regiment joined with Maj. General Philip Sheridan in the pursuit of Lee's army and was on the march for six days.

The pursuit of the Confederates was conducted along two lines. Maj. General Edward Ord, with the Army of the James, moved along the Lynchburg Railroad and Maj. General Sheridan, with the cavalry and the 5th Corps, followed by Maj. General George Meade and the 2nd and 6th Corps passed along the roads to the north toward Appomattox.

On April 8, the day before Lee's surrender, the regiment covered a distance of 60 miles in 36 hours. This ended the fighting service of the regiment. They had a period of rest until June 10 when as a part of the 25th Corps they sailed for

TEXAS

The regiment landed in Brazos de Santiago on June 22, 1865, marched to Brownsville and performed garrison duty until ordered to Connecticut for muster out on October 11. The regiment was finally mustered out at Hartford on December 1, 1865.

MODEL 1863 RIFLE MUSKET, TYPE II
CAL. 58

TOTAL CASUALTIES 30TH INFANTRY							
DATE	PLACE OF CASUALTY	TOTAL	K	M	W	W/C	C
1864							
March 25	Unknown	1	1				
May 30	Unknown	1			1		
July 30	Petersburg, VA	82	17	14	44	3	4
August 3	Petersburg, VA	1			1		
August 6	Petersburg, VA	1	1				
September 24	Roma, TX	1			1		
October 3	Petersburg, VA	1			1		
1865							
February 10	Bermuda Hundred, VA	1			1		

THE SOLDIER IN OUR CIVIL WAR

EXPLOSION OF THE MINE
PETERSBURG, VIRGINIA
JULY 30, 1864

TROOP MOVEMENTS 30TH INFANTRY

DATE	PLACE
1864	
May 18	Moved to Annapolis, MD
May 19	Consolidated with 31st U.S.C.I.
May-June	Campaign from Rapidan to James River
June 2-12	Guard trains of Army of the Potomac, near Cold Harbor, VA
June 15-19	Before Petersburg
June 16-April 2, 1865	Siege operations against Petersburg & Richmond
July 30	Mine explosion, Petersburg
August 18-21	Weldon Rail Road, VA
September 28	Fort Sedgewick
October 27-28	Hatcher's Run
Until March 1865	On the Bermuda Hundred front
1865	
March 26-28	Moved to Hatcher's Run
March 28-April 9	Appomattox Campaign
March 29-31	Hatcher's Run
April 2	Fall of Petersburg
April 3-9	Pursuit of Lee
April 9	Appomattox Court House
Until May	Surrender of Lee and duty in Dept. of Virginia
May-June	Moved to Texas
Until November	Duty on the Rio Grande, Texas
December 1	Mustered out

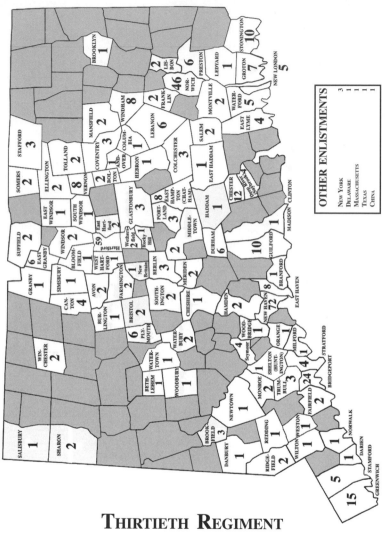

THIRTIETH REGIMENT
CONNECTICUT VOLUNTEER
COLORED INFANTRY

CONNECTICUT REGIMENTS BATTLES AND CAMPAIGNS

DATE	ACTION	PLACE	ST	REGIMENT
1861				
JUL 16-21	ADVANCE TO	MANASSAS	VA	1 2 3
JUL 17	OCCUPATION	FAIRFAX COURT HOUSE	VA	1 2 3
JUL 21	BATTLE OF	BULL RUN (MANASSAS)	VA	1 2 3
OCT 8	GUARD OUTPOST	HYATTSTOWN	MD	5
OCT 21- NOV 6	EXPEDITION TO	PORT ROYAL UNDER T W SHERMAN	SC	6,7
NOV 7	CAPTURE OF	FORTS WALKER & BEAUREGARD	SC	6,7
NOV 8	RECON. ON	HILTON HEAD ISLAND	SC	6,7
NOV 1-11	EXPEDITION	HILTON HEAD TO BRADOCK'S POINT	SC	6,7
NOV 11	EXPEDITION	TO BRADDOCK'S POINT	SC	6
NOV 12	EXPEDITION	BOSTON, MA TO SHIP IS	MS	9
DEC 3	OCCUPATION	SHIP ISLAND	MS	9
DEC 17-19	OPERATIONS	DAMS 4 AND 5	MD	5
1862				
JAN 1	EXPEDITION	NORTH CAROLINA	NC	8,10,11
JAN 28 – APR 11	OPERATIONS	AGAINST FOR FORT PULASKI	GA	6,7
FEB 8	BATTLE OF	ROANOKE ISLAND	NC	8
FEB 27	EXPEDITION	NEW YORK TO SHIP ISLAND	MS	12
MAR 5- 12	ADVANCE TO	WINCHESTER	VA	5
MAR 7	SKIRMISH	NEAR WINCHESTER	VA	5
MAR 17	MOVEMENT TO	NEW BERN	NC	8,10,11
MAR 12	OCCUPATION	WINCHESTER	VA	5
MAR 14	BATTLE OF	NEW BERN	NC	8,10,11
MAR 18	EXPEDITION	NEW YORK TO SHIP ISLAND	MS	13
MAR 18	OPERATIONS	ORDERED TO MANASSAS	VA	5
MAR 19	OPERATIONS	RETURNING TO WINCHESTER	VA	5
MAR 23	SIEGE	FORT MACON	NC	8
APR 26- MAY 23	SIEGE	FORT MACON	NC	8
APR 3	SKIRMISH	BILOXI	MS	9
APR 3	SKIRMISH	MOOREFIELD	WVA	1 Ca
APR 4	SKIRMISH	PASS CHRISTAIN	MS	9
APR 5 – MAY 30	SIEGE	YORKTOWN	VA	1 Ha
APR 10-11	BOMARDMENT	CAPTURE FORT PULASKI	GA	6,7
APR 12	SKIRMISH	FORT MACON	NC	8
APR 16	ACTION	COLUMBIA FURNACE	VA	5
MAY 1	OCCUPATION	NEW ORLEANS	LA	9,12
MAY 8	ENGAGEMENT	MCDOWELL, BULL PASTURE MT	VA	1 Ca
MAY 15-19	OPERATIONS	AT STRASBURG	VA	5
MAY 20-22	RETREAT	TO WINCHESTER	VA	5

DATE	ACTION	PLACE	ST	REGIMENTS
1862				
MAY 24-25	BATTLE OF	WINCHESTER	VA	5
MAY 24	ENGAGEMENT	MIDDLETOWN	VA	5
MAY 24	OPERATIONS	SHENANDOAH VALLEY	VA	5
MAY 24	RETREAT TO	WILLIAMSPORT	VA	5
MAY 25-26	RETREAT TO	MARTINSBURG AND WILLIAMSPORT	VA	5
MAY 27	ENGAGEMENT	HANOVER C H, SLASH CHURCH	VA	1 HA
MAY 27-29	OPERATIONS	ABOUT HANOVER COURT HOUSE	VA	1 HA
MAY 27 – JUN 5	OPERATIONS	MARTINSBURG AND WILLIAMSPORT	VA	5
JUN 1-28	OPERATIONS	JAMES ISLAND	SC	1 LB,6,7
JUN 6-9	OPERATIONS	AT WILLIAMSPORT	VA	5
JUN 7	SKIRMISH	HARRISONBURG	VA	1 CA
JUN 8	BATTLE OF	CROSS KEYS	VA	1 CA
JUN 8-9	ENGAGEMENT	PORT REPUBLIC	VA	1 CA
JUN 10	ACTION	JAMES ISLAND (GIMBALLS)	SC	6 (4 COS)
JUN 10-17	OPERATIONS	MOVED TO FRONT ROYAL	VA	5
JUN 16	ENGAGEMENT	SECESSIONVILLE, FT JOHNSON, JAMES IS	SC	1 LB,6,7
JUN 20- JUL 26	EXPEDITION	BATON ROUGE AGAINST VICKSBURG MS	LA	9
JUN 22	ACTION	ELLIS CLIFF	MS	9
JUN 22	SCOUT FROM	STRASBURG	VA	1 CA (CO B)
JUN 22-30	SKIRMISH	HAMILTON'S PLANT. NEAR GRAND GULF	MS	9
JUN 24	BATTLE OF	SEVEN DAYS RETREAT BEFORE RICHMOND	VA	1 HA
JUN 25-30	BATTLE OF	GAINES MILL, COLD HARBOR, CHICKAHOMINY	VA	1 HA
JUN 28 – JUL 7	EVACUATION	JAMES ISLAND	SC	1 LB,6,7
JUN 29-30	RECON. FROM	FRONT ROYAL TO LURAY	VA	5
JUN 30	SKIRMISH	LURAY	VA	5
JUL 1	BATTLE OF	MALVERN HILL, CREW'S/ POINDEXTER FARM	VA	1 HA
JUL 1	OPERATIONS	TO WARRENTON, GORDONSVILLE,CULPEPE	VA	5
JUL 25 – AUG 2	EXPEDITION	LK PONTCHARTRAIN, PASS MANCHAC	LA	12
JUL 27	SKIRMISH	MADISONVILLE AND NEAR COVINGTON	LA	12
JUL 29	RECON. TO	RACOON FORD	VA	5 (C0 I)
AUG 5	ENGAGEMENT	BATON ROUGE	LA	9

DATE	ACTION	PLACE	ST	REGIMENT
1862				
AUG 9	ENGAGEMENT	CEDAR MT, SLAUGHTER'S MT, CEDAR RUN	VA	5
AUG 16-SEP 2	CAMPAIGN	NORTHERN VIRGINIA (POPE'S)	VA	1 CA ,5
AUG 29-30	BATTLE OF	BULL RUN, MANASSAS, GROVETON HEIGHTS	VA	5
SEP 7-8	EXPEDITION	CARROLLTON TO ST CHARLES COURT HOUSE	LA	9
SEP 8	SKIRMISH	NEAR ST CHARLES COURT HOUSE	LA	9
SEP 13-15	EXPEDITION	PASS MANCHAC AND PONCHATOULA	LA	13 (DETACHMENT)
SEP 14	BATTLE OF	SOUTH MOUNTAIN	MD	11
SEP 16-17	BATTLE OF	ANTIETAM, SHARPSBURG	MD	8,11,14,16
SEP 30 – OCT 13	EXPEDITON	HILTON HEAD TO ST JOHN'S FL	SC	1 LB, 7
OCT 2	SKIRMISH	MAYPORT MILLS & NEAR ST JOHN'S BLUFF	FL	7
OCT 5	RECON. TO	JACKSONVILLE	FL	1 LB, 7
OCT 19	SKIRMISH	BONNETT CARRE, ST JOHN BABTIST PARISH	LA	9
OCT 21-23	EXPEDITION	POCOTALIGO	SC	1 LB,6,7
OCT 22	ENGAGEMENT	CASTON/FRAMPTON'S PLANT NEAR POCOTALIGO	SC	1 LB,6,7
OCT 24 – NOV 6	OPERATIONS	LA FOURCHE DISTRICT	LA	12,13
OCT 25	CAPTURE	DONALDSONVILLE	LA	12,13
OCT 27	ACTION	GEORGIA LANDING, NEAR LABADIEVILLE	LA	12,13
NOV 1-12	EXPEDITION	FROM NEW BERN	NC	10
NOV 2	ACTION	RAWLE'S MILL, LITTLE CREEK	NC	10
DEC 11-20	EXPEDITION	FROM NEW BERN TO GOLDSBORO	NC	10
DEC 12-15	BATTLE OF	FREDERICKSBURG	VA	1 HA (CO B M), 8,11 14,15,16,21,27
DEC 14	ENGAGEMENT	KINSTON	NC	10
DEC 16	ENGAGEMENT	WHITEHALL	NC	10
DEC 17	ENAGAGEMENT	GOLDSBORO BRIDGE	NC	10
DEC 21-23	RECON. FROM	STAFFORD CH TO KELLYSVILLE	VA	1 CA (DETACHED)
1863				
JAN 1	ENGAGEMENT	BAYOU TECHE, STEAMER COTTON	LA	12, 23
FEB 12-28	OPERATIONS	BAYOU PLAQUEMINE/ BLACK/ ATCHAFALAYA RIVER	LA	12
MAR 7-27	OPERATIONS	AGAINST PORT HUDSON	LA	12,13,24,25
MAR 21-30	EXPEDITION	NEW ORLEANS TO PONCHATOULA	LA	9 (DETACHMENT)

DATE	ACTION	PLACE	ST	REGIMENTS
1863				
MAR 21-31	OPERATIONS	NEAR JACKSONVILLE	FL	6
MAR 24	CAPTURE	PONCHATOULA	LA	9 (DETACHMENT)
MAR 28	ACTION	PATTERSONVILLE	LA	12 (DETACHMENT)
APR 9-MAY 14	OPERATIONS	IN WESTERN LOUISIANA	LA	12,13,24,25
APR 11-20	CAMPAIGN	TECHE CAMPAIGN	LA	12,13,24,25
APR 11-MAY 4	SEIGE	SUFFOLK	VA	8,11,15,16,21,22
APR 12-13	ENGAGEMENT	FT BISLAND, BETHEL PLACE,BAYOU TECHE	LA	12
APR 13	SKIRMISH	PORTER'S/MCWILLIAMS PLANT./ INDIAN BEND	LA	12
APR 14	ENGAGEMENT	IRISH BEND	LA	13,24,25
APR 14	SKIRMISH	JEANERETTE	LA	12
APR 17	ACTION	BAYOU VERMILLION	LA	13,24,25
APR 18	DESTRUCTION	OF SALT WORKS NEAR NEW IBERIA	LA	24
APR 19	ACTION	BATTERY HUGAR, HILL' POINT	VA	8 (DETACHMENT)
APR 19	RECON. FROM	WINCHESTER TO WARDENSVILLE,	VA	18
APR 24	ACTION	EDENTON ROAD, SUFFOLK	VA	11,15,16
APR 27 – MAY 6	CAMPAIGN	CHANCELLORSVILLE	VA	1 HA (C0 B M) 5,14 17,20,27
MAY 1-5	BATTLE OF	CHANCELLORSVILLE	VA	5,14,17,20,27
MAY 3	ACTION	REED'S FERRY, PROVIDENCE	VA	11 15 16
MAY 3	SKIRMISH	CHUCKATUCK AND REED'S FERRY	VA	21
MAY 3	SKIRMISH	CHURCH ROAD	VA	16
MAY 18	AFFAIR	NEAR CHENEYVILLE	LA	12
MAY 2 –18	OPERATIONS	TECHE ROAD/ BARRE'S LANDING/ BERWICK	LA	13 (1 CO)
MAY 24 – JUL 9	SEIGE	PORT HUDSON	LA	12,13,24,25,28
MAY 27	ASSAULT	PORT HUDSON	LA	12,13,24,25,26,28
JUN 13-14	SKIRMISH	WINCHESTER	VA	18
JUN 14	ASSAULT	PORT HUDSON	LA	12,13,24,25,26,28
JUN 15	BATTLE OF	WINCHESTER	VA	18
JUN 18	SKIRMISH	EDISTO ISLAND	SC	10
JUN 20	ACTION	LA FOURCHE CROSSING	LA	23
JUN 21	ACTION	LA FOURCHE CROSSING	LA	23
JUN 21	SKIRMISH	BRASHEAR CITY	LA	13 (DETACHMENT)

DATE	ACTION	PLACE	ST	REGIMENT
1863				
JUN 23	ACTION	CAPTURE, BRASHEAR CITY	LA	23 (DETACHMENT)
JUN 24-JUL 7	CAMPAIGN	DIX'S PENINSULA	VA	8,11,15,16
JUN 24	SKIRMISH	CHACKAHOULA STATION	LA	9 (COS C E G I K)
JUL 1-3	BATTLE OF	GETTYSBURG	PA	2 LB,5,14,17,20,27
JUL 1-7	EXPEDITION	FROM WHITE HOUSE TO SOUTH ANNA RIVER	VA	8,11,15,16
JUL 9	EXPEDITION	JAMES ISLAND	SC	1 LB, 10
JUL 10	ASSAULT	CAPTURE OF BATT. ON SOUTH END MORRIS IS	SC	6,7(COS A B I K)
JUL 10	ENGAGEMENT	WILLSTOWN BLUFF, PON PON RIVER	SC	1 LB (SECTION)
JUL 10-SEP 18	SEIGE	MORRIS ISLAND/ FT WAGNER/GREGG/SUMTER	SC	7,10,17
JUL 10-13	SKIRMISH	HAGERSTOWN	MD	17
JUL 13	ASSAULT	FORT WAGNER	SC	7 (COS A B L K)
JUL 12-13	ACTION	HAGERSTOWN	MD	5
JUL 12	CAMP	FUNKSTOWN	MD	5
JUL 12	SKIRMISH	FUNKSTOWN	MD	17
JUL 13	SKIRMISH	ROCKVILLE	MD	1 CA
JUL 16	ACTION	SECESSIONVILLE, JAMES ISLAND	SC	1 LB, 10
JUL 16	ASSAULT	FORT WAGNER	SC	6,7
JUL 19	ACTION	MORRIS ISLAND	SC	10
JUL 23	SKIRMISH	SNICKER' GAP	VA	5
AUG 8	SKIRMISH	WATERFORD	VA	1 CA
SEP 4-11	EXPEDITION	NEW ORLEANS TO SABINE PASS, TX	LA	12
SEP 7	OCCUPATION	FORTS WAGNER & GREGG, MORRIS ISLAND	SC	17
SEP 13-17	ADVANCE TO	FROM RAPPAHANNOCK TO RAPIDAN	VA	14
SEP 23-OCT 3	TRANSFER	11TH/12TH CORPS TO DEPT CUMBRERLAND	VA	5,20
SEP 24	GUARD DUTY	COWAN/CUMBERLAND TUNNELL NASHVILLE RR	AL	5,20
OCT 3-NOV 30	CAMPAIGN	WEST LA, OP IN TECHE COUNTRY	LA	12
0CT 9-22	CAMPAIGN	BRISTOE CAMPAIGN	VA	1 HA (CO B/M),14
OCT 14	BATTLE OF	BRISTOE STATION	VA	14
OCT 14	ENGAGEMENT	AUBURN/AUBURN MILLS/FORD	VA	14
OCT 18	ACTION	BERRYVILLE	VA	1 CA
NOV 7-8	ADVANCE TO	TO LINE OF RAPPAHANOCK	VA	1 HA (CO B/M), 14

DATE	ACTION	PLACE	ST	REGIMENT
1863				
NOV 8	ACTION	BRANDY STATION	VA	1 HA (CO B/M)
NOV 15-18	EXPEDITION	FRM CHARLESTOWN TO NEW MARKET, VA	WVA	1 CA
NOV 16	SKIRMISH	MOUNT JACKSON	VA	1 CA
NOV 26-DEC 2	CAMPAIGN	MINE RUN	VA	1 HA (CO B/M)
1864				
JAN 3	EXPEDITION	MADISONVILLE	LA	9
JAN 18-FEB 20	OPERATIONS	ABOUT NEW BERN AGAINST WHITING	NC	15,21
JAN 20	SKIRMISH	TRACY CITY	TN	20 (CO B)
JAN 22	SKIRMISH	HARRELLSVILLE	NC	15,16(DETACHED)
JAN 1 – FEB 7	OPERATIONS	IN HAMPSHIRE & HARDY CO.	WVA	1 CA
JAN 29	EXPEDITION	UP ROANOKE RIVER	NC	15 (DETACHED)
JAN 30	SKIRMISH	WINDSOR	NC	15,16(DETACHED)
FEB 1	ACTION	SMITHFIELD	VA	21
FEB 4	SKIRMISH	MOOREFIELD	WVA	1 CA
FEB 5-22	EXPEDITION	HILTON HEAD ISLAND TO FLORIDA	SC	7
FEB 6-7	DEMONSTRATION	ON THE RAPIDAN	VA	14
FEB 6-7	ENGAGEMENT	MORTON'S FORD	VA	14
FEB 6-14	EXPEDITION	JOHN'S & JAMES ISLANDS	SC	17
FEB 7-22	EXPEDITION	JACKSONVILLE TO LAKE CITY	FL	7
FEB 20	BATTLE OF	OLUSTEE OR OCEAN POND	FL	7
MAR 1	SKIRMISH	BALLAHOCK STATION	VA	8
MAR 10-MAY 22	CAMPAIGN	BANK'S RED RIVER	LA	13
MAR 17-18	RECONNOISSANCE	TOWARD SNICKER'S GAP	VA	18
APR 1	SKIRMISH	RAPPAHANNOCK RIVER	VA	1 CA
APR 5	AFFAIR	NEAR BLOUNT'S CREEK	NC	21
APR 17-20	ENGAGEMENT	SEIGE AND CAPTURE PLYMOUTH	NC	16
APR 23	ENGAGEMENT	MONETT'S FERRY, OR CANE RIVER CROSSING	LA	13
APR 30-JUL 22	CAMPAIGN	AGAINST ATLANTA	GA	5,20
APR 30-MAY 16	EXPEDITION	(SIGEL) MARTINSBURG TO NEW MARKET	WVA	18
MAY 4 –28	OPERATIONS	SOUTH SIDE JAMES PETERSBURG &	VA	1 HA, 1 LB, 6,7,8,10 11,21
MAY 5	COMBAT	CRAIG'S MEETING HOUSE	VA	1 CA

DATE	ACTION	PLACE	ST	REGIMENT
1864				
MAY 5-6	ENGAGEMENT	TODD'S TAVERN	VA	1 CA
MAY 5-7	BATTLE OF	WILDERNESS	VA	14
MAY 6-7	ACTION	WALTHAL JUNCTION & CHESTER STATION	VA	8,10,11
MAY 8-21	BATTLE OF	SPOTTSYLVANIA/ LAUREL HILL	VA	14
MAY 5	COMBAT	BUZZARD'S ROOST GAP OR MILL CREEK	GA	20
MAY 8	COMBAT	ALSOP'S FARM/ SPOTTSYLVANIA	VA	1 CA
MAY 8	COMBAT	LAUREL HILL	VA	14
MAY 8-11	DEMONSTRATION	AGAINST ROCKY FACED RIDGE	GA	5,20
MAY 9	COMABT	BUZZARD'S ROOST GAP OR MILL CREEK	GA	20
MAY 9	ENGAGEMENT	NORTH ANNA RIVER	VA	1 CA
MAY 9	ENGAGEMENT	SWIFT CREEK	VA	6,7,8,11,21
MAY 9-24	EXPEDITION	(SHERIDAN) TODD TAVERN & JAMES RIVER	VA	1 CA
MAY 9	SKIRMISH	BOYD'S TRAIL	GA	20
MAY 10	ACTION	CHESTER STATION	VA	6,7
MAY 10	OPERATIONS	BOYD'S TRAIL	GA	20
MAY 10-11	SKIRMISH	NEAR FRANKLIN	WVA	1 CA
MAY 11	ENGAGEMENT	YELLOW TAVERN	VA	1 CA
MAY 12	ASSAULT	SALIENT SPOTTSYLVANIA	VA	14
MAY 12	COMBAT	STRAWBERRY HILL	VA	1 CA
MAY 12	ENGAGEMENT	BROOK'S CHURCH & RICHMOND	VA	1 CA
MAY 12-16	BATTLE OF	PROCTOR'S CREEK & DREWRY'S BLUFF	VA	1 LB, 6,7,8,10,11,21
MAY 13-20	RETREAT	FROM ALEXANDRIA TO MORGANZA	LA	13
MAY 14-15	BATTLE OF	RESACA	GA	5,20
MAY 15	ENGAGEMENT	NEW MARKET	VA	18
MAY 17-30	OPERATIONS	ON BERMUDA HUNDRED FRONT	VA	1 HA,6,7
MAY 17-19	COMABT	NEAR CASSVILLE	GA	5,20
MAY 19	AFFAIR	WELAKA	FL	17
MAY 20	ACTION	WARE BOTTOM CHURCH	VA	6
MAY 22-26	OPERATIONS	ON LINE OF NORTH ANNA RIVER	VA	2 HA, 14
MAY 25-JUN 5	BATTLE OF	DALLAS/NEW HOPE/ ALLATOONA HILLS	GA	5,20
MAY26-JUL 1	EXPEDITION	LYNCHBURG (HUNTER'S)	VA	18

DATE	ACTION	PLACE	ST	REGIMENT
1864				
MAY 26-28	OPERATIONS	ON LINE OF PAMUNKEY RIVER	VA	2 HA, 14
MAY 27	DEMONSTRATION	ON LITTLE RUN	VA	1 CA
MAY 28-31	MOVEMENT	ARMY JAMES BERMUDA HUNDRED TO COLD	VA	8,11,21
MAY 28-31	SKIRMISH	ON LINE TOTOPOTOMOY RIVER	VA	1 CA, 2 HA
MAY 29	ACTION	HANOVER COURT HOUSE	VA	2 HA
MAY 30-JUN 12	CAMPAIGN	RAPIDAN TO JAMES RIVER	VA	1 CA, 8, 11, 14, 21
MAY 31	ACTION	MECHUMP'S CREEK	VA	1 CA
MAY31	ENGAGEMENT	HANOVER COURT HOUSE	VA	1 CA
MAY 31-JUN 3	EXPEDITION	JACKSONVILLE TO CAMP MILTON	FL	17
JUN 1-12	BATTLE OF	ABOUT COLD HARBOR	VA	1 CA,2 HA,8,11,14,21
JUN 1	ENGAGEMENT	ASHLAND	VA	1 CA
JUN 2-3	ACTION	HAWE'S STORE	VA	1 CA
JUN 2	CAPTURE	CAMP MILTON	FL	17
JUN 2	ENGAGEMENT	BERMUDA HUNDRED	VA	1 HA (CO L)
JUN 5	ENAGEMENT	PIEDMONT	VA	18
JUN 6	OCCUPATION	STAUNTON	VA	18
JUN 9	ENGAGEMENT	PETERSBURG	VA	6,7
JUN 10-JUL 2	OPERATIONS	MARIETTA/AGAINST KENESAW MT	GA	5
JUN 10-JUL 16	PROVOST DUTY	ACKWORTH	GA	20
JUN 11	ACTION	BETHESDA CHURCH	VA	1 CA
JUN 11-14	COMBAT	ABOUT PINE HILL	GA	5
JUN 12	ACTION	LONG BRIDGE	VA	1 CA
JUN 14	ACTION	BERMUDA HUNDRED	VA	7
JUN 15	PROVOST DUTY	AT MARIETTA	GA	20
JUN 15	ACTION	ST PETER'S CHURCH	VA	1 CA,1 HA,8,11,21
JUN 15-16	COMBAT	ABOUT LOST MOUNTAIN	GA	5
JUN 15	COMBAT	GILGAL OR GOLGOTHA CHURCH	GA	5
JUN 16	ACTION	BERMUDA HUNDRED FRONT	VA	1 LB, 6,7,10
JUN 16-APR 2	SIEGE	PETERSBURG/RICHMOND	VA	1 CA,1 HA,2 HA,1LB, 3LB, 6,7,8,10,11,14,21,29,30
JUN 17	ACTION	MUDDY CREEK & ABOUT LOST MOUNTAIN	GA	5
JUN 17-18	ASSAULT	ON PETERSBURG	VA	1 HA,8,11,14,21

DATE	ACTION	PLACE	ST	REGIMENT
1864				
JUN 17-18	ENGAGEMENT	LYNCHBURG	VA	18
JUN 18	SKIRMISH	COLD HARBOR	VA	1 CA
JUN 19	COMBAT	NOYE'S CREEK	GA	5
JUN 20	ACTION	WARE BOTTOM CHURCH BERMUDA HUNDRED	VA	6
JUN 20-23	EXPEDITION	BATCHELDER'S CREEK TO NEAR KINSTON	NC	15
JUN 22	COMBAT	KOLB'S FARM	GA	5
JUN 22	ENGAGEMENT	JERUSALEM PLNK RD WELDON RR	VA	2 HA, 14
JUN 22-JUL 2	EXPEDITION	(WILSON) SOUTH SIDE DANVILLE RR	VA	1 CA
JUN 22	SKIRMISH	SOUTHWEST CREEK	NC	15
JUN 23	ACTION	BLACK & WHITE STATION	VA	1 CA
JUN 23	ACTION	NOTTAWAY COURT HOUSE	VA	1 CA
JUN 24	ACTION	HARE'S HILL	VA	21
JUN 25	ACTION	STAUNTON RIVER BRIDGE ROANOKE STATION	VA	1 CA
JUN 27	GENERAL ASSAULT	KENESAW MOUNTAIN	GA	5
JUN 28	ACTION	HARE'S HILL	VA	21
JUN 28-29	ENGAGEMENT	SAPPONY CHURCH STONY CREEK	VA	1 CA
JUN 29	ENGAGEMENT	REAM'S STATION	VA	1 CA
JUL 4	COMBAT	RUFF'S STATION SMYRNA CAMP GROUND	GA	5
JUL 5-17	OPERATIONS	CHATTAHOOCHEE RIVER	GA	5
JUL 7	SKIRMISH	STAUNTON	VA	18
JUL 17-18	ENGAGEMENT	SNICKER'S FERRY PARKERS FORD	VA	18
JUL 19-20	BATTLE OF	PEACH TREE CREEK	GA	5,20
JUL 23-AUG 25	CAMPAIGN / SIEGE	AGAINST ATLANTA	GA	5,20
JUL 23-28	RAID	FROM JACKSONVILLE UPON BALDWIN	FL	17
JUL 24	ENGAGEMENT	KERNSTOWN OR WINCHESTER	VA	18
JUL 24	SKIRMISH	WHITESIDES	FL	17
JUL 27-29	DEMONSTRATION	N. SIDE JAMES/ DEEP BOTTOM /STRAWBERRY	VA	9.10,14
AG 1	ACTION	DEEP BOTTOM	VA	10
AUG 2-23	OPERATIONS	AGAINST FT GAINES & MORGAN	AL	2 LB
AUG 3-8	SIEGE	FT GAINES	AL	2 LB
AUG 13-20	DEMONSTRATION	NORTH SIDE OF JAMES ENGAGEMENTS	VA	1 LB,6,7,10,14,29

DATE	ACTION	PLACE	ST	REGIMENT
1864				
AUG 5-22	SIEGE	FT MORGAN	AL	2 LB
AUG 7-NOV 28	CAMPAIGN	(SHERIDAN'S) SHENENDOAH	VA	1 CA
AUG 9	CAPTURE	FT GAINES	AL	2 LB
AUG 15	SKIRMISH	ALLATOONA	GA	5
AUG 17	ACTION	WINCHESTER	VA	1 CA
AUG 23	CAPTURE	FT MORGAN	AL	2 LB
AUG 25	BATTLE OF	REAM'S STATION	VA	14
AUG 26-SEP 1	OPERATIONS	CHATTAHOOCHEE RIVER BRIDGE/ PACE'S	GA	5,20
SEP 2-7	OCCUPATION	OF ATLANTA	GA	5,20
SEP 13	ACTION	ABRAHAM'S CREEK NEAR WINCHESTER	VA	1 CA
SEP 19	BATTLE OF	WINCHESTER/OPEQUAN	VA	1 CA,2 HA,9,12,13
SEP 20	SKIRMISH	CEDARVILLE	VA	1 CA
SEP 21	ACTION	FRONT ROYAL	VA	1 CA
SEP 22	ACTION	MILFORD	VA	1 CA
SEP 23	BATTLE OF	FISHER'S HILL WOODSTOCK	VA	2 HA,9,12,13
SEP 25	SKIRMISH	WOODSTOCK	VA	2 HA
SEP 28	EXPEDITION	ENTERPRISE	FL	17
SEP 29-30	ENGAGEMENT	CHAFFIN'S FARM/FT HARRIS	VA	1 LB,6,7,8,10,21,29
OCT 1	ACTION	CHAFFIN'S FARM	VA	7
OCT 7	ACTION	DARBYTOWN/NEW MARKET ROADS	VA	6,7,10
OCT 8-9	ENGAGEMENT	TOM'S BROOK/FISHERS HILL	VA	1 CA
OCT 13	ACTION	CEDAR CREEK	VA	1 CA
OCT 13	ENGAGEMENT	DARBYTOWN ROAD	VA	7,10,20
OCT 17	SKIRMISH	CEDAR RUN CHURCH	VA	1 CA
OCT 19	BATTLE OF	CEDAR CREEK/MIDDLETOWN	VA	1 CA, 2HA,9,12,13
OCT 27	ENGAGEMENT	BOYDTON PLANK ROAD HATCHER'S RUN	VA	14
OCT 27-28	ENGAGEMENT	FAIR OAKS/ DARBYTOWN ROAD	VA	6,7,8,10,21,29
OCT 31	SKIRMISH	JOHNSON'S FARM	VA	10
NOV 12	ACTION	NEWTOWN/MIDDLETOWN CEDAR CREEK	VA	1 CA
NOV 15-DEC 10	CAMPAIGN	AGAINST SAVANNAH "MARCH TO SEA"	GA	5,20
NOV 22	ACTION	RUDE'S HILL NEAR MT JACKSON	VA	1 CA

DATE	ACTION	PLACE	ST	REGIMENT
1864				
DEC 9	SKIRMISH	MONTEITH SWAMP	GA	5
DEC 10-14	SCOUT FROM	CORE CREEK TO SOUTHWEST CREEK	NC	8
DEC 19-22	EXPEDITION	FRM KERNSTOWN TO LACEY'S SPRING	VA	1 CA
DEC 21	ACTION	LACEY'S SPRINGS	VA	1 CA
1865				
JAN 1-31	CAMPAIGN	OF THE CAROLINAS	NC	5,20
JAN 1-31	CAMPAIGN	OF THE CAROLINAS	SC	5,20
JAN 1-13	EXPEDITION	TO FORT FISHER	VA	1 HA (CO B,G,L) 6,7
JAN 15	ASSAULT	CAPTURE OF FORT FISHER	NC	1 HA (CO B G L),6,7
JAN 19	SKIRMISH	HALF MOON BATTERY	NC	7
JAN 23-24	ACTION	FORT BRADY	VA	1 HA
FEB 2	SKIRMISH	LAWTONVILLE	SC	20
FEB 4	EXPEDITION	FROM WINCHESTER TO MOOREFIELD WVA	VA	1 CA
FEB 5-7	BATTLE OF	DABNEY'S MILLS HATCHER'S RUN	VA	2 HA
FEB 4	EXPEDITION	FROM WINCHESTER TO MOOREFIELD WVA	VA	1 CA
FEB 11	ACTION	NEAR SUGAR LOAF BATTERY	NC	6,7
FEB 22	ACTION	NORTH EAST FERRY	NC	6,7
FEB 22	OCCUPATION	WILMINGTON	NC	6,7
FEB 22	SKIRMISH	SMITH'S CREEK	NC	7
FEB 27-MAR 2	EXPEDITION	(SHERIDAN) FROM WINCHESTER	VA	1 CA
MAR 2	ENGAGEMENT	WAYNESBORO	VA	1 CA
MAR 2	OCCUPATION	STAUNTON	VA	1 CA
MAR 2-3	SKIRMISH	THOMPSON'S CREEK, NEAR CHESTERFIELD	SC	5
MAR 3	OCCUPATION	CHARLOTTESVILLE	VA	1 CA
MAR 5-8	EXPEDITION	FROM FT MONROE TO FREDERICKSBURG	VA	21
MAR 8-10	BATTLE OF	KINSTON, OR WISE'S FORKS	NC	15
MAR 11-13	EXPEDITION	FROM FT MONROE TO WESTMORELAND CO	VA	21
MAR 14	RECON. FROM	FAYETTEVILLE/SILVER RUN CREEK/SKIRMISH	NC	20
MAR 15	SKIRMISH	ASHLAND	VA	1 CA
MAR 16	BATTLE OF	AVERYSBORO OR TAYLOR'S HOLE CREEK	NC	20
MAR 16	SKIRMISH	AVERYSBORO OR TAYLOR'S HOLE CREEK	NC	5

DATE	ACTION	PLACE	ST	REGIMENT
1865				
MAR 17-APR 12	CAMPAIGN	AGAINST MOBILE & DEFENCES	AL	2 LB
MAR 19-21	BATTLE OF	BENTONVILLE	NC	5,20
MAR 20-APR 1	EXPEDITION	BARRANCAS TO MOBILE BAY	FL	2 LB
MAR 24	OCCUPATION	GOLDSBORO	NC	5
MAR 25	ACTION	WATKIN'S HOUSE	VA	14
MAR 25	ASSAULT	FORT STEDMAN	VA	1 HA (E,K,L)
MAR 27	OCCUPATION	OF CANOE STATION	AL	2 LB
MAR 29-30	CAMPAIGN	OF APPOMATTOX	VA	1CA,1HA,2HA,1LB,3LB,8,10,11,14,21
MAR 30-31	SKIRMISH	ON LINE OF HATCHER'S GRAVELLY RUN	VA	10
MAR 31	ENGAGEMENT	DINWIDDIE COURT HOUSE	VA	1 CA
APR 1	ACTION	CROW'S HOUSE	VA	14
APR 2	BATTLE OF	FIVE FORKS	VA	1 CA
APR 3	ASSAULT	CAPTURE LINE BEFORE PETERSBURG	VA	1HA,2HA,10
APR 3	ACTION	NAMOZINE CHURCH	VA	1 CA
APR 3	OCCUPATION	RICHMOND	VA	8,11,21
APR 6	ENGAGEMENT	RICE'S STATION	VA	10
APR 6	ENGAGEMENT	SAILOR'S CREEK	VA	1 CA, 14
APR 7	ENGAGEMENT	FARMVILLE	VA	14
APR 7	ENGAGEMENT	HIGH BRIDGE	VA	14
APR 8	ENGAGEMENT	APPOMATTOX STATION	VA	1 CA
APR 9-13	ADVANCE TO	ON RALEIGH	NC	5
APR 9	CAPTURE	FT BLAKELY	AL	2 LB
APR 14	ENGAGEMENT	CLOVER HILL/ APPOMATTOX CH	VA	1 CA, 2 HA,10,14
APR 14	OCCUPATION	RALEIGH	NC	5
APR 26	EXPEDITION	FROM BURKESVILLE/ PETERSBRG/TO DANVILLE	VA	1 CA
APR 26	OPERATIONS	BENNETT'S HOUSE, SURRENDER JOHNSTONS	NC	5

WASHINGTON AND VICINITY

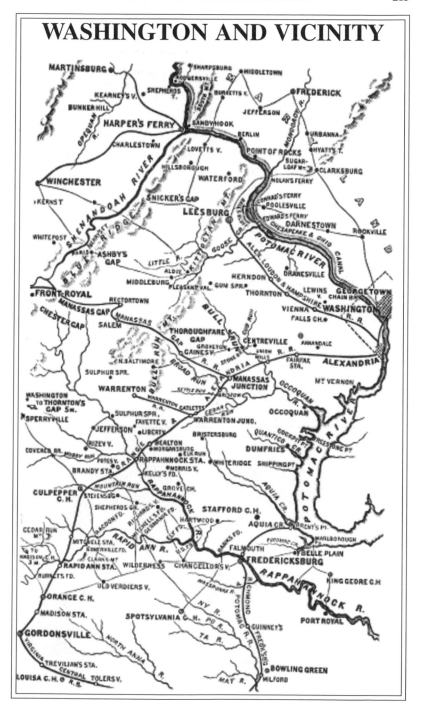

APPROACHES TO RICHMOND

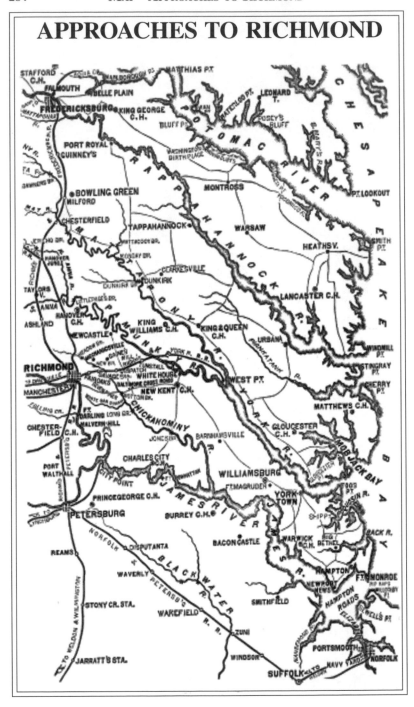

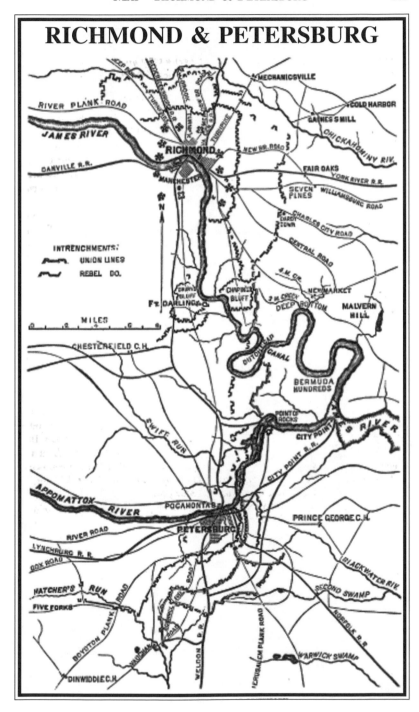

SOUTHERN GULF COAST

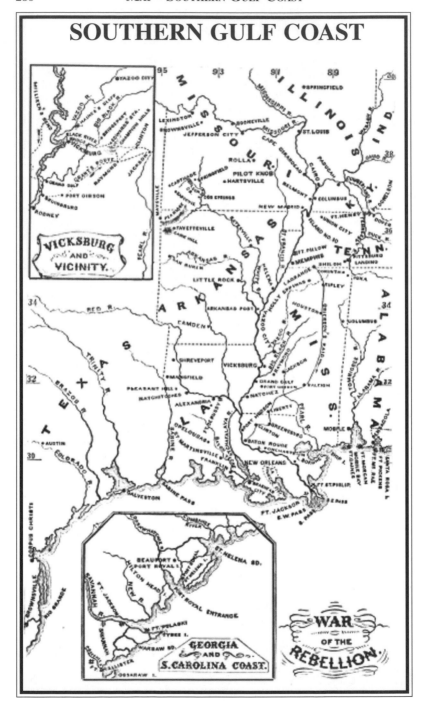

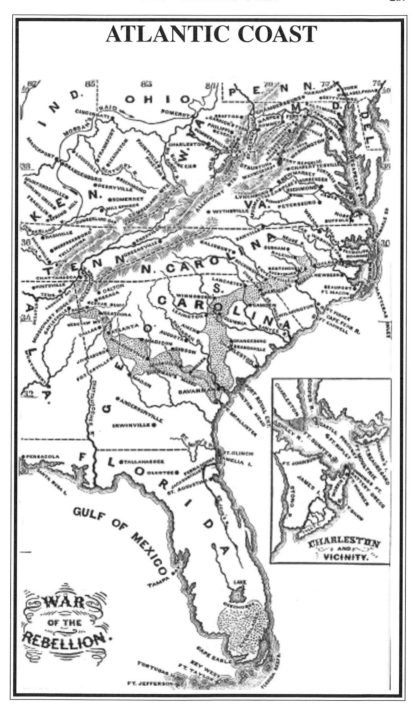

ATLANTIC COAST

CONNECTICUT TOWNS

ANDOVER
THE POPULATION IN 1860 WAS 517 (RANK 159)

THE MOST SIGNIFICANT
DAY OF THE CIVIL WAR

APRIL 14, 1863

IRISH BEND, LA

THE BATTLE WAS A PART OF
THE UNION ATTEMPT TO
SIEZE WESTERN LOUISIANA

More soldiers credited to Andover were listed as casaulties on April 14, 1863 at Irish Bend, LA (2) and on June 15, 1863 at Winchester, VA (2) than on any other days of the war. The casualties at Irish Bend were the most serious. Two soldiers were wounded in the 25TH Connecticut. Both survived the war.

The date April 14, 1863 ranks 17TH for total casualties (147) (18 killed, 120 wounded, 9 captured) for a single day for the State of Connecticut. There were 144 casualties at Irish Bend and the 3 other casualties were scattered about Louisiana.

The Battle of Irish Bend (April 14, 1863) ranks 18TH for total casualties (144) for an engagement for the State of Connecticut.

The Battle of Irish Bend, with 2 total casualties for Andover, was tied with the Second Battle of Winchester, VA (June 15, 1863) for the highest number of casualties for any single engagement of the war for the town.

Due to the lack of men, money, and supplies, the Confederate Army under General Richard Taylor fought a difficult fight to hold onto Louisiana. At the Battle of Irish Bend, in Bayou Tech, he held off a far larger Union force on two fronts until he could get his army to safety.

39 MEN CREDITED TO ANDOVER SERVED IN THE FOLLOWING CONNECTICUT ORGANIZATIONS

REGIMENT	TOTAL
18TH	6 (15%)
14TH	5 (13%)
10TH	4 (10%)
11TH	4 (10%)
25TH	4 (10%)
1ST HEAVY ARTILLERY	3 (8%)
6TH	3 (8%)
1ST LIGHT BATTERY	2 (5%)
1ST CAVALRY	2 (5%)
2ND HEAVY ARTILLERY	1
7TH	1
8TH	1
12TH	1
12TH BATTALION	1
16TH	1
30TH	1

8% OF POPULATION

TWO WERE KILLED

The first Andover soldier killed was Private Frederick Bohr of the 11ᵀᴴ Connecticut. He was killed at Petersburg, VA on June 16, 1864.

ANDOVER SOLDIERS KILLED

PLACE	DATE	NO.
Petersburg, VA (11ᵀᴴ)	6/16/64	1
Winchester, VA (2HA)	9/19/64	1

THREE WERE CAPTURED

No Andover soldiers died in captivity.

ANDOVER CAPTURED
NONE DIED IN CAPTIVITY

PLACE	DATE	NO.
Winchester, VA (18ᵀᴴ)	6/15/63	2
St. Augustine, FL(10ᵀᴴ)	12/30/63	1

TOTAL ANDOVER CASUALTIES

DIED	6	15%
KILLED	2	5%
WOUNDED	5	13%
CAPTURED	3	5%
DESERTED	8	21%

FIVE WERE WOUNDED

The first Andover soldier wounded was Private Edward S. Button of Company C, 11ᵀᴴ Connecticut. He was wounded at Kinston, NC on December 14, 1862 and recovered from his wound. No Andover soldiers died from a wound received during the war.

ANDOVER WOUNDED
NONE DIED FROM WOUNDS

PLACE	DATE	NO.
Kinston, NC (10ᵀᴴ)	12/14/62	1
Irish Bend, LA (25ᵀᴴ)	4/14/63	2
Snicker's Ford, VA (18ᵀᴴ)	7/18/64	1
Richmond, VA (7ᵀᴴ)	10/1/64	1

ASHFORD
THE POPULATION IN 1860 WAS 1,231 (RANK 117)

THE MOST IMPORTANT DAY OF THE CIVIL WAR

MAY 16, 1864

DREWRY'S BLUFF, VA

AN OBSTACLE ON THE WAY TO RICHMOND

More soldiers credited to Ashford were listed as casualties (7) on this day than on any other day of the war. Six soldiers were wounded in the 11TH and 21ST Connecticut at Drewry's Bluff and 1 was wounded at Deep Bottom, VA. All survived the war

The date May 16, 1864 ranks 4th for total casualties (560) (52 killed, 3 missing, 224 wounded, 243 captured, 38 wounded & captured) for a single day for the State of Connecticut. The Battle of Drewry's Bluff accounted for 545 casualties. The 15 other casualties were scattered about Virginia.

The Battle of Drewry's Bluff (May 13-17, 1864), also called Fort Darling, ranks 3rd for total casualties (634) for an engagement for the State of Connecticut. The most intense fighting developed on May 16. Ashford had no other casualties.

The Battle of Drewry's Bluff with 6 total casualties for Ashford was the highest number of casualties for any single engagement of the war for the town.

The Confederate attack at Drewry's Bluff forced the Union Army to retreat to Bermuda Hundred. The civil war would have concluded sooner had the Union Army been victorious.

81 MEN CREDITED TO ASHFORD SERVED IN THE FOLLOWING CONNECTICUT ORGANIZATIONS

REGIMENT	TOTAL
11TH	25 (31%)
21ST	20 (25%)
8TH	13 (16%)
12TH	5 (6%)
1ST SQUADRON CAVALRY	4 (5%)
26TH	4 (5%)
1ST HEAVY ARTILLERY	3 (4%)
1ST CAVALRY	3 (4%)
5TH	2 (2%)
6TH	2 (2%)
10TH	2 (2%)
2ND	1
2ND HEAVY ARTILLERY	1
7TH	1
13TH	1
22ND	1

7% OF POPULATION

TWO WERE KILLED

The first Ashford soldier killed in battle was 1ST Lieutenant Daniel Whitaker of Company B, 1ST Squadron Cavalry. He was killed at Aldie, VA on June 17, 1863.

ASHFORD SOLDIERS KILLED

PLACE	DATE	NO.
Railroad Accident, VA (1 SQ)	9/8/61	1
Aldie, VA (1 SQ)	6/17/63	1

TWO WERE CAPTURED

One Ashford soldier died in captivity at Salisbury, NC.

ASHFORD CAPTURED
*(1) DIED IN CAPTIVITY

PLACE	DATE	NO.
New Bern, NC (11TH)	3/20/62	1
Cedar Run Chrch, VA (1 CA)*	10/17/64	1

TOTAL ASHFORD CASUALTIES

DIED	10	12%
KILLED	2	2%
WOUNDED	24	30%
CAPTURED	2	2%
DESERTED	11	14%

TWENTY-FOUR WERE WOUNDED

The first Ashford soldiers wounded were Corporal William W. Scofield and Private Marcus N. Snell of Company B, 11TH Connecticut. Both were wounded at New Bern, NC on March 14, 1862 and both recovered from their wounds. One Ashford soldier died from a wound received during the war.

ASHFORD WOUNDED
*(1) DIED FROM WOUNDS

PLACE	DATE	NO.
New Bern, NC (11TH)	3/14/62	2
Antietam, MD (11TH)	9/17/62	4
Fredericksburg, VA (21ST)	12/10/62	1
Walthall Junction, VA (8TH)	5/7/64	1
Deep Bottom, VA (11TH)	5/16/64	1
Drewry's Bluff, VA (11TH,21ST)	5/16/64	6
Cold Harbor, VA (11TH ,21ST) *1	6/3/64	5
Cold Harbor, VA (8TH)	6/9/64	1
Petersburg, VA (8TH)	6/15/64	1
Petersburg, VA (21ST)	6/16/64	1
Chaffin's Farm, VA (21ST)	9/29/64	1

AVON
THE POPULATION IN 1860 WAS 1,059 (RANK 128)

THE MOST IMPORTANT DAY
OF THE CIVIL WAR

APRIL 20, 1864

PLYMOUTH, NC

THE CONFEDERATE PLAN
TO TAKE PLYMOUTH
ENDED WHEN 2,800 UNION
TROOPS SURRENDERED
THE CITY

More soldiers credited to Avon were listed as casualties (10) on this day than on any other day of the war. Ten soldiers were captured in the 16TH Connecticut. Three died in prison.

The date April 20, 1864 ranks 6TH for total casualties (433) (1 killed, 2 missing, 12 wounded & captured, 418 captured) for a single day for the State of Connecticut. All of the casualties were at Plymouth, NC

The Battle of Plymouth (April 20, 1864) ranks 9TH for total casualties (433) for an engagement for the State of Connecticut. Nearly half of all soldiers captured at Plymouth died in Southern prisons

The Battle of Plymouth with 10 total casualties for Avon was the highest number of casualties for any single engagement of the war for the town

When Confederate General Robert Hoke surrounded and captured the Union garrison at Plymouth, NC the Southern victory was the first in this military arena in quite some time. With aid from the two-gun ironclad *Albemarle* the Confederates were able to take advantage of the lack of suitable Union gunboats.

84 MEN CREDITED TO AVON
SERVED IN THE
FOLLOWING
CONNECTICUT
ORGANIZATIONS

REGIMENT	TOTAL
16TH	16 (19%)
25TH	16 (19%)
7TH	15 (18%)
14TH	7 (9%)
11TH	6 (7%)
1ST HEAVY ARTILLERY	5 (6%)
2ND HEAVY ARTILLERY	4 (5%)
12TH	4 (5%)
15TH	4 (5%)
29TH	3 (4%)
1ST CAVALRY	2 (2%)
10TH	2 (2%)
30TH	2 (2%)
1ST LIGHT BATTERY	1
5TH	1
6TH	1
12TH BATTALION	1
13TH	1

8% OF POPULATION

TWO WERE KILLED

The first Avon soldier killed was Corporal Henry D. Evans of Company F, 16TH Connecticut. He was killed at the Battle of Antietam, MD on September 17, 1862.

AVON SOLDIERS KILLED

PLACE	DATE	NO.
Antietam, MD (16TH)	9/17/62	1
Fort Wagner, SC (7TH)	7/11/63	1

TWELVE WERE CAPTURED

Three Avon soldiers died in captivity. One soldier died in each of the following prisons: Andersonville, GA, Charleston, SC and Florence, SC.

AVON CAPTURED
*(3) DIED IN CAPTIVITY

PLACE	DATE	NO.
Wreck of the *Union* , NC (7TH)	11/3/61	1
Plymouth, NC (16TH) *(3)	4/20/64	10
Kinston, NC (15TH)	3/8/65	1

TOTAL AVON CASUALTIES

DIED	18	21%
KILLED	2	2%
WOUNDED	15	18%
CAPTURED	12	14%
DESERTED	12	14%

FIFTEEN WERE WOUNDED

The first Avon soldier wounded was Private Job Beman of Company D, 11TH Connecticut. He was wounded at New Bern, NC on March 14, 1862 and recovered from his wound. Two Avon soldiers died from wounds received during the war.

AVON WOUNDED
*(2) DIED FROM WOUNDS

PLACE	DATE	NO.
New Bern, NC (11TH)	3/14/62	1
Antietam, MD (14,16[TH]) *(2)	9/17/62	6
Irish Bend, LA (25TH)	4/14/63	2
Morton's Ford, VA (14TH)	2/6/64	1
Swift's Creek, VA (11TH)	5/9/64	2
Cold Harbor, VA (14TH)	6/3/64	1
Newmarket, VA (7TH)	10/7/64	1
Cedar Creek, VA (12TH)	10/19/64	1

BARKHAMSTED
THE POPULATION IN 1860 WAS 1,272 (RANK 113)

THE MOST IMPORTANT DAY OF THE CIVIL WAR

JUNE 1, 1864

COLD HARBOR, VA

THE BATTLE WAS LEE'S LAST GREAT VICTORY

More soldiers credited to Barkhamsted were listed as casualties (3) on this day than on any other day of the war. Two soldiers were killed, and 1 was wounded in the 2ND Connecticut Heavy Artillery. The wounded soldier recovered.

The date June 1, 1864 ranks 8TH for total casualties (374) (89 killed, 10 missing, 246 wounded, 23 captured, 6 wounded & captured) for a single day for the State of Connecticut. There were 324 casualties at Cold Harbor, 41 casualties at Ashland, and 9 other casualties scattered about Virginia.

The battle and operations around Cold Harbor (May 31-June 12, 1864) rank 6TH for total casualties (557) for an engagement for the State of Connecticut. The most intense fighting developed on June 3 and Barkhamsted had no casualties.

The Battle of Cold Harbor with 3 total casualties for Barkhamsted was the highest number of casualties for any single engagement of the war for the town.

Approximately 117,000 Federal and 60,000 Confederate troops participated in operations from May 28 to June 3. Roughly 13,000 Union casualties were recorded and perhaps there were 5,000 Confederate casualties.

84 MEN CREDITED TO BARKHAMSTED SERVED IN THE FOLLOWING CONNECTICUT ORGANIZATIONS

REGIMENT	TOTAL
2ND HEAVY ARTILLERY	22 (27%)
8TH	9 (11%)
13TH	6 (7%)
28TH	5 (6%)
5TH	5 (6%)
1ST HEAVY ARTILLERY	5 (6%)
10TH	4 (5%)
13TH BATTALION	4 (5%)
1ST CAVALRY	3 (4%)
1ST SQUADRON CAVALRY	3 (4%)
12TH	3 (4%)
2ND	2 (2%)
6TH	2 (2%)
7TH	2 (2%)
11TH	2 (2%)
12TH BATTALION	2 (2%)
14TH	2 (2%)
16TH	2 (2%)
22ND	2 (2%)
25TH	2 (2%)
27TH	2 (2%)
1ST	1
15TH	1
17TH	1
29TH	1

7% OF POPULATION

FIVE WERE KILLED

The first Barkhamsted soldier killed was Corporal Elijah White of Company C, 8TH Connecticut. He was killed at the Battle of Antietam, MD on September 17, 1862.

BARKHAMSTED SOLDIERS KILLED

PLACE	DATE	NO.
Antietam, MD (8TH)	9/17/62	1
Cold Harbor, VA (2 HA)	6/1/64	2
Cedar Creek, VA (13TH)	10/19/64	1
Harper's Ferry, WVA (1 CA)	4/1/65	1

THREE WERE CAPTURED

One Barkhamsted soldier died in captivity at Salisbury, NC.

BARKHAMSTED CAPTURED
*(1) DIED IN CAPTIVITY

PLACE	DATE	NO.
Chancellorsville, VA (27TH)	5/3/63	1
Plymouth, NC (16TH)	4/20/64	1
Cedar Creek, VA (12TH) *	10/19/64	1

TOTAL BARKHAMSTED CASUALTIES

DIED	8	10%
KILLED	5	6%
WOUNDED	9	11%
CAPTURED	3	4%
DESERTED	12	15%

NINE WERE WOUNDED

The first Barkhamsted soldier wounded was Private James E. Pelton of Company C, 8TH Connecticut. He was wounded at the Battle of Antietam, MD on September 17, 1862. He died two years later from disease. Three Barkhamsted soldiers died from wounds received during the war.

BARKHAMSTED WOUNDED
*(3) DIED FROM WOUNDS

PLACE	DATE	NO.
Antietam, MD (8TH)	9/17/62	1
Fredericksburg, VA (14TH) *	12/13/62	1
Port Hudson, LA (28TH)	6/14/63	1
Fort Wagner, SC (6TH) *	7/18/63	1
Drewry's Bluff, VA (8TH) *	5/16/64	1
Cold Harbor, VA (2 HA)	6/1/64	1
Cedar Creek, VA (2 HA)	10/19/64	2
Harper's Ferry, WVA (1 CA)	4/1/65	1

BERLIN
THE POPULATION IN 1860 WAS 2,146 (RANK 69)

THE MOST IMPORTANT DAY OF THE CIVIL WAR

APRIL 20, 1864
PLYMOUTH, NC

THE CONFEDERATE PLAN TO TAKE PLYMOUTH ENDED WHEN 2,800 UNION TROOPS SURRENDERED THE CITY

More soldiers credited to Berlin were listed as casualties (19) on this day than on any other day of the war. Eighteen soldiers were captured, and 1 was wounded & captured in the 16TH Connecticut. Eight died in prison.

The date April 20, 1864 ranks 6TH for total casualties (433) (1 killed, 2 missing, 12 wounded & captured, 418 captured) for a single day for the State of Connecticut. All of the casualties were at Plymouth, NC.

The Battle of Plymouth (April 20, 1864) ranks 9TH for total casualties (433) for an engagement for the State of Connecticut. Nearly half of all soldiers captured at Plymouth died in Southern prisons

The Battle of Plymouth with 19 total casualties for Berlin was the highest number of casualties for any single engagement of the war for the town.

When Confederate General Robert Hoke surrounded and captured the Union garrison at Plymouth, NC the Southern victory was the first in this military arena in quite some time. With aid from the two-gun ironclad *Albemarle* the Confederates were able to take advantage of the lack of suitable Union gunboats.

209 MEN CREDITED TO BERLIN SERVED IN THE FOLLOWING CONNECTICUT ORGANIZATIONS

REGIMENT	TOTAL
1ST HEAVY ARTILLERY	43 (20%)
16TH	31 (15%)
14TH	21 (10%)
5TH	14 (7%)
8TH	13 (6%)
7TH	10 (5%)
2ND HEAVY ARTILLERY	9 (4%)
1ST SQUADRON CAVALRY	8 (4%)
12TH	8 (4%)
29TH	8 (4%)
20TH	7 (3%)
25TH	7 (3%)
1ST LIGHT BATTERY	5 (2%)
6TH	5 (2%)
13TH	5 (2%)
22ND	5 (2%)
1ST CAVALRY	4 (2%)
1ST	4 (2%)
9TH	3 (1%)
21ST	3 (1%)
30TH	3 (1%)
3RD	2
12TH BATTALION	2
15TH	2
18TH	2
11TH	1
13TH BATTALION	1
10% OF POPULATION	

298

TWELVE WERE KILLED AND ONE WAS MISSING

The first Berlin soldier killed was Private James L. Bailey of Company B, 5TH Connecticut. He was killed at Cedar Mountain, VA on August 9, 1862.

BERLIN SOLDIERS KILLED
*(1) MISSING

PLACE	DATE	NO.
Cedar Mountain, VA (5TH)	8/9/62	1
Antietam, MD (16TH)	9/17/62	2
Pocotaligo, SC (6TH)	10/22/62	1
Fredericksburg, VA (14TH)	12/13/62	2
Morton's Ford, VA (14TH) *	2/6/64	1
James River, VA (7TH)	5/6/64	1
Wilderness, VA (14TH)	5/6/64	1
Cold Harbor, VA (2HA)	6/1/64	1
Cold Harbor, VA (14TH)	6/7/64	1
Ream's Station, VA (14TH)	8/25/64	1
Richmond, VA (29TH)	10/13/64	1

THIRTY WERE CAPTURED

Ten Berlin soldiers died in captivity. Five soldiers died at Andersonville Prison, GA, two at Florence, SC, one at Charleston, SC one at Salisbury, NC, and one at Wilmington, NC.

BERLIN CAPTURED
*(10) DIED IN CAPTIVITY

PLACE	DATE	NO.
Cold Harbor, VA (1HA)	6/23/62	1
Cold Harbor, VA (1HA)	6/27/62	1
Gunboat "Diana" (12TH) (1 WOUNDED)	3/28/63	1
Plymouth, NC (16TH) *(8) (1 WOUNDED)	4/20/64	19
Ely's Ford, VA (14TH)	5/9/64	1
North Anna River, VA (14TH) *	5/25/64	1
Piedmont, VA (18TH)	6/5/64	1
Bermuda Hundred, VA (7TH)	7/26/64	1
Cox's Mills, VA (8TH) *	9/16/64	1
Kinston, NC (15TH)	3/8/65	2

TOTAL BERLIN CASUALTIES

DIED	34	16%
KILLED/MISSING	13	6%
WOUNDED	27	13%
CAPTURED	30	14%
DESERTED	26	12%

TWENTY-SEVEN WERE WOUNDED

The first Berlin soldiers wounded were Corporal Charles C. Bowers, and Privates George F. Chamberlain, Charles N. Penfield, Henry L. Porter, Edward Moore, and Walter E. Smith of the 16TH Connecticut. They were wounded at the Battle of Antietam, MD on September 17, 1862 and one soldier died from his wounds. Four Berlin soldiers died from wounds received during the war.

BERLIN WOUNDED
*(4) DIED FROM WOUNDS

PLACE	DATE	NO.
Antietam, MD (14TH,16TH) *1	9/17/62	7
Fredericksburg, VA (14TH)	12/13/62	2
Irish Bend, LA (25TH)	4/14/63	1
Gettysburg, PA (14TH)	7/3/63	1
Fort Wagner, SC (6TH)	7/18/63	1
Wilderness, VA (14TH)	5/6/64	1
Resaca, GA (5TH)	5/15/64	1
Drewry's Bluff, VA (6TH)	5/16/64	1
Cold Harbor, VA (2HA)	6/1/64	2
Bermuda Hundred, VA (6TH)	6/17/64	1
Culp's Farm, GA (5TH) *	6/22/64	1
Peach Tree Creek, GA (20TH)	7/20/64	1
Petersburg, VA (1HA)	7/24/64	1
Petersburg, VA (30TH)	7/30/64	1
Deep Bottom, VA (7TH)	8/16/64	1
Kell House, VA (29TH) *2	10/27/64	2
Summit Patrick, VA (12TH)	2/2/65	1
Silver Run, NC (20TH)	3/16/65	1

BETHANY
THE POPULATION IN 1860 WAS 974 (RANK 139)

THE MOST IMPORTANT DAY
OF THE CIVIL WAR
DECEMBER 14, 1862
KINSTON, NC
THE OUTNUMBERED
CONFEDERATES
RETREATED

More soldiers credited to Bethany were listed as casaulties on December 14, 1862 at Kinston, NC (3) and on May 3, 1863 at Chancellorsville, VA (3) than on any other days of the war. The casualties at Kinston were the most serious. One soldier was killed, and 2 were wounded in the 10TH Connecticut. One of the wounded soldiers died.

The date December 14, 1862 ranks 30TH for total casualties (104) (15 killed, 89 wounded) for a single day for the State of Connecticut. There were 103 casualties at Kinston, NC and 1 casualty at Fredericksburg, VA.

The First Battle of Kinston (December 14, 1862) ranks 22ND for total casualties (103) for an engagement for the State of Connecticut.

The First Battle of Kinston with three total casualties for Bethany, was tied with the Battle of Chancellorsville, VA (May 1863), the Battle of Gettysburg, PA (July 1863), and the Battle of Drewry's Bluff, VA (May 1864) for the highest number of casualties for any single engagement of the war for the town.

In December 1862, the Union Army under General John G. Foster undertook an expedition from New Bern, NC to destroy the Wilmington & Weldon Railroad at Goldsboro. A battle ensued on December 14 near Kinston Bridge. The Confederates were outnumbered and retreated North of the Neuse River.

70 MEN CREDITED TO BETHANY SERVED IN THE FOLLOWING CONNECTICUT ORGANIZATIONS

REGIMENT	TOTAL
10TH	11 (16%)
27TH	11 (16%)
2ND HEAVY ARTILLERY	6 (9%)
11TH	6 (9%)
1ST HEAVY ARTILLERY	5 (7%)
20TH	5 (7%)
29TH	5 (7%)
7TH	4 (6%)
13TH	4 (6%)
1ST CAVALRY	3 (4%)
5TH	3 (4%)
9TH	3 (4%)
6TH	2 (3%)
13TH BATTALION	2 (3%)
23RD	2 (3%)
3RD	1
15TH	1
21ST	1

7% OF POPULATION

THREE WERE KILLED

The first Bethany soldier killed was Private Sherald A. Brooks of Company K, 10TH Connecticut. He was killed at Kinston, NC on December 14, 1862.

BETHANY SOLDIERS KILLED

PLACE	DATE	NO.
Kinston, NC (10TH)	12/14/62	1
Stafford CH, VA (20TH)	12/2/63	1
Drewry's Bluff, VA (10TH)	5/14/64	1

FIVE WERE CAPTURED

One Bethany soldier died in captivity at Salisbury, NC.

BETHANY CAPTURED
*(1) DIED IN CAPTIVITY

PLACE	DATE	NO.
Chancellorsville, VA (27TH)	5/3/63	3
Drewry's Bluff, VA (11TH)	5/16/64	1
Cedar Creek, VA (13TH) *	10/19/64	1

TOTAL BETHANY CASUALTIES

DIED	8	11%
KILLED	3	4%
WOUNDED	9	13%
CAPTURED	5	7%
DESERTED	13	19%

NINE WERE WOUNDED

The first Bethany soldiers wounded were Privates Edgar Beecher and Luther Doolittle of Company K, 10TH Connecticut. Both were wounded at Kinston, NC on December 14, 1862. Private Doolittle died from his wound and Private Beecher died later from a wound received at Deep Bottom, VA in 1864. Two Bethany soldiers died from wounds received during the war.

BETHANY WOUNDED
*(2) DIED FROM WOUNDS

PLACE	DATE	NO.
Kinston, NC (10TH) *1	12/14/62	2
Gettysburg, PA (20TH)	7/3/63	2
Drewry's Bluff, VA (7TH)	5/16/64	1
Dallas, GA (5TH)	5/25/64	1
Deep Bottom, VA (10TH) *	8/1/64	1
Petersburg, VA (10TH)	9/13/64	1
Winchester, VA (13TH)	9/19/64	1

BETHEL

THE POPULATION IN 1860 WAS 1,711 (RANK 86)

THE MOST IMPORTANT DAY OF THE CIVIL WAR

MAY 2, 1863

CHANCELLORSVILLE, VA

THE SECOND DAY OF THE BATTLE

More soldiers credited to Bethel were listed as casualties (5) on this day than on any other day of the war. Two soldiers were wounded, 2 were captured, and 1 was wounded & captured in the 5TH and 17TH Connecticut. They all survived the war.

The date May 2, 1863 ranks 22ND for total casualties (121) (8 killed, 30 wounded, 62 captured, 21 wounded & captured) for the State of Connecticut. All of the casualties were at Chancellorsville.

The Battle of Chancellorsville (May 1-3, 1863) ranks 2ND for total casualties (677) for an engagement for the State of Connecticut.. The most intense fighting developed on May 3 and Bethel had no casualties on that day.

The Battle of Chancellorsville with 5 total casualties for Bethel was the highest number of casualties for any single engagement of the war for the town.

The Battle of Chancellorsville was an enormous defeat for the more than 70,000 Union soldiers who had moved against the flank and rear of 40,000 Confederate soldiers. Unfortunately, the Union Army had pulled back and had gone on the defensive around Chancellorsville. The Confederate victory was tainted however, by the loss of Confederate Major General "Stonewall" Jackson.

126 MEN CREDITED TO BETHEL SERVED IN THE FOLLOWING CONNECTICUT ORGANIZATIONS

REGIMENT	TOTAL
23RD	28 (22%)
17TH	26 (20%)
5TH	13 (10%)
6TH	12 (9%)
7TH	8 (6%)
2ND HEAVY ARTILLERY	6 (6%)
10TH	6 (5%)
11TH	5 (4%)
1ST CAVALRY	5 (4%)
1ST HEAVY ARTILLERY	4 (3%)
9TH	4 (3%)
15TH	4 (3%)
12TH	3 (2%)
13TH	3 (2%)
20TH	3 (2%)
3RD	2 (2%)
12TH BATTALION	2 (2%)
8TH	2 (2%)
29TH	2 (2%)
9TH BATTALION	1
13TH BATTALION	1
28TH	1

7% OF POPULATION

THREE WERE KILLED

The first Bethel soldier killed was Sergeant Bethel S. Barnum of Company C, 17TH Connecticut. He was killed on July 1, 1863 at the Battle of Gettysburg, PA.

BETHEL SOLDIERS KILLED

PLACE	DATE	NO.
Gettysburg, PA (17TH)	7/1/63	1
Gettysburg, PA (17TH)	7/2/63	1
Olustee, FL (7th)	2/20/64	1

SIXTEEN WERE CAPTURED

Four Bethel soldiers died in captivity. Two died in Andersonville Prison, GA and two died in Salisbury, NC.

BETHEL CAPTURED
* (4) DIED IN CAPTIVITY

PLACE	DATE	NO.
Cedar Mountain, VA (5TH)	8/9/62	2
Chancellorsville, VA (5,17[TH])	5/2/63	3
(1 WOUNDED)		
Brashear City, LA (23RD)	6/23/63	3
Drewry's Bluff, VA (6,7[TH]) *2	5/16/64	3
Cedar Creek, VA (2HA) *2	10/19/64	2
(2 WOUNDED)		
Dunn's Lake, FL (17TH)	2/5/65	2
Kinston, NC	3/8/65	1

TOTAL BETHEL CASUALTIES

DIED	15	12%
KILLED	3	2%
WOUNDED	22	17%
CAPTURED	16	13%
DESERTED	10	8%

TWENTY-TWO WERE WOUNDED

The first Bethel soldier wounded was Private Joseph Brotherton of Co. C, 11TH Connecticut. He was wounded at New Bern, NC on March 14, 1862 and recovered from his wound. Two Bethel soldiers died from a wound received in the war.

BETHEL WOUNDED
* (2) DIED FROM WOUNDS

PLACE	DATE	NO.
New Bern, NC (11TH)	3/14/62	1
Cedar Mountain, VA (5TH)	8/9/62	1
Antietam, MD (11TH)	9/17/62	1
Pocotaligo, SC (7TH)	10/22/62	1
Irish Bend, LA (13TH)	4/14/63	1
Chancellorsville, VA (5,17[TH])	5/2/63	2
Gettysburg, PA (17TH)	7/1/63	2
Gettysburg, PA (17TH)	7/3/63	1
Berwick, LA (23RD)	6/12/63	1
Drewry's Bluff, VA (6TH)	5/16/64	1
Cold Harbor, VA (2HA)	6/1/64	1
Cold Harbor, VA (11TH)	6/3/64	1
Petersburg, VA (7TH) *	6/6/64	1
Deep Bottom, VA (6,10[TH])	8/14/64	2
Newmarket Road, VA (6TH)	9/1/64	1
Winchester, VA (2HA)	9/19/64	1
Darbytown Road, VA (10TH)*	10/13/64	1
Goldsboro, NC (5TH)	3/19/65	1
Atlanta, GA (13TH)	6/1/65	1

BETHLEHEM
THE POPULATION IN 1860 WAS 815 (RANK 148)

THE MOST IMPORTANT DAY OF THE CIVIL WAR

MAY 16, 1864
DREWRY'S BLUFF , VA

AN OBSTACLE ON THE WAY TO RICHMOND

More soldiers credited to Bethlehem were listed as casualties (2) on September 17, 1862 at Antietam, MD and on May 16, 1864 at Drewry's Bluff, VA than on any other days of the war. The casualties at Drewry's Bluff were the most serious. One soldier was wounded, and 1 was captured in and 6TH and 11TH Connecticut. They both survived the war

The date May 16, 1864 ranks 4th for total casualties (560) (52 killed, 3 missing, 224 wounded, 243 captured, 38 wounded & captured) for a single day for the State of Connecticut. The Battle of Drewry's Bluff accounted for 545 casualties. The 15 other casualties were scattered about Virginia.

The Battle of Drewry's Bluff (May 13-17, 1864), also called Fort Darling, ranks 3rd for total casualties (634) for an engagement for the State of Connecticut. The most intense fighting developed on May 16. Bethlehem had no other casualties.

The Battle of Drewry's Bluff with 3 total casualties for Bethlehem was the highest number of casualties for any single engagement of the war for the town.

The Confederate attack at Drewry's Bluff forced the Union Army to retreat to Bermuda Hundred. The civil war would have concluded sooner had the Union Army been victorious.

46 MEN CREDITED TO BETHLEHEM SERVED IN THE FOLLOWING CONNECTICUT ORGANIZATIONS

REGIMENT	TOTAL
2ND HEAVY ARTILLERY	12 (26%)
8TH	7 (15%)
17TH	7 (15%)
11TH	6 (13%)
1ST CAVALRY	4 (9%)
6TH	4 (9%)
23RD	2 (4%)
1ST HEAVY ARTILLERY	1
5TH	1
10TH	1
15TH	1
27TH	1
30TH	1

7% OF POPULATION

TWO WERE KILLED

The first Bethlehem soldier killed was Private Felix Clary of Company F, 5TH Connecticut. He was killed at Atlanta, GA on July 30, 1864.

BETHLEHEM SOLDIERS KILLED

PLACE	DATE	NO.
Atlanta, GA (5TH)	7/30/64	1
Cedar Creek, VA (2HA)	10/19/64	1

FIVE WERE CAPTURED

No Bethlehem soldier died in captivity.

BETHLEHEM CAPTURED
NONE DIED IN CAPTIVITY

PLACE	DATE	NO.
Gettysburg, PA (17TH)	7/3/63	1
Drewry's Bluff, VA (6TH, 11TH) (1 WOUNDED)	5/16/64	2
Cedar Creek, VA (1CA)	11/12/64	1

TOTAL BETHLEHEM CASUALTIES

DIED	4	9%
KILLED	2	4%
WOUNDED	6	13%
CAPTURED	4	9%
DESERTED	12	26%

SIX WERE WOUNDED

The first Bethlehem soldiers wounded were Sergeant Major George W. Garthwait and Private Lucius S. Benton of the 11TH Connecticut. Both were wounded at the Battle of Antietam, MD on September 17, 1862 and both recovered from their wounds. One Bethlehem soldier died from a wound received during the war.

BETHLEHEM WOUNDED
*(1) DIED FROM WOUNDS

PLACE	DATE	NO.
Antietam, MD (11TH)	9/17/62	2
Bermuda Hundred, VA (6TH) *	6/17/64	1
Cedar Creek, VA (2HA)	9/20/64	1
Fort Harrison, VA (8TH)	10/2/64	1
Cedar Creek, VA (2HA)	10/19/64	1

BLOOMFIELD
THE POPULATION IN 1860 WAS 1,410 (RANK 104)

THE MOST IMPORTANT DAY OF THE CIVIL WAR

SEPTEMBER 17, 1862

SHARPSBURG, MD (ANTIETAM)

CONNECTICUT HAD MORE CASUALTIES FOR ONE DAY THAN ON ANY OTHER DAY OF THE WAR

124 MEN CREDITED TO BLOOMFIELD SERVED IN THE FOLLOWING CONNECTICUT ORGANIZATIONS

More soldiers credited to Bloomfield were listed as casualties (6) on this day than on any other day of the war. One soldier was killed and 5 were wounded in the 14TH and 16TH Connecticut. One of the wounded died.

The date September 17, 1862 ranks 1ST for total casualties (687) (131 killed, 2 missing, 515 wounded, 21 captured, 18 wounded & captured) for a single day for the State of Connecticut. All of the casualties were at Antietam.

The Battle of Antietam (September 16-17, 1862) ranks 1ST for total casualties (689) for an engagement for the State of Connecticut. The most intense fighting was on September 17. Bloomfield had all of its casualties on that day.

The Battle of Antietam with 6 total casualties for Bloomfield was the highest number of casualties for any single engagement of the war for the town.

Roughly 12,400 Union casualties were recorded and perhaps there were 10,300 Confederate casualties. Antietam proved to be one of the turning points of the war. It ended Lee's 1862 invasion of the North.

REGIMENT	TOTAL
22ND	44 (36%)
14TH	18 (15%)
10TH	9 (7%)
8TH	6 (5%)
29TH	6 (5%)
7TH	5 (4%)
6TH	5 (4%)
16TH	4 (3%)
1ST HEAVY ARTILLERY	3 (2%)
2ND HEAVY ARTILLERY	3 (2%)
11TH	3 (2%)
1ST CAVALRY	3 (2%)
21ST	3 (2%)
12TH BATTALION	2 (2%)
5TH	2 (2%)
12TH	2 (2%)
20TH	2 (2%)
13TH BATTALION	1
30TH	1
2ND	1
9TH	1
1ST SQUADRON CAVALRY	1
1ST LIGHT BATTERY	1
13TH	1

7% OF POPULATION

FOUR WERE KILLED

The first Bloomfield soldier killed was Sergeant Frederick R. Eno of Company F, 14TH Connecticut. He was killed at the Battle of Antietam, MD on September 17, 1862.

BLOOMFIELD SOLDIERS KILLED

PLACE	DATE	NO.
Antietam, MD (14TH)	9/17/62	1
Fredericksburg, VA (14TH)	12/13/62	1
Gettysburg, PA (14TH)	7/3/63	1
Drewry's Bluff, VA (21ST)	5/16/64	1

TWELVE WERE CAPTURED

No Bloomfield soldiers died in captivity.

BLOOMFIELDCAPTURED
NONE DIED IN CAPTIVITY

PLACE	DATE	NO.
Pattersonville, LA (12TH)	3/27/63	1
Brashear City, LA (12TH)	6/23/63	1
Fort Wagner, SC (7TH)	7/11/63	1
Plymouth, NC (16TH)	4/20/64	1
Craig's Church, VA (1CA)	5/5/64	1
Drewry's Bluff, VA (11TH)	5/16/64	2
Bermuda Hundred, VA (7TH)	6/2/64	1
Ream's Station, VA (14TH)	8/25/64	1
Cedar Creek, VA ((12TH)	10/19/64	1
Boydton Plank Rd, VA (14TH)	10/27/64	1
Madison, GA (5TH)	11/20/64	1

TOTAL BLOOMFIELD CASUALTIES

DIED	7	6%
KILLED	4	3%
WOUNDED	17	14%
CAPTURED	12	10%
DESERTED	20	16%

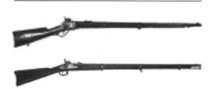

SEVENTEEN WERE WOUNDED

The first Bloomfield soldiers wounded was Privates Edmund I. Field, William Ashwell, J. Frank Smith, Moses G. Griswold and Martin D. Cowles of the 14TH Connecticut. They were wounded at the Battle of Antietam, MD on September 17, 1862. Private Field died from his wound. He was the only Bloomfield soldier who died from a wound received during the war.

BLOOMFIELD WOUNDED
*(1) DIED FROM WOUNDS

PLACE	DATE	NO.
Antietam, MD (14Th, 16TH) * 1	9/17/62	5
Fredericksburg, VA (14TH)	12/13/62	3
Chancellorsville, VA (14TH)	5/3/63	2
Morton's Ford, VA (14TH)	2/6/64	1
Drewry's Bluff, VA (7TH)	5/16/64	1
Strawberry Plains, VA (14TH)	7/26/64	1
Winchester, VA (12TH)	9/19/64	1
Darbytown Rd. VA (10TH)	10/13/64	1
Charles City Road, VA (7TH)	10/27/64	1
Petersburg, VA (10TH)	4/2/65	1

BOLTON
THE POPULATION IN 1860 WAS 683 (RANK 155)

THE MOST IMPORTANT DAY OF THE CIVIL WAR

JUNE 3, 1864

COLD HARBOR, VA

THE BATTLE WAS LEE'S LAST GREAT VICTORY

Bolton had no day in the war with more than 1 casualty. The soldiers of Bolton took part in 8 engagements. The most serious casualty was at Cold Harbor. One soldier was wounded in the 11TH Connecticut and he died from his wound.

The date June 3, 1864 ranks 12TH for total casualties (196) (24 killed, 2 missing, 168 wounded, 2 captured) for a single day for the State of Connecticut. Cold Harbor accounted for 190 casualties. There were also 4 casualties at Petersburg, VA and 2 at Dallas, GA.

The battle and operations around Cold Harbor (May 31-June 12, 1864) rank 6TH for total casualties (557) for an engagement for the State of Connecticut. The most intense fighting was on June 3. Bolton also had one casualty on June 1.

The Battle of Cold Harbor with 2 total casualties for Bolton was the highest number of casualties any single engagement of the war for the town.

Approximately 117,000 Federal and 60,000 Confederate troops participated in operations from May 28 to June 3. Roughly 13,000 Union casualties were recorded and perhaps there were 5,000 Confederate casualties.

48 MEN CREDITED TO BOLTON SERVED IN THE FOLLOWING CONNECTICUT ORGANIZATIONS

REGIMENT	TOTAL
16TH	12 (25%)
1ST HEAVY ARTILLERY	9 (19%)
22ND	8 (17%)
7TH	5 (10%)
2ND HEAVY ARTILLERY	3 (6%)
11TH	3 (6%)
1ST LIGHT BATTERY	2 (4%)
12TH	2 (4%)
12TH BATTALION	2 (4%)
25TH	2 (4%)
30TH	2 (4%)
5TH	1
6TH	1
14TH	1

7% OF POPULATION

NO BOLTON SOLDIERS WERE KILLED OR MISSING

TWO WERE CAPTURED

One Bolton soldier died in captivity at Andersonville Prison, GA.

BOLTON CAPTURED
*(1) DIED IN CAPTIVITY

PLACE	DATE	NO.
Charleston, SC (7TH) *	8/20/63	1
Plymouth, NC (16TH)	4/20/64	1

TOTAL BOLTON CASUALTIES

DIED	7	15%
KILLED	0	0%
WOUNDED	8	17%
CAPTURED	2	4%
DESERTED	4	8%

EIGHT WERE WOUNDED

The first Bolton soldier wounded was Private William Massey of Company H, 16TH Connecticut. He was wounded at the Battle of Antietam, MD on September 17, 1862 and recovered from his wound. Two Bolton soldier died from a wound received during the war.

BOLTON WOUNDED
*(2) DIED FROM WOUNDS

PLACE	DATE	NO.
Antietam, MD (16TH)	9/17/62	1
Proctor's Creek, VA (1LB)	5/14/64	1
Drewry's Bluff, VA (6TH)	5/15/64	1
Cold Harbor, VA (2HA)	6/1/64	1
Cold Harbor, VA (11TH) *	6/3/64	1
Bermuda Hundred, VA (7TH)	6/18/64	1
Winchester, VA (2HA)	9/19/64	1
Railroad Accident, VA (6TH)*	Unknown	1

BOZRAH
THE POPULATION IN 1860 WAS 1,216 (RANK 119)

THE MOST IMPORTANT DAY OF THE CIVIL WAR

JUNE 15 1863

WINCHESTER, VA

THE ENTIRE UNION ARMY WAS NEARLY CAPTURED AT THE SECOND BATTLE OF WINCHESTER

More soldiers credited to Bozrah were listed as casualties (8) on this day than on any other day of the war. Eight soldiers were captured in the 18TH Connecticut. One died in prison.

The date June 15, 1863 ranks 2ND for total casualties (595) (23 killed, 11 wounded, 520 captured, 41 wounded & captured) for a single day for the State of Connecticut. There were 592 casualties at Winchester, VA and 3 casualties at Port Hudson, LA.

The Second Battle of Winchester (June 13-15) ranks 5TH for total casualties (592) for an engagement for the State of Connecticut. The most intense fighting was on June 15. Bozrah had all its casualites on that day.

The Second Battle of Winchester with 8 total casualties for Bozrah was the highest number of casualties for any single engagement of the war for the town.

Winchester was one of the most contested locations in the Civil War. It changed hands seventy-two times.

56 MEN CREDITED TO BOZRAH SERVED IN THE FOLLOWING CONNECTICUT ORGANIZATIONS

REGIMENT	TOTAL
18TH	12 (21%)
7TH	6 (11%)
1ST HEAVY ARTILLERY	5 (9%)
1ST CAVALRY	5 (9%)
13TH	5 (9%)
3RD	4 (7%)
11TH	4 (7%)
21ST	4 (7%)
26TH	4 (7%)
8TH	3 (5%)
29TH	3 (5%)
2ND HEAVY ARTILLERY	2 (4%)
2ND	2 (4%)
5TH	1
13TH BATTALION	1
15TH	1

5% OF POPULATION

THREE WERE KILLED

The first Bozrah soldier killed was Private Thomas Lawlor of Company H, 11TH Connecticut. He was killed at the Battle of Antietam, MD on September 17, 1862.

BOZRAH SOLDIERS KILLED

PLACE	DATE	NO.
Antietam, MD (11TH)	9/17/62	1
Bermuda Hundred, VA (7TH)	6/17/64	1
Ream's Station, VA (1CA)	6/29/64	1

THIRTEEN WERE CAPTURED

Two Bozrah soldiers died in captivity at Andersonville Prison, GA.

BOZRAH CAPTURED
*(2) DIED IN CAPTIVITY

PLACE	DATE	NO.
Antietam, MD (8TH)	9/17/62	1
Winchester, VA (18TH) *1	6/15/63	8
Smithfield, VA (21ST) *	2/1/64	1
Bermuda Hundred, VA (7TH)	6/2/64	1
(WOUNDED)		
Winchester, VA (18TH)	7/24/64	1
(1 WOUNDED)		
Winchester, VA (13TH)	9/19/64	1

TOTAL BOZRAH CASUALTIES

DIED	**7**	**13%**
KILLED	**3**	**5%**
WOUNDED	**8**	**14%**
CAPTURED	**13**	**23%**
DESERTED	**2**	**4%**

EIGHT WERE WOUNDED

The first Bozrah soldier wounded was Sergeant John Brown of Company H, 11TH Connecticut. He was wounded at the Battle of Antietam, MD on September 17, 1862 and recovered from his wound. Three Bozrah soldiers died from wounds received during the war.

BOZRAH WOUNDED
*(3) DIED FROM WOUNDS

PLACE	DATE	NO.
Antietam, MD (11TH)	9/17/62	1
Port Hudson, LA (26TH) *	5/27/63	1
Port Hudson, LA (26TH) *	6/14/63	1
Fort Darling, VA (8TH) *	5/16/64	1
Cold Harbor, VA (2HA)	6/1/64	1
Piedmont, VA (18TH)	6/5/64	1
Bermuda Hundred, VA (7TH)	6/17/64	1
Cedar Creek, VA (2HA)	10/19/64	1

BRANFORD
THE POPULATION IN 1860 WAS 2,123 (RANK 72)

THE MOST IMPORTANT DAY OF THE CIVIL WAR

MAY 3, 1863

CHANCELLORSVILLE, VA

THE THIRD DAY OF THE BATTLE

More soldiers credited to Branford were listed as casualties (15) on this day than on any other day of the war. Fifteen soldiers were captured in the 27TH Connecticut. All survived the war.

The date May 3, 1863 ranks 3RD for total casualties (577) (36 killed, 1 missing, 138 wounded, 372 captured, 29 wounded & captured) for a single day for the State of Connecticut. The most casualties were at Chancellorsville (556) but there were also casualties at Providence Church Road, VA (12), Suffolk, VA (6), Port Hudson, LA (2) and Fredericksburg, VA (1).

The Battle of Chancellorsville (May 1-3, 1863) ranks 2ND for total casualties (677) for an engagement for the State of Connecticut. The most intense fighting developed on May 3 and Branford had all of its casualties on that date.

The Battle of Chancellorsville with 15 total casualties for Branford was the highest number of casualties for any single engagement of the war for the town.

The Battle of Chancellorsville was an enormous defeat for the more than 70,000 Union soldiers who had moved against the flank and rear of 40,000 Confederate soldiers. Unfortunately, the Union Army had pulled back and had gone on the defensive around Chancellorsville. The Confederate victory was tainted however, by the loss of Confederate Major General "Stonewall" Jackson.

199 MEN CREDITED TO BRANFORD SERVED IN THE FOLLOWING CONNECTICUT ORGANIZATIONS

REGIMENT	TOTAL
27TH	39 (20%)
15TH	22 (11%)
10TH	18 (9%)
11TH	14 (7%)
7TH	14 (7%)
1ST CAVALRY	13 (6%)
5TH	13 (4%)
1ST HEAVY ARTILLERY	12 (2%)
12TH	12 (2%)
29TH	12 (2%)
2ND HEAVY ARTILLERY	9 (2%)
20TH	8 (2%)
6TH	6 (3%)
14TH	6 (3%)
13TH	4 (2%)
1ST LIGHT BATTERY	3 (2%)
8TH	3 (2%)
9TH	3 (2%)
12TH BATTALION	3 (2%)
13TH BATTALION	2 (1%)
3RD	1
9TH BATTALION	1
17TH	1
30TH	1

9% OF POPULATION

THREE WERE KILLED

The first Branford soldier killed was Private Joseph Barker of Company K, 6TH Connecticut. He was killed at Drewry's Bluff, VA on May 16, 1864

BRANFORD SOLDIERS KILLED

PLACE	DATE	NO.
Drewry's Bluff, VA (6TH)	5/16/64	1
Darbytown Road, VA (10TH)	10/13/64	1
Cedar Creek, VA (2HA)	10/19/64	1

THIRTY-FOUR WERE CAPTURED

Three Branford soldiers died in captivity. Two died at Millen, GA and one died at Salisbury, NC.

BRANFORD CAPTURED
*(3) DIED IN CAPTIVITY

PLACE	DATE	NO.
Unknown Place (14TH)		1
Chancellorsville, VA (27TH)	5/3/63	15
Frederick, MD (1 CA)	6/20/63	1
Gettysburg, PA (27TH)	7/2/63	1
St Augustine, FLA (10TH) *	12/30/63	1
Drewry's Bluff, VA (7,11TH) *2	5/16/64	3
(1 WOUNDED)		
Richmond, VA (7TH)	10/1/64	1
Cedar Run Church, VA (1 CA)	10/17/64	1
Cedar Creek, VA (12TH)	10/19/64	2
Kinston, NC (15TH)	3/8/65	7
(1 WOUNDED)		
New Market, VA (1 CA)	3/9/65	1

TOTAL BRANFORD CASUALTIES

DIED	23	12%
KILLED	3	2%
WOUNDED	34	17%
CAPTURED	35	18%
DESERTED	28	14%

THIRTY-THREE WERE WOUNDED

The first Branford soldier wounded was Private Elizur C. Johnson of Company A, 10TH Connecticut. He was wounded at Roanoke Island, NC on February 8, 1862 and recovered from his wound. Four Branford soldiers died from wounds received during the war.

BRANFORD WOUNDED
*(4) DIED FROM WOUNDS

PLACE	DATE	NO.
Roanoke Island, NC (10TH)	2/8/62	1
Cedar Mountain, VA (5TH)	8/9/62	1
Antietam, MD (8TH) *	9/17/62	1
Pocotaligo, SC (7TH)	10/22/62	1
Georgia Landing, LA (12TH)	10/27/62	1
Fredericksburg, VA (27TH) *2	12/13/62	5
Kinston, NC (10TH)	12/14/62	3
Edenton Road, VA (15TH)	4/24/63	1
Port Hudson, LA (12TH)	6/10/63	1
Morton's Ford, VA (14TH)	2/6/64	2
Unknown Location (14TH)	5/10/64	1
Drewry's Bluff, VA (7TH)	5/14/64	2
Spottsylvania, VA (14TH)	5/19/64	1
Petersburg, VA (11TH)	6/16/64	1
Marietta, GA (5TH)	6/19/64	1
Petersburg, VA (2HA) *	6/22/64	1
Deep Bottom, VA (10TH)	8/1/64	1
Deep Bottom, VA (6TH)	8/14/64	1
Richmond, VA (10TH)	10/13/64	1
Cedar Creek, VA (13TH)	10/19/64	1
Fort Fisher, NC (7TH)	1/14/65	1
Petersburg, VA (10TH)	4/2/65	1
Fort Gregg, VA (10TH)	4/2/65	3

BRIDGEPORT
THE POPULATION IN 1860 WAS 13,299 (RANK 4)

THE MOST IMPORTANT DAY OF THE CIVIL WAR

OCTOBER 19, 1864

CEDAR CREEK, VA

THE LAST MAJOR BATTLE OF THE 1864 SHENANDOAH VALLEY CAMPAIGN WAS A UNION TRIUMPH

More soldiers credited to Bridgeport were listed as casualties (25) on this day than on any other day of the war. Three soldiers were killed, 4 were wounded, and 18 were captured in the 2ND Connecticut Heavy Artillery, 9TH, 12TH and 13TH Connecticut Infantry. Three eventually died.

The date October 19, 1864 ranks 7TH for total casualties (417) (48 killed, 2 missing, 204 wounded, 153 captured, 10 wounded & captured) for a single day for the State of Connecticut. The Battle of Cedar Creek accounted for 415 casualties. There were 2 other casualties in the neighboringing towns

The Battle of Cedar Creek (October 19, 1864) ranks 10TH for total casualties (415) for an engagement for the State of Connecticut.

The Battle of Cedar Creek with 25 total casualties for Bridgeport was the highest number of casualties for any single engagement of the war for the city.

The news of the Union triumph at Cedar Creek assured a Republican victory in the elections of November 1864 and the prosecution of the war to its end on President Abraham Lincoln's and Lieutenant General Ulysses S. Grant's terms.

1284 MEN CREDITED TO BRIDGEPORT SERVED IN THE FOLLOWING CONNECTICUT ORGANIZATIONS

REGIMENT	TOTAL
17TH	141 (11%)
2ND LIGHT BATTERY	131 (10%)
1ST	130 (10%)
6TH	127 (10%)
9TH	123 (10%)
2ND HEAVY ARTILLERY	102 (8%)
1ST CAVALRY	79 (6%)
14TH	74 (6%)
1ST HEAVY ARTILLERY	68 (5%)
12TH	59 (5%)
23RD	48 (4%)
9TH BATTALION	45 (3%)
3RD	40 (3%)
7TH	40 (3%)
10TH	37 (3%)
24TH	33 (2%)
8TH	28 (2%)
11TH	25 (2%)
30TH	24 (2%)
12TH BATTALION	22 (2%)
13TH	19 (1%)
5TH	15 (1%)
29TH	15 (1%)
13TH BATTALION	8
16TH	8
1ST LIGHT BATTERY	7
20TH	7
15TH	4
1ST SQUADRON CAVALRY	2
18TH	2
2ND	1
22ND	1
25TH	1
28TH	1

10% OF POPULATION

TOTAL BRIDGEPORT CASUALTIES

DIED	122	9%
KILLED/MISSING	41	3%
WOUNDED	175	14%
CAPTURED	100	8%
DESERTED	153	12%

THIRTY-FIVE WERE KILLED AND SIX WERE MISSING

The first Bridgeport soldiers killed were Privates Michael Maddigan and Thaddeus W. Lewis of Company A, 14TH Connecticut. They were killed at the Battle of Antietam, MD on September 17, 1862.

BRIDGEPORT SOLDIERS KILLED MISSING*

PLACE	DATE	NO.
Antietam, MD (14TH)	9/17/62	2
Pocotaligo, SC (6TH)	10/22/62	2
Fredericksburg, VA (14TH)	12/13/62	1
Chancellorsville, VA (17TH)	5/2/63	1
Chancellorsville, VA (20TH)	5/3/63	1
Brashear City, LA (23RD)	6/23/63	1
Gettysburg, PA (17TH) *(1)	7/1/63	3
Ft. Wagner, SC (7TH)	7/11/63	1
Ft. Wagner, SC (6TH) * (2)	7/18/63	4
New Orleans, LA (12TH) (DROWNED)	7/23/63	1
Alexandria, LA (13TH)	4/11/64	1
Wilderness, VA (14TH)	5/6/64	1
Strawberry Hill, VA (1 CA)	5/12/64	1
Ft. Darling, VA (8TH)	5/16/64	1
Drewry's Bluff, VA (10TH)	5/16/64	1
Cold Harbor, VA (2 HA)	6/1/64	1
Petersburg, VA (30TH) *	7/30/64	1
Deep Bottom, VA (6TH) *	8/16/64	1
Ream's Station, VA (14TH)*(1)	8/25/64	2
Petersburg, VA (7TH)	9/3/64	1
Cedar Creek, VA (2 HA)	10/19/64	1
Cedar Creek, VA (12TH)	10/19/64	1
Drowned at Sea (2 LB)	12/22/64	1
Dunn's Lake, FLA (17TH)	2/5/65	1
Hatcher's Run, VA (14TH)	2/5/65	1
Kinston, NC (15TH)	3/8/65	1
Ashland, VA (1 CA)	3/15/65	1
Ft. Gregg, VA (10TH)	4/2/65	1
Blakely, AL (2 LB)	4/9/65	1

ONE HUNDRED WERE CAPTURED

Twelve Bridgeport soldiers died in captivity. Seven died at Andersonville, GA Prison, three died at Salisbury, NC, two died at Libby Prison, Richmond, VA.

BRIDGEPORT CAPTURED (12) DIED IN CAPTIVITY

PLACE	DATE	NO.
Bull Run, VA (1ST, 3RD) (1 WOUNDED)	7/21/61	7
Wreck "Union", NC (7TH)	11/4/61	1
Cedar Mountain, VA (5TH)	8/9/62	1
Gloucester Point, VA (7TH) *	2/10/63	1
Pattersonville, LA (12TH)	3/29/63	1
Chancellorsville, VA (17TH) (3 WOUNDED)	5/2/63	5
Chancellorsville, VA (14TH)	5/3/63	1
Alexandria, LA (12TH)	5/16/63	1
Winchester, VA (18TH)	6/15/63	1
Brashear City, LA (23RD)	6/23/63	3
Gettysburg, PA (17TH)	7/1/63	7
Gettysburg, PA (14TH)	7/2/63	2
Gettysburg, PA (14, 17TH)	7/3/63	2
Fort Wagner, SC (7TH)	7/11/63	3
Fort Wagner, SC (6TH) *1	7/18/63	4
Warrenton, VA (14TH) *	7/20/63	1
Loudon County, VA (17TH)	7/21/63	1
Bristoe Station, VA (14TH)	10/14/63	1
Morton's Ford, VA (14TH) *1 (1 WOUNDED)	2/6/64	3
Craig's Church, VA (1 CA) *	5/5/64	1
Winchester, VA (14TH)	5/5/64	1
Drewry's Bluff,VA(6,7,8TH)*1	5/16/64	5
Bermuda Hundred, VA (6TH)	6/17/64	1
Ream's Station, VA (1 CA) *	6/29/64	2
Deep Run, VA (6,7TH) *2 (1 WOUNDED)	8/16/64	4
Petersburg, VA (8TH)	9/16/64	1
Richmond, VA (7TH)	10/1/64	1
Cedar Run Ch, VA (1CA) *1	10/17/64	2
Cedar Crk,VA(2HA,9,12,13TH)*1	10/19/64	18
Stony Creek, VA (14TH)	10/28/64	1
Dinwiddie CH, VA (14TH)	10/28/64	1
Newtown, VA (12TH)	11/4/64	1
Cedar Creek, VA (1 CA)	11/12/64	1
St John's County, FL (17TH)	12/24/64	1
St Augustine, FL (17TH)	2/1/65	1
St Augustine, FL (17TH)	2/4/65	3
Dunn's Lake, FL (17TH)	2/5/65	3
Kinston, NC (15TH)	3/8/65	1
Fisherville, VA (1 CA)	3/8/65	1
Burksville, VA (10TH)	4/6/65	1

ONE HUNDRED-SEVENTY FIVE WERE WOUNDED

The first Bridgeport soldiers wounded were Privates John N. Silleck and Theordore T. Winton of the 3RD Connecticut. They were wounded on July 21, 1861 at the Battle of Bull Run, VA and both recovered from their wounds. Twenty-six Bridgeport soldiers died from a wound received during the war.

BRIDGEPORT WOUNDED
* (26) DIED FROM WOUNDS

PLACE	DATE	NO.
Bull Run, VA (3RD)	7/21/61	1
Fort Richardson, VA (1 HA)	4/1/62	1
Fort Jackson, MS (9TH)	5/1/62	1
Vicksburg, MS (9TH)	6/1/62	1
Carlington, LA (9TH)	6/5/62	1
Cross Keys, VA (1 CA)	6/8/62	1
James Island, SC (7TH)	6/16/62	3
Antietam, MD (14TH)	9/17/62	8
Pocotaligo, SC (6TH) *2	10/22/62	4
Georgia Landing, LA (12TH)	10/27/62	1
New Haven, CT (23RD)	10/28/62	1
Antoich, VA (17TH)	11/14/62	1
Fredericksburg, VA (14TH)	12/13/62	3
Washington, DC (2 LB)	12/15/62	1
Fall Island, SC (6TH)	4/1/63	1
Chancellorsville, VA (17TH)	5/1/63	1
Chancellorsville, VA (17TH)	5/2/63	1
Chancellorsville, VA (14TH)	5/3/63	1
Port Hudson, LA (12,13[TH])*1	5/27/63	4
Port Hudson, LA (12TH)	6/10/63	1
La Fourche, LA (23RD)	6/21/63	1
Gettysburg, PA (17TH)	7/1/63	11
Gettysburg, PA (14TH) *	7/2/63	1
Gettysburg, PA (14,17[TH])	7/3/63	5
Fort Wagner, SC (6TH) *2	7/18/63	10
Fort Wagner, SC (17TH)	9/6/63	1
Mine Run, VA (1 HA)	11/30/63	1
Culpeper, VA (1 HA)	12/18/63	1
Morton's Ford, VA (14TH)	2/6/64	4
Olustee, FLA (7TH)	2/20/64	2
Wilderness, VA (14TH)	5/6/64	2
Walthall Junction, VA (8TH)	5/7/64	1
Chester Station, VA (7TH) *	5/10/64	1
Laurel Hill, VA (14TH)	5/10/64	1
Beaver Dam Station, VA (1 CA)	5/10/64	1
Drewry's Bluff, VA (6,7[TH]) *1	5/14/64	2
Drewry's Bluff, VA (6,7,11[TH])*	5/16/64	7

BRIDGEPORT WOUNDED CONTINUED

PLACE	DATE	NO.
Ware Bottom Church, VA (6TH)	5/20/64	1
Bermuda Hundred, VA (6TH)	5/20/64	2
Tolopotomy, VA (2 HA)	5/29/64	1
Haer Court House, VA (2 HA)*	5/30/64	1
Cold Harbor, VA (2 HA)*3	6/1/64	11
Petersburg, VA (2 HA)	6/1/64	1
Petersburg, VA (1 HA)	6/2/64	1
Bermuda Hundred, VA (7,10[TH])	6/2/64	2
Cold Harbor, VA (11TH)	6/3/64	3
Cold Harbor, VA (2 HA)*	6/5/64	1
Bermuda Hundred, VA (6TH)*	6/17/64	1
Bermuda Hundred, VA (6TH)	6/29/64	1
Peach Tree Creek, GA (5TH)	7/20/64	1
Rodney, MS (2 LB)	7/23/64	1
Petersburg, VA (1 HA)	7/24/64	1
Petersburg, VA (1HA,11,30[TH])	7/30/64	3
Dutch Gap, VA (6TH)*	8/1/64	1
Petersburg, VA (30TH)	8/3/64	1
Petersburg, VA (8TH)*	8/10/64	1
Deep Bottom, VA (6,14[TH])	8/16/64	3
Deep Run, VA (6,7,10[TH]) *3	8/16/64	9
Ream's Station, VA (14TH)	8/25/64	2
Berryville, VA (9TH)	9/5/64	1
Winchester, VA (2HA,12TH)*1	9/19/64	11
Fort Harrison, VA (8TH)	9/29/64	1
Chaffin's Farm, VA (7TH)	9/29/64	1
Richmond, VA (10TH)*	10/1/64	1
Darbytown Road, VA (10TH)	10/13/64	2
Cedar Creek, VA (2HA,12TH)*2	10/19/64	4
Strasburg, VA (2 HA) *	10/19/64	1
Hatcher's Run, VA (14TH)	10/28/64	1
Fort Harrison, VA (29TH)	11/10/64	1
Hatcher's Run, VA (14TH) *	3/25/65	1
Petersburg, VA (1 HA)	3/25/65	1
Petersburg, VA (2 HA)	4/2/65	1
Fort Gregg, VA (10TH)	4/2/65	2
Richmond, VA (29TH)	4/3/65	1
Sailor's Creek, VA (1 CA)	4/6/65	1

BRIDGEWATER
THE POPULATION IN 1860 WAS 1,048 (RANK 133)

THE MOST IMPORTANT DAY OF THE CIVIL WAR

JULY 20, 1864

PEACH TREE CREEK, GA

THE BATTLE WAS PART OF THE ATLANTA CAMPAIGN

Soldiers credited to Bridgewater had more casualties on May 3, 1863 at Chancellorsville, VA (4) and on July 20, 1864 at Peach Tree Creek and Atlanta, GA (4) than on any other days of the war. The casualtries at Peach Tree Creek were the most serious. Two soldiers were killed and 2 were wounded in the 5TH and 20TH Connecticut. The wounded survived the war.

The date July 20, 1864 ranks 23RD for total casualties (116) (23 killed, 91 wounded, 2 captured) for a single day for the State of Connecticut. The most casualties were at Peach Tree Creek (107) but there were also 6 casualties at Atlanta, GA and 3 at Petersburg, VA.

The Battle of Peach Tree Creek (July 20, 1864) ranks 21ST for total casualties (107) for an engagement for the State of Connecticut.

The Battle of Peach Tree Creek with 4 total casualties for Bridgewater was tied with the Battle of Chancellorsville (May 1863) for the highest number of casualties for any single engagement of the war for the town.

The Battle of Peach Tree Creek was fought in the hills north of Atlanta. The uncoordinated Confederate attacks and the good Union defensive postions sent the Confederates into retreat after desperate fighting. This set the stage for the next chapter: The Battle of Atlanta.

81 MEN CREDITED TO BRIDGEWATER SERVED IN THE FOLLOWING CONNECTICUT ORGANIZATIONS

REGIMENT	TOTAL
5TH	18 (22%)
28TH	17 (21%)
29TH	7 (9%)
10TH	6 (7%)
11TH	6 (7%)
2ND HEAVY ARTILLERY	5 (6%)
1ST HEAVY ARTILLERY	4 (5%)
27TH	4 (5%)
12TH	3 (4%)
20TH	3 (4%)
6TH	2 (2%)
1ST CAVALRY	1
7TH	1
8TH	1
9TH	1
12TH BATTALION	1
15TH	1
18TH	1
23RD	1

8% OF POPULATION

FOUR WERE KILLED

The first Bridgewater soldiers killed were Privates John Carr and Eugene H. Duffy of the 5TH Connecticut. Both were killed at Peach Tree Creek, GA on July 20, 1864.

TOTAL BRIDGEWATER CASUALTIES

DIED	4	5%
KILLED	4	5%
WOUNDED	9	11%
CAPTURED	5	6%
DESERTED	27	33%

BRIDGEWATER SOLDIERS KILLED

PLACE	DATE	NO.
Peach Tree Creek, GA (5TH)	7/20/64	2
Cedar Creek, VA (2 HA)	10/19/64	1
Kell House, VA (29TH)	10/27/64	1

FIVE WERE CAPTURED

No Bridgewater soldiers died in captivity.

BRIDGEWATER CAPTURED
NONE DIED IN CAPTIVITY

PLACE	DATE	NO.
Chancellorsville, VA (27TH)	5/3/63	4
Pedee River, NC (5TH)	3/6/65	1

NINE WERE WOUNDED

The first Bridgewater soldier wounded was Private Sidney R. Thompson of Company C, 27TH Connecticut. He was wounded at Fredericksburg, VA on December 13, 1862 and recovered from his wound. One Bridgewater soldier died from a wound received during the war.

BRIDGEWATER WOUNDED
*(1) DIED FROM WOUNDS

PLACE	DATE	NO.
Fredericksburg, VA (27TH)	12/13/62	1
Port Hudson, LA (28TH) *	6/14/63	2
Port Hudson, LA (12TH)	6/28/63	1
Culp's Farm, GA (5TH)	6/22/64	1
Petersburg, VA (2 HA)	6/22/64	1
Peach Tree Creek, GA (5, 20TH)	7/20/64	2
Petersburg, VA (29TH)	8/1/64	1

BRISTOL
THE POPULATION IN 1860 WAS 3,436 (RANK 28)

THE MOST IMPORTANT DAY OF THE CIVIL WAR

APRIL 20, 1864

PLYMOUTH, NC

THE CONFEDERATE PLAN TO TAKE PLYMOUTH ENDED WHEN 2,800 UNION TROOPS SURRENDERED THE CITY

More soldiers credited to Bristol were listed as casualties (42) on this day than on any other day of the war. Forty soldiers were captured, and 2 were wounded & captured in the 16TH Connecticut. Twenty-one died in prison and 2 died after release.

The date April 20, 1864 ranks 6TH for total casualties (433) (1 killed, 2 missing, 12 wounded & captured, 418 captured) for a single day for the State of Connecticut. All of the casualties were at Plymouth, NC.

The Battle of Plymouth (April 20, 1864) ranks 9TH for total casualties (433) for an engagement for the State of Connecticut. Nearly half of all soldiers captured at Plymouth died in Southern prisons

The Battle of Plymouth with 42 total casualties for Bristol was the greatest number of casualties for any single engagement of the war for the town.

When Confederate General Robert Hoke surrounded and captured the Union garrison at Plymouth, NC the Southern victory was the first in this military arena in quite some time. With aid from the two-gun ironclad *Albemarle* the Confederates were able to take advantage of the lack of suitable Union gunboats.

280 MEN CREDITED TO BRISTOL SERVED IN THE FOLLOWING CONNECTICUT ORGANIZATIONS

REGIMENT	TOTAL
16TH	78 (28%)
25TH	51 (18%)
5TH	26 (9%)
10TH	18 (6%)
11TH	16 (6%)
7TH	14 (5%)
1ST HEAVY ARTILLERY	12 (4%)
14TH	12 (4%)
6TH	11 (4%)
13TH	11 (4%)
1ST CAVALRY	10 (4%)
20TH	9 (3%)
2ND HEAVY ARTILLERY	8 (3%)
13TH BATTALION	7 (3%)
29TH	5 (2%)
12TH	4 (1%)
1ST SQUADRON CAVALRY	3 (1%)
8TH	3 (1%)
1ST LIGHT BATTERY	2
12TH BATTALION	2
30TH	2
2ND LIGHT BATTERY	1
9TH	1
18TH	1
22ND	1

8% OF POPULATION

TEN WERE KILLED AND ONE WAS MISSING

The first Bristol soldiers killed were Privates Charles W. Checkni and Robert O. Lane of Company B, 5ᵀᴴ Connecticut . Both were killed at Cedar Mountain, VA on August 9, 1862.

BRISTOL SOLDIERS KILLED
*(1) MISSING

PLACE	DATE	NO.
Cedar Mountain, VA (5ᵀᴴ)	8/9/62	2
Antietam, MD (16ᵀᴴ)	9/17/62	2
Pocotaligo, SC (6ᵀᴴ)	10/22/62	1
Irish Bend, LA (25ᵀᴴ)	4/14/63	1
Gettysburg, PA (1SQ) *	7/3/63	1
Fort Wagner, SC (7ᵀᴴ)	7/11/63	1
Cedar Run Church, VA(1 CA)	10/17/64	1
USS Lyons (16ᵀᴴ)	3/31/65	1
(Drowned)		
Potomac River (16ᵀᴴ)	4/24/65	1
(Drowned)		

SIXTY WERE CAPTURED

Twenty-five Bristol soldiers died in captivity. Twelve soldiers died at Andersonville Prison, GA, eight at Florence, SC, three at Charleston, SC one at Salisbury, NC, and one at Libby Prison Richmond, VA.

BRISTOL CAPTURED
*(25) DIED IN CAPTIVITY

PLACE	DATE	NO.
Winchester, VA (5ᵀᴴ)	5/24/62	1
James Island, SC (7ᵀᴴ)	6/7/62	1
Cedar Mountain, VA (5ᵀᴴ)	8/9/62	2
Warrenton, VA (5ᵀᴴ)	8/28/62	1
Brashear City, LA (25ᵀᴴ)	4/12/63	3
Brashear City, LA (25ᵀᴴ)	6/23/63	1
Bayou Boeuf, LA (25ᵀᴴ)	6/23/63	1
Bayou Boeuf, LA (25ᵀᴴ)	6/24/63	1
Bristoe Station, VA (14ᵀᴴ)	10/13/63	1
Plymouth, NC (16ᵀᴴ) *(21)	4/20/64	42
(2 WOUNDED)		
Drewry's Bluff, VA (11ᵀᴴ) *	5/16/64	2
Bermuda Hundred, VA (6ᵀᴴ)	5/20/64	1
Old Church Tavern, VA(1 CA) *6/10/64		1
Cedar Run Church, VA(1 CA) *10/17/64		1
Cedar Creek, VA (2 HA) *	10/19/64	1
Stony Creek, VA (14ᵀᴴ)	10/27/64	1

TOTAL BRISTOL
CASUALTIES

DIED	44	15%
KILLED/MISSING	11	4%
WOUNDED	34	12%
CAPTURED	60	21%
DESERTED	28	10%

THIRTY-FOUR WERE WOUNDED

The first Bristol soldiers wounded were Corporal Theodore Shubert and Privates Charles J. Hall and Henry F. Lardner of the 7ᵀᴴ Connecticut. They were wounded at James Island, SC on June 16, 1862 and recovered from their wounds. Three Bristol soldiers died from wounds received during the war.

BRISTOL WOUNDED
*(3) DIED FROM WOUNDS

PLACE	DATE	NO.
James Island, SC (7ᵀᴴ)	6/16/62	3
Cedar Mountain, VA (5ᵀᴴ)	8/9/62	1
Antietam, MD (16ᵀᴴ)	9/17/62	3
Kinston, NC (10ᵀᴴ)	12/14/62	1
Bayou Sara, LA (25ᵀᴴ) *	3/10/63	1
Irish Bend, LA (25ᵀᴴ) *	4/14/63	4
Chancellorsville, VA (5ᵀᴴ)	5/3/63	1
Port Hudson, LA (25ᵀᴴ)	5/27/63	1
Port Hudson, La (25ᵀᴴ)	6/27/63	1
Donaldsonville, LA (12ᵀᴴ)	7/13/63	1
Morton's Ford, VA (14ᵀᴴ)	2/6/64	2
Spottsylvania, VA (14ᵀᴴ)	5/12/64	1
Drewry's Bluff, VA (11ᵀᴴ)	5/16/64	1
Bermuda Hundred, VA (6ᵀᴴ)	5/20/64	1
Cold Harbor, VA (2 HA)	6/1/64	1
Cold Harbor, VA (14ᵀᴴ)	6/3/64	1
Petersburg, VA (1 HA) *	6/30/64	1
Ream's Station, VA (1 CA)	7/28/64	1
Deep Bottom, VA (10ᵀᴴ)	8/14/64	1
Deep Run (6ᵀᴴ, 10ᵀᴴ)	8/16/64	2
Winchester, VA (13ᵀᴴ)	9/19/64	3
Fort Harrison, VA (8ᵀᴴ)	9/29/64	1
Darbytown Road, VA (10ᵀᴴ)	10/13/64	1

BROOKFIELD
THE POPULATION IN 1860 WAS 1,224 (RANK 118)

THE MOST IMPORTANT DAY OF THE CIVIL WAR

SEPTEMBER 17, 1862

SHARPSBURG, MD (ANTIETAM)

CONNECTICUT HAD MORE CASUALTIES FOR ONE DAY THAN ON ANY OTHER DAY OF THE WAR

More soldiers credited to Brookfield were listed as casualties (4) on this day than on any other day of the war. Four soldiers were wounded in the 8TH Connecticut. All survived the war.

The date September 17, 1862 ranks 1ST for total casualties (687) (131 killed, 2 missing, 515 wounded, 21 captured, 18 wounded & captured) for a single day for the State of Connecticut. All of the casualties were at Antietam.

The Battle of Antietam (September 16-17) ranks 1ST for total casualties (689) for an engagement for the State of Connecticut. The most intense fighting developed on September 17. Brookfield had all of its casualties on that day.

The Battle of Antietam with 4 total casualties for Brookfield was the highest number of casualties for any single engagement of the war for the town.

Roughly 12,400 Union casualties were recorded and perhaps there were 10,300 Confederate casualties. Antietam proved to be one of the turning points of the war. It ended Lee's 1862 invasion of the North.

78 MEN CREDITED TO BOOKFIELD SERVED IN THE FOLLOWING CONNECTICUT ORGANIZATIONS

REGIMENT	TOTAL
8TH	25 (35%)
2ND HEAVY ARTILLERY	9 (12%)
12TH	8 (10%)
23RD	8 (10%)
17TH	7 (9%)
1ST HEAVY ARTILLERY	4 (5%)
13TH	4 (5%)
6TH	3 (4%)
15TH	3 (4%)
30TH	3 (4%)
5TH	2 (3%)
3RD	1
10TH	1
11TH	1
12TH BATTALION	1
13TH BATTALION	1
29TH	1

7% OF POPULATION

THREE WERE KILLED

The first Brookfield soldier killed was Private Albert Clark of Company I, 8TH Connecticut. He was killed at Drewry's Bluff, VA on May 16, 1864.

BROOKFIELD SOLDIERS KILLED

PLACE	DATE	NO.
Drewry's Bluff, VA (8TH)	5/16/64	1
Petersburg, VA (30TH)	7/30/64	1
Cedar Creek, VA (12TH)	10/19/64	1

FOUR WERE CAPTURED

No Brookfield soldiers died in captivity.

BROOKFIELD CAPTURED
NONE DIED IN CAPTIVITY

PLACE	DATE	NO.
Antietam, MD (8TH)	9/19/62	1
Cox's Mills, VA (8TH)	9/14/64	1
Cedar Creek, VA (2 HA)	9/19/64	1
Kinston, NC (15TH)	3/8/65	1

TOTAL BROOKFIELD CASUALTIES

DIED	14	18%
KILLED	3	4%
WOUNDED	15	19%
CAPTURED	4	5%
DESERTED	6	8%

FIFTEEN WERE WOUNDED

The first Brookfield soldier wounded was Private William B. Davis of Company D, 10TH Connecticut. He was wounded at Roanoke Island, NC on February 8, 1862 and recovered from his wound. No Brookfield soldiers died from a wound received during the war.

BROOKFIELD WOUNDED
NONE DIED FROM WOUNDS

PLACE	DATE	NO.
Roanoke Island, NC (10TH)	2/8/62	1
Antietam, MD (8TH)	9/17/62	4
New Orleans, LA (23RD)	12/1/62	1
Gettysburg, PA (17TH)	7/2/63	1
New Haven, CT (8TH)	2/24/64	1
Walthall Junction, VA (8TH)	6/10/63	1
Petersburg, VA (8TH)	6/15/64	1
Deep Run, VA (6TH)	8/16/64	1
Chaffin's Farm, VA (8TH)	9/29/64	1
Ft. Harrison, VA (8TH)	9/29/64	1
Cedar Creek, VA (2HA)	10/19/64	1
Richmond, VA (8TH)	10/1/65	1

BROOKLYN
THE POPULATION IN 1860 WAS 1,224 (RANK 118)

THE MOST IMPORTANT DAY OF THE CIVIL WAR

JUNE 15 1863

WINCHESTER, VA

THE ENTIRE UNION ARMY WAS NEARLY CAPTURED AT THE SECOND BATTLE OF WINCHESTER

More soldiers credited to Brooklyn were listed as casualties (7) on this day than on any other day of the war. One soldier was wounded and 6 were captured in the 18TH Connecticut. All survived the war.

The date June 15, 1863 ranks 2ND for total casualties (595) (23 killed, 11 wounded, 520 captured, 41 wounded & captured) for a single day for the State of Connecticut. There were 592 casualties at Winchester, VA and 3 casualties at Port Hudson, LA.

The Second Battle of Winchester (June 13-15, 1863) ranks 5TH for total casualties (592) for an engagement for the State of Connecticut. The most intense fighting developed on June 15. Brooklyn had all its casualites on that day.

The Second Battle of Winchester with 7 total casualties for Brooklyn was the highest number of casualties for any single engagement of the war for the town.

Winchester was one of the most contested locations in the Civil War. It changed hands seventy-two times.

109 MEN CREDITED TO BROOKLYN SERVED IN THE FOLLOWING CONNECTICUT ORGANIZATIONS

REGIMENT	TOTAL
18TH	17 (16%)
21ST	17 (16%)
11TH	16 (15%)
1ST HEAVY ARTILLERY	12 (11%)
1ST CAVALRY	10 (9%)
12TH	7 (6%)
5TH	6 (6%)
8TH	6 (6%)
6TH	5 (5%)
14TH	4 (4%)
20TH	3 (3%)
29TH	3 (3%)
2ND LIGHT BATTERY	1
7TH	1
9TH	1
10TH	1
12TH BATTALION	1
30TH	1

9% OF POPULATION

SEVEN WERE KILLED

The first Brooklyn soldier killed in combat was Private Daniel I. Tarbox of Company F, 11TH Connecticut. He was killed at the Battle of Antietam, MD on September 17, 1862.

BROOKLYN SOLDIERS KILLED

PLACE	DATE	NO.
Mississippi River (12TH) (Drowned)	6/14/62	1
Antietam, MD (11TH)	9/17/62	1
Spottsylvania, VA (14TH)	5/10/64	1
Cold Harbor, VA (11TH)	6/3/64	1
Petersburg, VA (30TH)	7/30/64	1
Petersburg, VA (6TH)	8/28/64	1
Cedar Creek, VA (12TH)	10/19/64	1

FOURTEEN WERE CAPTURED

One Brooklyn soldier died in captivity at Salisbury, NC.

BROOKLYN CAPTURED
(1) DIED IN CAPTIVITY

PLACE	DATE	NO.
Unknown (1 HA)	6/29/62	1
Antietam, MD (8TH) (WOUNDED)	9/17/62	1
Winchester, VA (18TH)	6/15/63	6
New Market, VA (18TH)	5/15/64	2
Ream's Station, VA (1 CA)	6/29/64	1
Winchester, VA (18TH) (WOUNDED)	7/24/64	1
Cedar Run Church, VA(1CA)*	10/17/64	2

TOTAL BROOKLYN CASUALTIES

DIED	18	17%
KILLED	7	6%
WOUNDED	18	17%
CAPTURED	14	14%
DESERTED	4	1%

EIGHTEEN WERE WOUNDED

The first Brooklyn soldiers wounded were Corporal James W. Kimball and Private Calvin H. Woodward of Company B, 5TH Connecticut. They were wounded at Cedar Moutain, VA on August 9, 1862 and recovered from their wounds. Five Brooklyn soldiers died from a wound received during the war.

BROOKLYN WOUNDED
*(5) DIED FROM WOUNDS

PLACE	DATE	NO.
Cedar Mountain, VA (5TH)	8/9/62	2
Antietam, MD (8,14TH) *2	9/17/62	3
Port Hudson, LA (12TH)	5/29/63	1
Winchester, VA (18TH)	6/15/63	1
Wilderness, VA (14TH) *	5/6/64	1
Drewry's Bluff, VA (6ST) *	5/15/64	1
Drewry's Bluff, VA (11,21ST)	5/16/64	4
Piedmont, VA (18TH)	6/5/64	1
Petersburg, VA (1 HA,29TH) *1	8/29/64	2
Fort Gregg, VA (10TH)	4/2/65	1
Richmond, VA (11TH)	4/15/65	1

BURLINGTON
THE POPULATION IN 1860 WAS 1,031 (RANK 135)

THE MOST IMPORTANT DAY OF THE CIVIL WAR

APRIL 20, 1864

PLYMOUTH, NC

THE CONFEDERATE PLAN TO TAKE PLYMOUTH ENDED WHEN 2,800 UNION TROOPS SURRENDERED THE CITY

More soldiers credited to Burlington were listed as casualties (6) on this day than on any other day of the war. Six soldiers were captured in the 16TH Connecticut. Three eventually died in prison.

The date April 20, 1864 ranks 6TH for total casualties (433) (1 killed, 2 missing, 12 wounded & captured, 418 captured) for a single day for the State of Connecticut. All of the casualties were at Plymouth, NC.

The Battle of Plymouth (April 20, 1864) ranks 9TH for total casualties (433) for an engagement for the State of Connecticut. Nearly half of all soldiers captured at Plymouth died in Southern prisons

The Battle of Plymouth with 6 total casualties for Burlington was the highest number of casualties for any single engagement of the war for the town.

When Confederate General Robert Hoke surrounded and captured the Union garrison at Plymouth, NC the Southern victory was the first in this military arena in quite some time. With aid from the two-gun ironclad *Albemarle* the Confederates were able to take advantage of the lack of suitable Union gunboats.

67 MEN CREDITED TO BURLINGTON SERVED IN THE FOLLOWING CONNECTICUT ORGANIZATIONS

REGIMENT	TOTAL
25TH	12 (18%)
1ST HEAVY ARTILLERY	9 (13%)
16TH	8 (12%)
2ND HEAVY ARTILLERY	5 (7%)
6TH	5 (7%)
7TH	5 (7%)
1ST SQUADRON CAVALRY	3 (4%)
10TH	3 (4%)
11TH	3 (4%)
12TH	3 (4%)
9TH	2 (3%)
12TH BATTALION	2 (3%)
14TH	2 (3%)
15TH	2 (3%)
29TH	2 (3%)
1ST CAVALRY	1
1ST LIGHT BATTERY	1
3RD	1
5TH	1
9TH BATTALION	1
22ND	1
30TH	1

6% OF POPULATION

ONE WAS KILLED

The only Burlington soldier killed was Private Edmund Rogers of Company B, 6TH Connecticut. He was killed at Morris Island, SC on July 18, 1863.

BURLINGTON SOLDIERS KILLED

PLACE	DATE	NO.
Morris Island, SC (6TH)	7/18/63	1

TEN WERE CAPTURED

Five Burlington soldiers died in captivity. Two soldiers died at Andersonville Prison, GA, one at Florence, SC, one at Charleston, SC and one at Savannah, GA.

BURLINGTON CAPTURED
*(5) DIED IN CAPTIVITY

PLACE	DATE	NO.
Bayou Boeuf, LA (25TH)	6/24/63	1
Richmond, VA (1 SQ) *	3/1/64	1
Plymouth, NC (16TH) *3	4/20/64	6
Bermuda Hundred, VA (7TH) *	6/2/64	1
Kinston, NC (15TH)	3/8/65	1

TOTAL BURLINGTON CASUALTIES

DIED	13	19%
KILLED	1	1%
WOUNDED	8	12%
CAPTURED	10	15%
DESERTED	6	9%

EIGHT WERE WOUNDED

The first Burlington soldier wounded was Private Gideon S. Barnes of Company K, 16TH Connecticut. He was wounded at the Battle of Antietam, MD on September 17, 1862 and died from his wound. Three Burlington soldiers died from a wound received during the war.

BURLINGTON WOUNDED
*(3) DIED FROM WOUNDS

PLACE	DATE	NO.
Antietam, MD (16TH) *	9/17/62	1
Pocotaligo, SC (6TH)	10/22/62	1
Kinston, NC (10TH)	12/14/62	1
Irish Bend, LA (25TH) *	4/14/63	1
Deep Run, VA (6TH)	8/16/64	1
Petersburg, VA (1 HA)	9/23/64	1
Roma, TX (30TH)	9/24/64	1
Cedar Creek, VA (2 HA) *	10/19/64	1

CANAAN
THE POPULATION IN 1860 WAS 2,834 (RANK 45)

THE MOST IMPORTANT
DAY OF THE CIVIL WAR

JUNE 1, 1864

COLD HARBOR, VA

THE BATTLE WAS LEE'S
LAST GREAT VICTORY

Canaan had more casualties on June 1, 1864 at Cold Harbor, VA (4) and on April 2, 1865 at Petersburg, VA (4) than on any other days of the war. The casualties at Cold Harbor were the most serious. Two soldiers were killed, and 2 were wounded in the 2ND Connecticut Heavy Artillery. One of the wounded died.

The date June 1, 1864 ranks 8TH for total casualties (374) (89 killed, 10 missing, 246 wounded, 23 captured, 6 wounded & captured) for a single day for the State of Connecticut. There were 324 casualties at Cold Harbor, 41 casualties at Ashland, and 9 other casualties scattered about Virginia.

The battle and operations around Cold Harbor (May 31-June 12, 1864) rank 6TH for total casualties (557) for an engagement for the State of Connecticut. The most intense fighting developed on June 3 and Canaan had 2 casualties.

The Battle of Cold Harbor with 6 total casualties for Canaan was the highest number of casualties for any single engagement of the war for the town.

Approximately 117,000 Federal and 60,000 Confederate troops participated in operations from May 28 to June 3. Roughly 13,000 Union casualties were recorded and perhaps there were 5,000 Confederate casualties.

120 MEN CREDITED TO CANAAN SERVED IN THE FOLLOWING CONNECTICUT ORGANIZATIONS

REGIMENT	TOTAL
2ND HEAVY ARTILLERY	41 (34%)
7TH	17 (14%)
11TH	17 (14%)
13TH	8 (7%)
5TH	7 (6%)
8TH	5 (4%)
29TH	5 (4%)
1ST CAVALRY	3 (3%)
6TH	3 (3%)
13TH BATTALION	3 (3%)
2ND LIGHT BATTERY	2 (2%)
9TH	2 (2%)
10TH	2 (2%)
1ST LIGHT BATTERY	1
1ST HEAVY ARTILLERY	1
9TH BATTALION	1
12TH	1
14TH	1
17TH	1
20TH	1

4% OF POPULATION

EIGHT WERE KILLED

The first Canaan soldiers killed were Privates Albert Todd and John Murray of Company I, 11TH Connecticut. Both were killed at the Battle of Antietam, MD on September 17, 1862.

CANAAN SOLDIERS KILLED

PLACE	DATE	NO.
Antietam, MD (11TH)	9/17/62	2
Fort Wagner, SC (7TH)	7/11/63	1
Drewry's Bluff, VA (7TH)	5/16/64	1
Cold Harbor, VA (2 HA)	6/1/64	2
Cold Harbor, VA (2 HA)	6/3/64	1
Railroad Accident, VA (2 HA)	Unknown	1

EIGHT WERE CAPTURED

One Canaan soldier died in captivity at Salisbury, NC.

CANAAN CAPTURED
*(1) DIED IN CAPTIVITY

PLACE	DATE	NO.
Suffolk, VA (11 TH)	5/4/63	1
Loudon County, VA (5TH)	7/21/63	1
Rapidan, VA (2 HA)	6/5/64	1
Fort Harrison, VA (8TH)	9/29/64	1
Hawkinstown, VA (13TH)	10/7/64	1
Cedar Creek, VA (2 HA) *	10/19/64	2
Fair Oaks, VA (8TH)	10/27/64	1

TOTAL CANAAN CASUALTIES

DIED	17	14%
KILLED	8	7%
WOUNDED	24	20%
CAPTURED	8	7%
DESERTED	20	17%

TWENTY-FOUR WERE WOUNDED

The first Canaan soldier wounded was Private Albert Todd of Company I, 11TH Connecticut. He was wounded at New Bern, NC on March 14, 1862 and recovered from his wound. He was killed six months later at the Battle of Antietam and was one of the first soldiers killed. Two Canaan soldiers died from a wound received during the war.

CANAAN WOUNDED
*(2) DIED FROM WOUNDS

PLACE	DATE	NO.
New Bern, NC (11TH)	3/14/62	1
Cedar Mountain, VA (5TH)	8/9/62	1
Antietam, MD (11TH)	9/17/62	1
Pocotaligo, SC (7TH)	10/22/62	1
Irish Bend, LA (13TH)	4/14/63	1
Chancellorsville, VA (5TH)	5/3/63	1
Cold Harbor, VA (2 HA)	6/1/64	2
Bermuda Hundred, VA (7TH)	6/2/64	1
Cold Harbor, VA (2 HA) *	6/3/64	1
Winchester, VA (2 HA)	9/19/64	1
Strasburg, VA (2 HA)	9/21/64	1
Fisher's Hill, VA (2 HA)	9/21/64	1
Fort Harrison, VA (8TH)	9/29/64	1
Cedar Creek, VA (2 HA)	10/19/64	1
Kell House, VA (29TH) *	10/27/64	1
Hatcher's Run, VA (2 HA)	2/2/65	1
Petersburg, VA (2 HA)	3/26/65	1
Petersburg, VA (2 HA)	4/2/65	4
Sailor's Creek, VA (2 HA)	4/6/65	1
Unknown (13TH)	Unknown	1

CANTERBURY
THE POPULATION IN 1860 WAS 1,591 (RANK 94)

THE MOST IMPORTANT DAY 0F THE CIVIL WAR

JUNE 15 1863
WINCHESTER, VA

THE ENTIRE UNION ARMY WAS NEARLY CAPTURED AT THE SECOND BATTLE OF WINCHESTER

More soldiers credited to Canterbury were listed as casualties (10) on this day than on any other day of the war. Nine soldiers were captured, and 1 was wounded & captured in the 18TH Connecticut. All survived the war.

The date June 15, 1863 ranks 2ND for total casualties (595) (23 killed, 11 wounded, 520 captured, 41 wounded & captured) for a single day for the State of Connecticut. There were 592 casualties at Winchester, VAand 3 casualties at Port Hudson, LA.

The Second Battle of Winchester (June 13-15, 1863) ranks 5TH for total casualties (592) for an engagement for the State of Connecticut. The most intense fighting developed on June 15. Canterbury had all its casualites on that day.

The Second Battle of Winchester with 10 total casualties for Canterbury was the highest number of casualties for any single engagement of the war for the town.

Winchester was one of the most contested locations in the Civil War. It changed hands seventy-two times.

97 MEN CREDITED TO CANTERBURY SERVED IN THE FOLLOWING CONNECTICUT ORGANIZATIONS

REGIMENT	TOTAL
18TH	22 (22%)
8TH	17 (17%)
12TH	13 (13%)
5TH	11 (11%)
11TH	9 (9%)
1ST CAVALRY	4 (4%)
2ND HEAVY ARTILLERY	4 (4%)
26TH	4 (4%)
3RD	3 (3%)
7TH	3 (3%)
10TH	3 (3%)
13TH	3 (3%)
20TH	3 (3%)
29TH	3 (3%)
14TH	2 (2%)
2ND	1
6TH	1
12TH BATTALION	1
13TH BATTALION	1
21ST	1

6% OF POPULATION

SEVEN WERE KILLED

The first Canterbury soldiers killed were Privates Dwight Carey, Henry H. Neff, and William A. Sweet of Company F, 8TH Connecticut. They were killed at the Battle of Antietam, MD on September 17, 1862.

CANTERBURY SOLDIERS KILLED

PLACE	DATE	NO.
Antietam, MD (8TH)	9/17/62	3
Port Hudson, LA (26TH)	6/14/63	1
Piedmont, VA (18TH)	6/5/64	1
Snicker's Ford, VA (18TH)	7/18/64	1
Deep Run, VA (7TH)	8/16/64	1

SEVENTEEN WERE CAPTURED

One Canterbury soldier died in captivity at Church Flats, SC.

CANTERBURY CAPTURED
*(1) DIED IN CAPTIVITY

PLACE	DATE	NO.
Winchester, VA (5TH)	5/24/62	1
Antietam, MD (8TH)	9/17/62	1
(WOUNDED)		
Seabrook Island, SC (10TH) *	3/28/63	1
(WOUNDED)		
Chancellorsville, VA (5TH)	5/2/63	1
Winchester, VA (18TH)	6/15/63	10
(1 WOUNDED)		
Drewry's Bluff, VA (7TH)	5/16/64	1
Petersburg, VA (11TH)	6/18/64	1
Bentonville, NC (20TH)	3/19/65	1

TOTAL CANTERBURY CASUALTIES

DIED	11	11%
KILLED	7	7%
WOUNDED	19	19%
CAPTURED	17	17%
DESERTED	3	3%

NINETEEN WERE WOUNDED

The first Canterbury soldiers wounded were Privates George A. Brown and Elijah Green of Company D, 11TH Connecticut. They were wounded at New Bern, NC on March 14, 1862 and both recovered from their wounds. One Canterbury soldier died from a wound received during the war.

CANTERBURY WOUNDED
*(1) DIED FROM WOUNDS

PLACE	DATE	NO.
New Bern, NC (11TH)	3/14/62	2
Ship Island, MS (13TH)	5/14/62	1
Cedar Mountain, VA (5TH)	8/9/62	1
Antietam, MD (8TH)	9/17/62	3
Georgia Landing, LA (12TH)	10/27/62	1
Port Hudson, LA (12TH)	6/10/63	1
Port Hudson, LA (12TH) *	7/5/63	1
Walthall Junction, VA (8TH)	5/7/64	1
New Market, VA (18TH)	5/15/64	2
Resaca, GA (5TH)	5/15/64	1
Cold Harbor, VA (8TH)	6/4/64	1
Piedmont, VA (18TH)	6/5/64	1
Peach Tree Creek, GA (5TH)	7/20/64	1
Fort Harrison, VA (8TH)	10/2/64	1
Cedar Creek, VA (12TH)	10/19/64	1

332

CANTON
THE POPULATION IN 1860 WAS 2,373 (RANK 59)

THE MOST IMPORTANT DAY OF THE CIVIL WAR

APRIL 20, 1864

PLYMOUTH, NC

THE CONFEDERATE PLAN TO TAKE PLYMOUTH ENDED WHEN 2,800 UNION TROOPS SURRENDERED THE CITY

244 MEN CREDITED TO CANTON SERVED IN THE FOLLOWING CONNECTICUT ORGANIZATIONS

More soldiers credited to Canton were listed as casualties (18) on this day than on any other day of the war. Sixteen soldiers were captured, and 2 were wounded & captured in the 16TH Connecticut. Six eventually died in prison.

The date April 20, 1864 ranks 6TH for total casualties (433) (1 killed, 2 missing, 12 wounded & captured, 418 captured) for a single day for the State of Connecticut. All of the casualties were at Plymouth, NC.

The Battle of Plymouth (April 20, 1864 ranks 9TH for total casualties (433) for an engagement for the State of Connecticut. Nearly half of all soldiers captured at Plymouth died in Southern prisons

The Battle of Plymouth with 18 total casualties for Canton was the highest number of casualties for any single engagement of the war for the town.

When Confederate General Robert Hoke surrounded and captured the Union garrison at Plymouth, NC the Southern victory was the first in this military arena in quite some time. With aid from the two-gun ironclad *Albemarle* the Confederates were able to take advantage of the lack of suitable Union gunboats.

REGIMENT	TOTAL
16TH	41 (17%)
1ST HEAVY ARTILLERY	33 (13%)
25TH	27 (11%)
12TH	25 (10%)
22ND	24 (10%)
2ND	22 (9%)
7TH	19 (8%)
8TH	15 (6%)
1ST SQUADRON CAVALRY	9 (4%)
29TH	9 (4%)
12TH BATTALION	8 (3%)
2ND HEAVY ARTILLERY	7 (3%)
14TH	6 (2%)
30TH	4 (2%)
15TH	3 (1%)
1ST CAVALRY	2
6TH	2
10TH	2
11TH	2
13TH	2
1ST LIGHT BATTERY	1
3RD	1
13TH BATTALION	1
17TH	1
20TH	1

10% OF POPULATION

TWELVE WERE KILLED

The first Canton soldier killed was Private William A. German of Company B, 1ST Squadron Cavalry. He was killed in a Virginia railroad accident on September 8, 1861.

CANTON SOLDIERS KILLED

PLACE	DATE	NO.
Railroad Accident, VA (1 SQ)	9/8/61	1
Rappahannock Sta., VA (1 SQ)	8/20/62	1
Gainesville, VA (1 SQ)	8/29/62	1
Antietam, MD (8TH,16TH)	9/17/62	3
Port Hudson, LA (25TH)	2/15/63	1
Wilderness, VA (14TH)	5/6/64	1
Drewry's Bluff, VA (11TH)	5/16/64	1
Cold Harbor, VA (2 HA)	6/1/64	1
Bermuda Hundred, VA (1 HA)	6/9/64	1
Petersburg, VA (30TH)	8/6/64	1

TWENTY-FIVE WERE CAPTURED

Nine Canton soldiers died in captivity. Four soldiers died at Andersonville Prison, GA, one at Plymouth, NC, one at Florence, SC, one at Charleston, SC, one at Libby Prison, Richmond, VA and one at an unknown place.

CANTON CAPTURED
*(9) DIED IN CAPTIVITY

PLACE	DATE	NO.
James Island, SC (7TH) *	6/16/62	1
Brashear City, LA (12TH)	6/23/63	1
Plymouth, NC (16TH) *6	4/20/64	18
(2 WOUNDED)		
Ream's Station, VA (1 SQ) *	6/30/64	1
Cedar Creek, VA (12TH)	10/19/64	1
Kinston, NC (15TH)	3/8/65	2
Virginia (1 SQ) *	Unknown	1

TOTAL CANTON CASUALTIES

DIED	28	11%
KILLED	12	5%
WOUNDED	26	11%
CAPTURED	25	10%
DESERTED	28	11%

TWENTY-SIX WERE WOUNDED

The first Canton soldier wounded was Private Thomas Sessions of Company B, 1ST Squadron Cavalry. He was wounded at Rappahannock Station, VA on August 20, 1862 and recovered from his wound. Six Canton soldiers died from wounds received during the war.

CANTON WOUNDED
*(6) DIED FROM WOUNDS

PLACE	DATE	NO.
Bull Run, VA (2ND)	7/21/61	1
Unknown (8TH)	3/14/62	1
Aquia Creek, VA (8TH)	8/31/62	1
Antietam, MD (16TH) *	9/17/62	5
Irish Bend, LA (25TH)	4/14/63	3
Bethel Place, LA (12TH) *	4/14/63	1
Port Hudson, LA (12TH)	5/27/63	2
Port Hudson, LA (25TH)	6/14/63	1
Aldie, VA (1 SQ) *	6/17/63	1
Sailor's Creek, GA (1 SQ)	9/1/63	1
Walthall Junction, VA (8TH)	5/7/64	1
Spottsylvania, VA (14TH)	5/12/64	1
Cold Harbor, VA (2 HA)	6/1/64	1
Petersburg, VA (1 HA) *	8/16/64	1
Fort Harrison, VA (8TH)	9/29/64	2
Cedar Creek, VA (12TH) *	10/19/64	1
Battery Morton, VA (1 HA) *	10/24/64	1
Chinquepin, NC (7TH)	4/1/65	1

CHAPLIN
THE POPULATION IN 1860 WAS 781 (RANK 150)

THE MOST IMPORTANT DAY OF THE CIVIL WAR

JUNE 15 1863

WINCHESTER, VA

THE ENTIRE UNION ARMY WAS NEARLY CAPTURED AT THE SECOND BATTLE OF WINCHESTER

More soldiers credited to Chaplin were listed as casualties (11) on this day than on any other day of the war. Two soldiers were killed, and 9 were captured in the 18TH Connecticut. One of the captured died in prison.

The date June 15, 1863 ranks 2ND for total casualties (595) (23 killed, 11 wounded, 520 captured, 41 wounded & captured) for a single day for the State of Connecticut. There were 592 casualties at Winchester, VA, and 3 casualties at Port Hudson, LA.

The Second Battle of Winchester (June 13-15, 1863) ranks 5TH for total casualties (592) for an engagement for the State of Connecticut. The most intense fighting developed on June 15. Chaplin had all its casualites on that day.

The Second Battle of Winchester with 11 total casualties for Chaplin was the highest number of casualties for any single engagement of the war for the town.

Winchester was one of the most contested locations in the Civil War. It changed hands seventy-two times.

50 MEN CREDITED TO CHAPLIN SERVED IN THE FOLLOWING CONNECTICUT ORGANIZATIONS

REGIMENT	TOTAL
18TH	11 (22%)
11TH	9 (18%)
12TH	7 (14%)
21ST	5 (10%)
8TH	4 (8%)
12TH BATTALION	4 (8%)
5TH	3 (6%)
7TH	3 (6%)
14TH	3 (6%)
1ST HEAVY ARTILLERY	2 (4%)
10TH	2 (4%)
29TH	1

6% OF POPULATION

FOUR WERE KILLED

The first Chaplin soldier killed was Private Lorenzo Button of Company F, 7TH Connecticut. He was killed at James Island, SC on June 16, 1862.

CHAPLIN SOLDIERS KILLED

PLACE	DATE	NO.
James Island,, SC (7TH)	6/16/62	1
Winchester, VA (18TH)	6/15/63	2
Drewry's Bluff, VA (10TH)	5/14/64	1

ELEVEN WERE CAPTURED

One Chaplin soldier died in captivity at Danville, VA.

CHAPLIN CAPTURED
*(1) DIED IN CAPTIVITY

PLACE	DATE	NO.
Cedar Mountain, VA (5TH)	8/9/62	1
Winchester, VA (18TH) *1	6/15/63	9
Cedar Creek, VA (12TH)	10/19/64	1

TOTAL CHAPLIN CASUALTIES

DIED	13	26%
KILLED	4	8%
WOUNDED	13	26%
CAPTURED	11	22%
DESERTED	4	8%

THIRTEEN WERE WOUNDED

The first Chaplin soldiers wounded were Corporal Edward M. Weaver and Privates Waterman Griggs and John M. Griggs of Company D, 11TH Connecticut. They were wounded at the Battle of Antietam, MD on September 17, 1862 and recovered from their wounds. No Chaplin soldier died from a wound received during the war.

CHAPLIN WOUNDED
NONE DIED FROM WOUNDS

PLACE	DATE	NO.
Antietam, MD (8TH, 11TH)	9/17/62	3
Pocotaligo, SC (7TH)	10/22/62	1
Drewry's Bluff, VA (21ST)	5/16/64	2
Cold Harbor, VA (11TH)	6/3/64	1
Cold Harbor, VA (8TH)	6/5/64	1
Bermuda Hundred, VA (7TH)	6/15/64	1
Snicker's Ford, VA (18TH)	7/18/64	1
Atlanta, GA (5TH)	7/20/64	1
Deep Bottom, VA (14TH)	8/15/64	1
Petersburg, VA (11TH)	8/15/64	1

CHESHIRE
THE POPULATION IN 1860 WAS 2,407 (RANK 58)

THE MOST IMPORTANT DAY OF THE CIVIL WAR

MAY 3, 1863

CHANCELLORSVILLE, VA

THE THIRD DAY OF THE BATTLE

More soldiers credited to Cheshire were listed as casualties (18) on this day than on any other day of the war. Four soldiers were killed, 6 were wounded, 7 were captured, and 1 was wounded & captured in the 20TH and 27TH Connecticut. One of the captured soldiers died in prison.

The date May 3, 1863 ranks 3RD for total casualties (577) (36 killed, 1 missing, 138 wounded, 372 captured, 29 wounded & captured) for a single day for the State of Connecticut. The most casualties were at Chancellorsville , VA (556). The other casualties were at Providence Church Road, VA (12), Suffolk, VA (6), Port Hudson, LA (2) and Fredericksburg, VA (1).

The Battle of Chancellorsville (May 1-3, 1863) ranks 2ND for total casualties (677) for an engagement for the State of Connecticut. The most intense fighting developed on May 3 and Cheshire had all of its casualties on that date.

The Battle of Chancellorsville with 18 total casualties for Cheshire was the highest number of casualties for any single engagement of the war for the town.

The Battle of Chancellorsville was an enormous defeat for the more than 70,000 Union soldiers who had moved against the flank and rear of 40,000 Confederate soldiers. Unfortunately, the Union Army had pulled back and had gone on the defensive around Chancellorsville. The Confederate victory was tainted however, by the loss of Confederate Major General "Stonewall" Jackson.

163 MEN CREDITED TO CHESHIRE SERVED IN THE FOLLOWING CONNECTICUT ORGANIZATIONS

REGIMENT	TOTAL
20TH	70 (43%)
11TH	13 (8%)
9TH	11 (7%)
5TH	10 (6%)
29TH	9 (6%)
15TH	8 (5%)
1ST HEAVY ARTILLERY	7 (4%)
1ST LIGHT BATTERY	6 (4%)
7TH	6 (4%)
1ST CAVALRY	5 (3%)
6TH	5 (3%)
10TH	4 (2%)
13TH	4 (2%)
8TH	3 (2%)
3RD	1
9TH BATTALION	1
12TH	1
12TH BATTALION	1
13TH BATTALION	1
16TH	1
23RD	1
27TH	1
30TH	1

7% OF POPULATION

SEVEN WERE KILLED

The first Cheshire soldiers killed were Corporal Titus Moss and Privates Reuben Benham, John L. Preston of Company A, 20TH Connecticut and William Burke of Company E, 27TH Connecticut. All were killed at Chancellorsville, VA on May 3, 1863.

CHESHIRE SOLDIERS KILLED

PLACE	DATE	NO.
Chancellorsville, VA (20,27TH)	5/3/63	4
Petersburg, VA (8TH)	6/15/64	1
Appomattox River, VA (1 HA) (DROWNED)	7/6/64	1
Kell House, VA (29TH)	10/27/64	1

THIRTEEN WERE CAPTURED

Two Cheshire soldiers died in captivity. One died at Andersonville Prison, GA and one died at Stevenson, AL.

CHESHIRE CAPTURED
*(2) DIED IN CAPTIVITY

PLACE	DATE	NO.
Chancellorsville, VA (20TH) *1 (1 WOUNDED)	5/3/63	8
Plymouth, NC (16TH) *	4/20/64	1
Drewry's Bluff, VA (11TH)	5/16/64	1
Kinston, NC (15TH) (1 WOUNDED)	3/8/65	2
Fayetteville, NC (20TH)	3/14/65	1

TOTAL CHESHIRE CASUALTIES

DIED	25	15%
KILLED	7	4%
WOUNDED	46	28%
CAPTURED	13	8%
DESERTED	23	14%

FORTY-SIX WERE WOUNDED

The first Cheshire soldier wounded was Private Martin Burke of Company B, 9TH Connecticut. He was wounded at Ship Island, MS on February 1, 1862 and recovered from his wound. Six Cheshire soldiers died from a wound received during the war.

CHESHIRE WOUNDED
*(6) DIED FROM WOUNDS

PLACE	DATE	NO.
Ship Island, MS (9TH)	2/1/62	1
Antietam, MD (8TH)	9/17/62	2
Irish Bend, LA (13TH)	4/14/63	1
Chancellorsville, VA (20TH)	5/3/63	6
Gettysburg, PA (20TH) *1	7/3/63	4
Walthall Junction, VA (8TH)	5/7/64	1
Bermuda Hundred, VA (6TH)	5/10/64	1
Drewry's Bluff, VA (7TH)	5/14/64	1
Resaca, GA (5TH) *	5/15/64	3
Drewry's Bluff, VA (11TH)	5/16/64	2
Cassville, GA (20TH)	5/19/64	2
Petersburg, VA (8TH)	6/15/64	1
Ream's Station, VA (1 CA)	6/29/64	1
Peach Tree Creek, GA (20TH)	7/20/64	1
Atlanta, GA (20TH) *	7/21/64	1
Virginia (1 CA)	7/28/64	1
Petersburg, VA (11,30TH) *1	7/30/64	2
Atlanta, GA (20TH)	8/15/64	1
Deep River, VA (6TH)	8/16/64	1
Atlanta, GA (20TH)	8/18/64	1
Strasburg, VA (9TH)	9/21/64	1
Cedar Creek, VA (12TH) *	10/19/64	1
Kell House, VA (29TH)	10/27/64	1
Richmond, VA (29TH)	10/27/64	1
Averysboro, NC (20TH)	3/15/65	1
Silver Run, NC (20TH)	3/16/65	2
Bentonville, NC (20TH) *1	3/19/65	4
Fort Gregg, VA (10TH)	4/2/65	1

CHESTER
THE POPULATION IN 1860 WAS 1,015 (RANK 136)

THE MOST IMPORTANT DAY OF THE CIVIL WAR

MAY 3, 1863

CHANCELLORSVILLE, VA

THE THIRD DAY OF THE BATTLE

More soldiers credited to Chester were listed as casualties (6) on this day than on any other day of the war. Five soldiers were wounded and 1 was wounded & captured in the 20TH Connecticut. All survived the war.

The date May 3, 1863 ranks 3RD for total casualties (577) (36 killed, 1 missing, 138 wounded, 372 captured, 29 wounded & captured) for a single day for the State of Connecticut. The most casualties were at Chancellorsville , VA(556). The other casualties were at Providence Church Road, VA (12), Suffolk, VA (6), Port Hudson, LA (2) and Fredericksburg, VA (1).

The Battle of Chancellorsville (May 1-3, 1863) ranks 2ND for total casualties (677) for an engagement for the State of Connecticut. The most intense fighting developed on May 3 and Chester had all of its casualties on that date.

The Battle of Chancellorsville with 6 total casualties for Chester was the highest number of casualties for any single engagement of the war for the town.

The Battle of Chancellorsville was an enormous defeat for the more than 70,000 Union soldiers who had moved against the flank and rear of 40,000 Confederate soldiers. Unfortunately, the Union Army had pulled back and had gone on the defensive around Chancellorsville. The Confederate victory was tainted however, by the loss of Confederate Major General "Stonewall" Jackson.

82 MEN CREDITED TO CHESTER SERVED IN THE FOLLOWING CONNECTICUT ORGANIZATIONS

REGIMENT	TOTAL
11TH	14 (17%)
20TH	12 (15%)
30TH	12 (15%)
1ST HEAVY ARTILLERY	11 (13%)
24TH	6 (7%)
29TH	6 (7%)
8TH	4 (5%)
7TH	3 (4%)
1ST CAVALRY	2 (2%)
3RD LIGHT BATTERY	2 (2%)
6TH	2 (2%)
10TH	2 (2%)
15TH	2 (2%)
26TH	2 (2%)
5TH	1
13TH	1
22ND	1
27TH	1

8% OF POPULATION

338

THREE WERE KILLED

The first Chester soldiers killed were Privates Joseph R. Barker and James Lombard of the 26ᵀᴴ Connecticut. Both were killed at Port Hudson, LA on May 27, 1863.

CHESTER SOLDIERS KILLED

PLACE	DATE	NO.
Port Hudson, LA (26ᵀᴴ)	5/27/63	2
Petersburg, VA (29ᵀᴴ)	8/29/64	1

THIRTEEN WERE CAPTURED

One Chester soldier died in captivity at Salisbury, NC.

CHESTER CAPTURED
*(1) DIED IN CAPTIVITY

PLACE	DATE	NO.
Culpeper, VA (5ᵀᴴ)	8/9/62	1
Chancellorsville, VA (5, 20ᵀᴴ)	5/3/63	5
(1 WOUNDED)		
Drewry's Bluff, VA (7,11ᵀᴴ)	5/16/64	2
Bermuda Hundred, VA (6ᵀᴴ)	6/17/64	1
Petersburg, VA (30ᵀᴴ)	7/30/64	1
(1 WOUNDED)		
Cedar Run Church, VA (1 CA)	10/17/64	1
Cedar Creek, VA (1 CA) *	10/19/64	1
Kinston, NC (15ᵀᴴ)	3/8/65	1

TOTAL CHESTER CASUALTIES

DIED	12	15%
KILLED	3	4%
WOUNDED	10	12%
CAPTURED	13	16%
DESERTED	4	5%

TEN WERE WOUNDED

The first Chester soldier wounded was Private Frederick D. Culver of Company K, 11ᵀᴴ Connecticut. He was wounded at the Battle of Antietam, MD on September 17, 1862 and recovered from his wound. Two Chester soldiers died from a wound received during the war.

CHESTER WOUNDED
*(2) DIED FROM WOUNDS

PLACE	DATE	NO.
Antietam, MD (11ᵀᴴ) *	9/17/62	1
Olustee, FL (7ᵀᴴ)	2/20/64	1
Chester Station, VA (6ᵀᴴ)	5/10/64	1
Resaca, GA (20ᵀᴴ)	5/15/64	1
Drewry's Bluff, VA (11ᵀᴴ)	5/16/64	1
Cold Harbor, VA (11ᵀᴴ)	6/2/64	1
Atlanta, GA (5ᵀᴴ)	7/20/64	1
Peach Tree Creek, GA (20ᵀᴴ)	7/20/64	1
Petersburg, VA (30ᵀᴴ)	7/30/64	1
Bentonville, NC (20ᵀᴴ) *	3/19/65	1

CLINTON
THE POPULATION IN 1860 WAS 1,427 (RANK 102)

THE MOST IMPORTANT DAY OF THE CIVIL WAR

SEPTEMBER 17, 1862
SHARPSBURG, MD (ANTIETAM)

CONNECTICUT HAD MORE CASUALTIES FOR ONE DAY THAN ON ANY OTHER DAY OF THE WAR

Clinton had more casualties on September 17, 1862 at the Battle of Antietam, MD (3) and on October 19, 1864 at the Battle of Cedar Creek, VA (3) than on any other days of the war. The casualties at Antietam were the most serious. Three soldiers were wounded in the 14TH Connecticut. One of the wounded soldiers died.

The date September 17, 1862 ranks 1ST for total casualties (687) (131 killed, 2 missing, 515 wounded, 21 captured, 18 wounded & captured) for a single day for the State of Connecticut. All of the casualties were at Antietam.

The Battle of Antietam (September 16-17, 1862) ranks 1ST for total casualties (689) for an engagement for the State of Connecticut. The most intense fighting developed on September 17. Clinton had all of its casualties on that day.

The Battle of Antietam with 3 total casualties for Clinton was tied with the Battle of Cedar Creek (October 1864) for the highest number of casualties for any single engagement of the war for the town.

Roughly 12,400 Union casualties were recorded and perhaps there were 10,300 Confederate casualties. Antietam proved to be one of the turning points of the war. It ended Lee's 1862 invasion of the North.

79 MEN CREDITED TO CLINTON SERVED IN THE FOLLOWING CONNECTICUT ORGANIZATIONS

REGIMENT	TOTAL
14TH	13 (17%)
24TH	11 (14%)
10TH	9 (13%)
1ST HEAVY ARTILLERY	6 (8%)
15TH	6 (8%)
29TH	6 (8%)
11TH	5 (6%)
27TH	5 (6%)
2ND HEAVY ARTILLERY	4 (5%)
6TH	4 (5%)
7TH	3 (4%)
12TH	3 (4%)
1ST SQUADRON CAVALRY	1
1ST CAVALRY	1
2ND LIGHT BATTERY	1
9TH	1
12TH BATTALION	1
13TH	1
12TH BATTALION	1
20TH	1

6% OF POPULATION

THREE WERE KILLED

The first Clinton soldier killed was Corporal Albert A. Bailey of Company C, 10TH Connecticut. He was killed at Kinston, NC on December 14, 1862.

CLINTON SOLDIERS KILLED

PLACE	DATE	NO.
Kinston, NC (10TH)	12/14/62	1
Cedar Creek, VA (12TH)	10/19/64	1
Fort Gregg, VA (10TH)	4/2/65	1

FOUR WERE CAPTURED

No Clinton soldier died in captivity.

CLINTON CAPTURED
NONE DIED IN CAPTIVITY

PLACE	DATE	NO.
Chancellorsville, VA (27TH)	5/3/63	1
Drewry's Bluff, VA (11TH)	5/16/64	1
Cold Harbor, VA (11TH)	6/3/64	1
Cedar Creek, VA (12TH)	10/19/64	1

TOTAL CLINTON CASUALTIES

DIED	5	6%
KILLED	3	4%
WOUNDED	10	13%
CAPTURED	4	5%
DESERTED	14	18%

TEN WERE WOUNDED

The first Clinton soldiers wounded were Privates John W. Parks, John A. Hurd, and George H. Doane of Company G, 14TH Connecticut. They were wounded at the Battle of Antietam, MD on September 17, 1862. Doane and Hurd recovered from their wounds however Parks died. Two Clinton soldiers died from a wound received during the war.

CLINTON WOUNDED
*(2) DIED FROM WOUNDS

PLACE	DATE	NO.
Antietam, MD (14TH) *1	9/17/62	3
Fredericksburg VA(14TH) *1	12/13/62	2
Kinston, NC (10TH)	12/14/62	1
Port Hudson, LA (24TH)	7/1/63	1
Deep Run, VA (10TH)	8/16/64	1
Winchester, VA (12TH)	9/19/64	1
Cedar Creek, VA (13TH)	10/19/64	1

COLCHESTER
THE POPULATION IN 1860 WAS 2,862 (RANK 44)

THE MOST IMPORTANT DAY OF THE CIVIL WAR

JUNE 15 1863

WINCHESTER, VA
THE ENTIRE UNION ARMY WAS NEARLY CAPTURED AT THE SECOND BATTLE OF WINCHESTER

More soldiers credited to Colchester were listed as casualties (20) on this day than on any other day of the war. Seventeen soldiers were captured, and 3 were wounded & captured in the 18TH Connecticut. All survived the war.

The date June 15, 1863 ranks 2ND for total casualties (595) (23 killed, 11 wounded, 520 captured, 41 wounded & captured) for a single day for the State of Connecticut. There were 592 casualties at Winchester, VA and 3 casualties at Port Hudson, LA.

The Second Battle of Winchester (June 13-15, 1863) ranks 5TH for total casualties (592) for an engagement for the State of Connecticut. The most intense fighting developed on June 15. Colchester had all its casualites on that day.

The Second Battle of Winchester with 20 total casualties for Colchester was the highest number of casualties for any single engagement of the war for the town.

Winchester was one of the most contested locations in the Civil War. It changed hands seventy-two times.

205 MEN CREDITED TO COLCHESTER SERVED IN THE FOLLOWING CONNECTICUT ORGANIZATIONS

REGIMENT	TOTAL
21ST	51 (25%)
18TH	34 (17%)
24TH	25 (12%)
5TH	16 (8%)
7TH	10 (5%)
1ST CAVALRY	10 (5%)
13TH	9 (4%)
10TH	8 (4%)
2ND HEAVY ARTILLERY	7 (3%)
14TH	7 (3%)
1ST HEAVY ARTILLERY	6 (3%)
8TH	4 (2%)
12TH	4 (2%)
29TH	4 (2%)
16TH	3 (1%)
20TH	3 (1%)
30TH	3 (1%)
2ND LIGHT BATTERY	2
11TH	2
12TH BATTALION	2
25TH	2
2ND	1
3RD	1
13TH BATTALION	1

7% OF POPULATION

NINE WERE KILLED

The first Colchester soldier killed in combat was Private Albert M. Fox of Company C, 1ST Connecticut Cavalry. He was killed at Waterford, VA on August 7, 1863.

COLCHESTER SOLDIERS KILLED

PLACE	DATE	NO.
New Orleans, LA (13TH)	7/22/63	1
(Drowned)		
Waterford, VA (1 CA)	8/7/63	1
Plymouth, NC (16TH)	4/20/64	1
Petersburg, VA (7TH)	5/14/64	1
Drewry's Bluff, VA (21ST)	5/16/64	1
Piedmont, VA (18TH)	6/5/64	1
Petersburg, VA (1 HA)	7/24/64	1
Darbytown Road, VA (7TH)	10/13/64	1
Petersburg, VA (7TH)	10/27/64	1

THIRTY-TWO WERE CAPTURED

Seven Colchester soldiers died in captivity. Three died at Andersonville Prison, GA, two at Staunton, VA, one at Charleston, SC and one at Libby Prison, Richmond, VA.

COLCHESTER CAPTURED
*(7) DIED IN CAPTIVITY

PLACE	DATE	NO.
Cedar Mountain, VA (5TH)	8/9/62	1
Winchester, VA (18TH)	6/15/63	20
(3 WOUNDED)		
Burnt Ordinary, VA (21ST)	7/9/63	1
Fort Wagner, SC (7TH) *2	7/11/63	2
(1 WOUNDED)		
Burnt Ordinary, VA (21ST)	7/14/63	1
Bristoe Station, VA (14TH) *	10/14/63	1
New Market, VA (18TH) * 2	5/15/64	2
(1 WOUNDED)		
Piedmont, VA (18TH) *	6/5/64	3
(2 WOUNDED)		
Stony Creek, VA (1 CA)	6/28/64	1

TOTAL COLCHESTER CASUALTIES

DIED	24	12%
KILLED	9	4%
WOUNDED	33	16%
CAPTURED	32	16%
DESERTED	23	11%

THIRTY-THREE WERE WOUNDED

The first Colchester soldier wounded was Private Alonzo Valentine of Company I, 7TH Connecticut. He was wounded at James Island, SC on June 16, 1862 and recovered from his wound. Five Colchester soldiers died from a wound received during the war.

COLCHESTER WOUNDED
*(5) DIED FROM WOUNDS

PLACE	DATE	NO.
James Island, SC (7TH)	6/16/62	1
Antietam, MD (11, 16TH)	9/17/62	3
Fredericksburg, VA (21ST) *	12/13/62	1
Port Hudson, LA (12TH) *	6/14/63	1
Port Hudson, LA (24TH)	6/26/63	1
Port Hudson, LA (24TH) *1	6/27/63	2
Little Washington, NC (21ST)	3/1/64	1
Little Washington, NC (21ST)	5/1/64	1
Resaca, GA (5TH)	5/15/64	1
Deep Run, VA (10TH)	5/16/64	1
Drewry's Bluff, VA (21ST)	5/16/64	3
Dallas, GA (5TH)	5/25/64	1
Cold Harbor, VA (2 HA)	6/1/64	1
Cold Harbor, VA (21ST) *1	6/3/64	5
Piedmont, VA (18TH)	6/5/64	2
Petersburg, VA (21ST) *	6/30/64	1
Atlanta, GA (5TH)	7/30/64	1
Petersburg, VA (21ST)	9/1/64	1
Chaffin's Farm, VA (21ST)	9/29/64	1
Darbytown Road, VA (10TH)	10/13/64	1
Kell House, VA (29TH)	10/27/64	1
Fort Gregg, VA (10TH)	4/2/65	2

COLEBROOK
THE POPULATION IN 1860 WAS 1,357 (RANK 106)

THE MOST IMPORTANT DAY OF THE CIVIL WAR

SEPTEMBER 17, 1862

SHARPSBURG, MD (ANTIETAM)

CONNECTICUT HAD MORE CASUALTIES FOR ONE DAY THAN ON ANY OTHER DAY OF THE WAR

More soldiers credited to Colebrook were listed as casualties (5) on this day than on any other day of the war. One soldier was killed and four were wounded in the 11TH and 16TH Connecticut. All of the wounded soldiers survived the war

The date September 17, 1862 ranks 1ST for total casualties (687) (131 killed, 2 missing, 515 wounded, 21 captured, 18 wounded & captured) for a single day for the State of Connecticut. All of the casualties were at Antietam.

The Battle of Antietam (September 16-17, 1862) ranks 1ST for total casualties (689) for an engagement for the State of Connecticut. The most intense fighting developed on September 17. Colebrook had all of its casualties on that day.

The Battle of Antietam with 5 total casualties for Colebrook was tied with the Battle of Cold Harbor (May-June 1864) for the highest number of casualties for any single engagement of the war for the town.

Roughly 12,400 Union casualties were recorded and perhaps there were 10,300 Confederate casualties. Antietam proved to be one of the turning points of the war. It ended Lee's 1862 invasion of the North.

106 MEN CREDITED TO COLEBROOK SERVED IN THE FOLLOWING CONNECTICUT ORGANIZATIONS

REGIMENT	TOTAL
2ND HEAVY ARTILLERY	25 (24%)
7TH	21 (20%)
11TH	12 (11%)
28TH	10 (9%)
1ST CAVALRY	7 (7%)
5STH	7 (7%)
29TH	6 (6%)
1ST HEAVY ARTILLERY	5 (5%)
13TH	5 (5%)
8TH	4 (4%)
13TH BATTALION	3 (3%)
2ND	1
9TH	1
16TH	1
20TH	1
23RD	1
25TH	1

8% OF POPULATION

SIX WERE KILLED

The first Colebrook soldier killed was Private Albert M. Hill of Company A, 16TH Connecticut. He was killed at the Battle of Antietam, MD on September 17, 1862.

COLEBROOK SOLDIERS KILLED

PLACE	DATE	NO.
Antietam, MD (16TH)	9/17/62	1
Cold Harbor, VA (2 HA)	6/1/64	2
Cedar Creek, VA (2 HA)	10/19/64	1
Kell House, VA (29TH)	10/27/64	1
Steamer *Fulton* Drowned (5TH)	1/10/65	1

ELEVEN WERE CAPTURED

Three Colebrook soldiers died in captivity. Two died at Andersonville Prison, GA and one died at Millen, GA.

COLEBROOK CAPTURED
*(3) DIED IN CAPTIVITY

PLACE	DATE	NO.
Winchester, VA (5TH)	5/25/62	1
(WOUNDED)		
Cedar Mountain, VA (5TH)	8/9/62	1
Washington, LA (13TH)	5/21/63	1
Olustee, FL (7TH) *2	2/20/64	3
Drewry's Bluff, VA (7TH) *1	5/16/64	2
(1 WOUNDED)		
Petersburg, VA (7TH)	6/2/64	1
Cedar Creek, VA (1 CA)	11/12/64	1
New Market, VA (1 CA)	3/9/65	1

TOTAL COLEBROOK CASUALTIES

DIED	15	14%
KILLED	6	6%
WOUNDED	18	17%
CAPTURED	11	10%
DESERTED	20	19%

EIGHTEEN WERE WOUNDED

The first Colebrook soldier wounded was Corporal Henry M. Gibbs of Company I, 5TH Connecticut. He was wounded at Winchester, VA on May 25, 1862 and recovered from his wound. Three Colebrook soldiers died from a wound received during the war.

COLEBROOK WOUNDED
*(3) DIED FROM WOUNDS

PLACE	DATE	NO.
Cedar Mountain, VA (5TH)	8/9/62	1
Antietam, MD (11TH)	9/17/62	4
Fort Hugar, VA (8TH)	4/19/63	1
Port Hudson, LA (28TH)	6/14/63	2
Walthall Junction, VA (8TH)	5/7/64	1
Bermuda Hundred, VA (7TH)	5/10/64	1
Drewry's Bluff, VA (7TH)	5/14/64	1
Cold Harbor, VA (2 HA)	6/1/64	2
Cold Harbor, VA (2 HA) *	6/3/64	1
Petersburg, VA (11TH)	8/2/64	1
Strasburg, VA (2 HA) *	9/22/64	1
Cedar Creek, VA (2 HA)	10/19/64	1
Kell House, VA (29TH) *	10/27/64	1

COLUMBIA
THE POPULATION IN 1860 WAS 832 (RANK 148)

THE MOST IMPORTANT DAY OF THE CIVIL WAR

JUNE 15 1863
WINCHESTER, VA

THE ENTIRE UNION ARMY WAS NEARLY CAPTURED AT THE SECOND BATTLE OF WINCHESTER

More soldiers credited to Columbia were listed as casualties (6) on this day than on any other day of the war. Six soldiers were captured in the 18TH Connecticut. All survived the war.

The date June 15, 1863 ranks 2ND for total casualties (595) (23 killed, 11 wounded, 520 captured, 41 wounded & captured) for a single day for the State of Connecticut. There were 592 casaulties at Winchester, VA, and 3 casualties at Port Hudson, LA.

The Second Battle of Winchester (June 13-15, 1863) ranks 5TH for total casualties (592) for an engagement for the State of Connecticut. The most intense fighting developed on June 15. Columbia had all its casualites on that day.

The Second Battle of Winchester with 6 total casualties for Columbia was the highest number of casualties for any single engagement of the war for the town.

Winchester was one of the most contested locations in the Civil War. It changed hands seventy-two times.

58 MEN CREDITED TO COLUMBIA SERVED IN THE FOLLOWING CONNECTICUT ORGANIZATIONS

REGIMENT	TOTAL
11TH	10 (17%)
18TH	8 (14%)
1ST CAVALRY	6 (10%)
1ST HEAVY ARTILLERY	5 (9%)
10TH	5 (9%)
1ST LIGHT BATTERY	3 (5%)
6TH	3 (5%)
13TH	3 (5%)
22ND	3 (5%)
29TH	3 (5%)
7TH	2 (3%)
24TH	2 (3%)
25TH	2 (3%)
26TH	2 (3%)
2ND HEAVY ARTILLERY	1
2ND LIGHT BATTERY	1
5TH	1
8TH	1
12TH	1
13TH BATTALION	1
15TH	1
30TH	1

7% OF POPULATION

ONE WAS KILLED AND ONE WAS MISSING

The first Columbia soldier killed was Private Nicholas Von Driest of Company C, 11TH Connecticut. He was killed at Cold Harbor, VA on June 3, 1864.

COLUMBIA SOLDIERS KILLED 0R MISSING*

PLACE	DATE	NO.
Cold Harbor, VA (11TH)	6/3/64	1
Ream's Station, VA (1 CA) *	6/21/64	1

TWELVE WERE CAPTURED

One Columbia soldier died in captivity at Camp Cross, TX.

COLUMBIA CAPTURED *(1) DIED IN CAPTIVITY

PLACE	DATE	NO.
Winchester, VA (18TH)	6/15/63	6
Grand Ecore, LA (13TH) *	4/21/64	1
New Market, VA (18TH)	5/15/64	2
(1 WOUNDED)		
Drewry's Bluff, VA (11TH)	5/16/64	1
Front Royal, VA (1CA)	9/24/64	1
Cedar Run Church, VA (1CA)	10/17/64	1

TOTAL COLUMBIA CASUALTIES

DIED	6	10%
KILLED/MISSING	2	3%
WOUNDED	5	9%
CAPTURED	12	21%
DESERTED	11	19%

FIVE WERE WOUNDED

The first Columbia soldier wounded was Private William Button of Company C, 25TH Connecticut. He was wounded at Irish Bend, LA on April 13, 1863 and died from his wound. He was the only Columbia soldier who died from a wound received during the war.

COLUMBIA WOUNDED *(1) DIED FROM WOUNDS

PLACE	DATE	NO.
Irish Bend, LA (25TH) *	4/14/63	1
Bermuda Hundred, VA (6TH)	6/17/64	1
Petersburg, VA (11TH)	6/18/64	1
Ream's Station, VA (1 CA)	6/29/64	1
Hatcher's Run, VA (14TH)	3/25/65	1

CORNWALL
THE POPULATION IN 1860 WAS 1,953 (RANK 77)

THE MOST IMPORTANT DAY OF THE CIVIL WAR
JUNE 1, 1864

COLD HARBOR, VA
THE BATTLE WAS LEE'S LAST GREAT VICTORY

More soldiers credited to Cornwall were listed as casualties (11) on this day than on any other day of the war. Eleven soldiers were wounded in the 2ND Connecticut Heavy Artillery. One of the soldiers died.

The date June 1, 1864 ranks 8TH for total casualties (374) (89 killed, 10 missing, 246 wounded, 23 captured, 6 wounded & captured) for a single day for the State of Connecticut. There were 324 casualties at Cold Harbor, 41 casualties at Ashland, and 9 casualties scattered throughout Virginia.

The battle and operations around Cold Harbor (May 31-June 12, 1864) rank 6TH for total casualties (557) for an engagement for the State of Connecticut. The most intense fighting developed on June 3 and Cornwall had 1 casualty.

The Battle of Cold Harbor with 12 total casualties for Cornwall was the highest number of casualties for any single engagement of the war for the town.

Approximately 117,000 Federal and 60,000 Confederate troops participated in operations from May 28 to June 3. Roughly 13,000 Union casualties were recorded and perhaps there were 5,000 Confederate casualties.

170 MEN CREDITED TO CORNWALL SERVED IN THE FOLLOWING CONNECTICUT ORGANIZATIONS

REGIMENT	TOTAL
2ND HEAVY ARTILLERY	66 (40%)
5TH	29 (17%)
11TH	16 (9%)
8TH	14 (8%)
13TH	14 (8%)
10TH	12 (7%)
14TH	12 (7%)
13TH BATTALION	6 (4%)
7TH	4 (2%)
29TH	4 (2%)
6TH	3 (2%)
1ST HEAVY ARTILLERY	2 (1%)
20TH	2 (1%)
1ST CAVALRY	1
12TH	1
28TH	1

9% OF POPULATION

SIX WERE KILLED

The first Cornwall soldier killed was Private Henry R. Morse of Company E, 8TH Connecticut. He was killed at the Battle of Antietam, MD on September 17,1862.

CORNWALL SOLDIERS KILLED

PLACE	DATE	NO.
Antietam, MD (8TH)	9/17/62	1
Irish Bend, LA (13TH)	4/14/63	1
Unknown (11TH)	1/24/64	1
Winchester, VA (2 HA)	9/19/64	1
Cedar Creek, VA (2 HA)	10/19/64	1
Potomac River (2 HA)	7/25/65	1

TWELVE WERE CAPTURED

Two Cornwall soldiers died in captivity at Libby Prison, Richmond, VA.

CORNWALL CAPTURED
*(2) DIED IN CAPTIVITY

PLACE	DATE	NO.
Winchester, VA (5TH)	5/25/62	1
Unknown (14TH)	Unknown	1
Cedar Mountain, VA (5TH)	8/9/62	2
Manassas Junction, VA (5TH)	9/1/62	1
Virginia (Unknown) (5TH)	7/28/63	1
Bristoe Station, VA (14TH) * (WOUNDED)	10/14/63	1
Bristoe Station, VA (14TH)	10/15/63	1
Drewry's Bluff, VA (11TH)	5/16/64	1
Snicker's Ford, VA (2 HA)	7/24/64	1
Savannah, GA (5TH) *	11/19/64	1
Wadesboro, NC (5TH)	3/5/65	1

TOTAL CORNWALL CASUALTIES

DIED	25	15%
KILLED	6	4%
WOUNDED	36	21%
CAPTURED	12	7%
DESERTED	26	15%

THIRTY-SIX WERE WOUNDED

The first Cornwall soldier wounded was Private Andrew Hall of Company D, 10TH Connecticut. He was wounded at New Bern, NC on March 8,1862 and recovered from his wound. Seven Cornwall soldiers died from a wound received during the war.

CORNWALL WOUNDED
*(7) DIED FROM WOUNDS

PLACE	DATE	NO.
New Bern, NC (10TH)	3/8/62	1
Cedar Mountain, VA (5TH) *1	8/9/62	4
Antietam, MD (11TH)	9/17/62	1
Olustee, FLA (7TH) *	2/20/64	1
Spottsylvania, VA (2 HA)	5/6/64	1
Walthall Junction, VA (8TH)	5/7/64	1
Resaca, GA (5TH) *	5/15/64	1
North Anna River, VA (2 HA)	5/24/64	1
Dallas, GA (5TH)	5/25/64	1
Cold Harbor, VA (2 HA) * 1	6/1/64	11
Cold Harbor, VA (11TH) *	6/3/64	1
Pine Mountain, GA (5TH)	6/17/64	1
Petersburg, VA (10TH)	9/15/65	1
Winchester, VA (2 HA) *2	9/19/64	2
Fort Harrison, VA (8TH)	9/29/64	1
Cedar Creek, VA (2 HA,13TH)	10/19/64	5
Petersburg, VA (2 HA)	3/25/65	1
Fort Gregg, VA (10TH)	4/2/65	1

COVENTRY
THE POPULATION IN 1860 WAS 2,085 (RANK 74)

THE MOST IMPORTANT DAY OF THE CIVIL WAR

JUNE 15 1863
WINCHESTER, VA

THE ENTIRE UNION ARMY WAS NEARLY CAPTURED AT THE SECOND BATTLE OF WINCHESTER

165 MEN CREDITED TO COVENTRY SERVED IN THE FOLLOWING CONNECTICUT ORGANIZATIONS

More soldiers credited to Coventry were listed as casualties (10) on this day than on any other day of the war. Two soldiers were wounded, and 8 were captured in the 18TH Connecticut. One of the captured soldiers died in prison.

The date June 15, 1863 ranks 2ND for total casualties (595) (23 killed, 11 wounded, 520 captured, 41 wounded & captured) for a single day for the State of Connecticut. There were 592 casualties at Winchester, VA, and 3 casualties at Port Hudson, LA.

The Second Battle of Winchester (June 13-15, 1863) ranks 5TH for total casualties (592) for an engagement. The most intense fighting developed on June 15. Coventry had all its casualites on that day.

The Second Battle of Winchester with 10 total casualties for Coventry was the highest number of casualties for any single engagement of the war for the town.

Winchester was one of the most contested locations in the Civil War. It changed hands seventy-two times.

REGIMENT	TOTAL
25TH	29 (18%)
10TH	19 (12%)
18TH	18 (11%)
11TH	13 (8%)
14TH	13 (8%)
12TH	11 (7%)
1ST HEAVY ARTILLERY	9 (5%)
2ND HEAVY ARTILLERY	9 (5%)
1ST CAVALRY	7 (4%)
5TH	7 (4%)
7TH	6 (4%)
6TH	4 (2%)
12TH BATTALION	4 (2%)
22ND	4 (2%)
8TH	3 (2%)
20TH	3 (2%)
21ST	3 (2%)
24TH	3 (2%)
29TH	3 (2%)
30TH	3 (2%)
16TH	2 (1%)
1ST	1
1ST LIGHT BATTERY	1
20TH	1

8% OF POPULATION

SIX WERE KILLED AND TWO WERE MISSING

The first Coventry soldier killed was 1ST Lieutenant Theron D. Hill of Company C, 10TH Connecticut. He was killed at Kinston, NC on December 14, 1862.

COVENTRY SOLDIERS KILLED OR MISSING *

PLACE	DATE	NO.
Kinston, NC (10TH)	12/14/62	1
Gettysburg, PA (14TH)	7/3/63	1
Drewry's Bluff, VA (11TH)	5/16/64	1
North Anna River, VA (14TH)	5/25/64	1
Cold Harbor, VA (2 HA) *	6/1/64	1
Petersburg, VA (30TH) *	7/30/64	1
Cedar Creek, VA (12TH)	10/19/64	1
Railroad Accident (20TH)	11/11/64	1

SIXTEEN WERE CAPTURED

Five Coventry soldiers died in captivity. One died at Andersonville Prison, GA, one at Danville, VA, one at Libby Prison, Richmond, VA, one at Florence, SC and one at Salisbury, NC.

COVENTRY CAPTURED *(5) DIED IN CAPTIVITY

PLACE	DATE	NO.
Winchester, VA (18TH) *1	6/15/63	8
Fort Wagner, SC (7TH) *	7/11/63	1
St. Augustine, FL (10TH) *	12/30/63	1
New Market, VA (18TH) *	5/15/64	2
Winchester, VA (18TH)	7/24/64	1
Cedar Creek, VA (12TH) *	10/19/64	2
Cedar Creek, VA (1 CA)	11/12/64	1

TOTAL COVENTRY CASUALTIES

DIED	24	15%
KILLED/MISSING	8	5%
WOUNDED	31	19%
CAPTURED	16	10%
DESERTED	28	17%

THIRTY-ONE WERE WOUNDED

The first Coventry soldier wounded was Corporal Eugene A. Root of the 10TH Connecticut. He was wounded at Roanoke Island, NC on February 8, 1862 and recovered from his wound. Seven Coventry soldiers died from a wound received during the war.

COVENTRY WOUNDED *(7) DIED FROM WOUNDS

PLACE	DATE	NO.
Roanoke Island, NC (10TH)	2/8/62	1
New Bern, NC (10TH)	3/14/62	1
Antietam, MD (14TH) *2	9/17/62	4
Kinston, NC (10TH) *	12/14/62	1
Irish Bend, LA (25TH)	4/14/63	2
Winchester, VA (18TH)	6/10/63	1
Port Hudson, LA (12TH)	6/10/63	1
Winchester, VA (18TH)	6/15/63	2
Port Hudson, LA (25TH)	6/27/63	1
Gettysburg, PA (14TH) *	7/3/63	1
Morton's Ford, VA (14TH)	2/6/64	1
Virginia (8TH)	3/17/64	1
Wilderness, VA (14TH)	5/7/64	1
Chester Station, VA (6TH)	5/10/64	1
Drewry's Bluff, VA (21ST)	5/16/64	1
Bermuda Hundred, VA (6TH)	5/20/64	1
Petersburg, VA (11TH)	6/3/64	1
Cold Harbor, VA (11TH) *	6/3/64	1
Petersburg, VA (11TH)	6/18/64	1
Snicker's Ford, VA (18TH)	7/18/64	1
Deep Run, VA (10TH)	8/16/64	1
Winchester, VA (12TH)	9/19/64	2
Darbytown Road, VA (10TH)	10/13/64	1
Hatcher's Run, VA (14TH)	2/7/65	1
North East Bridge (6TH)	4/22/65	1

CROMWELL
THE POPULATION IN 1860 WAS 1,617 (RANK 92)

THE MOST IMPORTANT DAY OF THE CIVIL WAR

MAY 3, 1863

CHANCELLORSVILLE, VA

THE THIRD DAY OF THE BATTLE

More soldiers credited to Cromwell were listed as casualties (4) on this day than on any other day of the war. Three soldiers were wounded and 1 was wounded & captured in the 20TH Connecticut. One of the wounded died.

The date May 3, 1863 ranks 3RD for total casualties (577) (36 killed, 1 missing, 138 wounded, 372 captured, 29 wounded & captured) for a single day for the State of Connecticut. The most casualties were at Chancellorsville, VA (556). The other casualties were at Providence Church Road, VA (12), Suffolk, VA (6), Port Hudson, LA (2) and Fredericksburg, VA (1).

The Battle of Chancellorsville (May 1-3, 1863) ranks 2ND for total casualties (677) for an engagement for the State of Connecticut. The most intense fighting developed on May 3 and Cromwell had all of its casualties on that day.

The Battle of Chancellorsville with 4 total casualties for Cromwell was the highest number of casualties for any single engagement of the war for the town.

The Battle of Chancellorsville was an enormous defeat for the more than 70,000 Union soldiers who had moved against the flank and rear of 40,000 Confederate soldiers. Unfortunately, the Union Army had pulled back and had gone on the defensive around Chancellorsville. The Confederate victory was tainted however, by the loss of Confederate Major General "Stonewall" Jackson.

112 MEN CREDITED TO CROMWELL SERVED IN THE FOLLOWING CONNECTICUT ORGANIZATIONS

REGIMENT	TOTAL
20TH	23 (21%)
24TH	21 (19%)
1ST HEAVY ARTILLERY	18 (16%)
11TH	13 (12%)
3RD LIGHT BATTERY	11 (10%)
7TH	7 (6%)
14TH	7 (6%)
2ND HEAVY ARTILLERY	3 (4%)
5TH	3 (2%)
6TH	2 (2%)
13TH	2 (2%)
17TH	1
1ST LIGHT BATTERY	1
3RD	1
12TH	1
12TH BATTALION	1
15TH	1
16TH	1
21ST	1

7% OF POPULATION

TWO WERE KILLED

The first Cromwell soldier killed was Private Edward Burke of the 11TH Connecticut. He was killed at Proctor's Creek, VA on May 12, 1864.

CROMWELL SOLDIERS KILLED

PLACE	DATE	NO.
Proctor's Creek, VA (11TH)	5/12/64	1
Fort Fisher, NC (6TH)	1/3/65	1

FIVE WERE CAPTURED

One Cromwell soldier died in captivity at Andersonville Prison, GA.

CROMWELL CAPTURED
*(1) DIED IN CAPTIVITY

PLACE	DATE	NO.
Harrisonburg, VA (5TH)	5/3/62	1
Chancellorsville, VA (20TH) (WOUNDED)	5/3/63	1
Plymouth, NC (16TH) *	4/20/64	1
Drewry's Bluff, VA (7TH)	5/16/64	1
Kinston, NC, (15TH)	3/8/65	1

TOTAL CROMWELL CASUALTIES

DIED	13	12%
KILLED	2	3%
WOUNDED	17	15%
CAPTURED	5	4%
DESERTED	17	15%

SEVENTEEN WERE WOUNDED

The first Cromwell soldiers wounded were Privates Robert J. Allison, Ralph James, Charles T. Penfield, and George B. Shoemaker of the 20TH Connecticut. They were wounded at Chancellorsville, VA on May 3, 1863 and one died from his wound. Five Cromwell soldiers died from a wound received during the war.

CROMWELL WOUNDED
*(5) DIED FROM WOUNDS

PLACE	DATE	NO.
Chancellorsville, VA(20TH)*1	5/3/63	3
Port Hudson, LA (24TH)	5/24/63	1
Port Hudson, LA (24TH)	6/20/63	1
New Haven, CT (20TH)	8/16/63	1
Morton's Ford, VA (14TH)	2/6/64	1
Bermuda Hundred, VA (6TH)	5/3/64	1
Drewry's Bluff, VA (7,11TH)*1	5/16/64	2
Bermuda Hundred, VA (7TH)	6/2/64	1
Cold Harbor, VA (11TH)	6/3/64	1
Petersburg, VA (11TH)	6/18/64	1
Peach Tree Creek, GA (20TH)*	7/20/64	1
Deep Run, VA (7TH)	8/16/64	1
Turner's Ford, GA (20TH) *	8/27/64	1
Winchester, VA (2 HA) *	9/19/64	1

354

DANBURY
THE POPULATION IN 1860 WAS 7,234 (RANK 10)

THE MOST IMPORTANT DAY OF THE CIVIL WAR

JULY 1, 1863

GETTYSBURG, PA

THE FIRST DAY OF THE BATTLE

More soldiers credited to Danbury were listed as casualties (21) on this day than on any other day of the war. Two soldiers were killed, 8 were wounded, and 11 were captured in the 17TH Connecticut. One of the wounded died.

The date July 1, 1863 ranks 16TH for total casualties (157) (18 killed, 4 missing, 70 wounded, 57 captured, 8 wounded & captured) for a single day for the State of Connecticut. The Battle of Gettysburg accounted for 143 casualties. The 14 other casualties were scattered about Virginia (6), Louisiana (6), and South Carolina (2).

The Battle of Gettysburg (July1-3, 1863) ranks 11TH for total casualties (360) for an engagement for the State of Connecticut. The most intense fighting developed on July 3. Danbury had 1 casualty on that day, and also had 1 casualty on July 2.

The Battle of Gettysburg with 23 total casualties for Danbury was the 2nd highest number of casualties for any single engagement of the war for the city. The highest number of casualties for an engagement was 27 at Drewry's Bluff, VA (May 13-17, 1864).

More than 170,00 men fought at the Battle of Gettysburg. Roughly 23,000 Union casualties were recorded and there were about 28,000 Confederate casualties. Gettysburg proved to be the great battle of the war. It ended Lee's 1863 invasion of the North. He was never able to launch a major offensive again

765 MEN CREDITED TO DANBURY SERVED IN THE FOLLOWING CONNECTICUT ORGANIZATIONS

REGIMENT	TOTAL
23RD	145 (19%)
1ST HEAVY ARTILLERY	93 (12%)
17TH	86 (11%)
11TH	84 (11%)
7TH	82 (11%)
1ST	65 (9%)
6TH	50 (7%)
3RD	48 (6%)
5TH	41 (5%)
1ST CAVALRY	27 (3%)
29TH	24 (3%)
8TH	20 (3%)
12TH	20 (3%)
15TH	14 (2%)
9TH	14 (2%)
2ND HEAVY ARTILLERY	11 (1%)
12TH BATTALION	8 (1%)
20TH	7 (1%)
9TH BATTALION	6
10TH	6
3RD LIGHT BATTERY	4
14TH	4
13TH	3
13TH BATTALION	2
24TH	1
28TH	1
30TH	1

11% OF POPULATION

SEVENTEEN WERE KILLED

The first Danbury soldier killed was First Sergeant John R. Marsh of Company C, 3RD Connecticut. He was killed at the Battle of Bull Run, VA on July 21, 1861.

DANBURY SOLDIERS KILLED

PLACE	DATE	NO.
Bull Run, VA (3RD)	7/21/61	1
James Island, SC (7TH)	6/16/62	1
Cedar Mountain, VA (5TH)	8/9/62	1
Brashear City, LA (23RD)	6/23/63	1
Gettysburg, PA (17TH)	7/1/63	2
Drewry's Bluff, VA (7TH)	5/14/64	1
Drewry's Bluff, VA (7TH)	5/16/64	2
Bermuda Hundred, VA (6TH)	5/20/64	1
Cold Harbor, VA (2 HA)	6/1/64	1
Bermuda Hundred, VA (7TH)	6/2/64	2
Cold Harbor, VA (11TH)	6/3/64	2
Deep Run, VA (6TH)	8/16/64	1
Richmond, VA (7TH)	10/13/64	1

FIFTY-THREE WERE CAPTURED

Thirteen Danbury soldiers died in captivity. Seven died at Andersonville Prison, GA, two at Salisbury, NC and one each at Charleston, SC, Charlottesville, VA, Florence, SC, and Millen, GA.

DANBURY CAPTURED
*(13) DIED IN CAPTIVITY

PLACE	DATE	NO.
Bull Run, VA (3RD)	7/21/61	1
Winchester, VA (5TH) (WOUNDED)	5/25/62	2
James Island, SC (7TH) * (WOUNDED)	6/16/62	1
Cedar Mountain, VA (5TH) (1*) (1 WOUNDED)	8/9/62	2
Chancellorsville, VA (17TH)	5/2/63	2
Brashear City, LA (23RD)	6/23/63	1
Gettysburg, PA (17TH)	7/1/63	11
Bradywine Creek, VA (11TH)	7/2/63	1
Bay St. Louis, MS (9TH) *	10/5/63	1
Olustee, FLA (7TH) *	4/26/64	1
Craig's Church, VA (1CA) * (2)	5/5/64	2
Drewry's Bluff, VA (7TH) *	5/14/64	1
Drewry's Bluff, VA (6,7,11TH) *2 (1 WOUNDED)	5/16/64	8
Ashland, VA (1 CA)	6/1/64	1
Bermuda Hundred, VA (7TH)	6/2/64	2
Petersburg, VA (11TH) *	6/18/64	1
Ft. Powhatan, VA (8TH)	9/18/64	1
Osborne, Pike, VA (6TH) *	10/2/64	1
Cedar Creek, VA (9TH,12TH) *(1)	10/19/64	3
Fair Oaks, VA (8TH)	10/29/64	1
St. Augustine, FLA (17TH)	2/4/65	3
Kinston, NC (15TH)	3/8/65	4
Ashland, VA (1 CA)	3/15/65	1

TOTAL DANBURY CASUALTIES

DIED	67	9%
KILLED	17	2%
WOUNDED	112	15%
CAPTURED	53	7%
DESERTED	71	9%

ONE HUNDRED-TWELVE WERE WOUNDED

The first Danbury soldiers wounded were Privates Patrick Foley and John Moore of Company I, 3RD Connecticut. Both recovered from their wounds. Thirteen Danbury soldiers died from a wound received in the war.

DANBURY WOUNDED
* (13) DIED FROM WOUNDS

PLACE	DATE	NO.
Bull Run, VA (3RD)	7/21/61	2
New Bern, NC (11TH) *	3/1/62	1
New Bern, NC (11TH)	3/14/62	1
James Island, SC (7TH) *(3)	6/16/64	5
Cedar Mountain, VA (5TH)	8/9/62	5
Antietam, MD (8TH, 11TH) *(1)	9/17/62	9
Providence Church RD, VA (11TH)	5/3/63	1
Brashear City, LA (23RD)	6/2/63	1
Port Hudson, LA (12TH)	6/10/63	1
La Fourche, LA (23RD) *(2)	6/21/63	9
Port Hudson, LA (12TH)	6/22/63	1
Brashear City, LA (23RD)	6/24/63	1
Gettysburg, PA (17TH) *(1)	7/1/63	8
Gettysburg, PA (17TH)	7/2/63	1
Gettysburg, PA (17TH)	7/3/63	1
Fort Wagner, SC (17TH)	8/19/63	1
Helena Island, SC (7TH)	12/20/63	1
Olustee, FLA (7TH)	2/20/64	4
Proctor's Creek, VA (6TH)	5/3/64	1
Chester Station, VA (7TH)	5/10/64	2
Drewry's Bluff, VA (7TH, 11TH)	5/14/64	5
Drewry's Bluff, VA (6, 7,11TH)*(1)	5/16/64	8
Bermuda Hundred, VA (7TH)	5/16/64	1
Bermuda Hundred, VA (6TH)	5/20/64	1
Bermuda Hundred, VA (6TH)	5/30/64	1
Cold Harbor, VA (2 HA)	6/1/64	1
Point of Rocks, VA (1 HA)	6/1/64	1
Cold Harbor, VA (11TH)	6/3/64	5
Petersburg, VA (7TH)	6/9/64	1
Bermuda Hundred, VA (7TH) *(1)	6/17/64	2
Petersburg, VA (11TH)	6/18/64	1
Culp's Farm, GA (5TH)	6/22/64	1
Peach Tree Creek, GA (5TH) *(1)	7/20/64	2
Atlanta, GA (5TH)	7/20/64	1
Petersburg, VA (11TH)	8/5/64	1
Deep Bottom, VA (6TH)	8/14/64	2
Deep Run, VA (,10TH)	8/16/64	1
Deep Run, VA (6TH) *(2)	8/16/64	3
Deep Bottom, VA (7TH)	8/16/64	1
Petersburg, VA (6TH)	9/8/64	1
Petersburg, VA (1 HA)	9/9/64	1
Petersburg, VA (29TH)	9/19/64	1
Petersburg, VA (7TH)	9/20/64	1
Chaffin's Farm, GA (8TH)	9/29/64	1
Ft. Harrison, VA (8TH)	9/29/64	1
Richmond, VA (6TH)	10/1/64	1
Richmond, VA (6TH)	10/7/64	1
Cedar Creek, VA (12TH)	10/19/64	1
Kell House, VA (29TH) *(1)	10/27/64	2
Ft. Fisher, NC (7TH)	1/15/65	1
Petersburg, VA (2 HA)	3/25/65	1
Petersburg, VA (1 HA,10TH)	4/2/65	2
Sailor's Creek, VA (2 HA) *	4/6/65	1
Harper's Farm, VA (1 CA)	4/6/65	1
Petersburg, VA (8TH)	8/27/65	1

DARIEN
THE POPULATION IN 1860 WAS 1,705 (RANK 87)

THE MOST IMPORTANT DAY OF THE CIVIL WAR

MAY 19, 1864
WELAKA, FL

ALMOST ALL OF COMPANY B, 17TH CONNECTICUT INFANTRY WERE CAPTURED IN NORTHERN FLORIDA

More soldiers credited to Darien were listed as casualties (18) on this day than on any other day of the war. Eighteeen soldiers in Company B, 17TH Connecticut were captured. They were imprisoned at Andersonville, GA, Millen, GA and Florence, SC. Four died in captivity and 4 others died after release.

The date May 19,1864 ranks 44TH for total casualties (49) (1 killed, 7 wounded, 41 captured) for the State of Connecticut. There were 42 casualties at Welaka and 7 casualties scattered about Georgia (4) and Virginia (3).

The incident at Welaka, FL (May19, 1864) ranks 41ST for total casualties (42) for an engagement for the State of Connecticut.

The incident at Welaka, FL with 18 total casualties for Darien was the highest number of casualties for any single engagement of the war for the town.

Florida was often referred to as the breadbasket of the Confederacy. With a location deep in the South and a favorable climate, Florida added greatly to the Southern cause. The principal products supplied were cattle, cotton and salt.

By 1864, the number of soldiers in the 17TH Connecticut had been greatly reduced. They did not have the strength to mount a strong fighting force and were placed in an out of the way outpost.

128 MEN CREDITED TO DARIEN SERVED IN THE FOLLOWING CONNECTICUT ORGANIZATIONS

REGIMENT	TOTAL
17TH	38 (30%)
28TH	21 (17%)
3RD	17 (14%)
10TH	17 (14%)
7TH	15 (12%)
11TH	9 (7%)
29TH	4 (3%)
1ST CAVALRY	3 (2%)
12TH	3 (2%)
2ND HEAVY ARTILLERY	2 (2%)
8TH	2 (2%)
13TH	2 (2%)
15TH	2 (2%)
23RD	2 (2%)
2ND LIGHT BATTERY	1
6TH	1
13TH BATTALION	1
18TH	1
20TH	1
30TH	1

7% OF POPULATION

THREE WERE KILLED AND TWO WERE MISSING

The first Darien soldier killed was Private Horace Curtis of Rifle Company F, 3RD Connecticut. He was reported missing on July 21, 1861 at the first Battle at Bull Run. His body was never recovered.

DARIEN SOLDIERS KILLED OR MISSING *

PLACE	DATE	NO.
Bull Run, VA (3RD) *	7/21/61	1
Port Hudson, LA (28TH)	6/17/63	1
Drewry's Bluff, VA (7TH) 1*	5/16/64	2
Kinston, NC (15TH)	3/8/65	1

TWENTY-EIGHT WERE CAPTURED

Eight Darien soldiers died in captivity. Five died at Andersonville Prison, GA, two at Millen, GA, and one at Florence, SC.

DARIEN CAPTURED
*(8) DIED IN CAPTIVITY

PLACE	DATE	NO.
Chancellorsville, VA (17TH)	5/2/63	1
Winchester, VA (18TH)	6/15/63	1
Gettysburg, PA (17TH)	7/1/63	1
Gettysburg, PA (17TH)	7/2/63	1
St. Augustine, FL (10TH) *	12/30/63	1
Olustee, FL (7TH) *	2/20/64	1
(WOUNDED)		
Welaka, FL (17TH) *4	5/19/64	18
Petersburg, VA (2HA) *	6/22/64	1
Dunn's Lake, FLA (17TH)	2/5/65	1
Kinston, NC (15TH)	3/8/65	1
Unknown (11TH) *	Unknown	1

TOTAL DARIEN CASUALTIES

DIED	26	20%
KILLED/MISSING	5	4%
WOUNDED	23	18%
CAPTURED	28	22%
DESERTED	17	13%

TWENTY-THREE WERE WOUNDED

The first Darien soldier wounded was Raymond Byxbee of Company G, 10th Connecticut. He was wounded at New Bern, NC on March 14, 1862 and recovered from his wound. Three Darien soldiers died from wounds received during the war.

DARIEN WOUNDED
* (3) DIED FROM WOUNDS

PLACE	DATE	NO.
New Bern, NC (8TH)	3/14/62	1
James Island, SC (7TH)	6/16/62	1
Kinston, NC (10TH) *1	12/14/62	2
Irish Bend, LA (13TH)	4/14/63	1
Chancellorsville, VA (17TH)	5/2/63	2
Port Hudson, LA (28TH)	6/14/63	2
Gettysburg, PA (17TH)	7/1/63	3
Gettysburg, PA (17TH)	7/2/63	1
Gettysburg, PA (17TH)	7/3/63	1
Walthall Junction, VA (8TH)	5/7/64	1
Drewry's Bluff, VA (7TH) *	5/14/64	1
Petersburg, VA (11TH)	6/18/64	1
Deep Run, VA (10TH)	8/16/64	1
Darbytown Road, VA (10TH)	8/18/64	1
Petersburg, VA (10TH)	9/13/64	1
Chaffin's Farm, VA (8TH) *	10/4/64	1
Newmarket Road, VA (10TH)	10/7/64	1
Fort Gregg, VA (10TH)	4/2/65	1

DEEP RIVER (SAYBROOK)
THE POPULATION IN 1860 WAS 1,427 (RANK 102)

THE MOST IMPORTANT DAY OF THE CIVIL WAR

SEPTEMBER 17, 1862

SHARPSBURG, MD (ANTIETAM)

CONNECTICUT HAD MORE CASUALTIES FOR ONE DAY THAN ON ANY OTHER DAY OF THE WAR

Deep River (Saybrook) had more casualties on September 17, 1862 at Antietam, MD (2) and on March 8, 1865 at Kinston, NC (2) than on any other days of the war. The casualties at Antietam were the most serious. Two soldiers were killed in the 11TH Connecticut.

The date September 17, 1862 ranks 1ST for total casualties (687) (131 killed, 2 missing, 515 wounded, 21 captured, 18 wounded & captured) for a single day for the State of Connecticut. All of the casualties were at Antietam.

The Battle of Antietam (September 16-17, 1862) ranks 1ST for total casualties (689) for an engagement for the State of Connecticut. The most intense fighting developed on September 17. Deep River (Saybrook) had all of its casualties on that day.

The Battle of Antietam with 2 total casualties for Deep River (Saybrook) was tied with the Second Battle of Kinston (March 8, 1865) for the 2nd highest number of casualties for any single engagement of the war for the town. The highest number of casualties was 4 at the Siege of Petersburg, VA (June1864-April1865).

Roughly 12,400 Union casualties were recorded and perhaps there were 10,300 Confederate casualties. Antietam proved to be one of the turning points of the war. It ended Lee's 1862 invasion of the North.

68 MEN CREDITED TO DEEP RIVER (SAYBROOK) SERVED IN THE FOLLOWING CONNECTICUT ORGANIZATIONS

REGIMENT	TOTAL
11TH	26 (38%)
8TH	6 (9%)
1ST CAVALRY	5 (7%)
7[STH]	5 (7%)
10 [TH]	4 (6%)
30TH	4 (6%)
12TH	3 (4%)
15TH	3 (4%)
21ST	3 (4%)
1ST HEAVY ARTILLERY	2 (3%)
2ND HEAVY ARTILLERY	2 (3%)
6TH	2 (3%)
16TH	2 (3%)
5TH	1
9TH	1
9TH BATTALION	1
14TH	1
16TH	1
20TH	1

6% OF POPULATION

FIVE WERE KILLED

The first Deep River (Saybrook) soldiers killed in the war were 1ST Sergeant George E. Bailey and Private William Lane of Company K, 11TH Connecticut. Both were killed at the Battle of Antietam, MD on September 17, 1862.

DEEP RIVER (SAYBROOK)
SOLDIERS KILLED

PLACE	DATE	NO.
Antietam, MD (11TH)	9/17/62	2
Bermuda Hundred, VA (7TH)	5/31/64	1
Petersburg, VA (30TH)	7/30/64	1
Winchester, VA (2 HA)	9/19/64	1

TWO WERE CAPTURED

No Deep River (Saybrook) soldier died in captivity.

DEEP RIVER (SAYBROOK)
CAPTURED
NONE DIED IN CAPTIVITY

PLACE	DATE	NO.
Plymouth, NC (16TH)	4/20/64	1
Kinston, NC (15TH)	3/8/65	1

TOTAL DEEP RIVER (SAYBROOK) CASUALTIES

DIED	7	10%
KILLED	5	7%
WOUNDED	8	12%
CAPTURED	2	3%
DESERTED	7	10%

EIGHT WERE WOUNDED

The first Deep River (Saybrook) soldier wounded was Corporal James A. Erwin of Company K, 10TH Connecticut. He was wounded at Kinston, NC on December 12, 1862 and recovered from his wound. No Deep River (Saybrook) soldier died from a wound received during the war.

DEEP RIVER (SAYBROOK) WOUNDED
NONE DIED FROM WOUNDS

PLACE	DATE	NO.
Kinston, NC (10TH)	12/14/62	1
Drewry's Bluff, VA (7TH)	5/16/64	1
Cold Harbor, VA (11TH)	6/3/64	1
Petersburg, VA (8TH)	6/15/64	1
Petersburg, VA (11TH)	6/18/64	1
Petersburg, VA (21ST)	8/3/64	1
Deep Run, VA (10TH)	8/16/64	1
Kinston, NC (15TH)	3/8/65	1

DERBY

THE POPULATION IN 1860 WAS 5443 (RANK 14)

THE MOST IMPORTANT DAY OF THE CIVIL WAR

MAY 3, 1863

CHANCELLORSVILLE, VA

THE THIRD DAY OF THE BATTLE

More soldiers credited to Derby were listed as casualties (20) on this day than on any other day of the war. Four soldiers were killed, 8 were wounded, 4 were captured, and 4 were wounded & captured in the 5TH and 20TH Connecticut. The wounded and captured survived the war.

The date May 3, 1863 ranks 3RD for total casualties (577) (36 killed, 1 missing, 138 wounded, 372 captured, 29 wounded & captured) for a single day for the State of Connecticut. The most casualties were at Chancellorsville, VA (556). The other casualties were at Providence Church Road, VA (12), Suffolk, VA (6), Port Hudson, LA (2) and Fredericksburg, VA (1).

The Battle of Chancellorsville (May 1-3, 1863) ranks 2ND for total casualties (677) for an engagement for the State of Connecticut. The most intense fighting developed on May 3 and Derby had all of its casualties on that day.

The Battle of Chancellorsville with 20 total casualties for Derby was the highest number of casualties for any single engagement of the war for the town.

The Battle of Chancellorsville was an enormous defeat for the more than 70,000 Union soldiers who had moved against the flank and rear of 40,000 Confederate soldiers. Unfortunately, the Union Army had pulled back and had gone on the defensive around Chancellorsville. The Confederate victory was tainted however, by the loss of Confederate Major General "Stonewall" Jackson.

511 MEN CREDITED TO DERBY SERVED IN THE FOLLOWING CONNECTICUT ORGANIZATIONS

REGIMENT	TOTAL
1ST HEAVY ARTILLERY	110 (22%)
20TH	110 (22%)
2ND	79 (16%)
3RD LIGHT BATTERY	47 (9%)
23RD	45 (9%)
5TH	31 (6%)
9TH	31 (6%)
1ST CAVALRY	30 (6%)
10TH	29 (6%)
7TH	22 (4%)
9TH BATTALION	13 (3%)
6TH	7 (1%)
11TH	7 (1%)
2ND HEAVY ARTILLERY	6 (1%)
13TH	6 (1%)
15TH	6 (1%)
1ST	4 (1%)
12TH	4 (1%)
8TH	3
29TH	3
1ST SQUADRON CAVALRY	2
12TH BATTALION	2
1ST LIGHT BATTERY	1
27TH	1
28TH	1

9% OF POPULATION

TWENTY-FIVE WERE KILLED AND ONE WAS MISSING

The first Derby soldier killed was Colonel Charles L. Russell. He was on the staff of the 10TH Connecticut and was killed at Roanoke Island, NC on February 8, 1862.

DERBY SOLDIERS KILLED OR MISSING *

PLACE	DATE	NO.
Roanoke Island, NC (10TH)	2/8/62	1
La Fourche Crossing, LA (12TH)	2/22/63	1
Chancellorsville, VA (20TH)	5/3/63	4
La Fourche, LA (23RD)	6/21/63	1
Gettysburg, PA (20TH)	7/3/63	1
Fort Wagner, SC (6TH)	7/18/63	1
Railroad Accident (20TH)	11/5/63	1
Tracy City, TN (20TH)	1/21/64	1
Resaca, GA (5TH)	5/15/64	1
Drewry's Bluff, VA (7TH)	5/16/64	1
Cold Harbor, VA (2HA)	6/1/64	1
Savage Station, VA (1 CA)	6/16/64	1
Peach Tree Creek, GA (20TH)	7/20/64	2
Atlanta, GA (20TH)	7/23/64	1
Ream's Station, VA (1 CA) *	7/29/64	1
Deep Run, VA (7TH)	8/16/64	2
Turner's Ford, GA (20TH)	8/30/64	1
Petersburg, VA (1 HA)	9/12/64	1
Richmond, VA (7TH)	10/13/64	1
Silver Run, NC (20TH)	3/16/65	1
Bentonville, NC (20TH)	3/19/65	1

TWENTY-NINE WERE CAPTURED

Two Derby soldiers died in captivity. One died at Andersonville Prison, GA and one died in Salisbury Prison, NC.

DANBURY CAPTURED * (2) DIED IN CAPTIVITY

PLACE	DATE	NO.
Fall Church, VA ((2ND)	6/19/61	1
Buckingham Co.,VA (5TH)	2/22/62	1
Winchester, VA (5TH)	5/25/62	1
Cross Keys, VA (1 CA)	6/8/62	1
Chancellorsville, VA (20TH) (4 WOUNDED)	5/3/63	8
Frederick, MD (1 CA)	6/20/63	1
Gettysburg, PA (5TH)	7/2/63	1
Bolivar Heights, VA (1 CA)	7/14/63	1
Craig's Church, VA (1 CA)	5/5/64	1
Drewry's Bluff, VA (7, 11TH)	5/16/64	2
White House, VA (1 CA) * (1)	5/23/64	1
Ashland, VA (1 CA) (1 WOUNDED)	6/1/64	2
Ream's Station, VA (1 CA)	6/29/64	2
Cedar Run Church, VA (1 CA)	10/17/64	1
Cedar Creek, VA (2 HA) *(1)	10/19/64	1
Madison, GA (5TH)	11/19/64	1
Kinston, NC (15TH)	3/8/65	3

TOTAL DERBY CASUALTIES

DIED	34	7%
KILLED/MISSING	26	5%
WOUNDED	55	11%
CAPTURED	29	6%
DESERTED	49	10%

FIFTY-FIVE WERE WOUNDED

The first Derby soldier wounded was Pliny Bartholomew of Company H, 10TH Connecticut. He was wounded at Roanoke Island, NC on February 8, 1862 and died from his wound. Four Derby soldiers died from wounds received during the war.

DERBY WOUNDED * (4) DIED FROM WOUNDS

PLACE	DATE	NO.
Roanoke Island, NC (10TH) *	2/8/62	1
New Bern, NC (10TH)	3/14/62	1
James Island, SC (7TH)	6/16/62	1
Chickahominy, VA (1 HA)	6/25/62	1
Baton Rouge, LA (9TH)	8/5/62	1
Antietam, MD (8TH) *	9/17/62	1
Pocotaligo, SC (7TH)	10/22/62	2
Kinston, NC (10TH)	12/14/62	3
Chancellorsville, VA (5, 20TH)	5/3/63	8
La Fourche, LA (23RD)	6/21/63	1
Brashear City, LA (23RD) *	6/23/63	1
Chattahoola Station, LA (9TH)	6/24/63	1
Gettysburg, PA (20TH)	7/2/63	1
Gettysburg, PA (20TH)	7/3/63	2
Fort Wagner, SC (6TH)	7/18/63	1
Unknown (1 SQ)	12/1/63	1
Olustee, FLA (7TH)	2/20/64	1
Drewry's Bluff, VA (10TH)	5/14/64	1
Drewry's Bluff, VA (7TH)	5/16/64	1
Cold Harbor, VA (2 HA)	6/1/64	1
Petersburg, VA (1 HA)	6/27/64	1
Ream's Station, VA (1 CA)	6/29/64	1
Andersonville, GA (1 CA)	7/1/64	2
Peach Tree Creek, GA (5,20[TH])	7/20/64	6
Atlanta, GA (20TH)	7/25/64	1
Petersburg, VA (10TH)	9/13/64	1
Fisher's Hill, VA (9TH)	9/22/64	1
Darbytown Road, VA (10TH)	10/13/64	1
Cedar Creek, VA (2 HA)	10/19/64	1
Fair Haven, CT (3RD LB)	10/31/64	1
Iversbury, NC (20TH)	3/14/65	1
Averysboro, NC (20TH)	3/16/65	1
Bentonville, NC (20TH) *(1)	3/19/65	6
Hatcher's Run, VA (10TH)	4/1/65	1

DURHAM
THE POPULATION IN 1860 WAS 1,130 (RANK 123)

THE MOST IMPORTANT DAY OF THE CIVIL WAR

MARCH 8, 1865
KINSTON, NC

THE CONFEDERATE ATTACK STALLED BECAUSE OF BAD COMMUNICATION

More soldiers credited to Durham were listed as casualties (17) on this day than on any other day of the war. One soldier was killed, 1 was wounded, 13 were captured, and 2 were wounded & captured in the 15TH Connecticut. The wounded and captured soldiers survived the war.

The date March 8, 1865 ranks 5TH for total casualties (496) (22 killed, 3 missing, 12 wounded, 410 captured, 49 wounded & captured) for a single day for the State of Connecticut. There were 494 casualties at Kinston, 1 casualty in Virginia, and 1 casualty at a railroad accident in an unknown place.

The Second Battle of Kinston (March 8, 1865) ranks 8TH for total casualties (494) for an engagement for the State of Connecticut.

The Second Battle of Kinston with 17 total casualties for Durham was the highest number of casualties for any single engagement of the war for the town

The military situation in North Carolina changed in early 1865. The Confederate forces in eastern North Carolina were called to help stop the advance of the Union Army coming out of Georgia. The Confederates attacked the Union flanks near Kinston on March 8 and failed.

95 MEN CREDITED TO DURHAM SERVED IN THE FOLLOWING CONNECTICUT ORGANIZATIONS

REGIMENT	TOTAL
15TH	32 (34%)
24TH	11 (12%)
7TH	9 (10%)
10TH	8 (9%)
14TH	7 (7%)
30TH	6 (6%)
29TH	6 (6%)
8TH	4 (4%)
13TH	4 (4%)
1ST HEAVY ARTILLERY	3 (3%)
20TH	3 (3%)
6TH	2 (2%)
1ST CAVALRY	1
2ND HEAVY ARTILLERY	1
5TH	1
11TH	1
12TH	1
13TH BATTALION	1
16TH	1
17TH	1
22ND	1
27TH	1

8% OF POPULATION

ONE WAS KILLED

The only Durham soldier killed was Private Calvin Albee of Company I, 15TH Connecticut. He was killed at Kinston, NC on March 8, 1865.

DURHAM SOLDIERS KILLED

PLACE	DATE	NO.
Kinston, NC (15TH)	3/8/65	1

SEVENTEEN WERE CAPTURED

One Durham soldier died in captivity at Libby Prison, Richmond, VA.

DURHAM CAPTURED
*(1) DIED IN CAPTIVITY

PLACE	DATE	NO.
Warrenton, VA (14TH)	11/17/62	1
Bermuda Hundred, VA (6TH) *	5/20/64	1
Kinston, NC (15TH)	3/8/65	15
(2 WOUNDED)		

TOTAL DURHAM CASUALTIES

DIED	5	5%
KILLED	1	1%
WOUNDED	13	14%
CAPTURED	17	18%
DESERTED	5	5%

THIRTEEN WERE WOUNDED

The first Durham soldiers wounded were Privates John Harren of Company K and Samuel G. Camp of Company B, 14TH Connecticut. Both were wounded at the Battle of Antietam, MD on September 17, 1862 and both recovered from their wounds. One Durham soldier died from a wound received during the war.

DURHAM WOUNDED
*(1) DIED FROM WOUNDS

PLACE	DATE	NO.
Antietam, MD (14TH)	9/17/62	2
Fredericksburg, VA (14TH)	12/13/62	1
Chancellorsville, VA (5TH)	5/3/63	1
Port Hudson, LA (13TH,24TH)	6/14/63	2
Cold Harbor, VA (8TH)	6/3/64	1
Petersburg, VA (8TH)	6/15/64	1
Deep Run, VA (7TH) *	8/16/64	2
Winchester, VA (13TH)	9/14/64	1
Hatcher's Run, VA (14TH)	2/5/65	1
Kinston, NC (15TH)	3/8/65	1

EAST GRANBY
THE POPULATION IN 1860 WAS 833 (RANK 145)

THE MOST SIGNIFICANT DAY OF THE CIVIL WAR

APRIL 14, 1863

IRISH BEND, LA

THE BATTLE WAS PART OF THE UNION ATTEMPT TO SIEZE WESTERN LOUISIANA

More soldiers credited to East Granby were listed as casualties (4) on this day than any other day of the war. One soldier was killed and 3 were wounded in the 25TH Connecticut. The wounded survived the war.

The date April 14, 1863 ranks 17TH for total casualties (147) (18 killed, 120 wounded, 9 captured) for a single day for the State of Connecticut. The Battle of Irish Bend accounted for 144 casualties. The 3 other casualties were also in Louisiana.

The Battle of Irish Bend (April 14, 1863) ranks 18TH for total casualties (144) for an engagement for the State of Connecticut

The Battle of Irish Bend with 4 total casualties for East Granby was the highest number of casualties for any single engagement of the war for the town.

Due to the lack of men, money, and supplies, the Confederate Army under General Richard Taylor fought a difficult fight to hold onto Louisiana. At the Battle of Irish Bend, in Bayou Tech, he held off a far larger Union force on two fronts until he could get his army to safety.

83 MEN CREDITED TO EAST GRANBY SERVED IN THE FOLLOWING CONNECTICUT ORGANIZATIONS

REGIMENT	TOTAL
25TH	24 (29%)
1ST HEAVY ARTILLERY	10 (12%)
16TH	7 (8%)
2ND HEAVY ARTILLERY	6 (7%)
30TH	6 (7%)
29TH	5 (6%)
1ST LIGHT BATTERY	4 (5%)
8TH	4 (5%)
11TH	4 (5%)
14TH	3 (4%)
15TH	3 (4%)
1ST SQUADRON CAVALRY	2 (2%)
1ST CAVALRY	2 (2%)
5TH	2 (2%)
10TH	2 (2%)
21ST	2 (2%)
1ST	1
6TH	1
7TH	1
22ND	1

10% OF POPULATION

TWO WERE KILLED

The first East Granby soldier killed was Corporal Edward Prindle of Company E, 25ᵀᴴ Connecticut. He was killed at Irish Bend, LA on April 14, 1863.

EAST GRANBY SOLDIERS KILLED

PLACE	DATE	NO.
Irish Bend, LA (25ᵀᴴ)	4/14/63	1
Petersburg, VA (30ᵀᴴ)	7/30/64	1

NINE WERE CAPTURED

No East Granby soldiers died in captivity.

EAST GRANBY CAPTURED
NONE DIED IN CAPTIVITY

PLACE	DATE	NO.
Smithburg, MD (1 SQ)	7/4/63	1
Plymouth, NC (16ᵀᴴ)	4/20/64	3
Ream's Station, VA (1 CA)	6/29/64	1
Kinston, NC (15ᵀᴴ)	3/8/65	3
Hatcher's Run, VA (14ᵀᴴ)	3/25/65	1

TOTAL EAST GRANBY CASUALTIES

DIED	10	12%
KILLED	2	2%
WOUNDED	10	12%
CAPTURED	9	11%
DESERTED	15	18%

TEN WERE WOUNDED

The first East Granby soldier wounded was Private Edward W. Pierce of Company I, 16ᵀᴴ Connecticut. He was wounded at the Battle of Antietam, MD on September 17, 1862 and recovered from his wound. One East Granby soldier died from a wound received during the war.

EAST GRANBY WOUNDED
*(1) DIED FROM WOUNDS

PLACE	DATE	NO.
Antietam, MD (16ᵀᴴ)	9/17/62	1
Irish Bend, LA (25ᵀᴴ)	4/14/63	3
Port Hudson, LA (25ᵀᴴ)	5/31/63	2
Cold Harbor, VA (8ᵀᴴ) *	6/3/64	1
Petersburg, VA (30ᵀᴴ)	7/30/64	1
Columbia, VA (1 CA)	3/3/65	1
Richmond, VA (1 HA)	6/1/65	1

EAST HADDAM
THE POPULATION IN 1860 WAS 3,056 (RANK 42)

THE MOST IMPORTANT DAY OF THE CIVIL WAR

MAY 16, 1864

DREWRY'S BLUFF , VA

AN OBSTACLE ON THE WAY TO RICHMOND

214 MEN CREDITED TO EAST HADDAM SERVED IN THE FOLLOWING CONNECTICUT ORGANIZATIONS

East Haddam had more casualties on May 3, 1863 at Chancellorsville, VA(4) May 16, 1864 at Drewry's Bluff, VA (4) and October 19, 1864 at Cedar Creek, VA (4) than on any other days of the war. The casualties at Drewry's Bluff were the most serious. Three soldiers were captured and 1 was wounded & captured in the 7TH and 11TH Connecticut. Two died in prison.

The date May 16, 1864 ranks 4th for total casualties (560) (52 killed, 3 missing, 224 wounded, 243 captured, 38 wounded & captured) for a single day for the State of Connecticut. The Battle of Drewry's Bluff accounted for 545 casualties. The 15 other casualties were scattered about Virginia.

The Battle of Drewry's Bluff (May 13-17, 1864), also called Fort Darling, ranks 3rd for total casualties (634) for an engagement for the State of Connecticut. The most intense fighting developed on May 16. East Haddam also had 1 casualty on May 14 and 1 on May 15

The Battle of Drewry's Bluff with 6 total casualties for East Haddam the highest number of casualties for an engagement of the war for the town.

The Confederate attack at Drewry's Bluff forced the Union Army to retreat to Bermuda Hundred. The civil war would have concluded sooner had the Union Army been victorious.

REGIMENT	TOTAL
1ST HEAVY ARTILLERY	29 (14%)
10TH	27 (13%)
20TH	25 (12%)
13TH	19 (9%)
14TH	18 (8%)
22ND	16 (7%)
12TH	15 (7%)
7TH	13 (6%)
11TH	12 (6%)
29TH	10 (5%)
26TH	8 (4%)
1ST CAVALRY	6 (3%)
6TH	6 (3%)
25TH	6 (3%)
2ND HEAVY ARTILLERY	5 (3%)
16TH	5 (3%)
27TH	5 (3%)
12TH BATTALION	4 (2%)
13TH BATTALION	4 (2%)
8TH	3 (1%)
24TH	3 (1%)
5TH	2 (1%)
15TH	2 (1%)
30TH	1
21ST	1

7% OF POPULATION

SIX WERE KILLED AND THREE WERE MISSING

The first East Haddam soldier killed was Private John F. Bingham of Company H, 16TH Connecticut. He was killed at the Battle of Antietam, MD on September 17, 1862.

EAST HADDAM SOLDIERS KILLED OR MISSING *

PLACE	DATE	NO.
Antietam, MD (16TH)	9/17/62	1
Wilderness, VA (14TH) *1	5/6/64	2
Drewry's Bluff, VA (10TH)	5/14/64	1
Atlanta, GA (20TH) *	7/21/64	1
Petersburg, VA (30TH) *	7/30/64	1
Fort Harrison, VA (8TH)	9/29/64	1
Hatcher's Run, VA (10TH)	4/1/65	1
Fort Gregg, VA (10TH)	4/2/65	1

EIGHTEEN WERE CAPTURED

Six East Haddam soldiers died in captivity. One died at Andersonville Prison, GA, one at Charleston Prison, SC, one at Salisbury Prison, NC, one at Millen, Prison, GA and two at Libby Prison Richmond, VA.

EAST HADDAM CAPTURED *(6) DIED IN CAPTIVITY

PLACE	DATE	NO.
Chancellorsville, VA (20,27TH) (1 WOUNDED)	5/3/63	4
Fort Wagner, SC (7TH) *	7/11/63	1
Bristoe Station, VA (14TH) *	10/14/63	2
Plymouth, NC (16TH) *	4/20/64	1
Drewry's Bluff, VA (7,11TH) *2 (1 WOUNDED)	5/16/64	4
Reams Station, VA (14TH) *	8/25/64	2
Cedar Creek, VA (12TH)	10/19/64	2
Kinston, NC (15TH)	3/8/65	1
Goldsboro, NC (20TH)	3/25/65	1

TOTAL EAST HADDAM CASUALTIES

DIED	29	14%
KILLED/MISSING	9	4%
WOUNDED	38	18%
CAPTURED	18	8%
DESERTED	31	14%

THIRTY-EIGHT WERE WOUNDED

The first East Haddam soldier wounded was Private Charles T. Hamilton of Company C, 14TH Connecticut. He was wounded at the Battle of Antietam, MD on September 17, 1862 and died from his wound. Six East Haddam soldiers died from a wound received during the war.

EAST HADDAM WOUNDED *(6) DIED FROM WOUNDS

PLACE	DATE	NO.
Antietam, MD (14TH) *	9/17/62	1
Stafford Court House, VA (20TH)	12/1/62	1
Fredericksburg, VA (27TH)	12/13/62	2
Port Hudson, LA (26TH)	5/27/63	1
Port Hudson, LA (26TH)	6/14/63	2
Gettysburg, PA (20TH)	7/3/63	1
Morris island, SC (7TH)	7/10/63	1
Fort Wagner, SC (7TH)	7/11/63	1
Morris Island, SC (7TH)	8/21/63	1
Morton's Ford, VA (14TH)	2/6/64	1
Cane River, LA (13TH) *	4/23/64	1
Wilderness, VA (14TH)	5/6/64	1
Wilderness, VA (14TH)	5/7/64	1
Drewry's Bluff, VA (6TH)	5/15/64	1
Cassville, GA (20TH)	5/19/64	1
Bermuda Hundred, VA (6TH) *	5/20/64	1
Peach Tree Creek, VA (20TH)	7/20/64	1
Deep Bottom, VA (7TH ,10TH)	8/14/64	2
Cedar Creek, VA (13TH)	9/18/64	1
Petersburg, VA (7TH)	10/1/64	1
Darbytown Rd, VA (10TH,29TH)	10/13/64	2
Cedar Creek, VA (12TH,13TH)	10/19/64	2
Kell House, VA (29TH)	10/27/64	1
Battery Morton, VA (1 HA) *	11/26/64	1
Petersburg, VA (1 HA)	11/28/64	1
Fort Fisher, NC (7TH)	1/15/65	1
Silver Run, NC (20TH) *	3/16/65	2

EAST HAMPTON (CHATHAM)
THE POPULATION IN 1860 WAS 1,231 (RANK 117)

THE MOST IMPORTANT DAY OF THE CIVIL WAR

MAY 16, 1864

DREWRY'S BLUFF , VA

AN OBSTACLE ON THE WAY TO RICHMOND

More soldiers credited to East Hampton (Chatham) were listed as casualties (7) on this day than on any other day of the war. Six soldiers were wounded and 1 was wounded & captured in the 21ST Connecticut. The captured soldier died in prison.

The date May 16, 1864 ranks 4th for total casualties (560) (52 killed, 3 missing, 224 wounded, 243 captured, 38 wounded & captured) for a single day for the State of Connecticut. The Battle of Drewry's Bluff accounted for 545 casualties. The 15 other casualties were scattered about Virginia.

The Battle of Drewry's Bluff (May 13-17, 1864), also called Fort Darling, ranks 3rd for total casualties (634) for an engagement for the State of Connecticut. The most intense fighting developed on May 16. East Hampton (Chatham) had no other casualties.

The Battle of Drewry's Bluff with 7 total casualties for East Hampton (Chatham) was tied with the Siege of Port Hudson, LA (May-July1863) for the highest number of casualties for an engagement of the war for the town.

The Confederate attack at Drewry's Bluff forced the Union Army to retreat to Bermuda Hundred. The civil war would have concluded sooner had the Union Army been victorious.

141 MEN CREDITED TO EAST HAMPTON (CHATHAM) SERVED IN THE FOLLOWING CONNECTICUT ORGANIZATIONS

REGIMENT	TOTAL
24TH	32 (23%)
21ST	30 (21%)
1ST HEAVY ARTILLERY	15 (11%)
14TH	15 (11%)
2ND HEAVY ARTILLERY	8 (6%)
29TH	8 (6%)
30TH	8 (6%)
12TH	7 (5%)
15TH	6 (4%)
10TH	4 (3%)
7TH	3 (2%)
11TH	2 (1%)
12TH BATTALION	2 (1%)
17TH	2 (1%)
1ST CAVALRY	1
1ST LIGHT BATTERY	1
1ST SQUADRON CAVALRY	1
5TH	1
6TH	1
20TH	1
25TH	1

8% OF POPULATION

THREE WERE KILLED

The first East Hampton (Chatham) soldier killed was Private Benjamin R. Fuller of Company K, 14TH Connecticut. He was killed at the Battle of Antietam, MD on September 17, 1862.

EAST HAMPTON (CHATHAM) SOLDIERS KILLED

PLACE	DATE	NO.
Antietam, MD (14TH)	9/17/62	1
Cold Harbor, VA (2 HA)	6/1/64	1
Petersburg, VA (30TH)	7/30/64	1

FIVE WERE CAPTURED

One East Hampton (Chatham) soldier died in captivity at Libby Prison, Richmond, VA.

EAST HAMPTON (CHATHAM) CAPTURED
*(1) DIED IN CAPTIVITY

PLACE	DATE	NO.
Drewry's Bluff, VA (21ST) * (WOUNDED)	5/16/64	1
Cedar Creek, VA (12TH)	10/19/64	1
Kinston, NC (15TH)	3/8/65	3

TOTAL EAST HAMPTON (CHATHAM) CASUALTIES

DIED	20	14%
KILLED	3	2%
WOUNDED	26	18%
CAPTURED	5	4%
DESERTED	7	5%

TWENTY-SIX WERE WOUNDED

The first East Hampton (Chatham) soldiers wounded were Corporal Jason H. Barton and Privates John Bayhan and Selden Fuller of the, 11TH and 14TH Connecticut. They were wounded at the Battle of Antietam, MD on September 17, 1862 and both recovered from their wounds. Corporal Barton died from a second wound he received at Petersburg, VA. He was the only East Hampton (Chatham) soldier who died from a wound received during the war.

EAST HAMPTON (CHATHAM) WOUNDED
*(1) DIED FROM WOUNDS

PLACE	DATE	NO.
Antietam, MD (11,14TH)	9/17/62	3
Port Hudson, LA (24TH)	5/27/63	1
Port Hudson, LA (24TH)	6/14/63	4
Port Hudson, LA (24TH)	6/17/63	1
Port Hudson, LA (24TH)	6/20/63	1
Bristoe Station, VA (14TH)	10/14/63	1
Drewry's Bluff, VA (21ST)	5/16/64	6
Cold Harbor, VA (2 HA)	6/1/64	1
Cold Harbor, VA (21ST)	6/3/64	1
Bermuda Hundred, VA (6TH)	6/17/64	1
Petersburg, VA (11TH) *	6/18/64	1
Petersburg, VA (21ST)	7/22/64	1
Petersburg, VA (21ST,30TH)	7/30/64	2
Kell House, VA (29TH)	10/27/64	1
Hatcher's Run, VA (14TH)	3/25/65	1

EAST HARTFORD
THE POPULATION IN 1860 WAS 2,951 (RANK 43)

THE MOST IMPORTANT DAY OF THE CIVIL WAR

MAY 16, 1864

DREWRY'S BLUFF , VA

AN OBSTACLE ON THE WAY TO RICHMOND

East Hartford had more casualties on May 16, 1864 at Drewry's Bluff, VA (4) and on June 3, 1864 at Cold Harbor, VA (4) than on any other days of the war. The casualties at Drewry's Bluff were the most serious. One soldier was killed, 2 were wounded, and 1 was captured in the 11TH and 21ST Connecticut. The wounded and captured survived the war.

The date May 16, 1864 ranks 4th for total casualties (560) (52 killed, 3 missing, 224 wounded, 243 captured, 38 wounded & captured) for a single day for the State of Connecticut. The Battle of Drewry's Bluff accounted for 545 casualties. The 15 other casualties were scattered about Virginia.

The Battle of Drewry's Bluff (May 13-17, 1864), also called Fort Darling, ranks 3rd for total casualties (634) for an engagement for the State of Connecticut. The most intense fighting developed on May 16. East Hartford also had 1 casualty on May 14.

The Battle of Drewry's Bluff with 5 total casualties for East Hartford was the highest number of casualties for any single engagement of the war for the town.

The Confederate attack at Drewry's Bluff forced the Union Army to retreat to Bermuda Hundred. The civil war would have concluded sooner had the Union Army been victorious.

227 MEN CREDITED TO EAST HARTFORD SERVED IN THE FOLLOWING CONNECTICUT ORGANIZATIONS

REGIMENT	TOTAL
21ST	47 (21%)
25TH	26 (11%)
13TH	22 (10%)
1ST HEAVY ARTILLERY	18 (8%)
7TH	17 (7%)
13TH BATTALION	17 (7%)
1ST CAVALRY	14 (6%)
12TH	14 (6%)
10TH	12 (5%)
5TH	9 (4%)
11TH	9 (4%)
6TH	7 (3%)
29TH	7 (3%)
16TH	6 (3%)
20TH	6 (3%)
22ND	6 (3%)
24TH	6 (3%)
2ND HEAVY ARTILLERY	3 (1%)
1ST	2 (1%)
1ST LIGHT BATTERY	2 (1%)
8TH	2 (1%)
12TH BATTALION	2 (1%)
14TH	2 (1%)
30TH	2 (1%)
1ST SQUADRON CAVALRY	1
15TH	1
27TH	1

8% OF POPULATION

SEVEN WERE KILLED AND ONE WAS MISSING

The first East Hartford soldier killed was 1st Sergeant John F. Carroll of Company K, 24TH Connecticut. He was killed at Port Hudson, LA on May 25, 1863.

EAST HARTFORD SOLDIERS KILLED OR MISSING *

PLACE	DATE	NO.
Port Hudson, LA (24TH)	5/25/63	1
Walthall Junction, VA (8TH)	5/7/64	1
Drewry's Bluff, VA (21ST)	5/16/64	1
Dallas, GA (5TH) *	5/25/64	1
Petersburg, VA (21ST)	7/30/64	1
Deep Bottom, VA (10TH)	8/14/64	1
Deep Run, VA (10TH)	8/16/64	1
Newmarket Road, VA (7TH)	10/7/64	1

SEVENTEEN WERE CAPTURED

Three East Hartford soldiers died in captivity. All three died at Andersonville Prison,GA.

EAST HARTFORD CAPTURED *(3) DIED IN CAPTIVITY

PLACE	DATE	NO.
2ND Bull Run, VA (5TH)	8/30/62	1
Pattersonville, LA (12TH) (WOUNDED)	3/27/63	1
Chancellorsville, VA (20TH)	5/3/63	1
Fort Wagner, SC (6TH) * (WOUNDED)	7/18/63	1
Smithfield, VA (21ST) *	2/1/64	1
Plymouth, NC (16TH)	4/20/64	3
Spottsylvania, VA (14TH)	5/12/64	1
Drewry's Bluff, VA (11TH)	5/16/64	1
Hatcher's Run, VA (7TH) *	6/2/64	1
Bermuda Hundred, VA (7TH)	6/2/64	1

TOTAL EAST HARTFORD CASUALTIES

DIED	14	6%
KILLED/MISSING	8	4%
WOUNDED	32	14%
CAPTURED	17	7%
DESERTED	21	9%

THIRTY-TWO WERE WOUNDED

The first East Hartford soldier wounded was Private Robert K. Reid of Company A, 7TH Connecticut. He was wounded at James Island, SC on June 16, 1862 and recovered from his wound. Two East Hartford soldiers died from a wound received during the war.

EAST HARTFORD WOUNDED *(2) DIED FROM WOUNDS

PLACE	DATE	NO.
James Island, SC (7TH)	6/16/62	1
James Island, SC (7TH)	6/17/62	1
2nd Bull Run, VA (5TH)	8/30/62	1
Antietam, MD (16TH)	9/17/62	2
Fredericksburg, VA (21ST)	12/13/62	1
Kinston, NC (10TH) *	12/14/62	1
Pattersonville, LA (12TH)	3/27/63	1
Irish Bend, LA (25TH)	4/14/63	2
Port Hudson, LA (25TH)	4/14/63	1
Port Hudson, LA (24TH)	5/27/63	1
Fort Wagner, SC (6TH)	7/18/63	1
Cane River, LA (13TH)	4/23/64	1
Drewry's Bluff, VA (7TH)	5/14/64	1
Drewry's Bluff, VA (11,7TH)	5/16/64	2
Bermuda Hundred, VA (11TH)	5/16/64	1
Ashland, VA (1 CA)	6/1/64	1
Cold Harbor, VA (21ST) *1	6/3/64	3
Petersburg, VA (21ST)	6/15/64	1
Petersburg, VA (21ST)	7/6/64	1
Petersburg, VA (10TH)	9/1/64	1
Winchester, VA (1 CA)	9/19/64	1
Fort Harrison, VA (21ST)	9/29/64	1
Chaffin's Farm, VA (21ST)	9/30/64	1
Darbytown Rd, VA (7,10TH)	10/13/64	2
Cedar Creek, VA (2 HA)	10/19/64	1
Fort Gregg, VA (10TH)	4/2/65	1

EAST HAVEN
THE POPULATION IN 1860 WAS 2,292 (RANK 63)

THE MOST IMPORTANT DAY
OF THE CIVIL WAR

MARCH 8, 1865

KINSTON, NC

THE CONFEDERATE
ATTACK STALLED
BECAUSE OF BAD
COMMUNICATION

More soldiers credited to East Haven were listed as casualties (10) on this day than on any other day of the war. One soldier was missing and 9 were captured in the 15TH Connecticut. The captured soldiers survived the war.

The date March 8, 1865 ranks 5TH for total casualties (496) (22 killed, 3 missing, 12 wounded, 410 captured, 49 wounded & captured) for a single day for the State of Connecticut. There were 494 casualties at Kinston, 1 casualty in Virginia, and 1 casualty at a railroad accident in an unknown place.

The Second Battle of Kinston (March 8, 1865) ranks 8TH for total casualties (494) for an engagement for the State of Connecticut.

The Second Battle of Kinston with 10 total casualties for East Haven was the highest number of casualties for any single engagement of the war for the town.

The military situation in North Carolina changed in early 1865. The Confederate forces in eastern North Carolina were called to help stop the advance of the Union Army coming out of Georgia. The Confederates attacked the Union flanks near Kinston on March 8 and failed.

191 MEN CREDITED TO EAST HAVEN SERVED IN THE FOLLOWING CONNECTICUT ORGANIZATIONS

REGIMENT	TOTAL
15TH	36 (20%)
27TH	27 (14%)
1ST HEAVY ARTILLERY	24 (13%)
5TH	19 (10%)
10TH	17 (9%)
20TH	14 (7%)
29TH	10 (5%)
1ST CAVALRY	8 (4%)
1ST LIGHT BATTERY	8 (4%)
7TH	8 (4%)
30TH	8 (4%)
2ND HEAVY ARTILLERY	6 (3%)
11TH	6 (3%)
6TH	5 (3%)
12TH	4 (2%)
8TH	3 (2%)
13TH	3 (2%)
12TH BATTALION	2 (1%)
13TH BATTALION	2 (1%)
14TH	2 (1%)
9TH	1 (1%)
17TH	1 (1%)

8% OF POPULATION

FOUR WERE KILLED AND ONE WAS MISSING

The first East Haven soldier killed was Private Augustus B. Fairchild of Company A, 27TH Connecticut. He was killed at Freddricksburg, VA on December 13, 1862..

EAST HAVEN SOLDIERS KILLED OR MISSING *

PLACE	DATE	NO.
Fredericksburg, VA (27TH)	12/13/62	1
Port Hudson, LA (12TH)	6/11/63	1
Proctor's Creek, VA (1 LB)	5/14/64	1
Drewry's Bluff, VA (11TH)	5/16/64	1
Kinston, NC (15TH) *	3/8/65	1

EIGHTEEN WERE CAPTURED

Two East Haven soldiers died in captivity. One died at Andersonville Prison, GA and one at Florence, SC.

**EAST HAVEN CAPTURED
*(2) DIED IN CAPTIVITY**

PLACE	DATE	NO.
Chancellorsville, VA (27TH)	5/3/63	1
Drewry's Bluff, VA (11TH) *2	5/16/64	2
(1 WOUNDED)		
Ream's Station, VA (1 CA)	6/28/64	1
Stony Creek, VA (1 CA)	6/28/64	1
Peach Tree Creek, GA (5TH)	7/20/64	1
Petersburg, VA (30TH)	7/30/64	1
(WOUNDED)		
Cedar Creek, VA (12TH)	10/19/64	1
Middletown, VA (2 HA)	10/19/64	1
Kinston, NC (15TH)	3/8/65	9

TOTAL EAST HAVEN CASUALTIES

DIED	11	6%
KILLED/MISSING	5	3%
WOUNDED	15	8%
CAPTURED	18	9%
DESERTED	32	17%

FIFTEEN WERE WOUNDED

The first East Haven soldiers wounded were Sergeant Henry D. Russell and Privates Charles Higgins, William A. Kelly and Leonard Russell of Company F, 27TH Connecticut. All were wounded at Fredericksburg, VA on December 13, 1862. Sergeant Russell died from his wound. He was the only East Haven soldier to die from a wound received during the war.

**EAST HAVEN WOUNDED
*(1) DIED FROM WOUNDS**

PLACE	DATE	NO.
Fredericksburg, VA (27TH) *1	12/13/62	4
Kinston, NC (10TH)	12/14/62	1
Fredericksburg, VA (15TH)	12/17/62	1
Gettysburg, PA (27TH)	7/2/63	3
Wilderness, VA (14TH)	5/6/64	1
Proctor's Creek, VA (1 LB)	5/14/64	1
Drewry's Bluff, VA (10TH)	5/16/64	1
Petersburg, VA (2 HA)	6/25/64	1
Darbytown Road, VA (10TH)	10/27/64	1
Fort Gregg, VA (10TH)	4/2/65	1

EAST LYME
THE POPULATION IN 1860 WAS 1,506 (RANK 98)

THE MOST IMPORTANT DAY OF THE CIVIL WAR

FEBRUARY 8, 1862

ROANOKE ISLAND, NC

THE OUTNUMBERED CONFEDERATES RETREATED

More soldiers credited to East Lyme were listed as casualties (3) on this day than on any other day of the war. Three soldiers were wounded in the 10TH Connecticut. Two of the wounded died.

The date February 8, 1862 ranks 42ND for total casualties (56) (4 killed, 52 wounded) for a single day for the State of Connecticut. All of the casualties were at Roanoke Island, NC.

The Battle of Roanoke Island (February 8, 1862) ranks 35TH for total casualties (56) for an engagement for the State of Connecticut

The Battle of Roanoke Island with 3 total casualties for East Lyme was tied with the Siege of Port Hudson, LA (May-July1863) for the highest number of casualties for any single engagement of the war for the town.

In January 1862, Union General Ambrose E. Burnside led a naval expedition to North Carolina with a mission to enter Albemarle and Pimlico Sounds and to capture Roanoke Island. A battle ensued on February 8 and Burnside's 15,000 man army forced the Confederates to retreat to the northwest point of the island where 2,500 Confederates were captured.

90 MEN CREDITED TO EAST LYME SERVED IN THE FOLLOWING CONNECTICUT ORGANIZATIONS

REGIMENT	TOTAL
26TH	31 (34%)
10TH	13 (15%)
5TH	10 (11%)
29TH	7 (8%)
14TH	6 (7%)
1ST HEAVY ARTILLERY	5 (6%)
1ST CAVALRY	4 (5%)
12TH	4 (5%)
30TH	4 (5%)
2ND HEAVY ARTILLERY	3 (3%)
21ST	2 (2%)
7TH	1
8TH	1
11TH	1
12TH BATTALION	1
13TH	1
13TH BATTALION	1

6% OF POPULATION

ONE WAS KILLED

The only East Lyme soldier killed was Corporal Silas S. Fox of Company H, 14TH Connecticut. He was killed at Morton's Ford, VA on February 6, 1864.

EAST LYME SOLDIERS KILLED

PLACE	DATE	NO.
Morton's Ford, VA (14TH)	2/6/64	1

NO EAST LYME SOLDIERS WERE CAPTURED

TOTAL EAST LYME CASUALTIES

DIED	12	13%
KILLED	1	1%
WOUNDED	22	24%
CAPTURED	0	0%
DESERTED	9	10%

TWENTY-TWO WERE WOUNDED

The first East Lyme soldiers wounded were Privates William H. Gorton, Joseph W. Huntley, and Milton Smith of Company H, 10TH Connecticut. All were wounded at Roanoke Island, NC on February 8, 1862 and two died from their wounds. Four East Lyme soldiers died from a wound received during the war.

EAST LYME WOUNDED
*(4) DIED FROM WOUNDS

PLACE	DATE	NO
Roanoke Island, NC (10TH) *2	2/8/62	3
Antietam, MD (14TH)	9/17/62	1
Georgia Landing, LA (12TH)	10/27/62	1
Fredericksburg, VA (14TH)	12/13/62	1
Kinston, NC (10TH)	12/14/62	1
Seabrook, SC (10TH)	5/1/63	1
Port Hudson, LA (26TH) *1	5/27/63	3
Port Hudson, LA (12TH)	6/10/63	1
Morton's Ford, VA (14TH) *	2/6/64	1
Drewry's Bluff, VA (7,21ST)	5/16/64	2
Cold Harbor, VA (2 HA)	6/1/64	1
Petersburg, VA (21ST)	6/22/64	1
Petersburg, VA (30TH)	7/30/64	1
Kell House, VA (30)	10/27/64	1
Darbytown Road, VA (10TH)	10/27/64	1
Fort Fisher, NC (7TH)	1/19/65	1
Fredericksburg, VA (10TH)	7/15/65	1

EAST WINDSOR
THE POPULATION IN 1860 WAS 2,580 (RANK 54)

THE MOST IMPORTANT DAY OF THE CIVIL WAR
SEPTEMBER 17, 1862
SHARPSBURG, MD
(ANTIETAM)

CONNECTICUT HAD MORE CASUALTIES FOR ONE DAY THAN ON ANY OTHER DAY OF THE WAR

More soldiers credited to East Windsor were listed as casualties (18) on this day than on any other day of the war. Seven soldiers were killed, 8 were wounded, and 3 were captured in the 8TH and 16TH Connecticut. One of the wounded died.

The date September 17, 1862 ranks 1ST for total casualties (687) (131 killed, 2 missing, 515 wounded, 21 captured, 18 wounded & captured) for a single day for the State of Connecticut. All of the casualties were at Antietam.

The Battle of Antietam (September 16-17, 1862) ranks 1ST for total casualties (689) for an engagement for the State of Connecticut. The most intense fighting developed on September 17. East Windsor had all of its casualties on that day.

The Battle of Antietam with 18 total casualties for East Windsor was the highest number of casualties for any single engagement of the war for the town.

Roughly 12,400 Union casualties were recorded and perhaps there were 10,300 Confederate casualties. Antietam proved to be one of the turning points of the war. It ended Lee's 1862 invasion of the North.

269 MEN CREDITED TO EAST WINDSOR SERVED IN THE FOLLOWING CONNECTICUT ORGANIZATIONS

REGIMENT	TOTAL
22ND	37 (14%)
16TH	34 (13%)
1ST HEAVY ARTILLERY	32 (12%)
25TH	32 (12%)
2ND HEAVY ARTILLERY	21 (8%)
20TH	16 (6%)
29TH	16 (6%)
8TH	12 (4%)
7TH	10 (4%)
1ST CAVALRY	9 (3%)
1ST LIGHT BATTERY	9 (3%)
5TH	9 (3%)
3RD	8 (3%)
6TH	8 (3%)
12TH	6 (2%)
12TH BATTALION	6 (2%)
11TH	5 (2%)
14TH	5 (2%)
10TH	4 (1%)
1ST SQUADRON CAVALRY	3 (1%)
13TH	3 (1%)
1ST	2
2ND	2
9TH	1
9TH BATTALION	1
21ST	1
23RD	1
24TH	1
26TH	1
30TH	1

10% OF POPULATION

FIFTEEN WERE KILLED

The first East Windsor soldier killed was Private Halsey F.D. Phelps of Company B, 8ᵀᴴ Connecticut. He was killed at New Bern, NC on March 14, 1862.

EAST WINDSOR SOLDIERS KILLED

PLACE	DATE	NO.
New Bern, NC (8ᵀᴴ)	3/14/62	1
Antietam, MD (8,16ᵀᴴ)	9/17/62	7
Irish Bend, LA (25ᵀᴴ)	4/14/63	1
Port Hudson, LA (13ᵀᴴ)	6/14/63	1
North Anna River, VA (2 HA)	5/24/64	1
Cold Harbor, VA (2 HA)	6/1/64	1
Ream's Station, VA (14ᵀᴴ)	8/25/64	1
Railroad Accident, VA (1 CA)	3/8/65	1
Potomac River (Drowned) (16ᵀᴴ)	4/24/65	1

TWENTY-ONE WERE CAPTURED

Five East Windsor soldiers died in captivity. Three died at Andersonville Prison, GA and two died at Florence, SC.

EAST WINDSOR CAPTURED
*(5) DIED IN CAPTIVITY

PLACE	DATE	NO.
Antietam, MD (16ᵀᴴ)	9/17/62	3
Opelousas, LA (13ᵀᴴ)	4/20/63	1
Fort Wagner, SC (7ᵀᴴ)	7/11/63	1
Plymouth, NC (16ᵀᴴ) *(4) (1 WOUNDED)	4/20/64	14
Craig's Church, VA (1 CA) *	5/5/64	1
Kinston, NC (15ᵀᴴ)	3/8/65	1

TOTAL EAST WINDSOR CASUALTIES

DIED	22	8%
KILLED	15	6%
WOUNDED	36	13%
CAPTURED	21	8%
DESERTED	41	15%

THIRTY-SIX WERE WOUNDED

The first East Windsor soldier wounded was Private John Ward of Company E, 10ᵀᴴ Connecticut. He was wounded at New Bern, NC on March 14, 1862 and recovered from his wound. Four East Windsor soldiers died from a wound received during the war.

EAST WINDSOR WOUNDED
*(4) DIED FROM WOUNDS

PLACE	DATE	NO.
New Bern, NC (10ᵀᴴ)	3/14/62	1
Antietam, MD (8,16ᵀᴴ) *	9/17/62	8
Pocotaligo, SC (6ᵀᴴ) *	10/22/62	1
Irish Bend, LA (25ᵀᴴ)	4/14/63	2
Port Hudson, LA (12ᵀᴴ)	6/10/63	1
Port Hudson, LA (25ᵀᴴ)	6/27/63	1
James Island, SC (1 LB)	7/16/63	1
Grove Church, VA (1 CA)	3/29/64	1
Wilderness, VA (14ᵀᴴ)	5/6/64	1
Resaca, GA (5ᵀᴴ)	5/15/64	2
Cold Harbor, VA (2 HA)	6/1/64	1
Cold Harbor, VA (8,14ᵀᴴ)	6/3/64	2
Piedmont, VA (18ᵀᴴ)	6/5/64	1
Old Church Tavern, VA (1 CA)	6/10/64	1
Petersburg, VA (1 HA)	7/15/64	1
Peach Tree Creek, GA (20ᵀᴴ)	7/20/64	1
Atlanta, GA (20ᵀᴴ)	7/22/64	1
Petersburg, VA (1 HA)	7/24/64	1
Petersburg, VA (1 HA)	8/24/64	1
Petersburg, VA (29ᵀᴴ) *	9/4/64	1
Winchester, VA (2 HA)	9/19/64	2
Fort Harrison, VA (8ᵀᴴ)	9/29/64	1
Cedar Creek, VA (12ᵀᴴ)	10/19/64	1
Kinston, NC (15ᵀᴴ) *	3/8/65	1
Fair Oaks, VA (29ᵀᴴ)	1865	1

EASTFORD
THE POPULATION IN 1860 WAS 1,005 (RANK 137)

THE MOST IMPORTANT DAY OF THE CIVIL WAR

JUNE 3, 1864

COLD HARBOR, VA

THE BATTLE WAS LEE'S LAST GREAT VICTORY

Eastford had more casualties on September 17, 1862 at Antietam, MD (4) and on June 3, 1864 at Cold Harbor (4) than on any other days of the war. The casualties at Cold Harbor were the most serious. Two were killed and 2 were wounded in the 11TH and 21ST Connecticut. The wounded survived the war.

The date June 3, 1864 ranks 12TH for total casualties (196) (24 killed, 2 missing, 168 wounded, 2 captured) for a single day for the State of Connecticut. The Battle of Cold Harbor accounted for 190 casualties. There were also 4 casualties at Petersburg, VA and 2 casualties at Dallas, GA.

The battle and operations around Cold Harbor (May 31-June 12, 1864) rank 6TH for total casualties (557) for an engagement for the State of Connecticut. The most intense fighting was on June 3. Eastford had one casualty on June 4 and 5.

The Battle of Cold Harbor with 6 total casualties for Eastford was the highest number of casualties any single engagement of the war for the town.

Approximately 117,000 Federal and 60,000 Confederate troops participated in operations from May 28 to June 3. Roughly 13,000 Union casualties were recorded and perhaps there were 5,000 Confederate casualties.

80 MEN CREDITED TO EASTFORD SERVED IN THE FOLLOWING CONNECTICUT ORGANIZATIONS

REGIMENT	TOTAL
11TH	20 (25%)
7TH	10 (13%)
18TH	10 (13%)
8TH	9 (11%)
1ST CAVALRY	8 (10%)
1ST HEAVY ARTILLERY	6 (8%)
6TH	5 (6%)
5TH	4 (5%)
10TH	3 (4%)
21ST	2 (3%)
1ST SQUADRON CAVALRY	1
12TH	1
14TH	1
22ND	1

8% OF POPULATION

SEVEN WERE KILLED

The first Eastford soldier killed was Private William H. Corey of Company H, 7TH Connecticut. He was killed at Petersburg, VA on May 14, 1864.

EASTFORD SOLDIERS KILLED

PLACE	DATE	NO.
Petersburg, VA (7TH)	5/14/64	1
New Market, VA (18TH)	5/15/64	1
Cold Harbor, VA (11TH)	6/3/64	2
Piedmont, VA (18TH)	6/5/64	1
Cold Harbor, VA (8TH)	6/5/64	1
Snicker's Ford, VA (18TH)	7/18/64	1

TWELVE WERE CAPTURED

Three Eastford soldiers died in captivity. One died at Petersburg, VA, one at Charleston, SC, and one at Florence, SC.

EASTFORD CAPTURED
*(3) DIED IN CAPTIVITY

PLACE	DATE	NO.
Winchester, VA (18TH)	6/15/63	2
Plymouth, NC (16TH)	4/20/64	1
New Market, VA (18TH) *	5/15/64	1
Drewry's Bluff, VA (11TH)	5/16/64	1
Bermuda Hundred, VA (7TH) *	6/2/64	1
Hatcher's Run, VA (7TH) *	6/2/64	1
Deep Bottom, VA (6TH)	8/16/64	1
Cedar Creek, VA (1 CA)	11/10/64	1
Cedar Creek, VA (1 CA)	11/12/64	1
Wilmington, NC (6TH)	1/18/65	1
Appomattox CH, VA (10TH)	4/9/65	1

TOTAL EASTFORD CASUALTIES

DIED	10	13%
KILLED	7	9%
WOUNDED	16	20%
CAPTURED	12	15%
DESERTED	10	13%

SIXTEEN WERE WOUNDED

The first Eastford soldiers wounded were Sergeant John B. Lewis and Privates Daniel Adams, Orrin E. Squires and Simon W. Tucker of Company F, 11TH Connecticut. They were wounded at the Battle of Antietam, MD on September 17, 1862 and all recovered from their wounds. Two Eastford soldiers died from a wound received during the war.

EASTFORD WOUNDED
*(2) DIED FROM WOUNDS

PLACE	DATE	NO.
Antietam, MD (11TH)	9/17/62	4
Pocotaligo, SC (7TH)	10/22/62	1
Morton's Ford, VA (14TH)	2/6/64	1
Drewry's Bluff, VA (7TH) *	5/14/64	1
Cold Harbor, VA (11,21ST)	6/3/64	2
Cold Harbor, VA (11TH)	6/4/64	1
Bermuda Hundred, VA (7TH)	6/17/64	1
Peach Tree Creek, GA (5TH)	7/20/64	1
Petersburg, VA (11TH) *	8/1/64	1
Deep Run, VA (7TH)	8/16/64	1
Richmond, VA (7TH)	10/13/64	1
Wilmington, NC (6TH)	4/1/65	1

EASTON
THE POPULATION IN 1860 WAS 1,350 (RANK 108)

THE MOST IMPORTANT DAY
OF THE CIVIL WAR

OCTOBER 19, 1864

CEDAR CREEK, VA

THE LAST MAJOR BATTLE OF THE 1864 SHENANDOAH VALLEY CAMPAIGN WAS A UNION TRIUMPH

109 MEN CREDITED TO EASTON SERVED IN THE FOLLOWING CONNECTICUT ORGANIZATIONS

More soldiers credited to Easton were listed as casualties (3) on this day than any other day of the war. One soldier was wounded, and 2 were captured in the 2ND Connecticut Heavy Artillery and 12TH Connecticut Infantry. One of the captured died in prison.

The date October 19, 1864 ranks 7TH for total casualties (417) (48 killed, 2 missing, 204 wounded, 153 captured, 10 wounded & captured) for a single day for the State of Connecticut. The Battle of Cedar Creek accounted for 415 casualties. The 2 other casualties were in the neighboring towns.

The Battle of Cedar Creek (October 19, 1864) ranks 10TH for total casualties (415) for an engagement for the State of Connecticut.

The Battle of Cedar Creek with 3 total casualties for Easton was the 2nd highest number of casualties for any single engagement of the war for the town. The Siege of Petersburg (June 1864-April 1865) ranks 1st with 5 casualties.

The news of the Union triumph at Cedar Creek assured a Republican victory in the elections of November 1864 and the prosecution of the war to its end on President Abraham Lincoln's and Lieutenant General Ulysses S. Grant's terms.

REGIMENT	TOTAL
23RD	21 (19%)
2ND HEAVY ARTILLERY	14 (13%)
17TH	12 (10%)
10TH	11 (10%)
2ND LIGHT BATTERY	10 (9%)
14TH	7 (6%)
29TH	7 (6%)
8TH	6 (6%)
11TH	6 (6%)
1ST HEAVY ARTILLERY	4 (4%)
5TH	3 (3%)
9TH	3 (3%)
7TH	2 (2%)
20TH	2 (2%)
1ST CAVALRY	1
6TH	1
9TH BATTALION	1
12TH	1
13TH	1
15TH	1
27TH	1
28TH	1

8% OF POPULATION

THREE WERE KILLED AND ONE WAS MISSING

The first Easton soldier killed was Private John Minor of Company A, 7TH Connecticut. He was reported missing and presumed dead at Drewry's Bluff, VA on May 16, 1864.

EASTON SOLDIERS KILLED OR MISSING *

PLACE	DATE	NO.
Drewry's Bluff, VA (7TH)*	5/16/64	1
Petersburg, VA (2 HA)	6/22/64	1
Fort Gregg, VA (10TH)	4/2/65	2

FIVE WERE CAPTURED

Three Easton soldiers died in captivity. Two died at Andersonville Prison, GA prison and one died at Salisbury Prison, NC.

EASTON CAPTURED
*(3) DIED IN CAPTIVITY

PLACE	DATE	NO.
Gettysburg, PA (17TH)	7/1/63	1
(WOUNDED)		
Warrenton, VA (14TH) *	7/20/63	1
Drewry's Bluff, VA (7TH)*	5/16/64	1
Cedar Creek, VA (2HA,12TH)*1	10/19/64	2

TOTAL EASTON CASUALTIES

DIED	6	6%
KILLED/MISSING	4	4%
WOUNDED	10	9%
CAPTURED	5	5%
DESERTED	25	25%

TEN WERE WOUNDED

The first Easton soldier wounded was Private Bradley Banks of the 2ND Connecticut Light Battery. He was wounded at Wolf Run Shoals, VA on February 1, 1863 and recovered from his wound. Two Easton soldiers died from a wound received during the war.

EASTON WOUNDED
*(2) DIED FROM WOUNDS

PLACE	DATE	NO.
Wolf Run Shoals, VA (2LB)	2/1/63	1
Gettysburg, PA (17TH)	7/1/63	1
Cold Harbor, VA (2HA)	6/1/64	1
Petersburg, VA (29TH) *	8/29/64	1
Petersburg, VA (6TH)	9/16/64	1
Winchester, VA (2HA)	9/19/64	1
Petersburg, VA (1HA)	10/15/64	1
Cedar Creek, VA (2HA)	10/19/64	1
Wilmington,NC (6TH) *	2/22/65	1
Petersburg, VA (1HA)	4/3/65	1

ELLINGTON
THE POPULATION IN 1860 WAS 1,510 (RANK 97)

THE MOST SIGNIFICANT DAY OF THE CIVIL WAR

APRIL 14, 1863

IRISH BEND, LA

THE BATTLE WAS PART OF THE UNION ATTEMPT TO SIEZE WESTERN LOUISIANA

Ellington had more casualties on September 17, 1862 at Antietam, MD (4), on April 14, 1863 at Irish Bend, LA (4), and on May 16, 1864 at Drewy's Bluff, VA (4) than on any other days of the war. The casualties at Irish Bend were the most serious. Four soldiers were wounded in the 25TH Connecticut. Two of the wounded died.

The date April 14, 1863 ranks 17TH for total casualties (147) (18 killed, 120 wounded, 9 captured) for a single day for the State of Connecticut. The Battle of Irish Bend accounted for 144 casualties. There were 3 other casualties scattered about Louisiana.

The Battle of Irish Bend (April 14, 1863) ranks 18TH for total casualties (144) for an engagement for the State of Connecticut.

The Battle of Irish Bend with 4 total casualties for Ellington was tied with the Battle of Antietam, MD (September 17, 1862), the Siege of Port Hudson, LA (May-July 1863), and the Battle of Drewry's Bluff, VA (May 13-17, 1864) for the highest number of casualties for any single engagement of the war for the town.

Due to the lack of men, money, and supplies, the Confederate Army under General Richard Taylor fought a difficult fight to hold onto Louisiana. At the Battle of Irish Bend, in Bayou Tech, he held off a far larger Union force on two fronts until he could get his army to safety.

143 MEN CREDITED TO ELLINGTON SERVED IN THE FOLLOWING CONNECTICUT ORGANIZATIONS

REGIMENT	TOTAL
25TH	37 (26%)
11TH	21 (15%)
1ST HEAVY ARTILLERY	15 (11%)
14TH	13 (9%)
7TH	11 (8%)
10TH	8 (6%)
2ND HEAVY ARTILLERY	6 (4%)
1ST CAVALRY	5 (4%)
6TH	5 (4%)
16TH	5 (4%)
12TH	4 (3%)
22ND	4 (3%)
1ST LIGHT BATTERY	3 (1%)
5TH	2 (1%)
30TH	2 (1%)
12TH BATTALION	1
13TH	1
13TH BATTALION	1
18TH	1
20TH	1
21ST	1
29TH	1

9% OF POPULATION

ONE WAS KILLED

The only Ellington soldier killed was Private Joseph Thompson of Company E, 11ᵀᴴ Connecticut. He was killed at Cold Harbor, VA on June 3, 1863.

ELLINGTON SOLDIERS KILLED

PLACE	DATE	NO.
Cold Harbor, VA (11ᵀᴴ)	6/3/64	1

FOUR WERE CAPTURED

No Ellington soldiers died in captivity.

ELLINGTON CAPTURED
NONE DIED IN CAPTIVITY

PLACE	DATE	NO.
Winchester, VA (18ᵀᴴ)	6/15/63	1
Drewry's Bluff, VA (7,11ᵀᴴ)	5/16/64	3

TOTAL ELLINGTON CASUALTIES

DIED	15	10%
KILLED	1	1%
WOUNDED	29	20%
CAPTURED	4	3%
DESERTED	27	19%

TWENTY-NINE WERE WOUNDED

The first Ellington soldiers wounded were Privates James Henderson, Ansel D. Newell, Alfred A. Taft and Joseph Allen of the 11ᵀᴴ and 16ᵀᴴ Connecticut. They were wounded at the Battle of Antietam, MD on September 17, 1862. One of the wounded soldiers died. Eight Ellington soldiers died from a wound received during the war.

ELLINGTON WOUNDED
*(8) DIED FROM WOUNDS

PLACE	DATE	NO.
Antietam, MD (11,14ᵀᴴ) *1	9/17/62	4
Long Island, NY (25ᵀᴴ)	12/1/62	1
Fredericksburg, VA (14ᵀᴴ)	12/13/62	2
Irish Bend, LA (25ᵀᴴ) *2	4/14/63	4
Port Hudson, LA (25ᵀᴴ) *1	5/3/63	2
Port Hudson, LA (25ᵀᴴ) *	5/27/63	1
Morton's Ford, VA (14ᵀᴴ)	2/6/64	1
Wilderness, VA (14ᵀᴴ)	5/6/64	1
Drewry's Bluff, VA (7ᵀᴴ)	5/16/64	1
Cold Harbor, VA (2 HA) *	6/1/64	1
Cold Harbor, VA (11ᵀᴴ)	6/3/64	1
Piedmont, VA (18ᵀᴴ) *	6/5/64	1
Petersburg, VA (14ᵀᴴ)	6/17/64	1
Petersburg, VA (11ᵀᴴ) *1	6/18/64	3
Strawberry Plains, VA (10ᵀᴴ)	7/26/64	1
Deep Bottom, VA (7ᵀᴴ)	8/16/64	1
Winchester, VA (2 HA)	9/19/64	1
Cedar Creek, VA (2 HA)	10/19/64	1
Hatcher's Run, VA (10ᵀᴴ)	3/31/65	1

ENFIELD
THE POPULATION IN 1860 WAS 4,997 (RANK 16)

THE MOST IMPORTANT DAY OF THE CIVIL WAR
SEPTEMBER 17, 1862
SHARPSBURG, MD (ANTIETAM)

CONNECTICUT HAD MORE CASUALTIES FOR ONE DAY THAN ON ANY OTHER DAY OF THE WAR

More soldiers credited to Enfield were listed as casualties (30) on this day than on any other day of the war. Three were killed, 22 were wounded, 1 was captured, and 4 were wounded & captured in the 8ᵀᴴ and 16ᵀᴴ Connecticut. Four of the wounded and one of the captured died.

The date September 17, 1862 ranks 1ˢᵀ for total casualties (687) (131 killed, 2 missing, 515 wounded, 21 captured, 18 wounded & captured) for a single day for the State of Connecticut. All of the casualties were at Antietam.

The Battle of Antietam (September 16-17, 1862) ranks 1ˢᵀ for total casualties (689) for an engagement for the State of Connecticut. The most intense fighting developed on September 17. Enfield had all of its casualties on that day.

The Battle of Antietam with 30 total casualties for Enfield was the highest number of casualties for any single engagement of the war for the town.

Roughly 12,400 Union casualties were recorded and perhaps there were 10,300 Confederate casualties. Antietam proved to be one of the turning points of the war. It ended Lee's 1862 invasion of the North.

402 MEN CREDITED TO ENFIELD SERVED IN THE FOLLOWING CONNECTICUT ORGANIZATIONS

REGIMENT	TOTAL
8ᵀᴴ	95 (24%)
22ᴺᴰ	79 (20%)
16ᵀᴴ	45 (11%)
5ᵀᴴ	40 (10%)
1ˢᵀ HEAVY ARTILLERY	30 (7%)
10ᵀᴴ	19 (5%)
29ᵀᴴ	17 (4%)
1ˢᵀ	15 (4%)
1ˢᵀ CAVALRY	13 (3%)
2ᴺᴰ HEAVY ARTILLERY	13 (3%)
12ᵀᴴ	9 (2%)
14ᵀᴴ	8 (2%)
1ˢᵀ LIGHT BATTERY	7 (2%)
3ᴿᴰ	6 (1%)
6ᵀᴴ	6 (1%)
11ᵀᴴ	6 (1%)
7ᵀᴴ	5 (1%)
20ᵀᴴ	5 (1%)
21ˢᵀ	4 (1%)
1ˢᵀ SQUADRON CAVALRY	3 (1%)
12ᵀᴴ BATTALION	3 (1%)
9ᵀᴴ	1
9ᵀᴴ BATTALION	1
13ᵀᴴ	1
13ᵀᴴ BATTALION	1
28ᵀᴴ	1

8% OF POPULATION

TEN WERE KILLED

The first Enfield soldiers killed were Captain Samuel Brown, Corporal Michael Grace and Private Michael Smith of the 8TH and 16TH Connecticut. They were killed at the Battle of Antietam, MD on September 17, 1862.

ENFIELD SOLDIERS KILLED

PLACE	DATE	NO.
Antietam, MD (8,16TH)	9/17/62	3
Kinston, NC (10TH)	12/14/62	1
Petersburg, VA (8TH)	7/2/64	1
Winchester, VA (2 HA)	9/19/64	1
Fort Harrison, VA (8TH)	9/29/64	1
Cedar Creek, VA (12TH)	10/19/64	1
Silver Run, NC (5TH)	3/16/65	1
Potomac (Drowned) (16TH)	4/24/65	1

THIRTY-SEVEN WERE CAPTURED

Thirteen Enfield soldiers died in captivity. Eleven died in Andersonville Prison, GA, one died in Florence Prison, SC and one died at Sharpsburg, MD.

ENFIELD CAPTURED
*(13) DIED IN CAPTIVITY

PLACE	DATE	NO.
Winchester, VA (5TH)	5/24/62	1
Antietam, MD (8,16TH) *1 (4 WOUNDED)	9/17/62	5
Port Hudson, LA (12TH)	3/27/63	1
Chancellorsville, VA (5TH)	5/2/63	1
Richmond, VA (1 SQ)	3/1/64	1
Plymouth, NC (16TH) *9	4/20/64	19
Craig's Church, VA (1 CA)	5/5/64	1
Virginia (1 SQ) *	Unknown	1
Drewry's Bluff, VA (8,11TH) *2 (1 WOUNDED)	5/16/64	2
Proctor's Creek, VA (8TH) (WOUNDED)	5/16/64	1
Winchester, VA (1 Ca)	8/18/64	1
Cox's Mills, VA (8TH)	8/25/64	1
Cedar Creek, VA (2 HA)	10/19/64	1
Madison, GA (5TH)	11/18/64	1

TOTAL ENFIELD CASUALTIES

DIED	40	10%
KILLED	10	2%
WOUNDED	59	15%
CAPTURED	37	9%
DESERTED	52	13%

FIFTY-NINE WERE WOUNDED

The first Enfield soldier wounded was Corporal Thomas Gordon of Company E, 10TH Connecticut. He was wounded at New Bern, NC on March 14, 1862 and recovered from his wound. Twelve Enfield soldiers died from a wound received during the war.

ENFIELD WOUNDED
*(12) DIED FROM WOUNDS

PLACE	DATE	NO.
New Bern, NC (10TH)	3/14/62	1
Winchester, VA (5TH)	5/25/62	1
South Mountain, MD (8TH)	9/14/62	1
Antietam, MD (8,16TH) *4	9/17/62	22
Kinston, NC (10TH)*	12/14/62	3
Irish Bend, LA (13TH)	4/14/63	1
Fort Hugar, VA (8TH)	4/19/63	1
Walthall Junction, VA (8TH) *2	5/7/64	2
Drewry's Bluff, VA (8TH)	5/16/64	1
Dallas, GA (5TH) *	5/25/64	1
Cold Harbor, VA (2 HA) *1	6/1/64	4
Cold Harbor, VA (8TH)	6/2/64	2
Cold Harbor, VA (8,21ST)	6/3/64	2
Dallas, GA (5TH) *	6/3/64	1
Petersburg, VA (8TH)	6/15/64	1
Petersburg, VA (8TH)	6/22/64	1
Peach Tree Creek, GA (5TH) *1	7/20/64	2
Petersburg, VA (29TH)	9/27/64	1
Fort Harrison, VA (8TH)	9/29/64	4
Chaffin's Farm, VA (8TH)	9/29/64	1
Richmond, VA (29TH)	9/30/64	1
Cedar Creek, VA (12TH,2 HA)	10/19/64	2
Kell House, VA (29TH)	10/27/64	1
Silver Run, NC (20TH)	3/16/65	1
Petersburg, VA (1 HA)*	3/25/65	1

ESSEX
THE POPULATION IN 1860 WAS 1,764 (RANK 84)

THE MOST IMPORTANT DAY
OF THE CIVIL WAR

MAY 16, 1864

DREWRY'S BLUFF , VA

AN OBSTACLE ON THE WAY
TO RICHMOND

More soldiers credited to Essex were listed as casualties (3) on this day than on any other day of the war. One soldier was killed, and 2 were captured in the 7TH and 11TH Connecticut. One of the captured soldiers died in prison.

The date May 16, 1864 ranks 4th for total casualties (560) (52 killed, 3 missing, 224 wounded, 243 captured, 38 wounded & captured) for a single day for the State of Connecticut. The Battle of Drewry's Bluff accounted for 545 casualties. The 15 other casualties were scattered about Virginia.

The Battle of Drewry's Bluff (May 13-17, 1864), also called Fort Darling, ranks 3rd for total casualties (634) for an engagement for the State of Connecticut. The most intense fighting developed on May 16. Essex had all of its casualties on that day.

The Battle of Drewry's Bluff with 3 total casualties for Essex was the 2nd highest number of casualties for an engagement for the town. The Siege of Port Hudson, LA (May-July1863) with 5 casualties was the highest number of casualties for an engagement for the town.

The Confederate attack at Drewry's Bluff forced the Union Army to retreat to Bermuda Hundred. The civil war would have concluded sooner had the Union Army been victorious.

105 MEN CREDITED TO ESSEX SERVED IN THE FOLLOWING CONNECTICUT ORGANIZATIONS

REGIMENT	TOTAL
24TH	48 (46%)
11TH	10 (10%)
2ND HEAVY ARTILLERY	9 (9%)
7TH	7 (7%)
20TH	5 (5%)
1ST LIGHT BATTERY	4 (4%)
15TH	4 (4%)
1ST CAVALRY	3 (3%)
10TH	3 (3%)
12TH	3 (3%)
1ST HEAVY ARTILLERY	2 (2%)
2ND LIGHT BATTERY	2 (2%)
8TH	2 (2%)
9TH	2 (2%)
6TH	1
16TH	1
18TH	1

6% OF POPULATION

FIVE WERE KILLED

The first Essex soldier killed was Private William Farris of the 7TH Connecticut. He was killed at Hampton Roads, VA on October 26, 1861.

ESSEX SOLDIERS KILLED

PLACE	DATE	NO.
Hampton Roads, VA (7TH)	10/26/61	1
Port Hudson, LA (24TH)	6/29/63	1
Drwery's Bluff, VA (7TH)	5/16/64	1
Atlanta, GA (20TH)	8/6/64	1
Near Petersburg, VA (1 LB)	8/13/64	1

FIVE WERE CAPTURED

Two Essex soldiers died in captivity. Both died at Andersonville, Prison GA.

ESSEX CAPTURED
*(2) DIED IN CAPTIVITY

PLACE	DATE	NO.
Plymouth, NC (16TH)	4/20/64	1
Craig's Church, VA (1 CA) *	5/5/64	1
Drewry's Bluff, VA (11TH) *1	5/16/64	2
Kinston, NC (15TH)	3/8/65	1

TOTAL ESSEX CASUALTIES

DIED	11	10%
KILLED	5	5%
WOUNDED	16	15%
CAPTURED	5	5%
DESERTED	19	18%

SIXTEEN WERE WOUNDED

The first Essex soldier wounded was 1ST Lieutenant Thomas J. Stillman of the 10TH Connecticut. He was wounded at Roanoke Island, NC on February 8, 1862 and recovered from his wound. Three Essex soldiers died from a wound received during the war.

ESSEX WOUNDED
*(3) DIED FROM WOUNDS

PLACE	DATE	NO.
Roanoke Island, NC (10TH)	2/8/62	1
Slocum's Creek, NC (11TH)	3/13/62	1
New Bern, NC (8TH)	3/14/62	1
James Island, SC (7TH)	6/16/62	1
Antietam, MD (11TH)	9/17/62	2
Brashear City, LA (12TH)	1/14/63	1
Port Hudson, LA (12TH) *	6/10/63	1
Port Hudson, LA (24TH)	6/14/63	1
Port Hudson, LA (12TH)	6/27/63	1
Port Hudson, LA (24TH) *	6/30/63	1
Proctor's Creek, VA (1 LB)	5/14/64	1
Petersburg, VA (8TH)	6/23/64	1
Peach Tree Creek, GA (20TH)	7/20/64	1
Petersburg, VA (1 HA) *	3/28/65	1
Fort Gregg, VA (10TH)	4/2/65	1

FAIRFIELD
THE POPULATION IN 1860 WAS 4,379 (RANK 20)

THE MOST IMPORTANT DAY OF THE CIVIL WAR

MAY 2, 1863

CHANCELLORSVILLE, VA

THE SECOND DAY OF THE BATTLE

More soldiers credited to Fairfield were listed as casualties (7) on this day than any other day of the war. One soldier was killed, 5 were captured, and 1 was wounded & captured in the 17TH Connecticut. The wounded and captured survived the war.

The date May 2, 1863 ranks 21ST for total casualties (121) (8 killed, 30 wounded, 62 captured, 21 wounded & captured) for the State of Connecticut. All of the casualties were at Chancellorsville.

The Battle of Chancellorsville (May1-3, 1863) ranks 2ND for total casualties (677) for an engagement for the State of Connecticut. The most intense fighting developed on May 3 and Fairfield had 2 casualties on that day.

The Battle of Chancellorsville with 9 total casualties for Fairfield was the highest number of casualties for any single engagement of the war for the town.

The Battle of Chancellorsville was an enormous defeat for the more than 70,000 Union soldiers who had moved against the flank and rear of 40,000 Confederate soldiers. Unfortunately, the Union Army had pulled back and had gone on the defensive around Chancellorsville. The Confederate victory was tainted however, by the loss of Confederate Major General "Stonewall" Jackson.

268 MEN CREDITED TO FAIRFIELD SERVED IN THE FOLLOWING CONNECTICUT ORGANIZATIONS

REGIMENT	TOTAL
23RD	68 (26%)
17TH	51 (19%)
29TH	33 (12%)
1ST CAVALRY	21 (8%)
1ST HEAVY ARTILLERY	14 (5%)
2ND LIGHT BATTERY	13 (5%)
8TH	11 (4%)
14TH	10 (4%)
5TH	9 (3%)
2ND HEAVY ARTILLERY	9 (3%)
9TH	6 (2%)
15TH	5 (2%)
24TH	5 (2%)
7TH	4 (1%)
11TH	4 (1%)
25TH	4 (1%)
10TH	3 (1%)
1ST	2 (1%)
13TH	2 (1%)
13TH BATTALION	2 (1%)
20TH	2 (1%)
30TH	2 (1%)
3RD	1
6TH	1
9TH BATTALION	1
28TH	1

6 % OF POPULATION

ONE WAS KILLED AND FOUR WERE MISSING

The first Fairfield soldier killed was Lieutenant Colonel Charles Walter of the 17TH Connecticut. He was killed on May 2, 1863 at Chancellorsville, VA.

FAIRFIELD SOLDIERS KILLED AND *MISSING

PLACE	DATE	NO.
Chancellorsville, VA (17TH)	5/2/63	1
Gettysburg, PA (17TH) *2	7/1/63	2
Ashland, VA (1 CA) *	3/14/65	1
Hatcher's Run, VA (10TH) *	4//1/65	1

EIGHTEEN WERE CAPTURED

Two Fairfield soldiers died in captivity. Both died at Andersonville Prison, GA.

FAIRFIELD CAPTURED *(2) DIED IN CAPTIVITY

PLACE	DATE	NO.
Bull Run, VA (1ST)	7/21/61	1
Cross Keys, VA (1 CA)	6/8/62	1
Chancellorsville, VA (17TH)	5/2/63	6
(1 WOUNDED)		
Chancellorsville, VA (17TH)	5/3/63	1
Frederick, MD (1 CA)	6/20/63	1
Gettysburg, PA (17TH)	7/1/63	1
Gettysburg, PA (17TH)	7/3/63	2
Winchester, VA (1 CA) *	1/24/64	1
Craig's Church, VA (1 CA) *	5/5/64	1
Walthall Junction, VA (8TH)	5/7/64	1
(WOUNDED)		
Kinston, NC (15TH)	3/8/65	1
Ashland, VA (1 CA)	3/15/65	1

TOTAL FAIRFIELD CASUALTIES

DIED	18	7%
KILLED/MISSING	5	2%
WOUNDED	23	9%
CAPTURED	18	7%
DESERTED	75	28%

TWENTY-THREE WERE WOUNDED

The first Fairfield soldier wounded was Private John Cavanaugh of Company I, 5TH Connecticut. He was wounded at Muddy Branch, MD on November 1, 1861 and recovered from his wound. Three Fairfield soldiers died from a wound received in the war.

FAIRFIELD WOUNDED * (3) DIED FROM WOUNDS

PLACE	DATE	NO.
Muddy Branch, MD (5TH)	11/1/61	1
Antietam, MD (8TH)	9/17/62	1
Bridgeport, CT (2 LB)	10/1/62	1
Fredericksburg, VA (14TH)	12/13/62	1
La Fourche, LA (23RD)	5/1/63	1
Chancellorsville, VA (5TH)	5/3/63	1
Port Hudson, LA (28TH)	6/14/63	1
Gettysburg, PA (17TH)	7/1/63	2
Port Hudson, LA (24TH)	7/1/63	1
Gettysburg, PA (17TH)	7/2/63	3
Virginia (29TH) *	4/9/64	1
Wilderness, VA (14TH) *	5/5/64	1
Wilderness, VA (14TH)	5/6/64	1
Drewry's Bluff, VA (8TH)	5/14/64	1
Ashland, VA (1 CA)	6/1/64	1
Ream's Station, VA (1 CA)	6/29/64	1
Dutch Gap, VA (1 HA)	8/31/64	1
Kell House, VA (29TH) *	10/27/64	2
Kinston, NC (15TH)	13/8/65	1
Appomattox CH, VA (29TH)	4/1/65	1

FARMINGTON
THE POPULATION IN 1860 WAS 2,373 (RANK 59)

THE MOST IMPORTANT DAY OF THE CIVIL WAR

APRIL 20, 1864

PLYMOUTH, NC

THE CONFEDERATE PLAN TO TAKE PLYMOUTH ENDED WHEN 2,800 UNION TROOPS SURRENDERED THE CITY

311 MEN CREDITED TO FARMINGTON SERVED IN THE FOLLOWING CONNECTICUT ORGANIZATIONS

More soldiers credited to Farmington were listed as casualties (22) on this day than on any other day of the war. Twenty-two soldiers in the 16TH Connecticut were captured. Nine of them eventually died in southern prisons.

The date April 20, 1864 ranks 6TH for total casualties (433) (1 killed, 2 missing, 12 wounded & captured, 418 captured) for a single day for the State of Connecticut. All of the casualties were at Plymouth, NC.

The Battle of Plymouth (April 20, 1864) ranks 9TH for total casualties (433) for an engagement for the State of Connecticut. Nearly half of all soldiers captured at Plymouth died in Southern prisons

The Battle of Plymouth with 22 total casualties for Farmington was the highest number of casualties for any single engagement of the war for the town.

When Confederate General Robert Hoke surrounded and captured the Union garrison at Plymouth, NC the Southern victory was the first in this military arena in quite some time. With aid from the two-gun ironclad *Albemarle* the Confederates were able to take advantage of the lack of suitable Union gunboats.

REGIMENT	TOTAL
16TH	60 (19%)
25TH	53 (17%)
7TH	33 (11%)
1ST HEAVY ARTILLERY	24 (8%)
1ST CAVALRY	22 (7%)
6TH	21 (7%)
20TH	18 (6%)
5TH	14 (5%)
1ST	11 (4%)
13TH	10 (3%)
14TH	10 (3%)
10TH	9 (3%)
11TH	8 (3%)
29TH	8 (3%)
12TH	7 (3%)
8TH	5 (2%)
2ND HEAVY ARTILLERY	4 (1%)
1ST LIGHT BATTERY	2
1ST SQUADRON CAVALRY	2
9TH	2
9TH BATTALION	2
15TH	2
22ND	2
27TH	2
30TH	2
13TH BATTALION	1
18TH	1

13% OF POPULATION

SEVEN WERE KILLED

The first Farmington soldier killed was Private Timothy Gladden of Company G, 16TH Connecticut. He was killed at the Battle of Antietam, MD on September 17,1862.

FARMINGTON SOLDIERS KILLED

PLACE	DATE	NO.
Antietam, MD (16TH)	9/17/62	1
Kinston, NC (10TH)	12/14/62	1
Drewry's Bluff, VA (7TH)	5/16/64	1
Bermuda Hundred, VA (7TH)	6/2/64	1
Cold Harbor, VA (14TH)	6/3/64	1
Peach Tree Creek, GA (5TH)	7/20/64	1
Deep Run, VA (7TH)	8/14/64	1

FORTY-SIX WERE CAPTURED

Twelve Farmington soldiers died in captivity. Five soldiers died at Andersonville Prison, GA, four at Florence Prison, SC, two at Libby Prison, Richmond, VA and one at Charleston Prison, SC.

FARMINGTON CAPTURED
*(12) DIED IN CAPTIVITY

PLACE	DATE	NO.
Winchester, VA (5TH)	5/25/62	1
Antietam, MD (16TH)	9/17/62	2
(1 WOUNDED)		
Pattersonville, LA (12TH)	3/27/63	1
Irish Bend, LA (25TH)	4/14/63	1
Kelly's Ford, VA (20TH)	4/29/63	1
Chancellorsville, VA (20,27[TH])	5/3/63	4
(1 WOUNDED)		
Fort Wagner, SC (7TH)	7/11/63	1
(WOUNDED)		
Mine Run, VA (14TH) *	12/1/63	1
St. Augustine, FL (10TH)	12/30/63	1
Olustee, FL (7TH)	2/20/64	1
Plymouth, NC (16TH) *9	4/20/64	22
Mechanicsville, VA (1 CA) *	5/13/64	1
Atlanta, GA (5TH)	5/25/64	1
Hatcher's Run, VA (7TH)	6/2/64	1
Bermuda Hundred, VA (7TH) *	6/2/64	2
Deep Run, VA (6TH)	8/16/64	1
Winchester, VA (13TH)	9/19/64	1
Cedar Creek, VA (1 CA)	11/12/64	2
Kinston, NC (15TH)	3/8/65	1

TOTAL FARMINGTON CASUALTIES

DIED	47	15%
KILLED	7	2%
WOUNDED	49	16%
CAPTURED	46	15%
DESERTED	26	8%

FORTY-NINE WERE WOUNDED

The first Farmington soldier wounded was Private John Manion of Company E, 7TH Connecticut. He was wounded at James Island, SC on June 16, 1862 and recovered from his wound. Six Farmington soldiers died from a wound received during the war.

FARMINGTON WOUNDED
*(6) DIED FROM WOUNDS

PLACE	DATE	NO.
James Island, SC (7TH)	6/16/62	1
James Island, SC (7TH)	6/30/62	1
Cedar Mountain, VA (5TH)	8/9/62	1
Antietam, MD (16TH) *2	9/17/62	7
Pocotaligo, SC (6TH)	10/22/62	1
Park Barracks, NY (25TH)	12/10/62	1
Fredericksburg, VA (14TH)	12/13/62	1
Kinston, NC (10TH)	12/14/62	1
Irish Bend, LA (25TH)	4/14/63	2
Suffolk, VA (16TH)	4/24/63	1
Port Hudson, LA (25TH)	4/25/63	1
Chancellorsville, VA (14TH)	5/3/63	1
Port Hudson, LA (12TH)	6/10/63	1
Port Hudson, LA (25TH)	6/14/63	3
Fort Wagner, SC (7TH)	7/11/63	1
Stevensburg, VA (1 CA)	4/1/64	1
Petersburg, VA (7TH)	5/1/64	1
Laurel Hill, VA (14TH)	5/10/64	1
Meadow Bridge, VA (1 CA)	5/12/64	1
Drewry's Bluff, VA (7TH)	5/14/64	1
Drewry's Bluff, VA (6TH) *	5/15/64	1
Bermuda Hundred, VA (6TH)	5/20/64	1
Culp's Farm, GA (5TH)	6/22/64	1
Atlanta, GA (20TH)	7/21/64	1
Petersburg, VA (30TH)	7/30/64	1
Atlanta, GA (20TH)	8/14/64	1
Deep Run, VA (6TH)	8/16/64	1
Winchester, VA (1 CA)	8/16/64	1
Petersburg, VA (8TH)	8/29/64	1
Petersburg, VA (10TH)	9/14/64	1
Winchester, VA (13TH)	9/19/64	1
Richmond, VA (29TH) *	9/29/64	1
Chaffin's Farm, VA (29TH)	9/29/64	2
Richmond, VA (29TH)	10/4/64	1
New Market, VA (7TH)	10/7/64	1
Darbytown Road, VA (7TH)	10/13/64	1
Wilmington, NC (6TH) *	2/2/65	1
Fort Gregg, VA (10TH) *	4/2/65	1
Unknown Place (16TH)	Unknown	1

FRANKLIN
THE POPULATION IN 1860 WAS 2,358 (RANK 60)

THE MOST IMPORTANT
DAY OF THE CIVIL WAR

MAY 27, 1863
PORT HUDSON, LA

THE FIRST MAJOR
ASSAULT

More soldiers credited to Franklin were listed as casualties (6) on this day than on any other day of the war. Six soldiers in the 26TH Connecticut were wounded and two eventually died from their wounds.

The date May 27, 1863 ranks 18TH for total casualties (145) (13 killed, 132 wounded) for a single day for the State of Connecticut. Port Hudson accounted for 144 casualties and 1 soldier died in a railroad accidcent at an unknown place.

The Siege of Port Hudson (May 2 - July 9, 1863) ranks 7TH for total casualties (520) for an engagement for the State of Connecticut. The most intense fighting developed on May 27 and June 14. Franklin had 1 casualty on June 14.

The siege of Port Hudson with 6 total casualties for Franklin was the highest number of casualties for any single engagement of the war for the town.

Control of the Mississippi was one of the major objectives of the Union army. Port Hudson was a formidable obstacle for control of the river. A siege began at Port Hudson on May 2, 1863 that lasted until July 9. On May 27, the Union force of 30,000 launched a major assault that failed.

79 MEN CREDITED TO FRANKLIN SERVED IN THE FOLLOWING CONNECTICUT ORGANIZATIONS

REGIMENT	TOTAL
26TH	21 (27%)
11TH	11 (14%)
29TH	11 (14%)
18TH	7 (9%)
10TH	6 (8%)
3RD	5 (6%)
5TH	5 (6%)
1ST CAVALRY	4 (5%)
2ND HEAVY ARTILLERY	3 (4%)
14TH	3 (4%)
2ND	2 (3%)
8TH	2 (3%)
13TH	2 (3%)
30TH	2 (3%)
1ST HEAVY ARTILLERY	1
12TH	1
21ST	1

3% OF POPULATION

TWO WERE KILLED AND ONE WAS MISSING

The first Franklin soldier killed was Corporal Oliver P. Ormsby of Company H, 11TH Connecticut. He was killed at the Battle of Antietam, MD on September 17, 1862.

FRANKLIN SOLDIERS KILLED OR MISSING *

PLACE	DATE	NO.
Antietam, MD (11TH)	9/17/62	1
Port Hudson, LA (26TH)	6/14/63	1
Petersburg, VA (30TH) *	7/30/64	1

FOUR WERE CAPTURED

No Franklin soldiers died in captivity.

FRANKLIN CAPTURED NONE DIED IN CAPTIVITY

PLACE	DATE	NO.
Winchester, LA (18TH)	6/15/63	2
Ream's Station, VA (14TH)	8/25/64	1
Cedar Creek, VA (2 HA)	10/19/64	1

TOTAL FRANKLIN CASUALTIES

DIED	9	11%
KILLED/MISSING	3	4%
WOUNDED	15	19%
CAPTURED	4	5%
DESERTED	6	8%

FIFTEEN WERE WOUNDED

The first Franklin soldier wounded was Musician Michael Driscoll of Rifle Company D, 3RD Connecticut. He was wounded at Falls Church, VA on July 14, 1861 and recovered from his wound. Five Franklin soldiers died from a wound received during the war.

FRANKLIN WOUNDED *(5) DIED FROM WOUNDS

PLACE	DATE	NO.
Falls Church, VA (3RD)	7/14/61	1
New Bern, NC (11TH)	3/14/62	1
Cedar Mountain, VA (5TH) *	8/9/62	1
Chancellorsville, VA (14TH)	5/3/63	1
Port Hudson, LA (26TH) *2	5/27/63	6
Port Hudson, LA (26TH)	6/14/63	1
Wilderness, VA (14TH)	5/5/64	1
Petersburg, VA (10TH)	9/1/64	1
Kell House, VA (29TH) *2	10/27/64	2

GLASTONBURY
THE POPULATION IN 1860 WAS 3,363 (RANK 30)

THE MOST IMPORTANT DAY OF THE CIVIL WAR

APRIL 20, 1864

PLYMOUTH, NC

THE CONFEDERATE PLAN TO TAKE PLYMOUTH ENDED WHEN 2,800 UNION TROOPS SURRENDERED THE CITY

296 MEN CREDITED TO GLASTONBURY SERVED IN THE FOLLOWING CONNECTICUT ORGANIZATIONS

More soldiers credited to Glastonbury were listed as casualties (7) on this day than on any other day of the war. Seven soldiers in the 16TH Connecticut were captured. Three of them eventually died in southern prisons.

The date April 20, 1864 ranks 6TH for total casualties (433) (1 killed, 2 missing, 12 wounded & captured, 418 captured) for a single day for the State of Connecticut. All of the casualties were at Plymouth, NC.

The Battle of Plymouth (April 20, 1864) ranks 9TH for total casualties (433) for an engagement for the State of Connecticut. Nearly half of all soldiers captured at Plymouth died in Southern prisons

The Battle of Plymouth with 7 total casualties for Glastonbury was the highest number of casualties for any single engagement of the war for the town

When Confederate General Robert Hoke surrounded and captured the Union garrison at Plymouth, NC the Southern victory was the first in this military arena in quite some time. With aid from the two-gun ironclad *Albemarle* the Confederates were able to take advantage of the lack of suitable Union gunboats.

REGIMENT	TOTAL
25TH	64 (22%)
1ST HEAVY ARTILLERY	43 (15%)
16TH	28 (10%)
10TH	22 (7%)
5TH	20 (7%)
14TH	18 (6%)
7TH	15 (5%)
21ST	14 (5%)
29TH	13 (4%)
2ND HEAVY ARTILLERY	12 (4%)
11TH	11 (4%)
12TH	11 (4%)
1ST CAVALRY	9 (3%)
20TH	8 (3%)
13TH	8 (3%)
8TH	7 (2%)
12TH BATTALION	5 (1%)
13TH BATTALION	4 (1%)
15TH	4 (1%)
1ST LIGHT BATTERY	3
1ST SQUADRON CAVALRY	3
3RD	3
30TH	3
2ND	1
17TH	1
22ND	1

9% OF POPULATION

SEVENTEEN WERE KILLED

The first Glastonbury soldier killed was Private Loren A. House of Company B, 10TH Connecticut. He was killed near New Bern, NC on April 3,1862.

GLASTONBURY SOLDIERS KILLED

PLACE	DATE	NO.
North Carolina, (10TH)	4/3/62	1
James Island, SC (7TH)	6/16/62	2
Cedar Mountain, VA (5TH)	8/9/62	1
Antietam, MD (11,16[TH])	9/17/62	2
Providence Church Rd, VA (16TH)5/3/63		1
Bristoe Station, VA (14TH)	10/14/63	1
Cold Harbor, VA (2 HA)	6/1/64	1
Bermuda Hundred, VA (7TH)	6/17/64	1
Peach Tree Creek, GA (5TH)	7/20/64	1
Atlanta, GA (20TH)	8/15/64	1
Petersburg, VA (1 HA)	9/18/64	1
Darbytown Road, VA (29TH)	10/13/64	1
Kell House, VA (29TH)	10/27/64	1
Petersburg, VA (1 HA)	3/25/65	1
Virginia (11TH)	4/20/65	1

EIGHTEEN WERE CAPTURED

Five Glastonbury soldiers died in captivity. Three soldiers died at Andersonville Prison, GA and two at Florence, SC.

GLASTONBURY CAPTURED
*(5) DIED IN CAPTIVITY

PLACE	DATE	NO.
Pattersonville, LA (12TH) *	3/27/63	1
Gunboat "Diana", LA (12TH)	3/28/63	1
Irish Bend, LA (25TH)	4/14/63	1
Chancellorsville, VA (20TH)	5/3/63	1
Fort Wagner, SC (7TH)	7/11/63	1
St. Augustine, FL (10TH)	12/30/63	1
Plymouth, NC (16TH) *3	4/20/64	7
Craig's Church, VA (1 CA)	5/5/64	2
Drewry's Bluff, VA (21ST) *1	5/16/64	3

TOTAL GLASTONBURY CASUALTIES

DIED	33	11%
KILLED	17	6%
WOUNDED	37	13%
CAPTURED	18	6%
DESERTED	47	16%

THIRTY-SEVEN WERE WOUNDED

The first Glastonbury soldier wounded was Private Eleazur Jones of Company D, 7TH Connecticut. He was wounded at Tybee Island, GA on March 1, 1862 and recovered from his wound. Ten Glastonbury soldiers died from a wound received during the war.

GLASTONBURY WOUNDED
*(10) DIED FROM WOUNDS

PLACE	DATE	NO.
Tybee Island, GA (7TH)	3/1/62	1
New Bern, NC (10TH) *	3/14/62	2
Cedar Mountain, VA (5TH)	8/9/62	1
New Haven, CT (20TH) *	9/10/62	1
Antietam, MD (16TH) *2	9/17/62	3
Port Elizabeth, NJ (25TH)	12/1/62	1
Irish Bend, LA (25TH)	4/14/63	4
Port Hudson, LA (25TH)	5/31/63	1
Portsmouth, VA (21ST)	7/30/63	1
Morton's Ford, VA (14TH)	2/6/64	1
Walthall Junction, VA (8TH)	5/7/64	1
Drewry's Bluff, VA (8TH)	5/16/64	2
Bermuda Hundred, VA (21ST)	5/19/64	1
Cold Harbor, VA (2 HA)	6/1/64	1
Petersburg, VA (14TH)	6/17/64	1
Strawberry Plains, VA (10TH)	*7/27/64	1
Deep Run, VA (7TH)	8/14/64	1
Ream's Station, VA (14TH)	8/25/64	1
Winchester, VA (2 HA)	9/19/64	2
Petersburg, VA (29TH) *	9/30/64	1
Cedar Creek, VA (12TH) *	10/19/64	1
Kell House, VA (29TH) *	10/27/64	1
Wilmington, NC (7TH)	2/22/65	1
Petersburg, VA (1 HA)	3/15/65	1
Bentonville, NC (20TH)	3/19/65	2
Hatcher's Run, VA (14TH) *	3/25/65	1
Fort Gregg, VA (10TH) *	4/2/65	2

GOSHEN
THE POPULATION IN 1860 WAS 1,381 (RANK 106)

THE MOST IMPORTANT DAY OF THE CIVIL WAR

OCTOBER 19, 1864

CEDAR CREEK, VA

THE LAST MAJOR BATTLE OF THE 1864 SHENANDOAH VALLEY CAMPAIGN WAS A UNION TRIUMPH

More soldiers credited to Goshen were listed as casualties (6) on this day than on any other day of the war. One soldier was killed, and 5 were wounded in the 2ND Connecticut Heavy Artillery. Two of the wounded died.

The date October 19, 1864 ranks 7TH for total casualties (417) (48 killed, 2 missing, 204 wounded, 153 captured, 10 wounded & captured) for a single day for the State of Connecticut. The Battle of Cedar Creek accounted for 415 casualties. The 2 other casualties were in the neighboring towns.

The Battle of Cedar Creek (October 19, 1864) ranks 10TH for total casualties (415) for an engagement for the State of Connecticut.

The Battle of Cedar Creek with 6 total casualties for Goshen was the highest number of casualties for any single engagement of the war for the town.

The news of the Union triumph at Cedar Creek assured a Republican victory in the elections of November 1864 and the prosecution of the war to its end on President Abraham Lincoln's and Lieutenant General Ulysses S. Grant's terms.

113 MEN CREDITED TO GOSHEN SERVED IN THE FOLLOWING CONNECTICUT ORGANIZATIONS

REGIMENT	TOTAL
2ND HEAVY ARTILLERY	60 (53%)
13TH	12 (11%)
7TH	10 (9%)
1ST HEAVY ARTILLERY	6 (5%)
11TH	6 (5%)
1ST CAVALRY	6 (5%)
29TH	4 (4%)
10TH	3 (3%)
13TH BATTALION	3 (3%)
14TH	2 (2%)
20TH	2 (2%)
1ST SQUADRON CAVALRY	1
5TH	1
6TH	1
8TH	1
17TH	1

8% OF POPULATION

SIX WERE KILLED

The first Goshen soldier killed was Private James Mooney of Company E, 2ND Heavy Artillery. He was killed at Cold Harbor, VA on June 1, 1864.

GOSHEN SOLDIERS KILLED

PLACE	DATE	NO.
Cold Harbor, VA (2 HA)	6/1/64	1
Bermuda Hundred, VA (7TH)	6/2/64	1
Petersburg, VA (2 HA)	6/22/64	1
Winchester, VA (2 HA)	9/19/64	2
Cedar Creek, VA (2 HA)	10/19/64	1

FOUR WERE CAPTURED

No Goshen soldiers died in captivity.

GOSHEN CAPTURED
NONE DIED IN CAPTIVITY

PLACE	DATE	NO.
Drewry's Bluff, VA (7TH)	5/16/64	1
Hatcher's Run, VA (7TH)	6/2/64	1
Winchester, VA (13TH)	9/19/64	1
New Market, VA (1 CA)	9/25/64	1

TOTAL GOSHEN CASUALTIES

DIED	22	19%
KILLED	6	5%
WOUNDED	20	18%
CAPTURED	4	4%
DESERTED	11	10%

TWENTY WERE WOUNDED

The first Goshen soldier wounded was Private Francis J. Bentley of Company E, 1ST Connecticut Heavy Artillery. He was wounded at Fort Richardson, VA on July 4, 1861 and recovered from his wound. Five Goshen soldiers died from a wound received during the war.

GOSHEN WOUNDED
*(5) DIED FROM WOUNDS

PLACE	DATE	NO.
Fort Richardson, VA (1 HA)	7/4/61	1
Antietam, MD (11TH)	9/17/62	1
Alexandria, VA (2 HA)	10/15/62	1
Irish Bend, LA (13TH)	4/14/63	1
North Anna River, VA (2 HA)	5/22/64	1
Bermuda Hundred, VA (7TH) *	5/31/64	1
Cold Harbor, VA (2 HA)	6/1/64	3
Bermuda Hundred, VA (7TH) *	6/17/64	1
Petersburg, VA (2 HA)	6/28/64	1
Deep Bottom, VA (6TH)	8/16/64	1
Winchester, VA (2 HA) *1	9/19/64	2
Darbytown Road, VA (29TH)	10/13/64	1
Cedar Creek, VA (2 HA) *2	10/19/64	5

398

GRANBY
THE POPULATION IN 1860 WAS 1,720 (RANK 85)

THE MOST IMPORTANT DAY OF THE CIVIL WAR

APRIL 20, 1864

PLYMOUTH, NC

THE CONFEDERATE PLAN TO TAKE PLYMOUTH ENDED WHEN 2,800 UNION TROOPS SURRENDERED THE CITY

133 MEN CREDITED TO GRANBY SERVED IN THE FOLLOWING CONNECTICUT ORGANIZATIONS

More soldiers credited to Granby were listed as casualties (8) on this day than on any other day of the war. Eight soldiers in the 16TH Connecticut were captured. Four of them eventually died in southern prisons.

The date April 20, 1864 ranks 6TH for total casualties (433) (1 killed, 2 missing, 12 wounded & captured, 418 captured) for a single day for the State of Connecticut. All of the casualties were at Plymouth, NC.

The Battle of Plymouth (April 20, 1864) ranks 9TH for total casualties (433) for an engagement for the State of Connecticut. Nearly half of all soldiers captured at Plymouth died in Southern prisons

The Battle of Plymouth with 8 total casualties for Granby was the highest number of casualties for any single engagement of the war for the town.

When Confederate General Robert Hoke surrounded and captured the Union garrison at Plymouth, NC the Southern victory was the first in this military arena in quite some time. With aid from the two-gun ironclad *Albemarle* the Confederates were able to take advantage of the lack of suitable Union gunboats.

REGIMENT	TOTAL
1ST HEAVY ARTILLERY	24 (18%)
10TH	21 (16%)
16TH	19 (14%)
7TH	11 (8%)
8TH	10 (8%)
1ST LIGHT BATTERY	8 (6%)
29TH	7 (5%)
14TH	6 (5%)
15TH	5 (4%)
25TH	5 (4%)
2ND HEAVY ARTILLERY	3 (2%)
13TH	4 (3%)
11TH	3 (2%)
13TH	3 (2%)
18TH	3 (2%)
6TH	2 (2%)
12TH	2 (2%)
1ST	1
1ST CAVALRY	1
2ND LIGHT BATTERY	1
3RD	1
5TH	1
12TH BATTALION	1
20TH	1
22ND	1
30TH	1

8% OF POPULATION

SIX WERE KILLED

The first Granby soldier killed was Corporal Lafayette Tillotson of Company C, 8ᵀᴴ Connecticut. He was killed at the Battle of Antietam, MD on September 17, 1862.

GRANBY SOLDIERS KILLED

PLACE	DATE	NO.
Antietam, MD (8ᵀᴴ)	9/17/62	1
Spottsylvania, VA (14ᵀᴴ)	5/12/64	1
North Anna River, VA (14ᵀᴴ)	5/24/64	1
Deep Run, VA (10ᵀᴴ)	8/16/64	1
Dutch Gap, VA (1 HA)	10/24/64	1
James River,VA(Drowned)(1HA)	5/3/65	1

NINE WERE CAPTURED

Four Granby soldiers died in captivity. Three soldiers died at Andersonville Prison, GA and one at Florence, SC.

GRANBY CAPTURED
*(4) DIED IN CAPTIVITY

PLACE	DATE	NO.
Plymouth, NC (16ᵀᴴ) *4	4/20/64	8
Bermuda Hundred, VA (7ᵀᴴ)	6/2/64	1

TOTAL GRANBY CASUALTIES

DIED	25	19%
KILLED	6	5%
WOUNDED	16	12%
CAPTURED	9	7%
DESERTED	16	12%

SIXTEEN WERE WOUNDED

The first Granby soldier wounded was Private Nelson Spellman of Company C, 1ˢᵀ Connecticut Heavy Artillery. He was wounded at Williamsport, MD on July 3, 1861 and recovered from his wound. Three Granby soldiers died from a wound received during the war.

GRANBY WOUNDED
*(3) DIED FROM WOUNDS

PLACE	DATE	NO.
Williamsport, MD (1 HA)	7/3/61	1
New Bern, NC (10ᵀᴴ)	3/14/62	1
Antietam, MD (16ᵀᴴ) *	9/17/62	1
Harper's Ferry, VA (16ᵀᴴ)	11/1/62	1
New Orleans, LA (13ᵀᴴ)	11/7/62	1
Kinston, NC (10ᵀᴴ) *	12/14/62	1
Irish Bend, LA (25ᵀᴴ)	4/14/63	1
Port Hudson, LA (12ᵀᴴ)	6/13/63	1
Olustee, FL (7ᵀᴴ)	2/20/64	1
Drewry's Bluff, VA (6ᵀᴴ)	5/14/64	1
Drewry's Bluff, VA (7ᵀᴴ)	5/16/64	1
Petersburg, VA (11ᵀᴴ) *	6/22/64	1
Petersburg, VA (29ᵀᴴ)	8/20/64	1
Deep Bottom, VA (29ᵀᴴ)	9/1/64	1
Fort Harrison, VA (8ᵀᴴ)	9/29/64	1
Darbytown Road, VA (10ᵀᴴ)	10/13/64	1

GREENWICH
THE POPULATION IN 1860 WAS 6,522 (RANK 12)

THE MOST IMPORTANT DAY OF THE CIVIL WAR

JULY 1, 1863
GETTYSBURG, PA

THE FIRST DAY OF THE BATTLE

More soldiers credited to Greenwich were listed as casualties (14) on this day than on any other day of the war. One soldier was killed, 5 were wounded, 1 was wounded & captured, and 7 were captured in the 17TH Connecticut. The wounded and captured survived the war.

The date July 1, 1863 ranks 16TH for total casualties (157) (18 killed, 4 missing, 70 wounded, 57 captured, 8 wounded & captured) for a single day for the State of Connecticut. The Battle of Gettysburg accounted for 143 casualties. The 14 other casualties were in Virginia (6), Louisiana (6), and South Carolina (2).

The Battle of Gettysburg (July1-3, 1863) ranks 11TH for total casualties (360) for an engagement for the State of Connecticut. The most intense fighting developed on July 3. Greenwich had no casualties on that day.

The Battle of Gettysburg with 14 total casualties for Greenwich was the highest number of casualties for any single engagement of the war for the town.

More than 170,00 men fought at the Battle of Gettysburg. Roughly 23,000 Union casualties were recorded and there were about 28,000 Confederate casualties. Gettysburg proved to be the great battle of the war. It ended Lee's 1863 invasion of the North. He was never able to launch a major offensive again.

437 MEN CREDITED TO GREENWICH SERVED IN THE FOLLOWING CONNECTICUT ORGANIZATIONS

REGIMENT	TOTAL
10TH	115 (26%)
17TH	94 (22%)
28TH	66 (15%)
2ND HEAVY ARTILLERY	25 (6%)
29TH	24 (6%)
6TH	20 (5%)
1ST CAVALRY	18 (4%)
7TH	15 (3%)
30TH	15 (3%)
5TH	9 (2%)
15TH	9 (2%)
1ST HEAVY ARTILLERY	8 (2%)
8TH	7 (2%)
20TH	6 (1%)
9TH	4 (1%)
9TH BATTALION	4 (1%)
2ND LIGHT BATTERY	3 (1%)
12TH	3 (1%)
13TH	3 (1%)
14TH	3 (1%)
8TH	2
23RD	2
11TH	1
13TH BATTALION	1
16TH	1
21ST	1

7% OF POPULATION

NINE WERE KILLED AND TWO WERE MISSING

The first Greenwich soldiers killed were Private James McDonald and Joseph A. Lombard of Company I, 10TH Connecticut. Both were killed on March 14, 1862 at New Bern, NC.

GREENWICH SOLDIERS KILLED AND MISSING *

PLACE	DATE	NO.
New Bern, NC (10TH)	3/14/62	2
Perdita Riv, FL(Drowned) (28TH)	3/26/63	1
Port Hudson, LA (28TH)	6/14/63	1
Gettysburg, PA (17TH)	7/1/63	1
Morris Island, SC (17TH)	8/20/63	1
St. Augustine, FLA (10TH)	12/30/63	1
Bermuda Hundred, VA (10TH)	6/18/64	1
Petersburg, VA (30TH) *	7/30/64	1
Darbytown Road, VA (10TH)	10/13/64	1
Petersburg, VA (2HA) *	4/2/65	1

FORTY-FOUR WERE CAPTURED

Two Greenwich soldiers died in captivity. One died at Andersonville Prison, GA and one died at Salisbury, NC.

GREENWICH CAPTURED
*(2) DIED IN CAPTIVITY

PLACE	DATE	NO.
Winchester, VA (5TH)	5/24/62	1
Dumfries, VA (17TH)	12/27/62	1
Chancellorsville, VA (17TH)	5/2/63	7
(3 WOUNDED)		
Chancellorsville, VA (17TH)	5/3/63	1
Gettysburg, PA (17TH)	7/1/63	8
(1 WOUNDED)		
St. Augustine, FL (10TH)	12/30/63	2
Olustee, FLA (7TH)	2/20/64	1
Winchester, VA (14TH)	5/6/64	1
Drewry's Bluff, VA *1	5/16/64	5
(6TH,7TH,10TH) (2 WOUNDED)		
Welaka, FLA (17TH)	5/19/64	2
Bermuda Hundred, VA (6TH)	6/17/64	2
Cold Harbor, VA (1CA)	6/29/64	1
(WOUNDED)		
Deep Bottom, VA (10TH)	8/16/64	1
Deep Run, VA (10TH) *	8/16/64	1
Darbytown Road, VA (10TH)	10/13/64	2
(1 WOUNDED)		
Cedar Creek, VA (2HA)	10/19/64	2
Winchester, VA (1CA)	1/30/65	1
St. Augustine, FLA (17TH)	2/4/65	1
Kinston, NC (15TH)	3/8/65	4
(1 WOUNDED)		

TOTAL GREENWICH CASUALTIES

DIED	58	13%
KILLED/MISSING	11	3%
WOUNDED	74	17%
CAPTURED	44	10%
DESERTED	67	15%

SEVENTY-FOUR WERE WOUNDED

The first Greenwich soldier wounded was Corporal George H. Dayton of Company I, 10TH Connecticut. He was wounded at Roanoke Island, NC on February 8,1862 and recovered from his wound. Nine Greenwich soldiers died from a wound received during the war.

GREENWICH WOUNDED
* (9) DIED FROM WOUNDS

PLACE	DATE	NO.
Roanoke Island, NC (10TH)	2/8/62	1
New Bern, NC (10TH) *1	3/14/62	3
Cedar Mountain, VA (5TH)	8/9/62	1
Pocotaligo, SC (6TH)	10/22/62	2
Kinston, NC (10TH) *2	12/14/62	9
Chancellorsville, VA (17TH)	5/2/63	1
Port Hudson, LA (28TH)	6/6/63	1
Port Hudson, LA (28TH) *1	6/14/63	6
Deep Bottom, VA (6TH)	6/14/63	1
Gettysburg, PA (17TH)	7/1/63	5
Fort Wagner, SC (6TH)	7/18/63	2
Olustee, FLA (7TH)	2/20/64	1
Drewry's Bluff, VA	5/14/64	5
Drewry's Bluff, VA *1	5/16/64	2
(6TH, 7TH, 10TH)		
Dallas, GA (5TH)	5/25/64	1
Cold Harbor, VA (2HA)	6/1/64	2
Strawberry Plains, VA (10TH)	7/26/64	1
Petersburg, VA (30TH) *1	7/30/64	3
Deep Bottom, VA (10TH)	8/14/64	2
Deep Run, VA (10TH) *1	8/16/64	10
Petersburg, VA (10TH)	8/31/64	1
Petersburg, VA (10TH)	9/1/64	1
Winchester, VA (1 HA)	9/19/64	1
Petersburg, VA (29TH) *	9/30/64	1
Laurel Hill, VA (10TH)	10/7/64	1
Fair Oaks, VA (29TH)	10/24/64	1
Kell House, VA (29TH)	10/27/64	4
Kinston, NC (15TH) *2	3/8/65	1
Petersburg, VA (2HA)	4/2/65	1
Fort Gregg, VA (10TH)	4/2/65	2
Camp Finnagan, FL (17TH)	5/15/65	1

GRISWOLD
THE POPULATION IN 1860 WAS 2,217 (RANK 65)

THE MOST IMPORTANT DAY OF THE CIVIL WAR

JUNE 15 1863

WINCHESTER, VA

THE ENTIRE UNION ARMY WAS NEARLY CAPTURED AT THE SECOND BATTLE OF WINCHESTER

More soldiers credited to Griswold were listed as casualties (13) on this day than on any other day of the war. Eleven soldiers were captured, and 2 were wounded & captured in the 18TH Connecticut. All survived the war.

The date June 15, 1863 ranks 2ND for total casualties (595) (23 killed, 11 wounded, 520 captured, 41 wounded & captured) for a single day for the State of Connecticut. There were 592 casualties at Winchester, VA, and 3 casualties at Port Hudson, LA.

The Second Battle of Winchester (June 13-15, 1863) ranks 5TH for total casualties (592) for an engagement for the State of Connecticut. The most intense fighting was on June 15. Griswold had all its casualites on that day.

The Second Battle of Winchester with 13 total casualties for Griswold was the highest number of casualties for any single engagement of the war for the town.

Winchester was one of the most contested locations in the Civil War. It changed hands seventy-two times.

151 MEN CREDITED TO GRISWOLD SERVED IN THE FOLLOWING CONNECTICUT ORGANIZATIONS

REGIMENT	TOTAL
18TH	28 (18%)
26TH	21 (14%)
5TH	14 (9%)
29TH	14 (9%)
8TH	13 (9%)
21ST	12 (8%)
10TH	11 (7%)
14TH	8 (5%)
2ND	7 (4%)
1ST HEAVY ARTILLERY	5 (3%)
1ST CAVALRY	5 (3%)
9TH	5 (3%)
7TH	4 (3%)
11TH	4 (3%)
12TH	4 (3%)
12TH BATTALION	3 (2%)
1ST	1
1ST SQUADRON CAVALRY	1
3RD	1
9TH BATTALION	1
16TH	1
20TH	1

7% OF POPULATION

THREE WERE KILLED

The first Griswold soldier killed was Sergeant Charles E. Lewis of Company F, 8TH Connecticut. He was killed at the Battle of Antietam, MD on September 17, 1862.

GRISWOLD SOLDIERS KILLED

PLACE	DATE	NO.
Antietam, MD (8TH)	9/17/62	1
Piedmont, VA (18TH)	6/5/64	2

TWENTY-FIVE WERE CAPTURED

Two Griswold soldiers died in captivity. One died at Charleston, SC and one died at Staunton, VA.

GRISWOLD CAPTURED
*(2) DIED IN CAPTIVITY

PLACE	DATE	NO.
Winchester, VA (5TH)	5/24/62	1
Cedar Run, VA (1 CA)	8/9/62	1
Chancellorsville, VA (5TH)	5/2/63	1
Winchester, VA (18TH)	6/15/63	13
(2 WOUNDED)		
Burnt Ordinary, VA (21ST)	7/9/63	1
Bermuda Hundred, VA (7TH) *	6/2/64	1
Piedmont, VA (18TH) *1	6/5/64	2
(2 WOUNDED)		
Staunton, VA (18TH)	6/11/64	1
Petersburg, VA (14TH)	6/22/64	1
Chaffin's Farm, VA (21ST)	9/29/64	1
Cedar Creek, VA (12TH)	10/19/64	1
Savannah, GA (5TH)	11/12/64	1

TOTAL GRISWOLD CASUALTIES

DIED	20	13%
KILLED	3	2%
WOUNDED	37	25%
CAPTURED	25	17%
DESERTED	10	7%

THIRTY-SEVEN WERE WOUNDED

The first Griswold soldier wounded was Private Robert McClure of Company B, 5TH Connecticut. He was wounded at Cedar Mountain, VA on August 9, 1862 and recovered from his wound. Six Griswold soldiers died from a wound received during the war.

GRISWOLD WOUNDED
*(6) DIED FROM WOUNDS

PLACE	DATE	NO.
Cedar Mountain, VA (5TH)	8/9/62	1
Antietam, MD (8,11TH)	9/17/62	4
Chancellorsville, VA (14TH)	5/3/63	1
Port Hudson, LA (12TH)	6/11/63	1
Port Hudson, LA (26TH) *	6/14/63	2
Morton's Ford, VA (14TH) *	2/6/64	1
Grove Church, VA (1 CA)	5/1/64	1
Walthall Junction, VA (8TH) *	5/7/64	1
Drewry's Bluff, VA (7TH)	5/14/64	1
Drewry's Bluff, VA (10TH,21ST)	5/16/64	2
Cold Harbor, VA (11,21ST) *	6/3/64	4
Piedmont, VA (18TH) *	6/5/64	3
Petersburg, VA (21ST)	7/30/64	1
Deep Bottom, VA (10TH)	8/14/64	1
Petersburg, VA (29TH)	8/27/64	1
Winchester, VA (12TH)	9/19/64	1
Petersburg, VA (21ST)	9/30/64	1
Petersburg, VA (29TH)	10/1/64	1
New Market, VA (10TH)	10/2/64	1
New Market, VA (10TH)	10/7/64	1
Darbytown Road, VA (10TH)	10/27/64	1
Kell House, VA (29TH) *	10/27/64	4
Cedar Creek, VA (1 CA)	11/12/64	1

GROTON
THE POPULATION IN 1860 WAS 4,450 (RANK 19)

THE MOST IMPORTANT DAY OF THE CIVIL WAR

MAY 16, 1864

DREWRY'S BLUFF , VA

AN OBSTACLE ON THE WAY TO RICHMOND

More soldiers credited to Groton were listed as casualties (16) on this day than on any other day of the war. Three soldiers were killed, 10 were wounded, 2 were wounded & captured, and 1 was captured in the 8TH ,10TH, 11TH and 21st Connecticut. Two of the wounded soldiers died and one of the captured died in prison.

The date May 16, 1864 ranks 4th for total casualties (560) (52 killed, 3 missing, 224 wounded, 243 captured, 38 wounded & captured) for a single day for the State of Connecticut. The Battle of Drewry's Bluff accounted for 545 casualties. The 15 other casualties were scattered about Vriginia.

The Battle of Drewry's Bluff (May 13-17, 1864), also called Fort Darling, ranks 3rd for total casualties (634) for an engagement for the State of Connecticut. The most intense fighting developed on May 16. Groton had all of its casualties on that date.

The Battle of Drewry's Bluff with 16 total casualties for Groton was tied with the Siege of Port Hudson, LA (May-July 1863) for the highest number of casualties for any single engagement of the war for the town.

The Confederate attack at Drewry's Bluff forced the Union Army to retreat to Bermuda Hundred. The civil war would have concluded sooner had the Union Army been victorious.

335 MEN CREDITED TO GROTON SERVED IN THE FOLLOWING CONNECTICUT ORGANIZATIONS

REGIMENT	TOTAL
21ST	98 (29%)
26TH	83 (25%)
14TH	29 (9%)
8TH	23 (7%)
1ST HEAVY ARTILLERY	19 (6%)
29TH	14 (4%)
10TH	14 (4%)
2ND HEAVY ARTILLERY	11 (3%)
5TH	11 (3%)
1ST CAVALRY	10 (3%)
9TH	10 (3%)
30TH	7 (2%)
9TH BATTALION	6 (2%)
11TH	6 (2%)
12TH	4 (1%)
13TH	3 (1%)
15TH	3 (1%)
7TH	1
12TH BATTALION	1
18TH	1
22ND	1
28TH	1

8% OF POPULATION

NINE WERE KILLED AND TWO WERE MISSING

The first Groton soldier killed was Private Thomas Fisher of Company F, 14TH Connecticut. He was killed at Bristoe Station on October 14, 1863.

GROTON SOLDIERS KILLED
*(2) MISSING

PLACE	DATE	NO.
Bristoe Station, VA (14TH)	10/14/63	1
Morton's Ford, VA (14TH)	2/6/64	1
Drewry's Bluff, VA (21ST)	5/16/64	3
Fort Harrison, VA (8TH)	9/29/64	1
Petersburg, VA (21ST)	9/29/64	1
Petersburg, VA (30TH) *2	7/30/64	2
Kinston, NC (15TH)	3/8/65	1
Brownsville, TX (29TH)	7/10/65	1

TWENTY WERE CAPTURED

Six Groton soldiers died in captivity. Two died at Salisbury Prison, NC, two at Libby Prison, Richmond , VA, one at Charleston, SC and one at Petersburg, VA.

GROTON CAPTURED
*(6) DIED IN CAPTIVITY

PLACE	DATE	NO.
McDowell, VA (1 CA)	5/14/62	1
Strasburg, VA (5TH)	5/24/62	1
Winchester, VA (5TH)	5/25/62	1
Cedar Mountain, VA (5TH)	8/9/62	1
Chancellorsville, VA (5TH)	5/2/63	2
Rapidan, VA (14TH)	12/1/63	1
Smithfield, VA (21ST) *	2/1/64	1
Winchester, VA (14TH)	5/6/64	1
Walthall Junction, VA (8TH) * (1 WOUNDED)	5/7/64	1
Drewry's Bluff, VA (11,21ST) * (2 WOUNDED)	5/16/64	3
Ashland, VA (1 CA)	6/1/64	1
Petersburg, VA (11TH) *	6/18/64	1
Ream's Station, VA (14TH) *	8/25/64	1
Petersburg, VA (8TH)	9/17/64	1
Cedar Creek, VA (9TH) *	10/19/64	1
Virginia, (14TH)	10/28/64	1
Kinston, NC (15TH)	3/8/65	1

TOTAL GROTON CASUALTIES

DIED	37	11%
KILLED/MISSING	11	3%
WOUNDED	66	20%
CAPTURED	20	6%
DESERTED	42	13%

SIXTY-SIX WERE WOUNDED

The first Groton soldiers wounded were Corporal Samuel J. Garland and Privates William F. Bailey, Charles H. Daniels, George F. Daniels and Patrick H. Denehey of Company H, 10TH Connecticut. They were wounded at Roanoke Island, NC on February 8, 1862 and all recovered from their wounds. Nine Groton soldiers died from a wound received during the war.

GROTON WOUNDED
*(9) DIED FROM WOUNDS

PLACE	DATE	NO.
Roanoke Island, NC (10TH)	2/8/62	5
New Bern, NC (10TH)	3/14/62	1
Fort Macon, NC (8TH)	4/26/62	1
Cedar Mountain, VA (5TH)	8/9/62	2
Norwich, CT (21ST)	8/16/62	1
Antietam, MD (8TH)	9/17/62	4
Fredericksburg, VA (21ST)	12/13/62	1
Kinston, NC (10TH)	12/14/62	1
Fredericksburg, VA (21ST)	12/30/62	1
Virginia, (21ST)	4/26/63	1
Port Hudson, LA (26TH) *3	5/27/63	13
Port Hudson, LA (26TH)	6/13/63	2
Port Hudson, LA (26TH)	6/14/63	1
Gettysburg, PA (5TH)	7/3/63	1
Grove Church, VA (1 CA) *	3/29/64	1
Wilderness, VA (14TH)	5/6/64	1
Walthall Junction, VA (8TH)	5/7/64	1
Laurel Hill, VA (14TH)	5/10/64	1
Drewry's Bluff, VA (8,10,21ST) *3	5/16/64	10
Cold Harbor, VA (21ST) *1	6/3/64	4
Petersburg, VA (21ST)	7/18/64	1
Petersburg, VA (30TH)	7/30/64	2
Petersburg, VA (29TH)	8/20/64	1
Petersburg, VA (21ST)	8/25/64	1
Petersburg, VA (10TH)	9/1/64	1
Fort Harrison, VA (8TH)	9/29/64	2
Petersburg, VA (21ST)	9/29/64	2
Chaffin's Farm, VA (21ST)	10/1/64	1
Boydton Plank Rd, VA (14TH) *	10/27/64	1
Darbytown Road, VA (10TH)	10/27/64	1

GUILFORD
THE POPULATION IN 1860 WAS 2,624 (RANK 52)

THE MOST IMPORTANT DAY OF THE CIVIL WAR

MARCH 8, 1865

KINSTON, NC

THE CONFEDERATE ATTACK STALLED BECAUSE OF BAD COMMUNICATION

More soldiers credited to Guilford were listed as casualties (13) on this day than on any other day of the war. Two soldiers were killed and 11 were captured in the 15TH Connecticut. The captured soldiers survived the war.

The date March 8, 1865 ranks 5TH for total casualties (496) (22 killed, 3 missing, 12 wounded, 410 captured, 49 wounded & captured) for a single day for the State of Connecticut. There were 494 casualties at Kinston, 1 casualty in Virginia, and 1 casualty at a railroad accident in an unknown place.

The Second Battle of Kinston (March 8, 1865) ranks 8TH for total casualties (494) for an engagement for the State of Connecticut.

The Second Battle of Kinston with 13 total casualties for Guilford was the highest number of casualties for any single engagement of the war for the town.

The military situation in North Carolina changed in early 1865. The Confederate forces in eastern North Carolina were called to help stop the advance of the Union Army coming out of Georgia. The Confederates attacked the Union flanks near Kinston on March 8 and failed.

253 MEN CREDITED TO GUILFORD SERVED IN THE FOLLOWING CONNECTICUT ORGANIZATIONS

REGIMENT	TOTAL
15TH	41 (16%)
14TH	37 (15%)
1ST LIGHT BATTERY	34 (13%)
10TH	18 (7%)
11TH	14 (6%)
16TH	14 (6%)
27TH	12 (5%)
20TH	11 (4%)
1ST HEAVY ARTILLERY	10 (4%)
5TH	10 (4%)
30TH	10 (4%)
1ST CAVALRY	9 (4%)
29TH	7 (3%)
2ND HEAVY ARTILLERY	6 (2%)
7TH	6 (2%)
23RD	6 (2%)
6TH	5 (2%)
3RD	4 (2%)
8TH	4 (2%)
9TH	4 (2%)
9TH BATTALION	2
12TH	2
13TH	2
2ND	1
3RD LIGHT BATTERY	1

10% OF POPULATION

THIRTEEN WERE KILLED

The first Guilford soldiers killed were Corporal Richard L. Hill and Private Joseph H. Grosvenor of the 14TH and 16TH Connecticut. They were killed at the Battle of Antietam, MD on September 17, 1862.

GUILFORD SOLDIERS KILLED

PLACE	DATE	NO.
Antietam, MD (14,16TH)	9/17/62	2
Fredericksburg, VA (27TH)	12/13/62	1
Chancellorsville, VA (14TH)	5/3/63	1
Gettysburg, PA (14TH)	7/3/63	1
Railroad Accident, VA (5TH)	10/5/63	1
Morton's Ford, VA (14TH)	2/6/64	1
Deep Bottom, VA (14TH)	8/15/64	1
Hatcher's Run, VA (14TH)	10/27/64	1
Kinston, NC (15TH)	3/8/65	2
Fort Gregg, VA (1 CA)	4/1/65	1
Potomac River (10TH) (Drowned)	4/2/65	1

TWENTY-NINE WERE CAPTURED

Three Guilford soldiers died in captivity. One died at Salisbury Prison, NC, one at Florence, SC and one at Winchester, VA.

GUILFORD CAPTURED
*(3) DIED IN CAPTIVITY

PLACE	DATE	NO.
Winchester, VA (5TH) * (WOUNDED)	5/25/62	1
Chancellorsville, VA (27TH)	5/3/63	5
Plymouth, NC (16TH) *1	4/20/64	6
Drewry's Bluff, VA (11TH)	5/16/64	1
Ashland, VA (1 CA)	6/1/64	1
Ream's Station, VA (14TH) *	8/25/64	1
Cedar Run Church, VA (1 CA)	10/17/64	1
Kinston, NC (15TH)	3/8/65	11
New Market, VA (1 CA)	3/10/65	1
Unknown Place (14TH)	Unknown	1

TOTAL GUILFORD CASUALTIES

DIED	34	13%
KILLED	13	5%
WOUNDED	29	11%
CAPTURED	29	11%
DESERTED	43	17%

TWENTY-NINE WERE WOUNDED

The first Guilford soldier wounded was Private George F. Remington of the 1ST Connecticut Light Battery. He was wounded by accident at Meriden, CT on December 20, 1861 and recovered from his wound. Ten Guilford soldiers died from a wound received during the war.

GUILFORD WOUNDED
*(10) DIED FROM WOUNDS

PLACE	DATE	NO.
Meriden, CT (1 LB)	12/20/61	1
Roanoke Island, NC (10TH) *	2/8/62	1
Antietam, MD (14,16TH) *1	9/17/62	3
Unknown (15TH)	Unknown	1
Fredericksburg, VA(14,27TH) *3	12/13/62	4
Kinston, NC (10TH)	12/14/62	1
Pompon, SC (1 LB)	6/1/63	1
Gettysburg, PA (14TH)	7/3/63	1
Fort Wagner, SC (6TH)	7/18/63	1
Morton's Ford, VA (14TH)	2/6/64	1
Chester Station, VA (1 LB)	5/10/64	1
Proctor's Creek, VA (1 LB)	5/14/64	1
Cold Harbor, VA (11TH)	6/3/64	1
Petersburg, VA (8TH)	6/15/64	1
Petersburg, VA (11TH) *	6/18/64	1
Peach Tree Creek, GA (20TH) *	7/20/64	1
Petersburg, VA (30TH) * 2	7/30/64	2
Atlanta, GA (5TH)	7/30/64	1
Deep Bottom, VA (10TH) *	8/14/64	1
Chaffin's Farm, VA (29TH)	9/30/64	1
Darbytown Rd, VA (10TH)	10/13/64	1
Unknown (10TH)	3/31/65	1
Fort Gregg, VA (10TH)	4/2/65	1

HADDAM
THE POPULATION IN 1860 WAS 2,307 (RANK 61)

THE MOST IMPORTANT DAY OF THE CIVIL WAR

MAY 16, 1864

DREWRY'S BLUFF , VA

AN OBSTACLE ON THE WAY TO RICHMOND

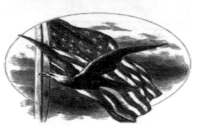

More soldiers credited to Haddam were listed as casualties (4) on this day than on any other day of the war. One soldier was killed, 1 was wounded, and 2 were captured in the 7TH & 11TH Connecticut. The wounded soldier died and one of the captured died following his release from captivity.

The date May 16, 1864 ranks 4th for total casualties (560) (52 killed, 3 missing, 224 wounded, 243 captured, 38 wounded & captured) for a single day for the State of Connecticut. The Battle of Drewry's Bluff accounted for 545 casualties. The 15 other casualties were scattered about Virginia.

The Battle of Drewry's Bluff (May 13-17, 1864), also called Fort Darling, ranks 3rd for total casualties (634) for an engagement for the State of Connecticut. The most intense fighting developed on May 16. Haddam had all of its casualties on that date.

The Battle of Drewry's Bluff with 4 total casualties for Haddam was tied with the Siege of Petersburg, VA (June 1864-April 1865) for the highest number of casualties for any single engagement of the war for the town.

The Confederate attack at Drewry's Bluff forced the Union Army to retreat to Bermuda Hundred. The civil war would have concluded sooner had the Union Army been victorious.

117 MEN CREDITED TO HADDAM SERVED IN THE FOLLOWING CONNECTICUT ORGANIZATIONS

REGIMENT	TOTAL
20TH	22 (19%)
24TH	19 (16%)
11TH	16 (14%)
1ST HEAVY ARTILLERY	11 (9%)
21ST	10 (9%)
29TH	7 (6%)
7TH	5 (4%)
15TH	5 (4%)
13TH	4 (3%)
13TH BATTALION	4 (3%)
16TH	4 (3%)
6TH	3 (3%)
8TH	3 (3%)
14TH	3 (3%)
2ND HEAVY ARTILLERY	2 (2%)
10TH	2 (2%)
12TH	2 (2%)
1ST CAVALRY	1 (1%)
1ST LIGHT BATTERY	1 (1%)
27TH	1 (1%)
30TH	1 (1%)

5% OF POPULATION

FOUR WERE KILLED AND ONE WAS MISSING

The first Haddam soldier killed was Private Aaron A. Clark of Company G, 14TH Connecticut. He was killed at the Battle of Gettysburg, PA on July 3,1863.

HADDAM SOLDIERS KILLED OR MISSING *

PLACE	DATE	NO.
Gettysburg, PA (14TH)	7/3/63	1
Drewry's Bluff, VA (7TH)	5/16/64	1
Cold Harbor, VA (2 HA)	6/1/64	1
Petersburg, VA (11TH)	8/8/64	1
Burksville, VA (10TH) *	4/7/65	1

TEN WERE CAPTURED

One Haddam soldier died in captivity at Andersonville Prison, GA.

HADDAM CAPTURED
*(1) DIED IN CAPTIVITY

PLACE	DATE	NO.
Fort Wagner, SC (7TH)	7/11/63	1
Plymouth, NC (16TH) *1	4/20/64	3
Drewry's Bluff, VA (11TH)	5/16/64	2
Bermuda Hundred, VA (7TH)	6/2/64	1
Winchester, VA (13TH)	9/19/64	1
Kinston, NC (15TH)	3/8/65	2
(1 WOUNDED)		

TOTAL HADDAM CASUALTIES

DIED	17	15%
KILLED/MISSING	5	4%
WOUNDED	19	16%
CAPTURED	10	9%
DESERTED	15	13%

NINETEEN WERE WOUNDED

The first Haddam soldier wounded was Private Charles L. Drake of Company K, 11TH Connecticut. He was wounded at the Battle of Antietam, MD on September 17, 1862 and recovered from his wound. Four Haddam soldiers died from a wound received during the war.

HADDAM WOUNDED
*(4) DIED FROM WOUNDS

PLACE	DATE	NO.
Antietam, MD (11TH)	9/17/62	1
Port Hudson, LA (24TH) *	6/14/63	3
Port Hudson, LA (24TH) *	6/22/63	1
Laurel Hill, VA (14TH)	5/10/64	1
Drewry's Bluff, VA (11TH) *	5/16/64	1
Cold Harbor, VA (21ST)	6/3/64	1
Petersburg, VA (11TH)	6/18/64	2
Petersburg, VA (21ST)	7/17/64	1
Peach Tree Creek, GA(20TH)*1	7/20/64	2
Deep Bottom, VA (14TH)	8/16/64	1
Deep Run, VA (6TH)	8/16/64	1
Winchester, VA (13TH)	9/19/64	1
Fort Harrison, VA (8TH)	9/29/64	1
Cedar Creek, VA (13TH)	10/19/64	1
Fayetteville, NC (20TH)	3/16/65	1

HAMDEN
THE POPULATION IN 1860 WAS 2,725 (RANK 49)

THE MOST IMPORTANT DAY OF THE CIVIL WAR

MARCH 8, 1865

KINSTON, NC

THE CONFEDERATE ATTACK STALLED BECAUSE OF BAD COMMUNICATION

More soldiers credited to Hamden were listed as casualties (12) on this day than on any other day of the war. One soldier was missing and 11 were captured in the 15TH Connecticut. The captured soldiers survived the war.

The date March 8, 1865 ranks 5TH for total casualties (496) (22 killed, 3 missing, 12 wounded, 410 captured, 49 wounded & captured) for a single day for the State of Connecticut. There were 494 casualties at Kinston, 1 casualty in Virginia, and 1 casualty at a railroad accident in an unknown place.

The Second Battle of Kinston (March 8, 1865) ranks 8TH for total casualties (494) for an engagement for the State of Connecticut.

The Second Battle of Kinston with 11 total casualties for Hamden was the highest number of casualties for any single engagement of the war for the town.

The military situation in North Carolina changed in early 1865. The Confederate forces in eastern North Carolina were called to help stop the advance of the Union Army coming out of Georgia. The Confederates attacked the Union flanks near Kinston on March 8 and failed.

245 MEN CREDITED TO HAMDEN SERVED IN THE FOLLOWING CONNECTICUT ORGANIZATIONS

REGIMENT	TOTAL
20TH	46 (19%)
24TH	34 (14%)
11TH	21 (9%)
15TH	21 (9%)
29TH	21 (9%)
1ST HEAVY ARTILLERY	20 (8%)
7TH	14 (6%)
2ND HEAVY ARTILLERY	13 (5%)
6TH	13 (5%)
10TH	12 (5%)
1ST CAVALRY	10 (4%)
13TH	8 (3%)
9TH	7 (3%)
9TH BATTALION	6 (2%)
3RD	5 (3%)
5TH	5 (3%)
8TH	3 (1%)
13TH BATTALION	2
27TH	2
30TH	2
2ND	1
12TH	1
14TH	1
18TH	1

9% OF POPULATION

EIGHT WERE KILLED AND TWO WERE MISSING

The first Hamden soldier killed was Corporal Edgar D. Ives of Company I, 24ᵀᴴ Connecticut. He was killed at Port Hudson, LA on June 14, 1863.

HAMDEN SOLDIERS KILLED OR MISSING *

PLACE	DATE	NO.
Port Hudson, LA (24ᵀᴴ)	6/14/63	2
Gettysburg, PA (20ᵀᴴ)	7/3/63	2
Unknown (Murdered) (9ᵀᴴ)	9/30/63	1
Cold Harbor, VA (11ᵀᴴ)	6/3/64	1
Petersburg, VA (11ᵀᴴ) *	6/18/64	1
Deep Bottom, VA (10ᵀᴴ)	8/14/64	1
Richmond, VA (29ᵀᴴ)	9/30/64	1
Kinston, NC (15ᵀᴴ) *	3/8/65	1

TWENTY-SEVEN WERE CAPTURED

Five Hamden soldiers died in captivity. Two died at Andersonville Prison GA, two at Libby Prison, Richmond, VA and one at Camp Ford, Tyler, TX.

HAMDEN CAPTURED *(5) DIED IN CAPTIVITY

PLACE	DATE	NO.
Chancellorsville, VA (20ᵀᴴ) (2 WOUNDED)	5/3/63	6
Olustee, FL (7ᵀᴴ)	2/24/64	1
Drewry's Bluff, VA (11ᵀᴴ) *3 (1 WOUNDED)	5/16/64	4
Marksville, LA (13ᵀᴴ) *	5/16/64	1
Ashland, VA (2 HA) * (WOUNDED)	6/1/64	1
Front Royal, VA (1 CA)	9/24/64	1
Fisher's Hill, VA (1 CA)	11/4/64	1
Kinston, NC (15ᵀᴴ)	3/8/65	11
Averysboro, NC (20ᵀᴴ)	3/24/65	1

TOTAL HAMDEN CASUALTIES

DIED	23	9%
KILLED/MISSING	10	4%
WOUNDED	37	15%
CAPTURED	27	11%
DESERTED	40	16%

THIRTY-SEVEN WERE WOUNDED

The first Hamden soldiers wounded were Corporal Ezra D. Dickerman and Private Andrew B. Dodd of Company A, 10ᵀᴴ Connecticut. Both were wounded at Roanoke Island, NC on February 8, 1862 and recovered from their wounds. Four Hamden soldiers died from a wound received during the war.

HAMDEN WOUNDED *(4) DIED FROM WOUNDS

PLACE	DATE	NO.
Roanoke Island, NC (10ᵀᴴ)	2/8/62	2
Harper's Ferry, WVA (20ᵀᴴ)	11/1/62	1
Chancellorsville, VA (20ᵀᴴ)	5/3/63	2
Port Hudson, LA (24ᵀᴴ) *	5/24/63	1
Port Hudson, LA (13,24ᵀᴴ)	6/14/63	2
Port Hudson, LA (24ᵀᴴ)	6/18/63	1
Port Hudson, LA (24ᵀᴴ)	6/24/63	1
Gettysburg, PA (20ᵀᴴ)	7/3/63	2
Fort Wagner, SC (6ᵀᴴ) *	7/18/63	1
Olustee, FL (7ᵀᴴ)	2/20/64	1
Resaca, GA (20ᵀᴴ) *	5/15/64	3
Drewry's Bluff, VA (11ᵀᴴ)	5/16/64	1
North Anna River, VA (14ᵀᴴ)	5/24/64	1
Cold Harbor, VA (2 HA)	6/1/64	1
Bermuda Hundred, VA (7ᵀᴴ)	6/2/64	1
Cold Harbor, VA (11ᵀᴴ)	6/3/64	1
Petersburg, VA (8ᵀᴴ)	6/17/64	1
Peach Tree Creek, VA (20ᵀᴴ)	7/20/64	5
Petersburg, VA (30ᵀᴴ)	7/30/64	1
Dutch Gap, VA (1 HA)	8/13/64	1
Deep Run, VA (10ᵀᴴ)	8/16/64	1
Deep Bottom, VA (7ᵀᴴ)	8/16/64	1
Winchester, VA (2 HA)	9/19/64	1
Chaffin's Farm, VA (29ᵀᴴ)	9/30/64	1
Richmond, VA (29ᵀᴴ) *	9/30/64	1
Silver Run, NC (20ᵀᴴ)	3/14/65	1
Bentonville, NC (20ᵀᴴ)	3/19/65	1

412

HAMPTON
THE POPULATION IN 1860 WAS 936 (RANK 140)

THE MOST IMPORTANT DAY OF THE CIVIL WAR

SEPTEMBER 17, 1862

SHARPSBURG, MD (ANTIETAM)

CONNECTICUT HAD MORE CASUALTIES FOR ONE DAY THAN ON ANY OTHER DAY OF THE WAR

Hampton had more casualties on September 17, 1862 at the Battle Antietam, MD (2), on June 15, 1863 at Winchester, VA (2) and on June 5, 1864 at Piedmont, VA (2) than on any other days of the war. The casualties at the Battle of Antietam were the most serious. Two soldiers were wounded in the 11TH Connecticut. Both survived the war.

The date September 17, 1862 ranks 1ST for total casualties (687) (131 killed, 2 missing, 515 wounded, 21 captured, 18 wounded & captured) for a single day for the State of Connecticut. All of the casualties were at Antietam.

The Battle of Antietam (September 16-17, 1862) ranks 1ST for total casualties (689) for an engagement for the State of Connecticut. The most intense fighting developed on September 17. Hampton had all of its casualties on that day.

The Battle of Antietam with 2 total casualties for Hampton was tied for the highest number of casualties for any single engagement of the war for the town with the battles of Winchester (June 15, 1863), and Piedmont (June 5, 1864).

Roughly 12,400 Union casualties were recorded and perhaps there were 10,300 Confederate casualties. Antietam proved to be one of the turning points of the war. It ended Lee's 1862 invasion of the North.

59 MEN CREDITED TO HAMPTON SERVED IN THE FOLLOWING CONNECTICUT ORGANIZATIONS

REGIMENT	TOTAL
12TH	9 (15%)
26TH	9 (15%)
18TH	8 (14%)
11TH	6 (10%)
1ST CAVALRY	5 (8%)
29TH	4 (7%)
1ST HEAVY ARTILLERY	4 (7%)
5TH	2 (3%)
7TH	2 (3%)
10TH	2 (3%)
13TH	2 (3%)
20TH	2 (3%)
1ST SQUADRON CAVALRY	1
2ND	1
8TH	1
9TH	1
12TH BATTALION	1
14TH	1
21ST	1

6% OF POPULATION

ONE WAS KILLED

The only Hampton soldier killed was Private Elisha L. Ashley of Company G, 12TH Connecticut. He was killed at Georgia Landing, LA on October 27, 1862.

HAMPTON SOLDIERS KILLED

PLACE	DATE	NO.
Georgia Landing, LA (12TH)	10/27/62	1

THREE WERE CAPTURED

One Hampton soldier died in captivity at Andersonville Prison, GA.

HAMPTON CAPTURED
***(1) DIED IN CAPTIVITY**

PLACE	DATE	NO.
Winchester, VA (18TH)	6/15/63	2
Waterford, VA (1 CA) *	8/7/63	1

TOTAL HAMPTON CASUALTIES

DIED	7	12%
KILLED	1	2%
WOUNDED	6	10%
CAPTURED	3	5%
DESERTED	5	8%

SIX WERE WOUNDED

The first Hampton soldiers wounded were Corporal Andrew J. Kimball and Private William E. Ford of Company F, 11TH Connecticut. Both were wounded at the Battle of Antietam, MD on September 17, 1862 and both recovered from their wounds. No Hampton soldiers died from a wound received during the war.

HAMPTON WOUNDED
NONE DIED FROM WOUNDS

PLACE	DATE	NO.
Antietam, MD (11TH)	9/17/62	2
Port Hudson, LA (26TH)	6/13/63	1
Piedmont, VA (18TH)	6/5/64	2
Deep Run, VA (10TH)	8/16/64	1

HARTFORD
THE POPULATION IN 1860 WAS 29,152 (RANK 2)

THE MOST IMPORTANT DAY OF THE CIVIL WAR

APRIL 20, 1864

PLYMOUTH, NC

THE CONFEDERATE PLAN TO TAKE PLYMOUTH ENDED WHEN 2,800 UNION TROOPS SURRENDERED THE CITY

More soldiers credited to Hartford were listed as casualties (106) on this day than on any other day of the war. Two soldiers were missing, 98 were captured, and 6 were wounded & captured in the 16TH Connecticut. Forty-four died in prison.

The date April 20, 1864 ranks 6TH for total casualties (433) (1 killed, 2 missing, 12 wounded & captured, 418 captured) for a single day for the State of Connecticut. All of the casualties were at Plymouth, NC.

The Battle of Plymouth (April 20, 1864) ranks 9TH for total casualties (433) for an engagement for the State of Connecticut. Nearly half of all soldiers captured at Plymouth died in Southern prisons

The Battle of Plymouth with 106 total casualties for Hartford was the highest number of casualties for any single engagement of the war for the city.

When Confederate General Robert Hoke surrounded and captured the Union garrison at Plymouth, NC the Southern victory was the first in this military arena in quite some time. With aid from the two-gun ironclad *Albemarle* the Confederates were able to take advantage of the lack of suitable Union gunboats.

3252 MEN CREDITED TO HARTFORD SERVED IN THE FOLLOWING CONNECTICUT ORGANIZATIONS

REGIMENT	TOTAL
1ST HEAVY ARTILLERY	385 (12%)
22ND	329 (10%)
16TH	275 (9%)
1ST CAVALRY	241 (7%)
14TH	218 (7%)
12TH	185 (6%)
1ST	170 (5%)
11TH	157 (5%)
25TH	153 (5%)
7TH	147 (5%)
5TH	146 (4%)
10TH	140 (4%)
3RD	131 (4%)
20TH	96 (3%)
9TH	96 (3%)
2ND HEAVY ARTILLERY	93 (3%)
21ST	89 (3%)
8TH	81 (3%)
29TH	73 (2%)
6TH	72 (2%)
12TH BATTALION	63 (2%)
30TH	59 (2%)
24TH	47 (2%)
13TH	48 (1%)
9TH BATTALION	37 (1%)
1ST SQUADRON CAVALRY	35 (1%)
2ND	26 (1%)
13TH BATTALION	12
1ST LIGHT BATTERY	11
15TH	9
18TH	6
2ND LIGHT BATTERY	5
23RD	3
26TH	1

11% OF POPULATION

ONE HUNDRED-ONE WERE KILLED AND TWELVE WERE MISSING

The first Hartford soldier killed was Private Jeremiah O. Leroy of Company E, 3RD Connecticut. He was killed at the Battle of Bull Run, VA on July 21, 1861.

TOTAL HARTFORD CASUALTIES

DIED	284	9%
KILLED/MISSING	113	3%
WOUNDED	411	13%
CAPTURED	319	10%
DESERTED	561	17%

HARTFORD SOLDIERS KILLED *MISSING

PLACE	DATE	NO.
Bull Run, VA (3RD)	7/21/61	1
New Bern, NC (11TH)	3/14/62	1
Falmouth, VA (1 SQ)	4/17/62	1
New Bern, NC (11TH)	7/3/62	1
Cedar Mountain, VA (5TH)	8/9/62	4
Antietam, MD (8,11,16TH) *1	9/17/62	15
Railroad Accident (22ND)	10/5/62	1
Unknown Place (12TH)	11/8/62	1
Fredericksburg, VA (14TH) *1	12/13/62	2
Kinston, NC (10TH)	12/14/62	1
Stafford Court House, VA (20TH) (ACCIDENT)	1/28/63	1
Alexandria, VA (1 HA)	3/2/63	1
Irish Bend, LA (25TH)	4/14/63	4
Siege Suffolk, VA (16TH)	4/24/63	1
Chancellorsville, VA (20TH)	5/3/63	1
Port Hudson, LA (25TH)	5/27/63	2
Port Hudson, LA (25TH)	5/28/63	1
Port Hudson, LA (12TH)	5/29/63	1
Port Hudson, LA (12TH)	6/9/63	1
Port Hudson, LA (24TH)	6/14/63	1
Gettysburg, PA (20TH)	7/3/63	1
Fort Wagner, SC (7TH)	7/11/63	3
Stono Inlet, SC (Drowned) (10TH)	7/18/63	1
Railroad Accident (5TH)	9/27/63	1
Fort Harrison, VA (8TH)	9/29/64	1
Bristoe Station, VA (14TH)	10/14/63	1
Trumbull, CT (Drowned) (10TH)	10/23/63	1
Gowan, TN (Accident) (5TH)	12/24/63	1
Unknown Place (29TH)	2/4/64	1
Morton's Ford, VA (14TH)	2/6/64	1
Olustee, FLA (7TH)	2/20/64	1
Plymouth, NC (16TH) *	4/20/64	2
Unknown Place (12TH)	5/3/64	1
Wilderness, VA (14TH)	5/6/64	1
Beaver Dam Station, VA (1 CA)	5/10/64	1
Spottsylvania, VA *	5/12/64	1
Proctor's Creek, VA (1 LB)	5/14/64	1
Resaca, GA (5TH)	5/15/64	1
Drewry's Bluff, VA (6,7TH)	5/16/64	2
Bermuda Hundred, VA (1 HA)	5/30/64	1
Cold Harbor, VA (2 HA) *1	6/1/64	2
Cold Harbor, VA (11TH)	6/3/64	1
Petersburg, VA (7TH)	6/9/64	1
Petersburg, VA (11TH)	6/18/64	1
Petersburg, VA (2 HA)	6/20/64	1
Culp's Farm, GA (5TH)	6/22/64	1
Ream's Station, VA (1CA) *	6/29/64	1
Peach Tree Creek, GA (5,20TH)	7/20/64	2
Petersburg, VA (21ST 30TH) *2	7/30/64	8
Petersburg, VA (11TH)	8/5/64	1
Petersburg, VA (11TH)	8/15/64	2
Deep Run, VA (7TH)	8/16/64	1
Ream's Station, VA (14TH)	8/25/64	1

HARTFORD SOLDIERS KILLED *MISSING (CONTINUED)

PLACE	DATE	NO.
Turner's Ford, GA (20TH)	8/27/64	1
Winchester, VA (2HA,12,13TH)	9/19/64	3
Fort Harrison, VA (8TH) *1	9/29/64	2
Marietta, GA (20TH)	10/4/64	1
Darbytown Road, VA (10TH) *1	10/13/64	2
Cedar Creek, VA (2HA,9,12TH)	10/19/64	4
Unknown (10TH)	1/17/65	1
Charlotte, NC (16TH)	2/2/65	1
Lyme, CT (Drowned) (14TH)	3/3/65	1
Bentonville, NC (20TH)	3/19/65	1
Petersburg, VA (1 HA)	3/25/65	2
Fort Gregg, VA (10TH)	4/2/65	2
Petersburg, VA (1 HA) *	4/2/65	1
Burksville, VA (10TH) *	4/7/65	1
Unknown Place (1 CA)	4/13/65	1
Potomac River (Drowned) (7TH)	4/24/65	1

THREE HUNDRED NINETEEN WERE CAPTURED

Ninety Hartford soldiers died in captivity. Fifty-four died at Andersonville Prison, GA, 16 at Florence, SC, 6 at Libby Prison, Richmond, VA, 4 at Charleston, SC, 3 at Salisbury, NC, and 1 each at Lake City, FL, Millen, GA, Raleigh, NC, Selma, AL, Sharpsburg, MD, and Wilmington, NC.

HARTFORD CAPTURED *(90) DIED IN CAPTIVITY

PLACE	DATE	NO.
Unknown Place (1 CA) *		1
Unknown Place (1 HA) *		1
Williamsport, MD (1 HA)	6/15/61	1
Bull Run, VA (2ND,3RD)	7/21/61	3
Edinburgh, VA	4/21/62	1
Winchester, VA (5TH)	5/24/62	1
Winchester, VA (5TH)	5/25/62	3
Cold Harbor, VA (1 HA)	6/27/62	1
Gaines' Mills, VA (1 HA)	6/27/62	1
Savage Station, VA (1 HA)	6/30/62	1
New Bern, NC (11TH) (Wounded)	7/3/62	1
Cedar Mountain, VA (5TH)	8/9/62	2
Cedar Run, VA (1 CA)	8/9/62	1
Virginia (5TH)	8/17/62	1
Antietam, MD (16TH)	9/17/62	1
Winchester, VA (16TH)	9/28/62	1
Lady's Island, SC (6TH)	10/19/62	1

HARTFORD CAPTURED (CONTINUED)

PLACE	DATE	NO.
Pattersonville, LA (12ᵀᴴ)	3/27/63	14
Pattersonville, LA (12ᵀᴴ)	3/28/63	4
Unknown Place (12ᵀᴴ)	3/30/63	1
Chancellorsville, VA (5ᵀᴴ)	5/2/63	1
Chancellorsville, VA (5,20ᵀᴴ)	5/3/63	9
(1 Wounded)		
Unknown Place (1 SQ) *	6/1/63	1
Brashear City, LA (12,25ᵀᴴ)	6/23/63	2
New Baltimore, VA (1 SQ) *	7/1/63	1
Gettysburg, PA (5ᵀᴴ)	7/2/63	1
Smithburg, MD (1 SQ)	7/4/63	1
King William's CH, VA (11ᵀᴴ)	7/5/63	1
Hanover Court House, VA (11ᵀᴴ)	7/6/63	1
Burnt Ordinary, VA (21ˢᵀ)	7/9/63	2
Fort Wagner, SC (7ᵀᴴ) *2	7/11/63	9
(2 Wounded)		
Bolivar Heights, VA (1CA) *4	7/14/63	7
(1 Wounded)		
Fort Wagner, SC (6ᵀᴴ) *2	7/18/63	2
Morris Island, SC (10ᵀᴴ)	7/19/63	2
Waterford, VA (1 CA)	8/7/63	1
Liberty Mills, VA (1 SQ)	9/22/63	1
Brandy Station, VA (1 SQ)	10/12/63	1
Rappahannock River, VA (14ᵀᴴ)	10/13/63	1
Bristoe Station, VA (14ᵀᴴ)	10/14/63	6
New Baltimore, VA (1 SQ)	10/19/63	1
Rapidan, VA (14ᵀᴴ) *	12/1/63	1
St Augustine, FL (10ᵀᴴ) *	12/30/63	1
New Bern, NC (21ˢᵀ)	2/1/64	1
Morton's Ford, VA (14ᵀᴴ) *1	2/6/64	2
Olustee, FL (7ᵀᴴ) *3	2/20/64	5
(2 Wounded)		
Plymouth, NC (16ᵀᴴ) *44	4/20/64	114
(6 Wounded)		
Cloutierville, LA (13ᵀᴴ)	4/23/64	1
Unknown Place (14ᵀᴴ) *	5/2/64	1
Craig's Church, VA (1CA) *1	5/5/64	2
Winchester, VA (14ᵀᴴ) *1	5/6/64	2
Drewry's Bluff, VA (7,11ᵀᴴ) *10	5/16/64	22
(1 Wounded)		
Ashland, VA (1 CA)	6/1/64	4
(1 Wounded)		
Bermuda Hundred, VA (7ᵀᴴ) *4	6/2/64	6
(1 Wounded)		
Hatcher's Run, VA (7ᵀᴴ)	6/2/64	2
Gaines' Mills, VA (2 HA) *	6/2/64	1
Piedmont, VA (18ᵀᴴ)	6/5/64	1
Bermuda Hundred, VA (7ᵀᴴ) *	6/5/64	1
Old Church Tavern, VA (1 CA) *1	6/10/64	4
Chester Station, VA (7ᵀᴴ)	6/17/64	1
Hatcher's Run, VA (7ᵀᴴ)	6/17/64	1
Petersburg, VA (11ᵀᴴ) *	6/18/64	1
Hatcher's Run, VA (7ᵀᴴ)	6/20/64	1
Culp's Farm, GA (7ᵀᴴ)	6/22/64	1
(1 Wounded)		
Notoway Court House, VA (1 CA)	6/24/64	1
Staunton, VA (1 CA)	6/25/64	1
Ream's Station, VA (1CA,1SQ) *2	6/29/64	9
(2 Wounded)		
Stony Creek, VA (1 CA)	6/29/64	1
Ream's Station, VA (1 SQ)	6/30/64	1
Cabin Point, VA (1 CA)	6/30/64	1
Ream's Station, VA (1 CA)	7/1/64	1
Peach Tree Creek, GA (20ᵀᴴ)	7/20/64	1
Ream's Station, VA (14ᵀᴴ)	8/25/64	2
Berryville, VA (1 CA)	9/7/64	1
Charlestown, VA (12ᵀᴴ)	9/11/64	1
Charlestown, VA (12ᵀᴴ)	9/12/64	1
Cox's Mills, VA (8ᵀᴴ)	9/16/64	1
Fair Oaks, VA (21ˢᵀ)	10/29/64	1
Cedar Creek, VA (1 CA)	11/12/64	4
Unknown Place (6ᵀᴴ)	3/6/65	1
Brunswick, NC (6ᵀᴴ)	3/6/65	1
Kinston, NC (15TH)	3/8/65	1
Ashland, VA (1 CA)	3/15/65	1
Petersburg, VA (1 HA)	3/25/65	1
Appomattox Court House, VA (10ᵀᴴ)	4/9/65	1

FOUR HUNDRED-ELEVEN SEVEN WERE WOUNDED

The first Hartford soldier wounded was Private George H. Bugbee of Company A, 1ˢᵀ Connecticut. He was wounded at Vienna, VA on July 15, 1861 and recovered from his wound. Forty-five Hartford soldiers died from a wound received during the war.

HARTFORD WOUNDED *(45) DIED FROM WOUNDS

PLACE	DATE	NO.
Unknown Place (6ᵀᴴ)		2
New Haven, CT (1 HA)	5/15/61	1
Vienna, VA (1ˢᵀ)	6/16/61	1
Bull Run, VA (1ˢᵀ, 3ᴿᴰ)	7/21/61	4
Harper's Ferry, WVA (1 HA)	7/26/61	1
Hyattstown, MD (5ᵀᴴ) *	10/8/61	1
Roanoke Island, NC (10ᵀᴴ)	2/8/62	1
New Bern, NC (10ᵀᴴ)	3/14/62	1
Pass Christian, LA (9ᵀᴴ)	4/3/62	1
Old Church, VA (1 HA)	5/24/62	1
Winchester, VA (5ᵀᴴ)	5/25/62	1
Antietam, MD (11ᵀᴴ)	6/1/62	1
James Island, SC (7ᵀᴴ)	6/16/62	7
New Orleans, LA (9ᵀᴴ)	8/3/62	1
Baton Rouge, LA (9ᵀᴴ)	8/4/62	1
Cedar Mountain, VA (5ᵀᴴ)	8/9/62	7
2 Bull Run, VA (1 CA)	8/30/62	1
Unknown Place (1 SQ)	9/7/62	1
South Mountain, MD (11ᵀᴴ)	9/14/62	1
Antietam, MD (8,11,14,16ᵀᴴ)	9/17/62	67
Pocotaligo, SC (6,7ᵀᴴ)	10/22/62	3
Georgia Landing, LA (12ᵀᴴ)	10/27/62	2
Fredericksburg, VA (14ᵀᴴ) *1	12/13/62	7
Kinston, NC (10ᵀᴴ) *	12/14/62	3
Bayou Teche, LA (12ᵀᴴ)	1/14/63	1
Pattersonville, LA (12ᵀᴴ) *1	3/27/63	2
Irish Bend, LA (13,25ᵀᴴ) *3	4/14/63	9
Siege Suffolk, VA (16ᵀᴴ)	4/24/63	2
Chancellorsville, VA (5,14ᵀᴴ) *1	5/2/63	2
Chancellorsville, VA (5,14,20ᵀᴴ)	5/3/63	14
Siege Suffolk, VA (16ᵀᴴ)	5/3/63	1
Providence Church Rd, VA (16ᵀᴴ) *1	5/3/63	4
Port Hudson, LA (25ᵀᴴ)	5/12/63	1
Port Hudson, LA (12,24,25,26ᵀᴴ)	5/27/63	7
Port Hudson, LA (25ᵀᴴ)	5/31/63	1
Port Hudson, LA (25ᵀᴴ)	6/1/63	1
Port Hudson, LA (12ᵀᴴ)	6/10/63	2
Port Hudson, LA (12,13,24,25ᵀᴴ)	6/14/63	7
Port Hudson, LA (25ᵀᴴ)	6/27/63	1
Gettysburg, PA (20ᵀᴴ)	7/2/63	1
Gettysburg, PA (14,20ᵀᴴ)	7/3/63	7
Fort Wagner, SC (7ᵀᴴ)	7/11/63	3
Fort Wagner, SC (6ᵀᴴ)	7/18/63	2

HARTFORD WOUNDED (CONTINUED)

PLACE	DATE	NO.
Port Hudson, LA (12,13,24,25[TH])	6/14/63	7
Port Hudson, LA (25TH)	6/27/63	1
Gettysburg, PA (20TH)	7/2/63	1
Gettysburg, PA (14,20[TH])	7/3/63	7
Fort Wagner, SC (7TH)	7/11/63	3
Fort Wagner, SC (6TH)	7/18/63	2
Unknown (5TH)	11/23/63	1
Bristoe Station, VA (14TH)	10/14/63	2
Morton's Ford, VA (14TH)	2/6/64	11
New Bern, NC (21ST)	2/17/64	1
Olustee, FL (7TH) *1	2/20/64	2
Petersburg, VA (1 HA)	3/9/64	1
Grove Church, VA (1 CA)	4/1/64	1
Cane River, LA (13TH)	4/23/64	1
Railroad Accident (14TH)	4/24/64	1
Siege Suffolk, VA (16TH)	4/24/64	1
Unknown Place (14TH)	5/4/64	1
Craig's Church, VA (1 CA)	5/5/6	2
Wilderness, VA (14TH)	5/6/64	7
Wilderness, VA (14TH)	5/7/64	1
Swift's Creek, VA (11TH)	5/9/64	2
Laurel Hill, VA (14TH)	5/10/64	1
Chester Station, VA (7TH)	5/10/64	1
Petersburg, VA (1 HA)	5/10/64	1
Spottsylvania, VA (14TH)	5/12/64	2
Meadow Bridge, VA (1 CA)	5/12/64	2
Cold Harbor, VA (1 CA)	5/12/64	1
Bermuda Hundred, VA (7,10[TH])	5/14/64	2
Drewry's Bluff, VA (7TH)	5/14/64	3
New Market, VA (18TH)	5/15/64	1
Resaca, GA (5,20[TH]) *1	5/15/64	5
Spottsylvania, VA (14TH)	5/15/64	1
Bermuda Hundred, VA (7TH)	5/16/64	1
Drewry's Bluff, VA (7,10,11[TH]21ST) *1	5/16/64	16
Drewry's Bluff, VA (6TH) *	5/17/64	1
Bermuda Hundred, VA (1 HA)	5/24/64	1
North Anna River, VA (14TH)	5/24/64	1
Atlanta, GA (5TH)	5/25/64	1
Dallas, GA (5TH)	5/25/64	3
Cold Harbor, VA (11TH)	6/1/64	1
Cold Harbor, VA (2 HA)	6/1/64	3
Bermuda Hundred, VA (7TH)	6/2/64	3
Petersburg, VA (11TH)	6/3/64	1
Cold Harbor, VA (8,11[TH],21ST)	6/3/64	16
Petersburg, VA (8TH,21ST)	6/16/64	2
Petersburg, VA (14TH) *	6/17/64	1
Snicker's Gap, VA (1 CA)	6/18/64	1
Petersburg, VA (1 HA)	6/18/64	1
Petersburg, VA (11TH)	6/18/64	1
Petersburg, VA (14TH)	6/20/64	1
Petersburg, VA (8TH)	6/23/64	1
Ream's Station, VA (1 CA)	6/28/64	1
Ream's Station, VA (1 CA)	6/29/64	1
Stony Creek, VA (1 CA)	6/29/64	1
Petersburg, VA (1 HA)	7/1/64	1
Petersburg, VA (1 HA)	7/5/64	1
Petersburg, VA (1 HA)	7/6/64	1
Peach Tree Creek, GA (5,20[TH])	7/20/64	9
Tennessee (5TH)	7/22/64	1
Petersburg, VA (1 HA)	7/24/64	1
Strawberry Plains, VA (10TH)	7/27/64	1
Atlanta, GA (5TH)	7/30/64	1
Petersburg, VA (1HA,8, 11,21,30)	7/30/64	11
City Point, VA (8TH)	8/1/64	1
Atlanta, GA (20TH)	8/7/64	1
Deep Run, VA (10TH)	8/14/64	1
Deep Run, VA (6,10[TH])	8/16/64	4
Petersburg, VA (1 HA)	8/19/64	1
Petersburg, VA (8TH)	8/25/64	1
Bermuda Hundred, VA (7TH)	9/1/64	1
Petersburg, VA (6TH)	9/12/64	1
Petersburg, VA (10TH)	9/14/64	1
Winchester, VA (2 HA,12TH)	9/19/64	11
Strasburg, VA (9TH)	9/21/64	1
Fisher's Hill, VA (2 HA)	9/22/64	1
Chaffin's Farm, VA (7,8[TH],21ST)	9/29/64	5
Fort Harrison, VA (8TH,21ST)	9/29/64	4
New Market Road, VA (7TH)	9/29/64	1
Richmond, VA (29TH)	9/30/64	1
Petersburg, VA (29TH)	9/30/64	1
Petersburg, VA (14TH)	10/2/64	1
Petersburg, VA (1 HA)	10/4/64	1
Darbytown Road, VA (6TH)	10/7/64	1
Darbytown Road, VA (7,10[TH]) *1	10/13/64	2
Chaffin's Farm, VA (29TH)	10/13/64	1
New Market Road, VA (10TH)	10/13/64	1
Cedar Run Church, VA (1 CA)	10/17/64	1
Cedar Creek,VA(1CA,2HA,9,12[TH]) *3	10/19/64	9
Kell House, VA (29TH)	10/27/64	6
Boydton Plank Road, VA (14TH)	10/27/64	1
Darbytown Road, VA (10TH) *	10/27/64	1
Petersburg, VA (1 HA)	11/2/64	1
Cedar Creek, VA (1 CA)	11/12/64	1
Petersburg, VA (1 HA)	11/27/64	1
Deep Bottom, VA (7TH)	12/10/64	1
Bermuda Hundred, VA (30TH)	2/10/65	1
Natural Bridge, FLA(12TH)	3/6/65	1
Bentonville, NC (20TH)	3/19/65	1
Petersburg, VA (1 HA) *1	3/25/65	5
Hatcher's Run, VA (14TH)	3/25/65	1
Petersburg, VA (1 HA)	3/30/65	1
Petersburg, VA (29TH)	4/1/65	1
Petersburg, VA (10TH)	4/2/65	1
Fort Gregg, VA (10TH) *1	4/2/65	3
Fort Mahone, VA (1 HA)	4/2/65	1
Petersburg, VA (1 HA)	4/3/65	2
Harper's Farm, VA (1 CA)	4/6/65	1
Gettysburg, PA (1 CA)	7/4/65	1
Atlanta, GA (5TH)	8/1/65	1

HARTLAND
THE POPULATION IN 1860 WAS 846 (RANK 144)

THE MOST SIGNIFICANT DAY OF THE CIVIL WAR

APRIL 14, 1863

IRISH BEND, LA

THE BATTLE WAS PART OF THE UNION ATTEMPT TO SIEZE WESTERN LOUISIANA

More soldiers credited to Hartland were listed as casualties (4) on this day than on any other day of the war. One soldier was killed and three were wounded in the 25TH Connecticut. One of the wounded died.

The date April 14, 1863 ranks 17TH for total casualties (147) (18 killed, 120 wounded, 9 captured) for a single day for the State of Connecticut. The Battle of Irish Bend accounted for 144 casualties. The 3 other casualties were scattered about Louisiana.

The Battle of Irish Bend (April 14, 1863) ranks 18TH for total casualties (144) for an engagement for the State of Connecticut.

The Battle of Irish Bend with 4 total casualties for Hartland was tied with the Siege of Port Hudson, LA (May-July 1863) for the highest number of casualties for any single engagement of the war for the town.

Due to the lack of men, money, and supplies, the Confederate Army under General Richard Taylor fought a difficult fight to hold onto Louisiana. At the Battle of Irish Bend, in Bayou Tech, he held off a far larger Union force on two fronts until he could get his army to safety.

66 MEN CREDITED TO HARTLAND SERVED IN THE FOLLOWING CONNECTICUT ORGANIZATIONS

REGIMENT	TOTAL
25TH	25 (40%)
16TH	8 (12%)
11TH	8 (12%)
7TH	5 (8%)
10TH	5 (8%)
5TH	3 (5%)
14TH	3 (5%)
2ND HEAVY ARTILLERY	2 (3%)
12TH	2 (3%)
13TH	2 (3%)
1ST LIGHT BATTERY	1
1ST HEAVY ARTILLERY	1
8TH	1
12TH BATTALION	1
20TH	1
22ND	1

8% OF POPULATION

TWO WERE KILLED

The first Hartland soldier killed was Private Samuel A. Lawton of Company E, 25TH Connecticut. He was killed at Irish Bend, LA on April 14, 1863.

HARTLAND SOLDIERS KILLED

PLACE	DATE	NO.
Irish Bend, LA (25TH)	4/14/63	1
Washington, DC (20TH)	6/4/65	1

FOUR WERE CAPTURED

One Hartland soldier died in captivity at Andersonville Prison, GA.

HARTLAND CAPTURED
*(1) DIED IN CAPTIVITY

PLACE	DATE	NO.
Plymouth, NC (16TH) *1	4/20/64	3
Petersburg, VA (7TH)	6/16/64	1

TOTAL HARTLAND CASUALTIES

DIED	14	21%
KILLED	2	3%
WOUNDED	11	17%
CAPTURED	4	6%
DESERTED	12	18%

ELEVEN WERE WOUNDED

The first Hartland soldier wounded was Private Solomon T. Bunnell of Company E, 16TH Connecticut. He was wounded at the Battle of Antietam, MD on September 17, 1862 and recovered from his wound. Three Hartland soldiers died from a wound received during the war.

HARTLAND WOUNDED
*(3) DIED FROM WOUNDS

PLACE	DATE	NO.
Antietam, MD (16TH)	9/17/62	1
Irish Bend, LA (25TH) *1	4/14/63	3
Port Hudson, LA (25TH) *	5/27/63	2
Port Hudson, LA (25TH)	6/6/63	1
Port Hudson, LA (25TH)	6/27/63	1
Noel's Station, VA (2 HA) *	5/26/64	1
Deep Bottom, VA (10TH)	8/14/64	1
Fort Gregg, VA (10TH)	4/2/65	1

HARWINTON
THE POPULATION IN 1860 WAS 1,044 (RANK 134)

THE MOST IMPORTANT
DAY OF THE CIVIL WAR

JUNE 1, 1864

COLD HARBOR, VA

THE BATTLE WAS LEE'S
LAST GREAT VICTORY

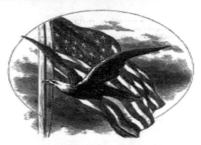

More soldiers credited to Harwinton were listed as casualties (5) on this day than on any other day of the war. Five soldiers were wounded in the 2ND Connecticut Heavy Artillery. Two of the wounded died.

The date June 1, 1864 ranks 8TH for total casualties (374) (89 killed, 10 missing, 246 wounded, 23 captured, 6 wounded & captured) for a single day for the State of Connecticut. There were 324 casualties at Cold Harbor, 41 casualties at Ashland, and 9 other casualties scattered about Virginia.

The Battle and operations around Cold Harbor (May 31-June 12, 1864) rank 6TH for total casualties (557) for an engagement for the State of Connecticut. The most intense fighting developed on June 3 and Harwinton had no casualties.

The Battle of Cold Harbor with 5 total casualties for Harwinton was the highest number of casualties for any single engagement of the war for the town.

Approximately 117,000 Federal and 60,000 Confederate troops participated in operations from May 28 to June 3. Roughly 13,000 Union casualties were recorded and perhaps there were 5,000 Confederate casualties.

82 MEN CREDITED TO HARWINTON SERVED IN THE FOLLOWING CONNECTICUT ORGANIZATIONS

REGIMENT	TOTAL
2ND HEAVY ARTILLERY	40 (49%)
1ST HEAVY ARTILLERY	14 (17%)
8TH	6 (7%)
11TH	4 (5%)
14TH	3 (4%)
1ST CAVALRY	2 (2%)
7TH	2 (2%)
15TH	2 (2%)
23RD	2 (2%)
27TH	2 (2%)
28TH	2 (2%)
2ND	1
3RD LIGHT BATTERY	1
6TH	1
10TH	1
12TH	1
13TH	1
17TH	1
20TH	1
29TH	1

8% OF POPULATION

THREE WERE KILLED

The first Harwinton soldier killed was Private James McLaughlin of Company A, 14TH Connecticut. He was killed at Bristoe Station, VA on October 14,1863.

HARWINTON SOLDIERS KILLED

PLACE	DATE	NO.
Bristoe Station, VA (14TH)	10/14/63	1
Battery Morton, VA (1 HA)	8/17/64	1
Cedar Creek, VA (2 HA)	10/19/64	1

THREE WERE CAPTURED

No Harwinton soldiers died in captivity.

HARWINTON CAPTURED
NONE DIED IN CAPTIVITY

PLACE	DATE	NO.
Chancellorsville, VA (27TH)	5/3/63	1
Spottsylvania, VA (14TH)	5/14/64	1
New Market, VA (1 CA)	3/9/65	1

TOTAL HARWINTON CASUALTIES

DIED	10	12%
KILLED	3	4%
WOUNDED	17	21%
CAPTURED	3	4%
DESERTED	10	12%

SEVENTEEN WERE WOUNDED

The first Harwinton soldier wounded was Private Emory Barber of Company F, 28TH Connecticut. He was wounded at Port Hudson, LA on June 14, 1863 and recovered from his wound. Four Harwinton soldiers died from a wound received during the war.

HARWINTON WOUNDED
*(4) DIED FROM WOUNDS

PLACE	DATE	NO.
Port Hudson, LA (28TH)	6/14/63	1
Fort Lyon, VA (2 HA)	8/15/63	1
Drewry's Bluff, VA (8,11TH)	5/16/64	2
North Anna River, VA (2 HA)	5/24/64	1
Cold Harbor, VA (2 HA) *2	6/1/64	5
Petersburg, VA (2 HA)	6/22/64	1
Winchester, VA (2 HA) *	9/19/64	2
Fisher's Hill, VA (2 HA)	9/22/64	2
Chaffin's Farm, VA (8TH)	9/29/64	1
Sailor's Creek, VA (2 HA) *	4/6/65	1

HEBRON
THE POPULATION IN 1860 WAS 1,425 (RANK 103)

THE MOST IMPORTANT DAY OF THE CIVIL WAR

MAY 14, 1864

PROCTOR'S CREEK, VA

THE ENGAGEMENT WAS A PART OF THE OPERATIONS NEAR THE JAMES RIVER TO CAPTURE RICHMOND

More soldiers credited to Hebron were listed as casualties (2) on this day than on any other day of the war. Two soldiers were wounded in the 1ST Connecticut Light Battery. Both soldiers survived the war.

The date May 14, 1864 ranks 31ST for total casualties (85) (13 killed, 70 wounded, 2 captured) for a single day for the State of Connecticut. All of the casualties were in Virginia: Drewry's Bluff (69), Proctor's Creek (23), Bermuda Hundred (2), Petersburg (2), Chester Station (1), and Spottsylvania (1).

The Engagement at Proctor's Creek (May 3-20, 1864) ranks 68TH for total casualties (23) for an engagement for the State of Connecticut.

The Engagement at Proctor's Creek with 2 total casualties for Hebron was the highest number of casualties for any single engagement of the war for the town.

In the Spring of 1864, the Union Army began a major offensive to capture Richmond and Petersburg, VA. Confederate General Pierre G.T. Beauregard, who commanded the forces at Petersburg, was able to deflect Union General Benjamin Butler's advances.

78 MEN CREDITED TO HEBRON SERVED IN THE FOLLOWING CONNECTICUT ORGANIZATIONS

REGIMENT	TOTAL
1ST LIGHT BATTERY	29 (37%)
13TH	8 (10%)
1ST HEAVY ARTILLERY	7 (9%)
29TH	7 (9%)
5TH	5 (6%)
1ST CAVALRY	4 (5%)
6TH	4 (5%)
21ST	4 (5%)
24TH	3 (5%)
7TH	2 (3%)
12TH	2 (3%)
14TH	2 (3%)
16TH	2 (3%)
2ND HEAVY ARTILLERY	1
8TH	1
10TH	1
12TH BATTALION	1
13TH BATTALION	1
30TH	1

6% OF POPULATION

ONE WAS KILLED

The only Hebron soldier killed was Captain Joseph Backus of Company K, 1ST Connecticut Cavalry. He was killed at Old Church Tavern, VA on June 10, 1864.

TOTAL HEBRON CASUALTIES

DIED	12	15%
KILLED	1	1%
WOUNDED	6	8%
CAPTURED	5	6%
DESERTED	5	6%

HEBRON SOLDIERS KILLED

PLACE	DATE	NO.
Old Church Tav., VA (1 CA)	6/10/64	1

FIVE WERE CAPTURED

Three Hebron soldiers died in captivity. Two died at Salisbury NC and one at Petersburg, VA.

HEBRON CAPTURED
*(3) DIED IN CAPTIVITY

PLACE	DATE	NO.
Darnestown, MD (5TH)	9/4/62	1
Bermuda Hundred, VA (6TH)	5/20/64	1
Petersburg, VA (30TH) *	7/30/64	1
Richmond, VA (6TH) *	10/7/64	1
Cedar Run Church, VA (1CA)*	10/17/64	1

SIX WERE WOUNDED

The first Hebron soldier wounded was Private John K. Lamphere of Company C, 24TH Connecticut. He was wounded at Port Hudson, LA on June 14, 1863 and recovered from his wound. One Hebron soldier died from a wound received during the war.

HEBRON WOUNDED
*(1) DIED FROM WOUNDS

PLACE	DATE	NO.
Port Hudson, LA (24TH)	6/14/63	1
Proctor's Creek, VA (1 LB)	5/14/64	2
Darbytown Road, VA (29TH) *	10/13/64	1
Charles City Road, VA (7TH)	10/27/64	1
Unknown (16TH)	Unknown	1

KENT
THE POPULATION IN 1860 WAS 1,855 (RANK 80)

THE MOST IMPORTANT DAY OF THE CIVIL WAR

JUNE 1, 1864

COLD HARBOR, VA

THE BATTLE WAS LEE'S LAST GREAT VICTORY

More soldiers credited to Kent were listed as casualties (15) on this day than on any other day of the war. Seven soldiers were killed, 7 wounded, and one wounded & captured in the 2ND Connecticut Heavy Artillery. One of the wounded died.

The date June 1, 1864 ranks 8TH for total casualties (374) (89 killed, 10 missing, 246 wounded, 23 captured, 6 wounded & captured) for a single day for the State of Connecticut. There were 324 casualties at Cold Harbor, 41 casualties at Ashland and 9 other casualties were scattered about Virginia.

The battle and operations around Cold Harbor (May 31-June 12, 1864) rank 6TH for total casualties (557) for an engagement for the State of Connecticut. The most intense fighting developed on June 3 and Kent had one wounded on that day.

The Battle of Cold Harbor with 16 total casualties for Kent was the highest number of casualties for any single engagement of the war for the town.

Approximately 117,000 Federal and 60,000 Confederate troops participated in operations from May 28 to June 3. Roughly 13,000 Union casualties were recorded and perhaps there were 5,000 Confederate casualties.

162 MEN CREDITED TO KENT SERVED IN THE FOLLOWING CONNECTICUT ORGANIZATIONS

REGIMENT	TOTAL
2ND HEAVY ARTILLERY	76 (47%)
13TH	37 (23%)
10TH	21 (13%)
11TH	8 (5%)
5TH	7 (4%)
13TH BATTALION	7 (4%)
8TH	6 (4%)
1ST HEAVY ARTILLERY	5 (3%)
6TH	2 (1%)
7TH	2 (1%)
15TH	1
29TH	1

9% OF POPULATION

TEN WERE KILLED

The first Kent soldier killed was Private Vivian Stowe of Company H, 11TH Connecticut. He was killed at Swift's Creek, VA on May 9, 1864.

KENT SOLDIERS KILLED

PLACE	DATE	NO.
Swift's Creek, VA (11TH)	5/9/64	1
Cold Harbor, VA (2 HA)	6/1/64	7
Winchester, VA (13TH)	9/19/64	1
Fort Gregg, VA (10TH)	4/2/65	1

FIVE WERE CAPTURED

Two Kent soldiers died in captivity at Salisbury NC.

KENT CAPTURED
*(2) DIED IN CAPTIVITY

PLACE	DATE	NO.
Cold Harbor, VA (2 HA) (WOUNDED)	6/1/64	1
Berryville, VA (13TH)	9/8/64	1
Winchester, VA (13TH) *2	9/19/64	3

TOTAL KENT CASUALTIES

DIED	20	12%
KILLED	10	6%
WOUNDED	22	14%
CAPTURED	5	3%
DESERTED	27	17%

TWENTY-TWO WERE WOUNDED

The first Kent soldier wounded was Private Leman G. Lane of Company D, 10TH Connecticut. He was wounded at Roanoke Island, NC on February 8, 1862 and recovered from his wound. Six Kent soldiers died from a wound received during the war.

KENT WOUNDED
*(6) DIED FROM WOUNDS

PLACE	DATE	NO.
Roanoke Island, NC (10TH) *	2/8/62	1
Algiers Opelousas RR,LA (13TH)	11/7/62	1
New Bern, NC (10TH)	3/14/63	1
Irish Bend, LA (13TH)	4/14/63	1
Port Hudson, LA (13TH) *	6/14/63	1
Fort Ward, VA (2 HA)	7/1/63	1
Fort Ellsworth, VA (2 HA)	6/1/64	1
Cold Harbor, VA (2 HA) *1	6/1/64	7
Cold Harbor, VA (2 HA)	6/3/64	1
Winchester, VA (2 HA,13TH) *2	9/19/64	4
Cedar Creek, VA (2 HA) *1	10/19/64	3

KILLINGLY
THE POPULATION IN 1860 WAS 4,926 (RANK 17)

THE MOST IMPORTANT DAY OF THE CIVIL WAR

JUNE 15 1863

WINCHESTER, VA

THE ENTIRE UNION ARMY WAS NEARLY CAPTURED AT THE SECOND BATTLE OF WINCHESTER

More soldiers credited to Killingly were listed as casualties (86) on this day than on any other day of the war. Five soldiers were killed, 76 captured, and 5 wounded & captured in the 18TH Connecticut. One of the captured soldiers died in prison.

The date June 15, 1863 ranks 2ND for total casualties (595) (23 killed, 11 wounded, 520 captured, 41 wounded & captured) for a single day for the State of Connecticut. There were 592 casualties at Winchester, VA and 3 casualties at Port Hudson, LA.

The Second Battle of Winchester (June 13-15, 1863) ranks 5TH for total casualties (592) for an engagement for the State of Connecticut. The most intense fighting developed on June 15. Killingly had all its casualites on that day.

The Second Battle of Winchester with 86 total casualties for Killingly was the highest number of casualties for any single engagement of the war for the town.

Winchester was one of the most contested locations in the Civil War. It changed hands seventy-two times.

407 MEN CREDITED TO KILLINGLY SERVED IN THE FOLLOWING CONNECTICUT ORGANIZATIONS

REGIMENT	TOTAL
18TH	166 (41%)
1ST HEAVY ARTILLERY	76 (19%)
11TH	31 (8%)
5TH	29 (7%)
7TH	27 (7%)
6TH	25 (6%)
20TH	15 (4%)
13TH	14 (3%)
1ST CAVALRY	11 (3%)
14TH	11 (3%)
21ST	5 (1%)
8TH	3 (1%)
2ND	2
12TH	2
13TH BATTALION	2
29TH	2
10TH	1
26TH	1

8% OF POPULATION

SEVENTEEN WERE KILLED AND TWO WERE MISSING

The first Killingly soldiers killed were Privates James Daggett, Thomas Simmons, Stephen H. Oatley, Robert Sharkey and Musician Daniel G. Bennett of the 18TH Connecticut. They were killed at Winchester, VA on June 15, 1863.

KILLINGLY SOLDIERS KILLED
MISSING *2

PLACE	DATE	NO.
Winchester, VA (18TH	6/15/63	5
Fort Wagner, SC (7TH)	7/11/63	1
Fort Wagner, SC (6TH) *1	7/18/63	2
Resaca, GA (5TH)	5/15/64	1
North Anna River, VA (14TH)	5/24/64	1
Cold Harbor, VA (11TH)	6/3/64	2
Bermuda Hundred, VA (6TH)	6/17/64	1
Ream's Station, VA (1CA) *	6/29/64	1
Petersburg, VA (1 HA)	7/15/64	1
Snicker's Ford, VA (18TH)	7/18/64	1
Petersburg, VA (29TH)	9/20/64	1
Cedar Creek, VA (13TH)	10/19/64	1
Unknown (7TH)	1/14/65	1

ONE HUNDRED-ONE WERE CAPTURED

Seven Killingly soldiers died in captivity. Four died at Andersonville Prison, GA, two at Libby Prison, Richmond, VA and one at Belle Island Prison, VA.

KILLINGLY CAPTURED
*(7) DIED IN CAPTIVITY

PLACE	DATE	NO.
Winchester, VA (5TH) *	5/24/62	2
Gaines Mills, VA (1 HA) (WOUNDED)	6/27/62	1
Winchester, VA (18TH) * (5 WOUNDED)	6/15/63	81
Fort Wagner, SC (7TH) *3 (1 WOUNDED)	7/11/63	5
Spottsylvania, VA (14TH) *	5/12/64	1
Ashland, VA (1 CA)	6/1/64	1
Bermuda Hundred, VA (7TH)	6/2/64	1
Piedmont, VA (18TH) *1 (1 WOUNDED DIED)	6/5/64	7
Cedar Run Church, VA (1 CA)	10/17/64	1
Cedar Creek, VA (12TH) (WOUNDED)	10/19/64	1

TOTAL KILLINGLY CASUALTIES

DIED	32	8%
KILLED/MISSING	19	5%
WOUNDED	59	14%
CAPTURED	101	25%
DESERTED	32	8%

FIFTY-NINE WERE WOUNDED

The first Killingly soldier wounded was Private James A. Howard of Company K, 7TH Connecticut. He was wounded at Tybee Island, GA on April 1, 1862 and recovered from his wound. Seven Killingly soldiers died from a wound received during the war.

KILLINGLY WOUNDED
*(7) DIED FROM WOUNDS

PLACE	DATE	NO.
Tybee Island, GA (7TH)	4/1/62	1
Antietam, MD (11, 14TH)	9/17/62	5
Fredericksburg, VA (14TH)	12/13/62	1
Havre de Grace, MD (18TH) *	1/4/63	1
Chancellorsville, VA (5TH)	5/3/63	1
Gettysburg, PA (14TH)	7/3/63	1
Morris Island, SC (6TH)	7/10/63	1
Fort Wagner, SC (7TH)	7/11/63	2
Fort Wagner, SC (6TH)	7/18/63	1
Morton's Ford, VA (14TH)	2/6/64	1
Martinsburg, WVA (18TH) *	2/7/64	1
Olustee, FL (7TH)	2/20/64	1
Cane River, LA (13TH)	4/23/64	1
Chester Station, VA (6TH)	5/10/64	1
Spottsylvania, VA (14TH)	5/13/64	1
Bermuda Hundred, VA (7TH)	5/16/64	1
Drewry's Bluff, VA (11TH)	5/16/64	5
Bermuda Hundred, VA (6TH) *	5/20/64	1
Bermuda Hundred, VA (6TH)	5/30/64	1
Winchester, VA (1 CA)	6/1/64	1
Cold Harbor, VA (11TH) *2	6/3/64	3
Piedmont, VA (18TH)	6/5/64	6
Petersburg, VA (11TH)	6/15/64	1
Bermuda Hundred, VA (6TH) *	6/17/64	1
Lynchburg, VA (18TH)	6/18/64	1
Petersburg, VA (11TH)	6/18/64	1
Petersburg, VA (1 HA)	6/30/64	1
Snicker's Ford, VA (18TH)	7/18/64	1
Peach Tree Creek, GA (5TH) *1	7/20/64	2
Atlanta, GA (20TH)	7/22/64	1
Petersburg, VA (1 HA)	7/24/64	1
Petersburg, VA (1 HA)	8/1/64	1
Petersburg, VA (1 HA)	8/5/64	1
Deep Run, VA (6TH)	8/16/64	1
Petersburg, VA (1 HA)	8/16/64	1
Petersburg, VA (1 HA)	8/17/64	1
Deep Bottom, VA (7TH)	8/18/64	1
Battery Anderson, VA (1 HA)	12/16/64	1
Hatcher's Run, VA (14TH)	2/5/65	1
Silver Run, VA (5TH)	3/16/65	1
Atlanta, GA (13TH)	3/5/66	1

KILLINGWORTH
THE POPULATION IN 1860 WAS 1,126 (RANK 124)

THE MOST IMPORTANT DAY OF THE CIVIL WAR

MARCH 8, 1865

KINSTON, NC

THE CONFEDERATE ATTACK STALLED BECAUSE OF BAD COMMUNICATION

More soldiers credited to Killingworth were listed as casualties (7) on this day than on any other day of the war. One soldier was wounded & captured, and 6 were captured in the 15TH Connecticut. The wounded soldier died and the others survived the war.

The date March 8, 1865 ranks 5TH for total casualties (496) (22 killed, 3 missing, 12 wounded, 410 captured, 49 wounded & captured) for a single day for the State of Connecticut. There were 494 casualties at Kinston, 1 casualty in Virginia, and 1 casualty at a railroad accident in an unknown place.

The Second Battle of Kinston (March 8, 1865) ranks 8TH for total casualties (494) for an engagement for the State of Connecticut.

The Second Battle of Kinston with 6 total casualties for Killingworth was the highest number of casualties for any single engagement of the war.

The military situation in North Carolina changed in early 1865. The Confederate forces in eastern North Carolina were called to help stop the advance of the Union Army coming out of Georgia. The Confederates attacked the Union flanks near Kinston on March 8 and failed.

82 MEN CREDITED TO KILLINGWORTH SERVED IN THE FOLLOWING CONNECTICUT ORGANIZATIONS

REGIMENT	TOTAL
24TH	13 (16%)
15TH	12 (15%)
12TH	11 (13%)
8TH	7 (9%)
1ST HEAVY ARTILLERY	6 (7%)
10TH	5 (6%)
29TH	5 (6%)
2ND HEAVY ARTILLERY	5 (6%)
11TH	5 (6%)
7TH	4 (5%)
12TH BATTALION	4 (5%)
20TH	4 (5%)
5TH	3 (4%)
14TH	3 (4%)
16TH	2 (2%)
1ST CAVALRY	1
6TH	1
13TH	1

7% OF POPULATION

TWO WERE KILLED

The first Killingworth soldier killed was Private Alonzo I. Richards of Company K, 8TH Connecticut. He was killed at the Battle of Antietam, MD on September 17, 1862.

KILLINGWORTH KILLED

PLACE	DATE	NO.
Antietam, MD (8TH)	9/17/62	1
Darbytown Road, VA (29TH)	10/13/64	1

ELEVEN WERE CAPTURED

One Killingworth soldier died in captivity at an unknown place.

KILLINGWORTH CAPTURED
*(1) DIED IN CAPTIVITY

PLACE	DATE	NO.
Chancellorsville, VA (14TH)	5/3/63	1
(WOUNDED)		
Carrion Crow Bayou, LA (12TH)	10/20/63	1
Drewry's Bluff, VA (8TH)	5/16/64	1
Cedar Creek, VA (12TH)	10/19/64	1
Kinston, NC (15TH) *1	3/8/65	7
(1 WOUNDED)		

TOTAL KILLINGWORTH CASUALTIES

DIED	14	17%
KILLED	2	2%
WOUNDED	6	7%
CAPTURED	11	13%
DESERTED	14	17%

SIX WERE WOUNDED

The first Killingworth soldier wounded was Private Ellis M. Stevens of the 8TH Connecticut. He was wounded at The Battle of Antietam, MD on September 17, 1862 and recovered from his wound. One Killingworth soldier died from a wound received during the war.

KILLINGWORTH WOUNDED
(1) * DIED FROM WOUNDS

PLACE	DATE	NO.
Antietam, MD (8TH)	9/17/62	1
Port Hudson, LA (12TH) *	5/28/63	1
Petersburg, VA (11TH)	6/18/64	1
Culp's Farm, GA (5TH)	6/22/64	1
Winchester, VA (12TH)	9/19/64	1
Cedar Creek, VA (2 HA)	10/19/64	1

LEBANON
THE POPULATION IN 1860 WAS 2,174 (RANK 68)

**THE MOST IMPORTANT
DAY OF THE CIVIL WAR**

JUNE 15, 1863

WINCHESTER, VA

**THE ENTIRE UNION ARMY
WAS NEARLY CAPTURED AT
THE SECOND BATTLE OF
WINCHESTER**

More soldiers credited to Lebanon were listed as casualties (24) on this day than on any other day of the war. Two soldiers were killed, 2 wounded & captured and 20 captured in the 18TH Connecticut. All of the wounded and captured survived the war.

The date June 15, 1863 ranks 2ND for total casualties (595) (23 killed, 11 wounded, 520 captured, 41 wounded & captured) for a single day for the State of Connecticut. There were 592 casualties at Winchester, VA and 3 casualties at Port Hudson, LA.

The Second Battle of Winchester (June 13-15, 1863) ranks 5TH for total casualties (592) for an engagement for the State of Connecticut. The most intense fighting developed on June 15. Lebanon had all its casualites on that day.

The Second Battle of Winchester with 24 total casualties for Lebanon was the highest number of casualties for any single engagement of the war for the town.

Winchester was one of the most contested locations in the Civil War. It changed hands seventy-two times.

**144 MEN CREDITED TO
LEBANON SERVED IN THE
FOLLOWING
CONNECTICUT
ORGANIZATIONS**

REGIMENT	TOTAL
18TH	49 (34%)
8TH	25 (17%)
2ND HEAVY ARTILLERY	14 (10%)
10TH	9 (6%)
13TH	9 (6%)
24TH	8 (6%)
14TH	7 (5%)
21ST	6 (4%)
30TH	6 (4%)
3RD	4 (3%)
12TH	4 (3%)
29TH	4 (3%)
1ST HEAVY ARTILLERY	3 (2%)
13TH BATTALION	3 (2%)
26TH	3 (2%)
2ND	2 (1%)
5TH	2 (1%)
1ST CAVALRY	1
12TH BATTALION	1

7% OF POPULATION

FIVE WERE KILLED

The first Lebanon soldiers killed were Privates Asher D. Holmes and Henry McCracken of the 18TH Connecticut. They were killed at Winchester, VA on June 15, 1863.

LEBANON SOLDIERS KILLED

PLACE	DATE	NO.
Winchester, VA (18TH)	6/15/63	2
Cold Harbor, VA (8TH)	6/4/64	1
Piedmont, VA (18TH)	6/5/64	1
Petersburg, VA (21ST)	7/20/64	1

TWENTY-NINE WERE CAPTURED

One Lebanon soldier died in captivity at Staunton VA.

LEBANON CAPTURED
*(1) DIED IN CAPTIVITY

PLACE	DATE	NO.
Winchester, VA (18TH) (2 WOUNDED)	6/15/63	22
Walthall Junction, VA (8TH) (WOUNDED)	5/7/64	1
New Market, VA (18TH) (WOUNDED)	5/15/64	1
Piedmont, VA (18TH) *1 (2 WOUNDED)	6/5/64	2
Petersburg, VA (30TH)	7/30/64	1
Cedar Creek, VA (2 HA)	10/19/64	2

TOTAL LEBANON CASUALTIES

DIED	17	12%
KILLED	5	3%
WOUNDED	32	22%
CAPTURED	29	20%
DESERTED	17	12%

THIRTY-TWO WERE WOUNDED

The first Lebanon soldier wounded was Private Diodate J. Mitchell of Company D, 8TH Connecticut. He was wounded at Bolivar Heights, VA on September 14, 1862 and died from his wound. Five Lebanon soldiers died from a wound received during the war.

LEBANON WOUNDED
*(5) DIED FROM WOUNDS

PLACE	DATE	NO.
Bolivar Heights, VA (8TH) *	9/14/62	1
Antietam, MD (8TH) *2	9/17/62	7
Georgia Landing, LA (12TH)	10/27/62	1
Port Hudson, LA (24TH)	3/13/63	1
Port Hudson, LA (24TH)	5/24/63	1
Port Hudson, LA (12TH) *	5/27/63	1
Port Hudson, LA (26TH)	6/13/63	2
Walthall Junction, VA (8TH)	5/7/64	3
New Market, VA (18TH)	5/15/64	2
Drewry's Bluff, VA (8T,21ST)*1	5/16/64	3
Totopotomy, VA (2 HA)	5/29/64	1
Cold Harbor, VA (2 HA)	6/1/64	1
Piedmont, VA (18TH)	6/5/64	6
Cold Harbor, VA (8TH)	6/5/64	1
Snicker's Ford, VA (18TH)	7/18/64	1
Cedar Creek, VA (2 HA)	10/19/64	1

432

LEDYARD
THE POPULATION IN 1860 WAS 1,615 (RANK 93)

**THE MOST IMPORTANT
DAY OF THE CIVIL WAR**

MAY 27, 1863

PORT HUDSON, LA

THE FIRST MAJOR ASSAULT

More soldiers credited to Ledyard were listed as casualties (6) on this day than on any other day of the war. Six soldiers in the 26TH Connecticut were wounded and two eventually died from their wounds.

The date May 27, 1863 ranks 18TH for total casualties (145) (13 killed, 132 wounded) for a single day for the State of Connecticut. Port Hudson accounted for 144 casualties. The other casualty was in Virginia.

The Siege of Port Hudson (May 2 - July 9, 1863) ranks 7TH for total casualties (520) for an engagement for the State of Connecticut. The most intense fighting developed on May 27 and June 14. Ledyard had 2 casualties on June 10 and 1 on June 13.

The Siege of Port Hudson with 9 total casualties for Ledyard was the highest number of casualties for any single engagement of the war for the town.

Control of the Mississippi was one of the major objectives of the Union army. Port Hudson was a formidable obstacle for control of the river. A siege began at Port Hudson on May 2, 1863 that lasted until July 9. On May 27, the Union force of 30,000 launched a major assault that failed.

91 MEN CREDITED TO LEDYARD SERVED IN THE FOLLOWING CONNECTICUT ORGANIZATIONS

REGIMENT	TOTAL
26TH	28 (31%)
12TH	14 (15%)
14TH	9 (10%)
21ST	9 (10%)
1ST CAVALRY	8 (9%)
1ST HEAVY ARTILLERY	5 (5%)
29TH	5 (5%)
11TH	3 (3%)
12TH BATTALION	3 (3%)
18TH	3 (3%)
2ND HEAVY ARTILLERY	2 (2%)
10TH	2 (2%)
8TH	1
13TH	1
13TH BATTALION	1
20TH	1
30TH	1

6% OF POPULATION

THREE WERE KILLED

The first Ledyard soldier killed was Private Samuel C. Rogers of Company H, 11TH Connecticut. He was killed at The Battle of Antietam, MD on September 17, 1862.

TOTAL LEDYARD CASUALTIES

DIED	18	20%
KILLED	3	3%
WOUNDED	20	22%
CAPTURED	4	4%
DESERTED	7	8%

LEDYARD SOLDIERS KILLED

PLACE	DATE	NO.
Antietam, MD (11TH)	9/17/62	1
Port Hudson, LA (26TH)	6/13/63	1
Cedar Creek, VA (12TH)	10/19/64	1

FOUR WERE CAPTURED

One Ledyard soldier died in captivity at Salisbury, NC.

LEDYARD CAPTURED
*(1) DIED IN CAPTIVITY

PLACE	DATE	NO.
Bristoe Station, VA (14TH)	10/14/63	1
Cedar Creek, VA (2HA,12TH)*	10/19/64	3

TWENTY WERE WOUNDED

The first Ledyard soldiers wounded were Privates Stephen D. Allyn, Erastus A. Maynard, and Jacob Dyetch of Company K, 14TH Connecticut. They were wounded at The Battle of Antietam, MD on September 17, 1862. Private Allyn died later in the war. The others recovered from their wounds. Five Ledyard soldiers died from wounds received during the war.

LEDYARD WOUNDED
*(5) DIED FROM WOUNDS

PLACE	DATE	NO.
Antietam, MD (14TH) *2	9/17/62	3
Port Hudson, LA (26TH) *2	5/27/63	6
Port Hudson, LA (12TH) *1	6/10/63	2
Morton's Ford, VA (14TH)	2/6/64	1
Spottsylvania, VA (14TH)	5/11/64	1
Spottsylvania, VA (14TH)	5/12/64	1
North Anna River, VA (14TH)	5/24/64	1
Cold Harbor, VA (21ST)	6/3/64	1
Petersburg, VA (30TH)	7/30/64	1
Winchester, VA (12TH)	9/19/64	2
Cedar Creek, VA (12TH)	10/19/64	1

LISBON
THE POPULATION IN 1860 WAS 1,262 (RANK 115)

**THE MOST IMPORTANT DAY
OF THE CIVIL WAR**

MAY 7, 1864

WALTHALL JUNCTION, VA

**THE UNION "ARMY OF THE
JAMES " FAILED TO MOVE
SWIFTLY**

Soldiers credited to Lisbon had 11 days in the war with one casualty. The casualty at Walthall Junction was the most serious A soldier in the 8th Connecticut was wounded and died later.

The date May 7, 1864 ranks 32ND for total casualties (80) (4 killed, 1 missing, 69 wounded, 3 captured, and 3 wounded & captured) for a single day for the State of Connecticut. All of the casualties were in Virginia. They were at Walthall Junction (70), Wilderness (6), Swift's Creek (3) and Petersburg (1).

The Action at Walthall Junction (May 7-9, 1964) ranks 27TH for total casualties (71) for an engagement for the State of Connecticut.

The Action at Walthall Junction with 1 casualty for Lisbon was tied with 10 others for the 2nd highest number of casualties for any single engagement of the war for the town. The Siege of Port Hudson, LA (May-July 1863) with 2 casualties was the highest number of casualties.

In May 1864, the Army of the James, under the command of General Benjamin Butler failed to move aggressively against the Confederates dug in near Richmond and Petersburg.

**42 MEN CREDITED TO
LISBON SERVED
IN THE FOLLOWING
CONNECTICUT
ORGANIZATIONS**

REGIMENT	TOTAL
26TH	7 (17%)
8TH	6 (14%)
29TH	5 (12%)
12TH	5 (12%)
2ND	3 (7%)
21ST	3 (7%)
5TH	2 (5%)
6TH	2 (5%)
14TH	2 (5%)
30TH	2 (5%)
1ST LIGHT BATTERY	1
1ST CAVALRY	1
2ND HEAVY ARTILLERY	1
7TH	1
10TH	1
12TH BATTALION	1
13TH	1
13TH BATTALION	1
15TH	1
18TH	1
20TH	1

3% OF POPULATION

NO LISBON SOLDIERS WERE KILLED IN THE WAR

THREE WERE CAPTURED

No Lisbon soldiers died in captivity

LISBON CAPTURED
NONE DIED IN CAPTIVITY

PLACE	DATE	NO.
Cedar Mountain, VA (5TH)	8/9/62	1
Winchester, VA (18TH)	6/15/63	1
Bermuda Hundred, VA (7TH) Wounded)	6/2/64	1

TOTAL LISBON CASUALTIES

DIED	7	17%
KILLED	0	0%
WOUNDED	10	24%
CAPTURED	3	7%
DESERTED	4	10%

TEN WERE WOUNDED

The first Lisbon soldier wounded was Corporal Charles H. Corey of Company G, 5TH Connecticut. He was wounded at Chancellorsville, VA on May 3, 1863 and recovered from his wound. One Lisbon soldier died from a wound received during the war.

LISBON WOUNDED
*(1) DIED FROM WOUNDS

PLACE	DATE	NO.
Chancellorsville, VA (5TH)	5/3/63	1
Port Hudson, LA (26TH)	5/27/63	1
Port Hudson, LA (26TH)	6/14/63	1
Fort Wagner, SC (6TH)	7/18/63	1
Morton's Ford, VA (14TH)	2/6/64	1
Walthall Junction, VA (8TH) *	5/7/64	1
Resaca, GA (5TH)	5/15/64	1
Cold Harbor, VA (8TH)	6/4/64	1
Peach Tree Creek, GA (5TH)	7/20/64	1
Chaffin's Farm, VA (29TH)	11/24/64	1

LITCHFIELD
THE POPULATION IN 1860 WAS 3,200 (RANK 39)

THE MOST IMPORTANT DAY OF THE CIVIL WAR

JUNE 1, 1864

COLD HARBOR, VA

THE BATTLE WAS LEE'S LAST GREAT VICTORY

More soldiers credited to Litchfield were listed as casualties (27) on this day than on any other day of the war. Nine soldiers were killed and 18 were wounded in the 2ND Connectcicut Heavy Artillery. Five of the wounded died.

The date June 1, 1864 ranks 8TH for total casualties (374) (89 killed, 10 missing, 246 wounded, 23 captured, 6 wounded & captured)) for a single day for the State of Connecticut. There were 324 casualties at Cold Harbor, 41 casualties at Ashland, and 9 casualties scattered about Virginia.

The battle and operations around Cold Harbor (May 31-June 12, 1864) rank 6TH for total casualties (557) for an engagement for the State of Connecticut. The most intense fighting developed on June 3 and Litchfield had one wounded on that day.

The Battle of Cold Harbor with 28 total casualties for Litchfield was the highest number of casualties for any single engagement of the war for the town.

Approximately 117,000 Federal and 60,000 Confederate troops participated in operations from May 28 to June 3. Roughly 13,000 Union casualties were recorded and perhaps there were 5,000 Confederate casualties.

294 MEN CREDITED TO LITCHFIELD SERVED IN THE FOLLOWING CONNECTICUT ORGANIZATIONS

REGIMENT	TOTAL
2ND HEAVY ARTILLERY	110 (37%)
13TH	46 (16%)
8TH	38 (13%)
1ST CAVALRY	17 (6%)
14TH	17 (6%)
1ST HEAVY ARTILLERY	16 (5%)
13TH BATTALION	16 (5%)
5TH	11 (4%)
10TH	11 (4%)
23RD	9 (3%)
29TH	7 (2%)
9TH	4 (1%)
11TH	4 (1%)
6TH	3 (1%)
2ND LIGHT BATTERY	2 (1%)
17TH	2 (1%)
3RD	1
3RD LIGHT BATTERY	1
15TH	1
16TH	1
20TH	1
24TH	1
25TH	1
27TH	1

7% OF POPULATION

NINETEEN WERE KILLED

The first Litchfield soldier killed was Private Enos Thompkins of Company A, 1ST Connecticut Cavalry. He was struck by lightning at Sperryville, VA on July 16, 1862.

LITCHFIELD SOLDIERS KILLED

PLACE	DATE	NO.
Sperryville, VA (1 CA)	7/16/62	1
Antietam, MD (8TH)	9/17/62	2
Unknown (13TH)	11/7/62	1
Chancellorsville, VA (20TH)	5/3/63	1
Fort Darling, VA (8TH)	5/16/64	1
North Anna River, VA (14TH)	5/24/64	1
Cold Harbor, VA (2 HA)	6/1/64	9
Petersburg, VA (14TH)	6/16/64	1
Fort Harrison, VA (8TH)	9/29/64	1
Petersburg, VA (2 HA)	3/25/65	1

THIRTEEN WERE CAPTURED

Five Litchfield soldiers died in captivity. Three died at Andersonville Prison, GA, one at Belle Isle Prison, VA, and one at Libby Prison, Richmond, VA.

LITCHFIELD CAPTURED
*(5) DIED IN CAPTIVITY

PLACE	DATE	NO.
Front Royal, VA (5TH) *	5/23/62	1
Unknown (2HA) *	Unknown	1
Cedar Mountain, VA (5TH)	8/9/62	1
(WOUNDED)		
Dumfires, VA (17TH)	12/9/62	1
Upperville, VA (1 CA) *	10/13/63	1
Bristoe Station, VA (14TH)	10/14/63	1
Craig's Church, VA (1 CA)	5/5/64	1
Mine Run, VA (1 CA) *	5/5/64	1
Winchester, VA (14TH)	5/6/64	1
Drewry's Bluff, VA (11TH) *	5/16/64	1
(WOUNDED)		
Welaka, FL (17TH)	5/19/64	1
Winchester, VA (13TH)	9/19/64	1
Kinston, NC (15TH)	3/8/65	1

TOTAL LITCHFIELD CASUALTIES

DIED	42	14%
KILLED	19	7%
WOUNDED	52	18%
CAPTURED	13	4%
DESERTED	39	13%

FIFTY-TWO WERE WOUNDED

Sergeant Edgar A. Alvord and Private Henry G. West of Companies D and E, 5TH Connecticut were the first Litchfield soldiers wounded. Both were wounded at Cedar Mountain, VA on August 9, 1862 and recovered from their wounds. Twelve Litchfield soldiers died from a wound received during the war.

LITCHFIELD WOUNDED
*(12) DIED FROM WOUNDS

PLACE	DATE	NO.
Cedar Mountain, VA (5TH)	8/9/62	1
New Orleans, LA (13TH) *	9/1/62	1
Antietam, MD (8TH) *2	9/17/62	3
Cedar Creek, VA (2 HA) *	4/8/64	1
Cane River, LA (13TH)	4/23/64	3
Walthall Junction, VA (8TH)	5/7/64	2
Resaca, GA (5TH)	5/15/64	1
Drewry's Bluff, VA (8TH)	5/16/64	1
Cold Harbor, VA (2 HA) *5	6/1/64	18
Petersburg, VA (2 HA) *	6/22/64	1
Cold Harbor, VA (8TH)	6/3/64	1
Ream's Station, VA (1 CA)	6/27/64	1
Winchester, VA (2HA,13TH) *	9/19/64	8
Chaffin's Farm, VA (29TH)	9/30/64	1
Chaffin's Farm, VA (29TH)	10/2/64	1
Cedar Creek, VA (2 HA) *	10/19/64	1
Hatcher's Run, VA (2 HA)	2/6/65	1
Petersburg, VA (2 HA)	3/5/65	1
Petersburg, VA (2 HA)	3/25/65	2
Hatcher's Run, VA (10TH)	4/1/65	1
Richmond, VA (8TH)	4/1/65	1
Fort Gregg, VA (10TH)	4/2/65	1

LYME
THE POPULATION IN 1860 WAS 1,246 (RANK 116)

**THE MOST IMPORTANT DAY
OF THE CIVIL WAR**

MAY 27, 1863

PORT HUDSON, LA

**THE FIRST MAJOR
ASSAULT**

More soldiers credited to Lyme were listed as casualties (8) on this day than on any other day of the war. Eight soldiers in the 26TH Connecticut were wounded and two eventually died from their wound.

The date May 27, 1863 ranks 18TH for total casualties (145) (12 killed, 132 wounded) for a single day for the State of Connecticut. Port Hudson accounted for 144 casualties. The other casualty was in Virginia.

The Siege of Port Hudson (May 2 - July 9, 1863) ranks 7TH for total casualties (517) for an engagement for the State of Connecticut. The most intense fighting developed on May 27 and June 14. Lyme had 6 casualties on June 14 and 1 on July 1.

The Siege of Port Hudson with 15 total casualties for Lyme was the highest number of casualties for any single engagement of the war for the town.

Control of the Mississippi was one of the major objectives of the Union army. Port Hudson was a formidable obstacle for control of the river. A siege began at Port Hudson on May 2, 1863 that lasted until July 9. On May 27, the Union force of 30,000 launched a major assault that failed.

**101 MEN CREDITED TO
LYME SERVED
IN THE FOLLOWING
CONNECTICUT
ORGANIZATIONS**

REGIMENT	TOTAL
26TH	35 (35%)
18TH	17 (17%)
5TH	10 (10%)
1ST CAVALRY	9 (9%)
1ST HEAVY ARTILLERY	9 (9%)
11TH	5 (5%)
12TH	5 (5%)
2ND	2 (2%)
6TH	2 (2%)
9TH	2 (2%)
14TH	2 (2%)
2ND HEAVY ARTILLERY	1
7TH	1
9TH BATTALION	1
10TH	1
12TH BATTALION	1
22ND	1
24TH	1
29TH	1

8% OF POPULATION

THREE WERE KILLED

The first Lyme soldier killed was Colonel Henry W. Kingsbury of the 11TH Connecticut. He was killed at the Battle of Antietam, MD on September 17, 1862..

LYME SOLDIERS KILLED

PLACE	DATE	NO.
Antietam, MD (11TH)	9/17/62	1
Piedmont, VA (18TH)	6/5/64	1
Fort Gregg, VA (1 CA)	4/1/65	1

THIRTEEN WERE CAPTURED

No Lyme soldiers died in captivity.

LYME CAPTURED
NONE DIED IN CAPTIVITY

PLACE	DATE	NO.
Winchester, VA (18TH)	6/15/63	7
Bristoe Station, VA (14TH)	10/14/63	1
Drewry's Bluff, VA (11TH)	5/16/64	1
Ream's Station, VA (1 CA)	6/29/64	1
Cedar Creek, VA (9TH)	10/19/64	1
Liberty Hill, SC (5TH)	2/28/65	1
Fort Stedman, VA (1 HA)	3/25/65	1

TOTAL LYME CASUALTIES

DIED	14	14%
KILLED	2	2%
WOUNDED	23	23%
CAPTURED	12	12%
DESERTED	8	9%

TWENTY-FOUR WERE WOUNDED

Private William S. Brockway of Company A, 10TH Connecticut was the first Lyme soldier wounded. He was wounded at Roanoke Island, NC on February 8, 1862 and recovered from his wound. Four Lyme soldiers died from a wound received during the war.

LYME WOUNDED
*(4) DIED FROM WOUNDS

PLACE	DATE	NO.
Roanoke Island, NC (10TH)	2/8/62	1
Port Hudson, LA (26TH) *2	5/27/63	8
Port Hudson, LA (26TH) *2	6/14/63	6
Port Hudson, LA (26TH)	7/1/63	1
Morton's Ford, VA (14TH)	2/6/64	1
Bermuda Hundred, VA (6TH)	5/20/64	1
Dallas, GA (5TH)	5/25/64	1
Piedmont, VA (18TH)	6/5/64	2
Peach Tree Creek, GA (5TH)	7/20/64	1
Dinwiddie CH, VA (1 CA)	4/1/65	1
Unknown (14TH)	Unknown	1

MADISON
THE POPULATION IN 1860 WAS 1,865 (RANK 79)

THE MOST IMPORTANT DAY OF THE CIVIL WAR

MAY 3, 1863

CHANCELLORSVILLE, VA

THE THIRD DAY OF THE BATTLE

More soldiers credited to Madison were listed as casualties (26) on this day than on any other day of the war. Three soldiers were wounded and 23 were captured in the 14TH and 27TH Connecticut. All survived the war.

The date May 3, 1863 ranks 3RD for total casualties (577) (36 killed, 1 missing, 138 wounded, 372 captured, 29 wounded & captured) for a single day for the State of Connecticut. The most casualties were at Chancellorsville, VA (556). The other casualties were at Providence Church Road, VA (12), Suffolk, VA (6), Port Hudson, LA (2) and Fredericksburg, VA (1).

The Battle of Chancellorsville (May 1-3, 1863) ranks 2ND for total casualties (677) for an engagement for the State of Connecticut. The most intense fighting developed on May 3 and Madison had all of its casualties on that date.

The Battle of Chancellorsville with 27 total casualties for Madison was the highest number of casualties for any single engagement of the war for the town.

The Battle of Chancellorsville was an enormous defeat for the more than 70,000 Union soldiers who had moved against the flank and rear of 40,000 Confederate soldiers. Unfortunately, the Union Army had pulled back and had gone on the defensive around Chancellorsville. The Confederate victory was tainted however, by the loss of Confederate Major General "Stonewall" Jackson.

207 MEN CREDITED TO MADISON SERVED IN THE FOLLOWING CONNECTICUT ORGANIZATIONS

REGIMENT	TOTAL
14TH	67 (32%)
27TH	43 (21%)
11TH	17 (8%)
15TH	16 (8%)
12TH	15 (7%)
20TH	11 (5%)
7TH	10 (5%)
5TH	8 (4%)
29TH	7 (3%)
2ND HEAVY ARTILLERY	5 (2%)
3RD	5 (2%)
12TH BATTALION	5 (2%)
1ST HEAVY ARTILLERY	3 (1%)
1ST LIGHT BATTERY	3 (1%)
6TH	3 (1%)
10TH	3 (1%)
13TH	3 (1%)
3RD LIGHT BATTERY	1
8TH	1
17TH	1
24TH	1
30TH	1

11% OF POPULATION

NINE WERE KILLED AND ONE WAS MISSING

The first Madison soldier killed was Private Richard Howard of Rifle Company A, 3RD Connecticut. He was accidently killed on June 18, 1861 at Washington, DC.

MADISON SOLDIERS KILLED MISSING *

PLACE	DATE	NO.
Washington, DC (3RD)	6/18/61	1
Antietam, MD (14TH)	9/17/62	2
Fredericksburg, VA (14,27TH)	12/13/62	3
Gettysburg, PA (14TH)	7/3/63	1
Wilderness, VA (14TH) *1	5/6/64	2
Petersburg, VA (11TH)	7/4/64	1

THIRTY-NINE WERE CAPTURED

Two Madison soldiers died in captivity. Both died at Andersonville Prison, GA.

MADISON CAPTURED *(2) DIED IN CAPTIVITY

PLACE	DATE	NO.
Fredericksburg, VA (14TH) (WOUNDED)	12/13/62	1
Chancellorsville, VA (14,27TH)	5/3/63	23
Winchester, VA (14TH)	5/6/64	1
Drewry's Bluff, VA (7,11TH)*2 (1 WOUNDED)	5/16/64	4
Culp's Farm, GA (5TH) (WOUNDED)	6/22/64	1
Cedar Creek, VA (12TH)	10/19/64	1
Boydton Plank Rd, VA (14TH)	10/27/64	1
Kinston, NC (15TH)	3/8/65	7

TOTAL MADISON CASUALTIES

DIED	27	13%
KILLED/MISSING	10	5%
WOUNDED	48	23%
CAPTURED	39	19%
DESERTED	28	14%

FORTY-EIGHT WERE WOUNDED

Sergeant Henry A. Pendleton and Corporal Sanford Foster of Company G, 14TH Connecticut were the first Madison soldiers wounded. Both were wounded at The Battle of Antietam, MD on September 17, 1862 and recovered from their wounds. Eight Madison soldiers died from a wound received during the war.

MADISON WOUNDED *(8) DIED FROM WOUNDS

PLACE	DATE	NO.
Antietam, MD (14TH)	9/17/62	2
Fredericksburg, VA (14,27TH)	12/13/62	10
Kinston, NC (10TH)	12/14/62	2
Bisland, LA (12TH)	4/14/63	1
Chancellorsville, VA (14, 27TH)	5/3/63	3
Siege Port Hudson, LA (12TH)	5/30/63	1
Siege Port Hudson, LA (24TH)	6/14/63	1
Gettysburg, PA (14TH)	7/3/63	2
Bristoe Station, VA (14TH)	10/14/63	1
Morton's Ford, VA (14TH)	2/6/64	1
Wilderness, VA (14TH) *	5/6/64	2
Laurel Hill, VA (14TH) *	5/10/64	1
Spottsylvania, VA (14TH)	5/12/64	2
Drewry's Bluff, VA (11TH)	5/16/64	1
Bermuda Hundred, VA (6TH) *2	5/20/64	2
North Anna River, VA (14TH)	5/24/64	1
Cold Harbor, VA (11TH) *	6/3/64	1
Cold Harbor, VA (14TH)	6/5/64	1
Siege Petersburg, VA (11TH) *	6/15/64	1
Siege Petersburg, VA (11TH)	6/23/64	1
Peach Tree Creek, GA (20TH)	7/20/64	1
Ream's Station, VA (14TH)	8/25/64	3
Winchester, VA (12TH)	9/19/64	1
Richmond, VA (29TH) *	9/30/64	1
Darbytown Road, VA (10TH)	10/13/64	1
Cedar Creek, VA (12TH)	10/19/64	2
Kinston, NC (15TH)	3/8/65	1
Bentonville, NC (20TH)	3/19/65	1
Hatcher's Run, VA (14TH) *	3/25/65	1

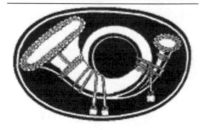

MANCHESTER
THE POPULATION IN 1860 WAS 3,294 (RANK 32)

THE MOST IMPORTANT DAY OF THE CIVIL WAR

SEPTEMBER 17, 1862

SHARPSBURG, MD (ANTIETAM)

CONNECTICUT HAD MORE CASUALTIES FOR ONE DAY THAN ON ANY OTHER DAY OF THE WAR

More soldiers credited to Manchester were listed as casualties (13) on this day than on any other day of the war. Two soldiers were killed, 9 were wounded, and 2 were captured in the 8TH and 16TH Connecticut. One of the wounded died.

The date September 17, 1862 ranks 1ST for total casualties (687) (131 killed, 2 missing, 515 wounded, 21 captured, 18 wounded & captured) for a single day for the State of Connecticut. All of the casualties were at Antietam.

The Battle of Antietam (September 16-17, 1862) ranks 1ST for total casualties (689) for an engagement for the State of Connecticut. The most intense fighting developed on September 17. Manchester had all of its casualties on that day.

The Battle of Antietam with 13 total casualties for Manchester was the highest number of casualties for any single engagement of the war for the town.

Roughly 12,400 Union casualties were recorded and perhaps there were 10,300 Confederate casualties. Antietam proved to be one of the turning points of the war. It ended Lee's 1862 invasion of the North.

236 MEN CREDITED TO MANCHESTER SERVED IN THE FOLLOWING CONNECTICUT ORGANIZATIONS

REGIMENT	TOTAL
16TH	46 (20%)
10TH	40 (17%)
1ST HEAVY ARTILLERY	40 (17%)
5TH	17 (7%)
12TH	12 (5%)
20TH	11 (5%)
1ST	9 (4%)
7TH	9 (4%)
14TH	9 (4%)
22ND	9 (4%)
2ND HEAVY ARTILLERY	8 (3%)
1ST CAVALRY	6 (3%)
11TH	6 (3%)
29TH	6 (3%)
8TH	5 (2%)
12TH BATTALION	5 (2%)
25TH	5 (2%)
1ST LIGHT BATTERY	4 (2%)
9TH	4 (2%)
1ST SQUADRON CAVALRY	3 (1%)
15TH	2
2ND	1
2ND LIGHT BATTERY	1
6TH	1
9TH BATTALION	1
21ST	1

7% OF POPULATION

SIX WERE KILLED

The first Manchester soldiers killed were Privates Julius C. Wilsey and Lucius Wheeler of the 8TH and 16TH Connecticut. Both were killed at The Battle of Antietam, MD on September 17, 1862.

MANCHESTER SOLDIERS KILLED

PLACE	DATE	NO.
Antietam, MD (8,16TH)	9/17/62	2
Proctor's Creek, VA (10TH)	5/16/64	1
Deep Run, VA (7TH)	8/18/64	1
Newmarket Road, VA (10TH)	10/7/64	2

SIXTEEN WERE CAPTURED

Two Manchester soldiers died in captivity. One died at Andersonville Prison, GA and one at Florence Prison, SC.

MANCHESTER CAPTURED
*(2) DIED IN CAPTIVITY

PLACE	DATE	NO.
Antietam, MD (16TH)	9/17/62	2
Brandy Station, VA (1 SQ)	6/9/63	1
Bolivar Heights, VA (1 CA)	7/14/63	1
Plymouth, NC (16TH) *1	4/20/64	5
Craig's Church, VA (1 CA)	5/5/64	1
Georgia, (20TH) *	6/6/64	1
Petersburg, VA (11TH)	7/30/64	1
Ream's Station, VA (14TH)	8/25/64	1
(WOUNDED)		
Cedar Creek, VA (12TH)	10/19/64	2
Kinston, NC (15TH)	3/8/65	1

TOTAL MANCHESTER CASUALTIES

DIED	33	14%
KILLED	6	3%
WOUNDED	39	17%
CAPTURED	16	7%
DESERTED	34	14%

THIRTY-NINE WERE WOUNDED

The first Manchester soldiers wounded were Colonel John L. Otis, Sergeant Watson G. Salter, Corporal Conrad Greges and Private Levi F. Lyman of the 10TH and 11TH Connecticut. They were wounded at New Bern, NC on March 14, 1862 and two died from their wounds. Six Manchester soldiers died from a wound received during the war.

MANCHESTER WOUNDED
*(6) DIED FROM WOUNDS

PLACE	DATE	NO.
New Bern, NC ((10,11TH) *2	3/14/62	4
Antietam, MD (8,16TH) *	9/17/62	9
Kinston, NC (10TH)	12/14/62	2
Fredericksburg, VA (1 HA)	4/1/63	1
Bisland, LA (12TH)	4/13/63	1
Suffolk, VA (16TH) *	4/24/63	1
Port Hudson, LA (12TH)	6/10/63	1
Morris Island, SC (7TH)	7/13/63	1
Gloucester Point, VA (10TH)	5/6/64	1
Wilderness, VA (14TH)	5/6/64	1
Drewry's Bluff, VA (21ST)	5/16/64	1
Dallas, GA (5TH)	5/25/64	1
Cold Harbor, VA (2 HA)	6/1/64	1
Peach Tree Crk, GA (5,20TH) *	7/20/64	2
Deep Bottom, VA (10TH)	8/14/64	1
Deep Run, VA (10TH) *1	8/16/64	3
Darbytown Rd, VA (10,29TH)	10/13/64	3
Cedar Creek, VA (9,12TH)	10/19/64	2
Fort Stedman, VA (1 HA)	3/25/65	1
Fort Gregg, VA (10TH)	4/2/65	1
Petersburg, VA (1 HA)	4/2/65	1

MANSFIELD
THE POPULATION IN 1860 WAS 1,697 (RANK 88)

THE MOST IMPORTANT DAY OF THE CIVIL WAR

JUNE 3, 1864

COLD HARBOR, VA

THE BATTLE WAS LEE'S LAST GREAT VICTORY

Soldiers credited to Mansfield had more casualties on June 15, 1863 at Winchester, VA (4), on May 16, 1864 at Drewry's Bluff, VA (4) and on June 3, 1864 at Cold Harbor, VA (4) than on any other days of the war. The casualties were the most serious at Cold Harbor. One soldier was killed and 3 were wounded in the 21ST Connecticut. The wounded survived the war.

The date June 3, 1864 ranks 12TH for total casualties (196) (24 killed, 2 missing, 168 wounded, 2 captured) for a single day for the State of Connecticut. Cold Harbor accounted for 190 casualties. There were also 4 casualties at Petersburg, VA and 2 casualties at Dallas, GA.

The battle and operations around Cold Harbor (May 31-June 12) rank 6TH for total casualties (557) for an engagement for the State of Connecticut. The most intense fighting developed on June 3. Mansfield had one casualty on June 4.

The Battle of Cold Harbor with 5 total casualties for Mansfield was the second highest number of casualties any single engagement of the war for the town. The highest number of casualties was the Siege of Petersburg (June 1864-April 1865) with 6.

Approximately 117,000 Federal and 60,000 Confederate troops participated in operations around Cold Harbor from May 31 to June 12. Roughly 13,000 Union casualties were recorded and perhaps there were 5,000 Confederate casualties.

148 MEN CREDITED TO MANSFIELD SERVED IN THE FOLLOWING CONNECTICUT ORGANIZATIONS

REGIMENT	TOTAL
21ST	41 (28%)
1ST HEAVY ARTILLERY	16 (11%)
7TH	16 (11%)
22ND	10 (7%)
5TH	9 (6%)
11TH	9 (6%)
10TH	8 (5%)
18TH	8 (5%)
29TH	8 (5%)
6TH	5 (3%)
1ST CAVALRY	4 (3%)
2ND HEAVY ARTILLERY	4 (3%)
8TH	3 (2%)
14TH	3 (2%)
15TH	3 (2%)
12TH	2 (1%)
30TH	2 (1%)
3RD	1
12TH BATTALION	1
16TH	1
24TH	1
25TH	1

9% OF POPULATION

SIX WERE KILLED

The first Mansfield soldiers killed were Privates William H. Hall and Asa Rouse of Company H, 11TH Connecticut. Both were killed at the Battle of Antietam, MD on September 17, 1862.

MANSFIELD SOLDIERS KILLED

PLACE	DATE	NO.
Antietam, MD (11TH)	9/17/62	2
Winchester, VA (18TH)	6/15/63	1
Drewry's Bluff, VA (21ST)	5/16/64	1
Cold Harbor, VA (21ST)	6/3/64	1
Petersburg, VA (29TH)	9/1/64	1

TWELVE WERE CAPTURED

One Mansfield soldier died in captivity at Florence, SC.

MANSFIELD CAPTURED
*(1) DIED IN CAPTIVITY

PLACE	DATE	NO.
Bull Run, VA (3RD)	7/21/61	1
Winchester, VA (18TH)	6/15/63	3
Plymouth, NC (16TH)	4/20/64	2
Drewry's Bluff, VA (6TH)	5/16/64	1
Hatcher's Run, VA (7TH)	6/2/64	1
(WOUNDED)		
James City, VA (1 CA)	6/13/64	1
Bermuda Hundred, VA (7TH)*	6/17/64	2
Ashland, VA (1 CA)	3/15/65	1

TOTAL MANSFIELD CASUALTIES

DIED	12	8%
KILLED	6	4%
WOUNDED	22	15%
CAPTURED	12	8%
DESERTED	25	17%

TWENTY-TWO WERE WOUNDED

Private James M. Perkins of Company H, 7TH Connecticut was the first Mansfield soldier wounded. He was wounded at James Island, SC on June 16, 1862 and recovered from his wound. Two Mansfield soldier died from a wound received during the war.

MANSFIELD WOUNDED
*(2) DIED FROM WOUNDS

PLACE	DATE	NO.
James Island, SC (7TH)	6/16/62	1
Antietam, MD (14TH)	9/17/62	1
Pocotaligo, SC (7TH)	10/22/62	2
Drewry's Bluff, VA (7TH)	5/14/64	1
Drewry's Bluff, VA (10TH,21ST)	5/16/64	2
Cold Harbor, VA (2 HA)	6/1/64	1
Cold Harbor, VA (21ST) *	6/3/64	3
Petersburg, VA (21ST) *	6/16/64	1
Petersburg, VA (14TH)	6/17/64	1
Petersburg, VA (21ST)	6/30/64	1
Petersburg, VA (21ST)	7/1/64	1
Atlanta, GA (5TH)	7/20/64	1
Petersburg, VA (30TH)	7/30/64	1
White's Tavern, VA (10TH)	8/16/64	1
Drewry's Bluff, VA (10TH)	8/16/64	1
New Market , VA (10TH)	10/7/64	1
Darbytown Road, VA (10TH)	10/12/64	1
Richmond, VA (21ST)	6/3/65	1

MARLBOROUGH
THE POPULATION IN 1860 WAS 682 (RANK 156)

THE MOST IMPORTANT DAY OF THE CIVIL WAR

AUGUST 16, 1864

DEEP RUN, VA

THE COMBAT WAS PART OF THE RICHMOND CAMPAIGN

Soldiers credited to Marlborough had more casualties on May 14, 1864 at Drewry's Bluff, VA (2), on August 16, 1864 at Deep Run, VA (2) and on October 19, 1864 at Cedar Creek, VA (2) than on any other days of the war. The casualties were the most serious at Deep Run. One soldier was killed and one was wounded in the 10TH Connecticut. The wounded soldier survived the war.

The date August 16, 1864 ranks 15TH for total casualties (163) (18 killed, 4 missing, 125 wounded, 14 captured, 2 wounded & captured) for a single day for the State of Connecticut. There were 129 casualties at Deep Run, VA 27 casualties at Deep Bottom, VA and the others were scattered about Virginia (6) and Georgia (1).

The Combat at Deep Run (August 16, 1864) ranks 19TH for total casualties (129) for an engagement for the State of Connecticut.

The Combat at Deep Run with 2 total casualties for Marlborough was tied with Drewry's Bluff, VA (May 13-17, 1864) and Cedar Creek, VA (October 19, 1864) for the second highest number of casualties for any single engagement of the war for the town. The highest number of casualties for an engagement was the Siege of Petersburg (June 1864-April 1865) with five.

77 MEN CREDITED TO MARLBOROUGH SERVED IN THE FOLLOWING CONNECTICUT ORGANIZATIONS

REGIMENT	TOTAL
10TH	21 (27%)
13TH	21 (27%)
20TH	7 (9%)
8TH	5 (6%)
21ST	5 (6%)
1ST HEAVY ARTILLERY	4 (5%)
13TH BATTALION	4 (5%)
14TH	4 (5%)
5TH	3 (5%)
29TH	3 (4%)
2ND HEAVY ARTILLERY	2 (3%)
15TH	2 (3%)
6TH	1
7TH	1
16TH	1
17TH	1
18TH	1
22ND	1

11% OF POPULATION

ONE WAS KILLED

The only Marlborough soldier killed was First Sergeant George I. Emily of Company B, 10TH Connecticut. He was killed at Deep Run, VA on August 16, 1864.

MARLBOROUGH SOLDIERS KILLED

PLACE	DATE	NO.
Deep Run, VA (10TH)	8/16/64	1

SIX WERE CAPTURED

Two Marlborough soldiers died in captivity. One died at Florence, SC. and one died at Petersburg, VA.

MARLBOROUGH CAPTURED
*(2) DIED IN CAPTIVITY

PLACE	DATE	NO.
Plymouth, NC (16TH) *	4/20/64	1
Cox's Mills, VA (8TH)	9/16/64	1
Cedar Creek, VA (13TH)	10/19/64	1
Petersburg, VA (14TH) *	10/27/64	1
Kinston, NC (15TH)	3/8/65	1
Goldsboro, NC (20TH)	3/24/65	1

TOTAL MARLBOROUGH CASUALTIES

DIED	7	6%
KILLED	1	4%
WOUNDED	14	18%
CAPTURED	6	8%
DESERTED	9	12%

FOURTEEN WERE WOUNDED

Private William G. Kelly of Company E, 14TH Connecticut was the first Marlborough soldier wounded. He was wounded at Fredericksburg, VA on December 13, 1862 and recovered from his wound. Two Marlborough soldiers died from a wound received during the war.

MARLBOROUGH WOUNDED
*(2) DIED FROM WOUNDS

PLACE	DATE	NO.
Fredericksburg, VA (14TH)	12/13/62	1
Kinston, NC (10TH)	12/14/62	1
Morris Island, SC (10TH) *	9/27/63	1
Drewry's Bluff, VA (8TH)	5/11/64	1
Drewry's Bluff, VA (10TH)	5/14/64	2
Petersburg, VA (8TH)	6/26/64	1
Deep Run, VA (10TH)	8/16/64	1
Winchester, VA (12TH)	9/19/64	1
Cedar Creek, VA (2 HA)	10/19/64	1
Kell House, VA (29TH)	10/27/64	1
Petersburg, VA (2 HA) *	3/25/65	1
Petersburg, VA (10TH)	4/2/65	1
Unknown (13TH)	Unknown	1

MERIDEN

THE POPULATION IN 1860 WAS 7,426 (RANK 9)

THE MOST IMPORTANT DAY OF THE CIVIL WAR

MARCH 8, 1865

KINSTON, NC

THE CONFEDERATE ATTACK STALLED

More soldiers credited to Meriden were listed as casualties (46) on this day than on any other day of the war. One soldier was killed, 42 were captured and 3 were wounded and captured in the 15TH Connecticut. One of the captured died at Goldsboro, NC.

The date March 8, 1865 ranks 5TH for total casualties (496) (22 killed, 3 missing, 12 wounded, 410 captured, 49 wounded & captured) for a single day for the State of Connecticut. There were 494 casualties at Kinston, 1 casualty in Virginia, and 1 casualty at a railroad accident in an unknown place.

The Second Battle of Kinston (March 8, 1865) ranks 8TH for total casualties (494) for an enagement for the State of Connecticut.

The Second Battle of Kinston with 46 total casualties for Meriden was the highest number of casualties for any single engagement of the war for the town.

The military situation in North Carolina changed in early 1865. The Confederate forces in eastern North Carolina were called to help stop the advance of the Union Army coming out of Georgia. The Confederates attempted to seize the initiative by attacking the Union flanks near Kinston on March 8 and failed.

826 MEN CREDITED TO MERIDEN SERVED IN THE FOLLOWING CONNECTICUT ORGANIZATIONS

REGIMENT	TOTAL
15TH	208 (25%)
8TH	119 (14%)
7TH	108 (13%)
3RD	84 (10%)
1ST	82 (10%)
1ST HEAVY ARTILLERY	73 (9%)
9TH	46 (6%)
14TH	41 (5%)
6TH	35 (4%)
1ST CAVALRY	35 (4%)
27TH	23 (3%)
5TH	20 (2%)
2ND HEAVY ARTILLERY	16 (2%)
9TH BATTALION	14 (2%)
1ST LIGHT BATTERY	12 (1%)
10TH	9 (1%)
11TH	6 (1%)
29TH	6 (1%)
20TH	5 (1%)
12TH	4
13TH	4
16TH	3
13TH BATTALION	3
1ST SQUADRON CAVALRY	2
17TH	2
18TH	2
30TH	2
3RD LIGHT BATTERY	1
12TH BATTALION	1
23RD	1
25TH	1

11% OF POPULATION

TWENTY-ONE WERE KILLED AND ONE WAS MISSING

The first Meriden soldier killed was Private Elihu Talmadge of Company K, 8ᵀᴴ Connecticut. He drowned in Albemarle Sound, NC on January 30, 1862.

MERIDEN SOLDIERS KILLED *MISSING

PLACE	DATE	NO.
Albemarle Sound, NC (8ᵀᴴ)	1/30/62	1
James Island, SC (7ᵀᴴ)	6/16/62	1
Antietam, MD (8ᵀᴴ)	9/17/62	2
Pocotaligo, SC (7ᵀᴴ)	10/22/62	1
Port Hudson, LA (13ᵀᴴ)	6/14/63	1
Fort Wagner, SC (7ᵀᴴ)	7/11/63	1
Swift's Creek, VA (8ᵀᴴ)	5/7/64	1
Swift's Creek, VA (8ᵀᴴ)	5/9/64	1
Drewry's Bluff, VA (7ᵀᴴ)	5/14/64	1
Drewry's Bluff, VA (7ᵀᴴ)	5/16/64	1
Bermuda Hundred, VA (6ᵀᴴ)	5/20/64	1
Cold Harbor, VA (2 HA)	6/1/64	1
Petersburg, VA (30ᵀᴴ) *	7/30/64	1
Deep Run, VA (7ᵀᴴ)	8/16/64	1
Winchester, VA (2 HA)	9/19/64	1
Cedar Creek, VA (2 HA,12ᵀᴴ)	10/19/64	2
Kinston, NC (15ᵀᴴ)	3/8/65	1
Petersburg, VA (1 HA)	3/25/65	2
Goldsboro, NC (7ᵀᴴ)	7/3/65	1

ONE HUNDRED-ONE WERE CAPTURED

Twenty-one Meriden soldiers died in captivity. Nine died at Andersonville Prison, GA, 4 at Florence Prison, SC, 3 at Libby Prison, Richmond, VA, 2 at Salisbury Prison, NC, 1 at Goldsboro, NC and 1 at Tallahassee, FL.

MERIDEN CAPTURED
*(21) DIED IN CAPTIVITY

PLACE	DATE	NO.
Wreck "Union", NC (7ᵀᴴ)	11/4/61	1
Antietam, MD (8ᵀᴴ)	9/17/62	2
(2 WOUNDED)		
Pass Manchac, LA (9ᵀᴴ)	4/18/63	1
Chancellorsville, VA (27ᵀᴴ)	5/3/63	7
Winchester, VA (18ᵀᴴ)	6/15/63	1
Fort Wagner, SC (7ᵀᴴ)	7/11/63	1
(WOUNDED)		
Bristoe Station, VA (14ᵀᴴ)	10/14/63	1
Orange County, TN (14ᵀᴴ)	11/17/63	1
Mine Run, VA (14ᵀᴴ) *	12/1/63	1
Rapidan, VA (14ᵀᴴ)*2	12/1/63	2
Rapidan, VA (14ᵀᴴ)*	2/6/64	1
Morton's Ford, VA (14ᵀᴴ)	2/6/64	1
Olustee, FL (7ᵀᴴ)*1	2/20/64	2
(WOUNDED)		
Plymouth, NC (15,16ᵀᴴ)*2	4/20/64	4
Winchester, VA (14ᵀᴴ)	5/5/64	1
Drewry's Bluff, VA (6,7,8ᵀᴴ)*3	5/16/64	4
(1 WOUNDED)		
Ashland, VA (1 CA)*	6/1/64	1
(WOUNDED)		
Bermuda Hundred, VA (7ᵀᴴ)*4	6/2/64	15
(2 WOUNDED)		
Ashland, VA (1 CA) *	6/10/64	1
Ream's Station, VA (1 CA)*	6/29/64	1
Shepardstown, VA (1 CA)	8/25/64	1
Cox's Mills, VA (8ᵀᴴ) *	9/16/64	1
Cedar Creek Church, VA (1CA)	10/17/64	1
Cedar Creek, VA (1 CA,9)*1	10/19/64	2
Cedar Creek, VA (1 CA)	11/12/64	1

ONE HUNDRED WERE WOUNDED

The first Meriden soldiers wounded were Privates Joseph Dainton, George Mecorney and James F. Lewis of the 3ᴿᴰ Connecticut. They were wounded at Bull Run, VA on July 21, 1861 and recovered from their wounds. Ten Meriden soldiers died from a wound received during the war.

MERIDEN WOUNDED
*(10) DIED FROM WOUNDS

PLACE	DATE	NO.
Bull Run, VA (3RD)	7/21/61	3
USS "Elwood Walter" (1 LB)	1/1/62	1
Stoddard's Plant., GA (7TH)	2/6/62	1
New Bern, SC (8TH)	3/14/62	1
James Island, SC (7TH)	6/16/62	2
Cedar Mountain, VA (5TH)	8/9/62	1
Antietam, MD (8,11TH) *5	9/17/62	9
Bona Casa, LA (9TH)	10/20/62	1
Pocotaligo, SC (7TH)	10/22/62	1
Fredericksburg, VA (15TH)	12/13/62	1
Suffolk, VA (15TH) *1	5/3/63	2
Suffolk, VA (15TH)	5/4/63	1
Gettysburg, PA (27TH)	7/2/63	1
Gettysburg, PA (14TH)	7/3/63	1
Morris Island, SC (6TH)	7/10/63	2
Fort Wagner, SC (6TH)	7/18/63	1
Unknown (15TH)	7/20/63	1
Getty's Station, VA (8TH)	8/1/63	1
Fort Wagner, SC (7TH)	9/18/63	1
Bristoe Station, VA (14TH)	10/14/63	1
Mine Run, VA (14TH)	11/29/63	1
Morton's Ford, VA (14TH)	2/6/64	2
Olustee, FL (7TH)	2/20/64	2
Wilderness, VA (14TH)	5/6/64	2
Walthall Junction, VA (8TH)*2	5/7/64	5
Petersburg, VA (8TH)	5/7/64	1
Chester Station, VA (1 LB)	5/10/64	1
Spottsylvania, VA (14TH)	5/12/64	2
Drewry's Bluff, VA (7TH)	5/14/64	2
Drewry's Bluff, VA (7,8TH)	5/16/64	5
Bermuda Hundred, VA (6TH)	5/20/64	1
Dallas, GA (5TH)	5/25/64	1
Cold Harbor, VA (2 HA)	6/1/64	1
Cold Harbor, VA (8TH)	6/2/64	1
Petersburg, VA (8TH)	6/16/64	1
Petersburg, VA (8TH)	6/23/64	2
Petersburg, VA (8TH)	7/1/64	1
Fort Stevens, DC (6TH)	7/12/64	1
Petersburg, VA (1 HA)	7/20/64	1
Peach Tree Creek, GA (20TH)	7/20/64	1
Petersburg, VA (1 HA)	7/24/64	1
Deep Run, VA (6TH)	8/14/64	1
Andersonville, GA (7TH)	8/15/64	1
Deep Run, VA (7TH)	8/16/64	2
Ream's Station, VA (14TH) *	8/25/64	1
Shepardstown, VA (1 CA)	8/25/64	1

PLACE	DATE	NO.
Petersburg, VA (7TH)	8/31/64	1
Antietam, MD (1 HA)	9/17/64	1
Fort Harrison, VA (8TH)	9/29/64	3
Deep Bottom, VA (7TH)	9/29/64	2
Richmond, VA (7TH)	10/1/64	1
Fort Harrison, VA (8TH)	10/1/64	1
Petersburg, VA (1 HA)	10/3/64	1
New Market, VA (7TH)	10/7/64	1
Richmond, VA (6TH) *	10/7/64	1
Richmond, VA (7TH)	10/13/64	1
Cedar Creek, VA (2 HA,6TH)	10/19/64	2
Chaffin's Farm, VA (7TH)	10/27/64	1
Columbia, SC (7TH)	12/1/64	1
Cedar Creek, VA (1 CA)	12/12/64	1
Petersburg, VA (6TH)	3/1/65	1
Bachelor's Creek, NC (15TH)	3/6/65	1
Petersburg, VA (2 HA)	3/25/65	1
Fort Gregg, VA (10TH)	4/2/65	2

TOTAL MERIDEN
CASUALTIES

DIED	**99**	**12%**
KILLED	**22**	**3%**
WOUNDED	**100**	**12%**
CAPTURED	**101**	**12%**
DESERTED	**79**	**10%**

LIBRARY OF CONGRESS

1ST CONNECTICUT VOLUNTEER HEAVY ARTILLERY
FORT RICHARDSON, VIRGINIA 1861

VIRGINIA 1863

LIBRARY OF CONGRESS

MIDDLEBURY
THE POPULATION IN 1860 WAS 696 (RANK 154)

**THE MOST IMPORTANT DAY
OF THE CIVIL WAR**

MARCH 8, 1865

KINSTON, NC

**THE CONFEDERATE
ATTACK STALLED**

More soldiers credited to Middlebury were listed as casualties (3) on this day than on any other day of the war. Three soldiers in the 15TH Connecticut were captured. They survived the war.

The date March 8, 1865 ranks 5TH for total casualties (496) (22 killed, 3 missing, 12 wounded, 410 captured, 49 wounded & captured) for a single day for the State of Connecticut. There were 494 casualties at Kinston, 1 casualty in Virginia, and 1 casualty at a railroad accident in an unknown place.

The Second Battle of Kinston (March 8. 1865) ranks 8TH for total casualties (494) for an engagement for the State of Connecticut.

The Second Battle of Kinston with 3 total casualties for Middlebury was the highest number of casualties for any single engagement of the war for the town.

The military situation in North Carolina changed in early 1865. The Confederate forces in eastern North Carolina were called to help stop the advance of the Union Army coming out of Georgia with Union General William T. Sherman. The Confederates attempted to seize the initiative by attacking the Union flanks near Kinston on March 8 and failed.

**30 MEN CREDITED TO
MIDDLEBURY SERVED IN
THE FOLLOWING
CONNECTICUT
ORGANIZATIONS**

REGIMENT	TOTAL
15TH	9 (30%)
7TH	5 (17%)
14TH	5 (17%)
23RD	4 (13%)
13TH	3 (10%)
1ST CAVALRY	3 (10%)
5TH	2 (7%)
1ST HEAVY ARTILLERY	1
8TH	1
13TH BATTALION	1
29TH	1

4% OF POPULATION

ONE WAS KILLED

The only Middlebury soldier killed was Private Eli B. Blackman of Company B, 13TH Connecticut. He was killed at Irish Bend, LA on April 14, 1863.

MIDDLEBURY SOLDIERS KILLED

PLACE	DATE	NO.
Irish Bend, LA (13TH)	4/14/63	1

SIX WERE CAPTURED

Two Middlebury soldiers died in captivity at Andersonville Prison, GA.

MIDDLEBURY CAPTURED
*(2) DIED IN CAPTIVITY

PLACE	DATE	NO.
Morton's Ford, VA (14TH) *	2/6/64	1
Craig's Church, VA (1 CA) *	5/5/64	2
Kinston, NC (15TH)	3/8/65	3

TOTAL MIDDLEBURY CASUALTIES

DIED	6	20%
KILLED	1	3%
WOUNDED	4	13%
CAPTURED	6	20%
DESERTED	5	17%

FOUR WERE WOUNDED

The first Middlebury soldiers wounded were Sergeant George W. Baldwin and Private James W. Benham of Company I, 14TH Connecticut. They were wounded at Gettysburg, PA on July 3, 1863 and Sergeant Baldwin died from his wound. Two Middlebury soldiers died from a wound received during the war.

MIDDLEBURY WOUNDED
*(2) DIED FROM WOUNDS

PLACE	DATE	NO.
Gettysburg, PA (14TH) *1	7/3/63	2
Ream's Station, VA (14TH) *	8/25/64	1
Five Forks, VA (1 CA)	4/1/65	1

MIDDLETOWN
THE POPULATION IN 1860 WAS 8,620 (RANK 7)

THE MOST IMPORTANT DAY OF THE CIVIL WAR

MAY 16, 1864

DREWRY'S BLUFF , VA

AN OBSTACLE ON THE WAY TO RICHMOND

More soldiers credited to Middletown were listed as casualties (31) on this day than on any other day of the war. One soldier was missing, 12 were wounded, 17 were captured, and 1 was wounded & captured in the 7th, 11th, and 21st Connecticut. One of the wounded died of his wound and 7 of the captured died in prison.

The date May 16, 1864 ranks 4th for total casualties (560) (52 killed, 3 missing, 224 wounded, 243 captured, 38 wounded & captured) for a single day for the State of Connecticut. The Battle of Drewry's Bluff accounted for 545 casualties. The 15 other casualties were scattered about Virginia.

The Battle of Drewry's Bluff (May 13-17, 1864), also called Fort Darling, ranks 3rd for total casualties (634) for an engagement for the State of Connecticut. The most intense fighting developed on May 16. Middletown had all of its casualties on that day.

The Battle of Drewry's Bluff with 30 total casualties for Middletown was the highest number of casualties for any single engagement of the war for the town.

The Confederate attack at Drewry's Bluff forced the Union Army to retreat to Bermuda Hundred. The civil war would have concluded sooner had the Union Army been victorious.

892 MEN CREDITED TO MIDDLETOWN SERVED IN THE FOLLOWING CONNECTICUT ORGANIZATIONS

REGIMENT	TOTAL
24TH	188 (21%)
14TH	125 (14%)
1ST HEAVY ARTILLERY	110 (12%)
11TH	84 (9%)
2ND	83 (9%)
21ST	60 (7%)
7TH	53 (6%)
13TH	44 (5%)
15TH	33 (4%)
10TH	23 (3%)
12TH	23 (3%)
1ST CAVALRY	21 (2%)
8TH	19 (2%)
20TH	18 (2%)
5TH	16 (2%)
29TH	16 (2%)
9TH	12 (1%)
6TH	10 (1%)
13TH BATTALION	10 (1%)
12TH BATTALION	9 (1%)
2ND HEAVY ARTILLERY	8 (1%)
3RD LIGHT BATTERY	6 (1%)
9TH BATTALION	5 (1%)
22ND	5 (1%)
18TH	4
16TH	3
25TH	3
30TH	2
1ST	1
1ST LIGHT BATTERY	1
17TH	1

10% OF POPULATION

TOTAL MIDDLETOWN CASUALTIES

DIED	66	7%
KILLED/MISSING	28	3%
WOUNDED	151	17%
CAPTURED	50	6%
DESERTED	153	17%

ONE HUNDRED FIFTY-ONE WERE WOUNDED

The first Middletown soldier wounded was Sergeant John A. Leeds of Company C, 7TH Regiment. He was wounded at James Island, SC on June 16, 1862 and recovered from his wound.

TWENTY- FIVE WERE KILLED AND THREE WERE MISSING

The first Middletown soldier killed was Private Curtiss S. Clark of Company A, 7th Connecticut. He was killed at James Island, SC on June 16, 1862.

MIDDLETOWN SOLDIERS KILLED *MISSING

PLACE	DATE	NO.
James Island, SC (7TH)	6/16/62	1
Antietam, MD (14TH) *1	9/17/62	2
Fredericksburg, VA (14TH)	12/13/62	5
Lake End, LA (9TH) Drowned	4/19/63	1
Port Hudson, LA (24TH)	5/24/63	1
Port Hudson, LA (24TH)	5/25/63	1
Baton Rouge, LA (24TH)	5/28/63	1
Port Hudson, LA (24TH)	6/14/63	3
Port Hudson, LA (24TH)	6/16/63	1
Gettysburg, PA (14TH)	7/3/63	1
Fort Wagner, SC (7TH)	7/11/63	2
Bristoe Station, VA (14TH)	10/14/63	1
Wilderness, VA (14TH)	5/6/64	2
Drewry's Bluff, VA (11TH)*	5/16/64	1
Ashland, VA (1 CA)	6/1/64	1
Cold Harbor, VA (11TH) *	6/3/64	1
Deep Bottom, VA (14TH)	8/16/64	1
Cedar Creek, VA (12TH)	10/19/64	1
Petersburg, VA (1 HA)	11/5/64	1

MIDDLETOWN WOUNDED
* (16) DIED FROM WOUNDS

PLACE	DATE	NO.
James Island, SC (7TH)	6/16/62	2
James Island, SC (7TH)	6/28/62	1
Antietam, MD (14TH, 16TH) *2	9/17/62	9
Fort Ethan Allen, VA (14TH)	9/23/62	1
Bayou La Fourche, LA (12TH)	10/27/62	1
Fredericksburg, VA (14, 21ST) *5	12/13/62	18
Irish Ben, LA (25TH)	4/14/63	1
Chancellorsville, VA (14TH) *	5/3/63	6
Port Hudson, LA (24TH)	5/27/63	1
Port Hudson, LA (13TH, 24TH	5/29/63	2
Port Hudson, LA (12TH)	6/10/63	1
Port Hudson, LA (24TH) *2	6/14/63	11
Port Hudson, LA (24TH)	6/15/63	1
Port Hudson, LA (24TH)	6/26/63	1
Port Hudson, LA (24TH)	6/27/63	1
Gettysburg, PA (14TH)	7/2/63	1
Gettysburg, PA (14TH)	7/3/63	9
Port Hudson, LA (24TH)	7/5/63	1
Port Hudson, LA (24TH)	7/6/63	1
Morris Island, SC (6TH)	7/10/63	1
Fort Wagner, SC (7TH)	7/11/63	1
Morton's Ford, VA (14TH)	2/6/64	5
Hatcher's Run, VA (14TH)	3/31/64	1
Wilderness, VA (14TH)	5/5/64	2
Wilderness, VA (14TH) *	5/6/64	9
Wilderness, VA (14TH)	5/7/64	1
Swift's Creek, VA (11TH)	5/9/64	1
Pomfret River, VA (14TH)	5/10/64	1
Laurel Hill, VA (14TH)	5/10/64	2
Spottsylvania, VA (14TH)	5/12/64	1
Spottsylvania, VA (14TH)	5/13/64	1
Drewry's Bluff, VA (7,11, 21ST)*1	5/16/64	12
Cold Harbor, VA (11, 21ST) *2	6/3/64	13
Petersburg, VA (21ST)	6/16/64	2
Petersburg, VA (11TH)	6/18/64	1
Petersburg, VA (21ST) *	6/23/64	1
Petersburg, VA (8TH)	7/17/64	1
Peach Tree Creek, GA (5TH) *	7/20/64	1
Petersburg, VA (21ST) *	7/30/64	3

MIDDLETOWN WOUNDED CONTINUED

PLACE	DATE	NO.
Atlanta, GA (5TH)	8/1/64	1
Deep Run, VA (6TH)	8/16/64	1
Petersburg, VA (11TH)	8/18/64	1
Fisher's Hill, VA (13TH)	9/22/64	1
Laurel Hill, VA (7TH)	9/29/64	1
New Market Heights, VA	9/29/64	1
Petersburg, VA (21ST)	9/30/64	1
Darbytown Road, VA (7TH)	10/13/64	1
Richmond, VA (29TH)	10/13/64	1
Darbytown Road, VA (29TH)	10/3/64	1
Cedar Creek, VA (12,13,2 HA)	10/19/64	3
Boydton Plank Rd, VA (14TH)	10/27/64	2
Kell House, VA (29TH)	10/27/64	3
Richmond, VA (7TH)	12/11/64	1
Fort Fisher, NC (7TH)	1/15/65	1
Beaufort, SC (29TH)	Unknown	1

FIFTY WERE CAPTURED

Ten Middletown soldiers died in captivity. Seven died at Andersonville Prison, GA, one at Salisbury, NC, one at Florence, SC, and one at Millen, GA.

MIDDLETOWN CAPTURED
*(10) DIED IN CAPTIVITY

PLACE	DATE	NO.
Bull Run, VA (2ND)	7/21/61	1
Harrisonburg, VA (1 CA)	6/12/62	1
Cedar Mountain, VA ((5TH)	8/9/62	1
Manassas, VA (10TH)	10/31/62	1
Pattersonville, LA (12TH)	3/27/63	1
Gettysburg, PA (5TH)	7/2/63	1
Long Island, SC (6TH)	7/8/63	1
Plymouth, NC (16TH) *1	4/20/64	2
Proctor's Creek, VA (11TH)	5/12/64	1
Drewry's Bluff, VA (11TH) *7 (1 WOUNDED)	5/16/64	18
Petersburg, VA (11TH) *1	5/16/64	1
Bermuda Hundred, VA (7TH)	6/2/64	1
Ream's Station, VA (1 CA)	6/30/64	1
Deep Bottom, VA (7TH) *1	8/16/64	1
Cedar Creek, VA (2 HA)	10/19/64	2
Boydton Plank Rd, VA (14TH)	10/27/64	1
Winchester, VA (1 CA)	1/30/65	1
Kinston, NC (15TH)	3/8/65	12
Hatcher's Run, VA (10TH)	4/2/65	1

USAMHI

1st Connecticut Heavy Artillery
Officer Group Cornwallis Cave
Yorktown Virginia 1863

USAMHI

1st Connecticut Heavy Artillery
Battery Abbot
South Side of James River, Virginia 1864

MILFORD
THE POPULATION IN 1860 WAS 2,828 (RANK 46)

THE MOST IMPORTANT DAY OF THE CIVIL WAR

MAY 3, 1863
CHANCELLORSVILLE, VA

THE THIRD DAY OF THE BATTLE

More soldiers credited to Milford were listed as casualties (13) on this day than on any other day of the war. One soldier was killed and 12 were captured in the 5, 20 and 27TH Connecticut. All survived the war.

The date May 3, 1863 ranks 3RD for total casualties (577) (36 killed, 1 missing, 138 wounded, 372 captured, 29 wounded & captured) for a single day for the State of Connecticut. The most casualties were at Chancellorsville, VA (556). The other casualties were at Providence Church Road, VA (12), Suffolk, VA (6), Port Hudson, LA (2) and Fredericksburg, VA (1).

The Battle of Chancellorsville (May 1-3, 1863) ranks 2ND for total casualties (677) for an engagement for the State of Connecticut. The most intense fighting developed on May 3 and Milford had all of its casualties on that date.

The Battle of Chancellorsville with 13 total casualties for Milford was the highest number of casualties for any single engagement of the war for the town.

The Battle of Chancellorsville was an enormous defeat for the more than 70,000 Union soldiers who had moved against the flank and rear of 40,000 Confederate soldiers. Unfortunately, the Union Army had pulled back and had gone on the defensive around Chancellorsville. The Confederate victory was tainted however, by the loss of Confederate Major General "Stonewall" Jackson.

167 MEN CREDITED TO MILFORD SERVED IN THE FOLLOWING CONNECTICUT ORGANIZATIONS

REGIMENT	TOTAL
27TH	30 (18%)
15TH	27 (16%)
10TH	26 (16%)
1ST HEAVY ARTILLERY	20 (12%)
1ST LIGHT BATTERY	12 (7%)
29TH	10 (6%)
5TH	8 (5%)
6TH	7 (4%)
11TH	7 (4%)
13TH	5 (3%)
7TH	4 (2%)
1ST CAVALRY	3 (2%)
8TH	3 (2%)
12TH	3 (2%)
14TH	3 (2%)
13TH BATTALION	2 (2%)
2ND LIGHT BATTERY	1
2ND HEAVY ARTILLERY	1
3RD	1
9TH	1
9TH BATTALION	1
12TH BATTALION	1
18TH	1
20TH	1
23RD	1
30TH	1

6% OF POPULATION

FIVE WERE KILLED AND ONE WAS MISSING

The first Milford soldier killed was Private Charles Michael of Company C, 27TH Connecticut. He was reported missing and presumed killed at Fredericksburg, VA on December 13, 1862.

MILFORD SOLDIERS KILLED MISSING *

PLACE	DATE	NO.
Fredericksburg, VA (27TH)	*12/13/62	1
Kinston, NC (10TH)	12/14/62	1
Chancellorsville, VA (27TH)	5/3/63	1
Gettysburg, PA (27TH)	7/2/63	2
Petersburg, VA (1 HA)	3/28/65	1

TWENTY-SEVEN WERE CAPTURED

Four Milford soldiers died in captivity. Two died at Andersonville Prison, GA, one died at Salisbury, NC and one died at Libby Prison, Richmond, VA.

MILFORD CAPTURED
*(4) DIED IN CAPTIVITY

PLACE	DATE	NO.
Culpeper, VA (5TH)	8/9/62	1
Chisolm, SC (6TH)	10/19/62	1
Chancellorsville, VA (5,20,27TH)	5/3/63	12
Gettysburg, PA (US 14TH) *	7/2/63	1
Unknown *	Unknown	1
Plymouth, NC (15TH) *	4/20/64	1
Kinston, NC (15TH) *	3/8/65	10
(3 WOUNDED)		

TOTAL MILFORD CASUALTIES

DIED	22	13%
KILLED/MISSING	6	4%
WOUNDED	16	10%
CAPTURED	27	16%
DESERTED	25	15%

SIXTEEN WERE WOUNDED

The first Milford soldier wounded was Private John Shine of the 1ST Connecticut Light Battery. He was wounded at Beaufort, SC on May 8, 1862 and recovered from his wound. One Milford soldier died from a wound received during the war.

MILFORD WOUNDED
*(1) DIED FROM WOUNDS

PLACE	DATE	NO.
Beaufort, SC (1 LB)	5/8/62	1
Winchester, VA (5TH)	5/25/62	1
Antietam, MD (11TH)	9/17/62	1
Fredericksburg, VA (27TH)	12/13/62	1
Fort Wagner, SC (6TH)	7/14/63	1
Fort Wagner, SC (6TH)	7/18/63	1
Morris Island, SC (7TH)	10/12/63	1
Dallas, GA (5TH)	5/25/64	1
Strawberry Plains, VA (10TH)	7/26/64	1
Deep Bottom, VA (7TH)	8/14/64	1
Deep Run, VA (6TH)	8/15/64	1
Strasburg, VA (9TH)	9/21/64	1
Kell House, VA (29TH)	10/27/64	1
Petersburg, VA (1 HA)	12/17/64	1
Fort Gregg, VA (10TH) *	4/2/65	1
Petersburg, VA (10TH)	4/2/65	1

MONROE
THE POPULATION IN 1860 WAS 1,382 (RANK 105)

THE MOST IMPORTANT DAY OF THE CIVIL WAR

OCTOBER 19, 1864

CEDAR CREEK, VA

THE LAST MAJOR BATTLE OF THE 1864 SHENANDOAH VALLEY CAMPAIGN WAS A UNION TRIUMPH

More soldiers credited to Monroe were listed as casualties (5) on this day than on any other day of the war. One soldier was killed, 2 were wounded and 2 were captured in the 2ND Connecticut Heavy Artillery and 13TH Connecticut Infantry. One of the wounded and one of the captured died.

The date October 19, 1864 ranks 7TH for total casualties (417) (48 killed, 2 missing, 204 wounded, 153 captured, 10 wounded & captured) for a single day for the State of Connecticut. The Battle of Cedar Creek accounted for 415 casualties. The 2 other casualties were in the neighboring towns.

The Battle of Cedar Creek (October 19, 1864) ranks 10TH for total casualties (415) for an engagement for the State of Connecticut.

The Battle of Cedar Creek with 5 total casualties for Monroe was the highest number of casualties for any single engagement of the war for the town.

The news of the Union triumph at Cedar Creek assured a Republican victory in the elections of November 1864 and the prosecution of the war to its end on President Abraham Lincoln's and Lieutenant General Ulysses S. Grant's terms.

90 MEN CREDITED TO MONROE SERVED IN THE FOLLOWING CONNECTICUT ORGANIZATIONS

REGIMENT	TOTAL
17TH	17 (19%)
2ND HEAVY ARTILLERY	13 (14%)
11TH	13 (14%)
1ST CAVLARY	9 (10%)
23RD	6 (7%)
13TH	5 (6%)
15TH	5 (6%)
9TH	4 (4%)
1ST HEAVY ARTILLERY	3 (3%)
8TH	3 (3%)
14TH	3 (3%)
5TH	2 (2%)
7TH	2 (2%)
10TH	2 (2%)
20TH	2 (2%)
30TH	2 (2%)
2ND LIGHT BATTERY	1
3RD LIGHT BATTERY	1
6TH	1
9TH BATTALION	1
12TH	1
12TH BATTALION	1
13TH BATTALION	1
29TH	1

7% OF POPULATION

THREE WERE KILLED

The first Monroe soldier killed was Private William S. Clark of Company D, 17TH Connecticut. He was killed at Chancellorsville, VA on May 2, 1863.

MONROE SOLDIERS KILLED

PLACE	DATE	NO.
Chancellorsville, VA (17TH)	5/2/63	1
Gettysburg, PA (17TH)	7/1/63	1
Cedar Creek, VA (2 HA)	10/19/64	1

THIRTEEN WERE CAPTURED

Two Monroe soldiers died in captivity. One died at Andersonville Prison, GA and one at Salisbury, NC.

MONROE CAPTURED
*(2) DIED IN CAPTIVITY

PLACE	DATE	NO.
Chancellorsville,VA (17TH)	5/2/62	2
Gettysburg, PA (17TH)	7/1/63	1
Gettysburg, PA (14TH)	7/2/63	1
Drewry's Bluff, VA *(1)	5/16/64	2
Bermuda Hundred, VA (11TH)	5/20/64	1
Cedar Creek, VA (2HA)*(1)	10/19/64	2
Hatcher's Run, VA (14TH)	10/27/64	1
Kinston, NC (15TH)	3/8/65	3

MONROE CASUALTIES

DIED	10	11%
KILLED	3	3%
WOUNDED	11	12%
CAPTURED	13	14%
DESERTED	19	21%

ELEVEN WERE WOUNDED

The first Monroe soldier wounded was Private Henry A. Smith of Company A 8TH Connecticut. He was wounded at The Battle of Antietam, MD on September 17, 1862 and recovered from his wound. Two Monroe soldiers died from a wound received during the war.

MONROE WOUNDED
*(2) DIED FROM WOUNDS

PLACE	DATE	NO.
Antietam, MD (8TH)	9/17/62	1
Baton Rouge, LA (13TH)	3/26/63	1
Cold Harbor, VA (2HA)	6/1/64	1
Petersburg, VA (11TH)	7/29/64	1
Petersburg, VA (30TH)	7/30/64	1
Winchester, VA (13TH)	9/19/64	1
Cedar Creek, VA (2HA,13TH)*1	10/19/64	2
Petersburg, VA (2HA)*	3/25/65	1
Richmond, VA (3LB)	4/22/65	1
Unknown (14TH)	Unknown	1

MONTVILLE
THE POPULATION IN 1860 WAS 2,141 (RANK 70)

THE MOST IMPORTANT DAY OF THE CIVIL WAR

MAY 16, 1864

DREWRY'S BLUFF , VA

AN OBSTACLE ON THE WAY TO RICHMOND

157 MEN CREDITED TO MONTVILLE SERVED IN THE FOLLOWING CONNECTICUT ORGANIZATIONS

More soldiers credited to Montville were listed as casualties (5) on this day than on any other day of the war. Five soldiers in the 21ST Connecticut were wounded. One of the wounded died.

The date May 16, 1864 ranks 4th for total casualties (560) (52 killed, 3 missing, 224 wounded, 243 captured, 38 wounded & captured) for a single day for the State of Connecticut. The Battle of Drewry's Bluff accounted for 545 casualties. The 15 other casualties were scattered about Virginia.

The Battle of Drewry's Bluff (May 13-17, 1864), also called Fort Darling, ranks 3rd for total casualties (634) for an engagement for the State of Connecticut. The most intense fighting developed on May 16. Montville had all of its casualties on that date.

The Battle of Drewry's Bluff with 5 total casualties for Montville was tied with the Siege of Petersburg, VA (June 1864-April -1865) for the second highest number of casualties. The Siege of Port Hudson, LA (May-July 1863) with 9 casualties was the highest number of casualties for any single engagement of the war for the town.

The Confederate attack at Drewry's Bluff forced the Union Army to retreat to Bermuda Hundred. The civil war would have concluded sooner had the Union Army been victorious.

REGIMENT	TOTAL
21ST	46 (29%)
26TH	25 (16%)
13TH	18 (11%)
1ST HEAVY ARTILLERY	13 (8%)
12TH	9 (6%)
13TH BATTALION	8 (5%)
1ST CAVALRY	6 (4%)
24TH	6 (4%)
7TH	5 (3%)
6TH	4 (3%)
8TH	4 (3%)
10TH	4 (3%)
11TH	4 (3%)
12TH BATTALION	4 (3%)
2ND HEAVY ARTILLERY	3 (2%)
18TH	3 (2%)
2ND	2 (1%)
14TH	2 (1%)
29TH	2 (1%)
30TH	2 (1%)

7% OF POPULATION

TWELVE WERE KILLED AND ONE WAS MISSING

The first Montville soldier killed was 1ST Lieutenant Andrew T. Johnson of Company A, 13TH Connecticut. He was wounded at Thibodeaux, LA on November 7, 1862.

MONTVILLE SOLDIERS KILLED MISSING *

PLACE	DATE	NO.
Thibodeaux, LA (13TH)	11/7/62	1
Kinston, NC (10TH)	12/14/62	1
Fort Hugar, VA (8TH)	4/19/63	1
Port Hudson, LA (26TH)	5/27/63	1
Port Hudson, LA (26TH)	6/14/63	2
Port Hudson, LA (26TH)	7/6/63	1
Cold Harbor, VA (11TH)	6/6/64	1
Virginia (1 CA) *	6/28/64	1
Petersburg, VA (30TH)	7/30/64	1
Winchester, VA (12TH)	9/19/64	1
Petersburg, VA (21ST)	9/29/64	1
Petersburg, VA (1 HA)	3/25/65	1

NINE WERE CAPTURED

Three Montville soldiers died in captivity. Two died at Andersonville Prison, GA and one at Florence, SC.

MONTVILLE CAPTURED *(3) DIED IN CAPTIVITY

PLACE	DATE	NO.
Harrisonburg, VA (1 CA)	6/6/62	1
Virginia (1 HA)	6/27/62	1
St. Augustine, FL (10TH) * (WOUNDED)	12/30/63	1
Bermuda Hundred, VA (7TH) *2	6/2/64	3
Ream's Station, VA (14TH)	8/25/64	1
Cedar Run Church, VA (1 CA)	10/17/64	1
Cedar Creek, VA (2 HA)	10/19/64	1

TOTAL MONTVILLE CASUALTIES

DIED	14	9%
KILLED/MISSING	13	8%
WOUNDED	23	15%
CAPTURED	9	6%
DESERTED	9	6%

TWENTY-THREE WERE WOUNDED

The first Montville soldier wounded was Corporal Jedediah R. Gay of Company H, 10TH Connecticut. He was wounded at Roanoke Island, NC on February 8, 1862 and recovered from his wound. Two Montville soldiers died from a wound received during the war.

MONTVILLE WOUNDED *(2) DIED FROM WOUNDS

PLACE	DATE	NO.
Roanoke Island, NC (10TH)	2/8/62	1
Antietam, MD (8,11TH)	9/17/62	2
Arlington Heights, VA (21ST)	10/26/62	1
Port Hudson, LA (26TH)	5/27/63	2
Port Hudson, LA (26TH) *1	6/14/63	2
Port Hudson, LA (12TH)	6/14/63	1
Drewry's Bluff, VA (21ST) *1	5/16/64	5
Cold Harbor, VA (21ST)	6/3/64	3
Petersburg, VA (1 HA)	7/23/64	1
Petersburg, VA (21ST)	7/30/64	1
Winchester, VA (12TH)	9/19/64	2
Chaffin's Farm, VA (21ST)	9/29/64	1
Chaffin's Farm, VA (21ST)	9/30/64	1

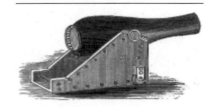

MORRIS
THE POPULATION IN 1860 WAS 796 (RANK149)

THE MOST IMPORTANT DAY
OF THE CIVIL WAR

JUNE 1, 1864

COLD HARBOR, VA

THE BATTLE WAS LEE'S
LAST GREAT VICTORY

More soldiers credited to Morris were listed as casualties (4) on this day than on any other day of the war. One soldier was killed and 3 were wounded in the 2ND Connecticut Heavy Artillery. None of the wounded died.

The date June 1, 1864 ranks 8TH for total casualties (374) (89 killed, 10 missing, 246 wounded, 23 captured, 6 wounded & captured)) for a single day for the State of Connecticut. There were 324 casualties at Cold Harbor, 41 casualties at Ashland, and 9 other casualties scattered about Virginia.

The battle and operations around Cold Harbor (May 31-June 12, 1864) rank 6TH for total casualties (557) for an engagement for the State of Connecticut. The most intense fighting developed on June 3. Morris had no casualties on that day.

The Battle of Cold Harbor with 4 total casualties for Morris was the highest number of casualties for any single engagement of the war for the town.

Approximately 117,000 Federal and 60,000 Confederate troops participated in operations from May 28 to June 3. Roughly 13,000 Union casualties were recorded and perhaps there were 5,000 Confederate casualties.

59 MEN CREDITED TO
MORRIS SERVED
IN THE FOLLOWING
CONNECTICUT
ORGANIZATIONS

REGIMENT	TOTAL
2ND HEAVY ARTILLERY	19 (32%)
11TH	11 (19%)
8TH	6 (10%)
23RD	5 (9%)
5TH	4 (7%)
1ST CAVALRY	3 (5%)
29TH	3 (5%)
9TH	2 (3%)
10TH	2 (3%)
13TH	2 (3%)
14TH	2 (3%)
1ST HEAVY ARTILLERY	1
7TH	1
9TH BATTALION	1
13TH BATTALION	1
20TH	1

7% OF POPULATION

THREE WERE KILLED

The first Morris soldier killed in was Private William Schofield of Company G, 23RD Connecticut. He was killed at St. Charles, LA on March 8, 1863.

MORRIS SOLDIERS KILLED

PLACE	DATE	NO.
St. Charles, LA (23RD)	3/8/63	1
Cold Harbor, VA (2 HA)	6/1/64	1
Hatcher's Run, VA (2 HA)	2/6/65	1

THREE WERE CAPTURED

Two Morris soldiers died in captivity. Both died at Andersonville Prison, GA.

MORRIS CAPTURED
*(2) DIED IN CAPTIVITY

PLACE	DATE	NO.
Walthall Junction, VA (8TH) *	5/7/64	1
Petersburg, VA (11TH)	5/15/64	1
Fort Darling, VA (8TH) *	5/16/64	1

TOTAL MORRIS CASUALTIES

DIED	7	12%
KILLED	3	5%
WOUNDED	7	12%
CAPTURED	3	5%
DESERTED	13	22%

SEVEN WERE WOUNDED

The first Morris soldier wounded was Private John L. Hine of Company E, 11TH Connecticut. He was wounded at The Battle of Antietam, MD on September 17, 1862 and recovered from his wound. No Morris soldiers died from a wound received during the war.

MORRIS WOUNDED
NONE DIED FROM WOUNDS

PLACE	DATE	NO.
Antietam, MD (11TH)	9/17/62	1
Drewry's Bluff, VA (8TH)	5/16/64	1
Cold Harbor, VA (2 HA)	6/1/64	3
Cedar Creek, VA (2 HA)	10/19/64	1
Petersburg, VA (2 HA)	3/25/65	1

NAUGATUCK
THE POPULATION IN 1860 WAS 2,295 (RANK 53)

THE MOST IMPORTANT DAY OF THE CIVIL WAR

MARCH 8, 1865

KINSTON, NC

THE CONFEDERATE ATTACK STALLED

More soldiers credited to Naugatuck were listed as casualties (27) on this day than on any other day of the war. One soldier was killed, 1 wounded, 19 captured and 6 wounded & captured in the 15TH Connecticut. One of the wounded soldiers died.

The date March 8, 1865 ranks 5TH for total casualties (496) (22 killed, 3 missing, 12 wounded, 410 captured, 49 wounded & captured) for a single day for the State of Connecticut. There were 494 casualties at Kinston, 1 casualty in Virginia, and 1 casualty at a railroad accident in an unknown place.

The Second Battle of Kinston (March 8, 1865) ranks 8TH for total casualties (494) for an engagement for the State of Connecticut.

The Second Battle of Kinston with 26 total casualties for Naugatuck was the highest number of casualties for any single engagement of the war for the town.

The military situation in North Carolina changed in early 1865. The Confederate forces in eastern North Carolina were called to help stop the advance of the Union Army coming out of Georgia with Union General William T. Sherman. The Confederates attempted to seize the initiative by attacking the Union flanks near Kinston on March 8 and failed.

219 MEN CREDITED TO NAUGATUCK SERVED IN THE FOLLOWING CONNECTICUT ORGANIZATIONS

REGIMENT	TOTAL
15TH	74 (34%)
23RD	44 (20%)
1ST HEAVY ARTILLERY	21 (10%)
6TH	20 (9%)
7TH	13 (6%)
3RD LIGHT BATTERY	11 (5%)
5TH	9 (4%)
8TH	8 (4%)
13TH	7 (3%)
1ST CAVALRY	5 (2%)
11TH	5 (2%)
20TH	5 (2%)
14TH	4 (2%)
1ST SQUADRON CAVALRY	3 (1%)
2ND HEAVY ARTILLERY	3 (1%)
13TH BATTALION	2 (1%)
9TH	1
10TH	1
17TH	1
25TH	1
27TH	1
29TH	1

9% OF POPULATION

THREE WERE KILLED

The first Naugatuck soldier killed was Private Oliver A. Hitchcock of Company A, 2ND Connecticut Heavy Artillery. He was killed at Cold Harbor, VA on June 1, 1864.

NAUGATUCK SOLDIERS KILLED

PLACE	DATE	NO.
Cold Harbor, VA (2 HA)	6/1/64	1
Deep Run, VA (6TH)	8/16/64	1
Kinston, NC (15TH)	3/8/65	1

THIRTY-TWO WERE CAPTURED

No Naugatuck soldiers died in captivity.

NAUGATUCK CAPTURED
NONE DIED IN CAPTIVITY

PLACE	DATE	NO.
Winchester, VA (5TH)	5/25/62	2
Antietam, MD (8TH)	9/17/62	1
Bayou Boeuf, LA (23RD)	6/24/63	1
New Baltimore, VA (1SQ)	7/1/63	1
Drewry's Bluff, VA (11TH)	5/16/64	1
Ashland, VA (1 CA)	6/1/64	1
Kinston, NC (15TH)	3/8/65	25
(6 WOUNDED)		

TOTAL NAUGATUCK CASUALTIES

DIED	20	8%
KILLED	3	1%
WOUNDED	17	8%
CAPTURED	32	15%
DESERTED	25	11%

SEVENTEEN WERE WOUNDED

The first Naugatuck soldier wounded was Corporal George L. Lewis of Company F, 1ST Connecticut Heavy Artillery. He was wounded at Hagerstown, MD on June 17, 1861 and recovered from his wound. Three Naugatuck soldiers died from a wound received during the war.

NAUGATUCK WOUNDED
***(3) DIED FROM WOUNDS**

PLACE	DATE	NO.
Hagerstown, MD (1 HA)	6/17/61	1
Cedar Mountain, VA (5TH)	8/9/62	1
Antietam, MD (14TH)	9/17/62	1
Colerain, NC (15TH)	Unknown	1
Suffolk, VA (15TH) *	4/24/63	1
Gettysburg, PA (20TH)	7/3/63	1
Fort Wagner, SC (6TH)	7/18/63	1
Bristoe Station, VA (14TH)	10/14/63	1
Petersburg, VA (2 HA)	3/25/64	1
Drewry's Bluff, VA (7TH)	5/16/64	1
Bermuda Hundred, VA (11TH)	5/20/64	1
Petersburg, VA (11TH)	6/16/64	1
Petersburg, VA (11TH)	6/18/64	1
Deep Run, VA (6TH) *	8/16/64	1
Dutch Gap, VA (29TH)	2/18/65	1
Kinston, NC (15TH) *1	3/8/65	1
Fort Gregg, VA (10TH)	4/2/65	1

NEW BRITAIN
THE POPULATION IN 1860 WAS 1,865 (RANK 79)

THE MOST IMPORTANT DAY OF THE CIVIL WAR

MAY 3, 1863

CHANCELLORSVILLE, VA

THE THIRD DAY OF THE BATTLE

More soldiers credited to New Britain were listed as casualties (13) on this day than on any other day of the war. Two soldiers were killed, 5 were wounded and 6 were captured in the 5TH,14TH and 20TH Connecticut. One of the wounded died.

The date May 3, 1863 ranks 3RD for total casualties (577) (36 killed, 1 missing, 138 wounded, 372 captured, 29 wounded & captured) for a single day for the State of Connecticut. The most casualties were at Chancellorsville, VA (556). The other casualties were at Providence Church Road, VA (12), Suffolk, VA (6), Port Hudson, LA (2) and Fredericksburg, VA (1).

The Battle of Chancellorsville (May 1-3, 1863) ranks 2ND for total casualties (677) for an engagement for the State of Connecticut. The most intense fighting developed on May 3. New Britain also had one casualty on May 2.

The Battle of Chancellorsville with 14 total casualties for New Britain was the highest number of casualties for any single engagement of the war for the town.

The Battle of Chancellorsville was an enormous defeat for the more than 70,000 Union soldiers who had moved against the flank and rear of 40,000 Confederate soldiers. Unfortunately, the Union Army had pulled back and had gone on the defensive around Chancellorsville. The Confederate victory was tainted however, by the loss of Confederate Major General "Stonewall" Jackson.

483 MEN CREDITED TO NEW BRITAIN SERVED IN THE FOLLOWING CONNECTICUT ORGANIZATIONS

REGIMENT	TOTAL
6TH	83 (17%)
14TH	76 (16%)
13TH	71 (15%)
1ST	59 (12%)
20TH	46 (10%)
1ST HEAVY ARTILLERY	36 (7%)
7TH	33 (7%)
13TH BATTALION	25 (5%)
5TH	14 (3%)
8TH	11 (2%)
1ST SQUAD CAVALRY	11 (2%)
29TH	10 (2%)
1ST CAVALRY	10 (2%)
16TH	9 (2%)
2ND HEAVY ARTILLERY	7 (1%)
9TH	7 (1%)
10TH	6 (1%)
11TH	6 (1%)
12TH	6 (1%)
22ND	6 (1%)
2ND	5 (1%)
1ST LIGHT BATTERY	3 (1%)
9TH BATTALION	3 (1%)
15TH	3 (1%)
12TH BATTALION	2
2ND LIGHT BATTERY	1
3RD LIGHT BATTERY	1
17TH	1
18TH	1
21ST	1
24TH	1
25TH	1
30TH	1

9% OF POPULATION

SIXTEEN WERE KILLED

The first New Britain soldier killed was Private Patrick McCluskey of Company C, 5TH Connecticut. He killed on August 9, 1862 at Cedar Mountain, VA.

NEW BRITAIN SOLDIERS KILLED

PLACE	DATE	NO.
Cedar Mountain, VA (16TH)	8/9/62	1
Antietam, MD (14,16TH)	9/17/62	4
Fredericksburg, VA (14TH)	12/13/62	1
Irish Bend, LA (13TH)	4/14/63	2
Chancellorsville, VA (20TH)	5/3/63	2
Fort Wagner, SC (7TH)	7/11/63	1
James Island (7TH)	8/22/63	1
Bristoe Station, VA (14TH)	10/14/63	1
Spottsylvania, VA (14TH)	5/12/64	1
Bentonville, NC (20TH)	3/19/65	1
Wilmington, NC (Drowned) (7TH)	5/2/65	1

THIRTY-EIGHT WERE CAPTURED

Nine New Britain soldiers died in captivity. Five died at Andersonville Prison, GA, two at Libby Prison Richmond, VA, one at Salisbury Prison, NC and one at Millen Prison, GA.

NEW BRITAIN CAPTURED
*(9) DIED IN CAPTIVITY

PLACE	DATE	NO.
Wreck "Union", NC (7TH)	11/4/61	1
Winchester, VA (5TH)	5/25/62	1
Cross Keys, VA (1 CA)	6/8/62	1
James Island, SC (7TH)	6/16/62	1
Cold Harbor, VA (1 HA)	6/27/62	1
Cedar Mountain, VA (5TH)	8/9/62	1
Beal's Station, VA (5TH)	8/20/62	1
Snicker's Gap, VA (14TH)	10/27/62	1
Bayou La Fourche, LA (13TH)	10/27/62	1
Chancellorsville, VA (5TH)	5/2/63	1
Chancellorsville, VA (5,14,20TH)	5/3/63	6
Fort Wagner, SC (7TH) *	7/11/63	2
Fort Wagner, SC (7TH) *	7/18/63	1
Mine Run, VA (14TH) *	12/1/63	1
Morton's Ford, VA (14TH) *	2/6/64	1
(WOUNDED)		
Plymouth, NC (16TH) *	4/20/64	3
Ellis Ford, VA (14TH)	5/8/64	1
Drewry's Bluff, VA (6,7TH) *2	5/16/64	4
Ackworth, GA (20TH) *	7/2/64	1
Deep Run, VA (6TH)	8/16/64	1
Ream's Station, VA (14TH) *	8/25/64	1
Cedar Creek, VA (12TH)	10/19/64	1
Winchester, VA (13TH)	9/19/64	1
Kinston, NC (15TH)	3/8/65	3
Ashland, VA (1 CA)	3/15/65	1

TOTAL NEW BRITAIN CASUALTIES

DIED	55	11%
KILLED	16	3%
WOUNDED	95	19%
CAPTURED	38	8%
DESERTED	35	7%

NINETY-FIVE WERE WOUNDED

The first New Britain soldier wounded was Private John Barker of Rifle Company D, 2ND Connecticut. He was wounded at Falls Church, VA on July 5, 1861 and recovered from his wound. Fourteen New Britain soldiers died from a wound received during the war.

NEW BRITAIN WOUNDED
*(14) DIED FROM WOUNDS

PLACE	DATE	NO.
Falls Church, VA (2ND)	7/5/61	1
Unknown (14TH)	Unknown	1
Germantown, VA (1ST)	7/17/61	1
Bull Run, VA (1ST)	7/21/61	1
Boyne Island, NC (7TH)	11/3/61	1
New Haven, CT (12TH)	3/11/62	1
Cedar Mountain, VA (5TH)	8/9/62	1
Antietam, MD (14TH)	9/17/62	5
Pocotaligo, SC (6TH)	10/22/62	3
Terre Bonne Station, LA (13TH)	11/7/62	1
Fredericksburg, VA (14TH) *1	12/13/62	8
Fairfax, VA (20TH)	1/4/63	1
Dumfries, VA (20TH)	1/21/63	1
Irish Bend, VA (13TH) *2	4/14/63	3
Chancellorsville, VA (14,20TH) *	5/3/63	5
Unknown, (20TH)	6/13/63	1
Gettysburg, PA (5TH)	7/2/63	1
Gettysburg, PA (14,20TH)	7/3/63	7
Morris Island, SC (6TH)	7/10/63	1
Port Hudson, LA (12TH)	7/13/63	1
Fort Wagner, SC ((6TH) *	7/18/63	9
Bristoe Station, VA (14TH)	10/14/63	1
Morton's Ford, VA (14TH) *1	2/6/64	2
Wilderness, VA (14TH)	5/6/64	1
Walthall Junction, VA (8TH)	5/7/64	1
Chester Station, VA (14TH)	5/12/64	1
Spottsylvania, VA (14TH) *	5/12/64	2
Drewry's Bluff, VA (6,7,11TH) *1	5/16/64	5
Drewry's Bluff, VA (8TH)	5/17/64	1
Bermuda Hundred, VA (6TH)	5/20/64	2
Dallas, GA (5TH) *	5/25/64	1
Petersburg, VA (11TH)	6/18/64	1
Peach Tree Creek, GA (20TH) *	7/20/64	2
Deep Run, VA (6TH) *	8/16/64	4
Ream's Station, VA (14TH)	8/25/64	1
Petersburg, VA (6TH)	8/26/64	1
James River, VA (1 HA)	8/29/64	1
Petersburg, VA (29TH) *	8/29/64	1
Winchester, VA (2 HA)	9/19/64	1
Fort Harrison, VA (8TH)	9/29/64	1
Petersburg, VA (1 HA) *	9/29/64	1
Chaffin's Farm, VA (8TH)	10/3/64	1
Cedar Creek, VA (2 HA,13TH) *	10/19/64	2
Fort Fisher, NC (7TH)	1/20/65	1
Averysboro, NC (20TH)	3/16/65	1
Bentonville, NC (20TH)	3/19/65	1
Fort George, VA (10TH)	4/2/65	2
Farmville, VA (14TH)	4/6/65	1
Fayetteville, NC (20TH)	3/14/65	1

NEW CANAAN
THE POPULATION IN 1860 WAS 2,771 (RANK 47)

THE MOST IMPORTANT DAY OF THE CIVIL WAR

JULY 1, 1863

GETTYSBURG, PA

THE FIRST DAY OF THE BATTLE

More soldiers credited to New Canaan were listed as casualties (14) on this day than on any other day of the war. One soldier was killed, 4 were wounded, 5 were captured, and 4 were wounded & captured in the 17TH Connecticut. The wounded and captured survived the war.

The date July 1, 1863 ranks 16TH for total casualties (157) (18 killed, 4 missing, 70 wounded, 57 captured, 8 wounded & captured) for a single day for the State of Connecticut. The Battle of Gettysburg accounted for 143 casualties. The other casualties were scattered about Louisiana (6), Virginia (6), and South Carolina (2).

The Battle of Gettysburg (July1-3, 1863) ranks 11TH for total casualties (360) for an engagement for the State of Connecticut. The most intense fighting developed on July 3. New Canaan had no casualties on that day, however, they did have 4 casualties on July 2.

The Battle of Gettysburg with 18 total casualties for New Canaan was the highest number of casualties for any single engagement of the war for the town.

More than 170,00 men fought at the Battle of Gettysburg. Roughly 23,000 Union casualties were recorded and there were about 28,000 Confederate casualties. Gettysburg proved to be the great battle of the war. It ended Lee's 1863 invasion of the North. He was never able to launch a major offensive again.

239 MEN CREDITED TO NEW CANAAN SERVED IN THE FOLLOWING CONNECTICUT ORGANIZATIONS

REGIMENT	TOTAL
17TH	93 (39%)
10TH	52 (22%)
13TH	17 (7%)
3RD	16 (7%)
2ND HEAVY ARTILLERY	15 (6%)
6TH	11 (5%)
8TH	9 (4%)
12TH	8 (3%)
29TH	8 (3%)
1ST HEAVY ARTILLERY	6 (3%)
12TH BATTALION	5 (2%)
13TH BATTALION	5 (2%)
7TH	4 (2%)
14TH	4 (2%)
1ST CAVALRY	3 (1%)
11TH	3 (1%)
5TH	2 (1%)
18TH	1
23RD	1
28TH	1

9% OF POPULATION

FIVE NEW WERE KILLED

The first New Canaan soldier killed was Eliphalet Mead of Company H, 17TH Connecticut. He was killed at Gettysburg, PA on July 1, 1863.

NEW CANAAN SOLDIERS KILLED

PLACE	DATE	NO.
Gettysburg, PA (17TH)	7/1/63	1
Cold Harbor, VA (2 HA)	6/1/64	1
Bermuda Hundred, VA (6TH)	6/9/64	1
Deep Run, VA (6TH)	8/16/64	1
Cedar Creek, VA (2 HA)	10/19/64	1

TWENTY-EIGHT WERE CAPTURED

No New Canaan soldier died in captivity.

NEW CANAAN CAPTURED
NONE DIED IN CAPTIVITY

PLACE	DATE	NO.
Bull Run, VA (3RD) (1 WOUNDED)	7/21/61	2
Chancellorsville, VA (17TH) (1 WOUNDED)	5/2/63	2
Chancellorsville, VA (17TH)	5/3/63	1
Gettysburg, PA (17TH) (4 WOUNDED)	7/1/63	9
Gettysburg, PA (17TH)	7/2/63	3
Bolivar Heights, VA (1CA)	7/14/63	1
St. Augustine, FL (10TH) (1 WOUNDED)	12/30/63	1
Welaka, FL (17TH)	5/19/64	2
Winchester, VA (13TH)	9/19/64	2
Boydton Plank Rd, VA (14TH)	10/27/64	1
Dunn's Lake, FL (17TH)	2/5/65	3
King William's CH, VA (1CA)	3/19/65	1

TOTAL NEW CANAAN CASUALTIES

DIED	23	10%
KILLED	5	2%
WOUNDED	42	18%
CAPTURED	28	12%
DESERTED	10	4%

FORTY-TWO WERE WOUNDED

The first New Canaan soldier wounded was John T. Fancher of Rifle Company F, 3RD Connecticut. He was wounded & captured at the Battle of Bull Run, VA on July 21, 1861 and recovered from his wound. Three New Canaan soldiers died from a wound received during the war.

NEW CANAAN WOUNDED
* (3) DIED FROM WOUNDS

PLACE	DATE	NO.
New Bern, NC (10TH)	3/14/62	1
James Island, SC (7TH)	6/10/62	1
Kinston, NC (10TH)	12/14/62	2
Chancellorsville, VA (17TH)	5/2/63	4
Port Hudson, LA (12TH)	5/27/63	1
Port Hudson, LA (13TH)	5/28/63	1
Gettysburg, PA (17TH)	7/1/63	4
Gettysburg, PA (17TH)	7/2/63	1
Morris Island, SC (6TH)	7/25/63	1
Cane River, LA (13TH)	4/23/64	1
Drewry's Bluff, VA (10TH)	5/14/64	1
Drewry's Bluff, VA (6TH)	5/15/64	1
Unknown (10TH)	5/25/64	1
Cold Harbor, VA (2HA)	6/1/64	1
Bermuda Hundred, VA (7TH)	6/2/64	1
Cold Harbor, VA (11TH,2HA)	6/3/64	2
Cold Harbor, VA (2HA)	6/8/64	1
Petersburg, VA (2HA) *	6/29/64	1
Deep Bottom, VA (10TH)	8/14/64	1
Deep Run, VA (10TH) *1	8/16/64	1
Petersburg, VA (29TH)	8/27/64	1
Petersburg, VA (10TH)	9/13/64	2
Richmond, VA (29TH)	9/29/64	1
Darbytown Road, VA (10TH)	10/13/64	2
Cedar Creek, VA (2HA) *1	10/19/64	4
Hatcher's Run, VA (2HA)	2/6/65	1
Petersburg, VA (10TH)	4/2/65	1
Fort Gregg, VA (10TH)	4/2/65	2

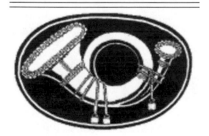

NEW FAIRFIELD
THE POPULATION IN 1860 WAS 915 (RANK 141)

THE MOST IMPORTANT DAY OF THE CIVIL WAR

JULY 21 1861

**BULL RUN, VA
(MANASSAS, VA)**

THE BATTLE SHOWED THAT THE WAR WOULD BE LONG

Soldiers credited to New Fairfield had more casualties on July 21, 1861 at Bull Run, VA (2), on June 1, 1864 at Cold Harbor, VA (2) and on June 2, 1864 at Bermuda Hundred, VA (2) than on any other days of the war. At Bull Run the casualties were the most serious. One soldier was wounded & captured and one was captured in the 3RD Connecticut. Both soldiers survived the war.

The date July 21, 1861 ranks 37TH for total casualties (66) (4 killed, 1 missing, 24 wounded, 33 captured, 4 wounded & captured) for a single day for the State of Connecticut. All of the casualties were at Bull Run.

The Battle of Bull Run (July 21, 1861) ranks 29TH for total casualties (66) for an engagement for the State of Connecticut.

The Battle of Bull Run with 2 total casualties for New Fairfield was tied with the Battle of Cold Harbor (May 31-June,12 1864) for the second highest number of casualties for any single engagement of the war for the town. The most casualties for an engagement were at La Fourche, LA (June 21-23, 1863) and the Siege of Petersburg (June 1864-April 1865) with three.

The Union defeat cast Major General Irwin McDowell as the scapegoat for the mistakes of many beside himself. As for the men on both sides, most had acquitted themselves as well as could have been expected, given their inexperience.

It took four long years and a great many battles far more horrible than Bull Run to bring an end to the American Civil War.

78 MEN CREDITED TO NEW FAIRIFELD SERVED IN THE FOLLOWING CONNECTICUT ORGANIZATIONS

REGIMENT	TOTAL
11TH	22 (28%)
23RD	19 (24%)
3RD	18 (23%)
2ND HEAVY ARTILLERY	9 (12%)
1ST HEAVY ARTILLERY	5 (6%)
17TH	4 (5%)
12TH	3 (4%)
7TH	3 (4%)
1ST	1
1ST CAVALRY	1
8TH	1
14TH	1

9% OF POPULATION

FOUR WERE KILLED

The first New Fairfield soldier killed was Corporal Fredrick C. Barnum of Company K, 23RD Connecticut. He was killed at La Fourche, LA on June 22, 1863.

NEW FAIRIFELD SOLDIERS KILLED

PLACE	DATE	NO.
La Fourche, LA (23RD)	6/22/63	1
Cold Harbor, VA (2 HA)	6/1/64	1
Petersburg, VA (2 HA)	6/22/64	1
Petersburg, VA (11TH)	7/12/64	1

SEVEN WERE CAPTURED

Two New Fairfield soldiers died in captivity. Both died at Florence, SC.

NEW FAIRFIELD CAPTURED
*(2) DIED IN CAPTIVITY

PLACE	DATE	NO.
Bull Run, VA (3RD) (1 WOUNDED)	7/21/61	2
La Fourche, LA (23RD)	6/23/63	1
Gettysburg, PA (17TH)	7/1/63	1
Bermuda Hundred, VA (7TH) * (WOUNDED)	6/2/64	1
Petersburg, VA (11TH) *	6/18/64	1
Fort Stedman, VA (1 HA)	3/25/65	1

TOTAL NEW FAIRFIELD CASUALTIES

DIED	5	6%
KILLED	4	5%
WOUNDED	5	6%
CAPTURED	7	9%
DESERTED	9	12%

FIVE WERE WOUNDED

The first New Fairfield soldier wounded was Private Alfred L. Benedict of Company C, 1ST Connecticut. He was wounded and captured at Bull Run, VA on July 21 1861 and recovered from his wound. One New Fairfield soldier died from a wound received during the war.

NEW FAIRFIELD WOUNDED
*(1) DIED FROM WOUNDS

PLACE	DATE	NO.
James Island, SC (7TH)	6/16/62	1
La Fourche, LA (23RD)	6/21/63	1
Swift's Creek, VA (11TH)	5/9/64	1
Cold Harbor, VA (2 HA)	6/1/64	1
Newmarket, VA (7TH) *	10/7/64	1

NEW HARTFORD
THE POPULATION IN 1860 WAS 2,758 (RANK 48)

THE MOST IMPORTANT DAY OF THE CIVIL WAR

SEPTEMBER 17, 1862
SHARPSBURG, MD (ANTIETAM)

CONNECTICUT HAD MORE CASUALTIES FOR ONE DAY THAN ON ANY OTHER DAY OF THE WAR

More soldiers credited to New Hartford soldiers were listed as casualties (18) on this day than on any other day of the war. Five soldiers were killed and 13 were wounded in the 8TH and 16TH Connecticut. Two of the wounded died.

The date September 17, 1862 ranks 1ST for total casualties (687) (131 killed, 2 missing, 515 wounded, 21 captured, 18 wounded & captured) for a single day for the State of Connecticut. All of the casualties were at Antietam.

The Battle of Antietam (September 16-17, 1862) ranks 1ST for total casualties (689) for an engagement for the State of Connecticut. The most intense fighting was on September 17. New Hartford had all of its casualties on that day.

The Battle of Antietam with 18 total casualties for New Hartford was the highest number of casualties for any single engagement of the war for the town.

Roughly 12,400 Union casualties were recorded and perhaps there were 10,300 Confederate casualties. Antietam proved to be one of the turning points of the war. It ended Lee's 1862 invasion of the North.

241 MEN CREDITED TO NEW HARTFORD SERVED IN THE FOLLOWING CONNECTICUT ORGANIZATIONS

REGIMENT	TOTAL
8TH	54 (22%)
2ND HEAVY ARTILLERY	51 (21%)
13TH	41 (17%)
2ND	25 (10%)
1ST HEAVY ARTILLERY	19 (8%)
16TH	15 (6%)
13TH BATTALION	12 (5%)
29TH	8 (3%)
10TH	7 (3%)
5TH	6 (3%)
7TH	5 (2%)
9TH	5 (2%)
12TH	5 (2%)
1ST CAVALRY	4 (2%)
1ST SQUADRON CAVALRY	4 (2%)
12TH BATTALION	3 (1%)
6TH	2 (1%)
11TH	2 (1%)
15TH	2 (1%)
3RD	1
3RD LIGHT BATTERY	1
17TH	1

9% OF POPULATION

THIRTEEN WERE KILLED

The first New Hartford soldier killed was Private George Barrett of Company H, 1ST Connecticut Heavy Artillery. He was killed in a Railroad accident in Maryland on June 12, 1861.

NEW HARTFORD SOLDIERS KILLED

PLACE	DATE	NO.
Railroad Accident, MD (1 HA)	6/12/61	1
Antietam, MD (8TH)	9/17/62	5
Fredericksburg, VA (8TH)	12/11/62	1
Port Hudson, LA (13TH)	6/14/63	2
Petersburg, VA (2 HA)	6/22/64	1
Cedar Creek, VA (2 HA)	10/19/64	2
Cedar Creek, VA (1 CA)	11/12/64	1

FOURTEEN WERE CAPTURED

Five New Hartford soldiers died in captivity. Three died at Andersonville Prison, GA and two at Salisbury, NC.

NEW HARTFORD CAPTURED
*(5) DIED IN CAPTIVITY

PLACE	DATE	NO.
Bull Run, VA (2ND)	7/21/61	1
Antietam, MD (8TH)	9/17/62	1
Opelousas, LA (13TH)	4/20/63	1
Plymouth, NC (16TH) *3	4/20/64	5
Drewry's Bluff, VA (8TH)	5/16/64	2
(2 WOUNDED)		
Fort Powhatan, VA (8TH) *	9/18/64	1
Winchester, VA (13TH) *	9/19/64	2

TOTAL NEW HARTFORD CASUALTIES

DIED	34	14%
KILLED	13	5%
WOUNDED	41	18%
CAPTURED	14	5%
DESERTED	17	7%

FORTY-ONE WERE WOUNDED

The first New Hartford soldier wounded was Musician Leonard Hart of the Band, 1ST Connecticut Heavy Artillery. He was wounded at Hagerstown, MD on August 1, 1861 and recovered from his wound. Four New Hartford soldiers died from a wound received during the war.

NEW HARTFORD WOUNDED
*(4) DIED FROM WOUNDS

PLACE	DATE	NO.
Hagerstown, MD (1 HA)	8/1/61	1
Franklin, VA (1 CA)	5/11/62	1
Louisiana, (13TH)	8/1/62	1
Antietam, MD (8,16TH) *2	9/17/62	13
Pocotaligo, SC (6TH)	10/22/62	1
Kinston, NC (10TH)	12/14/62	1
Irish Bend, LA (13TH)	4/14/63	1
Fort Wagner, SC (6TH)	7/18/63	1
Cane River, LA (13TH)	4/23/64	1
Walthall Junction, VA (8TH) *	5/7/64	2
Resaca, GA (5TH)	5/15/64	1
Drewry's Bluff, VA (8TH)	5/16/64	1
Cold Harbor, VA (2 HA) *1	6/1/64	4
Cold Harbor, VA (8TH)	6/5/64	1
Petersburg, VA (8TH)	7/23/64	1
Deep Bottom, VA (10TH)	8/1/64	1
Winchester, VA (2 HA)	9/19/64	4
Fort Harrison, VA (8TH)	9/29/64	1
Cedar Creek, VA (2 HA)	10/19/64	3
Amelia CH, VA (2 HA)	4/4/65	1

CONNECTICUT HISTORICAL SOCIETY

SOLDIERS ON NEW HAVEN GREEN 1865

NEW HAVEN
THE POPULATION IN 1860 WAS 39,267 (RANK 1)

THE MOST IMPORTANT DAY OF THE CIVIL WAR

DECEMBER 13, 1862

FREDERICKSBURG, VA

THE PRINCIPAL CITY BETWEEN WASHINGTON AND RICHMOND

Soldiers credited to New Haven had two days in the war with more casualties: May 3, 1863 at Chan-cellorsville, VA (185) and March 8, 1865 at Kinston, NC (172). The 85 casualties at Fredericksburg, VA however, were the most serious. Fourteen soldiers were killed, 67 were wounded, and 4 were captured in the 14TH, 15TH and 27TH Connecticut. Twelve of the wounded died.

The date December 13, 1862 ranks 10TH for total casualties (253) (40 killed, 5 missing, 200 wounded, 6 captured, 2 wounded & captured) for a single day for the State of Connecticut. All of the casualties were at Fredericksburg.

The Battle of Fredericksburg (December 11-15, 1862) ranks 13TH for total casualties (253) for an engagement for the State of Connecticut. The most intense fighting was on December 13. New Haven had all of its casualties on that day.

The Battle of Fredericksburg with 85 total casualties for New Haven was the 3RD highest number of casualties for any single engagement of the war for the city. The 2ND highest number of casualties (172) was at the Battle of Kinston, NC (March 8, 1865) and the highest number of casualties (187) was at the Battle of Chancellorsville, VA (May 1-3, 1863).

In November 1862, 120,000 Union troops under Ambrose Burnside met 75,000 Confederates under Robert E. Lee at Fredericksburg. After weeks of delay the Federals crossed the Rappahannock River and entered the city. After several furious Union attacks on the Confederate positions on the heights above the city, the Federal army was driven back with appalling loss.

4157 MEN CREDITED TO NEW HAVEN SERVED IN THE FOLLOWING CONNECTICUT ORGANIZATIONS

REGIMENT	TOTAL
15TH	545 (13%)
27TH	494 (12%)
1ST HEAVY ARTILLERY	375 (9%)
9TH	350 (8%)
6TH	315 (8%)
10TH	231 (6%)
7TH	221 (5%)
1ST CAVALRY	208 (5%)
20TH	169 (4%)
2ND	167 (4%)
13TH	155 (4%)
12TH	142 (3%)
29TH	137 (3%)
9TH BATTALION	136 (3%)
5TH	130 (3%)
14TH	127 (3%)
11TH	124 (3%)
3RD	120 (3%)
2ND HEAVY ARTILLERY	120 (3%)
24TH	111 (3%)
30TH	72 (2%)
12TH BATTALION	59 (1%)
1ST	54 (1%)
13TH BATTALION	42 (1%)
8TH	35 (1%)
1ST LIGHT BATTERY	33 (1%)
3RD LIGHT BATTERY	8
23RD	7
16TH	6
17TH	4
22ND	4
28TH	4
1ST SQUADRON CAVALRY	3
2ND LIGHT BATTERY	3
18TH	3
26TH	1

11% OF POPULATION

TOTAL NEW HAVEN CASUALTIES

DIED	372	9%
KILLED/MISSING	128	3%
WOUNDED	461	11%
CAPTURED	495	12%
DESERTED	540	13%

ONE HUNDRED-SEVENTEEN WERE KILLED AND ELEVEN WERE MISSING

The first New Haven soldier killed was Private James Fritz of Company I, 2ND Connecticut. He was killed at the First Battle of Bull Run, VA on July 21, 1861.

NEW HAVEN SOLDIERS KILLED AND *MISSING

PLACE	DATE	NO.
Bull Run, VA (2ND)	7/21/61	1
Roanoke Island, NC (10TH)	2/8/62	1
New Bern, NC (11TH)	3/14/62	1
Unknown (Accident) (9TH)	4/14/62	1
New Orleans, LA (9TH)	5/4/62	1
James Island, SC (7TH)	6/16/62	1
Golding's Farm, VA (1 HA)	6/27/62	1
Richmond, VA (1 HA) *	7/15/62	1
Cedar Mountain, VA (5TH)	8/9/62	6
Antietam, MD (8,11TH)	9/17/62	2
Pocotaligo, SC (6TH)	10/22/62	1
Thibodeaux, LA (13TH)	11/7/62	1
Fredericksburg, VA (27TH)	12/13/62	14
Kinston, NC (10TH)	12/14/62	2
Rappahannock, VA (1 HA) (DROWNED)	1/9/63	1
Unknown (Poisoned) (15TH)	2/3/63	1
Bisland, LA (12TH)	4/13/63	1
Irish Bend, LA (12TH)	4/14/63	1
Chancellorsville, VA (5,27TH)	5/3/63	2
Providence Church Rd, VA (15TH)	5/3/63	1
Port Hudson, LA (12TH)	5/27/63	1
Port Hudson, LA (12TH)	5/29/63	1
Port Hudson, LA (13,24TH)	6/14/63	2
Port Hudson, LA (12TH)	6/19/63	1
Gettysburg, PA (27TH) *1	7/2/63	8
Gettysburg, PA (20TH)	7/3/63	1
Fort Wagner, SC (6TH) *2	7/18/63	7

NEW HAVEN SOLDIERS KILLED AND *MISSING (Continued)

PLACE	DATE	NO.
James Island, SC (7TH)	8/16/63	1
Bristoe Station, VA (14TH)	10/14/63	1
Auburn, VA (14TH)	10/14/63	1
Morton's Ford, VA (14TH)	2/6/64	1
James River, VA (1 LB)	5/6/64	1
Wilderness, VA (14TH)	5/6/64	2
Spottsylvania, VA (14TH)	5/12/64	1
Wilderness, VA (10TH) *	5/12/64	1
Resaca, GA (5TH)	5/15/64	1
Drewry's Bluff, VA (7TH)	5/16/64	1
North Anna River, VA (14TH)	5/24/64	1
Dallas, GA (5TH)	5/25/64	1
Haer Court House, VA (1 CA)	5/31/64	1
Bermuda Hundred, VA (7TH)	5/31/64	1
Cold Harbor, VA (2 HA) *1	6/1/64	4
Cold Harbor, VA (11TH)	6/3/64	2
Cold Harbor, VA (14TH)	6/6/64	1
Bermuda Hundred, VA (6TH)	6/17/64	3
Petersburg, VA (11TH)	6/18/64	1
Ream's Station, VA (6TH,1 CA)	6/29/64	2
Peach Tree Creek, GA (5TH)	7/20/64	1
Peach Tree Creek, GA (20TH)	7/20/64	1
Petersburg, VA (30TH) *1	7/30/64	2
Petersburg, VA (1 HA)	7/30/64	1
Petersburg, VA (11TH)	8/13/64	1
Deep Run, VA (6TH)	8/16/64	1
Weldon Railroad, VA (6TH) *	8/19/64	1
Winchester, VA (12TH)	9/19/64	2
Cedar Creek, VA (9TH)	9/21/64	1
Darbytown Road, VA (10TH)	10/13/64	1
Cedar Creek, VA (12TH)	10/19/64	2
Ream's Station, VA (14TH) *	10/25/64	1
Kell House, VA (29TH)	10/27/64	3
Petersburg, VA (1 HA)	11/5/64	1
Cedar Creek, VA (1 CA) *	11/12/64	1
New Bern, NC (15TH)	12/27/64	1
Fort Fisher, NC (6TH)	1/16/65	1
Kinston, NC (15TH)	3/8/65	9
Unknown (Drowned) (12TH)	3/18/65	1
Bentonville, NC (20TH)	3/19/65	1
Harper's Farm, VA (1 CA)	4/6/65	2
Railroad Accident (15TH)	5/21/65	1

FOUR HUNDRED-NINETY FIVE WERE CAPTURED

Thirty seven New Haven soldiers died in captivity. Sixteen died at Andersonville Prison, GA, 7 died at Libby Prison, Richmond, VA, 7 died at Salisbury, NC, and one died at each of the following: Ashland, VA, Charleston, SC, Millen, GA, Petersburg, VA.

NEW HAVEN CAPTURED
*(37) DIED IN CAPTIVITY

PLACE	DATE	NO.
Unknown Place (14TH) *		1
Bull Run, VA (2ND,3RD)	7/21/61	2
Woodstock, VA (5TH)	4/21/62	1
Winchester, VA (5TH)	5/25/62	7
Cold Harbor, VA (1 HA) *1	6/27/62	3
Cold Harbor, VA (1 HA)	6/28/62	1
Near Richmond, VA (1 HA)	6/28/62	1
(WOUNDED)		
Gaines' Mills, VA (1 HA)	6/29/62	1
Haxall's Landing, VA (1 HA)	7/1/62	1
(WOUNDED)		
Madison C H, VA (1 CA)	7/29/62	2
Cedar Mountain, VA (5TH)	8/9/62	9
(1 WOUNDED)		
Culpeper, VA (5TH)	8/12/62	1
Fredericksburg, VA (27TH)	12/13/62	4
Dumfries, VA (20TH)	1/21/63	1
Pass Manchac, LA (9TH)	4/18/63	1
Chancellorsville, VA (5TH)	5/2/63	2
Chancellorsville, VA (5,20,27TH)	5/3/63	163
(5 WOUNDED) *2		
Alexandria, LA (12TH)	5/16/63	1
Winchester, VA (18TH)	6/15/63	1
Chattahoola Station, LA (9TH)	6/24/63	2
Port Hudson, LA (12TH,13TH) *1	6/27/63	2
Gettysburg, PA (5,27TH) *1	7/2/63	5
(1 WOUNDED)		
Danville, VA (5TH)	7/10/63	1
Fort Wagner, SC (7TH)	7/11/63	2
(1 WOUNDED)		
Bolivar Heights, VA (1 CA) *1	7/14/63	5
Fort Wagner, SC (6TH) *3	7/18/63	10
(2 WOUNDED)		
Culpeper, VA (14TH)	9/1/63	1
Bay St. Louis, MS (9TH) *	10/5/63	1
Fort Sumpter, SC (7TH)	10/10/63	1
Bristoe Station, VA (14TH) *3	10/14/63	5
Cedar Creek, VA (2 HA)	10/14/63	1
Rapidan, VA (14TH) *1	12/1/63	2
St Augustine, FL (10TH) *1	12/30/63	3

NEW HAVEN CAPTURED
*(38) DIED IN CAPTIVITY
(continued)

PLACE	DATE	NO.
Morton's Ford, VA (14TH) *	2/6/64	1
Richmond, VA (1 SQ) *	3/1/64	1
Grove Church, VA (1 CA)	3/29/64	1
(WOUNDED)		
Plymouth, NC (15, 16TH) *1	4/20/64	3
Plymouth, NC (15TH) *2	4/21/64	2
Craig's Church, VA (1 CA)	5/5/64	3
Winchester, VA (14TH) *	5/6/64	1
(WOUUNDED)		
Drewry's Bluff, VA (6,7,11TH) *7	5/16/64	22
(4 WOUNDED)		
Ashland, VA (1 CA) *2	6/1/64	2
(1 WOUNDED)		
Bermuda Hundred, VA (7TH) *2	6/2/64	3
(1 WOUNDED)		
Old Church Tav., VA (1 CA) *2	6/10/64	2
Cold Harbor, VA (2 HA)	6/14/64	1
Little Shop, VA (1 CA)	6/17/64	1
Ream's Station, VA (1 CA)	6/29/64	5
Unknown Place (1 LB)	7/10/64	1
Berryville, VA (1 CA) *	9/1/64	1
Winchester, VA (13TH)	9/19/64	2
Richmond, VA (6TH)	10/1/64	1
Darbytown Road, VA (7TH)	10/1/64	1
New Market Road, VA (7TH) *	10/1/64	1
Harrisonburg, VA (1 CA)	10/5/64	1
Darbytown Road, VA (10TH) *	10/13/64	1
Cedar Run Chrch, VA(1 CA) *1	10/17/64	2
Cedar Creek, VA (2HA,9,12TH)	10/19/64	18
(1 WOUNDED) *5		
Boydton Plank Rd, VA (14TH)	10/27/64	1
Stony Creek, VA (14TH)	10/27/64	1
Cedar Creek, VA (1 CA)	11/1/64	1
Cedar Creek, VA (1 CA) *1	11/12/64	4
Federal Point, NC (6TH)	1/18/65	1
Fort Fisher, NC (7TH)	1/19/65	1
Petersburg, VA (1 HA)	3/5/65	1
Kinston, NC (15TH) * 7	3/8/65	161
(22 WOUNDED)		
Petersburg, VA (1 HA)	3/25/65	1
Fort Stedman, VA (1 HA)	3/25/65	1
Appomattox CH, VA (10TH)	4/9/65	2

FOUR HUNDRED SIXTY-ONE WERE WOUNDED

The first New Haven soldiers wounded were Leonhardt Lyon of Rifle Company D, 1ST Connecticut Infantry and George C. Brandeau, Jacob Sneider of Company H, 3RD Connecticut Infantry. All were wounded at the First Battle of Bull Run, VA on July 21, 1861 and recovered from their wounds. Fifty-seven New Haven soldiers died from wounds received during the war.

NEW HAVEN WOUNDED
*(57) DIED FROM WOUNDS

PLACE	DATE	NO.
Unknown Place (1 CA)		1
Bull Run, VA (1ST, 3RD)	7/21/61	3
Stafford Court House, VA (20TH)	2/1/62	1
Roanoke Island, NC (10TH)	2/8/62	3
New Bern, NC (11TH)	3/1/62	1
Ship Island, MS (12TH)	3/12/62	1
Tybee Island, GA (7TH)	3/13/62	1
New Bern, NC (10TH)	3/14/62	2
Moorefield, VA (1 CA)	4/3/62	1
Unknown Place (10TH)	4/4/62	1
Savannah River, SC (6TH)	4/8/62	1
Malvern Hill, VA (1 HA) *	6/1/62	1
James Island, SC (7TH)	6/9/62	1
James Island, SC (6TH)	6/12/62	1
Hilton Head, SC (6TH)	6/15/62	1
James Island, SC (7TH) *1	6/16/62	9
Malvern Hill, VA (1 HA)	7/1/62	1
Cedar Mountain, VA (5TH) *3	8/9/62	7
Camp Parapet, LA (9TH)	9/8/62	1
Antietam, MD (11,14^{TH})	9/17/62	6
Antietam, MD (8TH)	9/17/62	1
St James Parish, LA (9TH)	10/1/62	1
Pocotaligo, SC (6,7^{TH}) *2	10/22/62	9
Arlington Heights, VA (27TH)	11/5/62	1
Thibodeaux, LA (13TH)	11/17/62	1
Fredericksburg, VA (15TH)	12/12/62	1
Fredericksburg, VA (14,15,27^{TH}) *12	12/13/62	67
Kinston, NC (10TH) *1	12/14/62	8
Fredericksburg, VA (15TH)	12/17/62	1
Falmouth, VA (27TH)	12/21/62	1
Brashear City, LA (12TH)	1/14/63	1
Jacksonville, FL (6TH)	3/1/63	1
Bethel Place, LA (12TH)	4/13/63	1
Bisland, LA (12TH)	4/13/63	1
Irish Bend, LA (13TH)	4/14/63	4
Edenton Road, VA (15TH)	4/24/63	1

NEW HAVEN WOUNDED
*(54) DIED FROM WOUNDS
(continued)

PLACE	DATE	NO.
Siege Suffolk, VA (15TH)	4/24/63	1
Chancellorsville, VA (5,14,20,27^{TH}) *2	5/3/63	20
Siege Suffolk, VA (15TH)	5/25/63	1
Port Hudson, LA (12TH)	5/27/63	1
Port Hudson, LA (12TH)	5/28/63	1
Port Hudson, LA (12TH)	6/10/63	5
Port Hudson, LA (12,13,24^{TH}) *1	6/14/63	6
Port Hudson, LA (13TH)	6/19/63	1
Brashear City, LA (23RD)	6/22/63	1
Chattahoola Station, LA (9TH)	6/24/63	2
Port Hudson, LA (24TH)	6/27/63	2
Fort Wagner, SC (6TH)	7/1/63	1
Morris Island, SC (10TH)	7/1/63	1
Gettysburg, PA (17TH)	7/1/63	1
Fort Lyon, VA (2 HA)	7/1/63	1
Fairfax, VA (1 CA)	7/1/63	1
Gettysburg, PA (27TH) *1	7/2/63	16
Gettysburg, PA (27TH)	7/3/63	1
Port Hudson, LA (12TH) *	7/3/63	1
Gettysburg, PA (20TH)	7/3/63	2
Gettysburg, PA (14TH)	7/3/63	1
Morris Island, SC (6,7^{TH})	7/10/63	4
Fort Wagner, SC (7TH)	7/11/63	1
Fort Wagner, SC (6TH) *2	7/18/63	23
Fort Wagner, SC (6TH)	7/25/63	1
Fort Wagner, SC (7TH)	9/5/63	1
Morris Island, SC (7TH)	9/7/63	1
Morris Island, SC (7TH)	9/20/63	1
Bay St. Louis, MS (9TH)	10/5/63	1
Bristoe Station, VA (14TH)	10/14/63	3
Summit Point, VA (12TH)	1/1/64	1
Morton's Ford, VA (14TH) *2	2/6/64	4
Olustee, FLA (7TH)	2/20/64	10
Olustee, FLA (7TH)	2/24/64	1
Cane River, LA (13TH) *1	4/23/64	3
Wilderness, VA (14TH)	5/6/64	5
Walthall Junction, VA (8TH)	5/7/64	1
Bermuda Hundred, VA (6TH)	5/9/64	1
Laurel Hill, VA (14TH)	5/10/64	2
Chester Station, VA (6TH) *	5/10/64	2
Drewry's Bluff, VA (6TH)	5/10/64	3
Spottsylvania, VA (1 CA,14TH)	5/12/64	3
Drewry's Bluff, VA (10TH)	5/13/64	1
Proctor's Creek, VA (1 LB)	5/14/64	2
Drewry's Bluff, VA (7,10^{TH})	5/14/64	7
Resaca, GA (20TH)	5/15/64	1
New Market, VA (18TH)	5/15/64	1

NEW HAVEN WOUNDED
*(54) DIED FROM WOUNDS
(continued)

PLACE	DATE	NO.
Resaca, GA (5TH)	5/15/64	4
Drewry's Bluff, VA (6,7,10TH)	5/16/64	9
Bermuda Hundred, VA (6TH)	5/18/64	1
Drewry's Bluff, VA (6TH)	5/20/64	1
Bermuda Hundred, VA (6,10TH)	5/20/64	6
Dallas, GA (5TH)	5/25/64	2
North Anna River, VA (14TH)	5/27/64	1
Haer Court House, VA (2 HA)	5/29/64	1
Haer Court House, VA (1 CA)	5/31/64	1
Ashland, VA (1 CA) *1	6/1/64	3
Cold Harbor, VA (2 HA)	6/1/64	9
Bermuda Hundred, VA (7TH)	6/2/64	3
Cold Harbor, VA (11TH) *	6/2/64	1
Cold Harbor, VA (14TH)	6/3/64	1
Cedar Creek, VA (12TH)	6/14/64	1
Hatcher's Run, VA (6TH)	6/17/64	1
Bermuda Hundred, VA	6/17/64	3
(1 CA, 6TH) *2		
Petersburg, VA (11TH) *1	6/18/64	2
Petersburg, VA (2 HA)	6/20/64	1
Bermuda Hundred, VA (6TH)	6/20/64	1
Culp's Farm, GA (5TH) *	6/22/64	1
Petersburg, VA (8TH)	6/25/64	1
Grand Gulf, MS (9TH)	6/26/64	1
Ream's Station, VA (1 CA)	6/29/64	1
Rockville, MD (1 CA)	7/12/64	1
Peach Tree Creek, GA (5TH)	7/19/64	1
Peach Tree Creek, GA (20TH) *2	7/20/64	4
Atlanta, GA (20TH)	7/24/64	1
Haxall's Landing, VA (10TH)	7/26/64	1
Petersburg, VA (11,30TH) *1	7/30/64	3
Petersburg, VA (1 HA) *	8/2/64	1
Petersburg, VA (1 HA)	8/5/64	1
Deep Bottom, VA (6,10TH) *1	8/14/64	3
Deep Run, VA (6,7TH)	8/14/64	3
Deep Run, VA (6,7,10TH) *2	8/16/64	6
Deep Bottom, VA (6TH)	8/16/64	1
Battery Morton, VA (1 HA)	8/17/64	1
Unknown Place (6TH)	8/24/64	1
Bolivar Heights, VA (9TH)	8/26/64	1
Unknown Place (29TH)	9/1/64	1
Petersburg, VA (6TH)	9/7/64	1
Petersburg, VA (10TH)	9/13/64	1
Winchester, VA *1	9/19/64	18
(1 CA,2 HA,12,13TH)		
Fisher's Hill, VA (9TH)	9/21/64	1
Fisher's Hill, VA (2 HA)	9/22/64	1
Deep Bottom, VA (7TH)	9/29/64	1

Fort Harrison, VA (8TH)	9/29/64	1
Chaffin's Farm, VA (29TH)	9/29/64	1
Petersburg, VA (29TH) *	9/30/64	1
Richmond, VA (29TH)	9/30/64	1
Richmond, VA (29TH)	10/1/64	1
Bunker's Hill, VA (1 CA)	10/6/64	1
Darbytown Road, VA (10TH)	10/13/64	4
Richmond, VA (29TH) *1	10/13/64	2
Cedar Creek, VA (9TH)	10/16/64	1
Cedar Creek, VA *1	10/19/64	11
(2 HA, 9,12TH)		
Petersburg, VA (1 HA)	10/24/64	1
Richmond, VA (6TH)	10/27/64	1
Strawberry Plains, VA (29TH)	10/27/64	1
Kell House, VA (29TH) *1	10/27/64	3
Boydton Plank Rd, VA (14TH) *	10/27/64	1
Darbytown Road, VA (10TH)	10/27/64	1
Cedar Creek, VA (1 CA)	11/12/64	1
Fort Fisher, NC (6TH)	1/15/65	1
Hatcher's Run, VA (2 HA)	2/6/65	1
Wilmington, NC (6TH)	2/22/65	1
Kinston, NC (15TH) *2	3/8/65	2
Averysboro, NC (20TH)	3/16/65	2
Silver Run, NC (20TH)	3/16/65	1
Petersburg, VA (1 HA)	3/25/65	1
Petersburg, VA (1 HA)	3/29/65	1
Hatcher's Run, VA (10TH) *1	3/31/65	2
Fort Gregg, VA (10TH) *2	4/2/65	9
Petersburg, VA (10TH, 2 HA)	4/2/65	3
Farmville, VA (1 CA)	4/3/65	1
South Side RR, VA (1 CA)	4/6/65	1
Sailor's Creek, VA (2 HA) *	4/6/65	1

NEW LONDON
THE POPULATION IN 1860 WAS 10,115 (RANK 5)

THE MOST IMPORTANT DAY OF THE CIVIL WAR

FEBRUARY 8, 1862

ROANOKE ISLAND, NC

THE OUTNUMBERED CONFEDERATES RETREATED

More soldiers credited to New London were listed as casualties (13) on this day than on any other day of the war. One soldier was killed and 12 were wounded in the 10TH Connecticut. Two of the wounded soldiers died.

The date February 8, 1862 ranks 42ND for total casualties (56) (4 killed, 52 wounded) for a single day for the State of Connecticut. All of the casualties were at Roanoke Island, NC.

The Battle of Roanoke Island (February 8, 1862) ranks 35TH for total casualties (56) for an engagement for the State of Connecticut.

The Battle of Roanoke Island with 13 total casualties for New London was the second highest number of casualties for any single engagement of the war for the town. The highest number of casualties for an engagement was the Siege of Port Hudson (May-July 1863) with 27.

In January 1862, Union General Ambrose E. Burnside led a naval expedition to North Carolina with a mission to enter Albemarle and Pimlico Sounds and to capture Roanoke Island. A battle ensued on February 8 and Burnside's 15,000 man army forced the Confederates to retreat to the northwest point of the island and 2,500 Confederates were captured.

576 MEN CREDITED TO NEW LONDON SERVED IN THE FOLLOWING CONNECTICUT ORGANIZATIONS

REGIMENT	TOTAL
26TH	138 (23%)
1ST HEAVY ARTILLERY	99 (17%)
14TH	67 (12%)
2ND	66 (11%)
10TH	52 (9%)
21ST	46 (8%)
12TH	44 (8%)
13TH	38 (7%)
5TH	24 (4%)
12TH BATTALION	23 (4%)
1ST CAVALRY	19 (3%)
13TH BATTALION	7 (1%)
29TH	7 (1%)
2ND HEAVY ARTILLERY	6 (1%)
8TH	5 (1%)
11TH	5 (1%)
30TH	5 (1%)
20TH	5 (1%)
18TH	4 (1%)
6TH	3
7TH	3
9TH	3
1ST LIGHT BATTERY	3
1ST	1
2ND LIGHT BATTERY	1
9TH BATTALION	1
15TH	1
17TH	1

6% OF POPULATION

EIGHTEEN WERE KILLED AND ONE WAS MISSING

The first New London soldier killed was Private Dwight T. Lester of Company H, 10TH Connecticut. He was killed at Roanoke Island, NC on February 8, 1862.

NEW LONDON SOLDIERS KILLED

PLACE	DATE	NO.
Roanoke Island, NC (10TH)	2/8/62	1
New Bern, NC (10TH)	3/14/62	1
New London, CT(Drowned) (10TH)	5/6/62	1
Cedar Mountain, VA (5TH)	8/9/62	1
Fredericksburg, VA (14TH)	12/13/62	3
Kinston, NC (10TH)	12/14/62	1
Irish Bend, LA (13TH)	4/14/63	1
Port Hudson, LA (26TH)	6/14/63	1
Port Hudson, LA (13TH)	6/14/63	1
Winchester, VA (18TH)	6/15/63	1
St. Augustine, FL (10TH) *	12/30/63	1
Wilderness, VA (14TH)	5/6/64	1
Peach Tree Creek, GA (5TH)	7/20/64	1
Deep Bottom, VA (10TH)	8/14/64	1
Petersburg, VA (21ST)	10/1/64	1
Hatcher's Run, VA (10TH)	3/13/65	1
Petersburg, VA (1 HA)	3/25/65	1

FIFTEEN WERE CAPTURED

One New London soldier died in captivity at Salisbury, NC.

NEW LONDON CAPTURED
*(1) DIED IN CAPTIVITY

PLACE	DATE	NO.
Bull Run, VA (2ND)	7/21/61	2
Winchester, VA (5TH)	5/25/62	2
Chancellorsville, VA (14TH)	5/3/63	1
Franklin, LA (12TH)	6/4/63	1
Burnt Ordinary (21ST)	7/9/63	1
Fort Wagner, SC (7TH)	7/11/63	1
Bristoe Station, VA (14TH)	10/14/63	1
Ashland, VA (1 CA)	6/1/64	1
Drewry's Bluff, VA (7TH)	5/16/64	1
Ream's Station, VA (14TH)	8/25/64	1
Cedar Creek, VA (12,13[TH])*1	10/19/64	3
(1 WOUNDED)		

TOTAL NEW LONDON CASUALTIES

DIED	60	10%
KILLED/MISSING	19	3%
WOUNDED	109	19%
CAPTURED	15	24%
DESERTED	65	11%

ONE HUNDRED-NINE WERE WOUNDED

The first New London soldiers wounded were at Roanoke Island, NC on February 8, 1862 and two died. Eighteen New London soldiers died from a wound received during the war.

NEW LONDON WOUNDED
*(18) DIED FROM WOUNDS

PLACE	DATE	NO.
Roanoke Island, NC (10TH) *2	2/8/62	12
New Bern, NC (10TH)	3/14/62	1
Richmond, VA (1 HA)	6/28/62	1
Sperryville, VA (1 CA)	8/6/62	1
Cedar Mountain, VA (5TH)	8/9/62	1
Beaufort, SC (1 LB)	9/1/62	1
Antietam, MD (11,14[TH]) *1	9/17/62	5
Pocotaligo, SC (7TH) *	10/22/62	1
Fredericksburg, VA (14,21[ST]) *1	12/13/62	6
Kinston, NC (10TH)	12/14/62	5
Newport News, VA (21ST)	1/18/63	1
Port Hudson, LA (26TH) *3	5/27/63	11
Port Hudson, LA (26TH)	5/28/63	1
Port Hudson, LA (12TH)	6/10/63	2
Port Hudson, LA (26TH)	6/13/63	1
Port Hudson, LA (13, 26TH) *2	6/14/63	10
Port Hudson, LA (13TH)	6/14/63	1
Gettysburg, PA (14TH)	7/3/63	1
Morris Island, SC (10TH)	7/26/63	1
Bristoe Station, VA (14TH) *	10/14/63	1
Morton's Ford, VA (14TH)	2/6/64	2
Cane River, LA (13TH)	4/23/64	2
Wilderness, VA (14TH)	5/6/64	1
Spottsylvania, VA (14TH)	5/10/64	1
Resaca, GA (5TH)	5/15/64	1
Drewry's Bluff, VA (6,8,10,21[ST])	5/16/64	5
North Anna River, VA (14TH)	5/24/64	1
Cold Harbor, VA (2 HA)	6/1/64	1
Ashland, VA (1 CA)	6/1/64	1
Cold Harbor, VA (2 HA)	6/2/64	1
Cold Harbor, VA (14TH)	6/3/64	1
Georgia (5TH)	6/3/64	1
Petersburg, VA (1 HA) *1	6/30/64	2
Petersburg, VA (21ST)	7/1/64	1
Petersburg, VA (1 HA)	7/2/64	1
Petersburg, VA (1 HA) *	7/10/64	1
Petersburg, VA (30, 21ST)	7/30/64	2
Deep Bottom, VA (10TH)	8/14/64	3
Petersburg, VA (10TH)	8/27/64	1
Winchester, VA (12,13[TH])	9/19/64	5
Chaffin's Farm, VA (21ST) *	9/29/64	1
Chaffin's Farm, VA (21ST)	9/30/64	1
Richmond, VA (29TH)	10/1/64	1
Battery Morton, VA (1 HA) *	10/12/64	1
Cedar Creek, VA (12, 13TH) *2	10/19/64	1
Boydton Plank Road, VA (14TH) *1	10/27/64	1
Petersburg, VA (1 HA)	3/29/65	1
Battery Anderson, VA (1 HA)	4/2/65	1

NEW MILFORD
THE POPULATION IN 1860 WAS 3,535 (RANK 26)

THE MOST IMPORTANT
DAY OF THE CIVIL WAR

JUNE 1, 1864

COLD HARBOR, VA

THE BATTLE WAS LEE'S
LAST GREAT VICTORY

More soldiers credited to New Milford were listed as casualties (14) on this day than on any other day of the war. Three soldiers were killed and 11 were wounded in the 2ND Connecticut Heavy Artillery. Two of the wounded died.

The date June 1, 1864 ranks 8TH for total casualties (374) (89 killed, 10 missing, 246 wounded, 23 captured, 6 wounded & captured) for a single day for the State of Connecticut. There were 324 casualties at Cold Harbor, VA, 41 casualties at Ashland, and 9 other casualties scattered about Virginia.

The battle and operations around Cold Harbor (May 31-June 12) rank 6TH for total casualties (557) for an engagement for the State of Connecticut The most intense fighting developed on June 3 and New Milford had one wounded on that day.

The Battle of Cold Harbor with 15 total casualties for New Milford was the highest number of casualties for any single engagement of the war for the town.

Approximately 117,000 Federal and 60,000 Confederate troops participated in operations from May 28 to June 3. Roughly 13,000 Union casualties were recorded and perhaps there were 5,000 Confederate casualties.

254 MEN CREDITED TO NEW MILFORD SERVED IN THE FOLLOWING CONNECTICUT ORGANIZATIONS

REGIMENT	TOTAL
2ND HEAVY ARTILLERY	88 (35%)
8TH	44 (17%)
28TH	37 (15%)
11TH	14 (6%)
13TH	14 (6%)
10TH	11 (4%)
29TH	11 (4%)
5TH	10 (4%)
6TH	7 (3%)
1ST HEAVY ARTILLERY	4 (2%)
7TH	4 (2%)
13TH BATTALION	4 (2%)
1ST CAVALRY	3 (1%)
14TH	3 (1%)
17TH	3 (1%)
20TH	3 (1%)
3RD	2
12TH	2
1ST LIGHT BATTERY	1
15TH	1

7% OF POPULATION

SIXTEEN WERE KILLED

The first New Milford soldiers killed were Sergeant David Lake, Corporal Henry Disbrow and Private George Birch of Company I, 8TH Connecticut. They were killed at The Battle of Antietam, MD on September 17, 1862.

NEW MILFORD SOLDIERS KILLED

PLACE	DATE	NO.
Antietam, MD (8TH)	9/17/62	3
Chancellorsville, VA (14TH)	5/3/63	1
Port Hudson, LA (28TH)	6/14/63	2
Swift's Creek, VA (8TH)	5/7/64	1
Cold Harbor, VA (2 HA)	6/1/64	3
Winchester, VA (2 HA)	9/19/64	1
Petersburg, VA (29TH)	9/23/64	1
Chaffin's Farm, VA (8TH)	9/29/64	1
Fort Harrison, VA (8TH)	9/29/64	2
Fort Gregg, VA (10TH)	4/2/65	1

FIVE WERE CAPTURED

One New Milford soldier died in captivity at Andersonville prison, GA.

NEW MILFORD CAPTURED
*(1) DIED IN CAPTIVITY

PLACE	DATE	NO.
Gordonsville, VA (1 CA)	8/7/62	1
((WOUNDED)		
Thoroughfare Gap, VA (1 CA)	3/7/63	1
Welaka, FL (17TH)	5/19/64	1
Ford's Mills, VA (2 HA) *	6/14/64	1
Cedar Creek, VA (1 CA)	11/12/64	1

TOTAL NEW MILFORD CASUALTIES

DIED	31	12%
KILLED	16	6%
WOUNDED	48	18%
CAPTURED	5	2%
DESERTED	50	20%

FORTY-SEVEN WERE WOUNDED

The first New Milford soldier wounded was Private Alvin Jennings of Company I, 8TH Connecticut. He was accidentally wounded at Jamaica, NY on October 21, 1861 and recovered from his wound. Two New Milford soldiers died from a wound received during the war.

NEW MILFORD WOUNDED
*(2) DIED FROM WOUNDS

PLACE	DATE	NO.
Jamaica, NY (8TH)	10/21/61	1
New Bern, NC (8TH)	3/14/62	1
Antietam, MD (8TH)	9/17/62	2
Alexandria, VA (2 HA)	11/20/62	1
Irish Bend, LA (13TH)	4/14/63	1
Fort Hugar, VA (8TH)	4/19/63	1
Port Hudson, LA (28TH)	6/14/63	2
Port Hudson, LA (28TH)	7/1/63	1
Petersburg, VA (2 HA)	4/1/64	1
Walthall Junction, VA (8TH)	5/7/64	1
Drewry's Bluff, VA (6TH)	5/16/64	1
Cold Harbor, VA (2 HA) *2	6/1/64	11
Cold Harbor, VA (2 HA)	6/3/64	1
Petersburg, VA (2 HA)	6/30/64	1
Petersburg, VA (2 HA)	8/31/64	1
Winchester, VA (2 HA,13TH)	9/19/64	6
Fort Harrison, VA (8TH)	9/29/64	2
Cedar Creek, VA (2 HA)	10/19/64	8
Fort Gregg, VA (10TH)	4/2/65	1
Sailor's Creek, VA (2 HA)	4/6/65	1
Atlanta, GA (13TH)	3/18/66	1

NEWTOWN
THE POPULATION IN 1860 WAS 3,578 (RANK 25)

THE MOST IMPORTANT DAY OF THE CIVIL WAR

JUNE 1, 1864

COLD HARBOR, VA

THE BATTLE WAS LEE'S LAST GREAT VICTORY

Soldiers credited to Newtown had more casualties on July 2, 1863 at Gettysburg, PA (5) and on June 1, 1864 at Cold Harbor, VA (5) than on any other days of the war. The casualties were the most serious at Cold Harbor. Two soldiers were killed and 3 were wounded in the 2ND Connecticut Heavy Artillery. The wounded survived the war.

The date June 1, 1864 ranks 8TH for total casualties (374) (89 killed, 10 missing, 246 wounded, 23 captured, 6 wounded & captured) for a single day for the State of Connecticut. There were 324 casualties at Cold Harbor, VA, 41 casualties at Ashland, and 9 other casualties scattered about Virginia.

The battle and operations around Cold Harbor (May 31-June 12) rank 6TH for total casualties (557) for an engagement for the State of Connecticut The most intense fighting developed on June 3 and Newtown had two wounded on that day. They also had one wounded on June 4.

The Battle of Cold Harbor with 8 total casualties for Newtown was the highest number of casualties for any single engagement of the war for the town.

Approximately 117,000 Federal and 60,000 Confederate troops participated in operations from May 28 to June 3. Roughly 13,000 Union casualties were recorded and perhaps there were 5,000 Confederate casualties.

234 MEN CREDITED TO NEWTOWN SERVED IN THE FOLLOWING CONNECTICUT ORGANIZATIONS

REGIMENT	TOTAL
23RD	45 (19%)
17TH	29 (12%)
2ND HEAVY ARTILLERY	23 (10%)
8TH	23 (10%)
11TH	19 (8%)
20TH	15 (6%)
13TH	13 (6%)
12TH	12 (5%)
1ST HEAVY ARTILLERY	9 (4%)
29TH	9 (4%)
5TH	7 (3%)
1ST CAVALRY	6 (3%)
7TH	6 (3%)
10TH	6 (3%)
6TH	4 (2%)
9TH	4 (2%)
12TH BATTALION	4 (2%)
3RD	3 (1%)
14TH	3 (1%)
15TH	3 (1%)
24TH	3 (1%)
2ND LIGHT BATTERY	2 (1%)
9TH BATTALION	2 (1%)
13TH BATTALION	2 (1%)
27TH	2 (1%)
3RD LIGHT BATTERY	1
30TH	1

7% OF POPULATION

EIGHT WERE KILLED AND TWO WERE MISSING

The first Newtown soldier killed was Sergeant David Andress of Company A, 11TH Connecticut. He was killed at Suffolk, VA on April 24, 1863.

NEWTOWN SOLDIERS KILLED MISSING *

PLACE	DATE	NO.
Suffolk, VA (11TH)	4/24/63	1
Chancellorsville, VA (20TH)	5/3/63	1
Port Hudson, LA (12TH)	5/27/63	1
Bayou Boeuf, LA (23RD)	6/6/63	1
Gettysburg, PA (17TH)	7/1/63	1
Gettysburg, PA (17TH) *	7/2/63	1
Cold Harbor, VA (2HA) *1	6/1/64	2
Cold Harbor, VA (8TH)	6/2/64	1
Petersburg, VA (8TH)	7/11/64	1

TWENTY-FIVE WERE CAPTURED

Two Newtown soldiers died in captivity. One died at Andersonville Prison, GA and one at Salisbury, NC.

NEWTOWN CAPTURED
*(2) DIED IN CAPTIVITY

PLACE	DATE	NO.
Moorefield, VA (1CA)	6/22/62	1
Chancellorsville, VA (17TH)	5/2/63	3
(1 WOUNDED)		
LaFourche, LA (23RD)	6/24/63	2
Gettysburg, PA (17TH)	7/1/63	1
(WOUNDED)		
Gettysburg, PA (17TH)	7/2/63	4
(1 WOUNDED)		
Bristoe Station, VA (14TH)	10/14/63	1
Drewry's Bluff, VA (8TH)	5/16/64	2
(1 WOUNDED)		
White Oak Swamp, VA (1CA)*	6/15/64	1
Fort Powhatan, VA (8TH)	9/19/64	1
Winchester, VA (2HA) *1	9/19/64	2
Cedar Creek, VA (12,13TH)	10/19/64	4
Dunn's Lake, FL (17TH)	2/5/65	1
Kinston, NC (15TH)	3/8/65	2

TOTAL NEWTOWN CASUALTIES

DIED	23	10%
KILLED/MISSING	10	4%
WOUNDED	30	13%
CAPTURED	25	11%
DESERTED	34	15%

THIRTY WERE WOUNDED

The first Newtown soldier wounded was Corporal George W. Ramsay of Company A, 10TH Connecticut. He was wounded at Roanoke Island, NC on February 8, 1862 and recovered from his wound. Four Newtown soldiers died from a wound received during the war.

NEWTOWN WOUNDED
*(4) DIED FROM WOUNDS

PLACE	DATE	NO.
Roanoke Island, NC (10TH)	2/8/62	1
Antietam, MD (8,11TH)	9/17/62	3
Chantilly, VA (17TH)	12/5/62	1
Fredricksburg, VA (11TH)	12/13/62	1
Chancellorsville, VA (17TH)	5/2/63	1
Port Hudson, LA (12TH)	6/10/63	2
Gettysburg, PA (20TH) *	7/3/63	1
Morris Island, SC (7TH)	10/8/63	1
Lakeport, LA (12TH)	4/8/64	1
Walthall Junction, VA (8TH)	5/7/64	1
Resaca, GA (5TH)	5/15/64	1
Drewry's Bluff, VA (8TH)	5/16/64	1
Virginia (7TH)	5/18/64	1
Cold Harbor, VA (2HA)	6/1/64	3
Cold Harbor, VA (8,11TH) *1	6/3/64	2
Cold Harbor, VA (8TH)	6/4/64	1
Peach Tree Creek, GA (20TH)	7/20/64	1
Winchester, VA (13TH) *1	9/19/64	2
Darbytown Road, VA (29TH)*	10/13/64	1
Kell House, VA (29TH)	10/27/64	1
Hatcher's Run, VA (2HA)	2/6/65	1
Kinston, NC (15TH)	3/8/65	1
Bentonville, NC (20TH)	3/19/65	1

NORFOLK
THE POPULATION IN 1860 WAS 1,803 (RANK 81)

THE MOST IMPORTANT
DAY OF THE CIVIL WAR

JUNE 1, 1864

COLD HARBOR, VA

THE BATTLE WAS LEE'S
LAST GREAT VICTORY

More soldiers credited to Norfolk were listed as casualties (7) on this day than on any other day of the war. Two soldiers were missing (killed) and 5 were wounded in the 2ND Connecticut Heavy Artillery. Two of the wounded died.

The date June 1, 1864 ranks 8TH for total casualties (374) (89 killed, 10 missing, 246 wounded, 23 captured, 6 wounded & captured) for a single day for the State of Connecticut. There were 324 casualties at Cold Harbor, 41 casualties at Ashland,and 9 other casualties scattered about Virginia.

The battle and operations around Cold Harbor (May 31-June 12) rank 6TH for total casualties (557) for an engagement for the State of Connecticut. The most intense fighting developed on June 3. Norfolk had 1 killed and 4 wounded.

The Battle of Cold Harbor with 12 total casualties for Norfolk was the highest number of casualties for any single engagement of the war for the town.

Approximately 117,000 Federal and 60,000 Confederate troops participated in operations from May 28 to June 3. Roughly 13,000 Union casualties were recorded and perhaps there were 5,000 Confederate casualties.

145 MEN CREDITED TO NORFOLK SERVED IN THE FOLLOWING CONNECTICUT ORGANIZATIONS

REGIMENT	TOTAL
11TH	48 (33%)
2ND HEAVY ARTILLERY	34 (23%)
5TH	11 (8%)
2ND	10 (7%)
1ST HEAVY ARTILLERY	7 (5%)
6TH	6 (4%)
7TH	6 (4%)
9TH	6 (4%)
10TH	6 (4%)
29TH	5 (3%)
1ST SQUADRON CAVALRY	4 (3%)
1ST CAVALRY	3 (2%)
9TH BATTALION	2 (1%)
14TH	2 (1%)
20TH	2 (1%)
28TH	2 (1%)
3RD	1
17TH	1

8% OF POPULATION

SEVEN WERE KILLED AND TWO WERE MISSING

The first Norfolk soldiers killed were Corporal Theodore S. Bates and Privates Theodore Parreit and Benjamin J. Beach of Company E, 11TH Connecticut. They were killed at The Battle of Antietam, MD on September 17, 1862.

NORFOLK SOLDIERS KILLED MISSING *

PLACE	DATE	NO.
Antietam, MD (11TH)	9/17/62	3
Drewry's Bluff, VA (7TH)	5/14/64	1
Cold Harbor, VA (2 HA) *	6/1/64	2
Cold Harbor, VA (11TH)	6/3/64	1
Petersburg, VA (11TH)	7/30/64	1
Petersburg, VA (11TH)	8/21/64	1

EIGHT WERE CAPTURED

Two Norfolk soldiers died in captivity. One died at Libby Prison Richmond, VA and one died at Salisbury, NC.

NORFOLK CAPTURED *(2) DIED IN CAPTIVITY

PLACE	DATE	NO.
Chancellorsville, VA (5TH)	5/3/63	1
Brashear City, LA (1 SQ)	6/9/63	1
Rapidan, VA (14TH) *	12/1/63	1
Drewry's Bluff, VA (11TH)	5/16/64	2
(WOUNDED)		
Bermuda Hundred, VA (7TH)	6/17/64	1
Cedar Run Church, VA (1 CA)	10/17/64	1
Cedar Creek, VA (2 HA) *	10/19/64	1

TOTAL NORFOLK CASUALTIES

DIED	21	14%
KILLED/MISSING	9	6%
WOUNDED	30	21%
CAPTURED	8	6%
DESERTED	12	8%

THIRTY WERE WOUNDED

The first Norfolk soldiers wounded were Corporal Daniel A. Keyes and Private John D. Barden of the 5TH Connecticut. They were wounded at Cedar Mountain, VA on August 9, 1862 and both recovered from their wounds. Eight Norfolk soldiers died from a wound received during the war.

NORFOLK WOUNDED *(8) DIED FROM WOUNDS

PLACE	DATE	NO.
Cedar Mountain, VA (5TH)	8/9/62	2
Antietam, MD (11TH) *1	9/17/62	3
Fredericksburg, VA (14TH)	12/13/62	1
Port Hudson, LA (28TH) *	6/14/63	1
Fort Wagner, SC (7TH)	7/11/63	1
Morris Island, SC (7TH)	10/14/63	1
Rapidan, VA (1 SQ) *	3/1/64	1
Petersburg, VA (11TH)	5/15/64	1
Drewry's Bluff, VA (11TH)	5/16/64	1
Cold Harbor, VA (2 HA) *2	6/1/64	5
Cold Harbor, VA (2 HA,11TH) *1	6/3/64	4
Culp's Farm, GA (5TH)	6/22/64	1
Petersburg, VA (11TH)	6/22/64	1
Petersburg, VA (11TH) *	6/28/64	1
Winchester, VA (2 HA) *	9/19/64	1
Cedar Creek, VA (2 HA)	10/19/64	2
Hatcher's Run, VA (10TH)	4/2/65	1
Fort Gregg, VA (10TH)	4/2/65	1
Sailor's Creek, VA (2 HA)	4/6/65	1

NORTH BRANFORD
THE POPULATION IN 1860 WAS 2,295 (RANK 53)

**THE MOST IMPORTANT DAY
OF THE CIVIL WAR**

MARCH 8, 1865

KINSTON, NC

**THE CONFEDERATE
ATTACK STALLED**

More soldiers credited to North Branford were listed as casualties (5) on this day than on any other day of the war. Five soldiers were captured in the 15TH Connecticut. All survived the war.

The date March 8, 1865 ranks 5TH for total casualties (496) (22 killed, 3 missing, 12 wounded, 410 captured, 49 wounded & captured) for a single day for the State of Connecticut. There were 494 casualties at Kinston, 1 casualty in Virginia, and 1 casualty at a railroad accident in an unknown place.

The Second Battle of Kinston (March 8, 1865) ranks 8TH for total casualties (494) for an engagement for the State of Connecticut.

The Second Battle of Kinston with 5 total casualties for North Branford was the highest number of casualties for any single engagement of the war for the town.

The military situation in North Carolina changed in early 1865. The Confederate forces in eastern North Carolina were called to help stop the advance of the Union Army coming out of Georgia with Union General William T. Sherman. The Confederates attempted to seize the initiative by attacking the Union flanks near Kinston on March 8 and failed.

**68 MEN CREDITED TO
NORTH BRANFORD SERVED
IN THE FOLLOWING
CONNECTICUT
ORGANIZATIONS**

REGIMENT	TOTAL
15TH	18 (26%)
27TH	9 (13%)
1ST HEAVY ARTILLERY	9 (13%)
7TH	8 (12%)
11TH	7 (10%)
10TH	5 (7%)
12TH	3 (4%)
13TH	3 (4%)
20TH	3 (4%)
1ST CAVALRY	2 (3%)
2ND	2 (3%)
1ST LIGHT BATTERY	1
2ND HEAVY ARTILLERY	1
13TH BATTALION	1
14TH	1

6% OF POPULATION

NO NORTH BRANFORD SOLDIERS WERE KILLED IN THE WAR

TWELVE WERE CAPTURED

One North Branford soldier died in captivity at Salisbury, NC.

NORTH BRANFORD CAPTURED
*(1) DIED IN CAPTIVITY

PLACE	DATE	NO.
Cold Harbor, VA (1 HA)	6/27/62	1
Chancellorsville, VA (27TH)	5/3/63	4
Drewry's Bluff, VA (7TH)	5/16/64	1
Cedar Creek, VA (12TH) *	10/19/64	1
Kinston, NC (15TH)	3/8/65	5

TOTAL NORTH BRANFORD CASUALTIES

DIED	9	13%
KILLED	0	0%
WOUNDED	11	16%
CAPTURED	12	18%
DESERTED	4	6%

ELEVEN WERE WOUNDED

The first North Branford soldier wounded was Private Josiah Johnson of Company B, 27TH Connecticut. He was wounded at Fredericksburg, VA on December 13, 1862 and recovered from his wound. Four North Branford soldiers died from a wound received during the war.

NORTH BRANFORD WOUNDED
*(4) DIED FROM WOUNDS

PLACE	DATE	NO.
Fredericksburg, VA (27TH) *	12/13/62	1
Kinston, NC (10TH) *1	12/14/62	2
Irish Bend, LA (13TH)	4/14/63	1
Port Hudson, LA (12TH) *	6/14/63	1
Strawberry Plains, VA (10TH)	7/26/64	1
Petersburg, VA (1 HA)	8/6/64	1
Winchester, VA (12TH)	9/19/64	1
Darbytown Road, VA (10TH)	10/13/64	1
Fort Gregg, VA (10TH) *	4/2/65	2

NORTH CANAAN
THE POPULATION IN 1860 WAS ESTIMATED AT 2,060

THE MOST IMPORTANT DAY OF THE CIVIL WAR

SEPTEMBER 17, 1862

SHARPSBURG, MD (ANTIETAM)

CONNECTICUT HAD MORE CASUALTIES FOR ONE DAY THAN ON ANY OTHER DAY OF THE WAR

More soldiers credited to North Canaan were listed as casualties (6) on this day than on any other day of the war. Six soldiers in the 11TH Connecticut were wounded. All survived the war.

The date September 17, 1862 ranks 1ST for total casualties (687) (131 killed, 2 missing, 515 wounded, 21 captured, 18 wounded & captured) for a single day for the State of Connecticut. All of the casualties were at Antietam.

The Battle of Antietam (September 16-17, 1862) ranks 1ST for total casualties (689) for an engagement for the State of Connecticut. The most intense fighting developed on September 17. North Canaan had all of its casualties on that day.

The Battle of Antietam with 6 total casualties for North Canaan was the highest number of casualties for any single engagement of the war for the town.

Roughly 12,400 Union casualties were recorded and perhaps there were 10,300 Confederate casualties. Antietam proved to be one of the turning points of the war. It ended Lee's 1862 invasion of the North.

104 MEN CREDITED TO NORTH CANAAN SERVED IN THE FOLLOWING CONNECTICUT ORGANIZATIONS

REGIMENT	TOTAL
2ND HEAVY ARTILLERY	35 (34%)
11TH	22 (22%)
7TH	11 (11%)
1ST CAVALRY	9 (9%)
1ST HEAVY ARTILLERY	7 (7%)
9TH	5 (5%)
8TH	4 (4%)
14TH	4 (4%)
23RD	3 (3%)
5TH	2 (2%)
9TH BATTALION	2 (2%)
10TH	2 (2%)
13TH BATTALION	2 (2%)
3RD LIGHT BATTERY	1
6TH	1
13TH	1
17TH	1
29TH	1

5% OF POPULATION

THREE WERE KILLED

The first North Canaan soldier killed was Private Clark Decker of Company I, 11TH Connecticut. He was killed at New Bern, NC on March 14, 1862.

NORTH CANAAN SOLDIERS KILLED

PLACE	DATE	NO.
New Bern, NC (11TH)	3/14/62	1
Cold Harbor, VA (2 HA)	6/1/64	1
Culp's Farm, GA (5TH)	6/22/64	1

ONE WAS CAPTURED

No North Canaan soldiers died in captivity.

NORTH CANAAN CAPTURED NONE DIED IN CAPTIVITY

PLACE	DATE	NO.
Ashland, VA (1 CA)	3/15/65	1

TOTAL NORTH CANAAN CASUALTIES

DIED	13	13%
KILLED	3	3%
WOUNDED	25	24%
CAPTURED	1	1%
DESERTED	17	16%

TWENTY-FIVE WERE WOUNDED

The first North Canaan soldier wounded was Private Robert Gardner of Company F, 7TH Connecticut. He was wounded at James Island, SC on June 16, 1862 and recovered from his wound. Three North Canaan soldiers died from a wound received during the war.

NORTH CANAAN WOUNDED *(3) DIED FROM WOUNDS

PLACE	DATE	NO.
James Island, SC (7TH)	6/16/62	2
Antietam, MD (11TH)	9/17/62	6
Morris Island, SC (7TH)	7/19/63	1
Bristoe Station, VA (14TH)	10/14/63	1
Dallas, GA (5TH)	5/25/64	1
Cold Harbor, VA (2 HA) *	6/1/64	1
Petersburg, VA (11TH)	6/16/64	1
Petersburg, VA (11TH)	6/18/64	1
Petersburg, VA (2 HA) *	6/20/64	1
Petersburg, VA (2 HA)	6/22/64	1
Petersburg, VA (2 HA)	7/2/64	1
Deep Run, VA (7TH)	8/16/64	1
Winchester, VA (2 HA) *1	9/19/64	3
Petersburg, VA (7TH)	8/25/64	1
Fisher's Hill, VA (2 HA)	9/21/64	1
Cedar Creek, VA (2 HA)	10/19/64	2

NORTH HAVEN
THE POPULATION IN 1860 WAS 1,865 (RANK 79)

THE MOST IMPORTANT DAY OF THE CIVIL WAR

MAY 3, 1863

CHANCELLORSVILLE, VA

THE THIRD DAY OF THE BATTLE

More soldiers credited to North Haven were listed as casualties (4) on this day than on any other day of the war. Four soldiers in the 27TH Connecticut were captured. All survived the war.

The date May 3, 1863 ranks 3RD for total casualties (577) (36 killed, 1 missing, 138 wounded, 372 captured, 29 wounded & captured) for a single day for the State of Connecticut. The most casualties were at Chancellorsville, VA (556). The other casualties were at Providence Church Road, VA (12), Suffolk, VA (6), Port Hudson, LA (2) and Fredericksburg, VA (1).

The Battle of Chancellorsville (May 1-3, 1863) ranks 2ND for total casualties (677) for an engagement for the State of Connecticut. The most intense fighting developed on May 3. North Haven had no other casualties in the battle other than on May 3.

The Battle of Chancellorsville with 4 total casualties for North Haven was the highest number of casualties for any single engagement of the war for the town.

The Battle of Chancellorsville was an enormous defeat for the more than 70,000 Union soldiers who had moved against the flank and rear of 40,000 Confederate soldiers. Unfortunately, the Union Army had pulled back and had gone on the defensive around Chancellorsville. The Confederate victory was tainted however, by the loss of Confederate Major General "Stonewall" Jackson.

102 MEN CREDITED TO NORTH HAVEN SERVED IN THE FOLLOWING CONNECTICUT ORGANIZATIONS

REGIMENT	TOTAL
15TH	39 (38%)
11TH	13 (13%)
1ST HEAVY ARTILLERY	8 (8%)
27TH	8 (8%)
10TH	7 (7%)
7TH	6 (6%)
2ND HEAVY ARTILLERY	4 (4%)
6TH	4 (4%)
1ST CAVALRY	3 (3%)
5TH	3 (3%)
8TH	2 (2%)
12TH	2 (2%)
2ND	1
14TH	1
20TH	1
23RD	1
29TH	1

9% OF POPULATION

SEVEN WERE KILLED

The first North Haven soldier killed was Corporal Joseph O. Blair of Company C, 5TH Connecticut. He was killed on August 9, 1862 at Cedar Mountain, VA.

NORTH HAVEN SOLDIERS KILLED

PLACE	DATE	NO.
Cedar Mountain, VA (5TH)	8/9/62	1
Pocotaligo, SC (7TH)	10/22/62	1
Kinston, NC (10TH)	12/14/62	1
Drewry's Bluff, VA (11TH)	5/16/64	2
Peach Tree Creek, GA (5TH)	7/20/64	1
Darbytown Road, VA (10TH)	10/13/64	1

ELEVEN WERE CAPTURED

No North Haven soldiers died in captivity.

NORTH HAVEN CAPTURED
NONE DIED IN CAPTIVITY

PLACE	DATE	NO.
Chancellorsville, VA (27TH)	5/3/63	4
Craig's Church, VA (1 CA)	5/5/64	1
Walthall Junction, VA (8TH)	5/7/64	1
Bermuda Hundred, VA (7TH)	6/17/64	1
Petersburg, VA (11TH)	6/18/64	1
Kinston, NC (15TH)	3/8/65	3
(1 WOUNDED)		

TOTAL NORTH HAVEN CASUALTIES

DIED	11	11%
KILLED	7	7%
WOUNDED	8	8%
CAPTURED	11	11%
DESERTED	16	16%

EIGHT WERE WOUNDED

The first North Haven soldier wounded was Private Theodore Bradley of Company H, 7TH Connecticut. He was wounded at James Island, SC on June 16, 1862 and recovered from his wound. One North Haven soldier died from a wound received during the war.

NORTH HAVEN WOUNDED
*(1) DIED FROM WOUNDS

PLACE	DATE	NO.
James Island, SC (7TH) *	6/16/62	1
Kinston, NC (10TH)	12/14/62	1
Laurel Hill, VA (14TH)	5/10/64	1
Bermuda Hundred, VA (7TH)	5/31/64	1
Cold Harbor, VA (2 HA)	6/1/64	1
Deep Bottom, VA (7TH)	8/16/64	1
Richmond, VA (29TH)	9/29/64	1
Fort Gregg, VA (10TH)	4/2/65	1

NORTH STONINGTON
THE POPULATION IN 1860 WAS 1,913 (RANK 78)

THE MOST IMPORTANT DAY OF THE CIVIL WAR

MAY 16, 1864

DREWRY'S BLUFF , VA

AN OBSTACLE ON THE WAY TO RICHMOND

More soldiers credited to North Stonington were listed as casualties (13) on this day than on any other day of the war. Three soldiers were wounded and 10 were captured in the 11TH and 21ST Connecticut. Five of the captured died in prison.

The date May 16, 1864 ranks 4th for total casualties (560) (52 killed, 3 missing, 224 wounded, 243 captured, 38 wounded & captured) for a single day for the State of Connecticut. The Battle of Drewry's Bluff accounted for 545 casualties. The 15 other casualties were scattered about Virginia.

The Battle of Drewry's Bluff (May 13-17, 1864), also called Fort Darling, ranks 3rd for total casualties (634) for an engagement for the State of Connecticut. The most intense fighting developed on May 16. North Stonington had all of its casualties on that day.

The Battle of Drewry's Bluff with 13 total casualties for North Stoning-ton was the highest number of casualties for any single engagement of the war for the town.

The Confederate attack at Drewry's Bluff forced the Union Army to retreat to Bermuda Hundred. The civil war would have concluded sooner had the Union Army been victorious.

138 MEN CREDITED TO NORTH STONINGTON SERVED IN THE FOLLOWING CONNECTICUT ORGANIZATIONS

REGIMENT	TOTAL
21ST	67 (49%)
29TH	25 (18%)
14TH	9 (7%)
11TH	7 (5%)
1ST CAVALRY	4 (3%)
8TH	4 (3%)
1ST HEAVY ARTILLERY	3 (2%)
2ND HEAVY ARTILLERY	3 (2%)
12TH	3 (2%)
15TH	3 (2%)
25TH	3 (2%)
3RD	2 (2%)
5TH	2 (2%)
7TH	2 (2%)
10TH	2 (2%)
13TH	2 (2%)
26TH	2 (2%)
6TH	1
12TH BATTALION	1
13TH BATTALION	1

7% OF POPULATION

FOUR WERE KILLED

The first North Stonington soldier killed was Private James M. Brown of Company G, 14TH Connecticut. He was killed at Cold Harbor, VA on June 9, 1864.

NORTH STONINGTON SOLDIERS KILLED

PLACE	DATE	NO.
Cold Harbor, VA (14TH)	6/9/64	1
Darbytown Road, VA (29TH)	10/13/64	1
Cedar Creek, VA (12TH)	10/19/64	1
Brownsville, TX (29TH)	7/5/65	1

SEVENTEEN WERE CAPTURED

Six North Stonington soldiers died in captivity. Two died at Florence, SC, one at Andersonville Prison, GA, one at Charleston, SC, one at Libby Prison Richmond, VA and one at Wilmington, NC.

NORTH STONINGTON CAPTURED *(6) DIED IN CAPTIVITY

PLACE	DATE	NO.
Sherman Mills, VA (21ST) *	7/11/63	1
Drewry's Bluff, VA (11,21ST)*5	5/16/64	10
Smithfield, VA (21ST)	2/1/64	1
(WOUNDED)		
Cold Harbor, VA (21ST)	6/3/64	1
Cedar Creek, VA (12TH)	10/19/64	1
Cedar Creek, VA (1 CA)	11/7/64	1
Cedar Creek, VA (1 CA)	11/12/64	1
Kinston, NC (15TH)	3/8/65	1

TOTAL NORTH STONINGTON CASUALTIES

DIED	26	19%
KILLED/MISSING	4	3%
WOUNDED	29	21%
CAPTURED	17	12%
DESERTED	14	10%

TWENTY-NINE WERE WOUNDED

The first North Stonington soldier wounded was Sergeant Burrows Partello of Company G, 5TH Connecticut. He was wounded at Chan-cellorsville, VA on May 3, 1863 and died from his wound. Three North Stonington soldiers died from a wound received during the war.

NORTH STONINGTON WOUNDED *(3) DIED FROM WOUNDS

PLACE	DATE	NO.
Chancellorsville, VA (5TH) *	5/3/63	1
Port Hudson, LA (26TH)	5/27/63	2
Morton's Ford, VA (14TH)	2/6/64	2
Drewry's Bluff, VA (21ST)	5/16/64	3
Hanover Junction, VA (14TH)	5/24/64	1
Dallas, GA (5TH)	5/25/64	1
Cold Harbor, VA (8TH)	6/1/64	1
Cold Harbor, VA (8,21ST) *1	6/3/64	2
Petersburg, VA (21ST)	6/26/64	1
Petersburg, VA (21ST)	7/1/64	1
Petersburg, VA (29TH)	8/29/64	1
Fort Harrison, VA (29TH)	9/1/64	1
Petersburg, VA (29TH)	9/3/64	1
Winchester, VA (12TH)	9/19/64	1
Winchester, VA (2 HA)	9/22/64	1
Chaffin's Farm, VA (21ST)	9/29/64	2
Chaffin's Farm, VA (21ST)	9/30/64	1
Darbytown Road, VA (29TH)	10/13/64	1
Kell House, VA (29TH) *1	10/27/64	5

498

NORWALK
THE POPULATION IN 1860 WAS 7,582 (RANK 8)

THE MOST IMPORTANT DAY OF THE CIVIL WAR

MAY 2, 1863
CHANCELLORSVILLE, VA

THE SECOND DAY OF THE BATTLE

More soldiers credited to Norwalk were listed as casualties (24) on this day than any other day of the war. Two soldiers were killed, 8 were wounded, 11 were captured, and 3 were wounded & captured in the 5TH and 17TH Connecticut. The wounded and captured survived the war.

The date May 2, 1863 ranks 22ND for total casualties (121) (8 killed, 30 wounded, 62 captured, 21 wounded & captured) for the State of Connecticut. All of the casualties were at Chancellorsville.

The Battle of Chancellorsville (May1-3, 1863) ranks 2ND for total casualties (677) for an engagement for the State of Connecticut. The most intense fighting developed on May 3. Norwalk had 13 casualties on that day.

The Battle of Chancellorsville with 36 total casualties for Norwalk was the highest number of casualties for any single engagement of the war for the city.

The Battle of Chancellorsville was an enormous defeat for the more than 70,000 Union soldiers who had moved against the flank and rear of 40,000 Confederate soldiers. Unfortunately, the Union Army had pulled back and had gone on the defensive around Chancellorsville. The Confederate victory was tainted however, by the loss of Confederate Major General "Stonewall" Jackson.

750 MEN CREDITED TO NORWALK SERVED IN THE FOLLOWING CONNECTICUT ORGANIZATIONS

REGIMENT	TOTAL
17TH	214 (29%)
3RD	83 (11%)
28TH	62 (8%)
8TH	61 (8%)
5TH	60 (8%)
6TH	59 (8%)
12TH	43 (6%)
2ND HEAVY ARTILLERY	32 (4%)
29TH	31 (4%)
1ST HEAVY ARTILLERY	30 (4%)
14TH	26 (3%)
7TH	22 (3%)
12TH BATTALION	19 (3%)
27TH	18 (3%)
1ST CAVALRY	17 (2%)
10TH	15 (2%)
13TH	15 (2%)
3RD LIGHT BATTERY	14 (2%)
11TH	10 (1%)
1ST	9 (1%)
15TH	5 (1%)
23RD	3
2ND LIGHT BATTERY	3
9TH	2
9TH BATTALION	2
20TH	2
2ND	1
13TH BATTALION	1
21ST	1
30TH	1

10% OF POPULATION

TWENTY-ONE WERE KILLED AND TWO WERE MISSING

The first Norwalk soldier killed was Private Thomas Hooton of Company D, 7TH Connecticut. He was killed at James Island, SC on June 16, 1862.

NORWALK SOLDIERS KILLED MISSING*

PLACE	DATE	NO.
James Island, SC (7TH)	6/16/	1
Cedar Mountain, VA (5TH)	8/9/62	3
Antietam, MD (11TH)	9/17/62	1
Fredricksburg, VA (27TH) *	12/13/62	1
Chancellorsville, VA (17TH)	5/2/63	2
Port Hudson, LA (12TH)	6/10/63	1
Brashear City, LA (12TH)	6/23/63	1
Gettysburg, PA (17TH)	7/1/63	2
Gettysburg, PA (17TH)	7/2/63	2
Drewry's Bluff, VA (7TH)	5/16/64	1
Cold Harbor, VA (2HA)	6/1/64	1
Cold Harbor, VA (8TH)	6/3/64	1
Bermuda Hun., VA (7TH)	6/17/64	1
James River, VA (Drowned) (6TH)	7/7/64	1
Winchester, VA (13TH)	9/19/64	1
Richmond, VA (29TH)	10/27/64	1
Fort Gregg, VA (10TH)	4/2/65	1
Petersburg, VA (10TH) *	4/15/65	1

TOTAL NORWALK CASUALTIES

DIED	62	8%
KILLED/MISSING	23	3%
WOUNDED	112	15%
CAPTURED	85	11%
DESERTED	84	11%

EIGHTY-FIVE WERE CAPTURED

Six Norwalk soldiers died in captivity. Five died at Andersonville Prison, GA and one died at Florence, SC.

NORWALK CAPTURED *(6) DIED IN CAPTIVITY

PLACE	DATE	NO.
Bull Run, VA (3RD)	7/21/61	1
Winchester, VA (5TH)	5/25/62	1
Cedar Moutain, VA (5TH)	8/9/62	6
(2 WOUNDED)		
Chancellorsville, VA (17TH)	5/2/63	14
(3 WOUNDED)		
Chancellorsville, VA (17,27TH)	5/3/63	11
(1 WOUNDED)		
Port Hudson, LA (28TH)	6/14/63	2
Gettysburg, PA (17TH)	7/1/63	11
(1 WOUNDED)		
Gettysburg, PA (17TH)	7/2/63	4
Darnesville, MD (5TH)	7/11/63	1
Bristoe Station, VA (14TH)	10/14/63	1
Olustee, FLA (7TH) *	2/20/64	1
Graig's Church, VA (1CA)	5/5/64	1
Spottyslvania, VA (14TH) *	5/12/64	2
Fort Darling, VA (8TH)	5/16/64	2
Drewry's Bluff, VA (6,7TH) *2	5/16/64	5
Petersburg, VA (2HA) *	6/19/64	1
Fort Harrison, VA (8TH)	9/29/64	1
Darbytown Road, VA (10TH)	10/13/64	1
(WOUNDED)		
Cedar Creek, VA (2HA, 12TH)	10/19/64	4
(2 WOUNDED)		
Madision, GA (5TH) *	11/20/64	2
Dunn's Lake, FL (17TH)	2/4/65	1
St. Augustine, FL (17TH)	2/4/65	2
Dunn's Lake, FL (17TH)	2/5/65	7
(1 WOUNDED)		
St. Augustine, FL (17TH)	2/5/65	1
Kinston, NC (15TH)	3/8/65	3

ONE HUNDRED TWELVE WERE WOUNDED

The first Norwalk soldiers wounded were Privates Abram Hendrickson and Ward B. Mead of the 3RD Connecticut. Both were wounded at the Battle of Bull Run, VA on July 21, 1861 and both recovered. Eleven Norwalk soldiers died from a wound received during the war

NORWALK WOUNDED
* (11) DIED FROM WOUNDS

PLACE	DATE	NO.
Bull Run, VA (3RD)	7/21/61	2
Roanoke Island, NC (8TH)	2/8/62	1
Newport News, VA (11TH)	7/27/62	1
Cedar Mountain, VA (5TH) *1	8/9/62	2
VA (Accident) (8TH)	9/7/62	1
Antietam, MD (8TH)	9/16/62	1
Antietam, MD (8,14TH)	9/17/62	1
Washington, VA (27TH)	11/20/62	1
Fredricksburg, VA (27TH)	12/13/62	3
Kinston, NC (10TH)	12/14/62	1
Suffolk, VA (8TH)	4/11/63	1
Fort Hugar, VA (8TH)	4/12/63	1
Chancellorsville, VA (5,17TH)	5/2/63	8
Chancellorsville,VA (14TH)	5/3/63	2
Port Hudson, LA (12,28TH) *2	6/14/63	8
Gettysburg, PA (17TH)	7/1/63	4
Gettysburg, PA (17TH) *2	7/2/63	8
Gettysburg, PA (17TH)	7/3/63	1
Morris Island, SC (17TH)	8/16/63	1
Fort Wagner, SC (7TH)	10/8/63	1
James Island, SC (17TH)	11/18/63	1
Morton's Ford, VA (3,14TH) *3	2/6/64	5
Grove Church, VA (1CA)	3/29/64	1
Walthall Junction, VA (8TH)	5/7/64	3
Bermuda Hundred, VA (6TH)	5/9/64	1
Petersburg, VA (6TH)	5/9/64	1
Chester Station, VA (7TH) *	5/10/64	1
Laurel Hill, VA (14TH)	5/10/64	2
Spottsylvania, VA (14TH)	5/11/64	1
Drewry's Bluff, VA (6TH)	5/14/64	2
Resaca, GA (5TH)	5/15/64	1
Fort Darling, VA (8TH)	5/16/64	1
Drewry's Bluff, VA (6,7TH)	5/16/64	4
Bermuda Hundred, VA (6TH)	5/20/64	1
Fontaine, VA (2HA)	5/24/64	1

PLACE	DATE	NO.
Dallas, GA (5TH)	5/25/64	1
Cold Harbor, VA (8TH)	6/2/64	1
Cold Harbor, VA (2HA)	6/6/64	1
Petersburg, VA (8TH)	6/15/64	1
Bermuda Hundred, VA (6,7TH)	6/17/64	2
Petersburg, VA (8TH)	6/22/64	1
Petersburg, VA (8TH)	6/29/64	1
Petersburg, VA (1HA, 8TH) *1	7/1/64	2
Petersburg, VA (8TH)	7/5/64	1
Peach Tree Creek, GA (5TH)	7/20/64	3
Petersburg, VA (1HA)	7/20/64	1
Deep Bottom, VA (6TH) *1	8/16/64	2
Deep Run, VA (6TH)	8/16/64	3
Kearneysville, VA (1CA)	8/25/64	1
Winchester, VA (2HA)	9/18/64	1
Winchester, VA (12,13TH)	9/19/64	2
Drewry's Bluff, VA (7TH)	9/29/64	1
Fort Harrison (8TH)	10/1/64	1
Richmond, VA (29TH)	10/1/64	2
Richmond, VA (6TH)	10/7/64	1
Cedar Creek, VA (2HA,12TH)	10/19/64	4
Boydton Plank Rd, VA (14TH)	10/27/64	1
Fort Fisher, NC (7TH)	1/19/65	1
Averysboro, NC (5TH)	3/10/65	1

NORWICH
THE POPULATION IN 1860 WAS 14,048 (RANK 3)

THE MOST IMPORTANT DAY OF THE CIVIL WAR

JUNE 15 1863

WINCHESTER, VA

THE ENTIRE UNION ARMY WAS NEARLY CAPTURED AT THE SECOND BATTLE OF WINCHESTER

More soldiers credited to Norwich were listed as casualties (170) on this day than on any other day of the war. Four soldiers were killed, 4 were wounded, 146 were captured, and 16 were wounded & captured in the 18TH Connecticut. Five soldiers died in captivity and 2 others died from wounds

The date June 15, 1863 ranks 2ND for total casualties (595) (23 killed, 11 wounded, 520 captured, 41 wounded & captured) for a single day for the State of Connecticut. There were 592 casualties at Winchester, VA and 3 casualties at Port Hudson, LA.

The Second Battle of Winchester (June 13-15, 1863) ranks 5TH for total casualties (592) for an engagement for the State of Connecticut. The most intense fighting was on June 15. Norwich had all its casualites on that day.

The Second Battle of Winchester with 169 total casualties for Norwich was the highest number of casualties for any single engagement of the war for the city.

Winchester was one of the most contested locations in the Civil War. It changed hands seventy-two times.

1248 MEN CREDITED TO NORWICH SERVED IN THE FOLLOWING CONNECTICUT ORGANIZATIONS

REGIMENT	TOTAL
18TH	282 (23%)
26TH	149 (12%)
2ND	97 (8%)
1ST CAVALRY	82 (7%)
2ND HEAVY ARTILLERY	82 (7%)
9TH	74 (6%)
14TH	68 (5%)
8TH	66 (5%)
1ST HEAVY ARTILLERY	64 (5%)
13TH	59 (5%)
3RD	48 (4%)
30TH	46 (4%)
11TH	41 (3%)
21ST	38 (3%)
29TH	32 (3%)
7TH	30 (2%)
9TH BATTALION	28 (2%)
5TH	23 (2%)
6TH	19 (1%)
12TH	15 (1%)
10TH	15 (1%)
13TH BATTALION	12 (1%)
20TH	10 (1%)
1ST	7
12TH BATTALION	5
17TH	4
1ST LIGHT BATTERY	2
1ST SQUADRON CAVALRY	1
15TH	1
16TH	1
22ND	1
24TH	1
27TH	1

9% OF POPULATION

FORTY-FIVE WERE KILLED

The first Norwich soldier killed was Private David C. Case of Company D, 3RD Connecticut. He was killed at the Battle of Bull Run, VA on July 21, 1861

NORWICH SOLDIERS KILLED

PLACE	DATE	NO.
Bull Run, VA (3RD)	7/21/61	1
Roanoke Island, NC (10TH)	2/8/62	1
New Bern, NC (10TH)	3/14/62	1
Cedar Mountain, VA (5TH)	8/9/62	1
Antietam, MD (8,11, 14TH)	9/17/62	4
Georgia Landing, LA (13TH)	10/27/62	1
Stafford CH, VA (1 CA)	1/3/63	1
Harewood Station, MD (18TH)	1/5/63	1
Port Hudson, LA (13TH)	5/24/63	1
Port Hudson, LA (26TH)	5/27/63	2
Winchester, VA (18TH)	6/15/63	4
Fort Wagner, SC (7TH)	7/11/63	1
Fort Wagner, SC (6TH)	7/18/63	2
Swift's Creek, VA (11TH)	5/9/64	1
Wilderness, VA (14TH)	5/11/64	1
Drewry's Bluff, VA (8TH)	5/16/64	1
Cold Harbor, VA (2 HA)	6/1/64	1
Cold Harbor, VA (11TH)	6/3/64	2
Piedmont, VA (18TH)	6/5/64	5
Petersburg, VA (2 HA)	6/22/64	1
Snicker's Ford, VA (18TH)	7/18/64	1
Petersburg, VA (30TH)	7/30/64	1
Winchester, VA (2HA,1CA13TH)	9/19/64	3
Cedar Creek, VA (9TH)	10/19/64	1
Kell House, VA (29TH)	10/27/64	1
Petersburg, VA (2 HA)	3/25/65	3
Fort Gregg, VA (10TH)	4/2/65	1

TOTAL NORWICH CASUALTIES

DIED	120	10%
KILLED	45	4%
WOUNDED	213	17%
CAPTURED	237	19%
DESERTED	172	14%

TWO HUNDRED-THIRTY SEVEN WERE CAPTURED

Twenty-seven Norwich soldiers died in captivity. Twelve died at Andersonville Prison, GA, three died at Winchester, VA, three died at Florence, SC, two died at Salisbury, NC, two died at Libby Prison, Richmond, VA, two died at Millen, GA, one died at Danville, VA, one died at Piedmont, VA, and one died at Staunton, VA.

NORWICH CAPTURED
*(27) DIED IN CAPTIVITY

PLACE	DATE	NO.
Falls Church, VA (2ND)	6/19/61	1
Bull Run, VA (2ND)	7/21/61	3
Wreck "Union", NC (7TH)	11/4/61	1
Winchester, VA (5TH)	5/25/62	1
Cold Harbor, VA (1 HA)	6/27/62	2
Sperryville, VA (1 CA)	8/6/62	1
Antietam, MD (8TH) (2 WOUNDED)	9/17/62	6
Bayou Sara, LA (13TH)	5/26/63	1
Winchester, VA (18TH)(16 WOUNDED) *6	6/15/63	162
Burnt Ordinary, VA (21ST)	7/9/63	1
Bolivar Heights, VA (1 CA)	7/14/63	1
Fort Wagner, SC (6TH) (1 WOUNDED)	7/18/63	3
Waterford, VA (1 CA)	8/7/63	1
Smithfield, VA (21ST) *	2/1/64	1
Morton's Ford, VA (14TH) *	2/6/64	1
Bristoe Station, VA (1 CA)	3/29/64	1
Craig's Church, VA(1CA)(2 WOUNDED)*4	5/5/64	4
Walthall Junction, VA (8TH) *	5/7/64	1
New Market, VA (18TH) *2	5/15/64	3
Drewry's Bluff, VA(1 WOUNDED)(7,11TH)*	5/16/64	2
Staunton, VA (18TH) *	6/1/64	1
Ashland, VA (1 CA) *3	6/1/64	4
Harrisonburg, VA (18TH)	6/1/64	1
Bermuda Hun., VA(2 WOUNDED)(7TH) *	6/2/64	2
Piedmont, VA (18TH) (8 WOUNDED)*3	6/5/64	11
Staunton, VA (18TH) (1 WOUNDED) *	6/11/64	1
Salem, VA (18TH)	6/29/64	1
Ream's Station, VA (1 CA)	6/29/64	3
Ream's Station, VA (1 CA)	7/1/64	1
Staunton, VA (18TH) *	7/8/64	1
Snicker's Ford, VA (18TH)	7/18/64	1
Winchester, VA (18TH)	7/24/64	1
Deep Run, VA (6TH)	8/16/64	1
Berryville, VA (1 CA) *	8/24/64	1
Winchester, VA (13TH)	9/19/64	1
Fort Harrison, VA (8TH)	9/29/64	1
Cedar Creek, VA (1CA, 2HA,12TH) *2	10/19/64	5
Boydton Plank Road, VA (14TH)	10/27/64	1

TWO HUNDRED-THIRTEEN WERE WOUNDED

The first Norwich soldiers wounded were Privates John Breed and Joseph Stokes of the 1ST and 3RD Connecticut. They were wounded at the Battle of Bull Run on July 21, 1861and Private Stokes died from his wound. Twenty-four Norwich soldiers died from a wound received during the war.

NORWCH WOUNDED
*(24) DIED FROM WOUNDS

PLACE	DATE	NO.
Bull Run, VA (2ND, 3RD) *1	7/21/61	2
Falls Church, VA (2ND)	8/1/61	1
Annapolis, MD (8TH)	11/6/61	1
Washington, DC (2ND)	12/22/61	1
Moorefield, VA (1 CA)	4/3/62	1
Antietam, MD ($8,11,14^{TH}$) *7	9/17/62	22
Washington, DC (21ST)	9/18/62	1
Pocotaligo, SC (7TH)	10/22/62	1
Georgia Landing, LA($12,13^{TH}$)*1	10/27/62	2
Fredericksburg, VA (14TH) *1	12/13/62	5
Baton Rouge, LA (9TH)	2/1/63	1
Irish Bend, LA (13TH)	4/14/63	3
Chancellorsville, VA ($14,20^{TH}$)	5/3/63	4
Havre De Grace, MD (18TH)	5/14/63	1
Port Hudson, LA (26TH)	5/22/63	1
Port Hudson, LA (26TH)	5/24/63	1
Port Hudson, LA (26TH) *1	5/27/63	16
Port Hudson, LA (26TH) *	6/13/63	1
Port Hudson, LA ($13,26^{TH}$) *1	6/14/63	16
Port Hudson, LA (26TH)	6/15/63	1
Winchester, VA (18TH)	6/15/63	3
Port Hudson, LA (26TH)	6/27/63	1
Port Hudson, LA (26TH)	7/1/63	1
Gettysburg, PA (14TH)	7/3/63	4
Fort Wagner, SC (6TH)	7/18/63	1
Winchester, VA (13TH)	8/18/63	1
Bay St. Louis, MS (9TH)	10/5/63	2
Morton's Ford, VA (14TH)	2/6/64	4
Cane River, LA (13TH)	4/23/64	2
Petersburg, VA (14TH)	5/6/64	1
Wilderness, VA (14TH)	5/6/64	3
Walthall Junction, VA (8TH) *1	5/7/64	3
Wilderness, VA (14TH)	5/7/64	1
Spottsylvania, VA (14TH)	5/10/64	3
Laurel Hill, VA (14TH)	5/10/64	1
Meadow Bridge, VA (1 CA)	5/12/64	1
Spottsylvania, VA (14TH)	5/13/64	2
Resaca, GA (5TH)	5/15/64	4
New Market, VA (18TH)	5/15/64	5
Drewry's Bluff, VA (21ST)	5/16/64	2
Hanover C H, VA (2 HA)	5/29/64	1
Cold Harbor, VA (2 HA)	6/1/64	3
Ashland, VA (1 CA)	6/1/64	1
Piedmont, VA (18TH)	6/5/64	21
Cold Harbor, VA (8TH)	6/5/64	1
Petersburg, VA (8TH)	6/15/64	1
Petersburg, VA (8TH)	6/16/64	1
Petersburg, VA (8TH)	6/17/64	1
Petersburg, VA (11TH)	6/18/64	1
Lynchburg, VA (18TH)	6/18/64	2

PLACE	DATE	NO.
Petersburg, VA (7TH)	6/20/64	1
Petersburg, VA (2 HA)	6/23/64	1
Stony Creek, VA (1 CA)	6/28/64	1
Petersburg, VA (21ST) *1	6/30/64	2
Light House Point, VA (1 CA)	7/17/64	1
Simsbury, CT (18TH)	7/18/64	1
Snicker's Ford, VA (18TH)	7/18/64	6
Winchester, VA (18TH)	7/24/64	1
Petersburg, VA ($21,30^{TH}$) *3	7/30/64	7
Petersburg, VA (11TH)	8/5/64	1
Deep Bottom, VA (14TH)	8/15/64	1
Deep Run, VA (6TH)	8/16/64	1
Deep Bottom, VA (14TH)	8/16/64	1
Petersburg, VA (21ST)	8/20/64	1
Ream's Station, VA (14TH) *1	8/25/64	2
Unknown Place (18TH)	9/4/64	1
Petersburg, VA (14TH)	9/6/64	1
Winchester, VA ($2HA,12,13^{TH}$)	9/19/64	5
Fort Harrison, VA (8TH)	9/29/64	3
Petersburg, VA (21ST)	10/2/64	1
Chaffin's Farm, VA (7TH)	10/7/64	1
Richmond, VA (29TH)	10/13/64	1
Cedar Creek, VA ($2HA,9,13^{TH}$)*1	10/19/64	7
Boydton Plank Rd, VA (14TH)	10/27/64	1
Fair Oaks, VA (8TH)	10/28/64	1
Broadway Landing, VA (11TH)	11/10/64	1
Cedar Creek, VA (1 CA)	11/12/64	1
Fort Gregg, VA ($1O^{TH}$) *	4/2/65	1
Petersburg, VA (2 HA)	4/2/65	1

OLD LYME
THE POPULATION IN 1860 WAS 1,304 (RANK 72)

THE MOST IMPORTANT DAY OF THE CIVIL WAR

JUNE 14, 1863

PORT HUDSON, LA

THE SECOND ASSAULT

More soldiers credited to Old Lyme were listed as casualties (5) on this day than on any other day of the war. Two soldiers were killed and 3 were wounded in the 26TH Connecticut.

The date June 14, 1863 ranks 11TH for total casualties (217) (32 killed, 179 wounded, 5 captured, 1 wounded & captured) for a single day for the State of Connecticut. Port Hudson accounted for 216 casualties. There was 1 casualty in Virginia.

The Siege of Port Hudson (May 2 - July 9) ranks 7TH for total casualties (520) for an engagement for the State of Connecticut. The most intense fighting developed on May 27 and June 14. Old Lyme had 2 casualties on May 27.

The siege of Port Hudson with 7 total casualties for Old Lyme was the highest number of casualties for any single engagement of the war for the town.

Control of the Mississippi was one of the major objectives of the Union army. Port Hudson was a formidable obstacle for control of the river. A siege began at Port Hudson on May 2, 1863 that lasted until July 9. On May 27 and June 14, the Union force of 30,000 launched major assaults that failed.

71 MEN CREDITED TO OLD LYME SERVED IN THE FOLLOWING CONNECTICUT ORGANIZATIONS

REGIMENT	TOTAL
26TH	40 (56%)
1ST HEAVY ARTILLERY	12 (17%)
11TH	6 (9%)
12TH	5 (7%)
14TH	4 (6%)
13TH	3 (4%)
5TH	2 (3%)
12TH BATTALION	2 (3%)
2ND HEAVY ARTILLERY	1
13TH BATTALION	1
24TH	1

6% OF POPULATION

FIVE WERE KILLED

The first Old Lyme soldier killed was Captain John D. Griswold of Company A, 11TH Connecticut. He was killed at The Battle of Antietam, MD on September 17, 1862.

OLD LYME SOLDIERS KILLED

PLACE	DATE	NO.
Antietam, MD (11TH)	9/17/62	1
Port Hudson, LA (26TH)	6/14/63	2
Port Hudson, LA (26TH)	6/17/63	1
Resaca, GA (5TH)	5/15/64	1

THREE WERE CAPTURED

One Old Lyme soldier died in captivity at Andersonville Prison, GA.

OLD LYME CAPTURED
*(1) DIED IN CAPTIVITY

PLACE	DATE	NO.
Grand Ecore, LA (13TH)	4/21/64	1
Unknown (14TH) *	Unknown	1
Drewry's Bluff, VA (11TH)	5/16/64	1

TOTAL OLD LYME CASUALTIES

DIED	10	14%
KILLED	5	7%
WOUNDED	8	11%
CAPTURED	3	4%
DESERTED	13	18%

EIGHT WERE WOUNDED

The first Old Lyme soldiers wounded were Privates Alonzo W. Rowland and Leroy Noon of Company C, 26TH Connecticut. Both were wounded at Port Hudson, LA on May 27, 1863. Private Rowland died from his wound. He was the only Old Lyme soldier who died from a wound received during the war.

OLD LYME WOUNDED
*(1) DIED FROM WOUNDS

PLACE	DATE	NO.
Port Hudson, LA (26TH) *1	5/27/63	2
Port Hudson, LA (26TH)	6/14/63	3
Cold Harbor, VA (11TH)	6/3/64	1
Battery Stevenson, VA (1 HA)	7/23/64	1
Cedar Creek, VA (12TH)	10/19/64	1

OLD SAYBROOK
THE POPULATION IN 1860 WAS 1,105 (RANK 126)

THE MOST IMPORTANT DAY OF THE CIVIL WAR

OCTOBER 19, 1864
CEDAR CREEK, VA

THE LAST MAJOR BATTLE OF THE 1864 SHENANDOAH VALLEY CAMPAIGN WAS A UNION TRIUMPH

Soldiers credited to Old Saybrook had 11 days in the war when they had one casualty. There were no other days with more. One soldier was killed in the 14th Connecticut on December 13, 1862 at Fredericksburg, VA and one soldier in the 12th Connecticut was killed on October 19, 1864 at Cedar Creek, VA. The casualties were greater at Cedar Creek for the State of Connecticut.

The date October 19, 1864 ranks 7TH for total casualties (417) (48 killed, 2 missing, 204 wounded, 153 captured, 10 wounded & captured) for a single day for the State of Connecticut. The Battle of Cedar Creek accounted for 415 casualties. The 2 other casualties were in the neighboring towns.

The Battle of Cedar Creek (October 19, 1864) ranks 10TH for total casualties (415) for an engagement for the State of Connecticut.

The Battle of Cedar Creek with 1 total casualty for Old Saybrook was tied with ten other engagements for the highest number of casualties for any single engagement of the war for the town.

The news of the Union triumph at Cedar Creek assured a Republican victory in the elections of November 1864 and the prosecution of the war to its end on President Abraham Lincoln's and Lieutenant General Ulysses S. Grant's terms.

46 MEN CREDITED TO OLD SAYBROOK SERVED IN THE FOLLOWING CONNECTICUT ORGANIZATIONS

REGIMENT	TOTAL
29TH	11 (24%)
14TH	9 (20%)
12TH	5 (11%)
24TH	4 (9%)
10TH	4 (9%)
11TH	3 (7%)
1ST HEAVY ARTILLERY	3 (7%)
6TH	2 (4%)
26TH	2 (4%)
8TH	1
5TH	1
2ND HEAVY ARTILLERY	1

4% OF POPULATION

THREE WERE KILLED

The first Old Saybrook soldier killed was Corporal Frederick S. Ward of Company G, 14TH Connecticut. He was killed on December 13, 1862 at Fredericksburg, VA.

OLD SAYBROOK SOLDIERS KILLED

PLACE	DATE	NO.
Fredericksburg, VA (14TH)	12/13/62	1
Petersburg, VA (10TH)	9/13/64	1
Cedar Creek, VA (12TH)	10/19/64	1

TWO WERE CAPTURED

No Old Saybrook soldiers died in captivity.

OLD SAYBROOK CAPTURED
NONE DIED IN CAPTIVITY

PLACE	DATE	NO.
Loudon, County, VA (14TH)	11/22/62	1
Chancellorsville, VA (14TH) (WOUNDED)	5/3/63	1

TOTAL OLD SAYBROOK CASUALTIES

DIED	7	15%
KILLED	3	7%
WOUNDED	7	15%
CAPTURED	2	4%
DESERTED	5	11%

SEVEN WERE WOUNDED

The first Old Saybrook soldier wounded was Sergeant Augustus L. Dibble of Company G, 14TH Connecticut. He was wounded at the Battle of Antietam, MD on September 17, 1862 and recovered from his wound. No Old Saybrook soldier died from a wound received during the war.

OLD SAYBROOK WOUNDED
NONE DIED FROM WOUNDS

PLACE	DATE	NO.
Antietam, MD (14TH)	9/17/62	1
Kinston, NC (10TH)	12/14/62	1
Wilderness, VA (14TH)	5/6/64	1
Drewry's Bluff, VA (6TH)	5/16/64	1
Petersburg, VA (11TH)	6/19/64	1
Winchester, VA (12TH)	9/19/64	1
Petersburg, VA (29TH)	9/29/64	1

ORANGE
THE POPULATION IN 1860 WAS 1,974 (RANK 76)

**THE MOST IMPORTANT DAY
OF THE CIVIL WAR**

MAY 3, 1863
CHANCELLORSVILLE, VA

**THE THIRD DAY OF THE
BATTLE**

More soldiers credited to Orange were listed as casualties (14) on this day than on any other day of the war. One soldier was killed and 13 were captured in the 20TH and 27TH Connecticut. The captured survived the war.

The date May 3, 1863 ranks 3RD for total casualties (577) (36 killed, 1 missing, 138 wounded, 372 captured, 29 wounded & captured) for a single day for the State of Connecticut. The most casualties were at Chancellorsville, VA (556). The other casualties were at Providence Church Road, VA (12), Suffolk, VA (6), Port Hudson, LA (2) and Fredericksburg, VA (1).

The Battle of Chancellorsville (May 1-3, 1863) ranks 2ND for total casualties (677) for an engagement for the State of Connecticut. The most intense fighting developed on May 3. Orange had no other casualties in the battle other than on May 3.

The Battle of Chancellorsville with 14 total casualties for Orange was the highest number of casualties for any single engagement of the war for the town.

The Battle of Chancellorsville was an enormous defeat for the more than 70,000 Union soldiers who had moved against the flank and rear of 40,000 Confederate soldiers. Unfortunately, the Union Army had pulled back and had gone on the defensive around Chancellorsville. The Confederate victory was tainted however, by the loss of Confederate Major General "Stonewall" Jackson.

161 MEN CREDITED TO ORANGE SERVED IN THE FOLLOWING CONNECTICUT ORGANIZATIONS

REGIMENT	TOTAL
15TH	34 (21%)
27TH	29 (18%)
29TH	29 (18%)
23RD	15 (9%)
7TH	8 (5%)
20TH	7 (4%)
10TH	6 (4%)
11TH	6 (4%)
1ST HEAVY ARTILLERY	5 (3%)
8TH	5 (3%)
6TH	4 (2%)
12TH	4 (2%)
1ST CAVALRY	3 (2%)
13TH	3 (2%)
14TH	3 (2%)
5TH	2 (1%)
2ND HEAVY ARTILLERY	1
30TH	1

9% OF POPULATION

THREE WERE KILLED

The first Orange soldier killed was First Sergeant Charles H. Smith of Company E, 20TH Connecticut. He was killed at Chancellorsville, VA on May 3, 1863.

ORANGE SOLDIERS KILLED

PLACE	DATE	NO.
Chancellorsville, VA (20TH)	5/3/63	1
Kell House, VA (29TH)	10/27/64	1
Kinston, NC (20TH)	3/8/65	1

TWENTY-SIX WERE CAPTURED

One Orange soldier died in captivity at Libby Prison, Richmond, VA.

ORANGE CAPTURED
*(1) DIED IN CAPTIVITY

PLACE	DATE	NO.
Winchester, VA (5TH)	5/25/62	1
Chancellorsville, VA (27TH)	5/3/63	13
Spottsylvania, VA (14TH) (WOUNDED)	5/12/64	1
Petersburg, VA (30TH) * (WOUNDED)	7/30/64	1
Kinston, NC (15TH)	3/8/65	10

TOTAL ORANGE CASUALTIES

DIED	15	9%
KILLED	3	2%
WOUNDED	18	12%
CAPTURED	26	16%
DESERTED	25	16%

EIGHTEEN WERE WOUNDED

The first Orange soldier wounded was Private Alexander Smith of Company E, 7TH Connecticut. He was wounded at Tallahatchie, FL on June 8, 1862 and recovered from his wound. One Orange soldier died from a wound received during the war.

ORANGE WOUNDED
*(1) DIED FROM WOUNDS

PLACE	DATE	NO.
Tallahatchie, FL (7TH)	6/18/62	1
Malvern Hill, VA (1 HA)	7/1/62	1
Fredericksburg, VA (14,15,27)	12/13/62	4
Morton's Ford, VA (14TH)	2/6/64	1
Gettysburg, PA (27TH)	7/2/63	1
Cold Harbor, VA (11TH)	6/3/64	2
Unknown (29TH)	8/1/64	1
Petersburg, VA (29TH)	9/19/64	1
Richmond, VA (29TH)	9/30/64	1
Darbytown Road, VA (29TH)	10/13/64	1
Kell House, VA (29TH) *	10/27/64	2
Fair Oaks, VA (29TH)	10/27/64	1
Bentonville, NC (20TH)	3/19/65	1

OXFORD
THE POPULATION IN 1860 WAS 1,269 (RANK 114)

THE MOST IMPORTANT DAY OF THE CIVIL WAR

MAY 3, 1863

CHANCELLORSVILLE, VA

THE THIRD DAY OF THE BATTLE

More soldiers credited to Oxford were listed as casualties (6) on this day than on any other day of the war. Two soldiers were killed, 3 were captured, and 1 was wounded & captured in the 20TH Connecticut. The wounded and captured survived the war.

The date May 3, 1863 ranks 3RD for total casualties (577) (36 killed, 1 missing, 138 wounded, 372 captured, 29 wounded & captured) for a single day for the State of Connecticut. The most casualties were at Chancellorsville, VA (556). The other casualties were at Providence Church Road, VA (12), Suffolk, VA (6), Port Hudson, LA (2) and Fredericksburg, VA (1).

The Battle of Chancellorsville (May 1-3, 1863) ranks 2ND for total casualties (677) for an engagement for the State of Connecticut. The most intense fighting developed on May 3. Oxford had no other casualties in the battle other than on May 3.

The Battle of Chancellorsville with 6 total casualties for Oxford was the highest number of casualties for any single engagement of the war for the town.

The Battle of Chancellorsville was an enormous defeat for the more than 70,000 Union soldiers who had moved against the flank and rear of 40,000 Confederate soldiers. Unfortunately, the Union Army had pulled back and had gone on the defensive around Chancellorsville. The Confederate victory was tainted however, by the loss of Confederate Major General "Stonewall" Jackson.

107 MEN CREDITED TO OXFORD SERVED IN THE FOLLOWING CONNECTICUT ORGANIZATIONS

REGIMENT	TOTAL
20TH	29 (27%)
3RD LIGHT BATTERY	14 (13%)
13TH	11 (10%)
11TH	10 (9%)
2ND HEAVY ARTILLERY	8 (7%)
15TH	7 (7%)
1ST HEAVY ARTILLERY	6 (5%)
7TH	5 (5%)
10TH	5 (5%)
6TH	4 (4%)
14TH	4 (4%)
1ST CAVALRY	3 (3%)
13TH BATTALION	3 (3%)
29TH	2 (2%)
5TH	1
9TH	1
12TH	1
23RD	1

8% OF POPULATION

FOUR WERE KILLED

The first Oxford soldiers killed were Privates John Powers and Joel Buckingham of Company H, 20ᵀᴴ Connecticut. They were killed at Chancellorsville, VA on May 3, 1863.

TOTAL OXFORD CASUALTIES

DIED	19	18%
KILLED	4	4%
WOUNDED	10	9%
CAPTURED	13	12%
DESERTED	19	18%

OXFORD SOLDIERS KILLED

PLACE	DATE	NO.
Chancellorsville, VA (20ᵀᴴ)	5/3/63	2
Bermuda Hundred, VA (7ᵀᴴ)	6/2/64	1
Kinston, NC (15ᵀᴴ)	3/8/65	1

THIRTEEN WERE CAPTURED

Four Oxford soldiers died in captivity. Two died at Andersonville Prison, GA, one died at Florence, SC and one at Salisbury, NC.

OXFORD CAPTURED
*(4) DIED IN CAPTIVITY

PLACE	DATE	NO.
Moorefield, VA (1 CA)	6/22/62	1
Chancellorsville, VA (20ᵀᴴ) (WOUNDED)	5/3/63	4
Bristoe Station, VA (14ᵀᴴ) *	10/14/63	1
Drewry's Bluff, VA (11ᵀᴴ) * (WOUNDED)	5/16/64	1
Hatcher's Run, VA (7ᵀᴴ) *	6/2/64	1
Cedar Creek, VA (2 HA) * (1 WOUNDED)	10/19/64	2
Kinston, NC (15ᵀᴴ)	3/8/65	3

TEN WERE WOUNDED

The first Oxford soldier wounded was Corporal Walter Skiff of Company D, 13ᵀᴴ Connecticut. He was wounded at Irish Bend, LA on April 14, 1863 and recovered from his wound. One Oxford soldier died from a wound received during the war.

OXFORD WOUNDED
*(1) DIED FROM WOUNDS

PLACE	DATE	NO.
Irish Bend, LA (13ᵀᴴ)	4/14/63	1
Port Hudson, LA (13ᵀᴴ)	6/14/63	1
Drewry's Bluff, VA (7ᵀᴴ)	5/14/64	1
Cold Harbor, VA (2 HA)	6/1/64	2
Peach Tree Creek, GA (20ᵀᴴ)	7/20/64	1
Fisher's Hill, VA (2 HA) *	9/21/64	1
Petersburg, VA (29ᵀᴴ)	9/29/64	1
Cedar Creek, VA (2 HA,13ᵀᴴ)	10/19/64	2

PLAINFIELD
THE POPULATION IN 1860 WAS 3,665 (RANK 23)

THE MOST IMPORTANT DAY OF THE CIVIL WAR

SEPTEMBER 17, 1862

SHARPSBURG, MD (ANTIETAM)

CONNECTICUT HAD MORE CASUALTIES FOR ONE DAY THAN ON ANY OTHER DAY OF THE WAR

Soldiers credited to Plainfield had more casualties on September 17, 1862 at Antietam, MD (13), June 15, 1863 at Winchester, VA (13), and May 16, 1864 at Drewry's Bluff, VA (13) than on any other days of the war. The casualties at the Battle of Antietam were the most serious. Four soldiers were killed and 9 were wounded in the 8TH and 11TH Connecticut. All of the wounded survived the war.

The date September 17, 1862 ranks 1ST for total casualties (687) (131 killed, 2 missing, 515 wounded, 21 captured, 18 wounded & captured) for a single day for the State of Connecticut. All of the casualties were at Antietam.

The Battle of Antietam (September 16-17) ranks 1ST for total casualties (689) for an engagement. The most intense fighting developed on September 17. Plainfield had all of its casualties on that day.

The Battle of Antietam with 13 total casualties for Plainfield was tied with the battles of Winchester (June 15, 1863), and Drewry's Bluff (May 12-17, 1864) for the highest number of casualties for any single engagement of the war for the town.

Roughly 12,400 Union casualties were recorded and perhaps there were 10,300 Confederate casualties. Antietam proved to be one of the turning points of the war. It ended Lee's 1862 invasion of the North.

256 MEN CREDITED TO PLAINFIELD SERVED IN THE FOLLOWING CONNECTICUT ORGANIZATIONS

REGIMENT	TOTAL
21ST	57 (22%)
11TH	40 (16%)
8TH	33 (13%)
18TH	33 (13%)
5TH	31 (12%)
1ST HEAVY ARTILLERY	16 (6%)
1ST CAVALRY	10 (4%)
6TH	8 (3%)
20TH	7 (3%)
12TH	6 (2%)
13TH	5 (2%)
14TH	4 (2%)
2ND HEAVY ARTILLERY	3 (1%)
12TH BATTALION	3 (1%)
29TH	3 (1%)
1ST SQUADRON CAVALRY	2
26TH	2
1ST LIGHT BATTERY	1
2ND	1
3RD	1
9TH	1
13TH BATTALION	1
16TH	1

7% OF POPULATION

NINE WERE KILLED

The first Plainfield soldiers killed were Davis Batty, George H. Heflin, Frank Trask, and Horace G. Rouse of the 8TH and 11TH Connecticut. They were killed at the Battle of Antietam on September 17, 1862

PLAINFIELD SOLDIERS KILLED

PLACE	DATE	NO.
Antietam, MD (8,11TH)	9/17/62	4
Fredericksburg, VA (14TH)	12/13/62	1
Drewry's Bluff, VA (21ST)	5/16/64	3
Piedmont, VA (18TH)	6/5/64	1

THIRTY WERE CAPTURED

Two Plainfield soldiers died in captivity. One died at Charleston Prison, SC and one at Salisbury Prison, NC.

PLAINFIELD CAPTURED
*(2) DIED IN CAPTIVITY

PLACE	DATE	NO.
Winchester, VA (5TH)	5/25/62	3
Winchester, VA (18TH) * (1 WOUNDED)	6/15/63	13
Brashear City, LA (12TH)	6/23/63	1
New Market, VA (18TH)	5/15/64	1
Drewry's Bluff, VA (8,11TH)	5/16/64	3
Bermuda Hundred, VA (7TH)	6/2/64	2
Virginia (18TH)	6/6/64	1
Ream's Station, VA (1 CA) *	6/29/64	1
Charlestown, VA (12TH)	9/4/64	1
Petersburg, VA (21ST)	9/29/64	1
Boydton Plank Rd, VA (14TH) (1 WOUNDED)	10/27/64	2
Georgia (5TH)	11/15/64	1

TOTAL PLAINFIELD CASUALTIES

DIED	21	8%
KILLED	9	4%
WOUNDED	48	19%
CAPTURED	30	12%
DESERTED	16	6%

FORTY-EIGHT WERE WOUNDED

The first Plainfield soldier wounded was Private David H. Kennedy of Company F, 8TH Connecticut. He was accidently wounded at Long Island, NY on October 16, 1861 and recovered from his wound. Five Plainfield soldiers died from a wound received during the war.

PLAINFIELD WOUNDED
*(5) DIED FROM WOUNDS

PLACE	DATE	NO.
Long Island, NY (8TH)	10/16/61	1
Winchester, VA (5TH) *	5/25/62	1
Cedar Mountain, VA (5TH)	8/9/62	2
Antietam, MD (8,11TH)	9/17/62	9
Providence Church Rd, VA(11TH)	5/4/63	1
Port Hudson, LA (12TH)	5/27/63	1
Port Hudson, LA (12TH)	6/13/63	1
Gettysburg, PA (5TH)	7/2/63	1
Fort Wagner, SC (6TH) *	7/18/63	1
Craig's Church, VA (1 CA)	5/5/64	1
Wilderness, VA (14TH)	5/6/64	1
Walthall Junction, VA (8TH)	5/7/64	1
Petersburg, VA (6TH)	5/10/64	1
Drewry's Bluff, VA (7TH)	5/14/64	2
Drewry's Bluff, VA (8,21ST)	5/16/64	7
Cold Harbor, VA (8TH)	6/2/64	1
Cold Harbor, VA (11,21ST) *2	6/3/64	4
Piedmont, VA (18TH)	6/5/64	1
Petersburg, VA (11TH)	6/18/64	1
Petersburg, VA (11TH)	7/1/64	1
Snicker's Ford, VA (18TH)	7/18/64	1
Peach Tree Creek, GA (5TH) *	7/20/64	1
Peretersburg, VA (21ST)	8/24/64	1
Winchester, VA (12TH)	9/19/64	1
Fort Harrison, VA (8TH)	9/29/64	2
Petersburg, VA (29TH)	9/30/64	1
Richmond, VA (6TH)	10/7/64	1
Wilmington, NC (8TH)	2/21/65	1

PLYMOUTH
THE POPULATION IN 1860 WAS 3,244 (RANK 37)

THE MOST IMPORTANT DAY OF THE CIVIL WAR
SEPTEMBER 19, 1864

WINCHESTER, VA

THIRD WINCHESTER (OPEQUON)WAS A UNION VICTORY

283 MEN CREDITED TO PLYMOUTH SERVED IN THE FOLLOWING CONNECTICUT ORGANIZATIONS

More soldiers credited to Plymouth were listed as casualties (14) on this day than on any other day of the war. Four soldiers were killed, 9 were wounded, and 1 was captured in the 9TH & 13TH Connecticut Infantry, and 2ND Connecticut Heavy Artillery. Two of the wounded died.

The date September 19, 1864 ranks 9TH for total casualties (279) (38 killed, 209 wounded, 32 captured) for a single day for the State of Connecticut. The Battle of Third Winchester accounted for 274 casualties. There were 2 other casualties in Virginia.

The Battle of Third Winchester (September 19, 1864) ranks 12TH for total casualties (274) for an engagement for the State of Connecticut.

The Battle of Third Winchester with 14 total casualties for Plymouth was the highest number of casualties for any single engagement of the war for the town.

The battle was not an overwhelming victory for the Union Army. As the Union force was approaching Winchester from the east they became bogged down and the attacks were uncoordinated. The Union army sustained heavier casualties but the Confederates moved to a stronger position at Fisher's Hill south of Strasburg. The total casualties were about 7,500.

REGIMENT	TOTAL
2ND HEAVY ARTILLERY	107 (38%)
1ST HEAVY ARTILLERY	37 (13%)
20TH	23 (8%)
5TH	20 (7%)
1ST CAVALRY	15 (5%)
10TH	14 (5%)
9TH	11 (4%)
13TH	10 (4%)
11TH	8 (3%)
14TH	8 (3%)
8TH	7 (2%)
6TH	6 (2%)
30TH	6 (2%)
25TH	5 (2%)
2ND LIGHT BATTERY	4 (1%)
1ST SQUADRON CAVALRY	3 (1%)
7TH	3 (1%)
9TH BATTALION	3 (1%)
17TH	3 (1%)
29TH	3 (1%)
16TH	2 (1%)
1ST LIGHT BATTERY	1
3RD	1
13TH BATTALION	1
15TH	1
23RD	1
27TH	1

9% OF POPULATION

TWELVE WERE KILLED AND ONE WAS MISSING

The first Plymouth soldier killed was Private Riley Marsh of Company I, 1ST Connecticut Heavy Artillery. He was killed at Gaines Mills, VA on June 20, 1862.

PLYMOUTH SOLDIERS KILLED *MISSING

PLACE	DATE	NO.
Gaines Mills, VA (1 HA)	6/20/62	1
Aldie, VA (1 SQ)	6/17/63	1
Albemarle Sound, NC (16TH) (Drowned)	3/8/64	1
Cold Harbor, VA (2 HA) *1	6/1/64	2
Deep Bottom, VA (1 HA)	8/16/64	1
Fisher's Hill, VA (2 HA)	9/2/64	1
Winchester, VA (2 HA)	9/19/64	4
Cedar Creek, VA (2 HA)	10/19/64	2

FOURTEEN WERE CAPTURED

Four Plymouth soldiers died in captivity. Two died at Andersonville Prison, GA, one at Salisbury, NC and one at Florence, SC.

PLYMOUTH CAPTURED *(4) DIED IN CAPTIVITY

PLACE	DATE	NO.
Hagerstown, VA (1 SQ)	7/6/63	1
Drewry's Bluff, VA (8,11TH)*1	5/16/64	3
Welaka, FL (17TH)	5/19/64	1
Cold Harbor, VA (2 HA) *	6/1/64	1
Petersburg, VA (2 HA) *	6/22/64	1
Ream's Station, VA (1 CA) *	6/27/64	1
Snicker's Ford, VA (2 HA)	7/21/64	1
Winchester, VA (13TH) (WOUNDED)	9/19/64	1
Cedar Run Church, VA (1 CA)	10/17/64	1
Cedar Creek, VA (2 HA)	10/19/64	1
Cedar Creek, VA (1 CA)	11/12/64	1
Kinston, NC (15TH)	3/8/54	1

TOTAL PLYMOUTH CASUALTIES

DIED	41	13%
KILLED/MISSING	13	5%
WOUNDED	46	16%
CAPTURED	14	5%
DESERTED	61	22%

FORTY-SIX WERE WOUNDED

The first Plymouth soldier wounded was Private Edward C. Blakeslee of Company A, 7TH Connecticut. He was wounded at Fort Wagner, SC on July 11, 1863 and died from his wound. Nine Plymouth soldiers died from a wound received during the war.

PLYMOUTH WOUNDED *(9) DIED FROM WOUNDS

PLACE	DATE	NO.
Fort Wagner, SC (7TH) *	7/11/63	1
Morton's Ford, VA (14TH)	2/6/64	1
Swift's Creek, VA (11TH)	5/9/64	2
Resaca, GA (5TH)	5/15/64	2
Cassville, GA (20TH) *	5/19/64	1
Cold Harbor, VA (1,2 HA) *2	6/1/64	8
Ashland, VA (1 CA)	6/1/64	1
Old Church Tav.,VA(1CA)	6/10/64	1
Pine Mountain, GA (5TH)	6/16/64	1
Petersburg, VA (2 HA) *1	6/20/64	2
Petersburg, VA (2 HA) *	6/22/64	1
Peach Tree Creek, GA (20TH)	7/20/64	1
Deep Run, VA (6TH)	8/16/64	1
Ream's Station, VA (14TH)	8/25/64	1
Winchester,VA(2HA,9,13TH)*2	9/19/64	8
Fisher's Hill, VA (2 HA)	9/22/64	3
Richmond, VA (29TH) *	9/29/64	1
Cedar Creek, VA (2 HA)	10/19/64	7
Kell House, VA (29TH)	10/27/64	1
Cedar Creek, VA (9TH)	11/1/64	1
Bentonville, NC (20TH)	3/19/65	1

POMFRET
THE POPULATION IN 1860 WAS 1,913 (RANK 78)

THE MOST IMPORTANT DAY OF THE CIVIL WAR

MAY 16, 1864

DREWRY'S BLUFF , VA

AN OBSTACLE ON THE WAY TO RICHMOND

More soldiers credited to Pomfret were listed as casualties (8) on this day than on any other day of the war. One soldier was killed, 5 were wounded, and 2 were wounded & captured in the 11TH and 21ST Connecticut. Both of the captured died in prison.

The date May 16, 1864 ranks 4th for total casualties (560) (52 killed, 3 missing, 224 wounded, 243 captured, 38 wounded & captured) for a single day for the State of Connecticut. The Battle of Drewry's Bluff accounted for 545 casualties. The 15 other casualties were scattered about Virginia.

The Battle of Drewry's Bluff (May 13-17, 1864), also called Fort Darling, ranks 3rd for total casualties (634) for an engagement for the State of Connecticut. The most intense fighting developed on May 16. Pomfret had all of its casualties on that date.

The Battle of Drewry's Bluff with 8 total casualties for Pomfret was the highest number of casualties for any single engagement of the war for the town.

The Confederate attack at Drewry's Bluff forced the Union Army to retreat to Bermuda Hundred. The civil war would have concluded sooner had the Union Army been victorious.

111 MEN CREDITED TO POMFRET SERVED IN THE FOLLOWING CONNECTICUT ORGANIZATIONS

REGIMENT	TOTAL
11TH	25 (23%)
18TH	21 (19%)
21ST	15 (14%)
7TH	10 (10%)
26TH	9 (8%)
1ST CAVALRY	8 (7%)
1ST HEAVY ARTILLERY	7 (6%)
6TH	7 (6%)
14TH	4 (4%)
2ND	3 (3%)
2ND HEAVY ARTILLERY	3 (3%)
29TH	3 (3%)
8TH	2 (2%)
12TH	1

7% OF POPULATION

FOUR WERE KILLED

The first Pomfret soldier killed was Sergeant Alfred E. Reynolds of Company K, 21ST Connecticut. He was killed at Drewry's Bluff, VA on May 16, 1864.

POMFRET SOLDIERS KILLED

PLACE	DATE	NO.
Drewry's Bluff, VA (21ST)	5/16/64	1
Ashland, VA (1 CA)	6/1/64	1
Piedmont, VA (18TH)	6/5/64	1
Fisher's Hill, VA (2 HA)	9/21/64	1

TEN WERE CAPTURED

Six Pomfret soldiers died in captivity. Four died at Libby Prison, Richmond, VA and two died at Andersonville Prison, GA.

POMFRET CAPTURED
*(6) DIED IN CAPTIVITY

PLACE	DATE	NO.
Winchester, VA (18TH)	6/15/63	3
Fort Wagner, SC (7TH) *2	7/11/63	3
(2 WOUNDED)		
Craig's Church, VA (1 CA) *	5/5/64	1
New Market, VA (18TH) *	5/15/64	1
Drewry's Bluff, VA (21ST) *2	5/16/64	2
(2 WOUNDED)		

TOTAL POMFRET CASUALTIES

DIED	21	19%
KILLED	4	4%
WOUNDED	20	18%
CAPTURED	10	9%
DESERTED	7	6%

TWENTY WERE WOUNDED

The first Pomfret soldier wounded was Sergeant Edward P. King of Company K, 7TH Connecticut. He was wounded at James Island, SC on June 14, 1862 and recovered from his wound. Three Pomfret soldiers died from a wound received during the war.

POMFRET WOUNDED
*(3) DIED FROM WOUNDS

PLACE	DATE	NO.
James Island, SC (7TH)	6/14/62	1
Antietam, MD (11TH)	9/17/62	2
Port Hudson, LA (26TH) *	5/27/63	1
Fort Wagner, SC (7TH)	7/11/63	1
Fort Wagner, SC (6TH)	7/18/63	1
Swift's Creek, VA (11TH)	5/9/64	1
New Market, VA (18TH)	5/15/64	1
Drewry's Bluff, VA (11,21ST)	5/16/64	5
Cold Harbor, VA (11TH) *1	6/3/64	2
Snicker's Ford, VA (18TH)	7/18/64	1
Petersburg, VA (11TH) *	7/25/64	1
Deep Run, VA (7TH)	8/16/64	1
Petersburg, VA (11TH)	8/25/64	1
Boydton Plank Rd, VA (14TH)	10/27/64	1

518

PORTLAND
THE POPULATION IN 1860 WAS 3,657 (RANK 24)

THE MOST IMPORTANT DAY OF THE CIVIL WAR
MAY 16, 1864
DREWRY'S BLUFF, VA

AN OBSTACLE ON THE WAY TO RICHMOND

More soldiers credited to Portland were listed as casualties (11) on this day than on any other day of the war. One soldier was killed, 1 was wounded and 9 were captured in the 7TH and 11TH Connecticut. Four of the captured died in prison.

The date May 16, 1864 ranks 4th for total casualties (560) (52 killed, 3 missing, 224 wounded, 243 captured, 38 wounded & captured) for a single day for the State of Connecticut. The Battle of Drewry's Bluff accounted for 545 casualties. The 15 other casualties were scattered about Virginia.

The Battle of Drewry's Bluff (May 13-17, 1864), also called Fort Darling, ranks 3rd for total casualties (634) for an engagement for the State of Connecticut. The most intense fighting developed on May 16. Portland had all of its casualties on that day.

The Battle of Drewry's Bluff with 11 total casualties for Portland was the highest number of casualties for any single engagement of the war for the town.

The Confederate attack at Drewry's Bluff forced the Union Army to retreat to Bermuda Hundred. The civil war would have concluded sooner had the Union Army been victorious.

192 MEN CREDITED TO PORTLAND SERVED IN THE FOLLOWING CONNECTICUT ORGANIZATIONS

REGIMENT	TOTAL
20TH	59 (31%)
11TH	37 (19%)
1ST HEAVY ARTILLERY	15 (8%)
9TH	14 (7%)
13TH	14 (7%)
7TH	10 (5%)
1ST CAVALRY	8 (4%)
15TH	7 (4%)
6TH	6 (3%)
10TH	5 (3%)
12TH	5 (3%)
9TH BATTALION	4 (2%)
13TH BATTALION	3 (2%)
21ST	3 (2%)
30TH	3 (2%)
8TH	2 (1%)
16TH	2 (1%)
18TH	2 (1%)
5TH	1
12TH BATTALION	1
14TH	1
24TH	1
22ND	1
29TH	1

5% OF POPULATION

EIGHT WERE KILLED

The first Portland soldiers killed were Privates Heman Demay, Thomas Francis and Samuel Potter of Company D, 20TH Connecticut. They were killed at Chancellorsville, VA on May 3, 1863.

PORTLAND SOLDIERS KILLED

PLACE	DATE	NO.
Chancellorsville, VA (20TH)	5/3/63	3
Louisiana (Drowned) (24TH)	8/4/63	1
Drewry's Bluff, VA (7TH)	5/16/64	1
Peach Tree Creek, GA (20TH)	7/20/64	1
Averysboro, NC (20TH)	3/16/65	1
Salem, VA (11TH)	10/9/65	1

EIGHTEEN WERE CAPTURED

Four Portland soldiers died in captivity. Three died at Andersonville Prison, GA, and one at Charleston Prison, SC.

PORTLAND CAPTURED
*(4) DIED IN CAPTIVITY

PLACE	DATE	NO.
Pattersonville, LA (12TH)	3/27/63	1
Chancellorsville, VA (20TH)	5/3/63	2
(1 WOUNDED)		
Plymouth, NC (16TH)	4/20/64	1
Drewry's Bluff, VA (11TH) *4	5/16/64	9
Hatcher's Run, VA (7TH)	6/2/64	1
Turner's Ford, GA (20TH)	8/27/64	1
Cedar Creek, VA (12TH)	10/19/64	1
Kinston, NC (15TH)	3/8/65	1
Goldsboro, NC (20TH)	3/24/65	1

TOTAL PORTLAND CASUALTIES

DIED	20	10%
KILLED	8	4%
WOUNDED	27	14%
CAPTURED	18	9%
DESERTED	34	18%

TWENTY-SEVEN WERE WOUNDED

The first Portland soldiers wounded were Corporal Halsay J. Tibbals and Privates William DeBank and Robert McKinley of Company D, 20TH Connecticut. They were wounded at Chancellorsville, VA on May 3, 1863. Private DeBank, who was also captured, died 7 months later. One Portland soldier died from a wound received during the war.

PORTLAND WOUNDED
*(1) DIED FROM WOUNDS

PLACE	DATE	NO.
Chancellorsville, VA (20TH)	5/3/63	3
Port Hudson, LA (24TH)	6/14/63	1
Gettysburg, PA (20TH)	7/3/63	2
Fort Wagner, SC (7TH)	7/11/63	1
Morton's Ford, VA (14TH)	2/6/64	1
Resaca, GA (20TH)	5/15/64	2
Drewry's Bluff, VA (11TH)	5/16/64	1
Bermuda Hundred, VA (7TH)	6/2/64	1
Cold Harbor, VA (11TH)	6/3/64	6
Peach Tree Creek, GA (20TH)	7/20/64	1
Petersburg, VA (21ST) *	7/30/64	1
Winchester, VA (13TH)	9/19/64	1
Dutch Gap, VA (7TH)	9/29/64	1
Fort Fisher, NC (6TH)	1/15/65	1
Bentonville, NC (20TH)	3/19/65	3
West Point, NC (15TH)	Uknown	1

PRESTON
THE POPULATION IN 1860 WAS 2,092 (RANK 73)

THE MOST IMPORTANT DAY OF THE CIVIL WAR

JUNE 15 1863

WINCHESTER, VA

THE ENTIRE UNION ARMY WAS NEARLY CAPTURED AT THE SECOND BATTLE OF WINCHESTER

More soldiers credited to Preston were listed as casualties (16) on this day than on any other day of the war. Sixteen soldiers in the 18TH Connecticut were captured. All survived the war.

The date June 15, 1863 ranks 2ND for total casualties (595) (23 killed, 11 wounded, 520 captured, 41 wounded & captured) for a single day for the State of Connecticut. There were 592 casualties at Winchester, VAand 3 casualties at Port Hudson, LA.

The Second Battle of Winchester (June 13-15, 1863) ranks 5TH for total casualties (592) for an engagement for the State of Connecticut. The most intense fighting developed on June 15. Preston had all its casualites on that day.

The Second Battle of Winchester with 16 total casualties for Preston was the highest number of casualties for any single engagement of the war for the town.

Winchester was one of the most contested locations in the Civil War. It changed hands seventy-two times.

146 MEN CREDITED TO PRESTON SERVED IN THE FOLLOWING CONNECTICUT ORGANIZATIONS

REGIMENT	TOTAL
26TH	35 (24%)
18TH	30 (21%)
29TH	22 (15%)
1ST CAVALRY	10 (7%)
14TH	10 (7%)
12TH	8 (5%)
2ND	7 (5%)
30TH	6 (4%)
7TH	5 (3%)
2ND HEAVY ARTILLERY	5 (3%)
1ST HEAVY ARTILLERY	4 (3%)
10TH	4 (3%)
15TH	2 (1%)
8TH	2 (1%)
5TH	2 (1%)
6TH	2 (1%)
21ST	2 (1%)
12TH BATTALION	2 (1%)
1ST	1
3RD	1
11TH	1
16TH	1

7% OF POPULATION

TWO WERE KILLED

The first Preston soldier killed was Private Frederick Smith of Company E, 14ᵀᴴ Connecticut. He was killed at Bristoe Station, VA on October 14, 1863.

PRESTON SOLDIERS KILLED

PLACE	DATE	NO.
Bristoe Station, VA (14ᵀᴴ)	10/14/63	1
Ashland, VA (1 CA)	6/1/64	1

TWENTY-SIX WERE CAPTURED

One Preston soldier died in captivity at Salisbury, NC.

PRESTON CAPTURED
*(1) DIED IN CAPTIVITY

PLACE	DATE	NO.
Cross Keys, VA (1 CA)	6/8/2	1
Cedar Mountain, VA (5ᵀᴴ)	8/9/62	1
Winchester, VA (18ᵀᴴ)	6/15/63	16
(WOUNDED)		
Waterford, VA (1 CA)	8/7/63	1
Craig's Church, VA (1 CA)	5/5/64	1
Piedmont, VA (18ᵀᴴ)	6/5/64	3
(3 WOUNDED)		
Lynchburg, VA (18ᵀᴴ)	6/18/64	1
(WOUNDED)		
Cedar Creek, VA (12ᵀᴴ) *	10/19/64	2

TOTAL PRESTON CASUALTIES

DIED	19	12%
KILLED	2	1%
WOUNDED	28	19%
CAPTURED	26	18%
DESERTED	11	7%

TWENTY-EIGHT WERE WOUNDED

The first Preston soldier wounded was 1ˢᵀ Sergeant Horace Gore of Company C, 1ˢᵀ Connecticut Cavalry. He was wounded at McDowell, VA on May 8, 1862 and recovered from his wound. Four Preston soldiers died from a wound received during the war.

PRESTON WOUNDED
*(4) DIED FROM WOUNDS

PLACE	DATE	NO.
McDowell, VA (1 CA)	5/8/62	1
2ᴺᴰ Bull Run, VA (1 CA)	8/30/62	1
Antietam, MD (8ᵀᴴ) *1	9/17/62	2
Camp Parapet, LA (26ᵀᴴ)	2/22/63	1
Bisland, LA (12ᵀᴴ)	4/13/63	1
Port Hudson, LA (26ᵀᴴ) *2	5/27/63	8
Virginia (18ᵀᴴ)	6/12/63	1
Port Hudson, LA (26ᵀᴴ)	6/14/63	4
Spottsylvania, VA (14ᵀᴴ)	5/12/64	1
Drewry's Bluff, VA (7ᵀᴴ) *	5/15/64	1
New Market, VA (18ᵀᴴ)	5/15/64	1
Cold Harbor, VA (8ᵀᴴ)	6/3/64	1
Piedmont, VA (18ᵀᴴ)	6/5/64	1
Snicker's Ford, VA (18ᵀᴴ)	7/18/64	1
Petersburg, VA (30ᵀᴴ) *	7/30/64	1
Winchester, VA (12ᵀᴴ)	9/19/64	1
Fort Gregg, VA (10ᵀᴴ)	4/2/65	1

PROSPECT
THE POPULATION IN 1860 WAS 574 (RANK 157)

THE MOST IMPORTANT DAY OF THE CIVIL WAR

MAY 3, 1863
CHANCELLORSVILLE, VA

THE THIRD DAY OF THE BATTLE

Soldiers credited to Prospect had more casualties on May 3, 1863 at Chancellorsville, VA (3) and on March 8, 1865 at Kinston, NC (3) than on any other days of the war. The casualties at Chancellorsville were the most serious. One soldier was killed, 1 was wounded, and 1 was captured in the 20TH Connecticut. The wounded soldier died from his wound.

The date May 3, 1863 ranks 3RD for total casualties (577) (36 killed, 1 missing, 138 wounded, 372 captured, 29 wounded & captured) for a single day for the State of Connecticut. The most casualties were at Chancellorsville, VA (556). The other casualties were at Providence Church Road, VA (12), Suffolk, VA (6), Port Hudson, LA (2) and Fredericksburg, VA (1).

The Battle of Chancellorsville (May 1-3, 1863) ranks 2ND for total casualties (677) for an engagement for the State of Connecticut. The most intense fighting developed on May 3. Prospect had no other casualties in the battle other than on May 3.

The Battle of Chancellorsville with 3 total casualties for Prospect was tied with the Second Battle of Kinston (March 8, 1865) for the highest number of casualties for any single engagement of the war for the town.

The Battle of Chancellorsville was an enormous defeat for the more than 70,000 Union soldiers who had moved against the flank and rear of 40,000 Confederate soldiers. Unfortunately, the Union Army had pulled back and had gone on the defensive around Chancellorsville. The Confederate victory was tainted however, by the loss of Confederate Major General "Stonewall" Jackson.

48 MEN CREDITED TO PROSPECT SERVED IN THE FOLLOWING CONNECTICUT ORGANIZATIONS

REGIMENT	TOTAL
20TH	19 (40%)
6TH	16 (38%)
15TH	4 (8%)
1ST CAVALRY	1
1ST LIGHT BATTERY	1
5TH	1
7TH	1
8TH	1
11TH	1
14TH	1
26TH	1
27TH	1
29TH	1

8% OF POPULATION

THREE WERE KILLED

The first Prospect soldier killed was Private Joel J. Brooks of Company A, 20TH Connecticut. He was killed at Chancellorsville, VA on May 3, 1863.

PROSPECT SOLDIERS KILLED

PLACE	DATE	NO.
Chancellorsville, VA (20TH)	5/3/63	1
Bermuda Hundred, VA (6TH)	6/1/64	1
Pikeville, NC (20TH)	3/25/65	1

FIVE WERE CAPTURED

No Prospect soldiers died in captivity.

PROSPECT CAPTURED
NONE DIED IN CAPTIVITY

PLACE	DATE	NO.
Antietam, MD (8TH) (WOUNDED)	9/17/62	1
Chancellorsville, VA (20TH)	5/3/63	1
New Market Road (6TH)	10/1/64	1
Kinston, NC (15TH)	3/8/65	2

TOTAL PROSPECT CASUALTIES

DIED	7	13%
KILLED	3	6%
WOUNDED	8	17%
CAPTURED	5	10%
DESERTED	5	10%

EIGHT WERE WOUNDED

The first Prospect soldier wounded was Private Philo D. Hotchkiss of Company E, 8TH Connecticut. He was wounded and captured at Antietam, MD on September 17, 1862 and recovered from his wound and captivity. Two Prospect soldiers died from a wound received during the war.

PROSPECT WOUNDED
*(2) DIED FROM WOUNDS

PLACE	DATE	NO.
Loudon Heights, VA (20TH)	11/1/62	1
Chancellorsville, VA (20TH) *	5/3/63	1
Morris Island, SC (6TH)	7/10/63	1
Fort Wagner, SC (6TH)	7/18/63	1
Atlanta, GA (20TH)	8/15/64	1
Bermuda Hundred, VA (6TH) *	8/23/64	1
Kinston, NC (15TH)	3/8/65	1
Bentonville, NC (20TH)	3/19/65	1

PUTNAM
THE POPULATION IN 1860 WAS 2,722 (RANK 50)

THE MOST IMPORTANT DAY 0F THE CIVIL WAR

JUNE 15 1863
WINCHESTER, VA

THE ENTIRE UNION ARMY WAS NEARLY CAPTURED AT THE SECOND BATTLE OF WINCHESTER

More soldiers credited to Putnam were listed as casualties (27) on this day than on any other day of the war. One soldier was killed and 26 were captured in the 18TH Connecticut. One of the captured soldiers died in prison.

The date June 15, 1863 ranks 2ND for total casualties (595) (23 killed, 11 wounded, 520 captured, 41 wounded & captured) for a single day for the State of Connecticut. There were 592 casualties at Winchester, VA and 3 casualties at Port Hudson, LA.

The Second Battle of Winchester (June 13-15, 1863) ranks 5TH for total casualties (592) for an engagement for the State of Connecticut. The most intense fighting developed on June 15. Putnam had all its casualites on that day.

The Second Battle of Winchester with 26 total casualties for Putnam was the highest number of casualties for any single engagement of the war for the town.

Winchester was one of the most contested locations in the Civil War. It changed hands seventy-two times.

193 MEN CREDITED TO PUTNAM SERVED IN THE FOLLOWING CONNECTICUT ORGANIZATIONS

REGIMENT	TOTAL
18TH	48 (25%)
6TH	35 (18%)
1ST CAVALRY	28 (14%)
5TH	18 (9%)
11TH	18 (9%)
13TH	15 (8%)
1ST HEAVY ARTILLERY	14 (7%)
14TH	12 (6%)
7TH	10 (5%)
2ND	4 (2%)
13TH BATTALION	4 (2%)
2ND HEAVY ARTILLERY	2 (1%)
8TH	1
20TH	1
26TH	1
29TH	1

7% OF POPULATION

NINE WERE KILLED AND THREE WERE MISSING

The first Putnam soldier killed was Private Charles H. Morse of the 18TH Connecticut. He was killed at The Battle of Antietam, MD on September 17, 1862.

PUTNAM SOLDIERS KILLED
*(3) MISSING

PLACE	DATE	NO.
Antietam, MD (11TH)	9/17/62	1
Winchester, VA (18TH)	6/15/63	1
Brashear City, LA (13TH)	6/21/63	1
Fort Wagner, SC (7TH)	7/11/63	1
Fort Wagner, SC (6TH) *1	7/18/63	2
Putnam, CT (5TH)	2/28/64	1
New Market, VA (18TH) *	5/15/64	1
Piedmont, VA (18TH)	6/5/64	1
Atlanta, GA (5TH)	7/30/64	1
Deep Run, VA (6TH) *	8/16/64	1
Unknown Place (11TH)	2/3/65	1

FORTY-SIX WERE CAPTURED

Five Putnam soldiers died in captivity. Two died at Andersonville Prison, GA, one died at Libby Prison Richmond, VA, one died at Salisbury, NC and one died at New Market, VA.

PUTNAM CAPTURED
*(5) DIED IN CAPTIVITY

PLACE	DATE	NO.
Chancellorsville, VA (5TH)	5/2/63	1
Chancellorsville, VA (14TH)	5/3/63	1
Fredericksburg, VA (14TH)	12/13/63	1
Winchester, VA (18TH) *1	6/15/63	26
Fort Wagner, SC (18TH) (1 WOUNDED)	7/11/63	2
Fort Wagner, SC (6TH)	7/18/63	1
Waterford, VA (1 CA) *	8/7/63	1
Bristoe Station, VA (14TH)	10/14/63	1
Grove Church, VA (1 CA)	3/29/64	1
Craig's Church, VA (1 CA)	5/5/64	1
Drewry's Bluff, VA (11TH)	5/16/64	1
Piedmont, VA (18TH) (3 WOUNDED)	6/5/64	3
Lynchburg, VA (18TH) *2 (2 WOUNDED)	6/18/64	2
Roanoke Station, VA (1 CA)	6/26/64	1
Cedar Run Church, VA (1 CA) *	10/17/64	2

TOTAL PUTNAM CASUALTIES

DIED	15	8%
KILLED/MISSING	12	6%
WOUNDED	37	19%
CAPTURED	46	23%
DESERTED	13	7%

THIRTY-SEVEN WERE WOUNDED

The first Putnam soldiers wounded were Privates Eugene Boudrie and Laughlin J. Braken of the 11TH Connecticut. They were wounded at New Bern, NC on March 14, 1862 and both recovered from their wounds. One Putnam soldier died from a wound received during the war.

PUTNAM WOUNDED
*(1) DIED FROM WOUNDS

PLACE	DATE	NO.
New Bern, NC (11TH)	3/14/62	2
Antietam, MD (11TH)	9/17/62	2
Siege Port Hudson, LA (13TH)	6/14/63	1
Gettysburg, PA (14TH)	7/3/63	1
Fort Wagner, SC (6TH)	7/18/63	6
Arlington Heights, VA (1 HA)	11/20/63	1
Ball's Cross Rd, VA (1 HA)	1/25/64	1
Suffolk, VA (11TH)	5/4/64	1
Drewry's Bluff, VA (6, 7TH)	5/14/64	2
New Market, VA (18TH)	5/15/64	2
Resaca, GA (5TH)	5/15/64	1
Drewry's Bluff, VA (6TH)	5/20/64	1
Proctor's Creek, VA (6TH)	5/20/64	1
Petersburg, VA (11TH)	6/3/64	1
Piedmont, VA (18TH)	6/5/64	1
Bermuda Hundred, VA (6TH)	6/6/64	1
Petersburg, VA (11TH)	6/16/64	1
Petersburg, VA (11TH)	6/18/64	2
Snicker's Ford, VA (18TH)	7/18/64	2
Deep Run, VA (6TH)	8/16/64	2
Petersburg, VA (11TH)	8/20/64	1
Winchester, VA (13TH)	9/19/64	3
Hatcher's Run, VA (14TH)	2/5/65	1

REDDING
THE POPULATION IN 1860 WAS 1,652 (RANK 91)

THE MOST IMPORTANT DAY OF THE CIVIL WAR

MAY 16, 1864

DREWRY'S BLUFF , VA

AN OBSTACLE ON THE WAY TO RICHMOND

More soldiers credited to Redding were listed as casualties (4) on this day than on any other day of the war. One soldier was killed, 1 was wounded & captured, and 2 were captured in the 7TH and 8TH Connecticut. The captured survived the war.

The date May 16, 1864 ranks 4th for total casualties (560) (52 killed, 3 missing, 224 wounded, 243 captured, 38 wounded & captured) for a single day for the State of Connecticut. The Battle of Drewry's Bluff accounted for 545 casualties. There were 15 other casualties scattered about Virginia.

The Battle of Drewry's Bluff (May 13-17, 1864), also called Fort Darling, ranks 3rd for total casualties (634) for an engagement for the State of Connecticut. The most intense fighting developed on May 16. Redding had all of its casualties on that day.

The Battle of Drewry's Bluff with 4 total casualties for Redding was the highest number of casualties for any single engagement of the war for the town.

The Confederate attack at Drewry's Bluff forced the Union Army to retreat to Bermuda Hundred. The civil war would have concluded sooner had the Union Army been victorious.

147 MEN CREDITED TO REDDING SERVED IN THE FOLLOWING CONNECTICUT ORGANIZATIONS

REGIMENT	TOTAL
23RD	48 (33%)
7TH	16 (11%)
17TH	16 (11%)
10TH	11 (8%)
1ST HEAVY ARTILLERY	10 (7%)
8TH	9 (6%)
29TH	8 (5%)
5TH	7 (5%)
2ND HEAVY ARTILLERY	6 (3%)
11TH	6 (4%)
6TH	3 (2%)
2ND LIGHT BATTERY	3 (2%)
1ST CAVALRY	2 (1%)
3RD	2 (1%)
9TH	2 (1%)
12TH	1
13TH	1
14TH	1
20TH	1
30TH	1

9% OF POPULATION

TWO WERE KILLED

The first Redding soldier killed was Private Jerome Dupoy of Company D, 7TH Connecticut. He was killed on February 20, 1864 at Olustee, FL.

REDDING SOLDIERS KILLED

PLACE	DATE	NO.
Olustee, FL (7TH)	2/20/64	1
Drewry's Bluff, VA (7TH)	5/16/64	1

ELEVEN WERE CAPTURED

No Redding soldier died in captivity.

REDDING CAPTURED
NONE DIED IN CAPTIVITY

PLACE	DATE	NO.
Winchester, VA (5TH)	5/25/62	1
Cedar Mountain, VA (5TH)	8/9/62	2
Gettysburg, PA (17TH)	7/1/63	1
Drewry's Bluff, VA (7, 8TH)	5/16/64	3
(1 WOUNDED)		
Spottsylvania, VA (14TH)	5/18/64	1
Petersburg, VA (11TH)	6/18/64	1
Dunn's Lake, FL (17TH)	2/5/65	2

TOTAL REDDING CASUALTIES

DIED	12	8%
KILLED	2	1%
WOUNDED	14	10%
CAPTURED	11	7%
DESERTED	23	16%

FOURTEEN WERE WOUNDED

The first Redding soldier wounded was Private Charles O. Morgan of Company A, 11TH Connecticut. He was wounded on April 23, 1863 at Suffolk, VA and recovered from his wound. One Redding soldier died from a wound received during the war.

REDDING WOUNDED
*(1) DIED FROM WOUNDS

PLACE	DATE	NO.
Suffolk, VA (11TH)	4/24/63	1
Port Hudson, LA (12TH) *	6/10/63	1
La Fourche, LA (23RD)	6/20/63	1
Gettysburg, PA (17TH)	7/1/63	1
Olustee, FL (7TH)	2/23/64	1
Proctor's Creek, VA (6TH)	5/3/64	1
Bermuda Hundred, VA (6TH)	5/20/64	1
Petersburg, VA (8TH)	6/15/64	1
Petersburg, VA (8TH)	7/5/64	1
Deep Run, VA (10TH)	8/16/64	1
Fort Hurricane, VA (29TH)	10/18/64	1
Fort Gregg, VA (10TH)	4/2/65	3

RIDGEFIELD
THE POPULATION IN 1860 WAS 2,213 (RANK 66)

THE MOST IMPORTANT DAY OF THE CIVIL WAR

JULY 1, 1863

GETTYSBURG, PA

THE FIRST DAY OF THE BATTLE

More soldiers credited to Ridgefield were listed as casualties (11) on this day than on any other day of the war. Two soldiers were killed, 5 were wounded, 1 was wounded & captured, and 3 were captured in the 17TH Connecticut. The wounded and captured survived the war.

The date July 1, 1863 ranks 16TH for total casualties (157) (18 killed, 4 missing, 70 wounded, 57 captured, 8 wounded & captured) for a single day for the State of Connecticut. The Battle of Gettysburg accounted for 143 casualties. The 14 other casualties were scattered about Virginia (6), Louisiana (6), and South Carolina (2).

The Battle of Gettysburg (July1-3, 1863) ranks 11TH for total casualties (360) for an engagement for the State of Connecticut. The most intense fighting developed on July 3. Ridgefield had no casualties on that day however, they did have 1 casualty on July 2.

The Battle of Gettysburg with 12 total casualties for Ridgefield was the highest number of casualties for any single engagement of the war for the town.

More than 170,00 men fought at the Battle of Gettysburg. Roughly 23,000 Union casualties were recorded and there were about 28,000 Confederate casualties. Gettysburg proved to be the great battle of the war. It ended Lee's 1863 invasion of the North. He was never able to launch a major offensive again

178 MEN CREDITED TO RIDGEFIELD SERVED IN THE FOLLOWING CONNECTICUT ORGANIZATIONS

REGIMENT	TOTAL
17TH	72 (41%)
1ST HEAVY ARTILLERY	13 (7%)
6TH	13 (7%)
5TH	12 (7%)
7TH	12 (7%)
8TH	9 (5%)
23RD	9 (5%)
11TH	8 (4%)
10TH	6 (3%)
13TH	6 (3%)
2ND HEAVY ARTILLERY	5 (3%)
1ST CAVALRY	4 (2%)
12TH	3 (2%)
12TH BATTALION	3 (2%)
15TH	3 (2%)
20TH	3 (2%)
13TH BATTALION	2 (1%)
29TH	2 (1%)
30TH	2 (1%)
9TH	1

8% OF POPULATION

THREE WERE KILLED AND TWO WERE MISSING

The first Ridgefield soldier killed was Corporal Andrew D. Couch of Company G, 17TH Connecticut. He was killed at Chancellorsville, VA on May 2, 1863.

RIDGEFIELD SOLDIERS KILLED MISSING *

PLACE	DATE	NO.
Chancellorsville, VA (17TH)	5/2/63	1
Gettysburg, PA (17TH)	7/1/63	2
Proctor's Creek, VA (7TH) *	6/13/64	1
North Carolina (15TH) *	9/27/64	1

TWENTY-SIX WERE CAPTURED

Three Ridgefield soldiers died in captivity. All three died at Andersonville Prison, GA.

RIDGEFIELD CAPTURED *(3) DIED IN CAPTIVITY

PLACE	DATE	NO.
Winchester, VA (5TH)	5/25/62	1
Cedar Mountain, VA (5TH)	8/9/62	2
Chancellorsville, VA (17TH)	5/2/63	6
(3 WOUNDED)		
Gettysburg, PA (17TH)	7/1/63	4
(1 WOUNDED)		
Gettysburg, PA (17TH)	7/2/63	1
Craig's Church, VA (1CA)	5/5/64	1
Drewry's Bluff, VA (7,8TH) *3	5/16/64	4
Welaka, FL (17TH)	5/19/64	1
St. Augustine, FL (17TH)	2/4/65	1
Dunn's Lake, FL (17TH)	2/5/65	3
Kinston, NC (15TH)	3/8/65	2
(1 WOUNDED)		

TOTAL RIDGEFIELD CASUALTIES

DIED	20	11%
KILLED/MISSING	5	3%
WOUNDED	27	15%
CAPTURED	26	15%
DESERTED	18	10%

TWENTY-SEVEN WERE WOUNDED

The first Ridgefield soldier wounded was Private Edwin Moffit of Company D, 7TH Connecticut. He was wounded at James Island, SC on June 1, 1862 and recovered from his wound. One Ridgefield soldier died from a wound received during the war.

RIDGEFIELD WOUNDED *(1) DIED FROM WOUNDS

PLACE	DATE	NO.
James Island, SC (7TH)	6/1/62	1
Cedar Mountain, VA (5TH)	8/9/62	2
Pocotaligo, SC (7TH)	10/22/62	1
Fredricksburg, VA (8TH)	12/11/62	1
Kinston, NC (10TH)	12/14/62	1
Chancellorsville, VA (17TH)	5/2/63	3
Chancellorsville, VA (17TH)	5/3/63	1
Gettysburg, PA (17TH)	7/1/63	5
Morris Island, SC (17TH)	8/1/63	1
Walthall Junction, VA (8TH)	5/7/64	1
Chester Station, VA (6TH)	5/10/64	2
Peach Tree Creek, GA (5TH)*	7/20/64	1
Petersburg, VA (29TH)	8/1/64	1
Deep Bottom, VA (10TH)	8/14/64	1
Deep Run, VA (6,7TH)	8/16/64	2
Deep Bottom, VA (6TH)	8/16/64	1
Winchester, VA (13TH)	9/19/64	1
Darbytown Road, VA (10TH)	10/13/64	1
Unknown Place (10TH)	Unknown	1

ROCKY HILL
THE POPULATION IN 1860 WAS 1,102 (RANK 127)

THE MOST IMPORTANT DAY OF THE CIVIL WAR

APRIL 20, 1864

PLYMOUTH, NC

THE CONFEDERATE PLAN TO TAKE PLYMOUTH ENDED WHEN 2,800 UNION TROOPS SURRENDERED THE CITY

More soldiers credited to Rocky Hill were listed as casualties (9) on this day than on any other day of the war. Nine soldiers in the 16TH Connecticut were captured. Four of them eventually died in prison.

The date April 20, 1864 ranks 6TH for total casualties (433) (1 killed, 2 missing, 12 wounded & captured, 418 captured) for a single day for the State of Connecticut. All of the casualties were at Plymouth, NC.

The Battle of Plymouth (April 20, 1864) ranks 9TH for total casualties (433) for an engagement for the State of Connecticut. Nearly half of all soldiers captured at Plymouth died in Southern prisons

The Battle of Plymouth with 9 total casualties for Rocky Hill was the highest number of casualties for any single engagement of the war for the town.

When Confederate General Robert Hoke surrounded and captured the Union garrison at Plymouth, NC the Southern victory was the first in this military arena in quite some time. With aid from the two-gun ironclad *Albemarle* the Confederates were able to take advantage of the lack of suitable Union gunboats.

100 MEN CREDITED TO ROCKY HILL SERVED IN THE FOLLOWING CONNECTICUT ORGANIZATIONS

REGIMENT	TOTAL
16TH	22 (22%)
25TH	17 (17%)
1ST HEAVY ARTILLERY	9 (9%)
8TH	9 (9%)
2ND	7 (7%)
14TH	6 (6%)
10TH	5 (5%)
11TH	5 (5%)
13TH	5 (5%)
29TH	5 (5%)
5TH	4 (4%)
7TH	3 (3%)
6TH	2 (2%)
15TH	2 (2%)
22ND	2 (2%)
1ST	1
1ST CAVALRY	1
1ST SQUADRON CAVALRY	1
13TH BATTALION	1
20TH	1
24TH	1
30TH	1

10% OF POPULATION

NO ROCKY HILL SOLDIERS WERE KILLED

TWELVE WERE CAPTURED

Four Rocky Hill soldiers died in captivity. Two soldiers died at Andersonville Prison, GA, one at Charleston, SC and one at Florence, SC.

ROCKY HILL CAPTURED
*(4) DIED IN CAPTIVITY

PLACE	DATE	NO.
Brandy Station, VA (1 SQ)	10/12/63	1
Plymouth, NC (16TH) *(4)	4/20/64	9
Brunswick, NC (6TH)	3/6/65	1
Kinston, NC (15TH)	3/8/65	1

TOTAL ROCKY HILL CASUALTIES

DIED	13	13%
KILLED	0	
WOUNDED	14	14%
CAPTURED	12	12%
DESERTED	15	15%

FOURTEEN WERE WOUNDED

The first Rocky Hill soldiers wounded were Corporal Albert S. Hatch, Musician John White, and Privates Charles H. Waterman and Donals Levaughn of the 8TH and 11TH Connecticut.They were wounded at The Battle of Antietam, MD on September 17, 1862. Private Waterman died from his wound. Two Rocky Hill soldiers died from a wound received during the war.

ROCKY HILL WOUNDED
*(2) DIED FROM WOUNDS

PLACE	DATE	NO.
Antietam, MD (8, 16TH) *1	9/17/62	4
Irish Bend, LA (25TH)	4/14/63	2
Suffolk, VA (16TH)	4/24/63	1
Providence Church Rd, VA (16TH)	5/3/63	1
Morton's Ford, VA (14TH)	2/6/64	2
Walthall Junction, VA (8TH)	5/7/64	1
North Anna River, VA (14TH)	5/24/64	1
Petersburg, VA (29TH)	7/5/64	1
Kell House, VA (29TH) *	10/27/64	1

ROXBURY
THE POPULATION IN 1860 WAS 992 (RANK 138)

THE MOST IMPORTANT DAY OF THE CIVIL WAR

SEPTEMBER 19, 1864

WINCHESTER, VA

THE BATTLE OF THIRD WINCHESTER (OPEQUON) WAS A UNION VICTORY

More soldiers credited to Roxbury were listed as casualties (4) on this day than on any other day of the war. Four soldiers were wounded in the 2ND Connecticut Heavy Artillery. All of the wounded survived the war.

The date September 19, 1864 ranks 9TH for total casualties (279) (38 killed, 209 wounded, 32 captured) for a single day for the State of Connecticut. The Battle of Third Winchester accounted for 274 casualties. The 5 other casualties were scattered about Virginia.

The Battle of Third Winchester (September 19, 1864) ranks 12TH for total casualties (274) for the State of Connecticut.

The Battle of Third Winchester with 4 total casualties for Roxbury was the highest number of casualties for any single engagement of the war for the town.

The battle was not an overwhelming victory for the Union Army. As the Union force was approaching Winchester from the east they became bogged down and the attacks were uncoordinated. The Union army sustained heavier casualties but the Confederates moved to a stronger position at Fisher's Hill south of Strasburg. The total casualties were about 7,500.

71 MEN CREDITED TO ROXBURY SERVED IN THE FOLLOWING CONNECTICUT ORGANIZATIONS

REGIMENT	TOTAL
10TH	17 (24%)
2ND HEAVY ARTILLERY	15 (21%)
5TH	12 (17%)
1ST HEAVY ARTILLERY	7 (10%)
13TH	7 (10%)
6TH	4 (6%)
11TH	3 (4%)
8TH	2 (3%)
13TH BATTALION	2 (3%)
17TH	2 (3%)
2ND LIGHT BATTERY	1
14TH	1
20TH	1
28TH	1

7% OF POPULATION

TWO WERE KILLED AND ONE WAS MISSING

The first Roxbury soldier killed was Private Charles Patterson of Company I, 8TH Connecticut. He was killed at New Bern, NC on March 14, 1862.

ROXBURY SOLDIERS KILLED MISSING *

PLACE	DATE	NO.
New Bern, NC (8TH)	3/14/62	1
Fort Wagner, SC (6TH) *	7/18/63	1
Culp's Farm, GA (5TH)	6/22/64	1

FOUR WERE CAPTURED

One Roxbury soldier died in captivity at Andersonville Prison, GA.

ROXBURY CAPTURED *(1) DIED IN CAPTIVITY

PLACE	DATE	NO.
Cedar Mountain, VA (5TH)	8/9/62	1
Gettysburg, PA (5TH)	7/2/63	1
Unknown (5TH) *	Unknown	1
Dunn's Lake, FLA (17TH)	2/5/65	1

TOTAL ROXBURY CASUALTIES

DIED	8	11%
KILLED/MISSING	3	4%
WOUNDED	15	21%
CAPTURED	4	6%
DESERTED	13	18%

FIFTEEN WERE WOUNDED

The first Roxbury soldier wounded was Private Roger L. Hurlburt of Company D, 10TH Connecticut. He was wounded at Roanoke Island, NC on April 1, 1862 and recovered from his wound. One Roxbury soldier died from a wound received during the war.

ROXBURY WOUNDED *(1) DIED FROM WOUNDS

PLACE	DATE	NO.
Roanoke Island, NC (10TH) *	2/8/62	1
Steamer "New York" (13TH)	Unknown	1
Richmond, VA (10TH)	6/1/64	1
Cold Harbor, VA (2 HA)	6/1/64	3
Petersburg, VA (2 HA)	6/24/64	1
Peach Tree Creek, GA (5TH)	7/20/64	1
Winchester, VA (2 HA)	9/19/64	4
Cedar Creek, VA (2 HA)	10/19/64	2
Unknown (6TH)	1/15/65	1

SALEM
THE POPULATION IN 1860 WAS 870 (RANK 147)

THE MOST IMPORTANT DAY OF THE CIVIL WAR

JUNE 15 1863

WINCHESTER, VA

THE ENTIRE UNION ARMY WAS NEARLY CAPTURED AT THE SECOND BATTLE OF WINCHESTER

More soldiers credited to Salem were listed as casualties (9) on this day than on any other day of the war. One soldier was wounded, 1 was wounded & captured, and 7 were captured in the 18TH Connecticut. All survived the war.

The date June 15, 1863 ranks 2ND for total casualties (595) (23 killed, 11 wounded, 520 captured, 41 wounded & captured) for a single day for the State of Connecticut. There were 592 casualties at Winchester, VA and 3 casualties at Port Hudson, LA.

The Second Battle of Winchester (June 13-15, 1863) ranks 5TH for total casualties (592) for an engagement for the State of Connecticut. The most intense fighting developed on June 15. Salem had all its casualties on that day.

The Second Battle of Winchester with 9 total casualties for Salem was the 2ND highest number of casualties for any single engagement of the war for the town. The Siege of Port Hudson, VA (May-July 1863) ranks 1ST with 11 casualties.

Winchester was one of the most contested locations in the Civil War. It changed hands seventy-two times.

65 MEN CREDITED TO SALEM SERVED IN THE FOLLOWING CONNECTICUT ORGANIZATIONS

REGIMENT	TOTAL
26TH	22 (34%)
18TH	14 (22%)
1ST HEAVY ARTILLERY	5 (8%)
13TH	5 (8%)
12TH	4 (6%)
1ST CAVALRY	3 (5%)
8TH	3 (5%)
12TH BATTALION	2 (3%)
14TH	2 (3%)
20TH	2 (3%)
21ST	2 (3%)
30TH	2 (3%)
10TH	1
11TH	1
13TH BATTALION	1

7% OF POPULATION

THREE WERE KILLED

The first Salem soldier killed was Private John O. Chapel of the 26TH Connecticut. He was killed at Port Hudson on June 14, 1863.

SALEM SOLDIERS KILLED

PLACE	DATE	NO.
Port Hudson, LA (26TH)	6/14/63	1
Piedmont, VA (18TH)	6/5/64	1
Charlestown, VA (1 CA)	12/7/64	1

TEN WERE CAPTURED

No Salem soldier died in captivity.

SALEM CAPTURED
NONE DIED IN CAPTIVITY

PLACE	DATE	NO.
Winchester, VA (18TH)	6/15/63	8
(1 WOUNDED)		
Piedmont, VA (18TH)	6/5/64	2
(1 WOUNDED)		

TOTAL SALEM CASUALTIES

DIED	8	12%
KILLED	3	5%
WOUNDED	18	28%
CAPTURED	10	15%
DESERTED	8	12%

EIGHTEEN WERE WOUNDED

The first Salem soldier wounded in combat was Private Charles H. Chapman of Company G, 13TH Connecticut. He was wounded at Bayou Boeuff, LA on March 14, 1862 and recovered from his wound. Two Salem soldiers died from a wound received during the war.

SALEM WOUNDED
*(2) DIED FROM WOUNDS

PLACE	DATE	NO.
New York, NY (26TH)	11/1/62	1
Bayou Boeuf, LA (13TH)	5/9/63	1
Port Hudson, LA (26TH) *2	5/27/63	5
Port Hudson, LA (26TH)	6/14/63	5
Winchester, VA (18TH)	6/15/63	1
Morton's Ford, VA (14TH)	2/6/64	1
Petersburg, VA (11TH)	6/16/64	1
Ream's Station, VA (1 CA)	6/29/64	1
Deep Run, VA (10TH)	8/16/64	1
Cedar Creek, VA (12TH)	10/19/64	1

SALISBURY
THE POPULATION IN 1860 WAS 3,100 (RANK 41)

THE MOST IMPORTANT DAY OF THE CIVIL WAR

JUNE 1, 1864

COLD HARBOR, VA

THE BATTLE WAS LEE'S LAST GREAT VICTORY

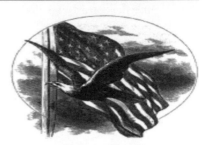

More soldiers credited to Salisbury were listed as casualties (22) on this day than on any other day of the war. Ten soldiers were killed and 12 were wounded in the 2ND Connecticut Heavy Artillery. Four of the wounded died.

The date June 1, 1864 ranks 8TH for total casualties (374) (89 killed, 10 missing, 246 wounded, 23 captured, 6 wounded & captured) for a single day for the State of Connecticut. There were 324 casualties at Cold Harbor, 41 casualties at Ashland, and 9 other casualties scattered about Virginia.

The battle and operations around Cold Harbor (May 31-June 12, 1864) rank 6TH for total casualties (557) for an engagement for the State of Connecticut. The most intense fighting developed on June 3. Salisbury had 1 missing and 3 wounded on that day. They also had 1 wounded on June 2

The Battle of Cold Harbor with 27 total casualties for Salisbury was the highest number of casualties for any single engagement of the war for the town.

Approximately 117,000 Federal and 60,000 Confederate troops participated in operations from May 28 to June 3. Roughly 13,000 Union casualties were recorded and perhaps there were 5,000 Confederate casualties.

344 MEN CREDITED SALISBURY SERVED IN THE FOLLOWING CONNECTICUT ORGANIZATIONS

REGIMENT	TOTAL
28TH	82 (24%)
2ND HEAVY ARTILLERY	79 (23%)
11TH	59 (17%)
5TH	21 (6%)
7TH	20 (6%)
10TH	17 (5%)
1ST HEAVY ARTILLERY	12 (4%)
29TH	12 (4%)
14TH	10 (3%)
6TH	8 (2%)
8TH	7 (2%)
12TH	7 (2%)
9TH	5 (1%)
15TH	5 (1%)
20TH	5 (1%)
12TH BATTALION	4 (1%)
13TH	4 (1%)
18TH	4 (1%)
23RD	3 (1%)
17TH	2
30TH	1

11% OF POPULATION

SEVENTEEN WERE KILLED AND ONE WAS MISSING

The first Salisbury soldier killed was Corporal Egbert F. Nott of the 28TH Connecticut. He was killed at Port Hudson, LA on June 14, 1863.

SALISBURY SOLDIERS KILLED

PLACE	DATE	NO.
Port Hudson, LA (28TH)	6/14/63	1
Olustee, FL (7TH)	2/20/64	1
Drewry's Bluff, VA (11TH)	5/16/64	1
Cold Harbor, VA (2 HA)	6/1/64	10
Cold Harbor, VA (11TH) *	6/3/64	1
Petersburg, VA (14TH)	6/17/64	1
Petersburg, VA (11TH)	6/18/64	1
Deep Run, VA (7TH)	8/16/64	1
Winchester, VA (2 HA)	9/19/64	1

ELEVEN WERE CAPTURED

Three Salisbury soldiers died in captivity. One died at Augusta, GA and two died at Salisbury, NC.

SALISBURY CAPTURED (3) DIED IN CAPTIVITY

PLACE	DATE	NO.
Chickahominy, VA (5TH)	6/10/62	1
Fort Wagner, SC (7TH)	7/11/63	1
Bristoe Station, VA (14TH) *	10/14/63	1
St Augustine, FL (10TH)	12/30/63	1
Drewry's Bluff, VA (11TH)	5/16/64	2
Petersburg, VA (11TH)	6/18/64	1
Cedar Creek, VA(2 HA, 12TH) *2	10/19/64	3
Kinston, NC (15TH)	3/8/65	1

TOTAL SALISBURY CASUALTIES

DIED	38	11%
KILLED/MISSING	18	6%
WOUNDED	56	16%
CAPTURED	11	3%
DESERTED	59	17%

FIFTY-SIX WERE WOUNDED

The first Salisbury soldiers wounded were Corporals Alexander Palmatier and George W. Newall and Privates Rueben R. Speed, John W. Speed and Orville D. Owen of Company D, 10TH Connecticut. They were wounded at Roanoke Island, NC on February 8, 1862. John Speed and Orville Owen died from their wounds. Eleven Salisbury soldiers died from a wound received during the war.

SALISBURY WOUNDED *(11) DIED FROM WOUNDS

PLACE	DATE	NO.
Roanoke Island, NC (10TH) *2	2/8/62	5
New Bern, NC (11TH)	3/14/62	1
Harrisonburg, VA (5TH)	5/3/62	1
James Island, SC (7TH)	6/16/62	1
Cedar Mountain, VA (5TH)	8/9/62	2
Antietam, MD (11TH)	9/17/62	2
Kinston, NC (10TH)	12/14/62	1
Port Hudson, LA (28TH)	5/22/63	1
Port Hudson, LA (28TH) *1	6/14/63	2
Fort Wagner, SC (7TH)	7/11/63	1
Drewry's Bluff, VA (7TH)	5/16/64	1
Bermuda Hundred, VA (6TH)	5/20/64	1
Haer Court House, VA (2 HA)	5/20/64	1
Tolopotomy, VA (2 HA) *	5/29/64	1
Cold Harbor, VA (2 HA) *4	6/1/64	12
Cold Harbor, VA (2 HA)	6/2/64	1
Cold Harbor, VA (11TH)	6/3/64	3
Petersburg, VA (11TH) *1	6/18/64	2
Petersburg, VA (2 HA) *	6/22/64	1
Petersburg, VA (11TH)	7/1/64	1
Atlanta, GA (5TH) *	7/30/64	1
Winchester, VA (2 HA,12TH)	9/19/64	2
Fisher's Hill, VA (2 HA)	9/21/64	2
Fisher's Hill, VA (2 HA)	9/22/64	1
Fort Harrison, VA (8TH)	9/29/64	1
Petersburg, VA (11TH)	10/2/64	1
Chaffin's Farm, VA (29TH)	10/12/64	1
Cedar Creek, VA (2 HA)	10/19/64	3
Kell House, VA (29TH)	10/27/64	1
Petersburg, VA (2 HA)	3/6/65	1
Petersburg, VA (2 HA)	4/2/65	1

SCOTLAND
THE POPULATION IN 1860 WAS 720 (RANK 152)

THE MOST IMPORTANT DAY OF THE CIVIL WAR

JUNE 15 1863

WINCHESTER, VA

THE ENTIRE UNION ARMY WAS NEARLY CAPTURED AT THE SECOND BATTLE OF WINCHESTER

More soldiers credited to Scotland were listed as casualties (4) on this day than on any other day of the war. Four soldiers in the 18TH Connecticut were captured and all survived the war.

The date June 15, 1863 ranks 2ND for total casualties (595) (23 killed, 11 wounded, 520 captured, 41 wounded & captured) for a single day for the State of Connecticut. There were 592 casualties at Winchester, VA and 3 casualties at Port Hudson, LA.

The Second Battle of Winchester (June 13-15, 1863) ranks 5TH for total casualties (592) for an engagement for the State of Connecticut. The most intense fighting developed on June 15. Scotland had all its casualties on that day.

The Second Battle of Winchester with 4 total casualties for Scotland was the highest number of casualties for any single engagement of the war for the town.

Winchester was one of the most contested locations in the Civil War. It changed hands seventy-two times.

46 MEN CREDITED TO SCOTLAND SERVED IN THE FOLLOWING CONNECTICUT ORGANIZATIONS

REGIMENT	TOTAL
26TH	9 (20%)
10TH	7 (15%)
18TH	6 (13%)
29TH	6 (13%)
11TH	4 (9%)
2ND HEAVY ARTILLERY	3 (7%)
12TH	3 (7%)
20TH	3 (7%)
5TH	2 (4%)
8TH	2 (4%)
1ST HEAVY ARTILLERY	1
21ST	1

6% OF POPULATION

ONE WAS KILLED

The only Scotland soldier killed was Private William Burton of the 29TH Connecticut. He was killed at Kell House, VA on October 27, 1864.

SCOTLAND SOLDIERS KILLED

PLACE	DATE	NO.
Kell House, VA (29TH)	10/27/64	1

FIVE WERE CAPTURED

One Scotland soldier died in captivity at Salisbury, NC.

SCOTLAND CAPTURED
*(1) DIED IN CAPTIVITY

PLACE	DATE	NO.
Winchester, VA (18TH)	6/15/63	4
Cedar Creek, VA (2 HA) *	10/19/64	1

TOTAL SCOTLAND CASUALTIES

DIED	6	13%
KILLED	1	2%
WOUNDED	11	24%
CAPTURED	5	11%
DESERTED	8	17%

ELEVEN WERE WOUNDED

The first Scotland soldier wounded was Private Humphrey Sheen of Company D, 11TH Connecticut. He was wounded after the Battle of Antietam, MD on September 20, 1862 and recovered from his wound. One Scotland soldier died from a wound received during the war.

SCOTLAND WOUNDED
*(1) DIED FROM WOUNDS

PLACE	DATE	NO.
Antietam, MD (11TH)	9/20/62	1
Kinston, NC (10TH) *	12/14/62	1
Portsmouth, VA (11TH)	6/1/63	1
Port Hudson, LA (26TH)	6/14/63	1
New Market, VA (18TH)	5/15/64	1
Drewry's Bluff, VA (21ST)	5/16/64	1
Deep Bottom, VA (10TH)	8/14/64	1
Deep Run, VA (10TH)	8/16/64	1
New Market, VA (10TH)	10/7/64	1
Kell House, VA (29TH)	10/27/64	2

SEYMOUR
THE POPULATION IN 1860 WAS 1,203 (RANK 121)

THE MOST IMPORTANT DAY OF THE CIVIL WAR

MAY 3, 1863

CHANCELLORSVILLE, VA

THE THIRD DAY OF THE BATTLE

More soldiers credited to Seymour were listed as casualties (11) on this day than on any other day of the war. Two soldiers were killed, 1 was wounded, 6 were captured, and 2 were wounded & captured in the 20TH & 27TH Connecticut. The wounded and captured survived the war.

The date May 3, 1863 ranks 3RD for total casualties (577) (36 killed, 1 missing, 138 wounded, 372 captured, 29 wounded & captured) for a single day for the State of Connecticut. The most casualties were at Chancellorsville, VA (556). The other casualties were at Providence Church Road, VA (12), Suffolk, VA (6), Port Hudson, LA (2) and Fredericksburg, VA (1).

The Battle of Chancellorsville (May 1-3, 1863) ranks 2ND for total casualties (677) for an engagement for the State of Connecticut. The most intense fighting developed on May 3. Seymour had no other casualties in the battle other than on May 3.

The Battle of Chancellorsville with 11 total casualties for Seymour was the highest number of casualties for any single engagement of the war for the town.

The Battle of Chancellorsville was an enormous defeat for the more than 70,000 Union soldiers who had moved against the flank and rear of 40,000 Confederate soldiers. Unfortunately, the Union Army had pulled back and had gone on the defensive around Chancellorsville. The Confederate victory was tainted however, by the loss of Confederate Major General "Stonewall" Jackson.

146 MEN CREDITED TO SEYMOUR SERVED IN THE FOLLOWING CONNECTICUT ORGANIZATIONS

REGIMENT	TOTAL
20TH	29 (20%)
3RD LIGHT BATTERY	23 (16%)
1ST HEAVY ARTILLERY	20 (14%)
5TH	16 (11%)
7TH	9 (6%)
10TH	9 (6%)
1TST CAVALRY	8 (5%)
29TH	8 (5%)
15TH	7 (5%)
11TH	6 (4%)
12TH	4 (3%)
30TH	4 (3%)
6TH	3 (2%)
27RD	3 (2%)
12TH BATTALION	2 (1%)
23TH	2 (1%)
1ST LIGHT BATTERY	1
2ND HEAVY ARTILLERY	1
3RD LIGHT BATTERY	1
3RD	1
8TH	1
9TH	1
9TH BATTALION	1
14TH	1

12% POPULATION

EIGHT WERE KILLED

The first Seymour soldier killed was Private Simon Lathrop of Company A, 10TH Connecticut. He was killed at Kinston, NC on December 14, 1862.

SEYMOUR SOLDIERS KILLED

PLACE	DATE	NO.
Kinston, NC (10TH)	12/14/62	1
Chancellorsville, VA (20TH)	5/3/63	2
Bristoe Station, VA (14TH)	10/14/63	1
Peach Tree Creek, GA (20TH)	7/20/64	1
Petersburg, VA (29TH)	9/3/64	1
Cedar Creek, VA (2 HA)	10/19/64	1
Kell House, VA (29TH)	10/27/64	1

EIGHTEEN WERE CAPTURED

No Seymour soldier died in captivity.

SEYMOUR CAPTURED
NONE DIED IN CAPTIVITY

PLACE	DATE	NO.
Malvern Hill, VA (1HA) (WOUNDED)	7/1/62	1
Cedar Mountain, VA (5TH)	8/9/62	1
Chancellorsville, VA (20, 27TH) (2 WOUNDED)	5/3/63	8
Gettysburg, PA (5TH)	7/2/63	1
Drewry's Bluff, VA (7TH) (WOUNDED)	5/16/64	1
Old Church Tavern, VA (1 CA)	6/10/64	1
Kinston, NC (15TH) (1 WOUNDED)	3/8/65	4
Ashland, VA (1 CA)	3/15/65	1

TOTAL SEYMOUR CASUALTIES

DIED	9	6%
KILLED	8	5%
WOUNDED	13	9%
CAPTURED	18	12%
DESERTED	14	10%

THIRTEEN WERE WOUNDED

The first Seymour soldier wounded was Private James Holeran of Company F, 5TH Connecticut. He was wounded at Winchester, VA on May 25, 1862 and recovered from his wound. Two Seymour soldiers died from a wound received during the war.

SEYMOUR WOUNDED
*(2) DIED FROM WOUNDS

PLACE	DATE	NO.
Winchester, VA (5TH)	5/25/62	1
Antietam, MD (8, 11TH) *1	9/17/62	2
Fredericksburg, VA (27TH)	12/13/62	1
Chancellorsville, VA (20TH)	5/3/63	1
Port Hudson, LA (12TH)	6/10/63	1
Gettysburg, PA (20TH)	7/3/63	1
Fort Wagner, SC (6TH)	7/18/63	1
Culp's Farm, GA (5TH)	6/22/64	1
Peach Tree Creek, GA (5,20[TH])	7/20/64	2
Kell House, VA (29TH) *	10/27/64	1
Bentonville, NC (20TH)	3/19/65	1

SHARON
THE POPULATION IN 1860 WAS 2,556 (RANK 55)

THE MOST IMPORTANT DAY OF THE CIVIL WAR
OCTOBER 19, 1864
CEDAR CREEK, VA
THE FINAL UNION VICTORY IN THE 1864 SHENENDOAH CAMPAIGN

More soldiers credited to Sharon were listed as casualties (8) on this day than on any other day of the war. Two soldiers were killed and 6 were wounded in the 2ND Connecticut Heavy Artillery. One of the wounded died.

The date October 19, 1864 ranks 7TH for total casualties (417) (48 killed, 2 missing, 204 wounded, 153 captured, 10 wounded & captured) for a single day for the State of Connecticut. There were 415 casualties at Cedar Creek, and 1 casualty at Strasburg, and Middletown VA.

The Battle of Cedar Creek (October 19, 1864) ranks 10TH for total casualties (415) for an engagement for the State of Connecticut.

The Battle of Cedar Creek with 8 total casualties for Sharon was the highest number of casualties for any single engagement of the war for the town.

The news of the Union victory is said to have assured a Republican victory in the upcoming November elections and the prosecution of the war to its end on President Lincoln's and General Grant's terms.

219 MEN CREDITED TO SHARON SERVED IN THE FOLLOWING CONNECTICUT ORGANIZATIONS

REGIMENT	TOTAL
2ND HEAVY ARTILLERY	56 (26%)
5TH	33 (15%)
23RD	29 (13%)
11TH	24 (11%)
13TH	15 (7%)
10TH	13 (6%)
8TH	12 (5%)
29TH	11 (5%)
6TH	7 (5%)
12TH	7 (5%)
1ST HEAVY ARTILLERY	4 (2%)
14TH	3 (1%)
7TH	3 (1%)
13TH BATTALION	2
17TH	2
20TH	2
30TH	2
3RD LIGHT BATTERY	1
15TH	1
16TH	1
28TH	1

9% OF POPULATION

ELEVEN WERE KILLED

The first Sharon soldiers killed were Privates James Doyle and James Malone of the 6TH Connecticut. They were killed at Drewry's Bluff, VA on May 15, 1864.

SHARON SOLDIERS KILLED

PLACE	DATE	NO.
Drewry's Bluff, VA (6TH)	5/15/64	2
Drewry's Bluff, VA (10TH)	5/16/64	1
Cold Harbor, VA (2 HA)	6/1/64	1
Atlanta, GA (5TH)	7/30/64	1
Petersburg, VA (30TH)	7/30/64	1
Winchester, VA (2 HA)	9/19/64	1
Cedar Creek, VA (2 HA)	10/19/64	2
Kell House, VA (29TH)	10/27/64	2

THIRTEEN WERE CAPTURED

Two Sharon soldiers died in captivity. Both died at Andersonville Prison, GA

SHARON CAPTURED
*(2) DIED IN CAPTIVITY

PLACE	DATE	NO.
Cedar Mountain, VA (5TH)	8/9/62	2
Brashear City, LA (23RD)	6/23/63	1
Plymouth, NC (16TH) *	4/20/64	1
Drewry's Bluff, VA (11TH) *1	5/16/64	4
Bermuda Hundred, VA (6TH)	6/17/64	1
Fort Powhatan, VA (8TH)	9/19/64	1
Madison, GA (5TH)	11/18/64	1
Dunn's Lake, FLA (17TH)	2/5/65	1
Burgan, NC (6TH)	4/8/65	1

TOTAL SHARON CASUALTIES

DIED	18	8%
KILLED	11	5%
WOUNDED	39	18%
CAPTURED	13	6%
DESERTED	45	21%

THIRTY-NINE WERE WOUNDED

The first Sharon soldier wounded was Sergeant William H. Waldron of Company I, 1ST Connecticut Heavy Artillery. He was wounded at Hagerstown, MD on June 1, 1861and recovered from his wound. Four Sharon soldiers died from a wound received during the war.

SHARON WOUNDED
*(4) DIED FROM WOUNDS

PLACE	DATE	NO.
Hagerstown, MD (1 HA)	6/1/61	1
Roanoke Island, NC (10TH)	2/8/62	1
Antietam, MD (11TH)	9/17/62	1
Kinston, NC (10TH)	12/14/62	1
Chancellorsville, VA (5TH)	5/3/63	1
Bristoe Station, VA (14TH) *	10/14/63	1
Walthall Junction, VA (8TH)	5/7/64	1
North Anna River, VA (2 HA)	5/23/64	1
Dallas, GA (5TH)	5/25/64	1
Dallas, GA (5TH)	5/27/64	1
Cold Harbor, VA (2 HA)	6/1/64	3
Cold Harbor, VA (11TH)	6/3/64	2
Cold Harbor, VA (11TH)	6/9/64	1
Petersburg, VA (11TH)	6/16/64	1
Petersburg, VA (11TH)	6/18/64	1
Petersburg, VA (8TH)	6/23/64	1
Peach Tree Creek, GA (5TH)	7/20/64	1
Petersburg, VA (6TH)	9/12/64	1
Winchester, VA (2 HA) *	9/19/64	2
Petersburg, VA (10TH)	9/20/64	1
Fisher's Hill, VA (2 HA)	9/22/64	1
Fort Harrison, VA (8TH)	10/3/64	1
Deep Bottom, VA (10TH)	10/13/64	1
Darbytown Road, VA (10TH)	10/13/64	1
Cedar Creek, VA (2 HA) *	10/19/64	6
Kell House, VA (29TH)	10/27/64	3
Petersburg, VA (2 HA) *	3/25/65	2

SHELTON (HUNTINGTON)
THE POPULATION IN 1860 WAS 1,477 (RANK 100)

THE MOST IMPORTANT DAY OF THE CIVIL WAR

JULY 1, 1863
GETTYSBURG, PA
THE FIRST DAY OF THE BATTLE

Soldiers credited to Shelton (Huntington) had more casualties on July 1, 1863 at Gettysburg, PA (3) and on May 16, 1864 at Drewry's Bluff, VA (3) than on any other days of the war. The casualties at Gettysburg were the most serious. Three soldiers were wounded in the 17TH Connecticut and all survived the war.

The date July 1, 1863 ranks 16TH for total casualties (157) (18 killed, 4 missing, 70 wounded, 57 captured, 8 wounded & captured) for a single day for the State of Connecticut. There were 143 casualties at Gettysburg. The 14 other casualties were scattered about Virginia (6), Louisiana (6), and South Carolina (2).

The Battle of Gettysburg (July1-3, 1863) ranks 11TH for total casualties (360) for an engagement for the State of Connecticut. The most intense fighting developed on July 3. Shelton (Huntington) had no casualties on that day.

The Battle of Gettysburg with 3 total casualties for Shelton (Huntington) was tied with the Battle of Drewry's Bluff (May 13-17, 1864) for the highest number of casualties for any single engagement of the war for the town.

More than 170,00 men fought at the Battle of Gettysburg. Roughly 23,000 Union casualties were recorded and there were about 28,000 Confederate casualties. Gettysburg proved to be the great battle of the war. It ended Lee's 1863 invasion of the North. He was never able to launch a major offensive again

96 MEN CREDITED TO SHELTON (HUNTINGTON) SERVED IN THE FOLLOWING CONNECTICUT ORGANIZATIONS

REGIMENT	TOTAL
23RD	26 (27%)
11TH	12 (13%)
17TH	10 (10%)
1ST HEAVY ARTILLERY	6 (6%)
6TH	6 (6%)
7TH	6 (6%)
1ST CAVALRY	5 (5%)
20TH	5 (5%)
8TH	4 (4%)
9TH	4 (4%)
9TH BATTALION	3 (3%)
10TH	3 (3%)
3RD LIGHT BATTERY	2 (2%)
22ND	2 (2%)
29TH	2 (2%)
2ND HEAVY ARTILLERY	1
12TH	1
13TH	1
14TH	1
15TH	1
27TH	1
30TH	1

6% OF POPULATION

THREE WERE KILLED

The first Shelton (Huntington) soldier killed was Private Thomas C. Cornell of Company D, 23RD Connecticut. He was killed at Brashear City, LA on June 23, 1863.

SHELTON (HUNTINGTON) SOLDIERS KILLED

PLACE	DATE	NO.
Brashear City, LA (23RD)	6/23/63	1
Atlanta, GA (20TH)	7/25/64	1
Wilmington, NC (6TH)	2/22/65	1

FOUR WERE CAPTURED

One Shelton (Huntington) soldier died in captivity at Smithville, NC.

SHELTON (HUNTINGTON) CAPTURED
*(1) DIED IN CAPTIVITY

PLACE	DATE	NO.
Chancellorsville, VA (17TH)	5/2/63	1
(WOUNDED)		
Drewry's Bluff, VA (6TH)	5/16/64	2
Bermuda Hundred, VA (7TH)*	6/16/64	1
(WOUNDED)		

TOTAL SHELTON (HUTINGTON) CASUALTIES

DIED	8	8%
KILLED	3	3%
WOUNDED	22	23%
CAPTURED	4	4%
DESERTED	18	19%

TWENTY-TWO WERE WOUNDED

The first Shelton (Huntington) soldier wounded was Private Joel N. Bradley of Company A, 14TH Connecticut. He was wounded at the Battle of Antietam on September 17, 1862 and recovered from his wound. Three Shelton (Huntington) soldiers died from a wound received during the war.

SHELTON (HUNTINGTON) WOUNDED
*(3) DIED FROM WOUNDS

PLACE	DATE	NO.
Antietam, MD (14TH)	9/17/62	1
Brashear City, LA (23RD) *	6/23/63	1
Gettysburg, PA (17TH)	7/1/63	3
Fort Wagner, SC (6TH)	7/18/63	1
Morton's Ford, VA (14TH)	2/6/64	1
Craig's Church, VA (1 CA)	5/5/64	1
Swift's Creek, VA (11TH)	5/9/64	1
Drewry's Bluff, VA (7TH)	5/14/64	1
Drewry's Bluff, VA (11TH)	5/16/64	1
Cold Harbor, VA (8TH) *	6/1/64	1
Peach Tree Creek, GA (20TH)	7/20/64	1
Petersburg, VA (11, 30TH)	7/30/64	2
Atlanta, GA (20TH)	8/12/64	1
Deep Run, VA (6TH)	8/15/64	1
Deep Run, VA (6TH) *	8/16/64	1
Cedar Creek, VA (12TH)	10/19/64	1
Richmond, VA (1 HA)	4/1/65	1
Five Forks, VA (1 CA)	4/1/65	1
Goldsboro, NC (6TH)	7/14/65	1

SHERMAN
THE POPULATION IN 1860 WAS 911 (RANK 142)

THE MOST IMPORTANT DAY OF THE CIVIL WAR
JUNE 1, 1864
COLD HARBOR, VA
THE BATTLE WAS LEE'S LAST GREAT VICTORY

Soldiers credited to Sherman had more casualties at Port Hudson, LA on June 14, 1863 (2), at Cold Harbor, VA on June 1, 1864 (2), at Fort Harrison, VA on September 29, 1864 (2), and at Cedar Creek, VA on October 19, 1864 (2) than on any other days of the war. The casualties at Cold Harbor were the most serious. One soldier was killed and 1 wounded in the 2ND Connecticut Heavy Artillery. The wounded soldier recovered.

The date June 1, 1864 ranks 8TH for total casualties (374) (89 killed, 10 missing, 246 wounded, 23 captured, 6 wounded & captured) for a single day for the State of Connecticut. There were 324 casualties at Cold Harbor, 41 casualties at Ashland, VA and 9 casualties scattered about Virginia.

The battle and operations around Cold Harbor (May 31-June 12, 1864) rank 6TH for total casualties (557) for an engagement for the State of Connecticut. The most intense fighting developed on June 3 and Sherman had no casualties.

The Battle of Cold Harbor with 2 total casualties for Sherman was tied with the Siege of Port Hudson, LA (May-July 1863), Siege of Petersburg, VA (June 1864-April 1865), Fort Harrison, VA (September 29, 1864), and Cedar Creek, VA (October 19, 1864) for the highest number of casualties for any single engagement of the war for the town.

Approximately 117,000 Federal and 60,000 Confederate troops participated in operations from May 28 to June 3. Roughly 13,000 Union casualties were recorded and perhaps there were 5,000 Confederate casualties.

62 MEN CREDITED TO SHERMAN SERVED IN THE FOLLOWING CONNECTICUT ORGANIZATIONS

REGIMENT	TOTAL
28TH	24 (39%)
2ND HEAVY ARTILLERY	15 (24%)
6TH	5 (8%)
8TH	5 (8%)
13TH	5 (8%)
10TH	4 (6%)
1ST	1
1ST HEAVY ARTILLERY	1
11TH	1
13TH BATTALION	1
17TH	1

7% POPULATION

ONE WAS KILLED

The only Sherman soldier killed was Corporal David D. Lake of Company K, 2ND Connecticut Heavy Artillery. He was killed at Cold Harbor, VA on June 1, 1864

SHERMAN SOLDIERS KILLED

PLACE	DATE	NO.
Cold Harbor, VA (2HA)	6/1/64	1

NO SHERMAN SOLDIERS WERE CAPTURED

TOTAL SHERMAN CASUALTIES

DIED	12	19%
KILLED	1	2%
WOUNDED	14	23%
CAPTURED	0	0%
DESERTED	8	13%

FOURTEEN WERE WOUNDED

The first Sherman soldier wounded was Private Robert Stuart of Company I, 8TH Connecticut. He was wounded at the Battle of Antietam on September 17, 1862 and recovered from his wound. Three Sherman soldiers died from a wound received during the war.

SHERMAN WOUNDED
*(3) DIED FROM WOUNDS

PLACE	DATE	NO.
Antietam, MD (8TH)	9/17/62	1
Port Hudson, LA (28TH)	6/14/63	2
Walthall Junction, VA (8TH)	5/7/64	1
Bermuda Hundred, VA (6TH) *	5/30/64	1
Cold Harbor, VA (2 HA)	6/1/64	1
Petersburg, VA (2 HA)	6/20/64	1
Petersburg, VA (2 HA)	6/21/64	1
Winchester, VA (13TH)	9/19/64	1
Fort Harrison, VA (8TH) *1	9/29/64	2
Richmond, VA (8TH)	10/9/64	1
Cedar Creek, VA (2 HA) *1	10/19/64	2

548

SIMSBURY
THE POPULATION IN 1860 WAS 2,410 (RANK 57)

THE MOST IMPORTANT DAY
OF THE CIVIL WAR

APRIL 20, 1864

PLYMOUTH, NC

THE CONFEDERATE PLAN
TO TAKE PLYMOUTH
ENDED WHEN 2,800 UNION
TROOPS SURRENDERED
THE CITY

204 MEN CREDITED TO
SIMSBURY SERVED
IN THE FOLLOWING
CONNECTICUT
ORGANIZATIONS

REGIMENT	TOTAL
16TH	31 (15%)
1ST HEAVY ARTILLERY	26 (13%)
25TH	24 (12%)
10TH	17 (8%)
7TH	14 (7%)
11TH	14 (7%)
5TH	12 (6%)
6TH	12 (6%)
8TH	12 (6%)
1ST	11 (5%)
12TH	9 (4%)
1ST LIGHT BATTERY	8 (4%)
29TH	8 (4%)
14TH	7 (3%)
22ND	5 (2%)
1ST CAVALRY	4 (2%)
2ND	4 (2%)
20TH	4 (2%)
9TH	3 (1%)
13TH	3 (1%)
2ND HEAVY ARTILLERY	2 (1%)
12TH BATTALION	2 (1%)
2ND LIGHT BATTERY	1
9TH BATTALION	1
13TH BATTALION	1
15TH	1
23RD	1
30TH	1

8% OF POPULATION

More soldiers credited to Simsbury were listed as casualties (19) on this day than on any other day of the war. Nineteen soldiers in the 16TH Connecticut were captured. Five of them eventually died in prison.

The date April 20, 1864 ranks 6TH for total casualties (433) (1 killed, 2 missing, 12 wounded & captured, 418 captured) for a single day for the State of Connecticut. All of the casualties were at Plymouth, NC.

The Battle of Plymouth (April 20, 1864) ranks 9TH for total casualties (433) for an engagement for the State of Connecticut. Nearly half of all soldiers captured at Plymouth died in Southern prisons

The Battle of Plymouth with 19 total casualties for Simsbury was the highest number of casualties for any single engagement of the war for the town.

When Confederate General Robert Hoke surrounded and captured the Union garrison at Plymouth, NC the Southern victory was the first in this military arena in quite some time. With aid from the two-gun ironclad *Albemarle* the Confederates were able to take advantage of the lack of suitable Union gunboats.

SIX WERE KILLED

The first Simsbury soldiers killed were Privates Oliver C. Case and James Grugan of the 8TH and 16TH Connecticut. Both were killed at the Battle of Antietam, MD on September 17, 1862.

SIMSBURY SOLDIERS KILLED

PLACE	DATE	NO.
Antietam, MD, (8, 16TH)	9/17/62	2
Kinston, NC (10TH)	12/14/62	1
Drewry's Bluff, VA (11TH)	5/16/64	1
Richmond, VA (7TH)	10/13/64	1
Petersburg, VA (1 HA)	1/16/65	1

TWENTY-TWO WERE CAPTURED

Eight Simsbury soldiers died in captivity. Seven soldiers died at Andersonville Prison, GA, and one died at Salisbury, NC.

SIMSBURY CAPTURED
*(8) DIED IN CAPTIVITY

PLACE	DATE	NO.
Antietam, MD (16TH)	9/17/62	1
Plymouth, NC (16TH) *5	4/20/64	19
Drewry's Bluff, VA (11TH) *2	5/16/64	2
Winchester, VA (13TH) *	9/19/64	1

TOTAL SIMSBURY CASUALTIES

DIED	29	14%
KILLED	6	3%
WOUNDED	34	17%
CAPTURED	22	11%
DESERTED	31	15%

THIRTY-FOUR WERE WOUNDED

The first Simsbury soldier wounded was Private Isaac Prindle of Company B, 5TH Connecticut. He was wounded in Virginia on October 8, 1861 and recovered from his wound. Four Simsbury soldiers died from a wound received during the war.

SIMSBURY WOUNDED
*(4) DIED FROM WOUNDS

PLACE	DATE	NO.
Virginia (5TH)	10/8/61	1
Annapolis, MD (8TH)	12/1/61	1
New Bern, NC (11TH) *	3/14/62	1
James Island, SC (7TH)	6/16/62	1
Antietam, MD (8, 16TH)	9/17/62	4
Georgia Landing, LA (12TH)	10/27/62	1
Kinston, NC (10TH)	12/14/62	1
Irish Bend, LA (25TH)	4/14/63	2
Chancellorsville, VA (5TH)	5/2/63	1
Port Hudson, LA (13TH)	5/24/63	1
Port Hudson, LA (12TH)	5/27/63	1
Port Hudson, LA (13,25TH)	6/14/63	3
Port Hudson, LA (25TH)	6/27/63	2
Bristoe Station, VA (14TH)	10/14/63	1
Olustee, FL (7TH) *	2/20/64	1
Proctor's Creek, VA (1 LB) *	5/15/64	1
Chester Station, VA (6TH)	5/16/64	1
North Anna River, VA (14TH)	5/24/64	1
Cold Harbor, VA (2 HA)	6/1/64	1
Cold Harbor, VA (11TH) *	6/3/64	1
Petersburg, VA (8TH)	6/16/64	1
Petersburg, VA (11TH)	7/30/64	1
Deep Run, VA (6TH)	8/16/64	1
Petersburg, VA (10TH)	9/13/64	1
Chaffin's Farm, VA (7TH)	9/29/64	1
Boydton Plank Rd, VA (14TH)	10/27/64	1
Petersburg, VA (1 HA)	3/25/65	1

SOMERS
THE POPULATION IN 1860 WAS 1,517 (RANK 96)

THE MOST IMPORTANT DAY OF THE CIVIL WAR

SEPTEMBER 17, 1862

SHARPSBURG, MD (ANTIETAM)

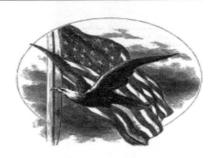

CONNECTICUT HAD MORE CASUALTIES FOR ONE DAY THAN ON ANY OTHER DAY OF THE WAR

More soldiers credited to Somers were listed as casualties (5) on this day than on any day of the war. One soldier was killed, 3 were wounded, and 1 was wounded & captured in the 14TH and 16TH Connecticut. One of the wounded died.

The date September 17, 1862 ranks 1ST for total casualties (687) (131 killed, 2 missing, 515 wounded, 21 captured, 18 wounded & captured) for a single day for the State of Connecticut. All of the casualties were at Antietam.

The Battle of Antietam (September 16-17, 1862) ranks 1ST for total casualties (689) for an engagement for the State of Connecticut. The most intense fighting dveloped on September 17. Somers had all of its casualties on that day.

The Battle of Antietam with 5 total casualties for Somers was the highest number of casualties for any single engagement of the war for the town.

Roughly 12,400 Union casualties were recorded and perhaps there were 10,300 Confederate casualties. Antietam proved to be one of the turning points of the war. It ended Lee's 1862 invasion of the North.

98 MEN CREDITED TO SOMERS SERVED IN THE FOLLOWING CONNECTICUT ORGANIZATIONS

REGIMENT	TOTAL
22ND	23 (23%)
1ST HEAVY ARTILLERY	13 (13%)
10TH	10 (10%)
16TH	9 (9%)
7TH	8 (8%)
1ST CAVALRY	7 (7%)
14TH	6 (6%)
8TH	5 (5%)
12TH	5 (5%)
11TH	3 (3%)
21ST	3 (3%)
6TH	2 (2%)
12TH BATTALION	2 (2%)
29TH	2 (2%)
30TH	2 (2%)
2ND HEAVY ARTILLERY	1
5TH	1
17TH	1
25TH	1

7% OF POPULATION

FOUR WERE KILLED

The first Somers soldier killed was Private Cornelius Wildman of Company A, 16TH Connecticut. He was killed at the Battle of Antietam, MD on September 17, 1862.

SOMERS SOLDIERS KILLED

PLACE	DATE	NO.
Antietam, MD (16TH)	9/17/62	1
Providence Church Rd, VA(16TH)	5/3/63	1
Laurel Hill, VA (14TH)	5/10/64	1
Bermuda Hundred, VA (7TH)	6/17/64	1

ELEVEN WERE CAPTURED

Seven Somers soldiers died in captivity. Two died at Andersonville Prison, GA, two died at Florence, SC, two died at Libby Prison Richmond, VA and one died at Charleston, SC.

SOMERS CAPTURED
*(7) DIED IN CAPTIVITY

PLACE	DATE	NO.
Antietam, MD (16TH) * (Wounded)	9/17/62	1
Fort Wagner, SC (7TH) (Wounded)	7/11/63	1
Plymouth, NC (16TH) *	4/20/64	1
Meadow Bridge, VA (1 CA) *	5/12/64	1
Drewry's Bluff, VA (7TH) *2	5/16/64	2
Proctor's Creek, VA (8TH) *	5/16/64	1
Petersburg, VA (6TH)	5/20/64	1
Ashland, VA (1 CA)	6/1/64	1
Ream's Station, VA (14TH)	8/25/64	1
Boydton Plank Rd, VA(14TH)* (Wounded)	10/27/64	1

TOTAL SOMERS CASUALTIES

DIED	15	15%
KILLED	4	4%
WOUNDED	6	6%
CAPTURED	11	11%
DESERTED	7	7%

SIX WERE WOUNDED

The first Somers soldier wounded was Private Lorin B Hurlburt of Company C, 10TH Connecticut. He was wounded at New Bern, NC on June 1, 1862 and recovered from his wound. One Somers soldier died from a wound received during the war.

SOMERS WOUNDED
*(1) DIED FROM WOUNDS

PLACE	DATE	NO.
New Bern, NC (16TH) *	6/1/62	1
Antietam, MD (14, 16TH)	9/17/62	3
Morton's Ford, VA (14TH)	2/6/64	1
Petersburg, VA (1 HA)	7/9/64	1

SOUTHBURY
THE POPULATION IN 1860 WAS 1,346 (RANK 109)

THE MOST IMPORTANT DAY OF THE CIVIL WAR

MAY 3, 1863

CHANCELLORSVILLE, VA

THE THIRD DAY OF THE BATTLE

More soldiers credited to Southbury were listed as casualties (5) on this day than any other day of the war. Five soldiers were captured in the 20TH & 27TH Connecticut. They survived the war.

The date May 3, 1863 ranks 3RD for total casualties (577) (36 killed, 1 missing, 138 wounded, 372 captured, 29 wounded & captured) for a single day for the State of Connecticut. The most casualties were at Chancellorsville, VA (556). The other casualties were at Providence Church Road, VA (12), Suffolk, VA (6), Port Hudson, LA (2) and Fredericksburg, VA (1).

The Battle of Chancellorsville (May 1-3, 1863) ranks 2ND for total casualties (677) for an engagement for the State of Connecticut. The most intense fighting developed on May 3. Southbury had no other casualties in the battle other than on May 3.

The Battle of Chancellorsville with 5 total casualties for Southbury was the highest number of casualties for any single engagement of the war for the town.

The Battle of Chancellorsville was an enormous defeat for the more than 70,000 Union soldiers who had moved against the flank and rear of 40,000 Confederate soldiers. Unfortunately, the Union Army had pulled back and had gone on the defensive around Chancellorsville. The Confederate victory was tainted however, by the loss of Confederate Major General "Stonewall" Jackson.

86 MEN CREDITED TO SOUTHBURY SERVED IN THE FOLLOWING CONNECTICUT ORGANIZATIONS

REGIMENT		TOTAL
20TH		15 (17%)
2ND HEAVY ARTILLERY		11 (13%)
13TH		10 (12%)
10TH		9 (10%)
11TH		8 (10%)
3RD LIGHT BATTERY		7 (8%)
12TH		5 (6%)
1ST HEAVY ARTILLERY		4 (5%)
1ST CAVALRY		3 (4%)
6TH		3 (4%)
8TH		3 (4%)
15TH		3 (4%)
5TH		2 (2%)
23RD		2 (2%)
29TH		2 (2%)
7TH		1
12TH	BATTALION	1
13TH	BATTALION	1
14TH		1
27TH		1

8% OF POPULATION

NO SOUTHBURY SOLDIERS WERE KILLED OR MISSING IN THE WAR

EIGHT WERE CAPTURED

No Southbury soldiers died in captivity.

PLACE	DATE	NO.
Chancellorsville, VA (20,27TH)	5/3/63	5
Drewry's Bluff, VA (11TH) (WOUNDED)	5/16/64	1
Cedar Creek, VA (12TH)	10/19/64	1
Kinston, NC (15TH)	3/8/65	1

TOTAL SOUTHBURY CASUALTIES

DIED	10	12%
KILLED	0	0%
WOUNDED	13	15%
CAPTURED	8	9%
DESERTED	15	18%

THIRTEEN WERE WOUNDED

The first Southbury soldiers wounded were Private Oscar Squires and George Wentz of the 8TH & 11TH Connecticut. Both were wounded at the Battle of Antietam, MD on September 17, 1862 and recovered from their wounds. Two Southbury soldiers died from a wound received during the war.

SOUTHBURY WOUNDED
*(2) DIED FROM WOUNDS

PLACE	DATE	NO.
Antietam, MD (8, 11TH)	9/17/62	2
Gettysburg, PA (20TH)	7/3/63	1
Morris Island, SC (6TH)	7/10/63	1
Morton's Ford, VA (14TH)	2/6/64	1
Drewry's Bluff, VA (11TH) *	5/16/64	1
North Anna River, VA (2 HA)	5/26/64	1
Cold Harbor, VA (2 HA)	6/1/64	2
Fort Harrison, VA (8TH)	10/1/64	1
Cedar Creek, VA (2 HA) *1	10/19/64	2
Silver Run, NC (20TH)	3/16/65	1

SOUTHINGTON
THE POPULATION IN 1860 WAS 3,315 (RANK 31)

THE MOST IMPORTANT DAY OF THE CIVIL WAR
MAY 3, 1863
CHANCELLORSVILLE, VA
THE THIRD DAY OF THE BATTLE

More soldiers credited to Southington were listed as casualties (15) on this day than on any other day of the war. One soldier was killed, 9 were wounded, and 5 were captured in the 20TH Connecticut. The wounded and captured survived the war.

The date May 3, 1863 ranks 3RD for total casualties (577) (36 killed, 1 missing, 138 wounded, 372 captured, 29 wounded & captured) for a single day for the State of Connecticut. The most casualties were at Chancellorsville, VA (556). The other casualties were at Providence Church Road, VA (12), Suffolk, VA (6), Port Hudson, LA (2) and Fredericksburg, VA (1).

The Battle of Chancellorsville (May 1-3, 1863) ranks 2ND for total casualties (677) for an engagement for the State of Connecticut. The most intense fighting developed on May 3 and Southington had all of their casualties on that day.

The Battle of Chancellorsville with 15 total casualties for Southington was the highest number of casualties for any single engagement of the war for the town.

The Battle of Chancellorsville was an enormous defeat for the more than 70,000 Union soldiers who had moved against the flank and rear of 40,000 Confederate soldiers. Unfortunately, the Union Army had pulled back and had gone on the defensive around Chancellorsville. The Confederate victory was tainted however, by the loss of Confederate Major General "Stonewall" Jackson.

294 MEN CREDITED TO SOUTHINGTON SERVED IN THE FOLLOWING CONNECTICUT ORGANIZATIONS

REGIMENT	TOTAL
20TH	82 (29%)
7TH	38 (13%)
12TH	26 (9%)
5TH	21 (7%)
1ST HEAVY ARTILLERY	18 (6%)
22ND	16 (6%)
8TH	16 (5%)
14TH	15 (5%)
1ST CAVALRY	14 (5%)
2ND HEAVY ARTILLERY	14 (5%)
10TH	9 (3%)
12TH BATTALION	9 (3%)
6TH	8 (3%)
29TH	5 (2%)
1ST	4 (1%)
1ST LIGHT BATTERY	4 (1%)
11TH	3 (1%)
2ND	2
9TH	2
13TH	2
15TH	2
23RD	2
30TH	2
1ST SQUADRON CAVALRY	1
9TH BATTALION	1
16TH	1
25TH	1

9% OF POPULATION

TEN WERE KILLED AND ONE WAS MISSING

The first Southington soldier killed was Private George B. Griffin of Company B, 5TH Connecticut. He was killed at Cedar Mountain, VA on August 9, 1862

SOUTHINGTON SOLDIERS KILLED MISSING *

PLACE	DATE	NO.
Cedar Mountain, VA (5TH)	8/9/62	1
Chancellorsville, VA (20TH)	5/3/63	1
Fort Wagner, SC (7TH)	7/11/63	1
Kelly's Ford, VA (Drowned)(5th)	8/12/63	1
Spottsylvania, VA (14TH)	5/12/64	1
Dallas, GA (5TH) *	5/25/64	1
Drewry's Bluff, VA (6,7[TH])	5/16/64	2
Cold Harbor, VA (2 HA)	6/1/64	1
Bermuda Hundred, VA (7TH)	6/17/64	1
Deep Run, VA (7TH)	8/16/64	1

THIRTY WERE CAPTURED

Eight Southington soldiers died in captivity. Three died at Libby Prison Richmond, VA, two died at Andersonville Prison, GA, two died at Salisbury, NC, and one died at Charleston, SC.

SOUTHINGTON CAPTURED *(8) DIED IN CAPTIVITY

PLACE	DATE	NO.
Unknown Place (14TH)	Unknown	1
Winchester, VA (5TH)	5/25/62	1
Cedar Mountain, VA (5TH)	8/9/62	1
Chancellorsville, VA (20TH)	5/3/63	5
Fort Wagner, SC (7TH) *1	7/11/63	5
(1 WOUNDED)		
Fort Wagner, SC (7TH)	7/18/63	1
(WOUNDED)		
Mine Run, VA (14TH) *	12/1/63	1
Rapidan, VA (14TH) *	12/1/63	1
Plymouth, NC (16TH) *	4/20/64	1
Brandy Station, VA (14TH)	5/4/64	1
Spottsylvania, VA (14TH)	5/12/64	1
Drewry's Bluff, VA (6,7[TH]) *1	5/16/64	3
Bermuda Hundred, VA (7TH) *	6/2/64	1
(WOUNDED)		
Cedar Creek, (1CA,2,12) *2	10/19/64	4
Cedar Creek, VA (1 CA)	11/2/64	1
Goldsboro, NC (5TH)	3/23/65	1
Petersburg, VA (1 HA)	3/25/65	1

TOTAL SOUTHINGTON CASUALTIES

DIED	42	14%
KILLED/MISSING	11	4%
WOUNDED	66	22%
CAPTURED	30	10%
DESERTED	41	14%

SIXTY-SIX WERE WOUNDED

The first Southington soldier wounded was Corporal Frank Racher of Company A, 10TH Connecticut. He was wounded at Roanoke Island, NC on February 8, 1862 and recovered from his wound. Two Southington soldiers died from a wound received during the war.

SOUTHINGTON WOUNDED *(2) DIED FROM WOUNDS

PLACE	DATE	NO.
Roanoke Island, NC (10TH)	2/8/62	1
Cross Keys, VA (1 CA)	6/8/62	1
James Island, SC (7TH)	6/16/62	6
Cedar Mountain, VA (5TH)	8/9/62	1
Antietam, MD (8TH)	9/17/62	2
Pocotaligo, SC (7TH)	10/22/62	2
Kinston, NC (10TH)	12/14/62	1
Chancellorsville, VA (20TH)	5/3/63	9
Port Hudson, LA (12TH)	5/27/63	1
Port Hudson, LA (12TH)	6/5/63	1
Port Hudson, LA (12TH)	6/14/63	1
Port Hudson, LA (12TH) *	6/15/63	1
Port Hudson, LA (12TH)	6/27/63	1
Gettysburg, PA (20TH)	7/3/63	2
Port Hudson, LA (12TH)	7/5/63	1
Fort Wagner, SC (7TH)	7/11/63	2
Tracy City, TN (20TH) *	1/20/64	1
Walthall Junction, VA (8TH)	5/7/64	3
Drewry's Bluff, VA (7TH)	5/14/64	3
Resaca, GA (20TH)	5/15/64	4
Dallas, GA (5TH)	5/25/64	1
Bermuda Hundred, VA (7TH)	6/2/64	1
Peach Tree Creek, GA (20TH)	7/20/64	1
Petersburg, VA (8TH)	7/27/64	1
Atlanta, GA (20TH)	8/15/64	1
Deep Run, VA (7, 10TH)	8/16/64	3
Petersburg, VA (7TH)	8/26/64	1
Winchester, VA (12TH)	9/19/64	1
Fort Harrison, VA (8TH)	9/29/64	1
New Market, VA (7TH)	10/7/64	1
Cedar Creek, VA (12TH)	10/19/64	2
Bentonville, NC (20TH)	3/19/65	5
Hatcher's Run, VA (10TH)	3/30/65	1
Fort Gregg, VA	4/2/65	2

SOUTH WINDSOR
THE POPULATION IN 1860 WAS 1,789 (RANK 82)

THE MOST IMPORTANT DAY OF THE CIVIL WAR

MAY 16, 1864

DREWRY'S BLUFF , VA

AN OBSTACLE ON THE WAY TO RICHMOND

More soldiers credited to South Windsor were listed as casualties (4) on this day than on any other day of the war. Four soldiers were captured in the 7TH and 11TH Connecticut. One of the captured died in prison.

The date May 16, 1864 ranks 4th for total casualties (560) (52 killed, 3 missing, 224 wounded, 243 captured, 38 wounded & captured) for a single day for the State of Connecticut. The Battle of Drewry's Bluff accounted for 545 casualties. There were 15 other casualties scattered about Virginia.

The Battle of Drewry's Bluff (May 13-17, 1864), also called Fort Darling, ranks 3rd for total casualties (634) for an engagement for the State of Connecticut. The most intense fighting developed on May 16. South Windsor had all of its casualties on that day.

The Battle of Drewry's Bluff with 4 total casualties for South Windsor was the highest number of casualties for any single engagement of the war for the town.

The Confederate attack at Drewry's Bluff forced the Union Army to retreat to Bermuda Hundred. The civil war would have concluded sooner had the Union Army been victorious.

123 MEN CREDITED TO SOUTH WINDSOR SERVED IN THE FOLLOWING CONNECTICUT ORGANIZATIONS

REGIMENT	TOTAL
11TH	20 (16%)
12TH	19 (15%)
25TH	16 (13%)
16TH	14 (11%)
22ND	10 (8%)
7TH	9 (7%)
12TH BATTALION	8 (7%)
1ST HEAVY ARTILLERY	6 (5%)
6TH	5 (4%)
5TH	4 (4%)
21ST	4 (3%)
10TH	3 (2%)
20TH	3 (2%)
29TH	3 (2%)
1ST	2 (2%)
1ST LIGHT BATTERY	2 (2%)
2ND LIGHT BATTERY	2 (2%)
14TH	2 (2%)
2ND HEAVY ARTILLERY	1
1ST CAVALRY	1
8TH	1
15TH	1
30TH	1

7% OF POPULATION

THREE WERE KILLED

The first South Windsor soldier killed was Private George Bills of Company D, 12TH Connecticut. He was killed at New Bern, NC on March 14, 1862.

SOUTH WINDSOR SOLDIERS KILLED

PLACE	DATE	NO.
New Bern, NC (11TH)	3/14/62	1
Antietam, MD (11TH)	9/17/62	1
Chancellorsville, VA (20TH)	5/3/63	1

ELEVEN WERE CAPTURED

One South Windsor soldier died in captivity at Andersonville Prison, GA.

SOUTH WINDSOR CAPTURED
*(1) DIED IN CAPTIVITY

PLACE	DATE	NO.
Pattersonville, LA (12TH)	3/27/63	1
Pattersonville, LA (12TH)	3/28/63	1
Brashear City, LA (25TH)	6/23/63	1
Drewry's Bluff, VA (7,11TH) *1	5/16/64	4
Cedar Creek, VA (12TH)	10/19/64	1
Federal Point, NC (6TH)	1/18/65	1
Petersburg, VA (1 HA)	3/5/65	1
Burgan, NC (6TH)	4/8/65	1

TOTAL SOUTH WINDSOR CASUALTIES

DIED	14	11%
KILLED	3	2%
WOUNDED	19	15%
CAPTURED	11	9%
DESERTED	19	15%

NINETEEEN WERE WOUNDED

The first South Windsor soldier wounded was Private Ezra Irish of Company D, 12TH Connecticut. He was wounded accidentally at West Hartford, CT on February 11, 1862 and died from his wound. Two South Windsor soldiers died from a wound received during the war.

SOUTH WINDSOR WOUNDED
*(2) DIED FROM WOUNDS

PLACE	DATE	NO.
West Hartford, CT (12TH) *	2/11/62	1
New Bern, NC (11TH)	3/20/62	1
James Island, SC (11TH) *	6/16/62	1
Antietam, MD (11, 16TH)	9/17/62	2
Fredericksburg, VA (14TH)	12/13/62	1
Baton Rouge, LA (25TH)	3/9/63	1
Irish Bend, LA (25TH)	4/14/63	2
Suffolk, VA (21ST)	5/3/63	1
Port Hudson, LA (12TH)	6/14/63	1
Port Hudson, LA (25TH)	6/27/63	1
Cold Harbor, VA (11TH)	6/3/64	2
Petersburg, VA (11TH)	6/18/64	1
Kenesaw Mountain, GA (5TH)	6/19/64	1
Cedar Creek, VA (12TH)	10/19/64	2
Kell House, VA (29TH)	10/27/64	1

SPRAGUE
THE POPULATION IN 1860 WAS 2,217 (RANK 65)

THE MOST IMPORTANT DAY 0F THE CIVIL WAR

JUNE 15 1863

WINCHESTER, VA

THE ENTIRE UNION ARMY WAS NEARLY CAPTURED AT THE SECOND BATTLE OF WINCHESTER

More soldiers credited to Sprague were listed as casualties (12) on this day than on any other day of the war. Twelve soldiers in the 18TH Connecticut were captured and all survived the war.

The date June 15, 1863 ranks 2ND for total casualties (595) (23 killed, 11 wounded, 520 captured, 41 wounded & captured) for a single day for the State of Connecticut. There were 592 casualties at Winchester, VA and 3 casualties at Port Hudson, LA.

The Second Battle of Winchester (June 13-15, 1863) ranks 5TH for total casualties (592) for an engagement for the State of Connecticut. The most intense fighting developed on June 15. Sprague had all its casualties on that day.

The Second Battle of Winchester with 12 total casualties for Sprague was the highest number of casualties for any single engagement of the war for the town.

Winchester was one of the most contested locations in the Civil War. It changed hands seventy-two times.

133 MEN CREDITED TO SPRAGUE SERVED IN THE FOLLOWING CONNECTICUT ORGANIZATIONS

REGIMENT	TOTAL
10TH	53 (40%)
18TH	17 (3%)
12TH	12 (9%)
7TH	11 (8%)
14TH	8 (6%)
2ND HEAVY ARTILLERY	7 (5%)
1ST CAVALRY	6 (5%)
5TH	6 (5%)
2ND	5 (4%)
21ST	5 (4%)
29TH	5 (4%)
12TH BATTALION	4 (3%)
1TH HEAVY ARTILLERY	2 (2%)
3RD	2 (2%)
13TH	2 (2%)
13TH BATTALION	2 (2%)
1ST SQUADRON CAVALRY	1
11TH	1
26TH	1

6% OF POPULATION

FOUR WERE KILLED

The first Sprague soldier killed was Corporal Walter F. Standish of Company E, 14TH Connecticut. He was killed at Gettysburg, PA on July 3, 1863.

SPRAGUE SOLDIERS KILLED

PLACE	DATE	NO.
Gettysburg, PA (14TH)	7/3/63	1
Deep Bottom, VA (10TH)	8/14/64	2
Winchester, VA (12TH)	9/19/64	1

TWENTY-TWO WERE CAPTURED

Three Sprague soldiers died in captivity. One died at Andersonville Prison, GA, Florence, SC and Salisbury, NC.

SPRAGUE CAPTURED
*(3) DIED IN CAPTIVITY

PLACE	DATE	NO.
Winchester, VA (5TH)	5/25/62	1
Winchester, VA (18TH)	6/15/63	12
St Augustine, FL (10TH) *	9/30/63	1
St Augustine, FL (10TH)	12/30/63	2
New Market, VA (18TH) *	5/15/64	1
Piedmont, VA (18TH)	6/5/64	1
(WOUNDED)		
Piedmont, VA (18TH)	6/10/64	1
Winchester, VA (18TH)	7/24/64	1
Winchester, VA (18TH)	7/25/64	1
Cedar Run Church, VA (1CA) *	10/17/64	1

TOTAL SPRAGUE CASUALTIES

DIED	15	11%
KILLED	4	3%
WOUNDED	30	23%
CAPTURED	22	17%
DESERTED	15	11%

THIRTY WERE WOUNDED

The first Sprague soldiers wounded were Privates Jeremiah Collins and Francis Standish of Company F, 10TH Connecticut. They were wounded at Roanoke Island, NC on February 8, 1862 and Private Collins died from his wound. He was the only Sprague soldier who died from a wound received during the war.

SPRAGUE WOUNDED
*(1) DIED FROM WOUNDS

PLACE	DATE	NO.
Roanoke Island, NC (10TH)*1	2/8/62	2
James Island, SC (7TH)	6/16/62	1
Pocotaligo, SC (7TH)	10/22/62	1
Kinston, NC (10TH)	12/14/62	4
Siege Suffolk, VA (21ST)	5/3/63	1
Chancellorsville, VA (14TH)	5/3/63	2
Spottsylvania, VA (14TH)	5/10/64	1
Laurel Hill, VA (14TH)	5/10/64	1
Drewry's Bluff, VA (7,10[TH])	5/14/64	2
Cedar Creek, VA (18TH)	5/25/64	1
Piedmont, VA (18TH)	6/5/64	1
Snicker's Ford, VA (18TH)	7/18/64	2
Strawberry Plains, VA (10TH)	7/27/64	1
Deep Bottom, VA (10TH)	8/14/64	2
Deep Bottom, VA (14TH)	8/15/64	1
Petersburg, VA (14TH)	9/5/64	1
Winchester, VA (2 HA)	9/19/64	1
Cedar Creek, VA (12TH)	10/19/64	2
Fort Gregg, VA (10TH)	4/2/65	2
Richmond, VA (10TH)	4/3/65	1

STAFFORD
THE POPULATION IN 1860 WAS 3,397 (RANK 29)

**THE MOST IMPORTANT DAY
OF THE CIVIL WAR**

APRIL 20, 1864

PLYMOUTH, NC

**THE CONFEDERATE PLAN
TO TAKE PLYMOUTH
ENDED WHEN 2,800 UNION
TROOPS SURRENDERED
THE CITY**

More soldiers credited to Stafford were listed as casualties (31) on this day than on any other day of the war. Thirty-one soldiers in the 16TH Connecticut were captured. Seven of them eventually died in prison.

The date April 20, 1864 ranks 6TH for total casualties (433) (1 killed, 2 missing, 12 wounded & captured, 418 captured) for a single day for the State of Connecticut. All of the casualties were at Plymouth, NC.

The Battle of Plymouth (April 20, 1864) ranks 9TH for total casualties (433) for an engagement for the State of Connecticut. Nearly half of all soldiers captured at Plymouth died in Southern prisons

The Battle of Plymouth with 31 total casualties for Stafford was the highest number of casualties for any single engagement of the war.

When Confederate General Robert Hoke surrounded and captured the Union garrison at Plymouth, NC the Southern victory was the first in this military arena in quite some time. With aid from the two-gun ironclad *Albemarle* the Confederates were able to take advantage of the lack of suitable Union gunboats.

**296 MEN CREDITED TO
STAFFORD SERVED
IN THE FOLLOWING
CONNECTICUT
ORGANIZATIONS**

REGIMENT	TOTAL
25TH	69 (23%)
16TH	67 (23%)
11TH	61 (21%)
1ST	20 (7%)
2ND HEAVY ARTILLERY	17 (6%)
1ST CAVALRY	16 (5%)
29TH	12 (4%)
7TH	10 (3%)
1ST HEAVY ARTILLERY	8 (3%)
12TH	7 (2%)
6TH	5 (2%)
5TH	3 (1%)
10TH	3 (1%)
22ND	3 (1%)
30TH	3 (1%)
1ST SQUADRON CAVALRY	2
1ST LIGHT BATTERY	1
2ND	1
3RD	1
8TH	1
9TH	1
12TH BATTALION	1
14TH	1
17TH	1

9% OF POPULATION

SEVEN WERE KILLED AND ONE WAS MISSING

The first Stafford soldiers killed were 1ST Lieutenant William Horton and Private Augustus Truesdell of Company I, 16TH Connecticut. Both were killed at the Battle of Antietam, MD on September 17, 1862.

STAFFORD SOLDIERS KILLED MISSING *

PLACE	DATE	NO.
Antietam, MD (16TH)	9/17/62	2
Irish Bend, LA (25TH)	4/14/63	1
Drewry's Bluff, VA (11TH)	5/16/64	2
Ream's Station, VA (1 CA) *	7/29/64	1
Silver Run, NC (5TH)	3/16/65	1
Potomac River(Drowned)(16TH)	4/20/65	1

FORTY-EIGHT WERE CAPTURED

Ten Stafford soldiers died in captivity. Five soldiers died at Florence, SC and five at Andersonville Prison, GA.

STAFFORD CAPTURED *(10) DIED IN CAPTIVITY

PLACE	DATE	NO.
Virginia (1 SQ) *	Unknown	1
New Bern, NC (11TH)	3/20/62	1
Antietam, MD (16TH)	9/17/62	2
Pattersonville, LA (12TH)	3/27/63	1
Irish Bend, LA (25TH)	4/14/63	3
Plymouth, NC (16TH) *7	4/20/64	31
Drewry's Bluff, VA (11TH) *2	5/16/64	3
Hatcher's Run, VA (7TH)	6/2/64	1
Ream's Station, VA (1CA)	6/29/64	1
Cedar Run Church, VA (1CA)	10/17/64	1
Cedar Creek, VA (2 HA)	10/19/64	3

TOTAL STAFFORD CASUALTIES

DIED	**34**	**11%**
KILLED/MISSING	**8**	**3%**
WOUNDED	**61**	**20%**
CAPTURED	**48**	**16%**
DESERTED	**37**	**13%**

SIXTY-ONE WERE WOUNDED

The first Stafford soldier wounded was Private Charles McElroy of Company C, 1ST Connecticut. He was wounded at the Battle of Bull Run, VA on July 21, 1861 and recovered from his wound. Four Stafford soldiers died from a wound received during the war.

STAFFORD WOUNDED *(4) DIED FROM WOUNDS

PLACE	DATE	NO.
Bull Run, VA (1ST)	7/21/61	1
Antietam, MD (11, 16TH) *2	9/17/62	18
Fredericksburg, VA (16TH)	12/17/62	1
Pensacola, FL (28TH)	3/22/63	1
Irish Bend, LA (25TH) *1	4/14/63	18
Port Hudson, LA (12,25TH)	6/14/63	3
Port Hudson, LA	6/27/63	3
Drewry's Bluff, VA (7TH)	5/14/64	1
Drewry's Bluff, VA (11TH)	5/16/64	1
Cold Harbor, VA (2 HA) *	6/1/64	1
Cold Harbor, VA (11TH)	6/3/64	2
Petersburg, VA (11TH)	6/16/64	1
Petersburg, VA (11TH)	6/18/64	1
Ream's Station, VA (1 CA)	6/29/64	1
Petersburg, VA (11TH)	8/25/64	1
Petersburg, VA (11TH)	9/11/64	1
Winchester, VA (2 HA)	9/19/64	1
Cedar Creek, VA (2 HA)	10/19/64	1
Malvern Hill, VA (29TH)	10/27/64	1
Kell House, VA (29TH	10/27/64	2
Dinwiddie Court House, VA	3/31/65	1

STAMFORD
THE POPULATION IN 1860 WAS 7,185 (RANK 11)

THE MOST IMPORTANT DAY OF THE CIVIL WAR
MAY 19, 1864
WELAKA, FL

ON OUTPOST DUTY IN NORTHERN FLORIDA ALMOST ALL OF COMPANY B, 17TH CONNECTICUT INFANTRY WERE CAPTURED

More Stamford soldiers were listed as casualties (16) on this day than on any other day of the war. Fifteeen soldiers in Company B, 17TH Connecticut were captured and 1 was wounded. The captured were imprisoned at Andersonville Prison, GA and all survived the captivity.

The date May 19,1864 ranks 45TH for total casualties (49) (1 killed, 7 wounded, 41 captured) for the State of Connecticut. There were 42 casualties at Welaka and 7 casualties scattered about Georgia (4) and Virginia (3).

The incident at Welaka, FL (May19, 1864) ranks 41ST for total casualties (42) for an engagement for the State of Connecticut.

The incident at Welaka, FL with 16 total casualties for Stamford was the highest number of casualties for any single engagement of the war for the town.

Florida was often referred to as the breadbasket of the Confederacy. With a location deep in the South and a favorable climate, Florida added greatly to the Southern cause. The principal products supplied were cattle, cotton and salt.

By 1864, the number of soldiers in the 17TH Connecticut had been greatly reduced. They did not have the strength to mount a strong fighting force and were placed in an out of the way yet important outpost.

550 MEN CREDITED TO STAMFORD SERVED IN THE FOLLOWING CONNECTICUT ORGANIZATIONS

REGIMENT	TOTAL
28TH	188 (34%)
6TH	110 (20%)
17TH	77 (14%)
3RD	41 (7%)
10TH	37 (7%)
13TH	23 (4%)
29TH	21 (4%)
1ST HEAVY ARTILLERY	19 (3%)
11TH	14 (3%)
2ND HEAVY ARTILLERY	14 (3%)
7TH	9 (2%)
8TH	6 (1%)
12TH	5 (1%)
30TH	5 (1%)
5TH	4 (1%)
9TH	4 (1%)
13TH BATTALION	3 (1%)
1ST CAVALRY	2
2ND LIGHT BATTERY	2
14TH	2
23RD	2
1ST	1
15TH	1
20TH	1

8% OF POPULATION

THIRTEEN WERE KILLED AND THREE WERE MISSING

The first Stamford soldier killed was Private Benjamin O. Searles of Company B, 13TH Connecticut. He was killed at the Battle of Irish Bend, LA on April 13, 1863.

STAMFORD SOLDIERS KILLED *MISSING

PLACE	DATE	NO.
Irish Bend, LA (13TH)	4/14/63	1
Chancellorsville, VA (17TH)	5/2/63	2
Chancellorsville, VA (17TH)	5/5/63	1
Port Hudson, LA (28TH)	6/14/63	3
Gettysburg, PA (17TH) *	7/1/63	1
Gettysburg, PA (17TH) *	7/2/63	1
Fort Wagner, SC (6TH) *1	7/18/63	2
Cold Harbor, VA (2 HA)	6/3/64	1
Deep Bottom, VA (6TH) *	8/16/64	1
Petersburg, VA (6TH)	9/22/64	1
Richmond, VA (7TH)	10/15/64	1
Kell House, VA (29TH)	10/27/64	1

FIFTY-ONE WERE CAPTURED

Three Stamford soldiers died in captivity. Two died at Andersonville Prison, GA and one died at Florence, SC.

STAMFORD CAPTURED *(3) DIED IN CAPTIVITY

PLACE	DATE	NO.
Bull Run, VA (3RD)	7/21/61	3
Chancellorsville, VA (17TH) (2 WOUNDED)	5/2/63	7
Chancellorsville, VA (17TH)	5/3/63	1
Port Hudson, LA (28TH)	6/14/63	1
Gettysburg, PA (17TH)	7/1/63	3
Fort Wagner, SC (6TH) *1	7/18/63	2
Drewry's Bluff, VA (6,1TH)	5/16/64	2
Proctors Creek, VA (10TH) * (WOUNDED)	5/16/64	1
Welaka, FL (17TH) (WOUNDED)	5/19/64	16
Bermuda Hundred, VA (6TH)	6/17/64	10
Deep Run, VA (6TH)	8/16/64	2
Deep Bottom, VA (10TH) *	8/16/64	1
Winchester, VA (13TH)	9/19/64	1
Braddock Farm, FL (17TH)	2/5/65	1

TOTAL STAMFORD CASUALTIES

DIED	84	15%
KILLED/MISSING	16	3%
WOUNDED	83	15%
CAPTURED	51	9%
DESERTED	53	10%

EIGHTY-THREE WERE WOUNDED

The first Stamford soldier wounded was Sergeant Henry Capper of Company G, 10TH Connecticut. He was wounded at New Bern, NC and recovered from his wound. Thirteen Stamford soldiers died from a wound received during the war.

STAMFORD WOUNDED *(13) DIED FROM WOUNDS

PLACE	DATE	NO.
New Bern, NC (10TH)	3/14/62	1
James Island, SC (7TH)	6/16/62	1
Pocotaligo, SC (6TH) *	10/22/62	7
Kinston, NC (10TH) *2	12/14/62	2
Chancellorsville, VA (17TH)	5/2/63	2
Port Hudson, LA (28TH) *	6/7/63	1
Port Hudson, LA (13TH28TH) *2	6/14/63	9
Gettysburg, PA (17TH)	7/1/63	3
Gettysburg, PA (17TH)	7/2/63	1
Gettysburg, PA (17TH)	7/3/63	1
Port Hudson, LA (28TH)	7/4/63	1
Port Hudson, LA (28TH)	7/8/63	1
Morris Island, SC (6TH) *	7/18/63	1
Fort Wagner, SC (6TH)	7/18/63	3
Morris Island, SC (6TH)	7/25/63	1
Walthall Junction, VA (8TH)	5/7/64	1
Petersburg, VA (6TH)	5/9/64	1
Chester Station, VA (6TH)	5/10/64	2
Drewry's Bluff, VA (10TH) *	5/13/64	1
Drewry's Bluff, VA (6TH) *1	5/15/64	5
Drewry's Bluff, VA (6TH)	5/16/64	7
Welaka, FL (17TH)	5/19/64	1
Bermuda Hundred, VA (6TH)	5/20/64	3
Unknown Place (30TH)	5/30/64	1
Cold Harbor, VA (2 HA) *	6/1/64	3
Petersburg, VA (11TH)	6/3/64	1
Cold Harbor, VA (11TH)	6/3/64	2
Bermuda Hundred, VA (6TH) *	6/6/64	1
Bermuda Hundred, VA (6TH)	6/17/64	1
Bermuda Hundred, VA (6TH)	6/19/64	1
Petersburg, VA (1 HA)	6/30/64	1
Petersburg, VA (11TH)	7/30/64	1
Deep Bottom, VA (10TH)	8/14/64	2
Deep Run, VA (6TH)	8/15/64	1
Deep Run, VA (6TH)	8/16/64	5
Petersburg, VA (29TH)	8/25/64	2
Strasburg, VA (2 HA)	9/22/64	1
Darbytown Road, VA (10TH)	10/13/64	1
Kell House, VA (29TH) *	10/27/64	1
Hatcher's Run, VA (10TH)	4/1/65	1
Petersburg, VA (10TH) *	4/2/65	2

STERLING
THE POPULATION IN 1860 WAS 1,051 (RANK 131)

THE MOST IMPORTANT DAY OF THE CIVIL WAR

SEPTEMBER 17, 1862

SHARPSBURG, MD (ANTIETAM)

CONNECTICUT HAD MORE CASUALTIES FOR ONE DAY THAN ON ANY OTHER DAY OF THE WAR

More soldiers credited to Sterling were listed as casualties (3) on this day than on any day of the war. One soldier was killed and 2 were wounded in the 11TH Connecticut. One of the wounded died.

The date September 17, 1862 ranks 1ST for total casualties (687) (131 killed, 2 missing, 515 wounded, 21 captured, 18 wounded & captured) for a single day for the State of Connecticut. All of the casualties were at Antietam.

The Battle of Antietam (September 16-17, 1862) ranks 1ST for total casualties (689) for an engagement for the State of Connecticut. The most intense fighting developed on September 17. Sterling had all of its casualties on that day.

The Battle of Antietam with 3 total casualties for Sterling was the highest number of casualties for any single engagement of the war for the town.

Roughly 12,400 Union casualties were recorded and perhaps there were 10,300 Confederate casualties. Antietam proved to be one of the turning points of the war. It ended Lee's 1862 invasion of the North.

74 MEN CREDITED TO STERLING SERVED IN THE FOLLOWING CONNECTICUT ORGANIZATIONS

REGIMENT	TOTAL
26TH	12 (17%)
21ST	11 (15%)
5TH	8 (11%)
8TH	8 (11%)
18TH	8 (11%)
11TH	6 (8%)
1ST HEAVY ARTILLERY	4 (5%)
13TH	4 (5%)
7TH	3 (4%)
12TH	3 (4%)
20TH	3 (4%)
1ST CAVALRY	2 (3%)
9TH	2 (3%)
12TH BATTALION	2 (3%)
13TH BATTALION	2 (3%)
14TH	2 (3%)
2ND HEAVY ARTILLERY	1
29TH	1

7% OF POPULATION

TWO WERE KILLED

The first Sterling soldier killed was Private Frank Chaffee of Company H, 11TH Connecticut. He was killed at the Battle of Antietam, MD on September 17, 1862.

STERLING SOLDIERS KILLED

PLACE	DATE	NO.
Antietam, MD (11TH)	9/17/62	1
Suffolk, VA (21ST)	5/3/63	1

THREE WERE CAPTURED

No Sterling soldiers died in captivity.

STERLING CAPTURED
NONE DIED IN CAPTIVITY

PLACE	DATE	NO.
Winchester, VA (18TH)	6/15/63	1
Lynchburg, VA (18TH)	6/18/64	1
Madison, GA (5TH)	11/19/64	1

TOTAL STERLING CASUALTIES

DIED	8	11%
KILLED	2	3%
WOUNDED	12	16%
CAPTURED	3	4%
DESERTED	10	14%

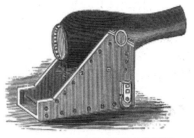

TWELVE WERE WOUNDED

The first Sterling soldiers wounded were Sergeant Henry O. Spalding and Private John Bently of Company F, 11TH Connecticut. They were wounded at the Battle of Antietam, MD on September 17, 1862 and Private Bently died from his wound. Two Sterling soldiers died from a wound received during the war.

STERLING WOUNDED
*(2) DIED FROM WOUNDS

PLACE	DATE	NO.
Antietam, MD (8TH) *1	9/17/62	2
Chancellorsville, VA (11TH) *	5/3/63	1
Port Hudson, LA (26TH)	6/14/63	2
Fort Wagner, SC (7TH)	8/3/63	1
New Bern, NC (21ST)	3/12/64	1
Petersburg, VA (11TH)	6/18/64	1
Winchester, VA (12TH)	9/19/64	1
Chaffin's Farm, VA (7TH)	10/7/64	1
Richmond, VA (29TH)	10/13/64	1
Richmond, VA (7TH)	11/15/64	1

STONINGTON
THE POPULATION IN 1860 WAS 5,827 (RANK 13)

THE MOST IMPORTANT DAY OF THE CIVIL WAR

MAY 16, 1864

DREWRY'S BLUFF , VA

AN OBSTACLE ON THE WAY TO RICHMOND

More soldiers credited to Stonington were listed as casualties (19) on this day than on any other day of the war. Four soldiers were killed, 5 were wounded, and 10 captured in the 8ᵀᴴ and 21ˢᵀ Connecticut. Six of the captured died in prison.

The date May 16, 1864 ranks 4th for total casualties (560) (52 killed, 3 missing, 224 wounded, 243 captured, 38 wounded & captured) for a single day for the State of Connecticut. The Battle of Drewry's Bluff accounted for 545 casualties. The 15 other casualties were scattered about Virginia.

The Battle of Drewry's Bluff (May 13-17, 1864), also called Fort Darling, ranks 3rd for total casualties (634) for an engagement for the State of Connecticut. The most intense fighting developed on May 16. Stonington also had one casualty on May 13 and 15.

The Battle of Drewry's Bluff with 21 total casualties for Stonington was the highest number of casualties for any single engagement of the war for the town.

The Confederate attack at Drewry's Bluff forced the Union Army to retreat to Bermuda Hundred. The civil war would have concluded sooner had the Union Army been victorious.

368 MEN CREDITED TO STONINGTON SERVED IN THE FOLLOWING CONNECTICUT ORGANIZATIONS

REGIMENT	TOTAL
8ᵀᴴ	92 (25%)
21ˢᵀ	79 (21%)
26ᵀᴴ	59 (16%)
1ˢᵀ CAVALRY	31 (8%)
12ᵀᴴ	27 (7%)
14ᵀᴴ	22 (6%)
5ᵀᴴ	19 (5%)
1ˢᵀ HEAVY ARTILLERY	12 (3%)
30ᵀᴴ	10 (3%)
12ᵀᴴ BATTALION	9 (2%)
2ᴺᴰ	7 (2%)
29ᵀᴴ	6 (2%)
10ᵀᴴ	5 (1%)
18ᵀᴴ	5 (1%)
2ᴺᴰ HEAVY ARTILLERY	4 (1%)
9ᵀᴴ	3 (1%)
20ᵀᴴ	3 (1%)
13ᵀᴴ	2
1ˢᵀ	1
3ᴿᴰ	1
6ᵀᴴ	1
13ᵀᴴ BATTALION	1

6% OF POPULATION

EIGHTEEN WERE KILLED AND ONE WAS MISSING

The first Stonington soldier killed was Corporal Oscar W. Hewitt of Company G, 8TH Connecticut. He was killed at the Battle of Antietam, MD on September 17, 1862.

STONINGTON SOLDIERS KILLED MISSING *

PLACE	DATE	NO.
Antietam, MD (8TH)	9/17/62	1
Georgia Landing, LA (12TH)	10/27/62	1
Baltimore,MD (1CA)(Accident)	3/20/63	1
Port Hudson, LA (26TH)	5/27/63	2
Winchester, VA (18TH)	6/15/63	1
Virginia ((1 CA) *	1/15/64	1
Newport News,VA(Drowned)21ST	2/3/64	1
Railroad Accident (12TH)	5/5/64	1
Drewry's Bluff, VA (8TH)	5/13/64	1
Drewry's Bluff, VA (8, 21ST)	5/16/64	4
Petersburg, VA (21ST)	6/30/64	1
Peach Tree Creek, GA (5TH)	7/20/64	2
Winchester, VA (12TH)	9/19/64	1
Fort Harrison, VA (8TH)	9/29/64	1

THIRTY-FOUR WERE CAPTURED

Eleven Stonington soldiers died in captivity. Six died at Andersonville Prison, GA., two died at Salisbury, NC, and one died at Savannah, GA.

STONINGTON CAPTURED *(11) DIED IN CAPTIVITY

PLACE	DATE	NO.
Winchester, VA (5TH)	5/25/62	1
Luray Valley, VA (5TH)	6/30/62	1
Cedar Mountain, VA (5TH)	8/9/62	1
Culpeper, VA (5TH)	8/20/62	1
Antietam, MD (8TH)	9/19/62	1
Brashear City, LA (12TH)	6/23/63	1
South Mills, NC (8TH)	8/25/63	1
Mine Run, VA (14TH) *	11/30/63	1
Morton's Ford, VA (14TH) *2	2/6/64	2
Monett's Ferry, LA (13TH)	4/23/64	1
Craig's Church, VA (1 CA)	5/5/64	1
Drewry's Bluff, VA (8, 21) *6	5/16/64	10
Berryville, VA (1 CA)	8/15/64	1
Ream's Station, VA (14TH)	8/25/64	1
Petersburg, VA (8TH)	9/17/64	1
Cedar Creek, VA (12TH) *2	10/19/64	8
Stony Creek, VA (14TH)	10/27/64	1

TOTAL STONINGTON CASUALTIES

DIED	62	17%
KILLED/MISSING	19	5%
WOUNDED	76	21%
CAPTURED	34	9%
DESERTED	39	11%

SEVENTY-SIX WERE WOUNDED

The first Stonington soldier wounded was Lieutenant Colonel Thomas D. Sheffield, 8TH Connecticut. He was wounded at Fort Macon, NC on April 12, 1862 and recovered from his wound. Thirteen Stonington soldiers died from a wound received during the war.

STONINGTON WOUNDED *(13) DIED FROM WOUNDS

PLACE	DATE	NO.
Fort Macon, NC (8TH)	4/12/62	1
Mt Jackson, VA (1 CA)	6/6/62	1
Antietam, MD (8TH)	9/17/62	14
Bisland, LA (12TH) *	4/13/63	1
Port Hudson, LA (12,26[TH]) *3	5/27/63	13
Port Hudson, LA (12TH)	5/28/63	1
Port Hudson, LA (12TH)	6/10/63	1
Port Hudson, LA (26TH)	6/13/63	1
Port Hudson, LA (12, 26TH)	6/14/63	4
Port Hudson, LA (12TH)	6/30/63	1
Bristoe Station, VA (14TH)	10/14/63	2
Walthall Junction, VA (8TH) *2	5/7/64	5
Drewry's Bluff, VA (8TH)	5/15/64	1
Drewry's Bluff, VA (21ST) *	5/16/64	5
Cold Harbor, VA (8TH)	6/2/64	1
Cold Harbor, VA (21ST)	6/3/64	4
Petersburg, VA (8TH) *1	6/16/64	3
Petersburg, VA (21ST) *1	6/30/64	2
Petersburg, VA (21ST)	7/9/64	1
Petersburg, VA (21ST)	7/17/64	1
Petersburg, VA (1 HA)	7/19/64	1
Peach Tree Creek, GA (5TH)	7/20/64	1
Petersburg, VA (21ST)	7/30/64	1
Petersburg, VA (21ST)	8/18/64	1
Winchester, VA (12TH)	9/19/64	3
Fort Harrison, VA (8TH) *1	9/29/64	3
Petersburg, VA (21ST) *	9/29/64	1
Cedar Run Chrch,VA (1 CA)*	10/17/64	1

568

STRATFORD
THE POPULATION IN 1860 WAS 2,294 (RANK 62)

THE MOST IMPORTANT DAY OF THE CIVIL WAR

JULY 1, 1863
GETTYSBURG, PA

THE FIRST DAY OF THE BATTLE

More soldiers credited to Stratford were listed as casualties (5) on this day than on any other day of the war. Two soldiers were killed, 2 were wounded, and 1 was captured in the 17TH Connecticut. The wounded and captured survived the war.

The date July 1, 1863 ranks 16TH for total casualties (157) (18 killed, 4 missing, 70 wounded, 57 captured, 8 wounded & captured) for a single day for the State of Connecticut. The Battle of Gettysburg accounted for 143 casualties. The 14 other casualties were scattered about Virginia (6), Louisiana (6), and South Carolina (2).

The Battle of Gettysburg (July1-3, 1863) ranks 11TH for total casualties (360) for an engagement for the State of Connecticut. The most intense fighting developed on July 3. Stratford had no casualties on that day.

The Battle of Gettysburg with 5 total casualties for Stratford was the highest number of casualties for any single engagement of the war for the town.

More than 170,00 men fought at the Battle of Gettysburg. Roughly 23,000 Union casualties were recorded and there were about 28,000 Confederate casualties. Gettysburg proved to be the great battle of the war. It ended Lee's 1863 invasion of the North. He was never able to launch a major offensive again

89 MEN CREDITED TO STRATFORD SERVED IN THE FOLLOWING CONNECTICUT ORGANIZATIONS

REGIMENT	TOTAL
2ND LIGHT BATTERY	12 (13%)
17TH	12 (13%)
6TH	10 (10%)
1ST HEAVY ARTILLERY	9 (10%)
2ND HEAVY ARTILLERY	6 (7%)
14TH	6 (7%)
1ST CAVALRY	5 (6%)
11TH	5 (6%)
29TH	5 (6%)
5TH	4 (4%)
30TH	4 (4%)
9TH	3 (3%)
12TH	3 (3%)
8TH	2 (2%)
15TH	2 (2%)
20TH	2 (2%)
9TH BATTALION	1
12TH BATTALION	1
23RD	1

4% OF POPULATION

FIVE WERE KILLED

The first Stratford soldier killed was Private Frederick N. Judson of Company C, 12TH Connecticut. He was killed at Georgia Landing, LA on October 27, 1862.

STRATFORD SOLDIERS KILLED

PLACE	DATE	NO.
Georgia Landing, LA (12TH)	10/27/62	1
Gettysburg, PA (17TH)	7/1/63	2
Petersburg, VA (30TH)	7/30/64	1
Cedar Creek, VA (12TH)	10/19/64	1

SIX WERE CAPTURED

One Stratford soldier died in captivity at Smithville, NC.

PLACE	DATE	NO.
Gettysburg, PA (17TH)	7/1/63	1
Fort Wagner, SC (6TH) *	7/18/63	1
Craig's Church, VA (1 CA)	5/5/64	1
Berryville, VA (1 CA)	9/12/64	1
Dunn's Lake, FLA (17TH)	2/5/65	1
Kinston, NC (15TH)	3/8/65	1

TOTAL STRATFORD CASUALTIES

DIED	12	13%
KILLED	5	6%
WOUNDED	13	15%
CAPTURED	6	7%
DESERTED	17	19%

THIRTEEN WERE WOUNDED

The first Stratford soldier wounded was Private Francis R. Curtis of Company A, 14TH Connecticut. He was wounded at the Battle of Antietam, MD on September 17, 1862 and recovered from his wound. Four Stratford soldiers died from a wound received during the war.

STRATFORD WOUNDED
*(4) DIED FROM WOUNDS

PLACE	DATE	NO.
Antietam, MD (14TH)	9/17/62	1
Bridgeport, CT (2LB)	9/20/62	1
Stafford CH, VA (17TH)	12/16/62	1
Chancellorsville, VA (14TH) *	5/3/63	1
Port Hudson, LA (12TH)	6/10/63	1
Gettysburg, PA (17TH)	7/1/63	2
Bermuda Hundred, VA (1 HA)	5/1/64	1
Drewry's Bluff, VA (6TH) *	5/16/64	1
Petersburg, VA (30TH)	7/30/64	1
Richmond, VA (29TH) *	9/30/64	1
Cedar Creek, VA (2HA, 9TH) *	10/19/64	2

SUFFIELD
THE POPULATION IN 1860 WAS 1,517 (RANK 96)

THE MOST IMPORTANT DAY OF THE CIVIL WAR

SEPTEMBER 17, 1862
SHARPSBURG, MD (ANTIETAM)

CONNECTICUT HAD MORE CASUALTIES FOR ONE DAY THAN ON ANY OTHER DAY OF THE WAR

More soldiers credited to Suffield were listed as casualties (24) on this day than on any day of the war. Four soldiers were killed, 17 were wounded, and 3 were captured in the 16TH Connecticut. The wounded and captured survived the war.

The date September 17, 1862 ranks 1ST for total casualties (687) (131 killed, 2 missing, 515 wounded, 21 captured, 18 wounded & captured) for a single day for the State of Connecticut. All of the casualties were at Antietam.

The Battle of Antietam (September 16-17, 1862) ranks 1ST for total casualties (689) for an engagement for the State of Connecticut. The most intense fighting developed on September 17. Suffield had all of its casualties on that day.

The Battle of Antietam with 24 total casualties for Suffield was the highest number of casualties for any single engagement of the war for the town.

Roughly 12,400 Union casualties were recorded and perhaps there were 10,300 Confederate casualties. Antietam proved to be one of the turning points of the war. It ended Lee's 1862 invasion of the North.

338 MEN CREDITED TO SUFFIELD SERVED IN THE FOLLOWING CONNECTICUT ORGANIZATIONS

REGIMENT	TOTAL
22ND	74 (22%)
16TH	70 (21%)
1ST HEAVY ARTILLERY	56 (17%)
29TH	35 (10%)
7TH	18 (5%)
5TH	12 (4%)
14TH	12 (4%)
11TH	11 (3%)
2ND HEAVY ARTILLERY	10 (3%)
1ST CAVALRY	8 (2%)
12TH	8 (2%)
8TH	7 (2%)
1ST LIGHT BATTERY	6 (2%)
13TH	5 (1%)
6TH	4 (1%)
1ST	3 (1%)
13TH BATTALION	3 (1%)
10TH	2
12TH BATTALION	2
15TH	2
30TH	2
1ST SQUADRON CAVALRY	1
3RD	1
20TH	1

10% OF POPULATION

TEN WERE KILLED AND TWO WERE MISSING

The first Suffield soldiers killed were Corporal Horace Warner and Privates Henry Barnett, George W. Allen, Nelson E. Snow of Company D, 16TH Connecticut. They were killed at the Battle of Antietam, MD on September 17, 1862.

SUFFIELD SOLDIERS KILLED MISSING *

PLACE	DATE	NO.
Antietam, MD (16TH)	9/17/62	4
Virginia (22ND)	4/12/63	1
Fort Wagner, SC (6,7TH)	7/11/63	2
Dallas, GA (5TH)	5/27/64	1
Petersburg, VA (1 HA)	7/12/64	1
Petersburg, VA (30TH) *	7/30/64	1
Deep Run, VA (6TH) *	8/16/64	1

THIRTY-FIVE WERE CAPTURED

Eight Suffield soldiers died in captivity. Six died at Andersonville Prison, GA, one died at Florence, SC and one died at Libby Prison Richmond, VA.

SUFFIELD CAPTURED *(8) DIED IN CAPTIVITY

PLACE	DATE	NO.
Antietam, MD (16TH)	9/17/62	3
Winchester, VA (16TH)	9/28/62	1
Fort Wagner, SC (7TH)	7/11/63	2
(1 WOUNDED)		
Plymouth, NC (16TH) *7	4/20/64	22
Drewry's Bluff, VA (7TH)	5/16/64	1
Petersburg, VA (8TH)	6/18/64	1
Cedar Creek, VA (2 HA)	10/19/64	2
Boydton Plank Rd,VA 14TH *	10/27/64	1
Madison, GA (5TH)	11/18/64	1
Kinston, NC (15TH)	3/8/65	1

TOTAL SUFFIELD CASUALTIES

DIED	24	7%
KILLED/MISSING	12	4%
WOUNDED	38	11%
CAPTURED	35	10%
DESERTED	47	14%

THIRTY-EIGHT WERE WOUNDED

The first Suffield soldier wounded was Private John H. Cline of Company C, 1ST Connecticut Heavy Artillery. He was wounded at Yorktown, VA on May 18, 1862 and recovered from his wound. Three Suffield soldiers died from a wound received during the war.

SUFFIELD WOUNDED *(3) DIED FROM WOUNDS

PLACE	DATE	NO.
Yorktown, VA (1 HA)	5/18/62	1
Antietam, MD (16TH)	9/17/62	17
Pocotaligo, SC (7TH) *	10/22/62	1
Georgia Landing, LA (12TH)	10/27/62	1
Unknown Place (16TH)	12/4/62	1
Fredericksburg, VA (14TH) *	12/13/62	1
Providence Ch. Rd, VA (16TH)*	5/3/63	1
Fort Wagner, SC (7TH)	7/11/63	1
Walthall Junction, VA (8TH)	5/7/64	1
Cold Harbor, VA (8TH)	6/2/64	1
Petersburg, VA (11TH)	6/19/64	1
Atlanta, GA (5TH)	8/16/64	1
Petersburg, VA (1 HA)	8/24/64	1
Petersburg, VA (29TH)	9/8/64	2
Richmond, VA (29TH)	9/30/64	1
Richmond, VA (7TH)	10/13/64	1
Cedar Creek, VA (13TH)	10/19/64	1
Kell House, VA (29TH)	10/27/64	3
Fort Brady, VA (1 HA)	1/1/65	1

THOMPSON
THE POPULATION IN 1860 WAS 3,259 (RANK 36)

THE MOST IMPORTANT DAY OF THE CIVIL WAR

JUNE 5, 1864

PIEDMONT, VA

A UNION VICTORY AT THE START OF THE 1864 SHENANDOAH VALLEY CAMPAIGN

215 MEN CREDITED TO THOMPSON SERVED IN THE FOLLOWING CONNECTICUT ORGANIZATIONS

More soldiers credited to Thompson were listed as casualties (18) on this day than on any day of the war. Four soldiers were killed, 4 were wounded, and 10 were wounded & captured in the 18TH Connecticut. Three died in prison and one died from his wound.

The date June 5, 1864 ranks 14TH for total casualties (166) (22 killed, 1 missing, 89 wounded, 29 captured, 25 wounded & captured) for a single day for the State of Connecticut. There were 156 casualties at Piedmont. The 10 other casualties were scattered about Virginia.

The Battle of Piedmont (June 5, 1864) ranks 10TH for total casualties (156) for an engagement for the State of Connecticut.

The Battle of Piedmont with 18 total casualties for Thompson was the highest number of casualties for any single engagement of the war for the town.

This was an important loss for the Confederate Dept. of Southwest Virginia under Brig. General W. E. Jones. Union Major General David Hunter's victory began the all important task of taking control of the Shenandoah Valley which was the breadbasket of the Confederacy.

REGIMENT	TOTAL
18TH	80 (37%)
13TH	27 (13%)
1ST HEAVY ARTILLERY	23 (11%)
1ST CAVALRY	15 (7%)
11TH	14 (7%)
6TH	12 (6%)
7TH	11 (5%)
5TH	10 (5%)
14TH	9 (4%)
29TH	6 (3%)
8TH	6 (3%)
2ND	3 (1%)
12TH	3 (1%)
13TH BATTALION	3 (1%)
1ST	2
1ST LIGHT BATTERY	1
2ND HEAVY ARTILLERY	1
3RD	1
10TH	1
12TH BATTALION	1
20TH	1

7% OF POPULATION

EIGHT WERE KILLED AND ONE WAS MISSING

The first Thompson soldier killed was Private Michael Keegan of Company C, 14TH Connecticut. He was killed at the Battle of Antietam, MD on September 17, 1862.

THOMPSON SOLDIERS KILLED MISSING *

PLACE	DATE	NO.
Antietam, MD (14TH)	9/17/62	1
Bermuda Hundred, VA (1 HA)	5/19/64	1
Piedmont, VA (18TH) *1	6/5/64	4
Snicker's Ford, VA (18TH)	7/18/64	1
Peach Tree Creek, GA (5TH)	7/20/64	1
Richmond, VA (7TH)	10/1/64	1

FORTY-FOUR WERE CAPTURED

Ten Thompson soldiers died in captivity. Five died at Andersonville Prison, GA, three died at Libby Prison Richmond, VA, and two died at Staunton, VA.

THOMPSON CAPTURED *(10) DIED IN CAPTIVITY

PLACE	DATE	NO.
Bull Run, VA (3RD)	7/21/61	2
Chancellorsville, VA (5TH)	5/2/63	1
Alexandria, LA (13TH)	5/14/63	1
Washington, LA (13TH)	5/21/63	2
Winchester, VA (18TH)	6/15/63	10
Fort Wagner, SC (7TH)	7/11/63	1
Fort Wagner, SC (6TH) *	7/18/63	1
Culpeper, VA (14TH) *	10/11/63	1
Bristoe Station, VA (14TH) *	10/14/63	1
Craig's Church, VA (1 CA) *	5/5/64	1
New Market, VA (18TH)	5/15/64	2
(2 WOUNDED)		
Drewry's Bluff, VA (6,11) *2	5/16/64	3
Gaines' Mills, VA (1 CA)	5/23/64	1
Piedmont, VA (18TH) *3	6/5/64	10
(10 WOUNDED)		
Bermuda Hundred, VA (7TH)	6/16/64	1
Ream's Station, VA (1 CA) *	7/1/64	1
Cedar Run Church,VA(1CA)	10/17/64	2
Cedar Creek, VA (13TH)	10/19/64	1
Cedar Creek, VA (1 CA)	11/12/64	1

TOTAL THOMPSON CASUALTIES

DIED	29	13%
KILLED/MISSING	9	4%
WOUNDED	30	14%
CAPTURED	44	20%
DESERTED	15	7%

THIRTY WERE WOUNDED

The first Thompson soldier wounded was Private Clinton Fessington of Company F, 11TH Connecticut. He was wounded at the Battle of Antietam, MD on September 17, 1862 and died from his wound. Four Thompson soldiers died from a wound received during the war.

THOMPSON WOUNDED *(4) DIED FROM WOUNDS

PLACE	DATE	NO.
Antietam, MD (11TH) *	9/17/62	1
Stemmer's Run, MD (18TH)	12/4/62	1
Chancellorsville, VA (5TH)	5/3/63	1
Morris Island, SC (7TH)	7/10/63	2
Morris Island, SC (7TH) *	7/11/63	1
Fort Wagner, SC (7TH)	7/11/63	2
Swift's Creek, VA (11TH)	5/9/64	1
New Market, VA (18TH)	5/15/64	4
Resaca, GA (5TH)	5/15/64	2
Drewry's Bluff, VA (8TH) *	5/16/64	1
Proctor's Creek, VA (6TH)	5/23/64	1
Cold Harbor, VA (11TH)	6/3/64	1
Piedmont, VA (18TH) *1	6/5/64	4
Petersburg, VA (14TH)	6/18/64	1
Petersburg, VA (11TH)	6/18/64	1
Snicker's Ford, VA (18TH)	7/18/64	4
Deep Run, VA (7TH)	8/16/64	1
Winchester, VA (12TH)	9/19/64	1

TOLLAND
THE POPULATION IN 1860 WAS 1,301 (RANK 111)

THE MOST IMPORTANT DAY 0F THE CIVIL WAR

JUNE 15 1863

WINCHESTER, VA

THE ENTIRE UNION ARMY WAS NEARLY CAPTURED AT THE SECOND BATTLE OF WINCHESTER

More soldiers credited to Tolland were listed as casualties (10) on this day than on any other day of the war. Two soldiers were killed, and 8 were captured in the 18TH Connecticut. The captured survived the war.

The date June 15, 1863 ranks 2ND for total casualties (595) (23 killed, 11 wounded, 520 captured, 41 wounded & captured) for a single day for the State of Connecticut. There were 592 casualties at Winchester, VA and 3 casualties at Port Hudson, LA.

The Second Battle of Winchester (June 13-15, 1863) ranks 5TH for total casualties (592) for an engagement for the State of Connecticut. The most intense fighting developed on June 15. Tolland had all its casualties on that day.

The Second Battle of Winchester with 10 total casualties for Tolland was the highest number of casualties for any single engagement of the war for the town.

Winchester was one of the most contested locations in the Civil War. It changed hands seventy-two times.

117 MEN CREDITED TO TOLLAND SERVED IN THE FOLLOWING CONNECTICUT ORGANIZATIONS

REGIMENT	TOTAL
22ND	42 (36%)
18TH	19 (16%)
2ND HEAVY ARTILLERY	12 (10%)
29TH	9 (8%)
1ST HEAVY ARTILLERY	6 (5%)
8TH	6 (5%)
10TH	6 (5%)
1ST CAVALRY	4 (4%)
11TH	4 (3%)
5TH	2 (2%)
7TH	2 (2%)
21ST	2 (2%)
30TH	2 (2%)
6TH	1
12TH	1
14TH	1
16TH	1
20TH	1
25TH	1

9% OF POPULATION

FOUR WERE KILLED

The first Tolland soldiers killed were Privates Charles A. Barber and Alfred E. Tracy of Company H, 18TH Connecticut. They were killed at Winchester, VA on June 15, 1863.

TOLLAND SOLDIERS KILLED

PLACE	DATE	NO.
Winchester, VA (18TH)	6/15/63	2
Cedar Creek, VA (12TH)	10/19/64	1
Fort Gregg, VA (10TH)	4/2/65	1

THIRTEEN WERE CAPTURED

One Tolland soldier died in captivity at Andersonville Prison, GA.

TOLLAND CAPTURED
*(1) DIED IN CAPTIVITY

PLACE	DATE	NO.
Winchester, VA (5TH)	5/25/62	1
Winchester, VA (18TH)	6/15/63	8
Piedmont, VA (18TH) *	6/5/64	2
(2 WOUNDED)		
Lynchburg, VA (18TH)	6/19/64	1
Strasburg, VA (2 HA)	9/24/64	1

TOTAL TOLLAND CASUALTIES

DIED	12	10%
KILLED	4	3%
WOUNDED	9	8%
CAPTURED	13	11%
DESERTED	15	13%

NINE WERE WOUNDED

The first Tolland soldier wounded was Private Thomas Wilkie of Company D, 14TH Connecticut. He was wounded at the Battle of Antietam, MD on September 17, 1862 and died from his wound. Two Tolland soldiers died from a wound received during the war.

TOLLAND WOUNDED
*(2) DIED FROM WOUNDS

PLACE	DATE	NO.
Antietam, MD (14TH) *	9/17/62	1
New Market, VA (18TH)	5/15/64	1
Cold Harbor, VA (8TH) *	6/2/64	1
Piedmont, VA (18TH)	6/5/64	2
Fort Dutton, VA (1 HA)	7/29/64	1
Richmond, VA (29TH)	9/29/64	1
Cedar Creek, VA (2 HA)	10/19/64	1
Petersburg, VA (1 HA)	3/15/65	1

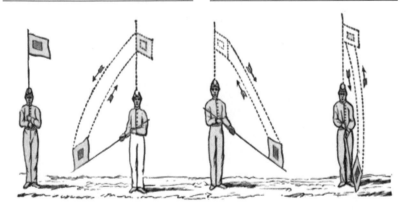

TORRINGTON
THE POPULATION IN 1860 WAS 2,278 (RANK 64)

THE MOST IMPORTANT
DAY OF THE CIVIL WAR

JUNE 1, 1864
COLD HARBOR, VA
ASHLAND, VA

COLD HARBOR WAS LEE'S LAST GREAT VICTORY ASHLAND WAS A VIRGINIA CAVALRY SKIRMISH

173 MEN CREDITED TO TORRINGTON SERVED IN THE FOLLOWING CONNECTICUT ORGANIZATIONS

More Soldiers credited to Torrington were listed as casualties (12) on this day than on any other day of the war. Two soldiers were killed and 8 were wounded in the 2ND Connecticut Heavy Artillery at Cold Harbor and 1 was wounded and 1 was captured at Ashland, VA in the 1ST Connecticut Cavalry. One of the wounded at Cold Harbor died.

The date June 1, 1864 ranks 8TH for total casualties (374) (89 killed, 10 missing, 246 wounded, 23 captured, 6 wounded & captured) for a single day for the State of Connecticut. There were 324 casualties at Cold Harbor, 41 casualties at Ashland and 9 casualties scattered about Virginia.

The battle and operations around Cold Harbor (May 31-June 12) rank 6TH for total casualties (557) for an engagement for the State of Connecticut. The action at Ashland (June 1) ranks 42ND with 41 casualties. The most intense fighting at Cold Harbor developed on June 3 and Torrington had 1 wounded on that day. They also had 1 wounded on June 2.

The Battle of Cold Harbor with 12 total casualties for Torrington was the highest number of casualties for any single engagement of the war for the town.

Approximately 117,000 Federal and 60,000 Confederate troops participated in operations from May 28 to June 3. Roughly 13,000 Union casualties were recorded and perhaps there were 5,000 Confederate casualties.

REGIMENT	TOTAL
2ND HEAVY ARTILLERY	61 (35%)
1ST HEAVY ARTILLERY	40 (23%)
11TH	15 (9%)
8TH	11 (6%)
14TH	10 (6%)
13TH	9 (5%)
1ST CAVALRY	7 (4%)
10TH	4 (2%)
28TH	4 (2%)
3RD	3 (2%)
20TH	3 (2%)
2ND	2 (1%)
6TH	2 (1%)
13TH BATTALION	2 (1%)
23RD	2 (1%)
29TH	2 (1%)
1ST	1
7TH	1
9TH	1
12TH	1
12TH BATTALION	1
15TH	1
16TH	1
17TH	1
22ND	1
25TH	1

8% OF POPULATION

SIX WERE KILLED AND THREE WERE MISSING

The first Torrington soldier killed was Private William T. Loomis of Company A, 1st Connecticut Heavy Artillery. He was killed in a Virginia railroad accident on January 29, 1863.

TORRINGTON SOLDIERS KILLED MISSING *

PLACE	DATE	NO.
Railroad Accident (1 HA)	1/29/63	1
Morton's Ford, VA (14TH) *	2/6/64	1
Cold Harbor, VA (2 HA)	6/1/64	2
Bermuda Hundred , VA (6TH) *	6/17/64	1
James River, VA (14TH) *	Unknown	1
Petersburg, VA (2 HA)	6/22/64	1
Winchester, VA (2 HA)	9/19/64	1
Harper's Farm, VA (1 CA)	4/6/65	1

SEVEN WERE CAPTURED

One Torrington soldier died in captivity at Libby Prison, Richmond, VA.

TORRINGTON CAPTURED *(1) DIED IN CAPTIVITY

PLACE	DATE	NO.
Cross Keys, VA (1 CA)	6/8/62	1
Golden Hill, VA (1 HA)*	6/27/62	1
Antietam, MD (8TH) (WOUNDED)	9/17/62	1
Morton's Ford, VA (14TH)	2/6/64	1
Drewry's Bluff, VA (11TH)	5/16/64	1
Ashland, VA (1 CA) (WOUNDED)	6/1/64	1
Kinston, NC (15TH)	3/8/65	1

TOTAL TORRINGTON CASUALTIES

DIED	19	11%
KILLED/MISSING	9	5%
WOUNDED	35	20%
CAPTURED	7	4%
DESERTED	24	14%

THIRTY-FIVE WERE WOUNDED

The first Torrington soldier wounded was Private Ansel E. Wheeler of Company E, 7TH Connecticut. He was wounded at Dawfuski Island, SC on February 10, 1862 and recovered from his wound. Four Torrington soldiers died from a wound received during the war.

TORRINGTON WOUNDED *(4) DIED OF WOUNDS

PLACE	DATE	NO.
Dawfuski Island, SC (7TH)	2/10/62	1
Antietam, MD (8,11TH)	9/17/62	2
Fredericksburg, VA (14TH)	12/13/62	1
Irish Bend, LA (13TH)	4/14/63	1
Gettysburg, PA (17TH)	7/2/63	1
Walthall Junction, VA (8TH)	5/7/64	1
Swift's Creek, VA (11TH)	5/9/64	2
Laurel Hill, VA (14TH)	5/10/64	1
Spottsylvania, VA (14TH)	5/12/64	1
Drewry's Bluff, VA (6,8TH)	5/16/64	2
Cold Harbor, VA (2 HA) *	6/1/64	8
Cold Harbor, VA (8TH)	6/2/64	1
Cold Harbor, VA (11TH)	6/3/64	1
Petersburg, VA (11TH)	6/18/64	1
Petersburg, VA (1 HA) *	6/30/64	1
Winchester, VA (2 HA) *1	9/19/64	3
Petersburg, VA (14TH)	9/30/64	1
Cedar Creek, VA (2 HA) *1	10/19/64	4
Boydton Plank Rd, VA (14TH)	10/27/64	1
Hatcher's Run, VA (10TH)	3/13/65	1

TRUMBULL
THE POPULATION IN 1860 WAS 1,474 (RANK 101)

THE MOST IMPORTANT DAY OF THE CIVIL WAR

JUNE 1, 1864
COLD HARBOR, VA

THE BATTLE WAS LEE'S LAST GREAT VICTORY

More soldiers credited to Trumbull were listed as casualties (5) on this day than on any other day of the war. Three soldiers were killed and 2 were wounded in the 2ND Connecticut Heavy Artillery. The wounded survived the war.

The date June 1, 1864 ranks 8TH for total casualties (374) (89 killed, 10 missing, 246 wounded, 23 captured, 6 wounded & captured) for a single day for the State of Connecticut. There were 324 casualties at Cold Harbor, 41 casualties at Ashland, and 9 other casualties scattered about Virginia.

The battle and operations around Cold Harbor (May 31-June 12, 1864) rank 6TH for total casualties (557) for an engagement for the State of Connecticut. The most intense fighting developed on June 3 and Trumbull had no casualties.

The Battle of Cold Harbor with 5 total casualties for Trumbull was the highest number of casualties for any single engagement of the war for the town.

Approximately 117,000 Federal and 60,000 Confederate troops participated in operations from May 28 to June 3. Roughly 13,000 Union casualties were recorded and perhaps there were 5,000 Confederate casualties.

119 MEN CREDITED TO TRUMBULL SERVED IN THE FOLLOWING CONNECTICUT ORGANIZATIONS

REGIMENT	TOTAL
23RD	19 (16%)
6TH	13 (11%)
9TH	11 (9%)
2ND HEAVY ARTILLERY	10 (9%)
1ST CAVALRY	9 (8%)
10TH	9 (8%)
14TH	8 (7%)
17TH	8 (7%)
1ST HEAVY ARTILLERY	7 (6%)
11TH	5 (4%)
2ND LIGHT BATTERY	4 (3%)
29TH	4 (3%)
8TH	3 (3%)
12TH	3 (3%)
30TH	3 (3%)
20TH	2 (2%)
5TH	2 (2%)
3RD	1
7TH	1
9TH BATTALION	1
12TH BATTALION	1

8% OF POPULATION

SEVEN WERE KILLED

The first Trumbull soldier killed was Private William H. Norton of Company A, 14TH Connecticut. He was killed at the Battle of Antietam on September 17, 1862.

TRUMBULL SOLDIERS KILLED

PLACE	DATE	NO.
Antietam, MD (14TH)	9/17/62	1
Brashear City, LA (23RD)	6/23/63	1
Cold Harbor, VA (2 HA)	6/1/64	3
Petersburg, VA (29TH)	9/1/64	1
Winchester, VA (2 HA)	9/19/64	1

FOUR WERE CAPTURED

One Trumbull soldier died in captivity at Libby Prison, Richmond, VA.

TRUMBULL CAPTURED
*(1) DIED IN CAPTIVITY

PLACE	DATE	NO.
Cross Keys, VA (1 CA)	6/8/62	1
Brashear City, LA (23RD)	6/23/63	1
Fort Wagner, SC (6TH) *	7/18/63	1
Dunn's Lake, FL (17TH)	2/5/65	1

TOTAL TRUMBULL CASUALTIES

DIED	7	6%
KILLED	7	6%
WOUNDED	14	12%
CAPTURED	4	3%
DESERTED	21	18%

FOURTEEN WERE WOUNDED

The first Trumbull soldier wounded was Private Henry B. Curtiss of Company A, 5TH Connecticut. He was wounded at Cedar Mountain, VA on August 9, 1862 and recovered from his wound. One Trumbull soldier died from a wound received during the war.

TRUMBULL WOUNDED
*(1) DIED FROM WOUNDS

PLACE	DATE	NO.
Unknown Place (1 CA)	Unknown	1
Cedar Mountain, VA (5TH)	8/9/62	1
Fredericksburg, VA (14TH)	12/13/62	1
Gettysburg, PA (17TH)	7/1/63	2
Morris Island, SC (6TH)	7/10/63	1
Fort Wagner, SC (6TH) *	7/18/63	1
Cold Harbor, VA (2 HA)	6/1/64	2
Richmond, VA (6TH)	10/7/64	1
Kell House, VA (29TH)	10/27/64	1
Petersburg, VA (1 HA)	3/25/65	1
Hatcher's Run, VA (10TH)	3/31/65	1
Fort Gregg, VA (10TH)	4/2/65	1

UNION
THE POPULATION IN 1860 WAS 732 (RANK 151)

THE MOST IMPORTANT DAY OF THE CIVIL WAR

SEPTEMBER 17, 1862
SHARPSBURG, MD (ANTIETAM)

CONNECTICUT HAD MORE CASUALTIES FOR ONE DAY THAN ON ANY OTHER DAY OF THE WAR

More soldiers credited to Union were listed as casualties (7) on this day than on any day of the war. One soldier was killed and 6 were wounded in the 16TH Connecticut. One of the wounded died.

The date September 17, 1862 ranks 1ST for total casualties (687) (131 killed, 2 missing, 515 wounded, 21 captured, 18 wounded & captured) for a single day for the State of Connecticut. All of the casualties were at Antietam.

The Battle of Antietam (September 16-17, 1862) ranks 1ST for total casualties (689) for an engagement. The most intense fighting developed on September 17. Union had all of its casualties on that day.

The Battle of Antietam with 7 total casualties for Union was the highest number of casualties for any single engagement of the war for the town.

Roughly 12,400 Union casualties were recorded and perhaps there were 10,300 Confederate casualties. Antietam proved to be one of the turning points of the war. It ended Lee's 1862 invasion of the North.

58 MEN CREDITED TO UNION SERVED IN THE FOLLOWING CONNECTICUT ORGANIZATIONS

REGIMENT	TOTAL
22ND	22 (39%)
16TH	10 (17%)
1ST LIGHT BATTERY	5 (8%)
10TH	4 (7%)
29TH	4 (7%)
11TH	3 (5%)
15TH	3 (5%)
5TH	2 (3%)
7TH	2 (3%)
14TH	2 (3%)
18TH	2 (3%)
1ST CAVALRY	1
2ND HEAVY ARTILLERY	1
3RD	1
12TH	1

8% OF POPULATION

ONE WAS KILLED

The only Union soldier killed was Private Stephen Himes of Company I, 16TH Connecticut. He was killed at the Battle of Antietam on September 17, 1862.

UNION SOLDIERS KILLED

PLACE	DATE	NO.
Antietam, MD (16TH)	9/17/62	1

SIX WERE CAPTURED

Two Union soldiers died in captivity at Andersonville Prison, GA.

UNION CAPTURED
*(2) DIED IN CAPTIVITY

PLACE	DATE	NO.
Unknown Place (14TH) *	Unknown	1
Winchester, VA (5TH)	5/25/62	1
Plymouth, NC (16TH) *	4/20/64	1
Cedar Creek, VA (12TH)	10/19/64	1
Kinston, NC (15TH)	3/8/65	2

TOTAL UNION CASUALTIES

DIED	7	12%
KILLED	1	2%
WOUNDED	12	21%
CAPTURED	6	10%
DESERTED	6	10%

TWELVE WERE WOUNDED

The first Union soldier wounded was Private Albert Hiscox of Company D, 3RD Connecticut. He was wounded at the Battle of Bull Run, VA on July 21, 1861 and recovered from his wound. Two Union soldiers died from a wound received during the war.

UNION WOUNDED
*(2) DIED FROM WOUNDS

PLACE	DATE	NO.
Bull Run, VA (3RD)	7/21/61	1
Antietam, MD (16TH) *1	9/17/62	6
Kinston, NC (10TH)	12/14/62	1
Providence Church Rd, VA (16TH)*	5/3/63	1
Alexandria, VA (14TH)	4/1/64	1
Piedmont, VA (18TH)	6/5/64	1
Snicker's Ford, VA (18TH)	7/18/64	1

VERNON
THE POPULATION IN 1860 WAS 3,838 (RANK 22)

THE MOST IMPORTANT DAY OF THE CIVIL WAR

SEPTEMBER 17, 1862

SHARPSBURG, MD (ANTIETAM)

CONNECTICUT HAD MORE CASUALTIES FOR ONE DAY THAN ON ANY OTHER DAY OF THE WAR

336 MEN CREDITED TO VERNON SERVED IN THE FOLLOWING CONNECTICUT ORGANIZATIONS

More soldiers credited to Vernon were listed as casualties (15) on this day than on any day of the war. Four soldiers were killed and 11 were wounded in the 14TH and 16TH Connecticut. Two of the wounded died.

The date September 17, 1862 ranks 1ST for total casualties (687) (131 killed, 2 missing, 515 wounded, 21 captured, 18 wounded & captured) for a single day for the State of Connecticut. All of the casualties were at Antietam.

The Battle of Antietam (September 16-17, 1862) ranks 1ST for total casualties (689) for an engagement for the State of Connecticut. The most intense fighting developed on September 17. Vernon had all of its casualties on that day.

The Battle of Antietam with 15 total casualties for Vernon was the highest number of casualties for any single engagement of the war for the town.

Roughly 12,400 Union casualties were recorded and perhaps there were 10,300 Confederate casualties. Antietam proved to be one of the turning points of the war. It ended Lee's 1862 invasion of the North.

REGIMENT	TOTAL
14TH	113 (34%)
7TH	46 (14%)
5TH	36 (11%)
11TH	27 (7%)
15TH	24 (7%)
1ST HEAVY ARTILLERY	22 (7%)
2ND HEAVY ARTILLERY	21 (6%)
16TH	11 (3%)
25TH	11 (3%)
29TH	10 (3%)
6TH	9 (3%)
20TH	9 (3%)
30TH	8 (2%)
1ST	5 (1%)
1ST LIGHT BATTERY	4 (1%)
1ST CAVALRY	4 (1%)
1ST SQUADRON CAVALRY	2 (1%)
8TH	2 (1%)
9TH	2 (1%)
10TH	2 (1%)
12TH	2 (1%)
21ST	2 (1%)
22ND	2 (1%)
9TH BATTALION	1
13TH	1
13TH BATTALION	1
27TH	1

9% OF POPULATION

TWELVE WERE KILLED AND TWO WERE MISSING

The first Vernon soldier killed was Private George Wind of Company H, 6TH Connecticut. He drowned at Dawfuski Lake, SC on April 15, 1862.

VERNON SOLDIERS KILLED MISSING *

PLACE	DATE	NO.
Dawfuskie Lake, SC (Drowned) (6TH)	4/15/62	1
Winchester, VA (5TH)	5/25/62	1
Antietam, MD (14,16TH)	9/17/62	4
Fredericksburg, VA (14TH) *1	12/13/62	2
Chancellorsville, VA (14TH) *	5/3/63	1
Gettysburg, PA (14TH)	7/3/63	1
Wilderness, VA (14TH)	5/6/64	1
Resaca, GA (5TH)	5/15/64	1
Ream's Station, VA (14TH)	8/25/64	1
Potomac River (Drowned)	4/24/65	1

THIRTY-NINE WERE CAPTURED

Eleven Vernon soldiers died in captivity. Seven died at Andersonville Prison, GA, two died at Libby Prison, Richmond, VA, one died at Charleston, SC and one died at Danville, VA.

VERNON CAPTURED *(11) DIED IN CAPTIVITY

PLACE	DATE	NO.
Unknown Place (14TH) *2	Unknown	2
Winchester, VA (5TH)	5/25/62	3
Rappahannock Station, VA (1 SQ) *	8/23/62	1
(WOUNDED)		
2 Bull Run, VA (5TH)	8/30/62	1
Irish Bend, LA (25TH)	4/14/63	1
Chancellorsville, VA (5TH)	5/2/63	2
Chancellorsville, VA (14,20TH)	5/3/63	3
Fort Wagner, SC (7TH)	7/11/63	1
Bristoe Station, VA (14TH)	10/14/63	1
Hartwood Church, VA (14TH) *	12/2/63	1
Olustee, FL (7TH) *	2/20/64	1
Plymouth, NC (16TH) *1	4/20/64	2
Craig's Church, VA (1 CA) *	5/5/64	2
Drewry's Bluff, VA (11TH) *1	5/16/64	5
(1 WOUNDED)		
Hanover Junction, VA (14TH) *	5/27/64	1
Hatcher's Run, VA (7TH)	6/2/64	1
Bermuda Hundred, VA (7TH)	6/2/64	1
Bermuda Hundred, VA (7TH)	6/17/64	1
Hatcher's Run, VA (7TH)	6/20/64	1
Petersburg, VA (30TH) *	7/30/64	1
Deep Run, VA (7TH)	8/16/64	1
(WOUNDED)		
Ream's Station, VA (14TH)	8/25/64	1
(WOUNDED)		
Richmond, VA (7TH)	10/1/64	1
Cedar Creek, VA (2 HA)	10/19/64	1
Kinston, NC (15TH)	3/8/65	3

TOTAL VERNON CASUALTIES

DIED	36	11%
KILLED/MISSING	14	4%
WOUNDED	72	21%
CAPTURED	39	12%
DESERTED	42	13%

SEVENTY-TWO WERE WOUNDED

The first Vernon soldier wounded was Private Charles L. Frerrard of Company B, 1ST Connecticut Heavy Artillery. He was wounded at the Silver Spring, MD on August 17, 1861 and recovered from his wound. Thirteen Vernon soldiers died from a wound received during the war.

VERNON WOUNDED *(13) DIED FROM WOUNDS

PLACE	DATE	NO.
Silver Spring, MD (1 HA)	8/17/61	1
Yorktown, VA (1 HA)	5/1/62	1
Winchester, VA (5TH)	5/25/62	1
Antietam, MD (14TH) *2	9/17/62	11
Fredericksburg, VA (14TH) *2	12/13/62	8
Kinston, NC (10TH) *	12/14/62	1
Irish Bend, LA (25TH)	4/14/63	2
Chancellorsville, VA (5,14TH) *1	5/3/63	3
Fort Gregg, VA (10TH)	7/3/63	1
Gettysburg, PA (14TH) *1	7/3/63	7
Morris Island, SC (7TH)	7/11/63	1
Fort Wagner, SC (6TH)	7/18/63	1
Bristoe Station, VA (14TH)	10/14/63	1
Morton's Ford, VA (14TH) *3	2/6/64	6
Wilderness, VA (14TH)	5/6/64	2
Swift's Creek, VA (11TH)	5/9/64	1
Spottsylvania, VA (14TH)	5/10/64	1
Po River, VA (14TH)	5/10/64	1
Chester Station, VA (7TH)	5/14/64	1
Resaca, GA (5TH)	5/15/64	2
Drewry's Bluff, VA (7,11TH) *1	5/16/64	2
Cold Harbor, VA (2 HA)	6/1/64	1
Cold Harbor, VA (11TH)	6/3/64	2
Cold Harbor, VA (21ST) *	6/9/64	1
Petersburg, VA (11TH)	6/18/64	2
Petersburg, VA (14TH)	6/22/64	1
Petersburg, VA (11TH)	7/1/64	1
Petersburg, VA (30TH)	7/30/64	3
Atlanta, GA (5TH)	7/30/64	1
Deep Run, VA (6TH)	8/16/64	1
Ream's Station, VA (14TH)	8/25/64	2
Winchester, VA (13TH)	9/19/64	1
Deer Creek, VA (14TH)	10/27/64	1

VOLUNTOWN
THE POPULATION IN 1860 WAS 1,055 (RANK 130)

THE MOST IMPORTANT DAY OF THE CIVIL WAR

MAY 16, 1864

DREWRY'S BLUFF , VA

AN OBSTACLE ON THE WAY TO RICHMOND

More soldiers credited to Voluntown were listed as casualties (5) on this day than on any other day of the war. One soldier was killed, 2 were wounded, and 2 were captured in the 6TH and 21ST Connecticut. The wounded and captured survived the war.

The date May 16, 1864 ranks 4th for total casualties (560) (52 killed, 3 missing, 224 wounded, 243 captured, 38 wounded & captured) for a single day for the State of Connecticut. The Battle of Drewry's Bluff accounted for 545 casualties. The 15 other casualties were scattered about Virginia.

The Battle of Drewry's Bluff (May 13-17, 1864), also called Fort Darling, ranks 3rd for total casualties (634) for an engagement for the State of Connecticut. The most intense fighting developed on May 16. Voluntown had all of its casualties on that day.

The Battle of Drewry's Bluff with 5 total casualties for Voluntown was the highest number of casualties for any single engagement of the war for the town.

The Confederate attack at Drewry's Bluff forced the Union Army to retreat to Bermuda Hundred. The civil war would have concluded sooner had the Union Army been victorious.

68 MEN CREDITED TO VOLUNTOWN SERVED IN THE FOLLOWING CONNECTICUT ORGANIZATIONS

REGIMENT	TOTAL
21ST	25 (37%)
26TH	13 (19%)
12TH	11 (15%)
10TH	8 (12%)
12TH BATTALION	6 (9%)
14TH	3 (4%)
1ST HEAVY ARTILLERY	2 (3%)
1ST CAVALRY	2 (3%)
8TH	2 (3%)
2ND HEAVY ARTILLERY	1
6TH	1
7TH	1
18TH	1

6% OF POPULATION

FOUR WERE KILLED

The first Voluntown soldier killed was Private William E. Sweet of Company G, 12TH Connecticut. He was killed at Port Hudson, LA on June 1, 1863.

VOLUNTOWN SOLDIERS KILLED

PLACE	DATE	NO.
Port Hudson, LA (12TH)	6/1/63	1
Drewry's Bluff, VA (21ST)	5/16/64	1
Cedar Creek, VA (12TH)	10/19/64	2

SEVEN WERE CAPTURED

No Voluntown soldiers died in captivity.

VOLUNTOWN CAPTURED
NONE DIED IN CAPTIVITY

PLACE	DATE	NO.
Antietam, MD (8TH) (WOUNDED)	9/17/62	1
Winchester, VA (18TH)	6/15/63	1
Bristoe Station, VA (14TH)	10/14/63	1
Drewry's Bluff, VA (21ST)	5/16/64	2
Bermuda Hundred, VA (7TH)	6/2/64	1
Cedar Creek, VA (12TH)	10/19/64	1

TOTAL VOLUNTOWN CASUALTIES

DIED	8	12%
KILLED	4	6%
WOUNDED	19	28%
CAPTURED	7	10%
DESERTED	5	7%

NINETEEN WERE WOUNDED

The first Voluntown soldier wounded was Private James R. Watson of Company F, 8TH Connecticut. He was wounded and captured at the Battle of Antietam, MD on September 17, 1862 and recovered from his wound. One Voluntown soldier died from a wound received during the war.

VOLUNTOWN WOUNDED
*(1) DIED FROM WOUNDS

PLACE	DATE	NO.
Fredericksburg, VA (21ST)	12/14/62	2
Kinston, NC (10TH)	12/14/62	1
Port Hudson, LA (26TH)	5/27/63	1
Port Hudson, LA (12TH)	5/29/63	1
Port Hudson, LA (12TH)	6/14/63	1
Port Hudson, LA (26TH)	6/25/63	1
Port Hudson, LA (12TH)	7/3/63	1
Drewry's Bluff, VA (6TH 21ST)	5/16/64	2
New Market, VA (10TH)	7/27/64	1
Deep Bottom, VA (10TH)	8/14/64	1
Deep Run, VA (10TH)	8/16/64	1
Petersburg, VA (21ST) *	8/18/64	1
Winchester, VA (12TH)	9/19/64	3
Chaffin's Farm, VA (21ST)	9/29/64	1
Cedar Creek, VA (12TH)	10/19/64	1

WALLINGFORD
THE POPULATION IN 1860 WAS 3,206 (RANK 38)

THE MOST IMPORTANT DAY OF THE CIVIL WAR

MAY 3, 1863

CHANCELLORSVILLE, VA

THE THIRD DAY OF THE BATTLE

More soldiers credited to Wallingford were listed as casualties (13) on this day than any other day of the war. One soldier was wounded and 12 were captured in the 27TH Connecticut. They survived the war.

The date May 3, 1863 ranks 3RD for total casualties (577) (36 killed, 1 missing, 138 wounded, 372 captured, 29 wounded & captured) for a single day for the State of Connecticut. The most casualties were at Chancellorsville, VA (556). The other casualties were at Providence Church Road, VA (12), Suffolk, VA (6), Port Hudson, LA (2) and Fredericksburg, VA (1).

The Battle of Chancellorsville (May 1-3, 1863) ranks 2ND for total casualties (677) for an engagement for the State of Connecticut. The most intense fighting developed on May 3. Wallingford had no other casualties in the battle other than on May 3.

The Battle of Chancellorsville with 13 total casualties for Wallingford was the highest number of casualties for any single engagement of the war for the town.

The Battle of Chancellorsville was an enormous defeat for the more than 70,000 Union soldiers who had moved against the flank and rear of 40,000 Confederate soldiers. Unfortunately, the Union Army had pulled back and had gone on the defensive around Chancellorsville. The Confederate victory was tainted however, by the loss of Confederate Major General "Stonewall" Jackson.

220 MEN CREDITED TO WALLINGFORD SERVED IN THE FOLLOWING CONNECTICUT ORGANIZATIONS

REGIMENT	TOTAL
15TH	83 (38%)
27TH	31 (14%)
7TH	24 (11%)
5TH	18 (8%)
6TH	11 (5%)
8TH	9 (4%)
1ST HEAVY ARTILLERY	7 (3%)
2ND HEAVY ARTILLERY	7 (3%)
10TH	7 (3%)
20TH	5 (2%)
29TH	5 (2%)
11TH	4 (2%)
1ST CAVALRY	3 (1%)
9TH	3 (1%)
13TH	3 (1%)
14TH	3 (1%)
9TH BATTALION	2
12TH	2
12TH BATTALION	2
17TH	2
21ST	2
1ST	1
3RD	1
13TH BATTALION	1
16TH	1

7% OF POPULATION

SIX WERE KILLED

The first Wallingford soldier killed was Private George V. Dagle of Company K, 8TH Connecticut. He was killed at the Battle of Antietam, MD on September 17, 1862.

WALLINGFORD SOLDIERS KILLED

PLACE	DATE	NO.
Antietam, MD (8TH)	9/17/62	1
Bona Casa, LA (9TH)	10/20/62	1
Gettysburg, PA (27TH)	7/2/63	1
Deep Bottom, VA (7TH)	8/16/64	1
Kinston, NC (15TH)	3/8/65	1
Brownsville, TX (29TH)	8/28/65	1
(Drowned)		

THIRTY WERE CAPTURED

Three Wallingford soldiers died in captivity. One died at Andersonville Prison, GA, one at Libby Prison, Richmond, VA, and one at Florence, SC.

WALLINGFORD CAPTURED
*(3) DIED IN CAPTIVITY

PLACE	DATE	NO.
Winchester, VA (5TH)	5/25/62	1
Cedar Mountain, VA (5TH)	8/9/62	1
Chancellorsville, VA (20,27TH)	5/3/63	12
Fort Wagner, SC (6TH) *	7/18/63	1
Plymouth, NC (16TH)	4/20/64	1
Drewry's Bluff, VA (7TH)	5/16/64	1
Cold Harbor, VA (2 HA)	6/16/64	1
Ream's Station, VA (1 CA) *1	6/29/64	2
Kinston, NC (15TH) *1	3/8/65	10
(1 WOUNDED		

TOTAL WALLINGFORD CASUALTIES

DIED	18	8%
KILLED	6	3%
WOUNDED	35	16%
CAPTURED	30	14%
DESERTED	18	8%

THIRTY-FIVE WERE WOUNDED

The first Wallingford soldier wounded was Private William A. Thrall of Company A, 10TH Connecticut. He was wounded at Roanoke Island, NC on February 8, 1862 and recovered from his wound. Four Wallingford soldiers died from a wound received during the war.

WALLINGFORD WOUNDED
*(4) DIED FROM WOUNDS

PLACE	DATE	NO.
Roanoke Island, NC (10TH)	2/8/62	1
Arlington Heights, VA (1 HA)	4/15/62	1
Middletown, VA (5TH)	5/25/62	1
James Island, SC (6TH) *	6/12/62	1
James Island, SC (7TH)	6/16/62	1
Cedar Mountain, VA (5TH)	8/9/62	1
Antietam, MD (8,14TH)	9/17/62	3
Fredericksburg (14,21,27)*1	12/13/62	5
Irish Bend, LA (13TH)	4/14/63	1
Providence Church Rd, VA(15TH)	5/3/63	1
Chancellorsville, VA (27TH)	5/3/63	1
Gettysburg, PA (27TH)	7/2/63	1
Fort Wagner, SC (7TH)	7/11/63	1
Fort Wagner, SC (6TH)	7/18/63	1
Morris Island, SC (7TH)	8/13/63	1
Morris Island, SC (7TH)	9/23/63	1
Olustee, FLA (7TH)	2/20/64	1
Cane River, LA (13TH)	4/23/64	1
Wilderness, VA (14TH)	5/6/64	1
Resaca, GA (20TH)	5/15/64	1
Petersburg, VA (21ST) *	5/26/64	1
Cold Harbor, VA (2 HA)	6/1/64	2
Deep Bottom, VA (7TH)	8/15/64	1
Deep Run, VA (6TH)	8/17/64	1
Petersburg, VA (10TH)	8/30/64	1
Winchester, VA (2 HA) *	9/19/64	1
Cedar Creek, VA (12TH)	10/19/64	1
Waynesville, NC (12TH)	2/5/65	1

WARREN
THE POPULATION IN 1860 WAS 710 (RANK 153)

THE MOST IMPORTANT DAY OF THE CIVIL WAR

OCTOBER 19, 1864

CEDAR CREEK, VA

THE LAST MAJOR BATTLE OF THE 1864 SHENANDOAH VALLEY CAMPAIGN WAS A UNION TRIUMPH

Soldiers credited to Warren had more casualties on September 22, 1864 at Fisher's Hill, VA (2) and on October 19, 1864 at Cedar Creek, VA (2) than on any other days of the war. The casualties at Cedar Creek were the most serious. Two soldiers were wounded in the 2ND Heavy Artillery. Both survived the war.

The date October 19, 1864 ranks 7TH for total casualties (417) (48 killed, 2 missing, 204 wounded, 153 captured, 10 wounded & captured) for a single day for the State of Connecticut. The Battle of Cedar Creek accounted for 415 casualties. The other 2 casualties were in the neighboring towns.

The Battle of Cedar Creek (October 19, 1864) ranks 10TH for total casualties (415) for an engagement for the State of Connecticut.

The Battle of Cedar Creek with 2 total casualties for Warren was tied with Fisher's Hill (September 22, 1864) for the 2ND highest number of casualties for any single engagement of the war. The Siege of Petersburg (June 1864-April 1865) ranks 1ST with 3 total casualties

The news of the Union triumph at Cedar Creek assured a Republican victory in the elections of November 1864 and the prosecution of the war to its end on President Abraham Lincoln's and Lieutenant General Ulysses S. Grant's terms.

52 MEN CREDITED TO WARREN SERVED IN THE FOLLOWING CONNECTICUT ORGANIZATIONS

REGIMENT	TOTAL
2ND HEAVY ARTILLERY	31 (60%)
11TH	6 (12%)
8TH	5 (10%)
5TH	4 (8%)
7TH	2 (4%)
13TH	2 (4%)
14TH	2 (4%)
1ST HEAVY ARTILLERY	1
13TH BATTALION	1
17TH	1

7% OF POPULATION

ONE WAS KILLED

The only Warren soldier killed was Private Charles Barney of Company I, 2ND Connecticut Heavy Artillery. He was killed at Winchester, VA on September 19, 1864.

WARREN SOLDIERS KILLED

PLACE	DATE	NO.
Winchester, VA (2 HA)	9/19/64	1

ONE WAS CAPTURED

No Warren soldiers died in captivity.

WARREN CAPTURED
NONE DIED IN CAPTIVITY

PLACE	DATE	NO.
Petersburg, VA (8TH)	9/18/64	1

TOTAL WARREN CASUALTIES

DIED	1	2%
KILLED	1	2%
WOUNDED	14	27%
CAPTURED	1	2%
DESERTED	10	19%

FOURTEEN WERE WOUNDED

The first Warren soldier wounded was Private Edward F. Brague of Company D, 10TH Connecticut. He was wounded at Roanoke Island, NC on February 8, 1862 and recovered from his wound. One Warren soldier died from a wound received during the war.

WARREN WOUNDED
*(1) DIED FROM WOUNDS

PLACE	DATE	NO.
Roanoke Island, NC (10TH)	2/8/62	1
Antietam, MD (8TH)	9/17/62	1
Pocotaligo, SC (7TH) *	10/22/62	1
Morton's Ford, VA (14TH)	2/6/64	1
Cold Harbor, VA (2 HA)	6/1/64	1
Petersburg, VA (2 HA)	6/22/64	1
Fisher's Hill, VA (2 HA)	9/22/64	2
Fort Harrison, VA (8TH)	9/29/64	1
Chaffin's Farm, VA (8TH)	9/29/64	1
Cedar Creek, VA (2 HA)	10/19/64	2
Petersburg, VA (2 HA)	4/2/65	1
Sailor's Creek, VA (2 HA)	4/6/65	1

WASHINGTON
THE POPULATION IN 1860 WAS 1,659 (RANK 90)

THE MOST IMPORTANT
DAY OF THE CIVIL WAR

JUNE 1, 1864
COLD HARBOR, VA

THE BATTLE WAS LEE'S
LAST GREAT VICTORY

More soldiers credited to Washington were listed as casualties (12) on this day than on any other day of the war. One soldier was killed, 1 was missing, and 10 were wounded in the 2ND Connecticut Heavy Artillery. Two of the wounded died.

The date June 1, 1864 ranks 8TH for total casualties (374) (89 killed, 10 missing, 246 wounded, 23 captured, 6 wounded & captured) for a single day for the State of Connecticut. There were 324 casualties at Cold Harbor, 41 casualties at Ashland, and 9 other casualties scattered about Virginia.

The battle and operations around Cold Harbor (May 31-June 12, 1864) rank 6TH for total casualties (557) for an engagement for the State of Connecticut. The most intense fighting developed on June 3 and Washington had 1 casualty.

The Battle of Cold Harbor with 13 total casualties for Washington was the highest number of casualties for any single engagement of the war for the town.

Approximately 117,000 Federal and 60,000 Confederate troops participated in operations from May 28 to June 3. Roughly 13,000 Union casualties were recorded and perhaps there were 5,000 Confederate casualties.

132 MEN CREDITED TO WASHINGTON SERVED IN THE FOLLOWING CONNECTICUT ORGANIZATIONS

REGIMENT	TOTAL
2ND HEAVY ARTILLERY	49 (37%)
28TH	16 (12%)
8TH	13 (10%)
10TH	7 (5%)
14TH	7 (5%)
11TH	6 (5%)
5TH	5 (4%)
6TH	5 (4%)
15TH	5 (4%)
1ST HEAVY ARTILLERY	4 (3%)
20TH	4 (3%)
1ST CAVALRY	3 (2%)
12TH	3 (2%)
13TH	3 (2%)
29TH	2
1ST LIGHT BATTERY	1
3RD	1
7TH	1
16TH	1
17TH	1

8% OF POPULATION

FOUR WERE KILLED AND ONE WAS MISSING

The first Washington soldier killed was Private James Mullen of Company H, 14TH Connecticut. He was killed at Bristoe Station, VA on October 14, 1863.

WASHINGTON SOLDIERS KILLED MISSING*

PLACE	DATE	NO.
Bristoe Station, VA (14TH)	10/14/63	1
Cold Harbor, VA (2 HA) *1	6/1/64	2
Petersburg, VA (8TH)	6/15/64	1
Winchester, VA (2 HA)	9/19/64	1

FOUR WERE CAPTURED

One Washington soldier died in captivity at Salisbury, NC.

WASHINGTON CAPTURED *(1) DIED IN CAPTIVITY

PLACE	DATE	NO.
Bull Run, VA (3RD)	7/21/61	1
Lexington, VA (14TH)	10/14/63	1
Drewry's Bluff, VA (11TH)	5/16/64	1
Winchester, VA (13TH) *	9/19/64	1

TOTAL WASHINGTON CASUALTIES

DIED	22	17%
KILLED/MISSING	5	4%
WOUNDED	31	24%
CAPTURED	4	3%
DESERTED	23	17%

THIRTY-ONE WERE WOUNDED

The first Washington soldier wounded was Corporal Livi A. Hamblin of Company D, 10TH Connecticut. He was wounded at Roanoke Island, NC on February 8, 1862 and recovered from his wound. Six Washington soldiers died from a wound received during the war.

WASHINGTON WOUNDED *(6) DIED OF WOUNDS

PLACE	DATE	NO.
Roanoke Island, NC (10TH) *	2/8/62	1
James Island, SC (7TH) *	6/16/62	1
Cedar Mountain, VA (5TH) *	8/9/62	1
Port Hudson, LA (13,28TH)	6/14/63	2
Fort Ellsworth, VA (2 HA)	10/1/63	1
Walthall Junction, VA (8TH)	5/7/64	1
Cold Harbor, VA (2 HA) *2	6/1/64	10
Cold Harbor, VA (8TH) *	6/3/64	1
Petersburg, VA (11TH)	7/12/64	1
Peach Tree Creek, GA (5TH)	7/20/64	1
Deep Run, VA (7TH) *	8/16/64	1
Deep Run, VA (6TH)	8/18/64	1
Winchester, VA (2 HA)	9/19/64	2
Cedar Creek, VA (2 HA)	10/19/64	5
Richmond, VA (29TH)	10/27/64	1
Shenandoah Valley, VA (2 HA)	7/7/65	1

WATERBURY
THE POPULATION IN 1860 WAS 10,004 (RANK 6)

THE MOST IMPORTANT DAY OF THE CIVIL WAR

MAY 3, 1863

CHANCELLORSVILLE, VA

THE THIRD DAY OF THE BATTLE

More soldiers credited Waterbury were listed as casualties (21) on this day than on any other day of the war. One soldier was killed, 6 were wounded, 9 were captured and 5 were wounded & captured in the 14TH and 20TH Connecticut. One of the wounded died.

The date May 3, 1863 ranks 3RD for total casualties (577) (36 killed, 1 missing, 138 wounded, 372 captured, 29 wounded & captured) for a single day for the State of Connecticut. The most casualties were at Chancellorsville, VA (556). The other casualties were at Providence Church Road, VA (12), Suffolk, VA (6), Port Hudson, LA (2) and Fredericksburg, VA (1).

The Battle of Chancellorsville (May 1-3, 1863) ranks 2ND for total casualties (677) for an engagement for the State of Connecticut. The most intense fighting developed on May 3. Waterbury also had 4 casualties on May 2.

The Battle of Chancellorsville with 25 total casualties for Waterbury was the highest number of casualties for any single engagement of the war for the city.

The Battle of Chancellorsville was an enormous defeat for the more than 70,000 Union soldiers who had moved against the flank and rear of 40,000 Confederate soldiers. Unfortunately, the Union Army had pulled back and had gone on the defensive around Chancellorsville. The Confederate victory was tainted however, by the loss of Confederate Major General "Stonewall" Jackson.

832 MEN CREDITED TO WATERBURY SERVED IN THE FOLLOWING CONNECTICUT ORGANIZATIONS

REGIMENT	TOTAL
14TH	148 (18%)
1ST	81 (10%)
6TH	79 (9%)
23RD	72 (9%)
9TH	68 (8%)
20TH	67 (8%)
1ST CAVALRY	64 (8%)
1ST HEAVY ARTILLERY	61 (7%)
2ND HEAVY ARTILLERY	47 (5%)
5TH	43 (5%)
8TH	40 (5%)
15TH	36 (4%)
7TH	27 (3%)
11TH	17 (2%)
13TH	15 (2%)
9TH BATTALION	12 (1%)
12TH	12 (1%)
3RD	10 (1%)
1ST SQUADRON CAVALRY	9 (1%)
10TH	8 (1%)
13TH BATTALION	8 (1%)
29TH	6 (1%)
3RD LIGHT BATTERY	3
1ST LIGHT BATTERY	2
2ND LIGHT BATTERY	2
27TH	2
30TH	2
2ND	1
12TH BATTALION	1
16TH	1
18TH	1

8% OF POPULATION

THIRTY-NINE WERE KILLED AND THREE WERE MISSING

The first Waterbury soldier killed was Corporal Cornelius Bailey of Company B, 1ST Connecticut Squadron Cavalry. He was killed at Washington, DC on October 21, 1861 by a kick from a horse.

WATERBURY SOLDIERS AND *MISSING

PLACE	DATE	NO.
Washington, DC (1 SQ)	10/12/61	1
(KICK FROM HORSE)		
North Edisto River, SC (6TH)	6/8/62	1
(DROWNED)		
Cedar Mountain, VA (5TH)	8/9/62	4
Antietam, MD (14TH)	9/17/62	3
Railroad Accident (20TH)	9/30/62	1
St John's Parish, LA (9TH)	10/19/62	1
Chancellorsville, VA (20TH)	5/3/63	1
Railroad Accident (9TH)	5/27/63	1
Fort Wagner, SC (6TH)	7/18/63	1
Rapidan Station, VA (1 SQ)	9/14/63	1
Morton's Ford, VA (14TH) *1	2/6/64	2
Railroad Accident (5TH)	2/17/64	1
Wilderness, VA (2 HA)	5/5/64	1
Wilderness, VA (14TH) *	5/6/64	1
Swift's Creek, VA (8TH)	5/7/64	1
Chester Station, VA (6TH)	5/10/64	1
Petersburg, VA (6TH)	5/10/64	1
Drewry's Bluff, VA (6TH)	5/15/64	1
North Anna River, VA (14TH)	5/26/64	1
Cold Harbor, VA (2 HA)	6/1/64	1
Ashland, VA (1 CA)	6/1/64	1
Cold Harbor, VA (14TH)	6/3/64	1
Bermuda Hundred, VA (6TH)	6/17/64	1
Petersburg, VA (11TH)	6/18/64	1
Peach Tree Creek, GA (20TH)	7/20/64	2
Peach Tree Creek, GA (5TH)	7/20/64	1
Petersburg, VA (30TH) *	7/30/64	1
Hartford, CT Drowned (14TH)	8/2/64	1
Fisher's Hill, VA (9TH)	9/22/64	1
Darbytown Road, VA (6TH)	10/7/64	2
Boydton Plank Rd, VA (14TH)	10/27/64	1
Kinston, NC (15TH)	3/8/65	2
Silver Run, NC (5TH)	3/16/65	1

NINETY-ONE WERE CAPTURED

Thirteen Waterbury soldiers died in captivity. Eight died at Andersonville Prison, GA, four at Libby Prison, Richmond, VA, and one at Florence, SC.

WATERBURY CAPTURED *(13) DIED IN CAPTIVITY

PLACE	DATE	NO.
Unknown Place (11TH) *	Unknown	1
Unknown Place (14TH) *2	Unknown	2
Bull Run, VA (2ND)	7/21/61	1
(WOUNDED)		
McDowell, VA (1 CA)	5/8/62	1
Winchester, VA (5TH)	5/25/62	1
Cedar Mountain, VA (5TH)	8/9/62	5
(1 WOUNDED)		
Chisholm, SC (6TH)	10/19/62	1
Cheatham Island, SC (6TH)	10/19/62	1
Fauquier, VA (8TH)	11/16/62	1
Falmouth, VA (14TH)	11/19/62	1
Fredericksburg, VA (14TH)	12/13/62	1
Chancellorsville, VA (5TH)	5/2/63	4
Chancellorsville, VA (20TH)	5/3/63	14
(5 WOUNDED)		
Bayou Boeuf, LA (23RD)	6/24/63	2
Bayou Boeuf, LA (23RD)	6/25/63	1
Fort Wagner, SC (6TH)	7/18/63	1
(WOUNDED)		
Manassas Gap, VA (5TH) *	7/21/63	1
Bristoe Station, VA (14TH) *1	10/14/63	4
Rapidan, VA (14TH) *2	12/1/63	2
Orange CH, VA (14TH)	12/1/63	1
Morton's Ford, VA (14TH)	2/6/64	1
Winchester, VA (1 CA,14TH) *1	5/5/64	2
Todds Tavern, VA (1 SQ) *	5/5/64	1
Craig's Church, VA (1 CA)	5/5/64	1
Drewry's Bluff, VA (6,7,8,11TH)*3	5/16/64	9
(1 WOUNDED)		
Cold Harbor, VA (2 HA) *	6/1/64	1
Bermuda Hundred, VA (6TH)	6/17/64	1
Bermuda Hundred, VA (7TH)	6/17/64	1
Stony Creek, VA (1 CA)	6/28/64	1
Ream's Station, VA (1 CA)	7/1/64	1
Leesburg, VA (2 HA)	7/21/64	1
Ream's Station, VA (14TH)	8/25/64	1
Spring Valley, VA (1 CA)	9/25/64	1
Cedar Creek, VA (12TH)	10/19/64	1
(WOUNDED)		
Kinston, NC (15TH)	3/8/65	16
(1 WOUNDED)		
Fayetteville, NC (20TH)	3/14/65	2
Ashland, VA (1 CA)	3/15/65	2
(WOUNDED)		

TOTAL WATERBURY CASUALTIES

DIED	79	9%
KILLED/MISSING	42	5%
WOUNDED	111	13%
CAPTURED	91	11%
DESERTED	119	14%

ONE HUNDRED-ELEVEN WERE WOUNDED

The first Waterbury soldier wounded was Private William H. Langdon of Company A, 5TH Connecticut. He was wounded at Winchester, VA on May 25, 1862 and recovered from his wound. Eight Waterbury soldiers died from a wound received during the war.

WATERBURY WOUNDED
*(8) DIED OF WOUNDS

PLACE	DATE	NO.
Unknown Place (1 CA)	Unknown	1
Winchester, VA (5TH)	5/25/62	1
James Island, SC (6TH)	6/12/62	1
Cedar Mountain, VA (5TH)	8/9/62	3
Antietam, MD (8,14TH) *2	9/17/62	14
St John's Parish, LA (9TH)	10/19/62	1
Pocotaligo, SC (6TH)	10/22/62	1
Fredericksburg, VA (14, 27TH)	12/13/62	9
Stafford CH, VA (20TH)	1/1/63	1
Fort Hugar, VA (8TH)	4/19/63	1
Chancellorsville, VA(14,20TH) *1	5/3/63	6
Gettysburg, PA (14TH)	7/2/63	1
Gettysburg, PA (14TH)	7/3/63	7
Fort Wagner, SC (6TH) *2	7/18/63	7
Morton's Ford, VA (14TH)	2/6/64	5
Wilderness, VA (14TH)	5/6/64	4
Wilderness, VA (14TH)	5/7/64	1
Walthall Junction, VA (8TH)	5/7/64	2
Laurel Hill, VA (14TH)	5/10/64	1
Spottsylvania, VA (14TH)	5/12/64	2
Drewry's Bluff, VA (6TH)	5/14/64	1
Resaca, GA (5,20TH)	5/15/64	3
Bermuda Hundred, VA (6TH) *	5/20/64	1
Ware Bottom Church,VA(6TH)	5/20/64	1
Cold Harbor, VA (2HA,11TH)	6/1/64	2
Ashland, VA (1 CA)	6/1/64	3
Cold Harbor, VA (14TH)	6/3/64	1
Petersburg, VA (11TH)	6/15/64	1
Hatcher's Run, VA (6TH)	6/17/64	1
Petersburg, VA (14TH)	6/18/64	1
Peach Tree Creek, GA (20TH)	7/20/64	3
Deep Run, VA (6,10TH) *1	8/16/64	2
Ream's Station, VA (14TH)	8/25/64	2
Winchester, VA (2HA,9,13TH)	9/19/64	3
Fort Harrison, VA (8TH)	9/29/64	1
Fort Harrison, VA (8TH)	9/30/64	1
Chaffin's Farm, VA (8TH)	9/29/64	1
Darbytown Road, VA (10TH)	10/13/64	1
Cedar Creek, VA(2HA,9,13TH)	10/19/64	4

PLACE	DATE	NO.
Petersburg, VA (14TH)	10/21/64	1
Chaffin's Farm, VA (11TH)	1/15/65	1
Richmond, VA (1 LB)	2/1/65	1
Kinston, NC (15TH) *	3/8/65	1
Silver Run, NC (20TH)	3/16/65	1
Bentonville, NC (20TH)	3/19/65	1
Hatcher's Run, VA (10TH)	3/31/65	1
Raleigh, NC (20TH)	4/15/65	1

1ST CONNECTICUT HEAVY ARTILLERY
OFFICER GROUP FORT DARLING
JAMES RIVER, VIRGINIA APRIL 1865

USAMHI

USAMHI

WATERFORD
THE POPULATION IN 1860 WAS 2,555 (RANK 56)

THE MOST IMPORTANT DAY OF THE CIVIL WAR
OCTOBER 19, 1864

CEDAR CREEK, VA

THE LAST MAJOR BATTLE OF THE 1864 SHENANDOAH VALLEY CAMPAIGN WAS A UNION TRIUMPH

Soldiers credited to Waterford had more casualties on May 3, 1863 at Chancellorsville, VA (4) and on October 19, 1864 at Cedar Creek, VA (4) than on any other days of the war. The casualties at the Battle of Cedar Creek were the most serious. Three soldiers were wounded and 1 was captured in the 12TH Connecticut. One of the wounded soldiers died.

The date October 19, 1864 ranks 7TH for total casualties (417) (48 killed, 2 missing, 204 wounded, 153 captured, 10 wounded & captured) for a single day for the State of Connecticut. The Battle of Cedar Creek accounted for 415 casualties. The 2 other casualties were in the neighboring towns.

The Battle of Cedar Creek (October 19, 1864) ranks 10TH for total casualties (415) for an engagement for the State of Connecticut.

The Battle of Cedar Creek with 4 total casualties for Waterford was tied with the Battle of Chancellorsville (May 1-3 1863) for the highest number of casualties for any single engagement of the war for the town.

The news of the Union triumph at Cedar Creek assured a Republican victory in the elections of November 1864 and the prosecution of the war to its end on President Abraham Lincoln's and Lieutenant General Ulysses S. Grant's terms.

121 MEN CREDITED TO WATERFORD SERVED IN THE FOLLOWING CONNECTICUT ORGANIZATIONS

REGIMENT	TOTAL
14TH	26 (21%)
1ST CAVALRY	17 (13%)
26TH	15 (12%)
12TH	15 (12%)
1ST HEAVY ARTILLERY	11 (9%)
5TH	8 (7%)
21ST	6 (5%)
12TH BATTALION	5 (4%)
30TH	5 (4%)
10TH	3 (2%)
7TH	3 (2%)
2ND HEAVY ARTILLERY	2 (2%)
6TH	2 (2%)
9TH	2 (2%)
9TH BATTALION	2 (2%)
11TH	2 (2%)
29TH	2 (2%)
3RD	1
8TH	1
13TH	1
18TH	1

5% OF POPULATION

SEVEN WERE KILLED AND ONE WAS MISSING

The first Waterford soldiers killed were Privates John H. Caulkins, John Green and Elias L. Jereome of Company H, 14TH Connecticut. They were killed at Fredericksburg, VA on December 13, 1862

WATERFORD SOLDIERS KILLED AND *MISSING

PLACE	DATE	NO.
Fredericksburg, VA (14TH)	12/13/62	3
Gettysburg, PA (14TH)	7/3/63	1
Mississippi River, LA (12TH) (DROWNED)	7/23/63	1
Petersburg, VA (11TH)	6/18/64	1
Petersburg, VA (30TH) *	7/30/64	1
Deep Run, VA (6TH)	8/16/64	1

ELEVEN WERE CAPTURED

Two Waterford soldiers died in captivity at Andersonville Prison, GA.

WATERFORD CAPTURED (*2) DIED IN CAPTIVITY

PLACE	DATE	NO.
Chancellorsville, VA (14TH	5/3/63	2
Winchester, VA (18TH) (WOUNDED)	6/15/63	1
Brashear City, LA (12TH)	6/23/63	1
Brashear City, LA (12TH)	6/26/63	1
Morton's Ford, VA (14TH)	2/6/64	1
Craig's Church, VA (1 CA)	5/5/64	1
Butler's Mills, VA (1 CA)	5/27/64	1
Ream's Station, VA (14TH) *	8/25/64	1
Atlanta, GA (5TH) *	8/26/64	1
Cedar Creek, VA (12TH)	10/19/64	1

TOTAL WATERFORD CASUALTIES

DIED	19	15%
KILLED/MISSING	8	7%
WOUNDED	17	14%
CAPTURED	11	9%
DESERTED	24	20%

SEVENTEEN WERE WOUNDED

The first Waterford soldier wounded was Corporal Thomas M. Ames of Company H, 14TH Connecticut. He was wounded at the Battle of Antietam, MD on September 17, 1862 and recovered from his wound. He was killed at Gettysburg, PA on July 3, 1861. Two Waterford soldiers died from a wound received during the war.

WATERFORD WOUNDED (*2) DIED OF WOUNDS

PLACE	DATE	NO.
Antietam, MD (14TH)	9/17/62	1
Georgia Landing, LA (12TH)	10/27/62	1
Kinston, NC (10TH)	12/14/62	1
Chancellorsville, VA (14TH)	5/3/63	2
Port Hudson, LA (12,26TH)	5/27/63	2
Port Hudson, LA (26TH) *	6/14/63	1
Gettysburg, PA (14TH)	7/3/63	1
Cold Harbor, VA (8TH)	6/2/64	1
Cold Harbor, VA (21ST)	6/3/64	1
Petersburg, VA (1 HA)	8/18/64	1
Winchester, VA (12TH)	9/19/64	1
Cedar Creek, VA (12TH) *1	10/19/64	3
Boydton Plank Rd, VA (14TH)	10/27/64	1

WATERTOWN
THE POPULATION IN 1860 WAS 1,587 (RANK 95)

THE MOST IMPORTANT DAY OF THE CIVIL WAR

JUNE 1, 1864

COLD HARBOR, VA

THE BATTLE WAS LEE'S LAST GREAT VICTORY

More soldiers credited to Watertown were listed as casualties (4) on this day than on any other day of the war. Two soldiers were killed, and 2 were wounded in the 2ND Connecticut Heavy Artillery. The wounded survived the war.

The date June 1, 1864 ranks 8TH for total casualties (374) (89 killed, 10 missing, 246 wounded, 23 captured, 6 wounded & captured) for a single day for the State of Connecticut. There were 324 casualties at Cold Harbor, 41 casualties at Ashland, and 9 casualties scattered about Virginia.

The battle and operations around Cold Harbor (May 31-June 12, 1864) rank 6TH for total casualties (557) for an engagement for the State of Connecticut. The most intense fighting developed on June 3 and Watertown had no casualties on that day. They did have 1 wounded on June 10.

The Battle of Cold Harbor with 5 total casualties for Watertown was the highest number of casualties for any single engagement of the war for the town.

Approximately 117,000 Federal and 60,000 Confederate troops participated in operations from May 28 to June 3. Roughly 13,000 Union casualties were recorded and perhaps there were 5,000 Confederate casualties.

142 MEN CREDITED TO WATERTOWN SERVED IN THE FOLLOWING CONNECTICUT ORGANIZATIONS

REGIMENT	TOTAL
23RD	32 (23%)
2ND HEAVY ARTILLERY	25 (18%)
5TH	20 (14%)
1ST HEAVY ARTILLERY	17 (12%)
29TH	13 (9%)
20TH	7 (5%)
1ST SQUADRON CAVALRY	4 (3%)
2ND LIGHT BATTERY	4 (3%)
7TH	4 (3%)
6TH	3 (2%)
11TH	3 (2%)
14TH	3 (2%)
8TH	2 (1%)
10TH	2 (1%)
3RD LIGHT BATTERY	1
9TH	1
22ND	1
30TH	1

9% OF POPULATION

SIX WERE KILLED AND ONE WAS MISSING

The first Watertown soldier killed was Private George S. Guilford of Company H, 20TH Connecticut. He was killed at Chancellorsville, VA on May 3, 1863.

WATERTOWN SOLDIERS KILLED MISSING *

PLACE	DATE	NO.
Chancellorsville, VA (20TH)	5/3/63	1
Fort Wagner, SC (7TH)	7/11/63	1
Cold Harbor, VA (2 HA)	6/1/64	2
Petersburg, VA (30TH)	7/30/64	1
Cedar Creek, VA (2 HA) *1	10/19/64	2

THREE WERE CAPTURED

One Watertown soldier died in captivity at Cold Harbor, VA.

WATERTOWN CAPTURED *(1) DIED IN CAPTIVITY

PLACE	DATE	NO.
Cold Harbor, VA (1 HA) *	6/27/62	1
(WOUNDED)		
Chancellorsville, VA (20TH)	5/3/63	1
Goldsboro, NC (20TH)	3/24/65	1

TOTAL WATERTOWN CASUALTIES

DIED	18	13%
KILLED/MISSING	7	5%
WOUNDED	11	8%
CAPTURED	3	2%
DESERTED	22	16%

ELEVEN WERE WOUNDED

The first Watertown soldier wounded was 1ST Lieutenant Nathan B. Abbott of Company H, 20TH Connecticut. He was wounded at Gettysburg, PA on July 3, 1863 and recovered from his wound. One Watertown soldier died from a wound received during the war.

WATERTOWN WOUNDED *(1) DIED FROM WOUNDS

PLACE	DATE	NO.
Gettysburg, PA (20TH)	7/3/63	1
Cold Harbor, VA (2 HA)	6/1/64	2
Dallas, GA (5TH)	6/2/64	1
Cold Harbor, VA (2 HA) *	6/10/64	1
Petersburg, VA (1 HA)	6/30/64	1
Winchester, VA (2 HA)	9/19/64	2
Cedar Creek, VA (2 HA)	10/19/64	1
Petersburg, VA (2 HA)	3/25/65	1
Fort Gregg, VA (10TH)	4/2/65	1

WESTBROOK
THE POPULATION IN 1860 WAS 1,056 (RANK 129)

THE MOST IMPORTANT DAY OF THE CIVIL WAR

JULY 3, 1863

GETTYSBURG, PA

THE THIRD DAY OF THE BATTLE

Soldiers credited to Westbrook had more casualties on July 3, 1863 at Gettysburg, PA (3) and on October 19, 1864 at Cedar Creek, VA (3) than on any other days of the war. At Gettysburg the casualties were the most serious. One soldier was killed and 2 were wounded in the 14TH Connecticut. One of the wounded died.

The date July 3, 1863 ranks 27TH for total casualties (112) (14 killed, 1 missing, 92 wounded, 5 captured) for a single day for the State of Connecticut. The Battle of Gettysburg accounted for 109 casualties. There were also 2 casualties at Port Hudson, LA and 1 at Ft. Gregg, VA.

The Battle of Gettysburg (July1-3, 1863) ranks 11TH for total casualties (360) for an engagement for the State of Connecticut. The most intense fighting developed on July 3. Westbrook had all its casualties on that day

The Battle of Gettysburg with 3 total casualties for Westbrook was tied with the Battle of Cedar Creek (October 19, 1864) for the highest number of casualties for any single engagement of the war for the town.

More than 170,00 men fought at the Battle of Gettysburg. Roughly 23,000 Union casualties were recorded and there were about 28,000 Confederate casualties. Gettysburg proved to be the great battle of the war. It ended Lee's 1863 invasion of the North. He was never able to launch a major offensive again

67 MEN CREDITED TO WESTBROOK SERVED IN THE FOLLOWING CONNECTICUT ORGANIZATIONS

REGIMENT	TOTAL
24TH	14 (21%)
12TH	12 (18%)
14TH	9 (13%)
7TH	7 (10%)
1ST CAVALRY	5 (7%)
12TH BATTALION	5 (7%)
13TH	5 (7%)
9TH	4 (6%)
9TH BATTALION	3 (4%)
2ND HEAVY ARTILLERY	2 (3%)
10TH	2 (3%)
11TH	2 (3%)
15TH	2 (3%)
1ST LIGHT BATTERY	1
1ST HEAVY ARTILLERY	1
5TH	1
8TH	1
13TH BATTALION	1
20TH	1
29TH	1

16% OF POPULATION

THREE WERE KILLED

The first Westbrook soldier killed was Private Alfred H. Dibble of Company G, 14TH Connecticut. He was killed at Gettysburg, PA on July 3, 1863.

WESTBROOK SOLDIERS KILLED

PLACE	DATE	NO.
Gettysburg, PA (14TH)	7/3/63	1
Ream's Station, VA (1 CA)	6/29/64	1
Cedar Creek, VA (12TH)	10/19/64	1

TWO WERE CAPTURED

No Westbrook soldiers died in captivity.

WESTBROOK CAPTURED
NONE DIED IN CAPTIVITY

PLACE	DATE	NO.
Cedar Creek, VA (12TH)	10/19/64	1
Kinston, NC (15TH)	3/8/65	1

TOTAL WESTBROOK CASUALTIES

DIED	14	21%
KILLED	3	4%
WOUNDED	13	19%
CAPTURED	2	3%
DESERTED	9	13%

THIRTEEN WERE WOUNDED

The first Westbrook soldier wounded was Private Levi M. Chapman of Company G, 14TH Connecticut. He was wounded at Chancellorsville, VA on May 3, 1863 and recovered from his wound. Two Westbrook soldiers died from a wound received during the war.

WESTBROOK WOUNDED
*(2) DIED FROM WOUNDS

PLACE	DATE	NO.
Chancellorsville, VA (14TH)	5/3/63	2
Port Hudson, LA (24TH) *	5/27/63	1
Port Hudson, LA (24TH)	6/14/63	1
Gettysburg, PA (14TH) *1	7/3/63	2
Drewry's Bluff, VA (7TH)	5/16/64	1
Cold Harbor (2 HA)	6/1/64	1
Winchester, VA (12TH)	9/19/64	2
Cedar Creek, VA (12TH)	10/19/64	1
Wallingford, CT (12TH)	3/15/65	1
(Accident)		
Five Forks, VA (1 CA)	4/1/65	1

WEST HARTFORD
THE POPULATION IN 1860 WAS 1,296 (RANK 112)

THE MOST IMPORTANT DAY OF THE CIVIL WAR

APRIL 20, 1864

PLYMOUTH, NC

THE CONFEDERATE PLAN TO TAKE PLYMOUTH ENDED WHEN 2,800 UNION TROOPS SURRENDERED THE CITY

142 MEN CREDITED TO WEST HARTFORD SERVED IN THE FOLLOWING CONNECTICUT ORGANIZATIONS

More soldiers credited to West Hartford were listed as casualties (4) on this day than on any other day of the war. Four soldiers in the 16TH Connecticut were captured. All survived the war.

The date April 20, 1864 ranks 6TH for total casualties (433) (1 killed, 2 missing, 12 wounded & captured, 418 captured) for a single day for the State of Connecticut. All of the casualties were at Plymouth, NC.

The Battle of Plymouth (April 20, 1864) ranks 9TH for total casualties (433) for an engagement for the State of Connecticut. Nearly half of all soldiers captured at Plymouth died in Southern prisons

The Battle of Plymouth with 4 total casualties for West Hartford was the highest number of casualties for any single engagement of the war for the town.

When Confederate General Robert Hoke surrounded and captured the Union garrison at Plymouth, NC the Southern victory was the first in this military arena in quite some time. With aid from the two-gun ironclad *Albemarle* the Confederates were able to take advantage of the lack of suitable Union gunboats.

REGIMENT	TOTAL
22ND	25 (18%)
1ST HEAVY ARTILLERY	23 (16%)
25TH	15 (11%)
16TH	12 (9%)
7TH	10 (7%)
2ND HEAVY ARTILLERY	9 (6%)
11TH	7 (5%)
20TH	6 (4%)
1ST CAVALRY	5 (4%)
14TH	5 (4%)
24TH	5 (4%)
29TH	5 (4%)
3RD	4 (3%)
8TH	3 (2%)
12TH	3 (2%)
13TH	3 (2%)
15TH	3 (2%)
1ST	2 (1%)
5TH	2 (1%)
13TH BATTALION	2 (1%)
9TH	1
9TH BATTALION	1
10TH	1
12TH BATTALION	1
30TH	1

11% OF POPULATION

FOUR WERE KILLED

The first West Hartford soldier killed was Corporal Edward Deming of Company D, 11TH Connecticut. He was killed at the Battle of Antietam on September 17, 1862.

WEST HARTFORD SOLDIERS KILLED

PLACE	DATE	NO.
Antietam, MD (11TH	9/17/62	1
Port Hudson, LA (24TH)	6/14/63	1
Bristoe Station, VA (14TH)	10/14/63	1
Drewry's Bluff, VA (7TH)	5/14/64	1

ELEVEN WERE CAPTURED

One West Hartford soldier died in captivity at Charleston, SC.

WEST HARTFORD CAPTURED
*(1) DIED IN CAPTIVITY

PLACE	DATE	NO.
Pattersonville, LA (12TH)	3/27/63	1
Chancellorsville, VA (20TH)	5/3/63	3
Fort Wagner, SC (7TH) *	7/11/63	1
(WOUNDED)		
Plymouth, NC (16TH)	4/20/64	4
Ream's Station, VA (14TH)	8/25/64	1
Kinston, NC (15TH)	3/8/65	1

TOTAL WEST HARTFORD CASUALTIES

DIED	7	5%
KILLED	4	7%
WOUNDED	17	12%
CAPTURED	11	8%
DESERTED	37	26%

SEVENTEEN WERE WOUNDED

The first West Hartford soldiers wounded were Privates William F. Sternberg and Arthur D. Talcott of Company A, 16TH Connecticut. They were wounded at the Battle of Antietam on September 17, 1862 and Private Talcott died from his wound. Two West Hartford soldiers died from a wound received during the war.

WEST HARTFORD WOUNDED
*(2) DIED FROM WOUNDS

PLACE	DATE	NO.
Antietam, MD (16TH) *1	9/17/62	2
Fredericksburg, VA (8TH)	12/13/62	1
Irish Bend, LA (25TH)	4/14/63	2
Port Hudson, LA (12TH)	6/10/63	1
Walthall Junction, VA (8TH)	5/7/64	1
Spottsylvania, VA (14TH)	5/13/64	1
Drewry's Bluff, VA (8TH)	5/15/64	1
Petersburg, VA (8TH)	6/14/64	1
Peach Tree Creek, GA (20TH)*	7/20/64	1
Richmond, VA (7TH)	10/7/64	1
Cedar Creek, VA (2 HA)	10/19/64	1
Kell House, VA (29TH)	10/27/64	2
Hatcher's Run, VA (2 HA)	2/6/65	1
Petersburg, VA (2 HA)	4/2/65	1

WESTON
THE POPULATION IN 1860 WAS 1,117 (RANK 125)

THE MOST IMPORTANT DAY OF THE CIVIL WAR

JUNE 1, 1864

COLD HARBOR, VA

THE BATTLE WAS LEE'S LAST GREAT VICTORY

Soldiers credited to Weston had more casualties on May 2, 1863 at Chancellorsville, VA (2) and on June 1, 1864 at Cold Harbor, VA (2) than on any other days of the war.. The casualties at Cold Harbor were the most serious. Two soldiers were wounded in the 2ND Connecticut Heavy Artillery. One of the wounded died.

The date June 1, 1864 ranks 8TH for total casualties (374) (89 killed, 10 missing, 246 wounded, 23 captured, 6 wounded & captured) for a single day for the State of Connecticut. There were 324 casualties at Cold Harbor, 41 casualties at Ashland, and 9 other casualties scattered about Virginia.

The battle and operations around Cold Harbor (May 31-June 12, 1864) rank 6TH for total casualties (557) for an engagement for the State of Connecticut. The most intense fighting developed on June 3 and Weston had 1 casualty.

The Battle of Cold Harbor with 3 total casualties for Weston was the highest number of casualties for any single engagement of the war for the town.

Approximately 117,000 Federal and 60,000 Confederate troops participated in operations from May 28 to June 3. Roughly 13,000 Union casualties were recorded and perhaps there were 5,000 Confederate casualties.

69 MEN CREDITED TO WESTON SERVED IN THE FOLLOWING CONNECTICUT ORGANIZATIONS

REGIMENT	TOTAL
23RD	20 (29%)
17TH	12 (17%)
2ND HEAVY ARTILLERY	10 (15%)
5TH	9 (13%)
1ST CAVALRY	3 (4%)
12TH	3 (4%)
1ST HEAVY ARTILLERY	2 (3%)
11TH	2 (3%)
20TH	2 (3%)
2ND LIGHT BATTERY	1
8TH	1
9TH	1
9TH BATTALION	1
12TH BATTALION	1
13TH	1
29TH	1
30TH	1

6% OF POPULATION

NO WESTON SOLDIERS WERE KILLED OR MISSING IN THE WAR

FOUR WERE CAPTURED

No Weston soldiers died in captivity.

WESTON CAPTURED
NONE DIED IN CAPTIVITY

PLACE	DATE	NO.
Chancellorsville, VA (17TH)	5/2/63	2
(1 WOUNDED)		
Gettysburg, PA (17TH)	7/2/63	1
White House, VA (1 CA)	5/18/64	1

TOTAL WESTON CASUALTIES

DIED	4	6%
KILLED	0	0%
WOUNDED	7	12%
CAPTURED	4	6%
DESERTED	12	17%

SEVEN WERE WOUNDED

The first Weston soldier wounded was Private George McCan of Company F, 5TH Connecticut. He was wounded at Cedar Mountain, VA on August 9, 1862 and recovered from his wound. One Weston soldier died from a wound received during the war.

WESTON WOUNDED
*(1) DIED FROM WOUNDS

PLACE	DATE	NO.
Cedar Mountain, VA (5TH)	8/9/62	1
Resaca, GA (5TH)	5/15/64	1
Cold Harbor, VA (2 HA) *1	6/1/64	2
Cold Harbor, VA (11TH)	6/3/64	1
Peach Tree Creek, GA (5TH)	7/20/64	1
Winchester, VA (2 HA)	9/19/64	1

WESTPORT
THE POPULATION IN 1860 WAS 3,293 (RANK 33)

THE MOST IMPORTANT DAY OF THE CIVIL WAR

JULY 2, 1863

GETTYSBURG, PA

THE SECOND DAY OF THE BATTLE

More soldiers credited to Westport were listed as casualties (10) on this day than on any other day of the war. Four soldiers were wounded and 6 were captured in the 17TH Connecticut. They all survived the war.

The date July 2, 1863 ranks 29TH for total casualties (108) (14 killed, 2 missing, 35 wounded, 36 captured, 1 wounded & captured) for a single day for the State of Connecticut. The Battle of Gettysburg accounted for 107 casualties. There was 1 casualty at Brandywine Creek, VA.

The Battle of Gettysburg (July1-3, 1863) ranks 11TH for total casualties (360) for an engagement for the State of Connecticut. The most intense fighting developed on July 3. Westport had no casualties on that day. However, they did have 2 killed and 1 wounded on July 1.

The Battle of Gettysburg with 13 total casualties for Westport was the highest number of casualties for any single engagement of the war for the town.

More than 170,00 men fought at the Battle of Gettysburg. Roughly 23,000 Union casualties were recorded and there were about 28,000 Confederate casualties. Gettysburg proved to be the great battle of the war. It ended Lee's 1863 invasion of the North. He was never able to launch a major offensive again

216 MEN CREDITED TO WESTPORT SERVED IN THE FOLLOWING CONNECTICUT ORGANIZATIONS

REGIMENT	TOTAL
28TH	61 (28%)
17TH	59 (27%)
8TH	14 (6%)
29TH	14 (6%)
5TH	13 (5%)
2ND HEAVY ARTILLERY	8 (4%)
1ST HEAVY ARTILLERY	7 (3%)
1ST CAVALRY	6 (3%)
12TH	6 (3%)
14TH	6 (3%)
11TH	5 (2%)
20TH	5 (2%)
6TH	4 (2%)
7TH	4 (2%)
3RD	3 (1%)
9TH	3 (1%)
23RD	3 (1%)
2ND LIGHT BATTERY	2 (1%)
12TH BATTALION	2 (1%)
13TH	2 (1%)
1ST SQUADRON CAVALRY	1
3RD LIGHT BATTERY	1
9TH BATTALION	1
10TH	1
13TH BATTALION	1

6% OF POPULATION

SEVEN WERE KILLED AND TWO WERE MISSING

The first Westport soldier killed was Private Robert R. Werner of Company A, 5TH Connecticut. He was killed at Cedar Mountain, VA on August 9, 1862

WESTPORT SOLDIERS KILLED

PLACE	DATE	NO.
Cedar Mountain, VA (5TH)	8/9/62	1
Bisland, LA (12TH)	4/13/63	1
Gettysburg, PA (17TH) *2	7/1/63	2
Bristoe Station, VA (14TH)	10/14/63	1
Petersburg, VA (8TH)	7/8/64	1
Deep Bottom, VA (10TH)	8/14/64	1
Ream's Station, VA (14TH)	8/25/64	1
Neuse River, NC (7TH)	6/16/65	1
(DROWNED)		

TWENTY-TWO WERE CAPTURED

One Westport soldier died in captivity at Millen, GA.

WESTPORT CAPTURED
*(1) DIED IN CAPTIVITY

PLACE	DATE	NO.
Buckingham County, VA (5TH)	4/22/62	1
Winchester, VA (5TH)	5/25/62	2
Chancellorsville, VA (17TH)	5/2/63	4
Chancellorsville, VA (17TH)	5/3/63	1
Port Hudson, LA (28TH)	6/14/63	3
(1 WOUNDED)		
Jackson, LA (28TH)	6/21/63	1
Gettysburg, PA (5, 17TH)	7/2/63	6
Drewry's Bluff, VA (11TH)	5/16/64	1
Ream's Station, VA (1 CA) *	6/29/64	1
Petersburg, VA (29TH)	8/26/64	1
Dunn's Lake, FLA (17TH)	2/5/65	1

TOTAL WESTPORT CASUALTIES

DIED	21	10%
KILLED	9	4%
WOUNDED	22	10%
CAPTURED	22	10%
DESERTED	43	20%

TWENTY WERE WOUNDED

The first Westport soldier wounded was Private John H. Fuller of Company A, 6TH Connecticut. He was wounded at Fort Pulaski, GA on March 1, 1862 and recovered from his wound. One Westport soldier died from a wound received during the war.

WESTPORT WOUNDED
*(1) DIED FROM WOUNDS

PLACE	DATE	NO.
Fort Pulaski, GA (6TH)	3/1/62	1
Cedar Mountain, VA (5TH) *	8/9/62	1
Hagerstown, MD (5TH)	5/1/63	1
Chancellorsville, VA (17TH)	5/2/63	1
Chancellorsville, VA (5TH)	5/3/63	1
Port Hudson, LA (28TH)	6/14/63	2
Port Hudson, LA (28TH)	7/1/63	1
Gettysburg, PA (17TH)	7/1/63	3
Gettysburg, PA (17TH)	7/2/63	4
Morris Island, SC (17TH)	8/20/63	1
Cold Harbor, VA (2 HA)	6/1/64	1
Cold Harbor, VA (8TH)	6/2/64	1
Dallas, GA (5TH)	6/3/64	1
Drewry's Bluff, VA (8TH)	5/16/64	1
Winchester, VA (2 HA)	9/19/64	1
Richmond, VA (29TH)	9/30/64	1

608

WETHERSFIELD
THE POPULATION IN 1860 WAS 2,705 (RANK 51)

THE MOST IMPORTANT DAY
OF THE CIVIL WAR

APRIL 20, 1864

PLYMOUTH, NC

THE CONFEDERATE PLAN
TO TAKE PLYMOUTH
ENDED WHEN 2,800 UNION
TROOPS SURRENDERED
THE CITY

213 MEN CREDITED TO
WETHERSFIELD SERVED
IN THE FOLLOWING
CONNECTICUT
ORGANIZATIONS

REGIMENT	TOTAL
22ND	41 (19%)
1ST HEAVY ARTILLERY	22 (10%)
7TH	22 (10%)
8TH	16 (8%)
25TH	15 (7%)
16TH	14 (7%)
10TH	11 (5%)
14TH	11 (5%)
11TH	9 (4%)
12TH	9 (4%)
29TH	9 (4%)
13TH	8 (4%)
2ND HEAVY ARTILLERY	7 (3%)
5TH	7 (3%)
12TH BATTALION	6 (3%)
21ST	5 (2%)
1ST CAVALRY	4 (2%)
20TH	4 (2%)
3RD	3 (1%)
1ST	2 (1%)
1ST LIGHT BATTERY	2 (1%)
9TH	2 (1%)
30TH	2 (1%)
6TH	1
9TH BATTALION	1
13TH BATTALION	1
18TH	1
27TH	1

8% OF POPULATION

More soldiers credited to Wethersfield were listed as casualties (8) on this day than on any other day of the war. Eight soldiers in the 16TH Connecticut were captured. Two of them eventually died in prison.

The date April 20, 1864 ranks 6TH for total casualties (433) (1 killed, 2 missing, 12 wounded & captured, 418 captured) for a single day for the State of Connecticut. All of the casualties were at Plymouth, NC.

The Battle of Plymouth (April 20, 1864) ranks 9TH for total casualties (433) for an engagement for the State of Connecticut. Nearly half of all soldiers captured at Plymouth died in Southern prisons

The Battle of Plymouth with 8 total casualties for Wethersfield was the highest number of casualties for any single engagement of the war for the town.

When Confederate General Robert Hoke surrounded and captured the Union garrison at Plymouth, NC the Southern victory was the first in this military arena in quite some time. With aid from the two-gun ironclad *Albemarle* the Confederates were able to take advantage of the lack of suitable Union gunboats.

FIVE WERE KILLED

The first Wethersfield soldiers killed were Privates Henry W. Davis and Henry Rising of the 11TH Connecticut. They were killed at the Battle of Antietam, MD on September 17, 1862.

WETHERSFIELD SOLDIERS KILLED

PLACE	DATE	NO.
Antietam, MD (11TH)	9/17/62	2
Fredericksburg, VA (14TH)	12/13/62	1
Cold Harbor, VA (8TH)	6/2/64	1
Cold Harbor, VA (8TH)	6/9/64	1

TWENTY-ONE WERE CAPTURED

Four Wethersfield soldiers died in captivity. Two died at Andersonville Prison, GA, one at Charleston, SC, and one at Salisbury, NC.

WETHERSFIELD CAPTURED
*(4) DIED IN CAPTIVITY

PLACE	DATE	NO.
Pattersonville, LA (12TH)	3/27/63	1
Irish Bend, LA (25TH)	4/14/63	1
Chancellorsville, VA (27TH)	5/3/63	1
Port Hudson, LA (13TH)	5/24/63	1
St Augustine, FL (10TH)	12/30/63	1
Morton's Ford, VA (14TH)	2/6/64	1
Plymouth, NC (16TH) *2	4/20/64	8
City Point, VA (8TH)	5/16/64	1
Drewry's Bluff, VA (7TH) *	5/16/64	1
Hatcher's Run, VA (7TH)	6/2/64	2
Ream's Station, VA (14TH) *	8/25/64	1
New Market Road, VA (7TH)	10/1/64	1
Cedar Creek, VA (12TH)	10/19/64	1
(WOUNDED)		

TOTAL WETHERSFIELD CASUALTIES

DIED	19	9%
KILLED	5	2%
WOUNDED	18	8%
CAPTURED	21	10%
DESERTED	45	21%

EIGHTEEN WERE WOUNDED

The first Wethersfield soldier wounded was Quartermaster Sergeant Edward D. Wells of Company B, 7TH Connecticut. He was wounded at James Island, SC on June 16, 1862 and recovered from his wound. One Wethersfield soldier died from a wound received during the war.

WETHERSFIELD WOUNDED
*(1) DIED FROM WOUNDS

PLACE	DATE	NO.
James Island, SC (7TH)	6/16/62	1
Kinston, NC (10TH)	12/14/62	1
Chancellorsville, VA (14TH)	5/3/63	1
Mine Run, VA (14TH)	11/27/63	1
Walthall Junction, VA (8TH)	5/7/64	1
Drewry's Bluff, VA (10TH)	5/14/64	1
Cold Harbor, VA (2 HA)	6/1/64	1
Cold Harbor, VA (8TH)	6/3/64	1
Cold Harbor, VA (21ST)	6/3/64	1
Petersburg, VA (11TH)	6/18/64	1
Peach Tree Creek, GA (5TH) *	7/20/64	1
Deep Run, VA (7TH)	8/16/64	1
Winchester, VA (12TH)	9/19/64	2
Chaffin's Farm, VA (7TH)	9/29/64	2
Unknown Place (14TH)	11/1/64	1
Unknown (1 LB)	Unknown	1

WILLINGTON
THE POPULATION IN 1860 WAS 1,166 (RANK 122)

THE MOST IMPORTANT
DAY OF THE CIVIL WAR

MARCH 14, 1862

NEW BERN, NC

THE UNION VICTORY
SECURED AN IMPORTANT
RAILROAD HUB

Soldiers credited to Willington had more soldiers listed as casualties on March 14, 1862 at New Bern, NC (2), September 17, 1862 at Antietam, MD (2), December 13, 1862 at Fredericksburg, VA (2), June 15, 1863 at Winchester, VA (2), April 20, 1864 at Plymouth, NC (2), and June 3, 1864 Cold Harbor, VA (2) than any others days of the war. The casualties at New Bern were the most serious. Two soldiers were killed in the 10TH and 11TH Connecticut.

The date March 14, 1862 ranks 43RD for total casualties (53) (13 killed, 40 wounded) for a single day for the State of Connecticut. All of the casualties except 1 were at New Bern, NC.

The Battle of New Bern (March 14, 1862) ranks 36TH for total casualties (52) for an engagement for the State of Connecticut

The Battle of New Bern with 2 total casualties for Willington was tied with 7 others for the highest number of casualties for any single engagement of the war for the town.

The victory boosted Union General Ambrose Burnside's reputation as a capable leader. It also gave the Union army a base of operations connected with the railroad to launch a campaign to gain control of the North Carolina coast

82 MEN CREDITED TO
WILLINGTON SERVED
IN THE FOLLOWING
CONNECTICUT
ORGANIZATIONS

REGIMENT	TOTAL
10TH	13 (16%)
11TH	10 (12%)
1ST HEAVY ARTILLERY	8 (10%)
5TH	6 (7%)
7TH	6 (7%)
16TH	6 (7%)
21ST	6 (7%)
14TH	5 (6%)
6TH	4 (5%)
12TH	4 (5%)
1ST CAVALRY	3 (4%)
18TH	3 (4%)
20TH	3 (4%)
29TH	3 (4%)
1ST SQUADRON CAVALRY	2 (2%)
8TH	1
25TH	1

7% OF POPULATION

FOUR WERE KILLED

The first Willington soldiers killed were Privates Charles Mitchell and James C. Smith of the 10TH and 11TH Connecticut. They were killed at New Bern, NC on March 14, 1862.

WILLINGTON SOLDIERS KILLED

PLACE	DATE	NO.
New Bern, NC (10,11TH)	3/14/62	2
Antietam, MD (16TH)	9/17/62	1
Kinston, NC (10TH)	12/14/62	1

TEN WERE CAPTURED

No Willington soldiers died in captivity.

WILLINGTON CAPTURED
NONE DIED IN CAPTIVITY

PLACE	DATE	NO.
Fredericksburg, VA (14TH)	12/13/62	1
Winchester, VA (18TH)	6/15/63	2
Plymouth, NC (16TH)	4/20/64	2
Drewry's Bluff, VA (6TH)	5/16/64	1
Piedmnt, VA (18TH)	6/5/64	1
(WOUNDED)		
Bermuda Hundred, VA (7TH)	6/16/64	1
(WOUNDED)		
Ream's Station, VA (14TH)	8/25/64	1
Fort Harrison, VA (21ST)	9/29/64	1

TOTAL WILLINGTON CASUALTIES

DIED	8	10%
KILLED	4	5%
WOUNDED	15	18%
CAPTURED	10	12%
DESERTED	18	22%

FIFTEEN WERE WOUNDED

The first Willington soldier wounded was Private Andrew M. Bartlett of Company I, 16TH Connecticut. He was wounded at the Battle of Antietam, MD on September 17, 1862 and recovered from his wound. One Willington soldier died from a wound received during the war.

WILLINGTON WOUNDED
*(1) DIED FROM WOUNDS

PLACE	DATE	NO.
Antietam, MD (16TH)	9/17/62	1
Fredericksburg, VA (14TH) *	12/13/62	1
Morton's Ford, VA (14TH)	2/6/64	1
Swift's Creek, VA (11TH)	5/9/64	1
Drewry's Bluff, VA (10TH)	5/16/64	1
Drewry's Bluff, VA (6TH)	5/20/64	1
Mechanicsville, VA (11TH)	6/1/64	1
Cold Harbor, VA (11TH)	6/3/64	2
Deep Bottom, VA (10TH)	8/14/64	1
Petersburg, VA (6TH)	9/21/64	1
Darbytown Road, VA (10TH)	10/13/64	1
Fort Fisher, NC (6TH)	1/15/65	1
Petersburg, VA (10TH)	4/2/65	1
Fort Gregg, VA (10TH)	4/2/65	1

WILTON
THE POPULATION IN 1860 WAS 2,208 (RANK 67)

THE MOST IMPORTANT DAY OF THE CIVIL WAR

JULY 1, 1863

GETTYSBURG, PA

THE FIRST DAY OF THE BATTLE

More soldiers credited to Wilton were listed as casualties (4) on this day than on any other day of the war. Three soldiers were wounded, and 1 was captured in the 17TH Connecticut. They survived the war.

The date July 1, 1863 ranks 16TH for total casualties (157) (18 killed, 4 missing, 70 wounded, 57 captured, 8 wounded & captured) for a single day for the State of Connecticut. There were 143 casualties at Gettysburg. The 14 other casualties were scattered about Louisiana (6), Virginia (6), and South Carolina (2).

The Battle of Gettysburg (July1-3, 1863) ranks 11TH for total casualties (360) for an engagement for the State of Connecticut. The most intense fighting developed on July 3. Wilton had no casualties on that day. However, they did have 3 casualties on July 2.

The Battle of Gettysburg with 7 total casualties for Wilton was the highest number of casualties for any single engagement of the war for the town.

More than 170,00 men fought at the Battle of Gettysburg. Roughly 23,000 Union casualties were recorded and there were about 28,000 Confederate casualties. Gettysburg proved to be the great battle of the war. It ended Lee's 1863 invasion of the North. He was never able to launch a major offensive again

157 MEN CREDITED TO WILTON SERVED IN THE FOLLOWING CONNECTICUT ORGANIZATIONS

REGIMENT	TOTAL
17TH	42 (28%)
23RD	27 (17%)
7TH	18 (11%)
1ST CAVALRY	15 (9%)
8TH	13 (8%)
1ST HEAVY ARTILLERY	8 (5%)
2ND HEAVY ARTILLERY	7 (4%)
12TH	6 (4%)
13TH	5 (3%)
5TH	4 (3%)
3RD	3 (2%)
9TH	3 (2%)
29TH	3 (2%)
3RD LIGHT BATTERY	2 (1%)
6TH	2 (1%)
10TH	2 (1%)
12TH BATTALION	2 (1%)
14TH	2 (1%)
15TH	2 (1%)
1ST	1
2ND LIGHT BATTERY	1
13TH BATTALION	1
20TH	1
25TH	1
28TH	1
30TH	1

7% OF POPULATION

FIVE WERE KILLED AND ONE WAS MISSING

The first Wilton soldiers killed were Sergeant Elijah B. Jones and Private Seth F. Mills of the 5TH Connecticut. They were killed at Cedar Mountain on August 9, 1862.

WILTON SOLDIERS KILLED AND MISSING *

PLACE	DATE	NO.
Cedar Mountain, VA (5TH)	8/9/62	2
Walthall Junction, VA (8TH)	5/7/64	1
Cold Harbor, VA (2 HA) *	6/1/64	1
Petersburg, VA (8TH)	7/10/64	1
Peach Tree Creek, GA (5TH)	7/20/64	1

TWENTY-ONE WERE CAPTURED

Three Wilton soldiers died in captivity at Andersonville Prison, GA.

WILTON CAPTURED *(3) DIED IN CAPTIVITY

PLACE	DATE	NO.
Gettysburg, PA (17TH)	7/1/63	1
Gettysburg, PA (17TH)	7/2/63	1
Olustee, FL(7TH) *1	2/20/64	3
(2 WOUNDED)		
Craig's Church, VA (1 CA) *	5/5/64	1
Spottsylvania, VA (7TH)	5/16/64	1
Drewry's Bluff, VA (7TH)	5/16/64	2
Cold Harbor, VA (2 HA)	6/14/64	1
Hungertown, VA (1 CA) *	6/23/64	1
Richmond, VA (7TH)	9/20/64	1
Cedar Creek, VA (12TH,1 CA)	10/19/64	3
Dunn's Lake, FLA (17TH)	2/5/65	3
Kinston, NC (15TH)	3/8/65	2
Ashland, VA (1 CA)	3/15/65	1

TOTAL WILTON CASUALTIES

DIED	22	14%
KILLED/MISSING	6	4%
WOUNDED	22	14%
CAPTURED	21	13%
DESERTED	18	11%

TWENTY-TWO WERE WOUNDED

The first Wilton soldier wounded was Private Leverett Campbell of Company A, 14TH Connecticut. He was wounded at the Battle of Antietam, MD on September 17, 1862 and recovered from his wound. Three Wilton soldiers died from a wound received during the war.

WILTON WOUNDED *(3) DIED FROM WOUNDS

PLACE	DATE	NO.
Antietam, MD (14TH)	9/17/62	1
Bisland, LA (12TH) *	4/13/63	1
Chancellorsville, VA (17TH)	5/2/63	1
La Fourche, LA (23RD)	6/21/63	1
Gettysburg, PA (17TH)	7/1/63	3
Gettysburg, PA (17TH)	7/2/63	2
Olustee, FLA (7TH)	2/24/64	1
Grove Church, VA (1 CA)	3/29/64	1
Walthall Junction, VA (8TH) *	5/7/64	1
Chester Station, VA (7TH)	5/10/64	1
Laurel Hill, VA (14TH)	5/10/64	1
Drewry's Bluff, VA (7TH) *1	5/14/64	2
Bermuda Hundred, VA (6TH)	5/30/64	1
Petersburg, VA (2 HA)	6/22/64	1
Deep Run, VA (10TH)	8/16/64	1
Darbytown Road, VA (10TH)	10/13/64	1
Petersburg, VA (7TH)	10/15/64	1
Fort Gregg, VA (10TH)	4/2/65	1

WINCHESTER
THE POPULATION IN 1860 WAS 3,513 (RANK 27)

THE MOST IMPORTANT DAY OF THE CIVIL WAR

JUNE 1, 1864

COLD HARBOR, VA

THE BATTLE WAS LEE'S LAST GREAT VICTORY

More soldiers credited to Winchester were listed as casualties (25) on this day than on any other day of the war. Eleven soldiers were killed, 2 were missing, and 12 were wounded in the 2ND Connecticut Heavy Artillery. One of the wounded died.

The date June 1, 1864 ranks 8TH for total casualties (374) (89 killed, 10 missing, 246 wounded, 23 captured, 6 wounded & captured) for a single day for the State of Connecticut. There were 324 casualties at Cold Harbor, 41 casualties at Ashland, and 9 other casualties scattered about Virginia.

The battle and operations around Cold Harbor (May 31-June 12, 1864) rank 6TH for total casualties (557) for an engagement for the State of Connecticut. The most intense fighting developed on June 3 and Winchester had 2 casualties.

The Battle of Cold Harbor with 27 total casualties for Winchester was the highest number of casualties for any single engagement of the war for the town.

Approximately 117,000 Federal and 60,000 Confederate troops participated in operations from May 28 to June 3. Roughly 13,000 Union casualties were recorded and perhaps there were 5,000 Confederate casualties.

394 MEN CREDITED TO WINCHESTER SERVED IN THE FOLLOWING CONNECTICUT ORGANIZATIONS

REGIMENT	TOTAL
2ND HEAVY ARTILLERY	102 (26%)
2ND	94 (24%)
28TH	68 (17%)
11TH	31 (8%)
5TH	22 (6%)
7TH	20 (5%)
1ST CAVALRY	15 (4%)
10TH	15 (4%)
8TH	13 (3%)
20TH	10 (3%)
1ST HEAVY ARTILLERY	8 (2%)
12TH	8 (2%)
13TH	8 (2%)
6TH	6 (2%)
15TH	6 (2%)
14TH	5 (1%)
12TH BATTALION	4 (1%)
9TH	3 (1%)
13TH BATTALION	3 (1%)
1ST SQUADRON CAVALRY	2 (1%)
30TH	2 (1%)
1ST LIGHT BATTERY	1
9TH BATTALION	1
16TH	1
17TH	1
21ST	1
25TH	1

11% OF POPULATION

TWENTY-THREE WERE KILLED AND THREE WERE MISSING

The first Winchester soldier killed was Private Gottlieb Arnold of Company I, 5TH Connecticut. He was killed at Cedar Mountain on August 9, 1862.

WINCHESTER SOLDIERS KILLED AND MISSING*

PLACE	DATE	NO.
Cedar Mountain, VA (5TH)	8/9/62	1
Antietam, MD (11,16TH)	9/17/62	4
Port Hudson, LA (28TH)	6/14/63	1
Olustee, FL (7TH)	2/20/64	1
Cold Harbor, VA (2 HA) *2	6/1/64	13
Cold Harbor, VA (11TH)	6/3/64	1
Winchester, VA (12TH)	9/19/64	1
Richmond, VA (7TH)	10/13/64	1
Cedar Creek, VA (2 HA)	10/19/64	1
Steamer "Fulton" (5TH)	1/10/65	1
Kinston, NC (15TH) *	3/8/65	1

SIXTEEN WERE CAPTURED

Three Winchester soldiers died in captivity. Two died at Libby Prison, Richmond, VA and one died at Salisbury, NC.

WINCHESTER CAPTURED *(3) DIED IN CAPTIVITY

PLACE	DATE	NO.
Bull Run, VA (2ND)	7/21/61	3
New Baltimore, VA (1 SQ)	7/1/63	1
Rapidan, VA (14TH) *	12/1/63	1
Drewry's Bluff, VA (7TH)	5/15/64	1
Drewry's Bluff, VA (11TH) *	5/16/64	1
(WOUNDED)		
Bermuda Hundred, VA (6TH)	6/17/64	1
Strasburg, VA (2 HA)	8/19/64	1
Fort Powhatan, VA (8TH)	9/18/64	1
Cedar Creek, VA (2 HA) *	10/19/64	2
Cedar Creek, VA (1 CA)	11/12/64	1
Kinston, NC (15TH)	3/8/65	2
(1 WOUNDED)		
Bentonville, NC (5TH)	3/19/65	1

TOTAL WINCHESTER CASUALTIES

DIED	32	8%
KILLED/MISSING	26	7%
WOUNDED	41	10%
CAPTURED	16	4%
DESERTED	50	13%

FORTY-ONE WERE WOUNDED

The first Winchester soldier wounded was Private William H. Slack of Company D, 11TH Connecticut. He was wounded at New Bern, NC on March 14, 1862 and died from his wound. Five Winchester soldiers died from a wound received during the war.

WINCHESTER WOUNDED *(5) DIED FROM WOUNDS

PLACE	DATE	NO.
New Bern, NC (11TH) *	3/14/62	1
James Island, SC (7TH)	6/16/62	1
Cedar Mountain, VA (5TH)	8/9/62	2
Antietam, MD (11TH)	9/17/62	1
Alexandria, VA (2 HA)	10/24/62	1
Port Hudson, LA (28TH)	6/14/63	4
Resaca, GA (5TH) *	5/15/64	1
Cold Harbor, VA (2 HA) *1	6/1/64	12
Cold Harbor, VA (11TH)	6/3/64	2
Petersburg, VA (8TH)	6/16/64	1
Petersburg, VA (11TH)	6/19/64	1
Petersburg, VA (2 HA)	6/22/64	1
Peach Tree Creek, GA (5TH)	7/20/64	1
Petersburg, VA (8TH)	7/26/64	1
Harper's Ferry, WVA (2 HA)	7/27/64	1
Winchester, VA (2 HA) *1	9/19/64	3
Chaffin's Farm, VA (11TH)	9/29/64	1
Richmond, VA (7TH) *	10/7/64	1
Richmond, VA (7TH)	10/13/64	1
Cedar Creek, VA (2 HA,9,12TH)	10/19/64	3
Petersburg, VA (2 HA)	4/2/65	1

WINDHAM
THE POPULATION IN 1860 WAS 4,711 (RANK 18)

THE MOST IMPORTANT DAY 0F THE CIVIL WAR

JUNE 15 1863

WINCHESTER, VA

THE ENTIRE UNION ARMY WAS NEARLY CAPTURED AT THE SECOND BATTLE OF WINCHESTER

More soldiers credited to Windham were listed as casualties (42) on this day than on any other day of the war. One soldier was killed, 5 were wounded & captured, and 36 were captured in the 18TH Connecticut. One of the captured died in prison.

The date June 15, 1863 ranks 2ND for total casualties (595) (23 killed, 11 wounded, 520 captured, 41 wounded & captured) for a single day for the State of Connecticut. There were 592 casualties at Winchester, VA and 3 casualties at Port Hudson, LA.

The Second Battle of Winchester (June 13-15, 1863) ranks 5TH for total casualties (592) for an engagement for the State of Connecticut. The most intense fighting developed on June 15. Windham had all its casualties on that day.

The Second Battle of Winchester with 42 total casualties for Windham was the highest number of casualties for any single engagement of the war for the town.

Winchester was one of the most contested locations in the Civil War. It changed hands seventy-two times.

318 MEN CREDITED TO WINDHAM SERVED IN THE FOLLOWING CONNECTICUT ORGANIZATIONS

REGIMENT	TOTAL
18TH	75 (24%)
5TH	45 (14%)
12TH	43 (14%)
8TH	33 (10%)
1ST HEAVY ARTILLERY	19 (6%)
21ST	19 (6%)
7TH	18 (6%)
12TH BATTALION	18 (6%)
10TH	14 (4%)
14TH	14 (4%)
2ND HEAVY ARTILLERY	12 (4%)
20TH	12 (4%)
11TH	9 (3%)
1ST CAVALRY	8 (3%)
30TH	8 (3%)
13TH	3 (1%)
1ST SQUAD CAVALRY	2 (1%)
1ST	1
1ST LIGHT BATTERY	1
2ND	1
3RD	1
6TH	1
13TH BATTALION	1
25TH	1
26TH	1
29TH	1

7% OF POPULATION

EIGHTEEN WERE KILLED

The first Windham soldiers killed were Privates Charles E. Thompson and Thomas Quinn of the 5TH Connecticut. They were killed at Cedar mountain, VA on August 9, 1862.

WINDHAM SOLDIERS KILLED

PLACE	DATE	NO.
Cedar Mountain, VA (5TH)	8/9/62	2
Port Hudson, LA (12TH)	5/28/63	1
Winchester, VA (18TH)	6/15/63	1
Gowan, TN (Accident) (5TH)	12/30/63	1
Drewry's Bluff, VA (7TH)	5/14/64	2
New Market, VA (18TH)	5/15/64	1
Drewry's Bluff, VA (7TH)	5/16/64	1
Bermuda Hundred, VA (1 HA)	5/20/64	1
Cold Harbor, VA (8TH)	6/2/64	1
Piedmont, VA (18TH)	6/5/64	1
Petersburg, VA (1 HA)	7/6/64	1
Petersburg, VA (8TH)	7/16/64	1
Snicker's Ford, VA (18TH)	7/18/64	1
Peach Tree Creek, GA (5TH)	7/20/64	1
Petersburg, VA (21ST)	7/30/64	1
Deep Run, VA (10TH)	8/16/64	1

EIGHTY-FIVE WERE CAPTURED

Eight Windham soldiers died in captivity. Three died at Salisbury, NC, two died at Andersonville Prison, GA, one died at Libby Prison, Richmond, VA, one died at Florence, SC, and one died at Charleston, SC

WINDHAM CAPTURED
*(8) DIED IN CAPTIVITY

PLACE	DATE	NO.
Winchester, VA (5TH)	5/24/62	1
Winchester, VA (5TH)	5/25/62	6
Cedar Mountain, VA (5TH)	8/9/62	3
Culpeper, VA (5TH)	8/9/62	2
Beal's Station, VA (5TH) (WOUNDED)	8/20/62	1
Antietam, MD (8TH)	9/17/62	1
Fredericksburg, VA (14TH) (WOUNDED)	12/13/62	1
Chancellorsville, VA (5TH)	5/2/63	1
Winchester, VA (18TH) * (5 WOUNDED)	6/15/63	41
Port Hudson, LA (12TH)	6/27/63	1
Fairfax, VA (5TH)	8/1/63	1
Kelly's Ford, VA (5TH)	8/4/63	1
Port Hudson, LA (12TH) (WOUNDED)	7/9/63	1
Rapidan, VA (14TH) *	12/1/63	1
Craig's Church, VA (1 CA) *	5/5/64	1
New Market, VA (18TH) *1 (3 WOUNDED)	5/15/64	4
Drewry's Bluff, VA (21ST) (WOUNDED)	5/16/64	1
Newtown, VA (18TH)	5/29/64	1
New Market, VA (18TH) *	5/29/64	1
Strasburg, VA (18TH)	5/30/64	1
Bermuda Hundred, VA (7TH)	6/2/64	2
Piedmont, VA (2 WOUNDED) (18TH)	6/5/64	2
Staunton, VA (18TH)	6/10/64	2
Lynchburg, VA (1 WOUNDED) (18TH) *	6/18/64	2
Front Royal, VA (1 CA)	9/24/64	1
Cedar Creek, VA (2HA,12TH) *1 (1 WOUNDED)	10/19/64	4
Cedar Creek, VA (1 CA) *	11/12/64	1

TOTAL WINDHAM CASUALTIES

DIED	29	9%
KILLED	18	6%
WOUNDED	64	20%
CAPTURED	85	27%
DESERTED	37	12%

SIXTY-FOUR WERE WOUNDED

The first Windham soldier wounded was Private Thomas Postle of Company H, 10TH Connecticut. He was wounded at Roanoke Island, NC on February 8, 1862 and recovered from his wound. Four Windham soldiers died from a wound received during the war.

WINDHAM WOUNDED
*(4) DIED FROM WOUNDS

PLACE	DATE	NO.
Roanoke Island, NC (10TH)	2/8/62	1
James Island, SC (7TH)	6/16/62	4
Cedar Mountain, VA (5TH)	8/9/62	3
Drewry's Bluff, VA (21ST)	9/15/62	1
Antietam, MD (8, 14TH) *1	9/17/62	7
Pocotaligo, SC (7TH)	10/22/62	3
Georgia Landing, LA (12TH)	10/27/62	2
Fredericksburg, VA (14TH)	12/13/62	1
Bisland, LA (12TH)	4/13/63	2
Chancellorsville, VA (5TH)	5/2/63	1
Port Hudson, LA (12TH)	5/28/63	1
Port Hudson, LA (12TH)	5/31/63	1
Port Hudson, LA (12TH)	6/4/63	1
Fort Wagner, SC (7TH)	9/4/63	1
Walthall Junction, VA (8TH)	5/7/64	1
Chester Station, VA (7TH)	5/10/64	1
Resaca, GA (5TH)	5/15/64	2
New Market, VA (18TH)	5/15/64	2
Drewry's Bluff, VA (21ST)	5/16/64	2
Cold Harbor, VA (11,14, 21ST)	6/3/64	3
Piedmont, VA (18TH)	6/5/64	2
Lynchburg, VA (18TH)	6/18/64	1
Petersburg, VA (21ST)	7/16/64	1
Lynchburg, VA (18TH)	7/18/64	1
Snicker's Ford, VA (18TH)	7/18/64	3
Petersburg, VA (1 HA)	7/19/64	1
Peach Tree Creek, GA (5TH) *	7/20/64	1
Petersburg, VA (30TH)	7/30/64	2
Deep Run, VA (7,10TH)	8/16/64	2
Atlanta, GA (20TH)	8/21/64	1
Winchester, VA (12, 13TH) *1	9/19/64	4
Darbytown Road, VA (10TH) *1	10/13/64	2
Cedar Creek, VA (12TH)	10/19/64	2
Hatcher's Run, VA (14TH)	2/5/65	1
Petersburg, VA (1 HA)	3/28/65	1
Fort Gregg, VA (10TH)	4/2/65	1

WINDSOR
THE POPULATION IN 1860 WAS 3,865 (RANK 21)

THE MOST IMPORTANT DAY
OF THE CIVIL WAR

APRIL 20, 1864

PLYMOUTH, NC

THE CONFEDERATE PLAN
TO TAKE PLYMOUTH
ENDED WHEN 2,800 UNION
TROOPS SURRENDERED
THE CITY

More soldiers credited to Windsor were listed as casualties (7) on this day than on any other day of the war. Seven soldiers in the 16TH Connecticut were captured. Five of them eventually died in prison.

The date April 20, 1864 ranks 6TH for total casualties (433) (1 killed, 2 missing, 12 wounded & captured, 418 captured) for a single day for the State of Connecticut. All of the casualties were at Plymouth, NC.

The Battle of Plymouth (April 20, 1864) ranks 9TH for total casualties (433) for an engagement for the State of Connecticut. Nearly half of all soldiers captured at Plymouth died in Southern prisons

The Battle of Plymouth with 7 total casualties for Windsor was the highest number of casualties for any single engagement of the war for the town.

When Confederate General Robert Hoke surrounded and captured the Union garrison at Plymouth, NC the Southern victory was the first in this military arena in quite some time. With aid from the two-gun ironclad *Albemarle* the Confederates were able to take advantage of the lack of suitable Union gunboats.

187 MEN CREDITED TO
WINDSOR SERVED
IN THE FOLLOWING
CONNECTICUT
ORGANIZATIONS

REGIMENT	TOTAL
22ND	63 (34%)
11TH	21 (11%)
10TH	13 (7%)
21ST	13 (7%)
7TH	12 (6%)
1ST HEAVY ARTILLERY	10 (5%)
16TH	10 (5%)
25TH	8 (4%)
12TH	7 (4%)
2ND HEAVY ARTILLERY	5 (3%)
1ST SQUADRON CAVALRY	5 (3%)
6TH	5 (3%)
1ST CAVALRY	4 (2%)
14TH	4 (2%)
8TH	3 (2%)
2ND LIGHT BATTERY	2 (1%)
5TH	2 (1%)
12TH BATTALION	2 (1%)
30TH	2 (1%)
1ST	1
3RD	1
9TH	1
9TH BATTALION	1
13TH	1
29TH	1

5% OF POPULATION

FIVE WERE KILLED AND ONE WAS MISSING

The first Windsor soldier killed was Private Henry W. Allyn of Company B, 1ST Connecticut Squadron Cavalry. He was killed at Aldie, VA on June 17, 1863.

WINDSOR SOLDIERS KILLED

PLACE	DATE	NO.
Aldie, VA (1 SQ)	6/17/63	1
Ft. Wagner, SC (6TH) *	7/18/63	1
Drewry's Bluff, VA (7TH)	5/16/64	1
Cold Harbor, VA (2 HA)	6/1/64	1
Winchester, VA (12TH)	9/19/64	1
Fort Fisher, NC (7TH)	1/15/65	1

TWELVE WERE CAPTURED

Six Windsor soldiers died in captivity. Three died at Andersonville Prison, GA, two at Florence, SC, and one died at Salisbury, NC.

WINDSOR CAPTURED
*(6) DIED IN CAPTIVITY

PLACE	DATE	NO.
Pattersonville, LA (12TH)	3/27/63	1
Irish Bend, LA (25TH)	4/14/63	1
Fort Wagner, SC (7TH)	7/11/63	1
Plymouth, NC (16TH) *5	4/20/64	7
Bermuda Hundred, VA (7TH)	6/2/64	1
Cedar Run Chch, VA (1 CA) *	10/17/64	1

TOTAL WINDSOR CASUALTIES

DIED	17	9%
KILLED/MISSING	6	3%
WOUNDED	27	14%
CAPTURED	12	6%
DESERTED	21	11%

TWENTY-SEVEN WERE WOUNDED

The first Windsor soldiers wounded were Sergeant James Shinners, Corporal William D. Warriner and Private Joseph J. Jones of the 8,11, 16TH Connecticut. They were wounded at the Battle of Antietam on September 17, 1862. Corporal Warriner died and Private Jones died in Andersonville Prison, GA after being captured later in the war at Plymouth, NC. Three Windsor soldiers died from wounds received during the war.

WINDSOR WOUNDED
*(3) DIED FROM WOUNDS

PLACE	DATE	NO.
Unknown Place (10TH)	Unnown	1
Antietam, MD (8,11,16TH) *1	9/17/62	3
Pocotaligo, SC (7TH)	10/22/62	1
Kinston, NC (10TH)	12/14/62	1
Irish Bend, LA (25TH)	4/14/63	2
Fort Wagner, SC (7TH)	7/11/63	1
White's Ford, VA (1 SQ)	9/22/63	1
Todd's Tavern, VA (1 SQ)	5/5/64	1
Wilderness, VA (14TH)	5/6/64	1
Drewry's Bluff, VA (11TH)	5/16/64	1
Drewry's Bluff, VA (10TH)	5/17/64	1
Bottom Bridge, VA (11TH)	5/31/64	1
Cold Harbor, VA (2 HA)	6/1/64	1
Bermuda Hundred, VA (7TH) *	6/2/64	1
Petersburg, VA (21ST)	7/17/64	1
Petersburg, VA (30TH)	7/30/64	1
Deep Bottom, VA (10TH)	8/14/64	1
Ream's Station, VA (14TH)	8/25/64	1
Fort Harrison, VA (21ST)	9/27/64	1
Fort Harrison, VA (8TH)	9/29/64	1
Chaffin's Farm, VA (29TH)	10/1/64	1
Cedar Creek, VA (12TH)	10/19/64	1
Battery Morton, VA (1 HA) *	11/26/64	1
Petersburg, VA (10TH)	4/2/65	1

WINDSOR LOCKS
THE POPULATION IN 1860 WAS 2,154   (RANK 68)

THE MOST IMPORTANT DAY OF THE CIVIL WAR

APRIL 14, 1863

IRISH BEND, LA

THE OUTNUMBERED CONFEDERATES HELD OFF THE UNION ARMY IN THE BAYOUS OF LOUISIANA

155 MEN CREDITED TO WINDSOR LOCKS SERVED IN THE FOLLOWING CONNECTICUT ORGANIZATIONS

More soldiers credited to Windsor Locks were listed as casualties (5) on this day than on any other day of the war. One soldier was killed, 3 were wounded, and 1 was captured in the 25TH Connecticut. The wounded and captured survived the war.

The date April 14, 1863 ranks 17TH for total casualties (147) (18 killed, 120 wounded, 9 captured) for a single day for the State of Connecticut. There were 144 casualties at Irish Bend. The 3 other casualties were scattered about Louisiana.

The Battle of Irish Bend (April 14, 1863) ranks 15TH for total casualties (144) for an engagement for the State of Connecticut.

The Battle of Irish Bend with 5 total casualties for Windsor Locks was the highest number of casualties for any single engagement of the war for the town.

The Union Army under the command of Major General Nathaniel P. Banks was greatly hindered in controlling Louisiana due to the great tactical ability of Confederate General Richard Taylor, son of former U.S. President Zachary Taylor. The western bayous of the state proved particularly difficult to control and it was only after the July 1863 surrender of Vicksburg, MS and Port Hudson, LA were the Confederates thwarted in the bayou country

REGIMENT	TOTAL
1ST HEAVY ARTILLERY	36 (23%)
25TH	34 (22%)
1ST	17 (11%)
12TH	16 (10%)
20TH	12 (8%)
1ST LIGHT BATTERY	11 (7%)
12TH BATTALION	9 (6%)
7TH	8 (5%)
22ND	7 (5%)
21ST	4 (3%)
6TH	3 (2%)
11TH	3 (2%)
16TH	3 (2%)
10TH	2 (1%)
13TH	2 (1%)
14TH	2 (1%)
1ST CAVALRY	1
2ND	1
2ND HEAVY ARTILLERY	1
8TH	1
9TH	1
13TH BATTALION	1
15TH	1
29TH	1

7% OF POPULATION

SIX WERE KILLED

The first Windsor Locks soldier killed was Captain Samuel S. Hayden of Company C, 25TH Connecticut. He was killed at Irish Bend, LA on April 14, 1863.

WINDSOR LOCKS KILLED

PLACE	DATE	NO.
Irish Bend, LA (25TH)	4/14/63	1
Port Hudson, LA (25TH)	5/27/63	1
Port Hudson, LA (12TH)	6/14/63	1
Fort Wagner, SC (7TH)	7/11/63	1
Cold Harbor, VA (11TH)	6/3/64	1
Cedar Creek, VA (12TH)	10/19/64	1

TWELVE WERE CAPTURED

One Windsor Locks soldier died in captivity at Millen, GA.

WINDSOR LOCKS CAPTURED
*(1) DIED IN CAPTIVITY

PLACE	DATE	NO.
Irish Bend, LA (25TH)	4/14/63	1
Chancellorsville, VA (20TH)	5/3/63	2
Brashear City, LA (12TH)	6/23/63	2
Fort Wagner, SC (7TH)	7/11/63	2
(2 WOUNDED)		
Ackworth, GA (20TH) *	7/2/64	1
Ackworth, GA (20TH)	7/4/64	1
Richmond, VA (7TH)	10/1/64	1
Cedar Creek, VA (13TH)	10/19/64	1
Bentonville, NC (20TH)	3/19/65	1

TOTAL WINDSOR LOCKS CASUALTIES

DIED	10	6%
KILLED	6	4%
WOUNDED	17	11%
CAPTURED	12	8%
DESERTED	20	13%

SEVENTEEN WERE WOUNDED

The first Windsor Locks soldier wounded was Private Otto Newport of Company C, 1ST Connecticut. He was wounded at the Battle of Bull Run, VA on July 21, 1861 and recovered from his wound. One Windsor Locks soldier died from a wound received during the war.

WINDSOR LOCKS WOUNDED
*(1) DIED FROM WOUNDS

PLACE	DATE	NO.
Bull Run, VA (1ST)	7/21/61	1
James Island, SC (7TH)	6/16/62	1
Antietam, MD (11TH)	9/17/62	2
Irish Bend, LA (25TH)	4/14/63	3
Port Hudson, LA (25TH)	5/28/63	1
Port Hudson, LA (25TH) *1	6/14/63	2
Drewry's Bluff, VA (6TH)	5/10/64	1
Ream's Station, VA (14TH)	8/25/64	1
Winchester, VA (12TH)	9/19/64	1
Petersburg, VA (1 HA)	9/20/64	1
Cedar Creek, VA (12TH)	10/19/64	2
Petersburg, VA (1 HA)	3/25/65	1

WOLCOTT
THE POPULATION IN 1860 WAS 574   (RANK 158)

THE MOST IMPORTANT DAY OF THE CIVIL WAR

JUNE 3, 1864

COLD HARBOR, VA

THE BATTLE WAS LEE'S LAST GREAT VICTORY

Soldiers credited to Wolcott had no day in the war with more than 1 casualty. There were 8 days with 1 casualty: August 9, 1862 at Cedar Mountain, VA, February 6, 1864 at Morton's Ford, VA, February 20, 1864 at Olustee, FL, May 15, 1864 at New Market, VA, June 1 & 3, 1864 at Cold Harbor, VA, October 27, 1864 at Boydton Plank Road, VA and March 25, 1865 at Petersburg, VA. At Cold Harbor, the casualty was more serious. One soldier was wounded in the 14TH Connecticut and he died from his wound.

The date June 3, 1864 ranks 12TH for total casualties (196) (24 killed, 2 missing, 168 wounded, 2 captured) for a single day for the State of Connecticut. Cold Harbor accounted for 190 casualties.There were 4 casualties at Petersburg, VA and 2 casualties at Dallas, GA.

The battle and operations around Cold Harbor (May 31-June 12, 1864) rank 6TH for total casualties (557) for an engagement for the State of Connecticut. The most intense fighting developed on June 3. Wolcott also had 1 casualty on June 1

The Battle of Cold Harbor with 2 total casualties for Wolcott was the highest number of casualties any single engagement of the war for the town.

Approximately 117,000 Federal and 60,000 Confederate troops participated in operations from May 28 to June 3. Roughly 13,000 Union casualties were recorded and perhaps there were 5,000 Confederate casualties.

38 MEN CREDITED TO WOLCOTT SERVED IN THE FOLLOWING CONNECTICUT ORGANIZATIONS

REGIMENT	TOTAL
1ST HEAVY ARTILLERY	7 (18%)
7TH	5 (12%)
8TH	4 (11%)
14TH	4 (11%)
5TH	3 (8%)
15TH	3 (8%)
2ND HEAVY ARTILLERY	2 (5%)
9TH	2 (5%)
11TH	2 (5%)
20TH	2 (5%)
29TH	2 (5%)
1ST LIGHT BATTERY	1
12TH	1
13TH	1
18TH	1
27TH	1

7% OF POPULATION

ONE WAS MISSING AND PRESUMED KILLED

The only Wolcott soldier killed was Private James P. Alcott of Company F, 14TH Connecticut. He was missing at Boydton Plank Road, VA on October 27, 1864. His body was never recovered.

WOLCOTT SOLDEIRS KILLED

PLACE	DATE	NO.
Boydton Plank Rd, VA (14TH)	10/27/64	1

THREE WERE CAPTURED

One Wolcott soldier died in captivity at Richmond, VA.

WOLCOTT CAPTURED
*(1) DIED IN CAPTIVITY

PLACE	DATE	NO.
Fort Wagner, SC (7TH) *	7/18/63	1
New Market, VA (18TH)	5/15/64	1
Petersburg, VA (1 HA)	3/25/65	1

TOTAL WOLCOTT CASUALTIES

DIED	5	13%
KILLED/MISSING	1	3%
WOUNDED	5	13%
CAPTURED	3	8%
DESERTED	7	18%

FIVE WERE WOUNDED

The first Wolcott soldier wounded was Private Amon L. Norton of Company D, 5TH Connecticut. He was wounded at Cedar Mountain, VA on August 9, 1862 and recovered from his wound. He was also wounded on February 6, 1864 at Morton's Ford and June 3, 1864 at Cold Harbor, VA while in the 14TH Connecticut. He died from the wound at Cold Harbor. Two Wolcott soldiers died from a wound received during the war.

WOLCOTT WOUNDED
*(2) DIED FROM WOUNDS

PLACE	DATE	NO.
Cedar Mountain, VA (5TH)	8/9/62	1
Morton's Ford, VA (14TH)	2/6/64	1
Olustee, FL (7TH) *	2/20/64	1
Cold Harbor, VA (11TH)	6/1/64	1
Cold Harbor, VA (14TH) *	6/3/64	1

624

WOODBRIDGE
THE POPULATION IN 1860 WAS 872 (RANK 143)

**THE MOST IMPORTANT DAY
OF THE CIVIL WAR**

MARCH 8, 1865

KINSTON, NC

**THE CONFEDERATE
ATTACK STALLED**

**60 MEN CREDITED TO
WOODBRIDGE SERVED IN
THE FOLLOWING
CONNECTICUT
ORGANIZATIONS**

More soldiers credited to Woodbridge were listed as casualties (5) on this day than on any other day of the war. Four soldiers were captured and 1 was wounded & captured in the 15TH Connecticut. The wounded & captured soldier died in prison.

The date March 8, 1865 ranks 5TH for total casualties (496) (22 killed, 3 missing, 12 wounded, 410 captured, 49 wounded & captured) for a single day for the State of Connecticut. There were 494 casualties at Kinston, 1 casualty in Virginia, and 1 casualty at a railroad accident in an unknown place.

The Second Battle of Kinston (March 8, 1865) ranks 8TH for total casualties (494) for an engagement for the State of Connecticut.

The Second Battle of Kinston with 5 total casualties for Woodbridge was the highest number of casualties for any single engagement of the war for the town.

The military situation in North Carolina changed in early 1865. The Confederate forces in eastern North Carolina were called to help stop the advance of the Union Army coming out of Georgia with Union General William T. Sherman. The Confederates attempted to seize the initiative by attacking the Union flanks near Kinston on March 8 and failed.

REGIMENT	TOTAL
10TH	9 (15%)
27TH	9 (15%)
6TH	7 (12%)
15TH	7 (12%)
1ST CAVALRY	5 (8%)
7TH	5 (8%)
1ST HEAVY ARTILLERY	4 (7%)
2ND HEAVY ARTILLERY	4 (7%)
5TH	3 (5%)
29TH	2 (3%)
8TH	1
9TH	1
9TH BATTALION	1
13TH	1
13TH BATTALION	1
14TH	1
23RD	1
30TH	1

7% 0F POPULATION

ONE WAS KILLED

The only Woodbridge soldier killed was Private Junius Payne of Company C, 30TH Connecticut. He was killed at Petersburg, VA on July 30, 1864.

WOODBRIDGE SOLDIERS KILLED

PLACE	DATE	NO.
Petersburg, VA (30TH)	7/30/64	1

EIGHT WERE CAPTURED

One Woodbridge soldier died in captivity at Guilford, NC.

PLACE	DATE	NO.
Chancellorsville, VA (27TH)	5/3/63	2
Luray Valley, VA (1 CA)	9/21/64	1
Kinston, NC (15TH) *1	3/8/65	5
(1 WOUNDED)		

TOTAL WOODBRIDGE CASUALTIES

DIED	8	13%
KILLED	1	2%
WOUNDED	7	12%
CAPTURED	8	13%
DESERTED	9	15%

SEVEN WERE WOUNDED

The first Woodbridge soldiers wounded were Privates Bruce Baldwin and Willis C. Thomas of the 6TH and 7TH Connecticut. They were wounded at Pocotaligo, SC on October 22, 1862. Both soldiers died from their wounds. They were the only Woodbridge soldiers who died from a wound received during the war.

WOODBRIDGE WOUNDED
*(2) DIED FROM WOUNDS

PLACE	DATE	NO.
Pocotaligo, SC (6,7TH) *2	10/22/62	2
Kinston, NC (10TH)	12/14/62	2
Drewry's Bluff, VA (7TH)	5/16/64	1
Cold Harbor, VA (2 HA)	6/1/64	1
Fort Gregg, VA (10TH)	4/2/65	1

WOODBURY
THE POPULATION IN 1860 WAS 2,037 (RANK 75)

THE MOST IMPORTANT DAY OF THE CIVIL WAR

SEPTEMBER 19, 1864

WINCHESTER, VA

THE BATTLE OF THIRD WINCHESTER (OPEQUON) WAS A UNION VICTORY

More soldiers credited to Woodbury were listed as casualties (11) on this day than on any other day of the war. Eleven soldiers were wounded in the 2ND Connecticut Heavy Artillery. Three of the wounded died.

The date September 19, 1864 ranks 9TH for total casualties (279) (38 killed, 209 wounded, 32 captured) for a single day for the State of Connecticut. There were 274 casualties at Winchester. The 5 other casualties were in the Petersburg, VA area.

The Battle of Third Winchester (September 19, 1864) ranks 12TH for total casualties (274) for an engagement for the State of Connecticut.

The Battle of Third Winchester with 11 total casualties for Woodbury was the highest number of casualties for any single engagement of the war for the town.

The battle was not an overwhelming victory for the Union Army. As the Union force was approaching Winchester from the east they became bogged down and the attacks were uncoordinated. The Union army sustained heavier casualties but the Confederates moved to a stronger position at Fisher's Hill south of Strasburg. The total casualties were about 7,500.

165 MEN CREDITED TO WOODBURY SERVED IN THE FOLLOWING CONNECTICUT ORGANIZATIONS

REGIMENT	TOTAL
2ND HEAVY ARTILLERY	78 (47%)
5TH	19 (12%)
8TH	17 (10%)
29TH	7 (4%)
6TH	7 (4%)
13TH	6 (4%)
1ST HEAVY ARTILLERY	5 (3%)
14TH	4 (2%)
1ST CAVALRY	3 (2%)
12TH	3 (2%)
20TH	3 (2%)
23RD	3 (2%)
7TH	2 (1%)
9TH	2 (1%)
11TH	2 (1%)
12TH BATTALION	2 (1%)
15TH	2 (1%)
2ND	1
2ND LIGHT BATTERY	1
10TH	1
13TH BATTALION	1
17TH	1
27TH	1
28TH	1
30TH	1

8% OF POPULATION

THREE WERE KILLED AND TWO WERE MISSING

The first Woodbury soldier killed was Private John E. Tuttle of Company E, 8TH Connecticut. He was killed at the Battle of Antietam, MD on September 17, 1862.

WOODBURY SOLDIERS KILLED AND *MISSING

PLACE	DATE	NO.
Antietam, MD (8TH)	9/17/62	1
Fredericksburg, VA (14TH) *	12/13/62	1
Cold Harbor, VA (2 HA)	6/1/64	2
Hatcher's Run, VA (2HA)*	2/6/65	1

FOUR WERE CAPTURED

One Woodbury soldier died in captivity at Salisbury, NC.

WOODBURY CAPTURED *(1) DIED IN CAPTIVITY

PLACE	DATE	NO.
Chancellorsville, VA (27TH)	5/3/63	1
Petersburg, VA (8TH) *	9/18/64	1
Kinston, NC (15TH)	3/8/65	2

TOTAL WOODBURY CASUALTIES

DIED	25	15%
KILLED/MISSING	5	3%
WOUNDED	38	23%
CAPTURED	4	2%
DESERTED	27	17%

THIRTY-EIGHT WERE WOUNDED

The first Woodbury soldiers wounded were Privates Wesley Bunnell, Thomas C. Galpin, and Frank J. Percy of the 8TH and 14TH Connecticut. They were wounded at the Battle of Antietam, MD on September 17, 1862 and survived their wounds. Private Percy was later reported missing and presumed dead at Fredericksburg, VA on December 13, 1862. Eight Woodbury soldiers died from a wound received during the war.

WOODBURY WOUNDED *(8) DIED FROM WOUNDS

PLACE	DATE	NO.
Fort Williams, VA (2 HA	Unknown	1
Antietam, MD (8,14TH)	9/17/62	3
Cold Harbor, VA (2 HA) *2	6/1/64	6
Cold Harbor, VA (2 HA) *	6/5/64	1
Culp's Farm, GA (5TH)	6/22/64	1
Peach Tree Creek, GA (5TH) *1	7/20/64	3
Winchester, VA (2 HA) *3	9/19/64	11
Chaffin's Farm, VA (8TH)	9/29/64	1
Chaffin's Farm, VA (8TH)	10/1/64	1
Darbytown Road, VA (6TH) *	10/7/64	1
Darbytown Road, VA (29TH)	10/13/64	1
Cedar Creek, VA (2 HA)	10/19/64	7
Petersburg, VA (2 HA)	3/25/65	1

WOODSTOCK
THE POPULATION IN 1860 WAS 3,285 (RANK 34)

THE MOST IMPORTANT DAY OF THE CIVIL WAR

JUNE 15 1863

WINCHESTER, VA

THE ENTIRE UNION ARMY WAS NEARLY CAPTURED AT THE SECOND BATTLE OF WINCHESTER

More soldiers credited to Woodstock were listed as casualties (38) on this day than on any other day of the war. Three soldiers were killed, 31 were captured, and 4 were wounded & captured in the 18TH Connecticut. One of the wounded soldiers died.

The date June 15, 1863 ranks 2ND for total casualties (595) (23 killed, 11 wounded, 520 captured, 41 wounded & captured) for a single day for the State of Connecticut. There were 592 casualties at Winchester, VA and 3 casualties at Port Hudson, LA.

The Second Battle of Winchester (June 13-15, 1863) ranks 5TH for total casualties (592) for an engagement for the State of Connecticut. The most intense fighting developed on June 15. Woodstock had all its casualties on that day.

The Second Battle of Winchester with 38 total casualties for Woodstock was the highest number of casualties for any single engagement of the war for the town.

Winchester was one of the most contested locations in the Civil War. It changed hands seventy-two times.

272 MEN CREDITED TO WOODSTOCK SERVED IN THE FOLLOWING CONNECTICUT ORGANIZATIONS

REGIMENT	TOTAL
18TH	77 (28%)
7TH	30 (11%)
11TH	30 (11%)
1ST CAVALRY	29 (11%)
26TH	23 (9%)
1ST HEAVY ARTILLERY	20 (7%)
14TH	14 (5%)
5TH	12 (4%)
6TH	11 (4%)
8TH	7 (3%)
29TH	7 (3%)
13TH	6 (2%)
10TH	5 (2%)
2ND	3 (1%)
2ND HEAVY ARTILLERY	3 (1%)
1ST LIGHT BATTERY	1
3RD	1
12TH	1
12TH BATTALION	1
13TH BATTALION	1
16TH	1
21ST	

8% OF POPULATION

TWELVE WERE KILLED AND ONE WAS MISSING

The first Woodstock soldier killed was Private Peter Fornnia of Company H, 11TH Connecticut. He was killed at New Bern, NC on March 14, 1862.

WOODSTOCK SOLDIERS KILLED MISSING *

PLACE	DATE	NO.
New Bern, NC (11TH)	3/14/62	1
James Island, SC (7TH)	6/16/62	2
Antietam, MD (11TH)	9/17/62	1
Drowned "West Point" (11TH) *	8/13/62	1
Winchester, VA (18TH)	6/15/63	3
James Island, SC (7TH)	8/12/63	1
Olustee, FL (7TH)	2/20/64	1
Piedmont, VA (18TH)	6/5/64	1
Winchester, VA (1 CA)	9/13/64	1
Harper's Farm, VA (1 CA)	4/6/65	1

FIFTY-EIGHT WERE CAPTURED

Six Woodstock soldiers died in captivity. Four died at Andersonville Prison, GA, one at Florence, SC and one died at Libby Prison, Richmond, VA.

WOODSTOCK CAPTURED *(6) DIED IN CAPTVITY

PLACE	DATE	NO.
2 Bull Run, VA (5TH)	8/30/62	1
Winchester, VA (18TH)	6/15/63	35
(4 WOUNDED)		
Fort Wagner, SC (7TH)	7/11/63	3
Bolivar Heights, VA (1 CA)	7/14/63	1
Waterford, VA (1 CA)	8/7/63	2
Bristoe Station, VA (14TH) *	10/14/63	1
Mine Run, VA (14TH)	12/2/63	1
Plymouth, NC (16TH)	4/20/64	1
Craig's Church, VA (1 CA) *	5/5/64	1
New Market, VA (18TH) *	5/15/64	2
Ashland, VA (1 CA)	6/1/64	1
Bermuda Hundred, VA (7TH)	6/2/64	1
Piedmont, VA (18TH)	6/5/64	2
(2 WOUNDED)		
Staunton, VA (18TH)	6/9/64	1
Lynchburg, VA (18TH)	6/18/64	1
(WOUNDED)		
Ream's Station, VA (1 CA)	6/29/64	2
Deep Bottom, VA (7TH)	8/16/64	1
Cedar Run Church, VA (1CA)	10/17/64	1
Boydton Plank Rd, VA (14TH) *	10/27/64	1

TOTAL WOODSTOCK CASUALTIES

DIED	41	15%
KILLED/MISSING	13	5%
WOUNDED	40	15%
CAPTURED	58	21%
DESERTED	24	9%

FORTY WERE WOUNDED

The first Woodstock soldiers wounded were Privates Henry C. Dodge, William H. Clements, Charles H. Moore and George D. Pike of the 11TH Connecticut. They were wounded at the Battle of Antietam, MD on September 17, 1862. Privates Dodge and Pike died from their wounds. Nine Woodstock soldiers died from a wound received during the war.

WOODSTOCK WOUNDED *(9) DIED FROM WOUNDS

PLACE	DATE	NO.
Antietam, MD (11TH) *2	9/17/62	4
Chancellorsville, VA (14TH)	5/3/63	1
Port Hudson, LA (26TH)	5/27/63	3
Morris Island, SC (7TH)	7/10/63	1
Fort Wagner, SC (7TH) *1	7/11/63	3
Bristoe Station, VA (14TH)	10/14/63	1
Tinsburg, WVA (18TH)	3/5/64	1
Wilderness, VA (14TH)	5/6/64	1
Drewry's Bluff, VA (7TH)	5/13/64	1
New Market, VA (18TH)	5/15/64	2
Drewry's Bluff, VA (6,11TH)	5/16/64	2
Bermuda Hundred, VA (7TH) *2	6/2/64	3
Cold Harbor, VA (11TH)	6/3/64	2
Piedmont, VA (18TH)	6/5/64	2
Lynchburg, VA (18TH)	6/14/64	1
Petersburg, VA (11TH)	6/18/64	2
Lynchburg, VA (18TH)	6/18/64	1
Culp's Farm, GA (5TH)	6/22/64	1
Snicker's Ford, VA (18TH) *	7/18/64	1
Winchester, VA (18TH)	7/24/64	1
Deep Bottom, VA (14TH) *	8/17/64	1
Petersburg, VA (29TH)	8/27/64	1
Darbytown Road, VA (10,29TH)	10/13/64	2
Railroad Accident (18TH) *	10/15/64	1
Cedar Creek, VA (1 CA) *	11/12/64	1

NOTES

The regimental histories presented in this book are based on the notes written by an individual veteran of the applicable Connecticut organization that was published in the *Record of Service of Connecticut Men in the Army and the Navy During the War of the Rebellion, 1889.* The names, dates, places, and events listed were checked against those referenced in the *The Official Records of the War of the Rebellion, The Connecticut War Record, The Military and Civil History of Connecticut During the War of 1861-65 Comprising a Detailed Account of the Various Regiments and Batteries,* and the various applicable published regimental histories and accounts. The number of recruits, and the number of casualties listed in the text are derived from the database created by the author from the *Record of Service of Connecticut Men ... 1889.*

1ST REGIMENT INFANTRY

1. From the notes of Col George S. Burnham in the *Record of Service of Connecticut Men During the War of the Rebellion, 1889*

1ST REGIMENT HEAVY ARTILLERY

1. From the notes of Col Henry L. Abbot in the *Record of Service of Connecticut Men During the War of the Rebellion, 1889*

1ST REGIMENT CAVALRY

1. From the notes of Lt Col Erastus Blakeslee in the in the *Record of Service of Connecticut Men During the War of the Rebellion, 1889*

1ST BATTERY LIGHT ARTILLERY

1. From the notes of 1st Lt. Theron Upson in the *Record of Service of Connecticut Men During the War of the Rebellion, 1889.*

1ST SQUADRON CAVALRY

1. From notes compiled by the Adjutant General in the *Record of Service of Connecticut Men During the War of the Rebellion, 1889*

2ND REGIMENT INFANTRY

1. From the notes of Private James B. Coit, Co B in the *Record of Service of Connecticut Men During the War of the Rebellion, 1889*

2ND REGIMENT HEAVY ARTILLERY

1. From the notes of Capt James N. Coe, Co H in the *Record of Service of Connecticut Men During the War of the Rebellion, 1889*

2ND BATTERY LIGHT ARTILLERY

1. From the notes of 1st Serg. David B. Lockwood in the *Record of Service of Connecticut Men During the War of the Rebellion, 1889*

3RD REGIMENT INFANTRY

1. From notes compiled by the Adjutant General in the *Record of Service of Connecticut Men During the War of the Rebellion, 1889*

3RD BATTERY LIGHT BATTERY

1. From the notes of Capt. Thomas S. Gilbert in the *Record of Service of Connecticut Men During the War of the Rebellion, 1889*

5TH REGIMENT INFANTRY

1. From the notes of Capt E.E. Marvin, Co F in the *Record of Service of Connecticut Men During the War of the Rebellion, 1889*

6TH REGIMENT INFANTRY

1. From the notes of Charles K. Cadwell, Co F in the *Record of Service of Connecticut Men During the War of the Rebellion, 1889*

7TH REGIMENT INFANTRY

1. From the notes of Capt. William H. Pierpont, Co D in the *Record of Service of Connecticut Men During the War of the Rebellion, 1889*

8TH REGIMENT INFANTRY

1. From the notes of QM Serg J. H. Vaill in the *Record of Service of Connecticut Men During the War of the Rebellion, 1889*

9TH REGIMENT INFANTRY

1. From the notes of Lt Col John G. Healy in the *Record of Service of Connecticut Men During the War of the Rebellion, 1889*

10TH REGIMENT INFANTRY

1. From the notes of Lt Col John L. Otis in the *Record of Service of Connecticut Men During the War of the Rebellion, 1889*

11TH REGIMENT INFANTRY

1.From the notes of Lt Col Charles Warren in the *Record of Service of Connecticut Men During the War of the Rebellion, 1889*

12TH REGIMENT INFANTRY

1. From the notes of Capt. L. A. Dickinson, Co G in the *Record of Service of Connecticut Men During the War of the Rebellion, 1889*

13TH REGIMENT INFANTRY

1. From the notes of 1st Lt. John C. Kinney, Co A
in the *Record of Service of Connecticut Men
During the War of the Rebellion, 1889*

14TH REGIMENT INFANTRY

1. From the notes of Chaplain Henry S. Stevens
in the *Record of Service of Connecticut Men
During the War of the Rebellion, 1889*

15TH REGIMENT INFANTRY

1. From the notes of Capt George M. White, Co E
in the *Record of Service of Connecticut Men
During the War of the Rebellion, 1889*

16TH REGIMENT INFANTRY

1. From the notes of 2Lt Bernard F. Blakeslee
in the *Record of Service of Connecticut Men
During the War of the Rebellion, 1889*

17TH REGIMENT INFANTRY

1. From the notes of Col. William H. Noble
in the *Record of Service of Connecticut Men
During the War of the Rebellion, 1889*

18TH REGIMENT INFANTRY

1. From the notes of Col. William G. Ely
in the *Record of Service of Connecticut Men
During the War of the Rebellion, 1889*

20TH REGIMENT INFANTRY

1. From the notes of 2nd Lt. Cecil A. Burleigh, Co C
in the *Record of Service of Connecticut Men
During the War of the Rebellion, 1889*

21ST REGIMENT INFANTRY

1. From the notes of Capt. Delos D. Brown, Co I
in the *Record of Service of Connecticut Men
During the War of the Rebellion, 1889*

22ND REGIMENT INFANTRY

1. From the notes of Capt. John K. Williams, Co H
in the *Record of Service of Connecticut Men
During the War of the Rebellion, 1889*

23RD REGIMENT INFANTRY

1. From the notes of Maj. David H. Miller
in the *Record of Service of Connecticut Men
During the War of the Rebellion, 1889*

24TH REGIMENT INFANTRY

1.From the notes of 1st Lt. Augustus H. Conklin, Co K
in the *Record of Service of Connecticut Men
During the War of the Rebellion, 1889*

25TH REGIMENT INFANTRY

1. From the notes of Col. George P. Bissell
in the *Record of Service of Connecticut Men
During the War of the Rebellion, 1889*

26TH REGIMENT INFANTRY

1. From the notes of Capt. Loren A. Gallup, Co F
in the *Record of Service of Connecticut Men
During the War of the Rebellion, 1889*

27TH REGIMENT INFANTRY

1.From the notes of Capt. Frank D. Sloat, Co A
in the *Record of Service of Connecticut Men
During the War of the Rebellion, 1889*

28TH REGIMENT INFANTRY

1. From the notes of Lt Col W. T. Batcheller
in the *Record of Service of Connecticut Men
During the War of the Rebellion, 1889*

29TH REGIMENT INFANTRY

1. From the notes of Capt. Henry G. Marshall, Co I
in the *Record of Service of Connecticut Men
During the War of the Rebellion, 1889*

30TH REGIMENT INFANTRY

1. From notes compiled by the Adjutant General
in the *Record of Service of Connecticut Men
During the War of the Rebellion, 1889*

REGIMENTAL TROOP MOVEMENT LISTS

1. From A Compendium of the War of the Rebellion by
Frederick Dyer

TOWN HISTORY SECTION BATTLEFIELD NOTES FOR THE MOST IMPORTANT DAY OF THE CIVIL WAR

1. Smithsonian's Great Battles & Battlefields of the Civil
War. New York: William Morrow and Company, Inc, 1997

2. The Civil War Battlefield Guide. Boston: Houghton
Mifflin Company, 1990.

3. The Civil War Dictionary. New York: Vintage Books,
1987

4. The Illustrated Atlas of the Civil War. Alexandria,
Virginia: Time Life Books 1996

Bibliography

Abbot, Henry L. *Siege Artillery in the Campaigns Against Richmond*. Washington, D.C. 1867

Anderson, Jospeh, *History of the Soldiers Monument in Waterbury*, Connecticut. Hartford:

Andrews, E. Benjamin, *A Private's Reminiscences of the First Year of the War*. Providence: 1886.

Bacon, Theodore. *The Veteran Soldier's Duty to His Country. An Address Delivered at Canandaigua, NY., on Decoration Day, May 30, 1884, before Albert M Murray Post No. 162, of the Grand Army of the Republic", by Theodore Bacon, Sometime of the Seventh Connecticut Volunteers...* Rochester: 1884.

Bailey, James Montgomery. *James M. Bailey's Civil War Humor, By Hamlin Hill*. Connecticut Historical Society Bulletin. XXVII (1962).

Beecher, Herbert W. *History of the First Light Battery Connecticut Volunteers 1861-1865. Personal Records and Reminiscences*. 2 vols. New York: A.T. De La Mare Printing and Publishing Co, Ltd., 1901.

Bennett, Edgar B. *First Connecticut Heavy Artillery; Historical Sketch and Present Addresses of Members*. Hartford: Star Printing Co., 1889.

Bissell, Lewis. *The Civil War Letters of Lewis Bissell, A Curriculum, By Mark Olcott With David Lear*. Washington, DC., The Field School Educational Foundation Press, 1981.

Blakeslee, Bernard F. *History of the Sixteenth Connecticut Volunteers*. Hartford: Case, Lockwood and Brainard Co., 1875.

Brownell, Henry Howard, *"The Battle of the Hartford and Tennessee"*. Connecticut Quarterly 3 (1897): 454-59.

Buckingham, Samuel Giles, *The War Governor of Connecticut*. Springfield: W.F. Adams, 1894.

Caldwell, Charles R., *The Old Sixth Regiment, Its War Record, 1861-5*. New Haven: Tuttle, Morehouse and Taylor, 1875.

Chapman, Horatio Dana, *Civil War Diary*. Hartford: 1929.

Clark, Henry, *Edward Crafts Hopson, A Biographical Sketch Read before the Vermont Historical Society, January 25, 1865.*

Cleaveland, Elisha Lord. *A Discourse in Commemoration of Colonel Frank Henry Peck, delivered at His Funeral in the Congregational Church, New Haven, October 7, 1864, By Elisha Lord Cleaveland*. New Haven, Thomas H. Pease, 1864.

Connecticut Adjutant-General, *Catalogue of the 6th, 7th, 8th, 9th, 10th, and 11th Regiments of Infantry, 1st Light Battery and 1st Battalion Cavalry, Connecticut Volunteers*. Hartford: 1869.

Connecticut Adjutant-General, *Catalogue of Connecticut Volunteer Organization, Infantry, Cavary, and Artillery Additional Enlistments, Casualties, Etc*. Hartford: Brown and Gross, 1869.

Connecticut Adjutant General, *Catalogue of Connecticut Volunteer Organizations, With Additonal Enlistments and Casualties to July 1, 1864*. Hartford: Case, Lockwood and Co., 1864.

Connecticut Adjutant General. *Record of Service of Connecticut Men in the Army and Navy of the United States During the War of the Rebellion*. Hartford: Case, Lockwood and Brainard Co., 1889.

Connecticut Adjutant General. *The Connecti cut Cavalry Volunteers In the War of the Rebellion, 1861-1865: Containing the History and Complete Rosters of the First Squadron and of the First Regiment Connecticut Cavalry Volunteers.* Hartford: Case, Lockwood and Brainard Co., 1889.

Connecticut General Assembly. *Addresses Delivered in the Senate and House of Representatives of Connecticut, in Honor of Colonel Charles L. Russell...* New Haven: Babcock & Sizer, State Printers, 1862.

Connecticut Infantry. 17th Regiment, 1862-1865., *17th Connecticut Volunteers at Gettysburg: June 30th and July 1st, 2nd and 3rd, 1884.*, 1884

Connecticut War Record. Vol 1, No. 1 1863-65 (Newspaper) New Haven: Peck and Peck, 1863-65.

Cowden, Joanna Dunlap. *Civil War and Reconstruction Politics in Connecticut, 1863-1868.* 1974.

Crofut, William Augustus, and Morris, John M., *Military and Civil History of Connecticut During the War of 1861-65 Comprising a Detailed Account of the Various Regiments and Batteries ...* New York: Ledyard Bill, 1868.

Dana, Malcolm McG., *The Norwich Memorial, The Annals of Norwich, New London County, Connecticut in the Great Rebellion 1861-1865.* Norwich: J.H. Jewett & Co., 1873.

Deforest, John William, *A Volunteers Adventures.* New Haven: 1946.

Deforest, John William. *Port Hudson.* Harper's Magazine XXXV (1867) 334-44.

Eberhardt, Nancy. *Plainville Men in the Civil War.* 1994.

Emmett, L.D., *"Connecticut and the Battlefield of Antietam".* CM 11 (1907): 614-16.

The 18th (Eighteenth) Regiment Connecticut Volunteer Infantry in the War of the Rebellion 1862-1865. Hartford 1889.

Fenton, E.B., *From the Rapidan to Atlanta Leaves From the Diary of E.B. Fenton.* Detroit: 1893.

Finian, William J., *Major Generaal Alfred Howe Terry (1827 - 1890) Hero of Fort Fisher.* Hartford: Connecticut Civil War Centennial Commission, 1965.

Fiske, Samuel Wheelock, *Mr. Dunn Brownes's Experiences in the Army.* Boston: 1866.

The First Regiment Connecticut Volunteers Heavy Artillery in the War of the Rebellion 1861-1865. Hartford: Case, Lockwood and Brainard Co., 1889.

Goddard, Henry P., *14th Connecticut Volunteers, Regimental Reminiscences of the War.* Middletown: 1877.

Goddard, Henry P., *Memorial of Deceased Officers of the 14th Regiment Connecticut Volunteers.* Middletown: 1877.

Griswold, Mary Hoadley. *"Connecticut Heroism in the Civil War".* CM 12 (1908) 330-32.

Hall, Marjory. *Beneath Another Sun.* 1970.

Hamblen, Charles P. *Connecticut Yankees at Gettysburg.* 1993.

Hart, E. Marvin. *The 15th Regiment Connecticut Volunteers a History.* Hartford: 1889.

Hartford (Conn.). City Guard. *The City Guard Register: Being a Complete Roster of the Hartford City Guard Since Its Organization in 1861.* 1880.

Hartford. Connecticut State Library *Record Group 13. Bounty Claim Papers. 1866-1877. List of Connecticut Men in Regiments of other States. Regimental Records and Histories. Requests for Certificates Attesting to Civil War Service 1868-1871.*

Helmreich, Charles G. *The Diary of Charles G. Lee in the Andersonville and Florence Prison Camps, 1864.* Connecticut Historical Society Bulletin XL I (1976) 12-28.

Hill, Isaac J. *A Sketch of the 29th Regiment of Connecticut Colored Troops Giving a Full Account of Its Formation, of All the Battles Through Which It Passed, and Its Final Disbandment.* Baltimore: Dougherty, Magazine and Co., 1867.

History of the First Connecticut Artillery and of the Siege Trains of the Armies Operating Against Richmond 1862-1865. Hartford: Case, Lockwood and Brainard Co., 1896.

History of the Twenty-Second Regiment Connecticut Volunteers Infantry, 1862-3. Hartford: Hartford Printing Co., 1896.

History of Battle Flag Day, September 17, 1879. Hartford: 1879.

Hitchcock, Henry Preston. *1000 Dollars Ex tra Bounty For One Hundred Men.*, 1862

Hoyt, Noah Webster. *The Civil War Diaries of Noah Webster: 28th Regiment Connecticut Volunteers.*, 1996

Idle, A.W. *A Sermon Preached October 8, 1862, at Stafford Springs, At the Funeral Of Lieutenant William Horton, of Company I, 16th Connecticut Regiment Volunteers, Who Was Killed At the Battle of Antietam, September 17, 1862, By Rev. A.W. Ide.* Holliston, Massachusetts, E.G. Plimpton, printer, 1862.

A Journal of Incidents Connected With the Travels of the 22nd Regiment Connecticut Volunteers for Nine Months, in Verse by an orderly Sergeant. Hartford: 1863.

Jurgin, Robert J., and Keller, Allan. *Major General John Sedgewick U.S. Volunteers (1813-64).* Hartford: Connecticut Civil War Centennial Commission, 1664.

Keller, Allan. *Andrew Hull Foote Gunboat Commodore (1806-1863).* Hartford: Connecticut Civil War Centennial Commission, 1964.

Kellogg, Robert H. *Life and Death in Rebel Prisons.* Hartford: 1865.

Kellogg, Robert H., et al. *Dedication of the Monument at Andersonville Georgia October 23, 1907. In memory of the Men of Connecticut who Suffered in Southern Military Prisons 1861-1865.* Hartford: Case, Lockwood and Brainard, Co., 1908.

Lane, Jarlath Robert. *A Political History of Connecticut During the Civil War.* Washington, DC: Catholic University of America, 1941.

Leddy, E.P. *Connecticut Military and Naval Leaders in the Civil War.* 1961.

Lucke, Jerome B. *History of the New Haven Grays.* New Haven: 1876.

Lynch, Chales H., *The Civil War Diary 1862-1865 of Charles H. Lynch 18th Connecticut Volunteers*: Hartford: 1915.

Marvin, Edwin E. *Official Record of the Service of the Men of the Fifth Regiment, Connecticut Infantry in the War of 1861.* Hartford: Wiley, Waterman and Eaton, 1889.

Mayer, Nathan. *A Poem Read by Surgeon Nathan Mayer, October 11, 1894, at the Dedication of a Monument By the Sixteenth Connecticut Where They Fought at Antietam, September 17, 1862.* 1894.

McGegor, Jeremiah S. *Life and Deeds of Dr. John McGregor, including Scenes of his Childhood, Also Scenes on the Battlefield of Bull Run, at the Prisons in Richmond, Charleston, Castle Pinckney, Columbia, Salisbury... By Jeremiah S. McGregor.* Foster, Rhode Island, Press of Fry Brothers, 1886.

McManus, Thomas. *Battlefields of Louisiana Revisited a Second Time.* 1898.

666635

McManus, Thomas. *Battle of Irish Bend: Interesting Reminiscences of That Terrible Combat... An Address Given Before the People of St. Patricks Church, Collinsville, April 23, 1891.* 1891.

McNamer, J.B. *Official Souvenir & Program of Monument, 1st Connecticut Heavy Artillery.* Hartford: 1902.

A Memorial of Lt. Daniel Perkins Dewey of the Twenty-Fifth Regiment Connecticut Volunteers. Hartford: 1864.

Murray, Thomas Hamilton. *History of the Ninth Regiment, Connecticut Volunteer Infantry, "The Irish Regiment", in the War of the Rebellion, 1861-65.* New Haven: Price, Lee and Adkins Co., 1903.

"Muster Rolls". Connecticut Historical Society Collections 15 (1914) 111-60.

"Nathan Whitings List of Soldiers Commissary Book". Connecticut Historical Society Collections 13 (1911) 68-83.

Newton, Alexander Heritage. *Out of the Briars, An Autobiography and Sketch of the Twenty-Ninth Regiment, Connecticut Volunteers.* Philadelphia: African Methodist Episcopal Book Concern, 1910.

Nichols, Joseph A. *A Very Varied Life.* University Place: Chaflin Print Co. 1915.

Niven, John. *Connecticut For the Union: The Role of the State in the Civil War.* New Haven: Yale University Press, 1965.

Olcott, Mark. *The Civil War Letters of Lewis Bissell.* Washington, DC: 1981.

Oviatt, George A. *A Memorial Address Delivered at the Funeral of Captain Samuel B. Hayden at Windsor Locks.* Hartford: 1863.

Page, Charles D. *History of the Fourteenth Regiment, Connecticut Volunteer Infantry.* Meriden: Horton, 1906.

Peck, Hiram T. Army Journal, *A Private Record of Life in the Federal Service During the Great Rebellion, By Hiram T. Peck, Company A, Tenth Regiment Connecticut Volunteer Infantry.* New Haven: 1874.

Preston, Francis W. *Port Hudson: A History of the Investment, Siege and Capture.* Brooklyn: 1892.

Quien, George. *Reminiscences of the Service and Experience of Lieutenant George Quien Co. K. 23rd Connecticut Volunteers.*

Rathburn, Julius G. *Trip of the First Regiment C.N.G. to Yorktown, VA and Charleston, SC.* Hartford: 1882.

Ray, Benjamin C. *The Old Battle Flags... Veteran Soldiers Souvenir Containing a Brief Historical Sketch of Each Connecticut Regiment, the Various Engagements Casualties, etc. During the War of the Rebellion.* 1879.

Roster, Muster Roll and Chronological Record of the Twenty-Sixth Regiment, Connecticut Volunteers, and Memoranda of the Association of the Twenty-Sixth Regiment, Connecticut Volunteers. Norwich: Frank Utley Print: 1888.

Roster of the Third Regiment, Connecticut Volunteers. Hartford: Calhoun Printing Co., 1861.

Schofield, Loomis. *History of the Twenty-Eighth Regiment Connecticut Volunteers.* New Canaan, Connecticut: New Canaan Advertiser, 1915.

Seventeenth Annual Reunion of the 17th Regiment Connecticut Volunteer Infantry. Bridgeport: 1884.

Sheldon, Winthop Dudley. *The Twenty-Seventh, A Regimental History.* New Haven: Morris and Benham, 1866.

Sherman, Andrew M. *In the Lowlands of Louisiana in 1863, An Address.* Morristown, New Jersey: 1908.

Simmons, Ichabod. *The Funeral Sermon of Captain Joseph R. Toy, Delivered in the Congregational Church, Simsbury, On the 16th of July, 1862, By Ichabod Simmons*. Hartford, Press of Case, Lockwood and Co., 1862.

"The Sixth Militia Company, Connecticut". Connecticut Historical Society Bulletin 25 (1960): 61-64.

Sixteenth Regiment Connecticut Volunteers, Excursion and Reunion at Antietam Battle-field September 17, 1889. Hartford: 1889.

Sixteenth Regiment Connecticut Volunteers, Report of the 23rd Annual Reunion. Hart ford: 1867.

Sprague, Homer Baxter, *History of the 13th Infantry Regiment of Connecticut Volun-teers, During the Great Rebellion*. Hart ford: Case, Lockwood and Co., 1867.

Sprague, Homer Baxter. *Lights and Shadows in Confederate Prisons, a Personal Experi-ence 1864-1865*. New York: 1915.

Stevens, Henry S. *Souvenir of Excursion of Battlefields by Society of Fourteenth Connecticut Regiment... 1891*. Washington, DC. 1893.

Storrs, John W. *The "Twentieth Connecticut" A Regimental History*. Ansonia: Naugatuck Valley Sentimental, 1886.

The Story of the Twenty-First Regiment, Connecticut Volunteer Infantry, During the Civil War 1861-1865. Middletown: Stewart Printing Co., 1900.

Talmadge, John E. *"A Peace Movement in Civil War Connecticut"*. NEQ 37 (1968): 306-21.

Taylor, Jeremiah. *The Sacrifice Consumed. Life of Edward Hamilton Brewer*.

Taylor, John C., Hatfield, Samuels P. *History of the First Connecticut Artillery and of the Siege Trains of the Armies Operating Against Richmond, 1862-1865*. Hartford:

Case, Lockwood and Brainard, 1893.

The Pledged Regiment. New York, American Temperance Union, 1861. (4th Infantry)

The Soldier Sacrifice. New York, American Temperance Union, 1862 (10th Infantry)

Thorpe, Sheldon Brainerd. *The History of the Fifteenth Connecticut Volunteers in the War For the Defense of the Union 1861-1865*. New Haven: Price, Lee and Adkins Co., 1893.

Tourtellotte, Jerome. *A History of Company K of the Seventh Connecticut Volunteer In-fantry in the Civil War, Compiled By a Member Who was Second in Rank in the Company When the Regiment Left the State For the Front and Second in Rank in the Regiment When It Returned to the State For Final Discharge*. N.P., 1910.

Townsend, P. *A Sermon Preached October 26, At Stafford Springs, At the Funeral Of James W. Brooks, Of Co. I, 16th Regiment Connecticut Volunteers Who Died October 11th, From Wounds Received At the Battle of Antietam, September 17th 1862, By Rev P. Townsend*. Palmer, Massachusetts, G.M. Fisk & Co., Printers, 1862.

Trecker, Janice Law. *Preachers, Rebels, and Traders: Connecticut 1818-1865*.

Trumbull, Henry Clay. *The Knightly Soldier, A Biography of Major Henry Ward Camp, Tenth Connecticut Volunteers*. Boston: 1865.

Trumbull, Henry Clay. *War Memories of an Army Chaplain*. New York: 1898.

Trumbull, Henry Clay. Good News. *A Sermon To the Veteran Volunteers of the 10th Connectciut Regiment, preached at St. Augustine, Florida, on Sabbath, February 7, 1864, By Chaplain H. Clay Trumbull*. Hartford, Press of Case, Lockwood and Co., 1864.

The 25th Regiment Connecticut Volunteers in the War of the Rebellion, History, Reminiscences, Description Battle Of Irish Bend, Carrying Of Payroll, Roster. Rockville, Connecticut: 1913.

Tyler, Elnathan B. *"Wooden Nutmegs" at Bull Run.* Hartford: G.L. Coburn, 1872.

U.S. National Archives and Record Service. *Index to Compiled Service Records of Volunteer Union Soldiers Who Served in Organizations From the State of Connecticut.* Microfilm Publication, No. 535. Washington, DC: 1964.

Vaill, Dudley Landon. *The County Regiment, A Sketch of the Second Regiment of Connecticut Volunteer Heavy Artillery, Origi nally the Nineteenth Volunteer Infantry in the Civil War.* Litchfield County University Club, 1908.

Vaill, Theodore Frelinghuysen. *History of the Second Connecticut Volunteer Heavy Artil lery, Originally the Nineteenth Connecticut Volunteers.* Winsted: Winsted Printing Co., 1868.

Walker, Edward A. *Our First Year of Army Life, An Anniversary Address Delivered to First Regiment of Connecticut Volunteer Heavy Artillery.* New Haven: 1862.

Walker, William Carey. *History of the Eighteenth Connecticut Volunteers in the War For the Union.* Norwich: The Committee, 1885.

Walkley, Stephen. *History of the Seventh Connecticut Infantry Hawley's Brigade, Terry's Division Tenth Army Corps, 1861-1865.* Hartford, Connecticut: 1905.

Waters, Elizur W. *An Allegory On the Members of Company E, 22nd Regiment, C.V.,* 1863.

Waters, Elizur W. *A Journal of Incidents Connected With the Travels of the 22nd Regiment Connecticut Volunteers For Nine Months, in Verse 1863.* Publisher Williams, Wiley and Waterman: 1863.

Weld, Stanley Buckingham. *Connecticut Physicians in the Civil War.* Hartford: Connecticut Civil War Centennial Commission, 1963.

GENERAL SOURCES

The Civil War CD-ROM v 1.5. Guild Press of Indiana, Inc, 1998

Boatner, Mark M. *The Civil War Dictionary.* Vintage Books, 1991.

Conservation Fund, Edited by Francis H. Kennedy. *The Civil War Battlefield Guide.* Houghton Mifflin Company, 1990.

Davis, George B., Perry, Leslie J., and Kirkley, Joseph W. *Atlas to Accompany the Official Records of the Union and Confederate Armies.* Arno Press, Inc. 1983

Guerney, Alfred H. and Alden, Henry M. *Harpers Pictorial History of the Civil War.* Star Publishing Co. 1894

Wert, Jay and Bearss, Edwin C. *Smithsonians Great Batles and Battlefields of the Civil War.* William Morrow and Company, Inc. 1997.

The Soldier In Our Civil War. Stanley Bradley Publishing Company. 1890.

INDEX

656

QUICK ORDER FORM

Postal orders: American Patriot Press
44 Fluker Street
Rm 157
Thomaston, ME 04861-3449

Please send the following number of books. I understand that I may return them for a full refund - for any reason, no questions asked. Please circle

1   2   3   4   5   Other _____

Name: _____

Address: _____

City: _____ **State:** _____ **Zip:** _____

Telephone: _____

email address: _____

Sales tax: Please add 6% for products shipped to Maine

Shipping: US: $4 for the first book and $2 for each
additional book. International: $9 for first book; $5 for
each additional book (estimate)

Payment: Cheque   Credit Card: Visa   Mastercard

Card number: _____

Name on card: _____

Exp. date: _____